# Lecture Notes of the Institute for Computer Sciences, Social Informatics and Telecommunications Engineering

562

The LNICST series publishes ICST's conferences, symposia and workshops.
LNICST reports state-of-the-art results in areas related to the scope of the Institute.
The type of material published includes

- Proceedings (published in time for the respective event)
- Other edited monographs (such as project reports or invited volumes)

LNICST topics span the following areas:

- General Computer Science
- E-Economy
- E-Medicine
- Knowledge Management
- Multimedia
- Operations, Management and Policy
- Social Informatics
- Systems

Honghao Gao · Xinheng Wang · Nikolaos Voros
Editors

# Collaborative Computing: Networking, Applications and Worksharing

19th EAI International Conference, CollaborateCom 2023
Corfu Island, Greece, October 4–6, 2023
Proceedings, Part II

 Springer

*Editors*
Honghao Gao
Shanghai University
Shanghai, China

Xinheng Wang
Xi'an Jiaotong-Liverpool
Suzhou, China

Nikolaos Voros
University of Peloponnese
Patra, Greece

ISSN 1867-8211            ISSN 1867-822X (electronic)
Lecture Notes of the Institute for Computer Sciences, Social Informatics
and Telecommunications Engineering
ISBN 978-3-031-54527-6       ISBN 978-3-031-54528-3 (eBook)
https://doi.org/10.1007/978-3-031-54528-3

This Springer imprint is published by the registered company Springer Nature Switzerland AG
The registered company address is: Gewerbestrasse 11, 6330 Cham, Switzerland

Paper in this product is recyclable.

# Preface

We are delighted to introduce the proceedings of the 19th European Alliance for Innovation (EAI) International Conference on Collaborative Computing: Networking, Applications and Worksharing (CollaborateCom 2023). This conference brought together researchers, developers and practitioners around the world who are interested in fully realizing the promises of electronic collaboration from the aspects of networking, technology and systems, user interfaces and interaction paradigms, and interoperation with application-specific components and tools.

This year's conference accepted 72 submissions. Each submission was reviewed by an average of 3 reviewers. The conference sessions were: Day 1 Session 1 – Collaborative Computing; Session 2 – Edge Computing & Collaborative Working; Session 3 – Blockchain Application; Session 4 – Code Search and Completion; Session 5 – Edge Computing Scheduling and Offloading; Session 6 – Deep Learning and Application; Session 7 – Graph Computing; Session 8 – Security and Privacy Protection; Session 9 – Processing and Recognition; Session 10 – Deep Learning and Application; Session 11 – Onsite Session. Day 2 Session 12 – Federated Learning and Application; Session 13 – Collaborative Working; Session 14 – Edge Computing; Session 15 – Security and Privacy Protection; Session 16 – Prediction, Optimization and Applications. Apart from high-quality technical paper presentations, the technical program also featured two keynote speeches that were delivered by Christos Masouros from University College London and Michael Hübner from Brandenburgische Technische Universität (BTU).

Coordination with the steering chair, Xinheng Wang, and steering members Song Guo, Bo Li, Xiaofei Liao, Honghao Gao, and Ning Gu was essential for the success of the conference. We sincerely appreciate their constant support and guidance. It was also a great pleasure to work with such an excellent organizing committee team for their hard work in organizing and supporting the conference. In particular, the Technical Program Committee, led by our General Chairs Nikolaos Voros and General Co-Chairs Tasos Dagiuklas, Xinheng Wang, and Honghao Gao, TPC Chairs Christos Antonopoulos, and Eleni Christopoulou, and TPC Co-Chair Dimitrios Ringas completed the peer-review process of technical papers and made a high-quality technical program. We are also grateful to the Conference Manager, Karolina Marcinova, for her support and to all the authors who submitted their papers to the CollaborateCom 2023 conference.

We strongly believe that CollaborateCom provides a good forum for all researchers, developers and practitioners to discuss all science and technology aspects that are relevant to collaborative computing. We also expect that the future CollaborateCom conferences will be as successful and stimulating, as indicated by the contributions presented in this volume.

Honghao Gao
Xinheng Wang
Nikolaos Voros

# Conference Organization

## Steering Committee

### Chair

Xinheng Wang                    Xi'an Jiaotong-Liverpool University

### Members

Bo Li                           Hong Kong University of Science and
                                    Technology, China
Honghao Gao                     Shanghai University, China
Ning Gu                         Fudan University, China
Song Guo                        University of Aizu, Japan
Xiaofei Liao                    Huazhong University of Science and Technology,
                                    China

## Organizing Committee

### General Chair

Nikolaos Voros                  University of the Peloponnese, Greece

### General Co-chairs

Tasos Dagiuklas                 London South Bank University, UK
Xinheng Wang                    Xi'an Jiaotong-Liverpool University, China
Honghao Gao                     Shanghai University, China

### TPC Chair and Co-chairs

Christos Antonopoulos           University of the Peloponnese, Greece
Eleni Christopoulou             Ionian University, Greece
Dimitrios Ringas                Ionian University, Greece

**Sponsorship and Exhibit Chair**

Christina Politi                    University of the Peloponnese, Greece

**Local Chair**

Eleni Christopoulou                 Ionian University, Greece

**Workshops Chair**

Georgios Keramidas                  Aristotle University of Thessaloniki, Greece

**Publicity and Social Media Chair**

Katerina Lamprakopoulou             University of the Peloponnese, Greece

**Publications Chair**

Christos Antonopoulos               University of the Peloponnese, Greece

**Web Chair**

Evi Faliagka                        University of the Peloponnese, Greece

## Technical Program Committee

| | |
|---|---|
| Zhongqin Bi | Shanghai University of Electric Power, China |
| Shizhan Chen | Tianjing University, China |
| Lizhen Cui | Shandong University, China |
| Weilong Ding | North China University of Technology, China |
| Yucong Duan | Hainan University, China |
| Honghao Gao | Shanghai University, China |
| Fan Guisheng | East China University of Science and Technology, China |
| Haiping Huang | Nanjing University of Posts and Telecommunications, China |
| Li Kuang | Central South University, China |
| Youhuizi Li | Hangzhou Dianzi University, China |
| Rui Li | Xidian University, China |
| Xuan Liu | Yangzhou University, China |

# Contents – Part II

**Deep Learning and Applications**

Task Offloading in UAV-to-Cell MEC Networks: Cell Clustering and Path
Planning .......................................................... 3
    *Mingchu Li, Wanying Qi, and Shuai Li*

LAMB: Label-Induced Mixed-Level Blending for Multimodal Multi-label
Emotion Detection ..................................................... 20
    *Shuwei Qian, Ming Guo, Zhicheng Fan, Mingcai Chen,*
    *and Chongjun Wang*

MSAM: Deep Semantic Interaction Network for Visual Question
Answering .......................................................... 39
    *Fan Wang, Bin Wang, Fuyong Xu, Jiaxin Li, and Peiyu Liu*

Defeating the Non-stationary Opponent Using Deep Reinforcement
Learning and Opponent Modeling ..................................... 57
    *Qian Yao, Xinli Xiong, Peng Wang, and Yongjie Wang*

A Multi-Agent Deep Reinforcement Learning-Based Approach
to Mobility-Aware Caching ........................................... 79
    *Han Zhao, Shiyun Shao, Yong Ma, Yunni Xia, Jiajun Su, Lingmeng Liu,*
    *Kaiwei Chen, and Qinglan Peng*

D-AE: A Discriminant Encode-Decode Nets for Data Generation ............ 96
    *Gongju Wang, Yulun Song, Yang Li, Mingjian Ni, Long Yan, Bowen Hu,*
    *Quanda Wang, Yixuan Li, and Xingru Huang*

ECCRG: A Emotion- and Content-Controllable Response Generation
Model ............................................................. 115
    *Hui Chen, Bo Wang, Ke Yang, and Yi Song*

Origin-Destination Convolution Recurrent Network: A Novel OD Matrix
Prediction Framework ................................................ 131
    *Jiayu Chang, Tian Liang, Wanzhi Xiao, and Li Kuang*

MD-TransUNet: TransUNet with Multi-attention and Dilated Convolution
for Brain Stroke Lesion Segmentation ................................. 151
    *Jie Xu, Jian Wan, and Xin Zhang*

## Graph Computing

DGFormer: An Effective Dynamic Graph Transformer Based Anomaly
Detection Model for IoT Time Series ..................................... 173
   *Hongxia He, Xi Li, Peng Chen, Juan Chen, Weijian Song, and Qinghui Xi*

STAPointGNN: Spatial-Temporal Attention Graph Neural Network
for Gesture Recognition Using Millimeter-Wave Radar .................... 189
   *Jun Zhang, Chunyu Wang, Shunli Wang, and Lihua Zhang*

NPGraph: An Efficient Graph Computing Model in NUMA-Based
Persistent Memory Systems ............................................. 205
   *Baoke Li, Cong Cao, Fangfang Yuan, Yuling Yang, Majing Su,
   Yanbing Liu, and Jianhui Fu*

tHR-Net: A Hybrid Reasoning Framework for Temporal Knowledge Graph .... 223
   *Yijing Zhao, Yumeng Liu, Zihang Wan, and Hongan Wang*

Improving Code Representation Learning via Multi-view Contrastive
Graph Pooling for Abstract Syntax Tree ................................ 242
   *Ruoting Wu, Yuxin Zhang, and Liang Chen*

## Security and Privacy Protection

Protect Applications and Data in Use in IoT Environment Using
Collaborative Computing ............................................... 265
   *Xincai Peng, Li Shan Cang, Shuai Zhang, and Muddesar Iqbal*

Robustness-Enhanced Assertion Generation Method Based on Code
Mutation and Attack Defense .......................................... 281
   *Min Li, Shizhan Chen, Guodong Fan, Lu Zhang, Hongyue Wu,
   Xiao Xue, and Zhiyong Feng*

Secure Traffic Data Sharing in UAV-Assisted VANETs ..................... 301
   *Yilin Liu, Yujue Wang, Chen Yi, Yong Ding, Changsong Yang,
   and Huiyong Wang*

A Lightweight PUF-Based Group Authentication Scheme
for Privacy-Preserving Metering Data Collection in Smart Grid .......... 321
   *Ya-Nan Cao, Yujue Wang, Yong Ding, Zhenwei Guo, Changsong Yang,
   and Hai Liang*

A Semi-supervised Learning Method for Malware Traffic Classification
with Raw Bitmaps ................................................... 341
  Jingrun Ma, Xiaolin Xu, Tianning Zang, Xi Wang, Beibei Feng,
  and Xiang Li

Secure and Private Approximated Coded Distributed Computing Using
Elliptic Curve Cryptography ......................................... 357
  Houming Qiu and Kun Zhu

A Novel Semi-supervised IoT Time Series Anomaly Detection Model
Using Graph Structure Learning ..................................... 375
  Weijian Song, Peng Chen, Juan Chen, Yunni Xia, Xi Li, Qinghui Xi,
  and Hongxia He

Structural Adversarial Attack for Code Representation Models ............... 392
  Yuxin Zhang, Ruoting Wu, Jie Liao, and Liang Chen

An Efficient Authentication and Key Agreement Scheme for CAV Internal
Applications ....................................................... 414
  Yang Li, Qingyang Zhang, Wenwen Cao, Jie Cui, and Hong Zhong

**Processing and Recognition**

SimBPG: A Comprehensive Similarity Evaluation Metric for Business
Process Graphs .................................................... 437
  Qinkai Jiang, Jiaxing Wang, Bin Cao, and Jing Fan

Probabilistic Inference Based Incremental Graph Index for Similarity
Search on Social Networks .......................................... 458
  Tong Lu, Zhiwei Qi, Kun Yue, and Liang Duan

Cloud-Edge-Device Collaborative Image Retrieval and Recognition
for Mobile Web .................................................... 474
  Yakun Huang, Wenwei Li, Shouyi Wu, Xiuquan Qiao, Meng Guo,
  Hongshun He, and Yang Li

Contrastive Learning-Based Finger-Vein Recognition with Automatic
Adversarial Augmentation ........................................... 495
  Shaojiang Deng, Huaxiu Luo, Huafeng Qin, and Yantao Li

Multi-dimensional Sequential Contrastive Learning for QoS Prediction . . . . . . . .   514
  *Yuyu Yin, Qianhui Di, Yuanqing Zhang, Tingting Liang, Youhuizi Li,*
  *and Yu Li*

**Author Index** . . . . . . . . . . . . . . . . . . . . . . . . . . . . . . . . . . . . . . . . . . . . . . . . . . . . . .   533

# Deep Learning and Applications

# Task Offloading in UAV-to-Cell MEC Networks: Cell Clustering and Path Planning

Mingchu Li$^{(\boxtimes)}$, Wanying Qi, and Shuai Li

School of Software Technology, Dalian University of Technology,
Dalian 116620, China
mingchul@dlut.edu.cn

**Abstract.** When a natural disaster occurs, ground base stations (BSs) are destroyed and cannot provide communication services. Rapid restoration of communication is of great significance to the lives of trapped persons. This paper studies the problem of unmanned aerial vehicle (UAV) equipped with mobile edge computing (MEC) servers to provide communication and computing services for ground users in the scenario where the ground infrastructure is destroyed. We designed a UAV-to-Cell offloading system, which provides services in units of cells. By determining the hover locations (HLs) and trajectories, the UAV can handle more tasks with limited battery energy. Since tasks have time limit requirements, the order of processing will affect the task data size of the system. We solve this problem by joint cell clustering and path planning. Among them, elliptic clustering is used to divide the cells, the 3D position of the UAV is determined according to the quality of user service, and the double deep Q-network (DDQN) algorithm is used to determine the trajectory of the UAV. Simulation experiments demonstrate the effectiveness and efficiency of our proposed strategy by comparing it with the baselines.

**Keywords:** Unmanned aerial vehicle · Mobile edge computing · Task offloading · UAV trajectory · Double deep Q network

## 1 Introduction

With the rapid development of mobile Internet, smartphones and IoT devices are increasing day by day. An estimated 4.9 billion people are using the Internet in 2021 [1]. In the 5G era, emerging applications are flourishing, such as mobile payment, smart medical care, and virtual reality. To solve the problems in mobile communication, a new concept, Mobile Edge Computing (MEC) [2] is introduced. MEC deploys computing and storage resources at the edge of the mobile network to provide users with low-latency, high-bandwidth services, with more flexible deployment methods and wider application scenarios.

The number of natural disasters in the world has risen alarmingly in the first two decades of the 21st century, with a total of 7,348 disaster events recorded,

© ICST Institute for Computer Sciences, Social Informatics and Telecommunications Engineering 2024
Published by Springer Nature Switzerland AG 2024. All Rights Reserved
H. Gao et al. (Eds.): CollaborateCom 2023, LNICST 562, pp. 3–19, 2024.
https://doi.org/10.1007/978-3-031-54528-3_1

resulting in 1.23 million deaths [3]. How restore the communication facilities as soon as possible after the disaster is of great significance to the rescue of the trapped people. Compared with a static edge server, an unmanned aerial vehicle (UAV) has high mobility and can be flexibly deployed in most scenarios. In addition, the wireless communication link between UAV and ground equipment (UE) generally uses line-of-sight (LoS) wireless transmission, which can improve computing performance. Therefore, the UAV equipped with a MEC server can solve the above problems very well. How to provide communication services to more users is a key problem that needs to be solved.

This paper considers that the UAV provides services in units of cells. On the one hand, users with similar geographical locations may have the same type of tasks, and clusters can be naturally formed according to task types and geographical locations. On the other hand, because the purpose is to provide services to more users and handle more tasks, it can encourage users to form clusters and form greater competitiveness [4]. When the UAV server provides services, it must determine a suitable hovering location (HL) to ensure that all users in the cell can be covered and guarantee the quality of service (QoS). Due to technical limitations, the number of UAV servers that can be deployed may be very limited, especially in the chaotic hours after a natural disaster. In this paper, it is assumed that there is only one UAV server in the area to provide services for cell users. Since the task data size of each UE is different, it is more scientific to examine the energy efficiency of the UAV by taking the number of CPU cycles required for the total tasks as a measure.

In this paper, a UAV-to-Cell network is designed. We propose the problem of maximizing the CPU cycles required for the total tasks handled by the UAV, which are constrained by battery capacity. The main contributions are summarized as follows:

1. We build a UAV-to-Cell offloading system without ground infrastructure. The UAV hovers over the HL above the cell to provide services for users. To solve this problem, the optimization problem is decomposed into three independent sub-problems, namely, the ellipse clustering problem, the UAV 3D position problem, and the UAV trajectory planning problem.
2. We fit the users in the cell into an ellipse, and the optimization problem is to minimize the area of the ellipse. We calculate the number of clusters by hierarchical clustering based on the contour index and then calculate the ellipse by using the Lagrange multiplier method.
3. The 3D position of the UAV is constrained by the range of altitude and QoS for the user. Without loss of generality, we only need to consider the QoS of the most marginal users to ensure the QoS of all users in the cell.
4. Since each task has a delay requirement, the order of UAV HL selection has a great influence on the optimization problem. We adopt the path planning algorithm based on DDQN to solve the optimal path.

The rest of the paper is structured as follows. Section 2 presents related work. Section 3 illustrates the system model. Section 4 addresses the problem to be solved by dividing it into three subproblems. Section 5 illustrates performance evaluation. Section 6 presents conclusions.

# 2   Related Work

## 2.1   UAV Coverage

At present, there have been many studies on the problem of UAV 3D deployment and coverage. In [5], by studying the effects of UAV-UE antenna beam width, movement speed, and cell association on coverage probability, a framework for evaluating UAV network coverage performance is proposed. In [6], the provided mathematical model aims to determine the optimal low-altitude aerial platform (LAP) height that maximizes ground coverage while adhering to the maximum allowable path loss defined by the International Telecommunication Union (ITU). This optimal altitude is determined as a function of various urban environment statistics parameters. In [7], the author of the research proposed a path loss modeling method specifically tailored for the air-to-ground communication scenario involving LAPs in urban environments. In [8], the approach considers the placement of UAVs to achieve the best possible coverage in a given area, taking into account factors such as the number of UAVs, antenna gain, and beam width. In [9], the author's proposal introduces an "ellipse clustering algorithm" for optimizing the deployment of UAVs in a wireless communication network. This algorithm leverages the concept of ellipses to represent the radiation beam pattern of the UAVs' antennas, ensuring that QoS requirements are met while optimizing various parameters, including UAV positions, transmission power levels, and deployment density. The ultimate goal is to minimize the total energy consumption of the UAVs. In [10], the author's proposal introduces an "ellipse clustering algorithm" for optimizing the deployment of UAVs in a wireless communication network. This algorithm leverages the concept of ellipses to represent the radiation beam pattern of the UAVs' antennas, ensuring that QoS requirements are met while optimizing various parameters, including UAV positions, transmission power levels, and deployment density. The ultimate goal is to minimize the total energy consumption of the UAVs.

Most of the UAV coverage issues focus on dividing an area into multiple subareas, and each subarea has a UAV to provide services. The main difference is the clustering method or the method of calculating the optimal height.

## 2.2   Path Planning

Path planning is an important issue in UAV-MEC networks. In recent years, many studies have focused on path planning. Most of the solutions to path planning use traditional optimization algorithms. In [11], the path planning is transformed into a multi-objective optimization task, and the goals of the total path length and terrain threat level are optimized, and the UAV precise path planning is based on the enhanced multi-objective intelligent algorithm. In [4,12], the author employs an auction algorithm and a gap-adjusted branch-and-bound algorithm for determining the trajectory of a UAV or vehicle server in a communication or service delivery context with a focus on maximizing average throughput. In [13], the author's approach involves modeling the sub-region division problem as a semi-discrete optimal transport problem and solving it iteratively. Additionally, the UAV trajectory optimization problem is modeled as a traveling salesman problem (TSP) to find the shortest route. Some studies also explore the use of reinforcement learning algorithms for solving path-planning problems. In [14], through the application of DRL, the author achieves optimal path planning and task assignment for UAVs while minimizing task completion time and maximizing system efficiency. This is accomplished by constructing both a Q-network and a policy network. In [15], the proposed framework addresses trajectory planning for multiple UAVs within a MEC network. It leverages DRL techniques to determine optimal trajectories for these UAVs with the specific objectives of minimizing energy consumption and reducing latency for MEC tasks.

These papers do not take into account the limitations of the flying height and coverage of UAVs. They usually assume that the flying height of UAVs is a fixed value, which does not conform to the actual use of UAVs.

## 3   System Model

We consider a UAV-to-Cell MEC network serving a finite area $\mathcal{D}$ as shown in Fig. 1, where ground BSs are destroyed due to the natural disaster. There are a UAV server and $k \in [K]$ cells in the area $\mathcal{D}$ following random distribution, and the user equipments (UEs) in the cell obey the normal distribution. There are

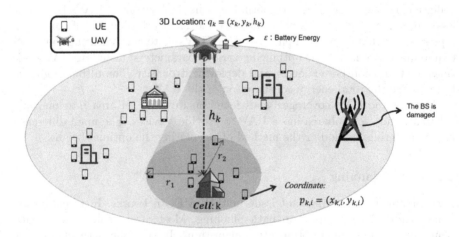

**Fig. 1.** Illusion of a UAV-to-Cell MEC network system.

$N$ UEs in area $\mathcal{D}$, and UE $i \in [N_k]$ in the cell $k$, it is obvious that $\sum_{i=1}^{k} N_i = N$. The UAV server stays at the hover locations (HLs) above each cell, and the UEs in this cell can offload tasks to the UAV. $q_k = (x_k, y_k, h_k)$ is a three-dimensional coordinate that represents the HL coordinate of the UAV server at the cell $s_k$. $p_{k,i} = (x_{k,i}, y_{k,i})$ represents the coordinates of UE $i$ in the cell $k$. In the cell $k$, the communication distance between the UAV server and UE $i$ is $d_{k,i} = \|q_k - p_{k,i}\|$. Each UE has a task $A_{k,i} = \{I_{k,i}, \beta_{k,i}, \tau_{k,i}\}$, where $I_{k,i}$ indicate the data size of the task, $\beta_{k,i}$ indicate the number of CPU cycles required per bit of the task, i.e., $I_{k,i} \cdot \beta_{k,i}$ indicate the total number of CPU cycles required to complete the task, $\tau_{k,i}$ indicate the task deadline. Beyond the deadline, the task can not be offloaded. We assume that the battery energy of the UAV server is not enough to handle the tasks of all cells, and when the remaining energy is not enough to handle the tasks of any cell, the UAV server will end the flight.

## 3.1 Communication Model

Non-orthogonal multiple access (NOMA) can improve spectral efficiency and is considered to be a promising multiple access technology for 5G networks. When the UAV server hovers over the cell $k$, the UEs in the cell $k$ offload their tasks to the UAV server for processing through NOMA technology. For the uplink link, we employ a probabilistic path loss model. The path loss between UE $i$ in the cell $k$ and the UAV server hovering over this cell is as follows:

$$PL_{k,i} = \begin{cases} FSPL_{k,i} + \varepsilon_{LoS}, & LoSLink \\ FSPL_{k,i} + \varepsilon_{NLoS}, & NLoSLink \end{cases} \tag{1}$$

where $FSPL_{k,i}$ is the free-space path loss between the $ith$ UE in the cell $k$ and the UAV server [7]. $FSPL_{k,i} = 20 log d_{k,i} + 20 \log (f_{MHz}) - 27.55$, where $f_{MHz}$ is the system center frequency in MHz. Variables $\varepsilon_{LoS}$ and $\varepsilon_{NLoS}$ are the additional path losses in dB. For the UAV-UE link, the LoS probability is $P_{k,i}^{LoS} = 1/(1 + a \cdot exp(-b[\theta_{k,i} - a]))$, where $\theta_{k,i}$ is the elevation angle between the UAV server and UE $i$ in the cell $k$, $a$ and $b$ are parameters reflecting the environmental impact. The NLOS probability is $P_{k,i}^{NLoS} = 1 - P_{k,i}^{LoS}$. The average path loss of the UAV-UE link:

$$\overline{PL}_{k,i} = FSPL_{k,i} + P_{k,i}^{LoS} \cdot \varepsilon_{LoS} + P_{k,i}^{NLoS} \cdot \varepsilon_{NLoS} \tag{2}$$

According to NOMA, sequential interference cancellation (SIC) is used by the user according to the channel condition. In the cell $k$, the channel between the UAV server and UE $i$ is represented by $h_{k,i} = \frac{g_{k,i}}{PL_{k,i}}$, where $g_{k,i}$ denotes Rayleigh fading channel gain [16]. The received signal-to-interference-plus-noise ratio (SINR) of UE $i$ can be expressed as

$$SINR_{k,i} = \frac{p_{k,i} \cdot |h_{k,i}|^2}{\sum_{j \neq i} p_{k,j} \cdot |h_{k,j}|^2 + \sigma^2} \tag{3}$$

where $p_{k,i}$ is the upload power of the UE, and $\sigma^2$ is the noise power, which represents the variance generated by all other signals and interference received during the receiving process. In this case, to guarantee QoS, $SINR_{k,i}$ of UE $i$ covered by UAV must be greater than the minimum SINR threshold $\delta_{th}$. Assume that the binary variable $a_{k,i}$ represents the permission control of UE $i$ task uploading in the cell $k$, if the processing completion time of UE $i$ does not exceed the task deadline, then $a_{k,i} = 1$, otherwise, $a_{k,i} = 0$. The achievable upload rate between UE $i$ and the UAV can be calculated:

$$
\begin{aligned}
R_{k,i}^u &= a_{k,i} \cdot B \cdot log(1 + SINR_{k,i}) \\
&= a_{k,i} \cdot B \cdot log(1 + \frac{p_{k,i} \cdot |h_{k,i}|^2}{\sum_{j \neq i} p_{k,j} \cdot |h_{k,j}|^2 + \sigma^2})
\end{aligned}
\tag{4}
$$

where $B$ is the wireless channel bandwidth. In the cell $k$, the transmission delay between UE $i$ and the UAV server is:

$$
t_{k,i}^u = \frac{a_{k,i} \cdot I_{k,i}}{R_{k,i}^u}
\tag{5}
$$

### 3.2 Computation Model

UAV energy consumption is composed of computing energy consumption, hovering energy consumption, flight energy consumption, and communication energy consumption. Since the proportion of communication energy consumption is very small compared with the other three parts [17], it is ignored in this paper.

**Computing Energy Consumption Model.** The computing energy consumption of the UAV server is determined by the task CPU cycles of the UE and the processing capacity of the UAV server. The CPU frequency of the UAV server is represented by $F_{UAV}$ (CPU cycles per second). The processing delay when the UAV server calculates the task $A_{k,i}$ is: $t_{k,i}^{com} = \frac{w_{k,i}}{F_{UAV}}$ where $w_{k,i} = a_{k,i} \cdot I_{k,i} \cdot \beta_{k,i}$ is the number of CPU cycles required to complete the task $A_{k,i}$.

In the cell $k$, the energy consumed by the UAV server to process the tasks of the UE $i$ is:

$$
E_{k,i}^{com} = P_{k,i}^{com} \cdot t_{k,i}^{com} = c \cdot w_{k,i} \cdot F_{UAV}^2
\tag{6}
$$

where $c$ is a constant that depends on the chip architecture of the UAV server [18]. The energy consumed by the UAV to process all UE tasks in the cell $k$ is:

$$
E_k^{com} = c \cdot \sum_{i=1}^{N_k} w_{k,i} \cdot F_{UAV}^2
\tag{7}
$$

**Hovering Energy Consumption Model.** When the UAV server hovers over the cell $k$, all qualified UEs will offload the task at the same time. Due to the different task data sizes and transmission rates of each UE, the arrival time of each task is different, and it needs to be queued for processing. First-come-first-serve (FCFS) queue schedule is adopted to ensure that tasks can be processed in a certain order. The time when the UE offloaded the last task is: $t^u_{k,last} = \max_i t^u_{k,i}$, the number of task CPU cycles completed by the UAV server is $w_{k,last} = t^u_{k,last}$ · $F_{UAV}$. Then the remaining task CPU cycles are $w_{k,res} = \sum_{i=1}^{N_k} w_{k,i} - w_{k,last}$, The hover delay of the UAV server at the cell $k$ is: $t^{hover}_k = t^u_{k,last} + w_{k,res}/F_{UAV}$. The hover energy consumption is:

$$E^{hover}_k = P_h \cdot t^{hover}_k$$

$$= P_h \cdot (\max_i t^u_{k,i} + \frac{\sum_{i=1}^{N_k} w_{k,i} - w_{k,last}}{F_{UAV}}) \tag{8}$$

where $P_h = \frac{F\sqrt{F}}{\eta\sqrt{\frac{1}{2}\pi cr^2 \rho}}$ is the hover power of the UAV [13].

**Flight Energy Consumption Model.** When the air resistance experienced by the UAV is equal to the weight of the UAV itself, the UAV's flight efficiency is the highest. This paper does not consider the acceleration changes when the UAV starts and stops, and the optimal flight speed of the UAV is: $v_{UAV} = \frac{2 \cdot o \cdot g}{\rho \cdot s \cdot \mu_f}$, where $o$ represents the weight of the UAV, $s$ represents the wing area, and $\mu_f$ represents the drag coefficient. The flight energy consumption of the UAV from the cell $k$ to $k+1$ is:

$$E^{fly}_{k,k+1} = P_m \cdot \frac{\|q_k - q_{k+1}\|}{v_{UAV}} \tag{9}$$

where $P_m = \frac{1}{2} \cdot \rho \cdot v_{UAV}^3 \cdot s \cdot \mu_f + v_{UAV} \cdot F_T$ is the flying power of the UAV. $F_T$ is the thrust of the UAV.

The total energy consumption of the UAV in area $\mathcal{D}$ is related to the path passed by the UAV. The path of the UAV is represented by the sequence of processed cells: $q_m, m \in [M], [M] \subseteq [K]$. The total energy consumption can be expressed as:

$$E_{total} = \sum_{m=1}^{M} (E^{com}_m + E^{hover}_m) + \sum_{m=1}^{M-1} E^{fly}_{m,m+1} \tag{10}$$

### 3.3  Problem Formulation

In the proposed UAV-to-Cell MEC network, processing as many task CPU cycles as possible is our goal. We maximize the total task CPU cycles handled by joint cell clustering and UAV path planning. Therefore, the optimization problem denoted by $P1$ can be formulated as:

$$P1: \quad \max_{k,m,q_k} \sum_{m=1}^{M} \sum_{i=1}^{N_m} w_{m,i}$$

$$s.t. \quad C1: \quad \sum_{k=1}^{K} |N_k| = N,$$

$$C2: \quad \text{SINR}_{k,i} \geq \delta_{\text{th}}, \quad (k \in K, i \in N_k)$$
$$C3: \quad h_{\min} \leq h_k \leq h_{\max}, \quad (k \in K)$$
$$C4: \quad E_{\text{total}} \leq \epsilon,$$
$$C5: \quad a_{k,i} \in \{0, 1\}, \quad (k \in K, i \in N_k)$$
$$C6: \quad (2) - (3), (7) - (10)$$

Constraint C1 ensures that the area division covers all UEs, and constraint C2 guarantees the QoS of UEs. Since the flying height of the UAV is limited, constraint C3 ensures that the flying height of the UAV is within the allowable range. Constraint C4 means that the total energy consumption of the UAV cannot exceed the total battery capacity of the UAV. Through the above formula, we can observe that the $SINR_{k,i}$ in C2 and the energy consumption in C4 are related to the UAV coordinates, so the constraints C2, C4, and C3 are coupled. Constraint C5 indicates whether the task $A_{k,i}$ can be offloaded to the UAV for processing.

# 4    Problem Analysis and Algorithm

Problem P1 is a MINLP problem, and it is very difficult to solve directly. The optimization variables $k$ and $m$ are independent of each other. We can use the coordinates of the UAV as an entry point, and we can convert problem $P1$ into three sub-problems, namely the ellipse clustering problem, the UAV 3D location problem, and the UAV path planning problem.

## 4.1    Ellipse Clustering Problem

Due to the practical radiation beam pattern being an ellipse, we consider the UAV server to cover the UEs in an ellipse by adjusting the orientation of the UAV and the HPBWs of the antenna [9]. In the process of rescuing trapped people, each user must be clustered into a cell. Firstly, the UEs on the ground are processed by hierarchical clustering based on the contour index, and the UEs can be merged into $K$ clusters according to the similarity of the user coordinates. After determining the number of clusters $K$, the users are fitted into an ellipse with the smallest area. For the $kth$ cluster, the problem $P2$ can be expressed as:

$$P2: \quad \min_{a_k, b_k, x_k, y_k} \pi \cdot a_k \cdot b_k$$
$$\text{s.t.} \quad \frac{(x_i - x_k)^2}{a_k^2} + \frac{(y_i - y_k)^2}{b_k^2} \leq 1 \quad i \in N_k$$

where $a_k, b_k$ is the semi-major axis and the semi-minor axis of the ellipse respectively, $(x_k, y_k)$ are the center coordinates of the ellipse, and $(x_i, y_i)$ are the coordinates of the UE $i$ in cluster $k$. This is a nonlinear optimization problem with constraints. The following Lagrangian function can be obtained by converting the constraints into the form of Lagrange multipliers: $L(a_k, b_k, x_k, y_k, \lambda_i) =$

$\pi a_k b_k + \sum_{i=1}^{N_k} \lambda_i \left(1 - \frac{(x_i - x_k)^2}{a_k^2} - \frac{(y_i - y_k)^2}{b_k^2}\right)$ where $\lambda_i$ is the Lagrange multiplier. Let $\frac{\partial L}{\partial a_k} = \frac{\partial L}{\partial b_k} = \frac{\partial L}{\partial x_k} = \frac{\partial L}{\partial y_k} = \frac{\partial L}{\partial \lambda_i} = 0$. This system of equations can be solved using the gradient descent method. The specific implementation process is shown in Algorithm 1.

---

**Algorithm 1.** Ellipse Clustering algorithm

---

**Input:** $U$ : Coordinates of UEs; $K_{max}$ : Maximum clusters; $\alpha$ : Learning rate; $I_{max}$ : Maximum iterations

**Output:** Number of clusters $K$; Ellipse fit parameters $(a_k, b_k, x_k, y_k)$

1: Calculate the distance matrix $M_d = Dist_{Matrix}(U)$
2: Initialize the list of silhouette coefficients $Silh_{scores} \leftarrow \{\}$
3: **for** $k = 2$ to $K_{max}$ **do**
4:     $M_{link} = Hierarchy_{Linkage}(M_d)$
5:     $clusters = Hierarchy_{Fcluster}(M_{link}, k)$
6:     $Silh_{scores} \leftarrow Silhouette_{Score}(M_d, clusters)$
7: **end for**
8: **if** $np.argmax(Silh_{scores}) \neq 0$ **then**
9:     $K = np.argmax(Silh_{scores}) + 2$
10: **else**
11:     $K = 2$
12: **end if**
13: $U_k = AgglomerativeClustering(K)$
14: **for** $k = 1$ to $K$ **do**
15:     **for** $i = 0$ to $I_{max}$ **do**
16:         $\lambda_{i+1} = \lambda_i - \alpha \frac{\partial L}{\partial \lambda}$,
17:         $a_{i+1} = a_i - \alpha \frac{\partial L}{\partial a}$, $b_{i+1} = b_i - \alpha \frac{\partial L}{\partial b}$, $x_{i+1} = x_i - \alpha \frac{\partial L}{\partial x}$, $y_{i+1} = y_i - \alpha \frac{\partial L}{\partial y}$
18:     **end for**
19:     $a_k = a_i, b_k = b_i, x_k = x_i, y_k = y_i$
20: **end for**

---

### 4.2 The UAV 3D Location Problem

The UEs of the cell are divided into an ellipse cluster according to the coordinates. We take the center of the ellipse cluster as the plane coordinates $(x_k, y_k)$ of the HL. We assume that the azimuth and elevation HPBWs of the UAV directional antenna are not equal, and they are expressed as $\theta_1, \theta_2 \in (0°, 90°)$, as shown in the Fig. 2.

Our goal is to determine a suitable UAV height and HPBWs angle, which minimizes the UAV's communication energy consumption and hovering energy consumption. We achieve this by minimizing the path loss between the UAV and the UEs. To guarantee the QoS of all UEs, we only need to guarantee the QoS between the farthest edge UE and the UAV of the cell. In the cell $k$, the UE farthest from the UAV is $N_e$, and its coordinates are $p_{k,e} = (x_{k,e}, y_{k,e})^T$.

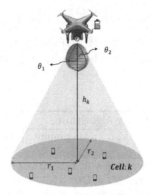

**Fig. 2.** Downlink between the UAV and UEs in the cell $k$.

$\overline{PL_e}$ is the average path loss of the cell edge UE which is farthest from the UAV. Problem $P3$ can be formulated as:

$$P3: \quad \min_{h_k} \overline{PL_e}$$

$$\text{s.t.} \quad h_{\min} \leq h_k \leq h_{\max} \quad (k \in K)$$

$$\text{SINR}_e \geq \delta_{\text{th}}$$

Figure 3 shows the average path loss for UAV heights for different environments and horizontal distances. From the Fig. 3, we can observe that the average path loss of UEs increases with the horizontal distance. But when the UAV height is too low, the influence of NLoS links dominates the path loss, which leads to a sharp increase in the average path loss. According to the quasi-convexity of $\overline{PL_e}$, we have to find $h^*$ that minimizes $\overline{PL_e}$ under $h_{min} \leq h^* \leq h_{max}$. Finally, using this result, we can also finalize the corresponding HPBWs for the UAV: $\theta_i = tan^{-1}(\frac{h^*}{r_i})$ $(i = 1, 2)$, where $r_i$ represents the major/minor axis of the ellipse.

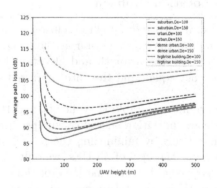

**Fig. 3.** The average path loss for UAV heights.

## 4.3    The UAV Path Planning Problem

---

**Algorithm 2.** DDQN-based Path Planning algorithm

---

**Input:** $M$ : Training rounds; $N$ : Training times; **batch_size** : Sample size
**Output:** DDQN model
 1: Initialize the weight parameters of the main network $Q(\delta, a)$ and the target network
     $Q'(\delta, a)$
 2: Initialize experience replay buffer $D$
 3: **for** $eposide = 0$ to $M$ **do**
 4:      Initialize the environment
 5:      Initialize state $\delta_0$
 6:      **for** $t = 0$ to $N$ **do**
 7:           Observe the current state of the environment $\delta_t$, and choosing an action based
     on the main network $a_t$.
 8:           Execute action $a_t$, observing reward $\imath_t$, the next state $\delta_{t+1}$ and end condition
     *done*.
 9:           **if** done **then**
10:                break
11:           **end if**
12:           $D \leftarrow (\delta_t, a_t, \imath_t, \delta_{t+1})$
13:      **end for**
14:      **if** $len(D) >$ **batch_size then**
15:           Randomly sample a batch of data from the experience replay buffer for
     training the main network $Q(\delta, a)$.
16:           Update the weight parameters of the main network according to the differ-
     ence between the $Q$ value and the target $Q$ value.
17:      **end if**
18:      **if** $epsoide\%10 = 0$ **then**
19:           Copy the weight parameters of the main network to the target network
20:      **end if**
21: **end for**

---

The coordinates of the HL in each cell have been determined, and the method of deep reinforcement learning can be used for path planning. In our DDQN model, the UAV acts as an agent that feeds back the current state in real time and determines the best action by interacting with the environment, to maximize the observed reward $\imath_t$ in the decision step. At each step $t$, the UAV observes the state $\delta_t$ from the state space, then selects an action $a_t$ based on the Q network. DDQN-based path planning algorithm is proposed as Algorithm 2. First, we define the state, action, and reward of the UAV environment.

- State $\delta$: The state represents a set of information about the current situation of the environment, including the current remaining battery energy of the UAV ($e^{res}$), the location of the UAV ($p^{UAV}$), the remaining task CPU cycles of each cell ($w_k$), and the positions of all HLs ($q_k$). In each episode, the initial state of the UAV is randomly determined.

- Action $a$: The action refers to the UAV choosing the next HL according to the current state $s$. We use the $\varepsilon$-greedy algorithm to select an action, and $\varepsilon$ will continue to decrease each round until it reaches a threshold.
- Reward $r$: The reward is a scalar indicating how good or bad the action $a$ is for the agent in its current state $s$. In our DDQN model, after the UAV determines the action $a$ according to the state $s$, we take the task CPU cycles in the selected cell $k$ as the reward. If the selected HL has been processed before, a penalty is given.

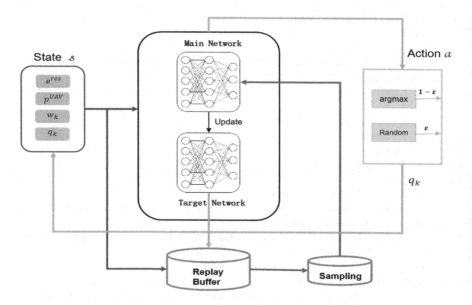

**Fig. 4.** Schematic of the proposed DDQN-based path planning algorithm.

The schematic of the proposed DDQN-based path planning algorithm is shown in Fig. 4. Then, preprocess the initial state $s_0$ to normalize the data. Then use a Deep-Learning Neural Network (DNN) to fit a function for generating the Q value. The input of the DNN is the state, and the output is an estimate of the value function for each possible action. During training, the reward is updated based on the current state, the action chosen, the reward obtained, and the next state. The updated formula is:

$$Q(s_t, a_t) \leftrightarrow r_t + \gamma Q'(s_{t+1}, \arg\max_a Q(s_{t+1}, a)) \tag{11}$$

where $s_t, a_t$ indicates the current state and action at step $t$. $r_t$ is the reward at the $t$ step. $\gamma$ is the discount factor ($0 \leq \gamma < 1$) which determines the importance of future rewards. It controls how the value function of the current state will be affected by future rewards.

We have introduced a penalty mechanism for some bad actions, for example, when the UAV is not moving or the UAV is flying to a HL that has been processed, we set the reward to a negative value. During the learning and updating process, we use the experience replay buffer to update and store the collected environment samples. At each step, the observed state, action, reward, and next state are stored in it. The sequence of states is then randomly sampled in mini-batches from the buffer to update the DDQN network.

## 5  Simulation and Experiment

**Table 1.** Simulation parameters

| Simulation parameters | Value |
|---|---|
| Bandwidth $B$ | 10 MHz |
| Noise power $\sigma^2$ | $-100$ dBm |
| CPU frequency $F_{UAV}$ | 1.2 GHz |
| Battery capacity $\epsilon$ | 30 kJ, 50 kJ |
| SINR threshold $\delta_{th}$ | 0 dB |
| Additional path losses $\varepsilon_{LoS}$, $\varepsilon_{NLoS}$ | 3 dB, 34 dB |
| Air density $\rho$ | 1.225 $kg/m^3$ |
| Weight $o$ [21] | 2 kg |
| Wing area $s$ | 0.5 $m^2$ |
| Drag coefficient $u_f$ | 0.05 |

In this section, we conduct simulation experiments to verify the effectiveness and efficiency of our solution, and numerical results are given. We assume that the UAV-to-Cell MEC network includes a UAV, and the number of UEs is 600, where these UEs are distributed in an area of $2 \times 2$ $km^2$ [4]. Each UE has one task waiting to be processed, the task data size varies between $[10, 30]$ MB, and the upload power of each UE varies between $[0.1, 0.6]$ W. Assuming that the computing resources of the UAV are sufficient, the CPU frequency of the UAV is $F_{UAV} = 1.2$ GHz [18]. The power of the UAV is insufficient to provide services for the UEs in all cells, and the battery capacity $\epsilon = 30$ kJ, the bandwidth $B = 10$ MHz [19], the noise power $\sigma^2 = -100$ dBm [18,20]. In the free-space path loss model, the additional path losses for LoS and NLoS are $\varepsilon_{LoS} = 3$ dB and $\varepsilon_{NLoS} = 34$ dB [9], respectively. The simulation environment parameters are shown in Table 1.

To verify the high efficiency of our proposed strategy (DDQN), we compare it with the following baselines.

- DDQN-FH: The HL height of the UAV is fixed at $h = 200$, and the DDQN algorithm is used for path planning. It should be noted that the flight power of horizontal flight is slightly less than that of oblique flight.

- Greedy-R: Determine the height of the HL of the UAV according to the SINR, and use the ratio of task CPU cycles to energy consumption as the optimal choice in the current state.
- Greedy-MD: The HL height of the UAV is determined according to the SINR, and the nearest HL is taken as the next choice.

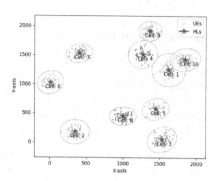

**Fig. 5.** UEs-UAV associations based on ellipse clustering.

Figure 5 shows the results of our proposed ellipse clustering. The UEs of each cell are fitted into an ellipse, and the center of the ellipse is the horizontal coordinate of the HL of the UAV. We assume that UAV only provides services for the currently hovering cells, even if the results of ellipse fitting may overlap and do not generate inter-cell interference.

The trajectory of the UAV is shown in the Fig. 6, which is a path calculated according to the algorithm proposed in this paper. The red point indicates the 3D HL of the UAV in different cells, and the blue line indicates the path of the UAV. The starting cell is 4 and the end cell is 7. Since the initial HL is randomly generated, we calculate the reward of each path, choose a path with the largest reward, and draw it, as shown in Fig. 7. The size of the HL in the figure indicates the relative number of task CPU cycles of the cell. It can be observed that the number of cells selected by the Greedy-MD and Greed-R algorithms is smaller than that of the reinforcement learning algorithm. The Greed-R algorithm tends to select cells with smaller energy consumption and larger task CPU cycles. The Greedy-MD algorithm selects the nearest HL as the next HL, without considering the task CPU cycle size of the hovering cell, resulting in performance loss. Both DDQN and DDQN-FH algorithms select cell 1 and cell 10, which are relatively closer and have larger task CPU cycles, which are relatively better.

Energy efficiency refers to the total task CPU cycles processed by the UAV divided by the energy consumption of the UAV, which can reflect the energy consumed by the UAV to process each task CPU cycle. Figure 8 shows the training results of average reward over different algorithms. Because the setting of the reward is the ratio of the task amount to the energy consumption, the Energy

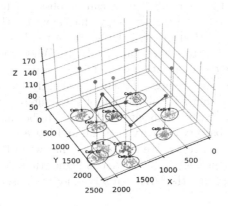

**Fig. 6.** The UAV 3D trajectory for DDQN.

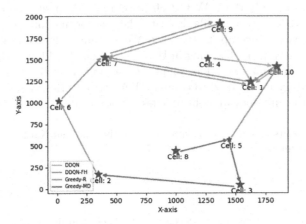

**Fig. 7.** Illustration of the UAV trajectories based on four algorithms.

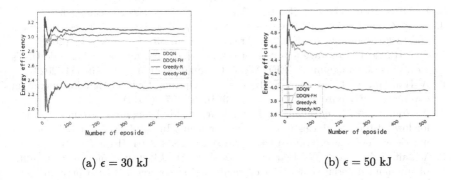

(a) $\epsilon = 30$ kJ                    (b) $\epsilon = 50$ kJ

**Fig. 8.** Comparison of the energy efficiency with four algorithms

efficiency is a value between $[1.8, 3.2]$. It can be observed from the figure that our proposed algorithm has a higher energy efficiency than the other three algorithms. In the DDQN-FH algorithm, the height of the UAV is fixed at 200 m, and the path loss is greater than that of DDQN. When the signal drops to a certain level, reliable communication cannot be carried out, and problems such as packet loss occur. The Energy efficiency is slightly lower than the DDQN algorithm. In order to meet the limitation of the limited power of the UAV in this paper, we set the battery capacity of the UAV to be small. Figure 8a is the case where the UAV battery capacity is 30 kJ, and Fig. 8b is the case where the UAV battery capacity is 50 kJ. We can observe that when the battery capacity is 50 kJ, the energy efficiency of the system is higher than 30 kJ. Because of the increased battery capacity, the UAV can serve more cell users.

## 6   Conclusion

In this paper, we study the UAV-to-Cell MEC network in situations where the ground infrastructure is unavailable, with the goal of maximizing the number of task CPU cycles to complete the task. We combine cell clustering and path planning to achieve task offloading in UAV networks. Considering the radiation pattern of the antenna, we adopt elliptic clustering to realize unit clustering. A DDQN strategy is proposed to compute UAV trajectories. Simulation results demonstrate the efficiency and effectiveness of our strategy.

**Acknowledgments.** This paper is supported by the National Nature Science Foundation of China under grant number: T2350710232.

## References

1. ITU, DBM.: Measuring digital development - Facts and figures 2021. ITU Publication (2021)
2. Luo, Q., Hu, S., Li, C., Li, G., Shi, W.: Resource scheduling in edge computing: a survey. IEEE Commun. Surv. Tutor. **23**(4), 2131–2165 (2021)
3. UNDRR: Human cost of disaster - An overview of the last 20 years (2020)
4. Ning, Z., et al.: 5G-enabled UAV-to-community offloading: joint trajectory design and task scheduling. IEEE J. Sel. Areas Commun. **39**(11), 3306–3320 (2021)
5. Sun, H., et al.: Coverage analysis for cellular-connected random 3D mobile UAVs with directional antennas. IEEE Wirel. Commun. Lett. **12**(3), 550–554 (2023)
6. Al-Hourani, A., Kandeepan, S., Lardner, S.: Optimal LAP altitude for maximum coverage. IEEE Wirel. Commun. Lett. **3**(6), 569–572 (2014)
7. Al-Hourani, A., Kandeepan, S., Jamalipour, A.: Modeling air-to-ground path loss for low altitude platforms in urban environments. In: 2014 IEEE Global Communications Conference (GLOBECOM 2014), pp. 2898–2904. IEEE (2014)
8. Mozaffari, M., Saad, W., Bennis, M., Debbah, M.: Efficient deployment of multiple unmanned aerial vehicles for optimal wireless coverage. IEEE Commun. Lett. **20**(8), 1647–1650 (2016)

9. Noh, S.C., Jeon, H.B., Chae, C.B.: Energy-efficient deployment of multiple UAVs using ellipse clustering to establish base stations. IEEE Wirel. Commun. Lett. **9**(8), 1155–1159 (2020)
10. Babu, N., Virgili, M., Papadias, C.B., Popovski, P., Forsyth, A.J.: Cost- and energy-efficient aerial communication networks with interleaved hovering and flying. IEEE Trans. Veh. Technol. **70**(9), 9077–9087 (2021)
11. Wan, Y., Zhong, Y., Ma, A., Zhang, L.: An accurate UAV 3-D path planning method for disaster emergency response based on an improved multiobjective swarm intelligence algorithm. IEEE Trans. Cybern. **53**(4), 2658–2671 (2023)
12. Liu, Y., Li, Y., Niu, Y., Jin, D.: Joint optimization of path planning and resource allocation in mobile edge computing. IEEE Trans. Mob. Comput. **19**(9), 2129–2144 (2020)
13. Wang, D., Tian, J., Zhang, H., Wu, D.: Task offloading and trajectory scheduling for UAV-enabled MEC networks: an optimal transport theory perspective. IEEE Wirel. Commun. Lett. **11**(1), 150–154 (2022)
14. Chang, H., Chen, Y., Zhang, B., Doermann, D.: Multi-UAV mobile edge computing and path planning platform based on reinforcement learning. IEEE Trans. Emerg. Top. Comput. Intell. **6**(3), 489–498 (2021)
15. Wang, L., Wang, K., Pan, C., Xu, W., Aslam, N., Hanzo, L.: Multi-agent deep reinforcement learning-based trajectory planning for multi-UAV assisted mobile edge computing. IEEE Trans. Cogn. Commun. Netw. **7**(1), 73–84 (2021)
16. Zhang, N., Wang, J., Kang, G., Liu, Y.: Uplink nonorthogonal multiple access in 5G systems. IEEE Commun. Lett. **20**(3), 458–461 (2016)
17. Zeng, Y., Zhang, R.: Energy-efficient UAV communication with trajectory optimization. IEEE Trans. Wirel. Commun. **16**(6), 3747–3760 (2017)
18. Hu, Q., Cai, Y., Yu, G., Qin, Z., Zhao, M., Li, G.Y.: Joint offloading and trajectory design for UAV-enabled mobile edge computing systems. IEEE Internet Things J. **6**(2), 1879–1892 (2019)
19. Zhang, T., Xu, Y., Loo, J., Yang, D., Xiao, L.: Joint computation and communication design for UAV-assisted mobile edge computing in IoT. IEEE Trans. Industr. Inf. **16**(8), 5505–5516 (2019)
20. Zhang, K., Gui, X., Ren, D., Li, D.: Energy-latency tradeoff for computation offloading in UAV-assisted multiaccess edge computing system. IEEE Internet Things J. **8**(8), 6709–6719 (2020)
21. Lyu, L., Zeng, F., Xiao, Z., Zhang, C., Jiang, H., Havyarimana, V.: Computation bits maximization in UAV-enabled mobile-edge computing system. IEEE Internet Things J. **9**(13), 10640–10651 (2021)

# LAMB: Label-Induced Mixed-Level Blending for Multimodal Multi-label Emotion Detection

Shuwei Qian[1,2](✉) , Ming Guo[1,2] , Zhicheng Fan[1,2] , Mingcai Chen[1,2] ,
and Chongjun Wang[1,2]

[1] State Key Laboratory for Novel Software Technology, Nanjing University,
Nanjing, China
{gm,fanzc,chenmc}@smail.nju.edu.cn,
chjwang@nju.edu.cn, qiansw@smail.nju.edu.cn
[2] Department of Computer Science and Technology, Nanjing University,
Nanjing, China

**Abstract.** To better understand complex human emotions, there is
growing interest in utilizing heterogeneous sensory data to detect multiple co-occurring emotions. However, existing studies have focused on
extracting static information from each modality, while overlooking various interactions within and between modalities. Additionally, the label-
to-modality and label-to-label dependencies still lack exploration. In
this paper, we propose **LA**bel-induced Mixed-level **B**lending (**LAMB**)
to address these challenges. Mixed-level blending leverages shallow but
manifold self-attention and cross-attention encoders in parallel to model
unimodal context dependency and cross-modal interaction simultaneously. This is in contrast to previous works either use one of them or
cascade them successively, which ignores the diversity of interaction in
multimodal data. LAMB also employs label-induced aggregation to allow
different labels to attend to the most relevant blended tokens adaptively
using a transformer-based decoder, which facilitates the exploration of
label-to-modality dependency. Unlike common low-order strategies in
multi-label learning, correlations among multiple labels can be learned by
self-attention in label embedding space before being treated as queries.
Comprehensive experiments demonstrate the effectiveness of our methods for multimodal multi-label emotion detection.

**Keywords:** multimodal fusion · multi-label classification · emotion
detection

## 1 Introduction

Detecting emotions plays a vital role in many real-world applications. For example, accurate recognition of emotions is crucial to maintain the high quality
of user interaction in some dialogue systems and virtual reality. Moreover, the

H. Gao et al. (Eds.): CollaborateCom 2023, LNICST 562, pp. 20–38, 2024.
https://doi.org/10.1007/978-3-031-54528-3_2

emotional tendencies of the population towards a specific topic on social media can be used to predict large-scale events, such as the general election. With the massive multimodal data accumulated on the Internet, multimodal learning has become a leading approach to this problem. The core challenge of multimodal learning comes from various modality heterogeneity in representation, structure, and semantics.

Since transformer prevails in machine learning, attention mechanisms [23] have become the de-facto paradigm for multimodal representation, alignment, and fusion [1]. Attention mechanisms aggregate values based on the compatibility or similarity between the corresponding keys and the queries. When queries are selected from different modalities, the aggregation patterns of values vary. However, previous works have utilized either self-attention [23] to extract unimodal features or cross-attention [21] to capture cross-modal long-term dependency, ignoring the diverse nature of interaction in multimodal data. In some cases, the context of language modality dominates the labels of the utterance. Taking non-language modality as queries will introduce noise impeding the learning process in such situations. Conversely, utilizing self-attention independently for each modality overlooks the potential interactions among modalities in other cases. Preserving interactions as manifold as possible contributes to a more flexible and powerful fusion.

In addition, most approaches in multimodal emotion detection focus on single-label classification or regression [28, 29]. When it comes to the multi-label setting, two additional challenges arise: label-to-modality dependency and label-to-label dependency. Individual labels are influenced by various interactions differently, whereas single-label methods use the same representation for all label classifications. Some emotions, such as anger, often rely more on the coordination of facial expressions and tone of voice than others, which implies different labels depend on different multimodal interactions. Two-stage methods that cascade a multi-label classifier immediately after the unified representation fail to capture the label-to-modality dependency. Besides, some labels tend to co-occur together frequently. For example, people often experience several negative emotions simultaneously when feeling down. This correlation among labels can be used as a priori to guide feature extraction and fusion. Current low-order strategies for multi-label learning discard label correlations [3,5,37] or explore simple pairwise correlations [7,9,10,18] and cannot capture complex correlations among multiple labels.

To tackle these challenges, we propose a method known as **LA**bel-induced **M**ixed-level **B**lending (**LAMB**) for multimodal multi-label emotion detection. Mixed-level blending leverages shallow but diverse self-attention and cross-attention encoders in parallel to model unimodal context dependencies and cross-modal interaction simultaneously. This parallel architecture differs from approaches that stack layers deeply. In this way is retained the diversity of the interactions in multimodal data. Furthermore, LAMB also employs label-induced aggregation to acquire label-specific representations via a transformer-based decoder, which enables the exploration of label-to-modality dependency. Each label embedding selectively attends to the most relevant blended tokens via cross-attention, adapting to the discriminative information of different emotions. In contrast to common low-order strategies in multi-label learning, correlations among multiple labels are learned by self-attention in label embedding space before being treated as queries to the cross-attention.

Our main contributions can be summarised as follows:

- We propose mixed-level blending, a shallow but manifold architecture with multiple parallel encoders, to preserve diverse interactions of multimodal data, which is essential to a more flexible and powerful fusion.
- We design label-induced aggregation that learns label-specific representations for multiple labels via a transformer-based decoder with self-attention among labels, to explore label-to-modality and label-to-label dependencies.
- Extensive experiments on aligned and unaligned settings demonstrate the superiority of the proposed LAMB and validate the dependencies among modalities and labels.

## 2 Related Works

### 2.1 Multimodal Emotion Detection

Relevant works of multimodal emotion detection mainly focus on three challenges: representation, alignment, and fusion.

Representation aims to turn data from different sources with distinct structures into an informative and learnable format to facilitate the coordination of modalities. FDMER [28] and MFSA [29] learn modality-specific and modality-agnostic representations, improving task predictions from the holistic and disentangled views. Self-MM [31] aids the multimodal task via acquiring independent unimodal representations with a self-supervised learning strategy. The vast majority of current works first adopt heterogeneous models to extract unimodal representations from each modality independently, such as LSTM networks for audio and CNN for vision, and leave multimodal representations to the fusion stage.

Alignment refers to identifying the corresponding relationship between subcomponents from one or more modalities of the same instance, which helps to explore the commonality among modalities for a robust prediction. The challenge arises from asynchronous sampling rates and semantic gaps in modalities. CTC network [11] is a typical explicit alignment method that models a probability distribution over all possible label sequences by RNN without pre-segmented data and maximizes the probabilities of the correct one. In order to reuse pretrained language models, MAG+ [40] proposes an adapter module consisting of cross-modal attention and dynamic gating to align audio and vision with language. PMR [16] introduces a message hub to exchange information across all modalities and progressively reinforces unaligned features. Apart from utilizing alignment modules, there are some works performing alignment by additional objectives. MICA [14] designs a loss function that maximizes mean discrepancy to align the marginal distribution.

Fusion integrates the complementarity of the multimodal data to get a more comprehensive view of the downstream tasks. Previous works have explored various sophisticated fusion mechanisms to achieve this goal, including tensor-based, graph-based, gating-based [19], attention-based methods, etc. TFN [32] and LMF [15] use the outer product between vectors to fuse different levels of multimodal interactions but suffer from large memory costs and computational load. DFG [33] builds a graph where vertices are modal sets and edges denote their inclusion relationship, and fuse modalities via an output vertex connected to all vertices. MISA [12] performs a multi-head self-attention on a concatenation of all the transformed modality vectors to make each vector aware of other modal representations.

There are some noticeable differences between our work and these available works. LAMB exploits multiple label-specific representations for multi-label classification rather than a fixed representation for all labels. Before fusion, it preserves more multimodal dynamics than static modality-specific representations. Besides, our method does not assume alignment between modalities and can be naturally extended to asynchronous multimodal data thanks to the attention mechanism.

## 2.2  Multi-label Learning

The key challenge of multi-label Learning lies in how to cope with the exponentially growing output space. Although the output space of multi-label data is intimidatingly enormous, labels are not completely separate from each other. Relevant strategies that take advantage of label correlations could be broadly divided into three categories according to the order of label correlations: first-order strategies, second-order strategies, and high-order strategies.

First-order strategies explore labels one-by-one, without considering the relationships among them [3]. The simplest one is a linear classifier with a sigmoid function. Second-order strategies introduce pairwise relations of multiple labels but fail to manage complex real-world applications due to the limitation of their hypothesis [9]. High-order strategies build more complicated label relations to discover effective exploitation of the label correlations [20].

It has been demonstrated in various studies [8,24,38,41] that modeling label correlations can significantly improve classification performance. One example is the use of MLGCN [4], which constructs a label correlation matrix that facilitates the dissemination of information among the nodes in GCN. Other works [13,35,36] have explored label-specific strategies that are efficient for multi-label learning. For instance, LSAN [27] learns the label-specific representation for each document by grabbing the label-related component and computing semantic relations between document words and labels.

In contrast to the above studies, LAMB focuses on multi-label emotion detection in multimodal application scenarios. In addition to label-to-label coexistence, LAMB empowers labels to guide multimodal fusion. Allowing labels to attend diverse multimodal dynamics adaptively is beneficial to exploring label-to-modality dependency, an aspect that remains underdeveloped in other relevant works.

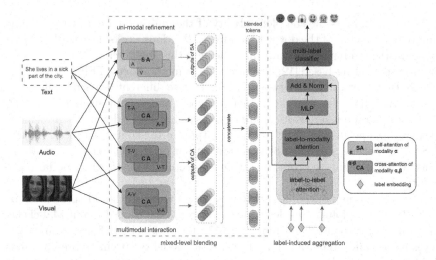

**Fig. 1.** The overall structure of LAMB. It first encoders different modality tokens by mixed-level blending consisting of unimodal refinement and multimodal interaction modules. All the outputted tokens of both modules are concatenated as blended tokens. Then, these blended tokens and learnable label embeddings are fed into a decoder followed by a linear multi-label classifier.

## 3 Approach

### 3.1 Problem Formulation

The goal of multimodal multi-label emotion detection is to predict a set of emotions by utilizing text $T$, audio $A$, and visual frames $V$. We denote a training dataset with $N$ instances as $\mathcal{D} = \{((\mathbf{X}_T, \mathbf{X}_A, \mathbf{X}_V)_i, \mathbf{Y}_i)\}_{i=1}^N$. Individual elements in the $i$th instance $(\mathbf{X}_T, \mathbf{X}_A, \mathbf{X}_V)_i$ are from the original text space $\mathcal{X}^T = \mathbb{R}^{\tau_T \times d_T}$, audio space $\mathcal{X}^A = \mathbb{R}^{\tau_A \times d_A}$, visual space $\mathcal{X}^V = \mathbb{R}^{\tau_V \times d_V}$ respectively, where $\tau_\alpha$ and $d_\alpha$ are the maximum sequence length and dimension of modality $\alpha \in \{T, A, V\}$. The label set is $\mathcal{Y} = \{1, 2, \cdots, c\}$, where $c = |\mathcal{Y}|$ is the total number of labels. The task aims to learn a mapping $\mathcal{F} : \mathcal{X}^T \times \mathcal{X}^A \times \mathcal{X}^V \to 2^{\mathcal{Y}}$ from multiple modalities' joint space to the label space's power set. Since each instance may contain varying numbers of labels, its label set is a subset of $\mathcal{Y}$.

### 3.2 Overview

As depicted in Fig. 1, LAMB primarily comprises two components: mixed-level blending and label-induced aggregation. In the initial stage, the multimodal data is passed through parallel encoders in mixed-level blending, namely unimodal refinement and multimodal interaction modules, and their outputs are concatenated together as blended tokens. Subsequently, in the label-induced aggregation, trainable label embeddings first attend to each other and then query the blended tokens that encapsulate diverse multimodal dynamics to obtain label-specific representations. Ultimately, these representations are fed into a linear classifier which outputs a probability distribution over all the labels.

### 3.3   Mixed-Level Blending

**Temporal Convolutions.** To bridge the modality gap, we project multimodal data in the original modality space to a unified space $\mathbb{R}^d$, where $d$ is the common dimension for all modalities. Considering the following dot-product attention mechanism utilizes a point-wise similarity to aggregate vectors, it does not give enough attention to the local neighborhood information. LAMB exploits 1D convolutions to alleviate this problem. The following is a description of the process:

$$\hat{\mathbf{X}}_\alpha = \text{Conv1D}(\mathbf{X}_\alpha, \text{kernel}_\alpha), \alpha \in \{T, A, V\} \tag{1}$$

Here, $\text{kernel}_\alpha$ is the kernel size of modality $\alpha$. The attention mechanism which is applied to tokens embedded with local information becomes segment-aware.

**Unimodal Refinement Module.** Each modality encapsulates distinct and discriminative information, establishing the fundamental basis for prediction. To enhance the predictive capability, it is imperative to fully extract valuable unimodal features from them. Certain pieces of information are contingent upon long-term contextual dependencies, and refining contextual information within each modality facilitates a holistic comprehension of the task at hand. For instance, consider the sentences *'She lives in a sick part of the city. It is full of restaurants.'* If the model fails to grasp the context, it may misinterpret the emotional connotation of 'sick' in the sentence as negative. Conversely, a context-sensitive model would discern that this expression reflects a positive or impressive sentiment in American parlance. To capture the contextual interdependencies within each modality, we utilize self-attention encoders to implement unimodal refinement.

Given queries $\mathbf{Q} \in \mathbb{R}^{n_q \times d_k}$, keys $\mathbf{K} \in \mathbb{R}^{n_k \times d_k}$ and values $\mathbf{V} \in \mathbb{R}^{n_k \times d_v}$, multi-head attention with $h$ heads is employed in accordance with the definition outlined in Transformer [23]:

$$\text{head}_i = \text{softmax}(\frac{\mathbf{Q}\mathbf{W}_i^Q(\mathbf{K}\mathbf{W}_i^K)^T}{\sqrt{\bar{d}_k}})\mathbf{V}\mathbf{W}_i^V$$

$$\text{MHA}(\mathbf{Q}, \mathbf{K}, \mathbf{V}) = \text{Concat}(\text{head}_1, \cdots, \text{head}_h)\mathbf{W}^O \tag{2}$$

where $\mathbf{W}_i^Q \in \mathbb{R}^{d_k \times \bar{d}_k}$, $\mathbf{W}_i^K \in \mathbb{R}^{d_k \times \bar{d}_k}$, $\mathbf{W}_i^V \in \mathbb{R}^{d_v \times \bar{d}_v}$, $\mathbf{W}^O \in \mathbb{R}^{h\bar{d}_v \times d_v}$ are the parameter matrices of linear projections. Furthermore, a unimodal refinement module consisting of multi-head attention (MHA), layer normalization (LN), and multilayer perceptron (MLP) of modality $\alpha$ is defined as follows:

$$\mathbf{U}_\alpha^0 = \hat{\mathbf{X}}_\alpha$$

$$\hat{\mathbf{U}}_\alpha^l = \text{LN}(\text{MHA}(\mathbf{U}_\alpha^l, \mathbf{U}_\alpha^l, \mathbf{U}_\alpha^l) + \mathbf{U}_\alpha^l)$$

$$\mathbf{U}_\alpha^{l+1} = \text{LN}(\text{MLP}(\hat{\mathbf{U}}_\alpha^l) + \hat{\mathbf{U}}_\alpha^l) \tag{3}$$

where $l$ represents the number of the layer. The simplified notation $\mathbf{U}_\alpha$ refers to the outcomes of the last layer.

**Multimodal Interaction Module.** Unlike intra-modality context refinement, inter-modality interaction forms new information not involved in a single modality, thus improving predictive performance. For example, *'The movie is very nice'* may convey a negative emotional polarity with an ironic tone. Through the utilization of cross-modal transformers, we model these inter-modality interactions. The cross-modal attention mechanism takes one modality as queries and another modality as key-value pairs. Since queries and key-value pairs originate from distinct modalities, the multimodal interaction module could explore cross-modal long-term dependency without relying on intra-modal context. Concretely, the outputs possess the same length as queries and share identical dimensions with key-value pairs. In other words, the key modality is weighted and averaged based on the query modality rather than itself. Analogous to the unimodal module, a multimodal interaction module that characterizes modality $\alpha$ attending to modality $\beta(\beta \neq \alpha)$ computes the following equations for $l = 0, 1, \cdots$ layers:

$$
\begin{aligned}
\mathbf{Z}^0_{\alpha \to \beta} &= \hat{\mathbf{X}}_\alpha, \\
\hat{\mathbf{Z}}^l_{\alpha \to \beta} &= \mathrm{LN}(\mathrm{MHA}(\mathbf{Z}^l_{\alpha \to \beta}, \hat{\mathbf{X}}_\beta, \hat{\mathbf{X}}_\beta) + \mathbf{Z}^l_{\alpha \to \beta}) \\
\mathbf{Z}^{l+1}_{\alpha \to \beta} &= \mathrm{LN}(\mathrm{MLP}(\hat{\mathbf{Z}}^l_{\alpha \to \beta}) + \hat{\mathbf{Z}}^l_{\alpha \to \beta})
\end{aligned}
\tag{4}
$$

We use $\mathbf{Z}_{\alpha \to \beta}$ to denote the final outputs of the multimodal interaction module.

To preserve the diversity of multimodal dynamics, LAMB concatenates all the tokens outputted from both unimodal refinement and multimodal interaction modules into a new tensor $\ddot{\mathbf{X}}$, namely

$$
\begin{aligned}
\ddot{\mathbf{X}} = \mathrm{Concat}(\mathbf{U}_T, \mathbf{U}_A, \mathbf{U}_V, \mathbf{Z}_{T \to A}, \mathbf{Z}_{T \to V}, \\
\mathbf{Z}_{A \to T}, \mathbf{Z}_{A \to V}, \mathbf{Z}_{V \to T}, \mathbf{Z}_{V \to A})
\end{aligned}
\tag{5}
$$

The pertinent discriminative information of all the blended tokens is left for label-induced aggregation to extract in a label-specific manner.

### 3.4  Label-Induced Aggregation

First-order strategies adopt the label-by-label style, thus neglecting correlations of the other labels. Second-order strategies employ label coexistence, but they are limited to pairwise relations. In contrast, label-induced aggregation explores high-order label-to-label correlations via attention mechanism. Label latent representations enrich the label semantics by allowing each label to attend to all labels, which helps to explore more complicated relations among labels. The initial discrete labels $[1, 2, \cdots, c]$ are first mapped to one-hot vectors $[\mathbf{e}_1, \mathbf{e}_2, \cdots, \mathbf{e}_c]$ where $i$ denotes the location of element $1$ in $\mathbf{e}_i$. By looking up a learnable table $\mathbf{W}^E$ that stores embeddings, these one-hot vectors transform into label embeddings $\mathbf{E} = [\mathbf{e}_1, \mathbf{e}_2, \cdots, \mathbf{e}_c]\mathbf{W}^E$. Then, the embeddings are passed through the label-to-label self-attention architecture which provides information about all labels to each particular label. After that, label embeddings are treated as queries and fed into the label-to-modality module along with blended tokens as key-value pairs. It is worth mentioning that multimodal tokens $\ddot{\mathbf{X}}$ here are outputs of mixed-level blending. These tokens contain serviceable specific unimodal extraction and complementary multimodal interaction. Unlike relevant works focusing on the CLS token or the last token [21], the label-induced aggregation module retains all tokens. Without token-grained screening, latent representations can be learned and extracted adaptively, thus facilitating the following multiple classifications. The label-to-modality multi-head attention receives label queries alongside modality key-value pairs. Under the guidance of labels, discriminative information is selected to capture potential correlations from modality space to label space. The label-induced aggregation implemented by a transformer-based decoder can be formulated as:

$$\begin{aligned}
\mathbf{D}^0 &= \mathbf{E} \\
\tilde{\mathbf{D}}^l_{L \to L} &= \mathrm{MHA}(\mathbf{D}^l, \mathbf{D}^l, \mathbf{D}^l) \\
\hat{\mathbf{D}}^l_{L \to M} &= \mathrm{MHA}(\tilde{\mathbf{D}}^l_{L \to L}, \ddot{\mathbf{X}}, \ddot{\mathbf{X}}) \\
\mathbf{D}^{l+1} &= \mathrm{LN}(\mathrm{MLP}(\hat{\mathbf{D}}^l_{L \to M}) + \hat{\mathbf{D}}^l_{L \to M})
\end{aligned} \tag{6}$$

where $\mathbf{D}^0$ refers to the initial state of the first layer in the label-induced aggregation decoder. Similarly, $\mathbf{D}^l$ and $\mathbf{D}^{l+1}$ denote the outputs of the $l$th and $(l+1)$th layers in the decoder. $\tilde{\mathbf{D}}^l_{L \to L}$ and $\hat{\mathbf{D}}^l_{L \to M}$ are two intermediate states. The self-attention in computing $\tilde{\mathbf{D}}^l_{L \to L}$ and the cross-attention in computing $\hat{\mathbf{D}}^l_{L \to M}$ explore the label-to-label and label-to-modality dependencies respectively.

### 3.5  Multi-label Classifier

After obtaining the label-specific representations $\mathbf{D}_{L \to M} \in \mathbb{R}^{N \times c \times d}$, LAMB feeds them into a linear classifier with weight matrix $\mathbf{W}^f \in \mathbb{R}^{d \times 1}$, bias $b \in \mathbb{R}$, and sigmoid function to infer label sets. The predicted probabilities of each label are written as:

$$\hat{\mathbf{Y}} = f(\mathbf{D}_{L \to M}) = \mathrm{sigmoid}(\mathbf{D}_{L \to M}\mathbf{W}^f + b^f) \tag{7}$$

Finally, we use binary Cross-entropy loss which is a classical optimization objective for multi-label learning to guide our model globally for classification. Formally, it can be calculated as:

$$\mathrm{BCELoss}(\mathbf{Y}, \hat{\mathbf{Y}}) = -\frac{1}{N}\sum_{i=1}^{N}\left[\mathbf{Y}_i \log(\hat{\mathbf{Y}}_i) + (1 - \mathbf{Y}_i)\log(1 - \hat{\mathbf{Y}}_i)\right] \tag{8}$$

# 4   Experiments

## 4.1   Experimental Settings

**Dataset.** The CMU-MOSEI [33] dataset is a widely used benchmark for multimodal sentiment analysis and emotion recognition. It comprises 3,229 full-length videos of 1,000 speakers, divided into 22,856 video segments at the utterance level. Each video segment consists of three modalities: text, audio, and visual, and covers six emotion categories: anger, disgust, fear, happiness, sadness, and surprise. To extract features from the visual modality, FACET [2] employs a facial expression recognition system that generates 35-dimensional features from video frames. For the audio modality, COVAREP [6] extracts 74-dimensional features from acoustic signals. Lastly, GloVe [17] provides 300-dimensional features from the video transcripts for the text modality.

**Evaluation Criteria.** Since multimodal multi-label emotion detection is a classification task, we report the performance of all approaches with four classical metrics and a typical multi-label loss function, i.e., accuracy (Acc), precision (P), recall (R), micro-F1 (F1), and Hamming loss (HL). Superior performance is indicated by higher accuracy, precision, recall, and micro-F1 scores, while lower values of Hamming loss are desirable outcomes.

**Implement Details.** We implement the LAMB model using Pytorch and conduct all evaluations on an NVIDIA RTX 3090 GPU. The model is trained by Adam optimizer with default parameters. In unimodal refinement modules, multimodal interaction modules, and the label-induced aggregation decoder, the number of layers is set to 1, as LAMB prioritizes diversity over depth. The attention heads in all attention layers are fixed to 5. The dimension of the unified modality space, as well as the hidden sizes of the transformer encoders and the decoder, have been configured to 30. Notably, the hidden size of the intermediate layer within the transformer block's multilayer perceptron is set to 120 for the encoders and 256 for the decoder.

Additionally, we employ label smoothing to prevent overfitting and clip the gradients to the maximum norm of 0.8. During training, we train each model for a fixed number of epochs 50 with an early-stopping strategy and schedule the learning rate from 1e-3 by its performance on the validation set. After the training process, we select the model with the highest accuracy on the validation set as our final model and evaluate its performance on the test set.

## 4.2   Baselines

Based on the degree of modality contribution and label correlation participation, the baselines in our study can be categorized into four groups. Firstly, classical methods transform multi-label learning problems into other sophisticated learning scenarios. Regardless of modality heterogeneity, the multimodal inputs are concatenated as new inputs. **BR** [3] decomposes the multi-label task into independent binary classification problems, ignoring the correlations between labels. **LP** [22] converts the original multi-label set into small random subsets and tackles the modified single-label classification problem. **CC** [20] transforms the multi-label learning problem into a chain of binary classification problems, considering high-order label correlations. Secondly, text-based or image-based algorithms solely utilize information from the text or image modality. **SGM** [30] treats multi-label classification as a sequence generation problem to exploit label relations for text data. **LSAN** [27] constructs label-specific document representation by simultaneously using document content and label text. **ML-GCN** [4] proposes a graph convolutional network-based model to capture label dependencies for multi-label image recognition. Thirdly, this group of baselines mainly focuses on solving multimodal issues but lacks the utilization of label correlation. **DFG** [33] analyzes the mechanism of modality interaction in sentiment analysis and emotion recognition by taking advantage of the interpretable dynamic fusion graph algorithm. **RAVEN** [25] investigates the fine-grained structure of nonverbal subword sequences and constructs multimodal-shifted word representations to dynamically capture changes in non-linguistic context. **MulT** [21] introduces a cross-modal attention mechanism to provide a latent cross-modal adaptation for multimodal fusion, while capturing long-range contingencies. **SIMM** [26] develops shared subspace and extracts view-specific information to strengthen communication between views while preserving individual-specific

**Table 1.** Performance comparison on aligned and unaligned settings. The best results are in bold. LAMB outperforms other state-of-the-art approaches, indicating the effectiveness of our method.

| Approaches | Aligned | | | | Unaligned | | | |
|---|---|---|---|---|---|---|---|---|
| | Acc ↑ | P ↑ | R ↑ | F1 ↑ | Acc ↑ | P ↑ | R ↑ | F1 ↑ |
| BR [3] | 0.222 | 0.309 | 0.515 | 0.386 | 0.233 | 0.321 | 0.545 | 0.404 |
| LP [22] | 0.159 | 0.231 | 0.377 | 0.286 | 0.185 | 0.252 | 0.427 | 0.317 |
| CC [20] | 0.225 | 0.306 | 0.523 | 0.386 | 0.235 | 0.320 | 0.550 | 0.404 |
| SGM [30] | 0.455 | 0.595 | 0.467 | 0.523 | 0.449 | 0.584 | 0.476 | 0.524 |
| LSAN [27] | 0.393 | 0.550 | 0.459 | 0.501 | 0.403 | 0.582 | 0.460 | 0.514 |
| ML-GCN [4] | 0.411 | 0.546 | 0.476 | 0.509 | 0.437 | 0.573 | 0.482 | 0.524 |
| DFG [33] | 0.396 | 0.595 | 0.457 | 0.517 | 0.386 | 0.534 | 0.456 | 0.494 |
| RAVEN [25] | 0.416 | 0.588 | 0.461 | 0.517 | 0.403 | 0.633 | 0.429 | 0.511 |
| MulT [21] | 0.445 | 0.619 | 0.465 | 0.531 | 0.423 | 0.636 | 0.445 | 0.523 |
| SIMM [26] | 0.432 | 0.561 | 0.495 | 0.525 | 0.418 | 0.482 | 0.486 | 0.484 |
| MISA [12] | 0.430 | 0.453 | **0.582** | 0.509 | 0.398 | 0.371 | **0.571** | 0.450 |
| HHMPN [34] | 0.459 | 0.602 | 0.496 | 0.556 | 0.434 | 0.591 | 0.476 | 0.528 |
| TAILOR [39] | 0.488 | 0.641 | 0.512 | 0.569 | 0.460 | 0.639 | 0.452 | 0.529 |
| LAMB (Ours) | **0.490** | **0.643** | 0.517 | **0.573** | **0.463** | **0.656** | 0.454 | **0.536** |

characteristics. **MISA** [12] obtains modality-invariant and modality-specific features that are fused to estimate affective states by considering the holistic view of the multimodal data. Fourthly, multimodal multi-label approaches validate the significance of exploring modalities and labels comprehensively. **HHMPN** [34] effectively handles both complete and partial time series data. The feature-to-label, label-to-label and modality-to-label dependencies are modeled simultaneously by means of the graph message passing. **TAILOR** [39] extracts private and common representations adversarially and leverages label semantics to construct label-specific representations for multimodal fusion at different granularity.

## 5    Results and Analysis

### 5.1    Comparison Experiment

Table 1 shows the performance of representative approaches to multimodal multi-label emotion detection on CMU-MOSEI in both aligned and unaligned settings. Due to the heterogeneity of modalities, different modalities are obtained at different sampling rates. As a result, the three modalities possess varying sequence lengths for the same utterance in the unaligned setting. In the aligned setting, preprocessed video and audio data are aligned with the words in the text, ensuring that all modalities have the same sequence length. For methods incapable of directly handling non-aligned data, we report the results of their modified version that contain an additional CTC module [11] and corresponding training loss in the unaligned setting. Based on the comparison results, there are some observations:

1. CC achieves the best performance among the three classical multi-label methods, validating the utilization of label correlation is beneficial for multi-label learning.
2. The classical multi-label approaches BR, LP, and CC show much worse performance than the text-based or image-based algorithms SGM, LSAN, and ML-GCN, which indicates that methods employing fully exploited unimodal features are comparable with classical multi-label approaches.
3. Most of the multimodal baselines surpass text-based or image-based. Specifically, MulT outperforms SGM except for accuracy, ML-GCN except for recall, and beats LSAN through all metrics in the aligned setting, demonstrating the necessity of exploiting intra-modal and inter-modal dynamics.
4. Multimodal multi-label methods, such as TAILOR, display even better outcomes than the approaches mentioned above, suggesting the effectiveness of simultaneously leveraging modalities and labels.
5. In both settings, our proposed LAMB demonstrates superior performance in addressing multi-label emotion detection across three metrics, albeit with suboptimal recall results. This is attributed to our approach effectively exploring label-to-label and label-to-modality dependencies while preserving the diversity of multimodal interactions.

## 5.2   Ablation Study

With the purpose of figuring out the role of individual components in LAMB, we further conduct ablation experiments on CMU-MOSEI. By selectively removing different parts while keeping the basic structure, the performance variations of specific components reveal their impact. Table 2 presents the evaluation results. We report four typical multi-label evaluation metrics: Accuracy, Hamming loss, Recall, and Micro-F1.

**Table 2.** Ablation study on aligned CMU-MOSEI dataset. The best results are in bold. "w/o" denotes removing the component.

| Approches | Acc ↑ | R ↑ | F1 ↑ | HL ↓ |
|---|---|---|---|---|
| only text | 0.456 | 0.452 | 0.544 | 0.260 |
| only audio | 0.418 | 0.435 | 0.498 | 0.266 |
| only visual | 0.429 | 0.413 | 0.502 | 0.287 |
| only text-audio | 0.458 | 0.466 | 0.546 | 0.248 |
| only text-visual | 0.460 | 0.456 | 0.551 | 0.257 |
| only audio-text | 0.472 | 0.477 | 0.553 | 0.241 |
| only audio-visual | 0.445 | 0.452 | 0.518 | 0.256 |
| only visual-text | 0.481 | 0.489 | 0.556 | 0.233 |
| only visual-audio | 0.436 | 0.437 | 0.507 | 0.266 |
| only unimodal | 0.482 | 0.512 | 0.566 | 0.220 |
| only multimodal | 0.480 | 0.496 | 0.563 | 0.229 |
| w/o decoder | 0.474 | 0.479 | 0.565 | 0.241 |
| w/o label correlations | 0.478 | 0.512 | 0.552 | 0.220 |
| w/o label embeddings | 0.479 | 0.491 | 0.561 | 0.232 |
| LAMB (Ours) | **0.490** | **0.517** | **0.573** | **0.217** |

**Role of Individual Modalities.** Avoiding the mutual influence among modalities, three variants using only a single modality as input are scrutinized. *'only text'*, *'only audio'*, and *'only visual'* in Table 2 denote experiments to explore the role of individual modalities with models that only use a single unimodal refinement module and do not use multimodal interaction modules. For instance, *'only text'* represents the model only using a text unimodal refinement module without any multimodal interaction modules followed by a label-induced aggregation directly. As is exhibited, the result obtained by using only one modality input is the worst among all the results, which fully reflects the importance of utilizing information from multiple modalities. Multimodal complementarity has a powerful impetus on emotion recognition tasks.

**Role of Paired Modality Interaction.** We perform experiments to explore the role of paired modality interaction with models that only use one multimodal interaction module and do not use unimodal refinement modules. As two arbitrary modalities serve as either queries or key-value pairs in the cross-attention mechanism, this results in six different variants. For example, *'only text-audio'* denotes the model that takes text as queries and audio as key-value pairs. As illustrated in Table 2, our LAMB surpasses all the variants. We can conclude that preserving the diversity of different multimodal interactions is crucial to a more flexible and powerful fusion.

**Role of Mixed-Level Blending.** To explore the role of unimodal refinement and multimodal interaction in mixed-level blending, we conduct experiments denoted by *'only unimodal'* and *'only multimodal'*. *'only unimodal'* represents the variant where three unimodal refinement modules of text, audio, and visual modalities are followed by a label-induced aggregation without any multimodal interaction modules, while *'only multimodal'* represents the model with all six multimodal interaction modules followed by label-induced aggregation directly. The poor performance of these two variants implies the effectiveness of exploiting the intra-modality context in a single modality and exploring long-term inter-modality dependency.

**Role of Label-Induced Aggregation.** Furthermore, label induction is under evaluation. The first variant, as is demonstrated in the *'w/o decoder'* of Table 2, corresponds to the whole decoder being removed. Instead, the first element of the tokens from self-attention and cross-modal attention are concatenated directly. This variant is the worst result among the three in this label impact detection section, signifying the indispensability of the whole label-induced aggregation. In other words, only taking advantage of modality information is inadequate. In order to probe the necessity of label correlations, we replace the regular attention masks with an identity matrix in the label-to-label self-attention so that each label can only attend to itself without any correlations. *'w/o label correlations'* displays the performance of this variant which treats each label independently. By comparison, we can conclude that the attention mechanism indeed makes contributions to label-to-label correlations. For the sake of proving the mutual effect between labels and modalities, we use identical rather than label-specific embeddings to fuse modalities for all the labels as the third variant. As is shown in *'w/o label embeddings'*, the defective consequence of eliminating label-specific guidance shows the importance of label-to-modality dependency.

As is demonstrated in Table 2, all measurements decline consistently, regardless of the component being removed. It reveals that each part plays an irreplaceable role in achieving the remarkable performance of LAMB. The complete version encompassing all elements is better than other variants, underscoring the mutual enhancement among all components.

## 5.3   Visualization

**Analysis on Label-to-modality Dependency.** To further investigate the label-to-modality dependency, we select the tokens that receive the highest five attention values across all the heads for each emotion. These tokens contain the most discriminative information for the corresponding labels. Then, we count the number of these tokens each encoder generates and plot the distribution in the histogram. The higher the number is, the more important this kind of multimodal dynamics is for the specific emotion. In Fig. 2, 't', 'a', and 'v' denote unimodal refinement modules from text, audio, and visual respectively. Similarly, 'ta' refers to the multimodal interaction module with text as queries, audio as key-value pairs, and so on. The highest bars of different labels have different colors, demonstrating that emotions tend to depend on different multimodal

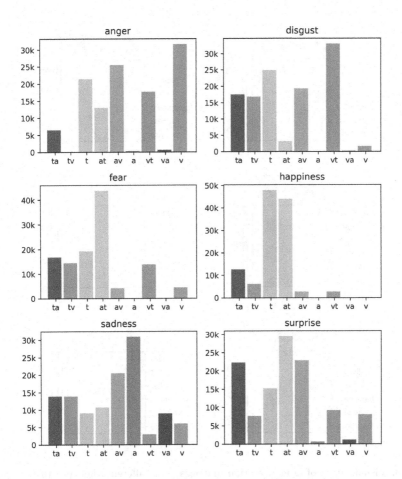

**Fig. 2.** Histogram of the encoders from which the top-5 attended tokens are over six emotions. The highest bar differs in each chart, which indicates labels have distinct associations with different multimodal dynamics and LAMB adaptively learns it.

dynamics. For example, facial expression is vital to recognize anger, while audio-text interactions are more crucial for fear. Thanks to label-induced aggregation, LAMB explores the label-to-modality dependency adaptively.

**Analysis on Label-to-Label Dependency.** In order to delve into the label-to-label dependency, we extract all the attention matrices in the label self-attention of the decoder and visualize them in heatmaps. As shown in Fig. 3, (a) - (e) are the dependence among different labels learned by five attention heads, and (f) is the outcome of using the identity matrix. The label-to-label self-attention models complicated label correlations compared to utilizing the identity matrix. Furthermore, different attention heads learn diverse label co-existence to enrich the semantic information from various perspectives. For instance, anger has a

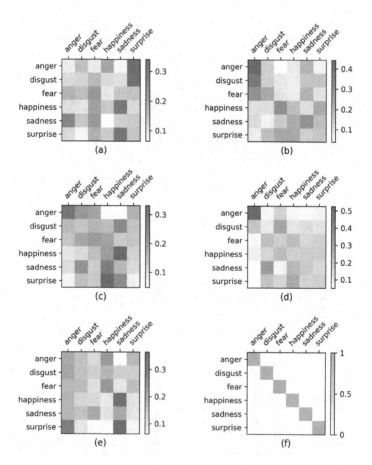

**Fig. 3.** Visualization of label attention matrices. The difference between (a) - (e) and the identity matrix (f) demonstrates LAMB can capture complex label correlations.

higher correlation with surprise in the first head (a), while it pays more attention to itself in other heads.

## 6    Conclusion

In this paper, we propose LAMB, a novel approach for multimodal multi-label emotion detection that addresses the inefficiency of static modality information extraction, as well as the limited exploration of label-to-modality and label-to-label dependencies. LAMB mainly consists of mixed-level blending and label-induced aggregation. Mixed-level blending involves multiple parallel encoders to preserve modality interaction diversity for better fusion. Label-induced aggregation obtains label-specific representation by employing learnable label embeddings to query blended tokens. It allows the model to capture label-to-modality and label-to-label dependencies, which are essential for accurate emotion detection.

Experimental evaluations and analysis of aligned and unaligned data certify the effectiveness of our proposed LAMB. Individual component of LAMB plays an indispensable role and coordinates with each other. Label correlations are explored by self-attention in label embedding space. Under the induction of labels, tokens from different encoders provide unequal discriminative information for different emotions, validating the dependencies between modalities and labels.

Emotion detection models often lack interpretability, making it difficult to understand the reasoning behind their predictions. Future work could delve into techniques for interpreting and explaining the decisions made by the LAMB framework. This could enable users to gain insights into the model's decision-making process and enhance trust and transparency in its applications.

**Acknowledgments.** This paper is supported by the National Natural Science Foundation of China (Grant No. 62192783, 62376117), the Collaborative Innovation Center of Novel Software Technology and Industrialization at Nanjing University.

## References

1. Baltrusaitis, T., Ahuja, C., Morency, L.P.: Multimodal machine learning: a survey and taxonomy. IEEE Trans. Pattern Anal. Mach. Intell. **41**, 423–443 (2019)
2. Baltrusaitis, T., Robinson, P., Morency, L.P.: OpenFace: an open source facial behavior analysis toolkit. In: Proceedings of the IEEE Winter Conference on Applications of Computer Vision, pp. 1–10 (2016)
3. Boutell, M.R., Luo, J., Shen, X., Brown, C.M.: Learning multi-label scene classification. Pattern Recogn. **37**, 1757–1771 (2004)
4. Chen, Z.M., Wei, X.S., Wang, P., Guo, Y.: Multi-label image recognition with graph convolutional networks. In: Proceedings of the IEEE International Conference on Computer Vision, pp. 5177–5186 (2019)
5. Clare, A., King, R.D.: Knowledge discovery in multi-label phenotype data. In: Proceedings of the European Conference on Principles of Data Mining and Knowledge Discovery, pp. 42–53 (2001)

6. Degottex, G., Kane, J., Drugman, T., Raitio, T., Scherer, S.: COVAREP - A collaborative voice analysis repository for speech technologies. In: Proceedings of the IEEE International Conference on Acoustics, Speech and Signal Processing, pp. 960–964 (2014)
7. Elisseeff, A., Weston, J.: A kernel method for multi-labelled classification. In: Proceedings of the Conference on Neural Information Processing Systems, pp. 681–687 (2001)
8. Feng, L., An, B., He, S.: Collaboration based multi-label learning. In: Proceedings of the AAAI Conference on Artificial Intelligence, pp. 3550–3557 (2019)
9. Fürnkranz, J., Hüllermeier, E., Mencía, E.L., Brinker, K.: Multilabel classification via calibrated label ranking. Mach. Learn. **73**, 133–153 (2008)
10. Ghamrawi, N., McCallum, A.: Collective multi-label classification. In: Proceedings of the ACM International Conference on Information and Knowledge Management, pp. 195–200 (2005)
11. Graves, A., Fernández, S., Gomez, F.J., Schmidhuber, J.: Connectionist temporal classification: labelling unsegmented sequence data with recurrent neural networks. In: Proceedings of the International Conference on Machine Learning, pp. 369–376 (2006)
12. Hazarika, D., Zimmermann, R., Poria, S.: MISA: modality-invariant and -specific representations for multimodal sentiment analysis. In: Proceedings of the ACM International Conference on Multimedia, pp. 1122–1131 (2020)
13. Huang, J., Li, G., Huang, Q., Wu, X.: Learning label-specific features and class-dependent labels for multi-label classification. IEEE Trans. Knowl. Data Eng. **28**, 3309–3323 (2016)
14. Liang, T., Lin, G., Feng, L., Zhang, Y., Lv, F.: Attention is not Enough: mitigating the distribution discrepancy in asynchronous multimodal sequence fusion. In: Proceedings of the IEEE International Conference on Computer Vision, pp. 8128–8136 (2021)
15. Liu, Z., Shen, Y., Lakshminarasimhan, V.B., Liang, P.P., Zadeh, A., Morency, L.P.: Efficient low-rank multimodal fusion with modality-specific factors. In: Proceedings of the Annual Meeting of the Association for Computational Linguistics, vol. 1, pp. 2247–2256 (2018)
16. Lv, F., Chen, X., Huang, Y., Duan, L., Lin, G.: Progressive modality reinforcement for human multimodal emotion recognition from unaligned multimodal sequences. In: Proceedings of the IEEE Conference on Computer Vision and Pattern Recognition, pp. 2554–2562 (2021)
17. Pennington, J., Socher, R., Manning, C.D.: GloVe: global vectors for word representation. In: Proceedings of the Conference on Empirical Methods in Natural Language Processing, pp. 1532–1543 (2014)
18. Qi, G.J., Hua, X.S., Rui, Y., Tang, J., Mei, T., Zhang, H.J.: Correlative multi-label video annotation. In: Proceedings of the ACM International Conference on Multimedia, pp. 17–26 (2007)
19. Rahman, W., et al.: Integrating multimodal information in large pretrained transformers. In: Proceedings of the Annual Meeting of the Association for Computational Linguistics, vol. 1, pp. 2359–2369 (2020)
20. Read, J., Pfahringer, B., Holmes, G., Frank, E.: Classifier chains for multi-label classification. Mach. Learn. **85**, 333–359 (2011)
21. Tsai, Y.H.H., Bai, S., Liang, P.P., Kolter, J.Z., Morency, L.P., Salakhutdinov, R.: Multimodal transformer for unaligned multimodal language sequences. In: Proceedings of the Annual Meeting of the Association for Computational Linguistics, vol. 1, pp. 6558–6569 (2019)

22. Tsoumakas, G., Katakis, I.: Multi-label classification: an overview. Int. J. Data Warehouse. Min. **3**, 1–13 (2007)
23. Vaswani, A., et al.: Attention is all you need. In: Advances in Neural Information Processing Systems, pp. 5998–6008 (2017)
24. Wang, H., et al.: Collaboration based multi-label propagation for fraud detection. In: Proceedings of the International Joint Conference on Artificial Intelligence, pp. 2477–2483 (2020)
25. Wang, Y., Shen, Y., Liu, Z., Liang, P.P., Zadeh, A., Morency, L.P.: Words Can Shift: dynamically adjusting word representations using nonverbal behaviors. In: Proceedings of the AAAI Conference on Artificial Intelligence, pp. 7216–7223 (2019)
26. Wu, X., et al.: Multi-View Multi-label learning with view-specific information extraction. In: Proceedings of the International Joint Conference on Artificial Intelligence, pp. 3884–3890 (2019)
27. Xiao, L., Huang, X., Chen, B., Jing, L.: Label-specific document representation for multi-label text classification. In: Proceedings of the Conference on Empirical Methods in Natural Language Processing, pp. 466–475 (2019)
28. Yang, D., Huang, S., Kuang, H., Du, Y., Zhang, L.: Disentangled representation learning for multimodal emotion recognition. In: Proceedings of the ACM International Conference on Multimedia, pp. 1642–1651 (2022)
29. Yang, D., Kuang, H., Huang, S., Zhang, L.: Learning modality-specific and - agnostic representations for asynchronous multimodal language sequences. In: Proceedings of the ACM International Conference on Multimedia, pp. 1708–1717 (2022)
30. Yang, P., Sun, X., Li, W., Ma, S., Wu, W., Wang, H.: SGM: sequence generation model for multi-label classification. In: Proceedings of the International Conference on Computational Linguistics, pp. 3915–3926 (2018)
31. Yu, W., Xu, H., Yuan, Z., Wu, J.: learning modality-specific representations with self-supervised multi-task learning for multimodal sentiment analysis. In: Proceedings of the AAAI Conference on Artificial Intelligence, pp. 10790–10797 (2021)
32. Zadeh, A., Chen, M., Poria, S., Cambria, E., Morency, L.P.: Tensor fusion network for multimodal sentiment analysis. In: Proceedings of the Conference on Empirical Methods in Natural Language Processing, pp. 1103–1114 (2017)
33. Zadeh, A., Liang, P.P., Poria, S., Cambria, E., Morency, L.P.: Multimodal language analysis in the wild: CMU-MOSEI dataset and interpretable dynamic fusion graph. In: Proceedings of the Annual Meeting of the Association for Computational Linguistics, vol. 1, pp. 2236–2246 (2018)
34. Zhang, D., et al.: Multi-modal multi-label emotion recognition with heterogeneous hierarchical message passing. In: Proceedings of the AAAI Conference on Artificial Intelligence, pp. 14338–14346 (2021)
35. Zhang, M.L., Fang, J.P., Wang, Y.B.: BiLabel-specific features for multi-label classification. ACM Trans. Knowl. Discov. Data **16**, 1–23 (2022)
36. Zhang, M.L., Wu, L.: Lift: multi-label learning with label-specific features. IEEE Trans. Knowl. Data Eng. **37**, 107–120 (2015)
37. Zhang, M.L., Zhou, Z.H.: ML-KNN: A lazy learning approach to multi-label learning. Pattern Recogn. **40**, 2038–2048 (2007)
38. Zhang, M.L., Zhou, Z.H.: A review on multi-label learning algorithms. IEEE Trans. Knowl. Data Eng. **26**, 1819–1837 (2014)
39. Zhang, Y., Chen, M., Shen, J., Wang, C.: Tailor versatile multi-modal learning for multi-label emotion recognition. In: Proceedings of the AAAI Conference on Artificial Intelligence, pp. 9100–9108 (2022)

40. Zhao, X., Chen, Y., Li, W., Gao, L., Tang, B.: MAG+: an extended multimodal adaptation gate for multimodal sentiment analysis. In: Proceedings of the IEEE International Conference on Acoustics, Speech and Signal Processing, pp. 4753–4757 (2022)
41. Zhu, Y., Kwok, J.T., Zhou, Z.H.: Multi-label learning with global and local label correlation. IEEE Trans. Knowl. Data Eng. **30**, 1081–1094 (2018)

# MSAM: Deep Semantic Interaction Network for Visual Question Answering

Fan Wang, Bin Wang, Fuyong Xu, Jiaxin Li, and Peiyu Liu[✉]

Shandong Normal University, Jinan 250358, China
liupy@sdnu.edu.cn

**Abstract.** In Visual Question Answering (VQA) task, extracting semantic information from multimodalities and effectively utilizing this information for interaction is crucial. Existing VQA methods mostly focus on attention mechanism to reason about answers, but do not fully utilize the semantic information of modalities. Furthermore, the question and the image relation description through attention mechanism may cover some conflicting information, which weakens multi-modal semantic information relevance. Based on the above issues, this paper proposes a Multi-layer Semantics Awareness Model (MSAM) to fill the lack of multi-modal semantic understanding. We design a Bi-affine space projection method to construct multi-modal semantic space to effectively understand modal features at the semantic level. Then, we propose to utilize contrastive learning to achieve semantic alignment, which effectively brings modalities with the same semantics closer together and improves multi-modal information relevance. We conduct extensive experiments on the VQA2.0 dataset, and our model boosts the metrics even further compared to the baseline, improving the performance of the VQA task.

**Keywords:** Visual Question and Answering · Contrastive Learning · Semantic Alignment · Semantic Information

## 1 Introduction

The goal of the Visual Question Answering (VQA) task is to predict answers based on given questions and relevant images. There are two main variants of VQA, Free Form Open End (FFOE) and Multiple Choice (MC). In FFOE, the answers are free response to given image-question input pairs, whereas in MC, the answers are chosen from a predefined list of ground truths. In both cases, extracting meaningful features from both images and questions plays a key role. In addition, semantic features mapped from images and questions can strongly influence the results [1]. Most of the existing VQA task solutions rely on visual relations [2,3], attention mechanism [4,5] and external knowledge [6].

© ICST Institute for Computer Sciences, Social Informatics and Telecommunications Engineering 2024
Published by Springer Nature Switzerland AG 2024. All Rights Reserved
H. Gao et al. (Eds.): CollaborateCom 2023, LNICST 562, pp. 39–56, 2024.
https://doi.org/10.1007/978-3-031-54528-3_3

VQA modeling process often involves feature extraction, cross-modal interaction, cross-modal feature fusion, and answer prediction. Feature extraction involves extracting visual and textual features from raw data. Cross-modal interaction mechanisms (such as attention mechanism) enable the model to reason about the relations between visual and textual features. Cross-modal feature fusion aims to integrate the complementary information from questions and images, enhancing the overall representation of the input. Finally, after obtaining the fused features from questions and images, the VQA task predicts techniques such as classification or generation to predict the answers.

Most of the current VQA methods extract rich features from questions and images through attention mechanism. Yang et al. [7] propose a method to obtain features in key regions of images by stacking attention networks, which aims to solve the problem of too extensive feature regions. Based on this, Nguyen et al. [8] design a co-attention learning method that alternates image attention and question attention to obtain fine-grained key feature representations. Yu et al. [9] introduce the Self-Attention and the Guided-Attention, which result in more detailed representations of the question keywords and the image key regions, facilitating multi-modal interaction. Thus attention mechanism plays a crucial role in VQA task by allowing the model to focus on relevant parts of questions and images. By attending to specific regions, the model can gather more informative features. There are also some VQA approaches that focus on the importance of multi-modal semantic information [10] fusion. Nguyen et al. [11] design fusion for multi-modal at different semantic levels. Chen et al. [12] emphasize the importance of contextual semantic information in the fusion process. Tu et al. [13] propose internal contextual information to enhance memory in an attentional model.

Although there are many approaches to VQA, VQA is still challenging: 1). While attention mechanism has been effective in improving the performance of VQA task, they have limitations in terms of fully understanding the semantic multi-modal information. For example, the question is "What is this person doing?", and the image shows a person standing in a kitchen. Although attention mechanism can focus on the image region of the person, it cannot understand the specific activity of the person in the kitchen, such as whether he is cooking, washing dishes, or cleaning. 2). Existing semantic fusion methods usually focus on combining visual and textual features without explicitly resolving conflicts. This may result in the fusion process ignoring conflicting information and failing to effectively capture the relevance of multi-modal information.

To address the above issues, we propose the MSAM model, in which the self-private semantic space and the co-public semantic space are constructed to further understand multi-modal from the semantic level. Then, we utilize contrastive learning to deeply mine the multi-modal semantic space. By constructing positive pairs (aligned question-image pairs from co-public semantic space) and negative pairs (question-image pairs from self-private semantic space) of multi-modal samples, the method can stretch positive pairs in the semantic space closer together and negative pairs farther apart. In the multi-modal fusion stage,

Self-Attention(SA) and Guided-Attention(GA) [9] are used to achieve multi-modal interaction.

Our contributions are summarized as follows:

- To bridge the difficulty of attention mechanism in understanding multi-modal features at the semantic level, we design the MSAM model, which constructs the modal semantic space by Bi-affine projection to understand modal features at the semantic level.
- To alleviate the problem of conflicting information affecting the relevance of multi-modal semantic information, we employ contrastive learning to achieve semantic alignment. The distance between multi-modal features with identical semantics is further narrowed, thus enhancing the multi-modal semantic relevance.
- Our method is validated on the VQA2.0 dataset and the results confirm that our method outperforms previous methods.

The rest of the paper is organized as follows: Sect. 2 presents related work; Sect. 3 describes the paper methodology; Sect. 4 presents the experiments of our method on the VQA2.0 dataset; Sect. 5 presents conclusion.

## 2   Related Work

### 2.1   Multi-modal Feature Representation for VQA

The basis of the VQA task is to extract visual features of images and textual features of questions accurately and effectively. In early VQA methods, the Visual Geometry Group (VGG) [15] network is commonly applied to extract visual features. With the ResNet (Residual Network) network proposed by Kaiming et al. [16], the researchers gradually shift to the ResNet network that performs better than VGG in visual feature extraction. Recently, the bottom-up attention network [17] derives from Faster R-CNN [18] outperforms better than ResNet. By using the bottom-up attention network, the VQA model can focus on relevant regions in images, allowing it to better understand the visual context of questions. For the extraction of question features, the Long Short-Term Memory network (LSTM) [19] and the Gated Recurrent Unit (GRU) network [20] are commonly applied. Additionally, pre-training methods on Global Vectors for Word Representation (GLoVe) [21] or Bidirectional Encoder Representations from Transformers (Bert) [22] are also applied to obtain better features. Usually, VQA methods combine GLoVe and LSTM for the question features extraction. Multi-modal feature representation is crucial for improving the performance of VQA task. VQA task involves understanding both the visual content of images and the textual information conveyed by questions. By effectively representing multi-modal features, VQA models can better capture the relations between images and questions, leading to accurate answers.

## 2.2   Multi-modal Semantic Information for VQA

VQA aims to answer questions about images. To do so effectively, it needs to understand the semantics of both questions and images. In this regard, researchers present a number of approaches. The first one is the attention based approach, Peng et al. [23] propose a new Cross Fusion Network (CF-Net) for fast and efficient extraction of multi-scale semantic information. Tian et al. [24] introduce a Multi-level Semantic Context Information (MSCI) network with an overall symmetrical structure. The interconnections between three different semantic layers are utilized to extract contextual information between multi-modalities. Secondly, based on graph structure methods, Li et al. [25] design a graph embedding method that introduces pointwise mutual information to compute the semantic similarity between nodes. The correlation between the question and the image is measured by calculating the similarity. Adhikari et al. [26] present a new semantic fusion network that fuses the semantic information of questions and images by constructing a semantic graph. The above works focus on the importance of semantic information in the multi-modal fusion process, but ignore the fact that unimodal plays a complementary role in multi-modal semantic fusion. The individual modals themselves carry specific and important semantic information that can contribute to the overall understanding and answering of questions. Therefore, we propose to construct semantic space by Bi-affine space projection, constructing self-private semantic space for each modality separately and co-public semantic space for multi-modality at the same time. By constructing self-private semantic space for each modality, we can capture the unique semantic information of each modality. By building co-public semantic space, we can capture the relation between multi-modal semantic.

## 2.3   Multi-modal Semantic Alignment for VQA

Semantic alignment refers to the process of aligning the semantic information from multi-modal, to facilitate understanding and interaction between them. In recent years, there has been significant research progress in addressing the challenge of multi-modal semantic alignment in the VQA task. Li et al. [27] introduce a dynamic interaction network that combines Self-Attention and Cross-modal Attention. The ability to dynamically explore the various semantic depths of these different modal representations and fuse them together at a matching semantic level. Bao et al. [28] propose a method is designed for multi-task learning, i.e., learning shared semantic representations of different modals and introducing constraints to narrow the semantic distance between different modals. Based on previous works, we design a method to deeply mine the semantic space utilizing contrastive learning [14]. This approach enables semantic alignment, bridges the semantic distance that exists between modalities, and improves multi-modal semantic information relevance. Semantic Information relevance refers to the degree of semantic matching due to representational differences between heterogeneous modal features. We compute the similarity of image-question pairs and select sample pairs with high similarity as inputs for subsequent modal fusion, so that semantically similar multi-modal feature representations are more compact, while semantically different ones are mutually exclusive, thus improves the information relevance of the multi-modal.

## 2.4   Multi-modal Feature Fusion for VQA

Multi-modal feature fusion is an indispensable process in VQA task that combines information from different modalities to generate better representations for answering questions. Early stages utilize simple joint modal representations [10] for multi-modal feature fusion to capture high-level interactions between images and questions. Fukui et al. [29] apply MCB, a bilinear ensemble-based feature fusion method for VQA. This method improves the accuracy of VQA task by bilinear interaction of questions and answers. Kim et al. [30] propose the MLB method, which has a performance equal to MCB but with fewer weighting parameters. Nowadays, most of the multi-modal fusion in VQA task is done in an attention-based manner. Yu et al. [31] propose the MHF method which is superior to the above methods. MFH utilizes the correlation between multimodal features to achieve more effective multi-modal feature fusion. Yang et al. [7] propose a stacked attention network based on simple fusion to learn attention to image regions through multiple iterations. Chowdhury et al. [8] propose a coattentive learning method that alternates image attention and question attention based on attention to unimodal. Yu et al. [9] reduce co-attention to two steps, one for self-attentive learning of the question and the other for question-guided attention learning of the image. Based on the above work, we chose to introduce the fusion method of Modular Co-Attention (MCA) [9]. Before fusion, we narrow the semantic distance between multi-modal features through modal semantic alignment, which improves the information relevance between modal features. This approach addresses a limitation of the fusion model mentioned in MCA [9], which is the lack of ability to infer correlations between the question words and the image regions.

Unlike other models that focus on enriching images and questions information. In our work, we consider interacting with multi-modal from semantic perspective. Narrowing the semantic distance between multi-modal can lead to a more compact relations between multi-modal. Our model provides better results compared to other methods while maintaining a reasonable computational cost for the network.

## 3   Methodology

### 3.1   Overview

Figure 1 illustrates our MSAM model. Our model first maps the image features obtained after Faster-RCNN (Sect. 3.2) and the question features obtained after GLoVe+LSTM (Sect. 3.2) by means of a Bi-affine space projection method. The

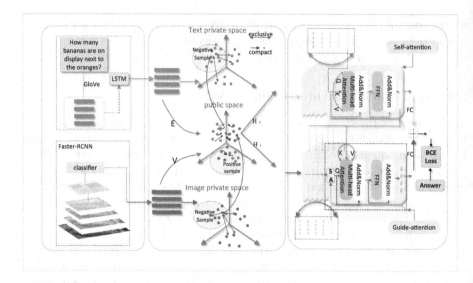

**Fig. 1.** MSAM model. On the left side of the MSAM model is multi-modal feature extraction. In the middle is semantic space building and multi-modal semantic alignment through contrastive learning. The right side is multi-modal feature fusion.

projections are made to self-private semantic spaces and simultaneously to co-public semantic space (Sect. 3.3). After semantic level alignment (Sect. 3.3), question features and image features with similar semantics are obtained. Finally, the obtained question features and image features with similar semantics are fused (Sect. 3.4) and the fused features are fed to the multi-label classifier to predict the correct answer (Sect. 3.4).

### 3.2    Images and Questions Representation

**Image Representation.** Following [32], the input image is represented as a set of image region features. These features are extracted from a Faster R-CNN [33] model pre-trained on the Visual Genome dataset [34]. Give an image I, the image features of I are represented as $V \in \mathbb{R}^{k \times 2048}$. where $k \in [10, 100]$ is the number of object regions. For the i-th word, it is represented as a feature $v_i \in \mathbb{R}^{2048}$.

**Question Representation.** Firstly, we give a question Q that is tokenized into words. Then, each word of the question is transformed into a vector, and pre-trained on a large-scare corpus by using the 300-dimensional GLoVe word embeddings [35] to get the final size of words $u \times 300$, where $u \in [1, 14]$ is the number of words in question. Finally, the word embeddings are passed through a one-layer and 512-dimensional LSTM network to obtain the question features $E \in \mathbb{R}^{u \times 512}$. This LSTM layer takes as input a sequence of embedded vectors and processes the sequence step-by-step through time steps. For the j-th word, it is represented as a feature $e_j \in \mathbb{R}^{512}$.

In practice, to handle the different number of object regions k and the variable number of words u, following [9], both of V and E are filled to their maximum sizes (i.e., k = 100, u = 14) by zero-padding. Especially, we conduct a linear transformation of V to make its dimension consistent with the question features.

### 3.3 Contrastive Learning Deep Mining of Multi-modal Semantic Space

**Bi-affine Space Projection.** The Bi-affine space projection method can be divided into two steps, first the affine space followed by the affine transformation also known as projection. Affine transformations differ from linear transformations in that they not only maintain the linear nature of vector spaces, but also preserve translation invariance. Based on comprehensive consideration, we choose to obtain the semantic space by affine transformation.

We first store question features E and image features V extracted in Sect. 3.2 into the Bi-affine space. Due to the different modal features of the inputs, they are mapped to different semantic spaces after Bi-affine transformation, which are called question private semantic space and image private semantic space, respectively. Since this space is built on a semantic level, a representation of the distribution of the different modal features in their respective private semantic spaces is obtained at this point. Complementary evidence for subsequent multi-modal semantic fusion is provided. In the subsequent operations we will seize contrastive learning to achieve multi-modal alignment at the semantic level, and therefore use modal features in the private semantic space as negative samples. The unimodal *Hidden representation* obtained in the private semantic space is denoted as $H$. The output of the text private semantic space is denoted by $H_t$ and the output of the image private semantic space is represented by $H_i$.

The question features E and image features V extracted in Sect. 3.2 are stored into the affine space. After affine projected into the same semantic space, which is called the co-public semantic space, we obtain representations of different modalities in the same semantic space. Since the spatial construction is de-constructed based on semantic information, there is a partial aggregation of different modal features. The aggregation of different modalities realizes a multi-modal fusion representation at the semantic level, which reduces some noise. However, despite the similarity of certain problem features and image features at some semantic levels, due to the semantic gaps between heterogeneous modalities, these modal features are close in the semantic space but still at a certain distance. Therefore it is difficult to provide a good representation of the semantic information correlation of multi-modal. In the previous section, the modal features in the private space are used as negative samples, and we use the modal features in the co-public semantic space as positive samples at this point. The modal *Hidden representation* obtained in the co-public semantic space is denoted as $H^P$. The question output features in the public semantic space are denoted by $H_T^P$, and the image output features are represented by $H_I^P$.

**Contrastive Learning for Semantic Alignment.** Contrastive learning is called self-supervised learning [36] in some papers and unsupervised learning [37] in others, and self-supervised learning is a form of unsupervised learning. Through contrastive learning, we compute the similarity of the question-image pairs in the batch and obtain sample pairs with the highest possible similarity. Multi-modal semantic alignment is achieved on this basis, shrinking the modal distance that exists. Therefore, multi-modal features with similar semantics lead to more compact modalities, while ones with different semantics are mutually exclusive. For a batch with N training samples, the unsupervised comparison loss for all samples in the batch can be expressed as follows:

$$L = \sum_{m \in M} -\frac{1}{|P(m)|} \sum_{p \in P(m)} \log \frac{\exp(H_m \cdot H_p/\tau)}{\sum_{c \in A(m)} \exp(H_m \cdot H_c/\tau)} \tag{1}$$

where $m \in M = \{1, 2, ..., N\}$ indicates the index of the samples, $\tau \in \mathbb{R}^+$ denotes the temperature coefficients introduced to control the distance between instances, $P(m) = I_{j=m} - \{m\}$ represents samples with the same category as $m$ while excluding itself, $A(m) = M - \{m, N+m\}$ indicates samples in a batch except itself.

### 3.4   Cross-Modal Fusion and Answer Prediction

**Cross-Modal Deep Interaction Networks.** We are inspired by the previous work of [9] to introduce Self-Attention (SA), Guide-Attention (GA), and their combined Modular Co-Attention (MCA). The SA module consists of a multi-head attention and a feedforward layer, where the multi-head attention is introduced to further improve the representation of the participating features. A set of input features $H_T^P = [H_{T1}^P; H_{T2}^P; ...; H_{Tm}^P]$ as samples, the multi-head attention learns the pairwise relations between the paired samples $\left(H_{T_i}^P, H_{T_j}^P\right)$ in the samples $H_T^P$, and outputs the participating output features by weighting the sum of all instances in the $H_T^P$. Multi-headed attention consists of $h$ parallel "heads", where each head corresponds to an independently scaled dot-product attention function, and the attended output features $f$ is given by:

$$f = \text{softmax}\left(\frac{QK}{\sqrt{d}}\right) V \tag{2}$$

$$Mf = [\text{head}_1, \text{head}_2, ..., \text{head}_h] \, \mathbf{W}^o \tag{3}$$

$$\text{head}_j = f\left(Q\mathbf{W}_j^Q, K\mathbf{W}_j^K, V\mathbf{W}_j^V\right) \tag{4}$$

where $\mathbf{W}_j^Q$, $\mathbf{W}_j^K$, $\mathbf{W}_j^V \in \mathbb{R}^{d \times d_h}$ are the projection matrices for the $d$ head, and $\mathbf{W}^o \in \mathbb{R}^{h \times d_h \times d}$. $d_h$ is the dimensionality of the output features from each head.

The input of scaled dot-product attention consists of Queries and Keys with dimension $d_{key}$, and Values with dimension $d_{value}$. For simplicity, $d_{key}$ and $d_{value}$ are usually set to the same number $d$. We are given a Query $Q \in \mathbb{R}^{1 \times d}$, $n$ Key-Value pairs(packed into a key matrix $K \in \mathbb{R}^{n \times d}$ and a value matrix $V \in \mathbb{R}^{n \times d}$), $f \in \mathbb{R}^{1 \times d}$.

The feedforward layer applies the output characteristics of multi-attention, and further transforms them through two fully-connected layers with ReLU activation and dropout (FC$(\cdot)$-ReLU-Dropout(0.1)-FC$(\cdot)$). Moreover, residual connection followed by layer normalization [38] is applied to the outputs of the two layers to facilitate optimization.

The GA module applies two sets of input features $H_T^P$ and $H_I^P = \left[ H_{I1}^P; H_{I2}^P; ...; H_{Im}^P \right]$ as samples, where $H_T^P$ guides the attention learning for $H_I^P$. Note that the shapes of $H_T^P$ and $H_I^P$ are flexible, so they can be applied to represent the features for different modalities. The GA units simulates the pairwise relations between the paired samples $\left( H_{T_i}^P, H_{I_j}^P \right)$ from $H_T^P$ and $H_I^P$, respectively.

Based on the two attention modules mentioned above, they are combined to obtain MCA layer, which can be utilized to process multi-modal features. Any MCA layer is deeply cascaded [39], and the output of the previous MCA layer is utilized as the input to the next MCA layer. This means that the number of input characteristics is equal to the number of output characteristics without reducing any instances.

$$\left[ H_T^{\text{out}(L)}, H_I^{\text{out}(L)} \right] = \text{MCA}^{(L-1)} \left[ H_T^{\text{out}(L-1)}, H_I^{\text{out}(L-1)} \right] \qquad (5)$$

We take the image features $H_I^P$ and question features $H_T^P$ obtained by contrastive learning as input, and pass the input features through a deep co-attention model composed of L-MCA layer to perform deep concentrative learning (denoted by MCA(1), MCA(2)... MCA(L)). Denoting the input features for MCA(L) as $H_T^{\text{out}(L-1)}$ and $H_I^{\text{out}(L-1)}$ respectively, their output features are denoted by $H_T^{\text{out}(L)}$ and $H_I^{\text{out}(L)}$, which are further fed to the MCA(L+1) as its inputs in a recursive manner.

**Answering Prediction.** After passing through the six layers of SA module and MCA module, the question features $H_T^{\text{fina-out}(L)}$ and image features $H_I^{\text{fina-out}(L)}$ already contain rich and accurate informations, so it is also important to fuse the features to predict the correct answer. In this process, a two-layer MLP(FC$(\cdot)$-ReLU-Dropout(0.1)-FC$(\cdot)$) structure is introduced to obtain the participation features, and the formula is as follows (seizing the image features as an example):

$$a = \text{softmax} \left( \text{MLP} \left( H_I^{\text{out}(L)} \right) \right) \qquad (6)$$

$$H_I^{\text{fina-out}(L)} = \sum_{i=1}^{m} a_i H_I^{\text{out}(L)} \qquad (7)$$

where $a = [a_1, a_2, ..., a_m] \in \mathbb{R}^m$ are the learned attention weights.

Using the computed $H_T^{\text{fina-out}}$ and $H_I^{\text{fina-out}}$, we apply the linear multi-modal fusion function as follows:

$$Z = \text{LayerNorm}\left(\mathbf{W}_t^T H_T^{\text{fina-out}(L)} + \mathbf{W}_i^T H_I^{\text{fina-out}(L)}\right) \qquad (8)$$

where $\mathbf{W}_t, \mathbf{W}_i \in \mathbb{R}^{d \times d_z}$ are two linear projection matrices, $d_z$ is the common dimensionality of the fused features. LayerNorm is introduced here to stabilize training. Z represents the fusion features.

The fused features Z is projected into vector $\mathbf{s} \in \mathbb{R}^D$ followed by a sigmoid function, where D is the number of the most frequent answers in the training set. Following [40], we utilize binary cross-entropy (BCE) as the loss function to train an D-way classifier on top of the fused features Z.

## 4 Experiments

In this section, we conduct experiments to evaluate the performance of our model on the largest VQA benchmark dataset. After introducing contrastive learning in our model, we learn that the temperature coefficients in contrastive learning can have an impact on the experimental results. Therefore, we conduct a number of quantitative and qualitative abatement experiments to explore the conditions under which our model MSAM performs best. Finally, we introduce optimal hyperparameters to compare MSAM with current methods.

### 4.1 Datasets

VQA2.0 is the most commonly used VQA benchmark dataset [41]. It contains human-annotated question-answer pairs relating to the images from the MS-COCO dataset [42], with 3 questions per image and 10 answers per question. The dataset is divided into three parts: train split (80k images and 444k QA pairs), val split (40k images and 214k QA pairs) and test split (80k images and 448k QA pairs). Additionally, there are two test subsets called test-dev and test-standard to evaluate model performance online. The results consist of three per-type accuracies (Yes/No, Number, and Other) and an overall accuracy.

### 4.2 Implementation Details

The model hyperparameters used in the experiments are shown below. The dimensions of input image features, input question features, public semantic space output image features, public semantic space output question features and fused multi-modal features are 2048, 512, 512, 512 and 1024, respectively.

The potential dimension of multihead attention is 512 and the number of heads h is set to 8. The potential dimension of each header is $d_h = d/h = 64$. The size of the answer vocabulary is set to 3129. The number of layers of MCA is set to L = 6. To train this model, we still apply the same Adam solver [43] $\beta_1 = 0.9$ and $\beta_2 = 0.98$ introduced in the MCAN model. The basic learning rate in the model is set to a minimum value ($2.5e^{-5}$, $1e^{-4}$) and the current epoch experienced starting from 1. The learning rate decreases according to the epoch experienced. All models are trained in the same batch of 15 epochs with a batch size of 64.

## 4.3  Baselines

In order to verify the effectiveness and generalization of our proposed approach to the VQA task, we compare it with the following models.

- **UpDn** [44]. This model is able to combine bottom-up and top-down attention mechanism and can compute attention at the level of objects and other salient image regions.
- **BAN** [21]. This model is able to compute the similarity between the image and the question using bilinear ensemble operations, and weight the features of the image and the question using the attention mechanism.
- **MUTAN** [45]. This model can be efficiently parameterized in a visual and textual bilinear interaction models (bilinear models) based on multi-modal tensor Tucker decomposition.
- **TRN+UpDn** [46]. This model maximizes the likelihood of estimating the joint distribution between observed questions and predicted answers.
- **DFAF** [1]. This model is used to dynamically fuse multi-modal features so that information is transmitted alternately between the image and the question modality.
- **DOG** [47]. It is able to learn an end-to-end VQA model from pixels directly to answers, and demonstrates good performance without the use of any region annotations in pre-training.
- **MLIN** [48]. The model is capable of utilizing multi-modal information, fusing sensitive information from each modality, and updating visual and textual features using multi-modal information.
- **HAN** [49]. This model is enabled to add semantic and structural information (hypergraph subgraph matching) to construct common concern graphs.
- **SUPER** [50]. The model is customized by five powerful specialized modules and dynamic routers to build a compact routing space. A variety of routing customizables can be used through explicitly calibrated visual semantic representations.
- **Co-VQA** [51]. This model is able to break down a complex question into a series of simple sub-questions and ultimately arrive at an answer to the question.
- **MRA-Net** [52]. The model explores both textual and visual relationships to improve performance and interpretation.
- **CAM** [53]. The Cascading Answer Model (CAM) is proposed, which extends the traditional single-stage VQA model to a two-stage model.
- **COB** [54]. A new regularization method is proposed for the VQA model, which exploits the theory of baroque (COB) to improve the information content of the joint space by minimizing redundancy.

- **CCC** [55]. The model divides questions into skills and concepts and combines them in new ways to improve the generalization of the VQA model.
- **DAQC** [56]. The model solves the VQA problem based on the visual problem construction of double attention and question categorization.
- **ALSA** [57]. The model is freeform and detection-based and aims to utilize prior knowledge for attention distribution learning.

### 4.4   Results

**Validation Results on VQA2.0.** Table 1 summarizes the results of our comparison with different methods in the VQA task. On the VQA2.0 dataset, Since our model focuses more on deeper understanding of multi-modal information at the semantic level, we have a fuller understanding of questions and images. The more comprehensively understood question and image features are fed into the fusion model to accomplish answer prediction. On the VQA2.0 dataset, our model outperforms the existing new model in terms of overall accuracy and accuracy in other categories. Since most of the existing papers validate the effect of online testing on the test set, we further compare it with the existing new method in Table 4. It shows that our model MSAM works better than the existing models.

**Table 1.** Results of MSAM compared with the new current models on VQA2.0 val. All Accuracy represents the overall accuracy, Yes/No represents the accuracy of the question type where the answer to the question is yes/no, Number represents the accuracy of the question with numeric answers, and Other represents the accuracy of the question with other question types.

| Model | All Accuracy | Other | Yes/No | Number |
|---|---|---|---|---|
| UpDn [44] | 63.15 | 55.81 | 80.07 | 42.87 |
| BAN [21] | 66.04 | – | – | – |
| MUTAN [45] | 63.61 | – | – | – |
| TRN+UpDn [46] | 65.10 | 57.10 | 82.61 | 45.10 |
| DFAF [1] | 66.20 | – | – | – |
| DOG [47] | 64.29 | 55.70 | 82.16 | 45.45 |
| MLIN [48] | 66.53 | – | – | – |
| HAN [49] | 65.50 | – | – | – |
| MCAN [9] | 66.88 | 58.04 | 84.62 | 49.00 |
| SUPER [50] | 66.59 | 58.07 | 85.15 | 48.27 |
| COB [54] | 63.80 | 55.86 | 81.36 | 43.30 |
| Ours | **67.27** | **58.53** | **85.00** | **49.73** |

**Results of Introducing Hard Samples.** With the addition of contrastive learning, we introduce hard samples. The role of hard samples is to enhance modal alignment. By enhancing modal alignment, question-image pairs with the same semantics are made better distinguishable from other sample pairs that do not have the same semantics. Table 2 shows the effect of adding hard samples and changing the number of hard samples on the results. Based on the results, it can be seen that as the number of hard sample increases to some extent, the various metrics are improved. However, due to the limitation of the number of batches, the number of hard samples cannot be increased without limit. Figure 2 visualizes the changes produced by various indicators by changing the number of hard samples.

**Table 2.** The effect of the number of hard samples on MSAM.

| Model | All Accuracy | Other | Yes/No | Number |
|---|---|---|---|---|
| $\text{Ours}_{\tau=15}$ | 67.03 | 58.31 | 84.53 | 49.41 |
| $\text{Ours+hard10 sample}_{\tau=15}$ | 67.25 | 58.45 | 84.91 | 49.45 |
| $\text{Ours+hard16 sample}_{\tau=15}$ | 67.27 | 58.53 | 85.00 | 49.73 |
| $\text{Ours+hard24 sample}_{\tau=15}$ | 67.24 | 58.43 | 84.92 | 49.40 |

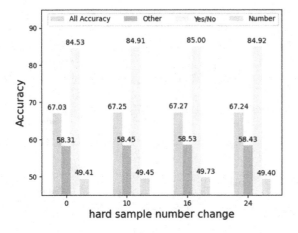

**Fig. 2.** Purple represents the All Accuracy indicator, blue represents the Other indicator, yellow represents the Yes/No indicator, and pink represents the Number indicator. (Color figure online)

**Results of Changing Temperature Coefficients.** With the introduction of contrastive learning, we learn that the presence of temperature coefficients in the contrastive learning formulation affects the extent to which comparative loss focuses on hard samples. For this reason, we conduct the following experiments to explore the effect of varying different temperature coefficients on the accuracy of the model. By setting the temperature coefficients to {1, 15, 50, 75, 100}, we obtain that the model is optimal when the temperature coefficient is 15. The results are shown in Table 3. In order to express more clearly the variation of the experimental results due to the temperature coefficients, we plot the following line graph (as shown in the Fig. 3).

**Table 3.** The effect of temperature coefficient variation on MSAM.

| Model | All Accuracy | Other | Yes/No | Number |
|---|---|---|---|---|
| Ours$_{\tau=1}$ | 67.20 | 58.32 | 84.75 | 49.42 |
| Ours$_{\tau=15}$ | 67.27 | 58.53 | 85.00 | 49.73 |
| Ours$_{\tau=50}$ | 67.25 | 58.39 | 84.90 | 49.63 |
| Ours$_{\tau=75}$ | 67.22 | 58.43 | 84.89 | 49.60 |
| Ours$_{\tau=100}$ | 67.21 | 58.36 | 84.87 | 49.55 |

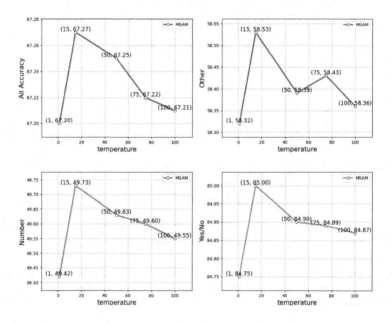

**Fig. 3.** The four line graphs show the effect on the various metrics as the temperature coefficients change.

**Online Test for VQA2.0.** Finally, we evaluate our results on the test-dev and test-std sets. The results show that our model MSAM can be used for modal interactions by digging deeper into the multi-modal semantic information from the semantic point of view. The VQA task is accomplished by deeply understanding the modal semantic information and combining the semantic information. As shown in Table 4.

**Table 4.** Results of MSAM compared with the new current models on test-dev and test-std sets.

| Model | test-dev | | | | test-std |
|---|---|---|---|---|---|
| | All Accuracy | Other | Yes/No | Number | All Accuracy |
| TRN+UpDn [46] | 67.00 | 57.44 | 83.83 | 45.61 | 67.21 |
| MRA-Net [52] | 69.06 | 59.62 | 86.79 | 43.89 | 69.22 |
| CCC [55] | 69.78 | – | – | – | 70.09 |
| SUPER [50] | 69.23 | 59.35 | 85.42 | 51.16 | 69.69 |
| Co-VQA [51] | – | – | – | – | 70.39 |
| CAM [53] | 68.82 | 59.76 | 85.18 | 47.35 | 68.99 |
| DAQC [56] | 64.51 | 56.39 | 82.15 | 43.57 | – |
| ALSA [57] | 69.21 | 59.17 | 85.73 | 48.98 | – |
| ours | **70.38** | **60.12** | **87.35** | **51.70** | **70.65** |

# 5   Conclusions

In this paper, we design the MSAM for deep mining multi-modal semantics for VQA task. By constructing semantic space, we understand the information deeply at the semantic level. Multi-modal semantic alignment is achieved through contrastive learning, which reduces the distance between heterogeneous modalities and improves the relevance of semantic information. The attention mechanism, which is widely used in VQA task, has limited ability in deep semantic understanding, and it does not has the ability of multi-modal semantic alignment and reasoning to deeply understand the semantic relationship between different modalities. Our propose method well compensates the deficiencies existing in the attention mechanism. Extensive experiments on the VQA2.0 dataset show that our approach achieves competitive results compared to current methods.

# References

1. Gao, P., Jiang, Z., You, H., et al.: Dynamic fusion with intra-and inter-modality attention flow for visual question answering. In: Proceedings of the IEEE/CVF Conference on Computer Vision and Pattern Recognition, pp. 6639–6648 (2019)
2. Zhang, W., Yu, J., Hu, H., et al.: Multimodal feature fusion by relational reasoning and attention for visual question answering. Inf. Fusion **55**, 116–126 (2020)

3.  Chen, T., Yu, W., Chen, R., et al.: Knowledge-embedded routing network for scene graph generation. In: Proceedings of the IEEE/CVF Conference on Computer Vision and Pattern Recognition, pp. 6163–6171 (2019)
4.  Zhou, H., Du, J., Zhang, Y., et al.: Information fusion in attention networks using adaptive and multi-level factorized bilinear pooling for audio-visual emotion recognition. IEEE/ACM Trans. Audio Speech Lang. Process. **29**, 2617–2629 (2021)
5.  Tan, H., Bansal, M.: LXMERT: learning cross-modality encoder representations from transformers. arXiv preprint arXiv:1908.07490 (2019)
6.  Gu, J., Zhao, H., Lin, Z., et al.: Scene graph generation with external knowledge and image reconstruction. In: Proceedings of the IEEE/CVF Conference on Computer Vision and Pattern Recognition, pp. 1969–1978 (2019)
7.  Yang, Z., He, X., Gao, J., et al.: Stacked attention networks for image question answering. In: Proceedings of the IEEE Conference on Computer Vision and Pattern Recognition, pp. 21–29 (2016)
8.  Chowdhury, M.I.H., Nguyen, K., Sridharan, S., et al.: Hierarchical relational attention for video question answering. In: 2018 25th IEEE International Conference on Image Processing (ICIP), pp. 599–603. IEEE (2018)
9.  Yu, Z., Yu, J., Cui, Y., et al.: Deep modular co-attention networks for visual question answering. In: Proceedings of the IEEE/CVF Conference on Computer Vision and Pattern Recognition, pp. 6281–6290 (2019)
10. Chang, L., Zhang, C.: Vehicle taillight detection based on semantic information fusion. In: Mantoro, T., Lee, M., Ayu, M.A., Wong, K.W., Hidayanto, A.N. (eds.) ICONIP 2021. CCIS, vol. 1517, pp. 528–536. Springer, Cham (2021). https://doi.org/10.1007/978-3-030-92310-5_61
11. Nguyen, B.X., Do, T., Tran, H., et al.: Coarse-to-fine reasoning for visual question answering. In: Proceedings of the IEEE/CVF Conference on Computer Vision and Pattern Recognition, pp. 4558–4566 (2022)
12. Chen, C., Han, D., Chang, C.C.: CAAN: context-aware attention network for visual question answering. Pattern Recogn. **132**, 108980 (2022)
13. Tu, G., Wen, J., Liu, C., et al.: Context-and sentiment-aware networks for emotion recognition in conversation. IEEE Trans. Artif. Intell. **3**(5), 699–708 (2022)
14. Xiong, L., Xiong, C., Li, Y., et al.: Approximate nearest neighbor negative contrastive learning for dense text retrieval. arXiv preprint arXiv:2007.00808 (2020)
15. Donahue, J., Anne Hendricks, L., Guadarrama, S., et al.: Long-term recurrent convolutional networks for visual recognition and description. In: Proceedings of the IEEE Conference on Computer Vision and Pattern Recognition, pp. 2625–2634 (2015)
16. Xu, K., Ba, J., Kiros, R., et al.: Neural image caption generation with visual attention. In: Proceedings of the ICML, pp. 2048–2057 (2015)
17. Nam, H., Ha, J.W., Kim, J.: Dual attention networks for multimodal reasoning and matching. In: Proceedings of the IEEE Conference on Computer Vision and Pattern Recognition, pp. 299–307 (2017)
18. Wang, Y., Yasunaga, M., Ren, H., et al.: VQA-GNN: reasoning with multimodal semantic graph for visual question answering. arXiv preprint arXiv:2205.11501 (2022)
19. Malinowski, M., Fritz, M.: A multi-world approach to question answering about real-world scenes based on uncertain input. In: Advances in Neural Information Processing Systems, vol. 27 (2014)
20. Zhao, Z., Zhang, Z., Xiao, S., et al.: Open-ended long-form video question answering via adaptive hierarchical reinforced networks. IJCAI **2**, 8 (2018)

21. Kim, J.H., Jun, J., Zhang, B.T.: Bilinear attention networks. In: Advances in Neural Information Processing Systems, vol. 31 (2018)

22. Simonyan, K., Zisserman, A.: Very deep convolutional networks for large-scale image recognition. arXiv preprint arXiv:1409.1556 (2014)

23. Peng, C., Zhang, K., Ma, Y., et al.: Cross fusion net: a fast semantic segmentation network for small-scale semantic information capturing in aerial scenes. IEEE Trans. Geosci. Remote Sens. **60**, 1–13 (2021)

24. Tian, P., Mo, H., Jiang, L.: Image caption generation using multi-level semantic context information. Symmetry **13**(7), 1184 (2021)

25. Li, D., Li, D., Wang, C., et al.: Network embedding method based on semantic information. In: Proceedings of the 3rd International Conference on Advanced Information Science and System, pp. 1–6 (2021)

26. Adhikari, A., Dutta, B., Dutta, A., et al.: Semantic similarity measurement: an intrinsic information content model. Int. J. Metadata Semant. Ontol. **14**(3), 218–233 (2020)

27. Li, B., Lukasiewicz, T.: Learning to model multimodal semantic alignment for story visualization. arXiv preprint arXiv:2211.07289 (2022)

28. Bao, Y., Lattimer, B.M., Chai, J.: Human inspired progressive alignment and comparative learning for grounded word acquisition. arXiv preprint arXiv:2307.02615 (2023)

29. Fukui, A., Park, D.H., Yang, D., et al.: Multimodal compact bilinear pooling for visual question answering and visual grounding. arXiv preprint arXiv:1606.01847 (2016)

30. Kim, J.H., On, K.W., Lim, W., et al.: Hadamard product for low-rank bilinear pooling. arXiv preprint arXiv:1610.04325 (2016)

31. Yu, Z., Yu, J., Xiang, C., et al.: Beyond bilinear: generalized multimodal factorized high-order pooling for visual question answering. IEEE Trans. Neural Networks Learn. Syst. **29**(12), 5947–5959 (2018)

32. Chen, C., Han, D., Wang, J.: Multimodal encoder-decoder attention networks for visual question answering. IEEE Access **8**, 35662–35671 (2020)

33. Ren, S., He, K., Girshick, R., et al.: Faster R-CNN: towards real-time object detection with region proposal networks. In: Advances in Neural Information Processing Systems, vol. 28 (2015)

34. Krishna, R., Zhu, Y., Groth, O., et al.: Visual genome: connecting language and vision using crowdsourced dense image annotations. Int. J. Comput. Vision **123**, 32–73 (2017)

35. Pennington, J., Socher, R., Manning, C.D.: Glove: global vectors for word representation. In: Proceedings of the 2014 Conference on Empirical Methods in Natural Language Processing (EMNLP), pp. 1532–1543 (2014)

36. Li, L., Liang, Y., Shao, M., et al.: Self-supervised learning-based Multi-Scale feature Fusion Network for survival analysis from whole slide images. Comput. Biol. Med. **153**, 106482 (2023)

37. Zheng, Z., Feng, X., Yu, H., et al.: Unsupervised few-shot image classification via one-vs-all contrastive learning. Appl. Intell. **53**(7), 7833–7847 (2023)

38. Yeo, Y.J., Sagong, M.C., Park, S., et al.: Image generation with self pixel-wise normalization. Appl. Intell. **53**(8), 9409–9423 (2023)

39. Ye, Y., Pan, Y., Liang, Y., et al.: A cascaded spatiotemporal attention network for dynamic facial expression recognition. Appl. Intell. **53**(5), 5402–5415 (2023)

40. Kulkarni, C., Rajesh, M,. Shylaja, S.S.: Dynamic binary cross entropy: an effective and quick method for model convergence. In: 2022 21st IEEE International

Conference on Machine Learning and Applications (ICMLA), pp. 814–818. IEEE (2022)

41. Goyal, Y., Khot, T., Summers-Stay, D., et al.: Making the v in VQA matter: elevating the role of image understanding in visual question answering. In: Proceedings of the IEEE Conference on Computer Vision and Pattern Recognition, pp. 6904–6913 (2017)

42. Lin, T.-Y., et al.: Microsoft COCO: common objects in context. In: Fleet, D., Pajdla, T., Schiele, B., Tuytelaars, T. (eds.) ECCV 2014, Part V. LNCS, vol. 8693, pp. 740–755. Springer, Cham (2014). https://doi.org/10.1007/978-3-319-10602-1_48

43. Kingma, D.P., Ba, J.: Adam: a method for stochastic optimization. arXiv preprint arXiv:1412.6980 (2014)

44. Anderson, P., He, X., Buehler, C., et al.: Bottom-up and top-down attention for image captioning and visual question answering. In: Proceedings of the IEEE Conference on Computer Vision and Pattern Recognition, pp. 6077–6086 (2018)

45. Ben-Younes, H., Cadene, R., Cord, M., et al.: MUTAN: multimodal tucker fusion for visual question answering. In: Proceedings of the IEEE International Conference on Computer Vision, pp. 2612–2620 (2017)

46. Han, X., Wang, S., Su, C., Zhang, W., Huang, Q., Tian, Q.: Interpretable visual reasoning via probabilistic formulation under natural supervision. In: Vedaldi, A., Bischof, H., Brox, T., Frahm, J.-M. (eds.) ECCV 2020, Part IX. LNCS, vol. 12354, pp. 553–570. Springer, Cham (2020). https://doi.org/10.1007/978-3-030-58545-7_32

47. Jiang, H., Misra, I., Rohrbach, M., et al.: In defense of grid features for visual question answering. In: Proceedings of the IEEE/CVF Conference on Computer Vision and Pattern Recognition, pp. 10267–10276 (2020)

48. Gao, P., You, H., Zhang, Z., et al.: Multi-modality latent interaction network for visual question answering. In: Proceedings of the IEEE/CVF International Conference on Computer Vision, pp. 5825–5835 (2019)

49. Kim, E.S., Kang, W.Y., On, K.W., et al.: Hypergraph attention networks for multimodal learning. In: Proceedings of the IEEE/CVF Conference on Computer Vision and Pattern Recognition, pp. 14581–14590 (2020)

50. Han, Y., Yin, J., Wu, J., et al.: Semantic-aware modular capsule routing for visual question answering. arXiv preprint arXiv:2207.10404 (2022)

51. Wang, R., et al.: Co-VQA: answering by interactive sub question sequence. In: Findings of the Association for Computational Linguistics: ACL (2022)

52. Peng, L., Yang, Y., Wang, Z., et al.: MRA-Net: improving VQA via multi-modal relation attention network. IEEE Trans. Pattern Anal. Mach. Intell. **44**(1), 318–329 (2020)

53. Peng, L., Yang, Y., Zhang, X., et al.: Answer again: improving VQA with Cascaded-Answering model. IEEE Trans. Knowl. Data Eng. **34**(04), 1644–1655 (2022)

54. Jha, A., Patro, B., Van Gool, L., et al.: Barlow constrained optimization for visual question answering. In: Proceedings of the IEEE/CVF Winter Conference on Applications of Computer Vision, pp. 1084–1093 (2023)

55. Whitehead, S., Wu, H., Ji, H., et al.: Separating skills and concepts for novel visual question answering. In: Proceedings of the IEEE/CVF Conference on Computer Vision and Pattern Recognition, pp. 5632–5641 (2021)

56. Mishra, A., Anand, A., Guha, P.: Dual attention and question categorization-based visual question answering. IEEE Trans. Artif. Intell. **4**(1), 81–91 (2022)

57. Liu, Y., Zhang, X., Zhao, Z., et al.: ALSA: adversarial learning of supervised attentions for visual question answering. IEEE Trans. Cybern. **52**(6), 4520–4533 (2022)

# Defeating the Non-stationary Opponent Using Deep Reinforcement Learning and Opponent Modeling

Qian Yao[1,2], Xinli Xiong[1,2], Peng Wang[1,2], and Yongjie Wang[1,2(✉)]

[1] College of Electronic Engineering, National University of Defense Technology, Hefei 230037, China
{yaoqian21,xiongxinli_,wangpeng21e,wangyongjie17}@nudt.edu.cn
[2] Anhui Province Key Laboratory of Cyberspace Security Situation Awareness and Evaluation, Hefei 230037, China

**Abstract.** In the cyber attack and defense process, the opponent's strategy is often dynamic, random, and uncertain. Especially in an advanced persistent threat scenario, it is not easy to capture its behavior strategy when confronted with a long-term latent, highly dynamic and unpredictable opponent. FlipIt game can model the stealth interaction of advanced persistent threat. However, it is insufficient for traditional reinforcement learning approach to solve real-time and non-stationary game model. Therefore, how to model a non-stationary opponent implicitly and keep the defense agent's advantage continuously is essential. In this paper, we propose an extended FlipIt game model incorporating opponent modeling. And then we propose an approach that combines deep reinforcement learning, opponent modeling, and dropout technology to perceive the behavior of a non-stationary opponent and defeat it. Instead of explicitly identifying the opponent's intention, the defense agent observes the opponent's last move actions from the game environment, stores the information in its knowledge, then perceives the opponent's strategy and finally makes a decision to maximize its benefits. We show the excellent performance of our approach whether the opponent adopts traditional, random or composite strategies. The experimental results demonstrated that our approach can perceive the opponent quickly and maintain the superiority of suppressing the opponent.

**Keywords:** Deep reinforcement learning · Opponent modeling · FlipIt game · Non-stationary environment

## 1 Introduction

In recent years, cyberspace incidents have occurred frequently. One of the most serious attacks is advanced persistent threats (APT) [21]. Through long-term reconnaissance and investigation of the target, APT attackers usually adjust their attack policies correspondingly. The automated and intelligent cyber attack

H. Gao et al. (Eds.): CollaborateCom 2023, LNICST 562, pp. 57–78, 2024.
https://doi.org/10.1007/978-3-031-54528-3_4

tools [1,11,22] constantly emerging. If attackers exploit these tools to launch APT attacks, it will bring disastrous consequences.

It is essential to model APT attacks and study defense strategies against intelligent attacks. FlipIt game [12,23] can model the continuous cyber attack and defense process, which can characterize the stealth interaction characteristics of APT attacks. In a FlipIt game, the attacker and defender compete for sensitive resources without knowing the opponent's behavior. Some researchers have improved the modeling of FlipIt game [10,27]. However, the modeling of highly dynamic and non-stationary opponents is insufficient. Therefore, We proposed an extended FlipIt game model combined with opponent modeling.

As the cyber modeling becomes more fine-grained, the complexity problem comes with it. When confronted with the real-time and complex cyber attacks, it is not easy for humans to make correct decisions immediately. Therefore, the solution method [5,15,28] of FlipIt game is also a research hotspot. At present, it's recommended to train a reinforcement learning agent to execute the cyber defense decision-making tasks. On the one hand, reinforcement learning agent can observe and interact with the game environment, and then make sequential decisions without prior knowledge. On the other hand, reinforcement learning agent has shown excellent performance in both human-agent confrontation [18] and agent-agent confrontation [20]. However, the classic reinforcement learning algorithms have a shared limitation of over-fitting and over-estimation, and cannot adapt to the non-stationary game environment. In this work, we proposed an improved Deep Q-Network (DQN) [14] approach to learn the opponent's strategy in a FlipIt game.

At the same time, the FlipIt game environment is non-stationary due to the influence of the opponent's behavior. Opponent modeling [6,7,26] are the main solutions to deal with the non-stationary problem. It mainly refers to modeling the behavior of the opponent by using interactive information and exploring the opponent's weakness.

Overall, due to intelligent attack tools, APT attacks may become more unpredictable and disastrous. FlipIt game can be used to model APT attacks. However, the exited FlipIt game models without modeling the non-stationary opponent well. Reinforcement learning is widely used to solve FlipIt game model, but the shortcomings such as over-fitting and over-estimation need to be further improved.

In this paper, we construct an extended FlipIt game model with opponent modeling. And we incorporate an perception vector into DQN, which stores the observation of the opponent's last move actions into the knowledge of the defense agent. And then defense agent analyzes the opponent's strategy to maintain a long-term advantage over the opponent. For adapting to the non-stationary game environment and preventing the over-fitting problem of the reinforcement learning, we adopt the dropout technology in the DQN. Simultaneously, we adopt Constrained Q-Learning to overcome the over-estimation problem. Meanwhile, the proposed method can be further extended to multi-agent collaborative decision-making problems. The contributions of this work are as follows:

- Given the cyber attack and defense environment is dynamic and random, we introduce a controllable random factor and propose random strategies for the FlipIt game. To adapt the non-stationary game environment, we construct an extended FlipIt game model with opponent modeling, called FlipIt-OM.
- We propose an improved deep reinforcement learning approach to solve the FlipIt-OM game, called ND3QN. ND3QN combines NoisyNet, Dueling Q-Network, Dropout technology and Constrained Q-Learning. It solves the problems of over-estimation, over-fitting and insufficient exploration.
- The experimental results show the superior performance of ND3QN to the baseline DQN, PER-DQN. Through stealth interaction with the environment, ND3QN agent can model the opponent's strategy well and maintain its advantage over its opponents. ND3QN is more suitable for the non-stationary game environment.

The rest of this paper is structured as follows. Section 2 introduced the related works about FlipIt game and opponent modeling. Section 3 presented the extended FlipIt game model. Section 4 elaborated on the basic architecture and technical implementation details. Section 5 analyzed the experimental results. Section 6 summarized the paper and pointed out the future research direction.

## 2   Related Work

FlipIt game aims at simulating an APT-like scenario. The defender and opponent fight for controlling a sensitive resource, such as a private key, a password, etc. Laszka et al. [10] introduced two control models (AND and OR models) and proposed the FlipThem model. The attacker tries to destroy one or all of the resources. The existing FlipIt game models without considering model a non-stationary opponent.

It is a research hotspot to solve the FlipIt game with reinforcement learning algorithms. Lisa et al. [15] introduced QFlip, an adaptive strategy based on Q-Learning for the FlipIt game. Deep reinforcement learning integrates the powerful perceiving ability of deep learning (DL) and decision-making ability of reinforcement learning (RL). Laura et al. [5] used DQN to maximize the defender's rewards in a FlipIt game, and extended to an n-player security game. However, a common limitation is that Q-Learning or DQN can't adapt to the non-stationary environment well. Zhu et al. [28] presented adaptive DQN to apply to a non-stationary FlipIt game. The approach can realize the rebalance of exploration and exploitation quickly by tracking the variance changes of Q-value distribution. However, this work only considers the non-stationary problem of the game environment, the opponent still adopts the fixed period and exponential strategy. Furthermore, our proposed FlipIt-OM models a non-stationary opponent.

There are inevitable defects in the classic RL approach, such as over-fitting, over-estimation and insufficient exploration. Dropout [19] is proposed to overcome the over-fitting problem. Dropout drops some units from the neural network randomly during the training process, which breaks up the co-adaptations among specific hidden units. Co-adaptation means that the units depend on each other. Conservative Q-Learning [9] and Double Q-Learning [24] are proposed to address the over-estimation problem. To enhance the exploration ability of the agent to induce stochasticity of its strategy, NoisyNet [4] adds Gaussian noise to the neural network. Dueling Q-Network [25] divides the last layer in two streams. One of them estimates the state value function for state $s$ and the other one estimates the advantage function for each action $a$. Finally, both parts are combined into a single stream to calculate the Q-values.

Given the non-stationary problem, the researchers pay attention to the method of opponent modeling, including explicit and implicit modeling categories. Explicit modeling identifies the opponent's behavior directly. Richard et al. [2] combined DRL and opponent modeling and proposed a Switching Agent Model. Jakob et al. [3] presents Learning with Opponent-Learning Awareness(LOLA). Yuxi et al. [13] proposed an opponent portrait approach using MADDPG in a competitive environment. Roberta et al. [16] proposed Self Other-Modeling. An agent can predict the other agent's actions. Zhang et al. [8] added a policy inferring module into the DQN, called DPIQN. DPIQN models the observation of opponents into the Q-value learning process. While implicit modeling attempts to take a strategy through implicit reasoning. He et al. [6] presented deep reinforcement opponent network and encoded the opponent's behavior into DQN, instead explicitly predicting the opponent's action. In this paper, ND3QN perceives the strategy of opponent and stores the opponent's behavior data, and then makes defensive decisions.

In summary, RL is the mainstream method to solve the FlipIt game. However, RL has the problem of over-fitting, which can't adapt to the non-stationary game environment. In addition, the existing FlipIt game models without considering model the non-stationary opponent. And we often can't accurately identify the opponent's behavior, especially in the APT-like scenario. How to implicitly perceive and reason the opponent's policy through stealth interaction with the game environment is worth to research.

## 3  FlipIt-OM Game Model

In this Section, we introduce the proposed FlipIt-OM game model. Section 3.1 makes the assumptions of the FlipIt-OM game model. Section 3.2 elaborates on the FlipIt-OM model. Section 3.3 introduces the strategies adopted by the opponent.

### 3.1  Assumptions

FlipIt-OM game model makes the following assumptions.

- Assuming that the defense agent can observe the last move actions of the opponent.
- Assuming that when the defense agent and the opponent compete for resources at the same time, the control power belongs to the defense agent.

## 3.2   Model

We adopt the Last Move (LM) [23] version of the FlipIt game. The players are in stealth interaction with the environment. Specifically, the defense agent and opponent can neither know who controls the sensitive resource currently, nor observe all the actions of the opponent, they can only capture the opponent's last flip action. The illustration of the FlipIt game (LM) is shown in Fig. 1.

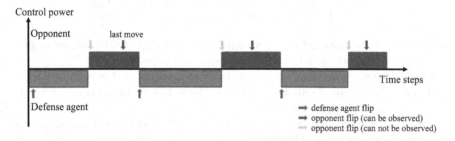

**Fig. 1.** illustration of FlipIt-OM game (LM)

Here, the red area indicates the time steps that the opponent controls, and the blue area indicates the defense agent controls. Based on the LM observation mechanism, the light red flip will never be perceived by the defense agent, while the dark red flip opportunity can be caught. For each step the agent decides to flip, it will control the resource and know the opponent's last flip opportunity. And it will spend flip cost at the same time.

In the FlipIt game (LM), $\mathcal{N}^d$ is a defense agent and $\mathcal{N}^o$ is the opponent. $T_{LM}^i$ is the time interval since the last flip of $\mathcal{N}^i$ at step $t$. $\mathcal{N}^d$ has full knowledge of $T_{LM}^d$, but only has last-move knowledge of $T_{LM}^o$. Then, $\mathcal{N}^d$ can perceive the opponent's strategy $\pi^{\rho^o}$ from observed opponent actions $a_t^o$. $\rho$ is a perceptual vector. Finally, $\mathcal{N}^d$ decide whether to flip the resources at each step $t$ based on the perceived knowledge $\pi^{\rho^o}$.

FlipIt-OM game models the opponent into FlipIt game. In a FlipIt-OM game, the observation space is influenced by the joint action of both sides. FlipIt-OM game model can be defined as a 8-tuple $(\mathcal{N}, \mathcal{S}, \mathcal{A}, \tau, \mathcal{R}, \gamma, \mathcal{K}, \pi)$.

- $\mathcal{N} = \{\mathcal{N}^d, \mathcal{N}^o\}$ represents the defense agent and opponent respectively.
- $\mathcal{S} = \{s_1, s_2, \cdots, s_n\}$ denotes the states observed by the defense agent $\mathcal{N}^d$, represented by $s_t = (T_{LM}^d, T_{LM}^o \mid \pi^{\rho^o}) \in \mathcal{S}$.
- $\mathcal{A} = \{\mathcal{A}^d, \mathcal{A}^o\}$, $\mathcal{A}^d$ and $\mathcal{A}^o$ represent the action space available to the defense agent and opponent, denoted as $a_t^d = \{flip, notflip\} \in \mathcal{A}^d$, $a_t^o = \{flip, notflip\} \in \mathcal{A}^o$.
- $\tau \{s, a^d, a^o, s'\}$ represents the transferring probability to a state $s'$ from the state $s$ when the defense agent selects $a^d$ and opponent selects $a^o$ .
- $\mathcal{R} = \{\mathcal{R}^d, \mathcal{R}^o\}$, $\mathcal{R}^d(s, a^d, a^o, s')$ and $\mathcal{R}^o(s, a^d, a^o, s')$ represent the reward of defense agent and opponent respectively. Three situations [28] are as follows. (1) If a player decides not to flip, the reward is empty. (2) If a player decides

to flip and $T_{LM}^d \leq T_{LM}^o$, the player will not obtain benefits $bef$ but need to spend the cost $cos$, for the reason that the control power originally belongs to it. (3) If a player decides to flip and $T_{LM}^d > T_{LM}^o$, the player regains control from opponent $\mathcal{N}^o$. Then the player will obtain the benefits $bef$ and spend the cost $cos$ at the same time. In conclusion, $r_t$ is represented as follows.

$$r_t = \begin{cases} 0 & if \ a_t \ = \ not \ flip \\ -cos & if \ a_t \ = \ flip \ and \ T_{LM}^d \leq T_{LM}^o \\ bef - cos & if \ a_t \ = \ flip \ and \ T_{LM}^d > T_{LM}^o \end{cases} \tag{1}$$

- $\gamma \in [0, 1)$ is the discount factor, which decides whether the defense agent pays attention to short-term interests or long-term interests.
- $\mathcal{K}$ is the knowledge about opponent. Defense agent stores the opponent's last flipping opportunity into knowledge $\mathcal{K}$. Thus the observation space of the defense agent is expanded.
- $\pi = \{\pi^d, \pi^o\}$ denotes the flipping strategy decided by defense agent and opponent respectively. The defense agent perceives the opponent's flip strategy $\pi^{\rho^o}$ through the knowledge $\mathcal{K}$. Then defense agent makes decisions $\pi^d$ correspondingly.

The descriptions of the symbols used in this paper are shown in Table 1.

**Table 1.** The descriptions of symbols used in this paper.

| Symbols | Descriptions |
|---------|-------------|
| $S_t$ | state space |
| $A_t$ | action space |
| $R_t$ | reward function |
| $Q(s, t)$ | action-value function |
| $\tau$ | state transferring probability |
| $\gamma$ | discount factor |
| $\rho$ | perception vector |
| $\mathcal{K}$ | knowledge about opponent |
| $\pi^o$ | opponent strategy |
| $\pi^d$ | defense agent strategy |
| $a^o$ | opponent actions |
| $a^d$ | defense agent actions |
| $\delta$ | flipping with fixed $\delta$ steps (period strategy) |
| $\lambda$ | flipping with an exponential distribution (exponential strategy) |
| $\zeta$ | flipping with fixed $\delta + \zeta$ steps (random period strategy) |
| $c$ | a constant floating number $c \in [0, 1)$ (random strategy) |
| $q$ | a random floating number $q \in [0, 1)$ (random strategy) |

The FlipIt-OM game model perceives the opponent's actions and stores the perceived information in its knowledge, therefore, the state space of the RL agent is expanded. It means that the state space observed by the defense agent is non-stationary. The Q-function of the defense agent is dependent on the strategy of the opponent. It is necessary to adjust the definition of Q-function so that the actions of other agents are considered. We consider a 1 vs. 1 scenario in a FlipIt game. The defense agent needs to perceive the opponent's strategy $\pi^o$ by observing its actions $a^o$. The Q function can be represented as Eq. 2.

$$Q(s, a | \pi^o) = \sum_{a^o} \pi^o(a^o | s) \sum_{s'} \tau\left(s, a^d, a^o, s'\right) \left[R(s, a^d, a^o, s') + \gamma E_{a'}\left[Q(s', a' \mid \pi^o)\right]\right]$$

(2)

The FlipIt-OM game model is updated by batch gradient descent to minimize the Mean Squared Error loss.

### 3.3 Opponent Strategies

Traditional strategies of the FlipIt game include period and exponential strategies. However, the opponent's behavior is random and dynamic in the real world. Therefore, we introduce a random factor and propose two new random strategies, called random period strategy and random strategy. Opponents can also adopt a composite strategy that contains more than two mentioned strategies. Therefore, the opponent adopts the following five strategies in this work.

- **Period.** Period strategy represents the opponent flips the resources with fixed $\delta$ time steps, represented as

$$\pi_{pe}^o = \begin{cases} flip & if\ T_{LM}^o = \delta \\ notflip & otherwise \end{cases}$$

(3)

where, $T_{LM}^o$ is the time interval since the last flip of $\mathcal{N}^o$ at step $t$.
- **Exponential.** Exponential strategy returns flipping opportunities with an exponential distribution. The probability density function is expressed as

$$p(x) = \begin{cases} \lambda e^{-\lambda x} & x > 0 \\ 0 & otherwise \end{cases}$$

(4)

$$\pi_{exp}^o = \begin{cases} flip & if\ T_{LM}^o \sim E(\lambda) \\ notflip & otherwise \end{cases}$$

(5)

where, $x$ is the value of random variables.
- **Random Period.** We introduce a random factor $\zeta(|\zeta| < \delta)$, which can be positive or negative. Then the flipping strategy becomes $\delta + \zeta$. $\zeta$ makes the flipping opportunity of period strategy no longer fixed, which aggravates the non-stationary of the FlipIt game environment.

$$\pi^o_{ran\_pe} = \begin{cases} flip & if \ T^o_{LM} = \delta + \zeta \\ notflip & otherwise \end{cases} \tag{6}$$

- **Random.** Random strategy returns a random floating number $q \in [0, 1)$ with uniform distribution. Then the opponent compares the values of $q$ and $c$ $(c \in [0, 1))$ to decide whether to flip the resources. Random strategy can be formally expressed as

$$\pi^o_{ran} = \begin{cases} flip & if \ q \le c \\ notflip & otherwise \end{cases} \tag{7}$$

- **Composite.** Composite strategy refers to the opponent's random choice of the above strategies to form a new composite strategy. Composite strategy is more unstable. This strategy poses greater challenges and requirements for defense agents.

## 4 ND3QN Decision-Making Approach

RL can be used to solve the solution of the FlipIt-OM game. To solve the non-stationary FlipIt-OM game, we propose ND3QN. In this Section, we elaborate on the architecture and implementation details of ND3QN. Section 4.1 outlines the architecture of ND3QN. Section 4.2 introduces the Constrained Q-Learning. Section 4.3 presents the process of interacting with opponents and environment. Section 4.4 explains the training procedure of ND3QN in detail.

### 4.1 The Architecture of NLD3QN

Due to the influence of the opponent's strategy, the process of FlipIt-OM game is dynamic and non-stationary. Therefore, we propose an approach called ND3QN to adapt to the non-stationary FlipIt game environment. The main objective of ND3QN is to defend against the potential opponent agent in a non-stationary game environment, such as an APT scenario. The approach combines NoisyNet, Dropout, Dueling Q-Network and Constrained Q-Learning into DQN to obtain a strategy that adapts to a non-stationary environment. ND3QN can learn a better reward function in a non-stationary environment than the classic DQN algorithm. The architecture of ND3QN is shown in Fig. 2.

The classic problems faced by reinforcement learning are over-fitting, over-estimation and insufficient exploration. ND3QN addresses these classic problems.

- To overcome the over-fitting problem, dropout is adopted during the training process of ND3QN. With dropout training, ND3QN is more suitable for a non-stationary environment.
- To enhance the exploring ability of ND3QN and make optimal decisions, NoisyNet is added in front of the action output layer. The Gassian noise is defined as $\xi \equiv (\mu + \sigma) \odot \epsilon$, where $(\mu + \sigma)$ is a set of learnable parameter vectors, $\epsilon$ denotes the zero-mean noise.

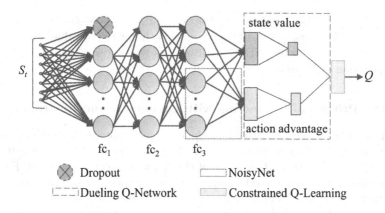

**Fig. 2.** The architecture of ND3QN.

- To improve the performance of ND3QN, Dueling Q-Network is incorporated to split the last layer of the same neural network in two streams: the state-value function $S$ and the advantage function $A$.

Simultaneously, we have also made specific improvements for the non-stationary FlipIt-OM game environment appropriately.

- To solve the over-estimation problem of classic DQN, we propose Constrained Q-Learning(Cons-QL). The design of Cons-QL is introduced in Sect. 4.2.
- To adapt to the stealth interaction in an APT scenario, ND3QN is able to perceive the opponent's behavior. The implementation details of the perception process are presented in Sect. 4.3.

ND3QN can quickly achieve the balance between exploring and exploiting the environment, and continue to maintain its advantages over its opponent. Then we introduce the detail of Cons-QL and the perception process in the following subsections.

### 4.2   Constrained Q-Learning

The Bellman-style Q function of reinforcement learning is as follows:

$$Q(s_t, a_t) = Q(s_t, a_t) + \alpha(r_t + \gamma \max Q(s_{t+1}, a_{t+1}) - Q(s_t, a_t)) \tag{8}$$

where $\alpha$ is the learning rate. However, due to the influence of $\max Q(s_{t+1}, a_{t+1})$, the value of $Q(s, a)$ in Eq. 8 may be overestimated. Cons-QL takes a constrained mean value as the lower bounds of Q value, as shown in Eq. 9.

$$Q(s_t, a_t) = Q(s_t, a_t) - \omega * (Q(s_t, a_t) - Q_{mean})^2 \tag{9}$$

where $\omega \in [0,1)$ is a balance factor, $Q_{mean} = \frac{(Q_{last}+Q(s_t,a_t))}{2}$, $Q_{last} = Q(s_{t-1}, a_{t-1})$. After using Cons-QL, it can smooth out the Q-value spike caused by over-fitting. As a result, ND3QN will reduce wrong decisions caused by the over-estimation of Q value.

### 4.3   The Process of Interacting with Opponents and Environment

A diagram of the process of perceiving opponents and interacting with the environment using ND3QN is shown in Fig. 3. In the process of the FlipIt-OM real-time game, the observation space of the ND3QN agent is extended. Firstly, the ND3QN agent stores the information of the opponent's last move actions $a^o$ in its knowledge base $\mathcal{K}$. Perceptual vector $\rho^o$ analyzes a series of actions of the opponent from the knowledge base $\mathcal{K}$. Then ND3QN agent learns the opponent's strategy $\pi^o$ through perception vector $\rho^o$. According to the perceived opponent's strategy $\pi^{\rho^o}$, the ND3QN agent makes its strategy $\pi^d$ and then does defensive actions $a^d$.

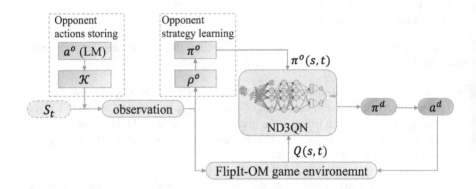

**Fig. 3.** Diagram of perception process of ND3QN.

### 4.4   The Training Procedure of ND3QN

Because of the concealment, latency, and unpredictability of APT attacks, it is essential to perceive opponents' behavior from the environment for learning agents. DRL can learn from the environment and make sequential decisions without given prior knowledge. DRL is accordance with the stealth interaction characteristics of APT attacks. A novel algorithm called ND3QN was proposed. The perception vector is set in the observation space of the ND3QN agent to capture the flipping opportunity of the opponent's last move actions and store it in the knowledge of the ND3QN agent. The training procedure of ND3QN is shown in Algorithm 1.

---

**Algorithm 1:** The training procedure of ND3QN.

---

1  Initialize replay memory $D$, environment $env$, and observation $s$
2  Initialize network with random weights $\theta$, dropout $p$ and noise $\xi$
3  Initialize target network with weights $\theta^-$
4  Initialize the advantage function parameter $\alpha$, the state-value function parameter $\beta$
5  **for** $t = 1$ $to$ $T$ **do**
6  $\quad$ Select an action $a_d \leftarrow Q(s, a, \xi; \theta, \alpha, \beta)$
7  $\quad$ Execute $a_d$ in $env$ and observe $a^o, r, s'$
8  $\quad$ Store $a^o$ in knowledge $k^d$
9  $\quad$ Perceive $\pi^o$ using perception vector $\rho^o$
10 $\quad$ Store transition $\tau \{s, a^d, a^o, s'\}$ in $D$
11 $\quad$ Sample random minibatch of transitions $\tau \{s_j, a_j^d, a_j^o, s_j'\}$ from $D$
12 $\quad$ **for** $j = 1$ $to$ $minibatch$ **do**
13 $\quad\quad$ **if** $s_j'$ *is a terminal state* **then**
14 $\quad\quad\quad$ $Q(s_j, a_j^d | \pi^o) \leftarrow R(s_j, a_j^d, a_j^o, s_j')$
15 $\quad\quad$ **end**
16 $\quad\quad$ $Q(s_j, a_j^d \mid \pi^o) \leftarrow \sum_{a^o} \pi^o(a^o \mid s_j) \sum_{s'} \tau(s_j, a_j^d, a_j^o, s_j')$
$\quad\quad\quad [R(s_j, a_j^d, a_j^o, s_j') + \gamma E_{a'} [Q(s_j', a_j', \xi'; \theta^-, \alpha, \beta \mid \pi^o)]]$
17 $\quad\quad$ Calculate constrained Q value $Q(s_j, a_j^d \mid \pi^o)$
18 $\quad\quad$ Perform a gradient descent step with loss
$\quad\quad\quad \frac{1}{m} \sum_{i=1}^{m} (Q(s_j, a_j^d \mid \pi^o) - Q_E(s, a \mid \pi^o))^2$
19 $\quad$ **end**
20 $\quad$ Every $C$ steps update the target network $\theta^- \leftarrow \theta$
21 **end**

---

## 5 Experiments

The experiments were conducted in a FlipIt game simulator. Section 5.1 describes the environmental settings. Section 5.2 introduces the baseline algorithms. Section 5.3 analyzes the experimental results.

### 5.1 Environmental Settings

Experiments were conducted in the FlipIt-OM (LM) game environment. Generally speaking, the resources are limited. Thus the cost of flipping the resources by the players is higher than the benefit. In the experiments, the flipping cost is 5, the flipping reward is 1. And the numbers of training episodes are 10000, the steps of per episodes are 200.

### 5.2 Baseline

In this section, we introduce two baseline algorithms (DQN and PER-DQN), and then we show the hyperparameters used in this experiment.

- **DQN.** Deep Q-Network stores the experience into the replay buffer, and then evenly samples a mini-batch of samples from the replay buffer for a Q-learning update in each time step $t$.
- **PER-DQN.** Prioritized Experience Replay (PER) [17] improves the sampling problem of DQN. PER samples a batch of experiences from memory based on the priority. The sampling probability of state transition $i$ can be calculated as follows.

$$P(i) = \frac{p_i^\alpha}{\sum_k p_k^\alpha} \tag{10}$$

where $p_i$ is the priority of $i$. $\alpha \in [0, 1]$ is a factor to adjust random sampling or prior sampling. PER adjusts the weight in importance sampling to correct the deviation of $i$ with $\beta \in [0, 1]$. $N$ is the size of the replay buffer.

$$w_i = N P(i)^{-\beta} \tag{11}$$

Table 2 shows the hyperparameters of the three algorithms. Where, $p$ denotes the proportion of dropped units in the fully connected layer to prevent overfitting.

**Table 2.** Hyperparameters of three algorithms.

| Hyperparameters | ND3QN | DQN | PER-DQN |
|---|---|---|---|
| buffer_size | 2000 | 2000 | 2000 |
| batch_size | 32 | 32 | 32 |
| learning rate | 0.003 | 0.003 | 0.003 |
| $\tau$ | 0.003 | 0.003 | 0.003 |
| $\gamma$ | 0.99 | 0.99 | 0.99 |
| eps_start | 1 | 1 | 1 |
| eps_end | 0.01 | 0.01 | 0.01 |
| eps_decay | 0.995 | 0.995 | 0.995 |
| update_network | 5 | 5 | 5 |
| p | 0.05 | – | – |
| $\alpha$ | – | – | 0.2 |
| $\beta$ | – | – | 0.2 |

– indicates that there are no values.

## 5.3   Analysis of Experimental Results

To validate the effectiveness and efficiency of ND3QN, we adopted a series of experiments. Section 5.3.1 introduced the evaluation index. Section 5.3.2 compared the three methods against the opponent with traditional strategies, including period and exponential strategies. Section 5.3.3 compared the three methods against an opponent with non-stationary strategies, including random period and random strategies. Section 5.3.4 compared the three methods against an opponent with a composite strategy.

**Evaluation Index.** The average score, last score, and winning rate are selected as evaluation indexes. The criteria for judging the effectiveness of defense agents are as follows: (1) defeating the attack agent is the premise of the defense agent; (2) if (1) is satisfied, the higher last score of the defense agent is better.

- **Average score.** The average rewards obtained by the players from the FlipIt-OM game environment every 100 episodes.
- **Last score.** The average rewards of last 100 episodes obtained by the players in 10000 episodes of the FlipIt-OM game.
- **Winning rate.** The probability of the defense agent defeating the opponent in the total times.

**ND3QN Against an Opponent with Traditional Strategies.** In this section, we compare the performance of the three algorithms against an opponent with traditional strategies, including period and exponential strategies.

- **ND3QN against an opponent with period strategy.**

The average scores of the three algorithms against an opponent with a period strategy are shown in Fig. 4.

Due to the integration of Dueling Q-Network and Noisynet, the performance of the ND3QN agent is improved. And dropout solves the co-adaption between units. Especially, the ND3QN agent almost always maintains its advantage over the opponent owing to the perception vector. Combined with these advantages, the performance of the ND3QN agent is the best. However, the DQN agent can't adapt to the opponent's strategy, and the convergence process is unstable. The standard deviation of ND3QN is 16.58 after 1000 episodes, while DQN is 27.87 ($\delta$ = 10). This is because without opponent modeling, DQN needs to relearn from experience. The performance of PER-DQN is the worst, and it's not able to take effect. This is because PER-DQN adds priority experience replay to evaluate a priority of historical experience. PER may work in a static environment, but it is difficult to take effect in a continuous game process.

The last scores against a period opponent with different $\delta$ is shown in Fig. 5. The ND3QN agent always keeps its advantage even if the opponent's flipping opportunity changes. If the opponent flips the resource at regular intervals, the DQN agent also performs well, but the learning progress of the DQN agent is relatively slow and the convergence is unstable during the game process. PER-DQN agent neither adapts to the game environment nor learns the optimal strategy, and it always loses to the opponent.

- **ND3QN against an opponent with exponential strategy.**

As shown in Fig. 6 and Fig. 7, exponential strategy is more difficult to capture its flipping opportunity compared with period strategy.

However, we still come to a similar conclusion. The ND3QN agent can always beat the opponent and obtain a higher reward. It can be seen that the ND3QN

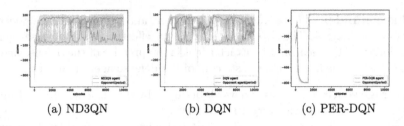

**Fig. 4.** Average scores against an opponent with period strategies ($\delta = 10$).

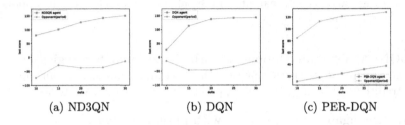

**Fig. 5.** Last score against a period opponent. ($\delta = 10, 15, 20, 25, 30$.)

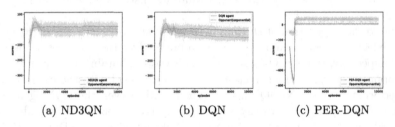

**Fig. 6.** Average scores against an opponent with exponential strategies ($\lambda = 0.02$).

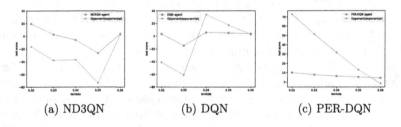

**Fig. 7.** Last score against an exponential opponent. ($\lambda = 0.02, 0.03, 0.04, 0.05, 0.06$.)

agent has strong adaptability to the opponent's strategy, and can learn the optimal flipping strategy through opponent modeling. Overall, the DQN agent is unable to adapt to the opponent's different strategies. Sometimes DQN agent beats its opponent but sometimes loses to its opponent. Because the DQN agent has the defects of over-fitting and over-estimation, it can't quickly adjust its strategy when the opponent's strategies change. PER-DQN agent still doesn't work, and it can't learn a strategy to beat its opponent.

The comparison of the last scores of the three algorithms against an opponent with traditional strategies is shown in Table 3. When the opponent adopts the period strategy, the efficiency of ND3QN and DQN is similar, because the period strategy is relatively stable. While when the opponent adopts exponential strategy, the advantage of ND3QN is more obvious, and DQN sometimes fails to analyze the law of exponential strategy and loses to the opponent.

**Table 3.** Comparison of the last scores of the three algorithms against an opponent with traditional strategies.

| Opponent strategy | Last score of the defense agent vs. opponent | | |
|---|---|---|---|
| | ND3QN | DQN | PER-DQN |
| Period ($\delta = 10$) | **80.38/−73.48** | 26.70/−13.55 | 11.22/84.88 |
| Period ($\delta = 15$) | 100.84/−27.79 | **112.95/−46.25** | 18.29/112.81 |
| Period ($\delta = 20$) | 126.50/−37.55 | **137.68/−45.98** | 24.70/121.40 |
| Period ($\delta = 25$) | 141.96/−36.61 | **142.16/−34.06** | 31.97/124.13 |
| Period ($\delta = 30$) | **150.19/−14.14** | 143.18/−13.73 | 37.69/128.41 |
| Exponential ($\lambda = 0.02$) | **19.30/−16.55** | 3.44/−40.99 | 10.03/72.97 |
| Exponential ($\lambda = 0.03$) | **2.64/−37.74** | −15.01/−60.94 | 7.80/51.20 |
| Exponential ($\lambda = 0.04$) | **−6.04/−36.86** | 5.70/34.10 | 6.25/31.55 |
| Exponential ($\lambda = 0.05$) | **−26.66/−73.49** | 4.81/17.14 | 5.31/13.09 |
| Exponential ($\lambda = 0.06$) | **3.70/2.25** | 3.70/2.25 | 4.38/−1.63 |

**ND3QN Against an Opponent with Non-stationary Strategies.** In this section, we compare the performance of the three algorithms against an opponent with non-stationary strategies, including random period and random strategies.

- **ND3QN against an opponent with a random period strategy.**

As described in Sect. 3.3, random period is represented as $T^o_{LM} = \delta + \zeta$. As shown in Fig. 8 and Fig. 9, the advantages of ND3QN are more obvious confronted with a non-stationary opponent. ND3QN has the highest average scores and keeps a stable convergence. However, the last score of DQN is lower than ND3QN. In addition, DQN has an unstable convergence, and in some cases it can't learn a decision-making strategy and eventually loses to its opponent. In contrast, PER-DQN can't learn the opponent's behavior.

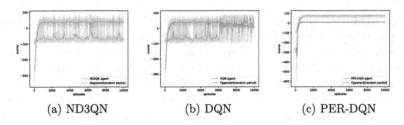

**Fig. 8.** Average scores against an opponent with random period strategies ($\delta = 10$, $\zeta = 3$).

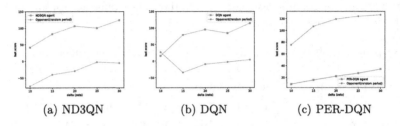

**Fig. 9.** Last score against a random period opponent. ($\delta = 10, 15, 20, 25, 30$; $\zeta = 3$, 4, 5, 7, 8.)

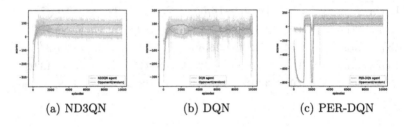

**Fig. 10.** Average scores against an opponent with random strategies ($c = 0.04$).

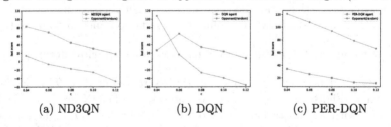

**Fig. 11.** Last score against a random opponent. ($c = 0.04, 0.06, 0.08, 0.10, 0.12$.)

- **ND3QN against an opponent with a random strategy.**

Random strategy returns a random floating number $q \in [0,1)$ with uniform distribution. Then the opponent compares the values of $q$ and $c$ to decide whether to flip the resources. As shown in Fig. 10 and Fig. 11, similarly, ND3QN continues to maintain an advantage over its opponent and has the highest average scores. DQN can learn an optimal strategy in most cases. However, the unstable convergence of DQN is more severe, and sometimes it even loses to its opponent. PER-DQN utilizes the acquired historical experience for priority sampling, it still can't defeat the opponent who adopts a random strategy.

The comparison of the last scores of the three algorithms against an opponent with non-stationary strategies is shown in Table 4. ND3QN has an extraordinary performance when the opponent adopts random strategy. ND3QN has the highest last score and good convergence, and it can continue to beat opponents. Because ND3QN can perceive and analyze the opponent's strategy, it can quickly find the optimal strategy to defeat the opponent. However, DQN agent is unstable in convergence and sometimes loses to its opponents.

**Table 4.** Comparison of the last scores of the three algorithms against an opponent with non-stationary strategies.

| Opponent strategy | Last score of the defense agent vs. opponent | | |
|---|---|---|---|
| | ND3QN | DQN | PER-DQN |
| Random Period ($\delta = 10, \zeta = 3$) | **41.72/−74.72** | 15.75/27.10 | 8.83/75.32 |
| Random Period ($\delta = 15, \zeta = 4$) | **81.54/−40.49** | 78.91/−34.16 | 15.75/106.95 |
| Random Period ($\delta = 20, \zeta = 5$) | **105.88/−29.68** | 95.38/−9.38 | 22.21/119.44 |
| Random Period ($\delta = 25, \zeta = 7$) | **99.89/−2.94** | 84.41/−2.71 | 27.31/124.24 |
| Random Period ($\delta = 30, \zeta = 8$) | **123.76/−5.46** | 114.61/4.14 | 34.40/126.70 |
| Random ($c = 0.04$) | **82.78/13.82** | 26.34/107.71 | 34.31/120.94 |
| Random ($c = 0.06$) | **69.05/−6.60** | 65.40/16.60 | 25.72/107.78 |
| Random ($c = 0.08$) | **44.31/−17.56** | 33.81/−26.66 | 19.95/93.90 |
| Random ($c = 0.10$) | **30.61/−25.76** | 23.49/−39.34 | 12.89/78.61 |
| Random ($c = 0.12$) | **17.74/−46.69** | 7.46/−56.11 | 11.54/66.36 |

**ND3QN Against an Opponent with a Composite Strategy.** Assuming that the opponent adopts a composite strategy of random ($c = 0.05$) and random period strategy ($\delta = 20, \zeta = 3$). It's more difficult to catch the flipping opportunities of composite strategy. Average scores against the opponent are shown in Fig. 12.

As can be seen from Fig. 12(a) and 12(b), the opponent defeats all the defense agent after approximately 1000 epsisodes. ND3QN can perceive the opponent's behavior and learn the strategy of defeating its opponent, while DQN cannot learn the strategy and eventually loses to the opponent. Opponent modeling becoming more important when faced with opponents of composite strategies. The standard deviation of ND3QN scores is 2.49 after 1000 episodes, while the value of DQN is 10.45. It indicates that the convergence of ND3QN is better.

For another example, when the opponent adopts a random ($c = 0.01$) and random period strategy ($\delta = 10, \zeta = 4$). The last score of the ND3QN vs. its opponent is $3.62/-31.82$, the value of DQN is $65.05/15.60$, and the value of PER-DQN is $24.68/73.58$. Although the performance of DQN is the best in this case, ND3QN can still learn the strategy of defeating the opponent quickly. When the opponent adopts random $(c = 0.04)$ and exponential strategy $(\lambda = 0.03)$. The last score of ND3QN vs. its opponent is $17.53/-21.23$, the value of DQN is $15.85/-37.35$, and the value of PER-DQN is $11.56/79.39$. The standard deviation of ND3QN scores is 2.30 after 1000 episodes, the value of DQN is 3.49. ND3QN is slightly better than DQN in this case.

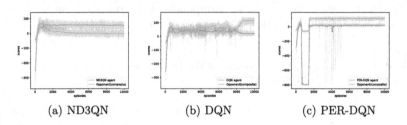

(a) ND3QN              (b) DQN              (c) PER-DQN

**Fig. 12.** Average scores against an opponent with composite strategies $(c = 0.05, \delta = 20, \zeta = 3.)$

The comparison of the last scores against an opponent with non-stationary strategies is shown in Table 5.

**Table 5.** Comparison of the last scores of the three algorithms against an opponent with composite strategies.

| Opponent strategy | Last score of the defense agent vs. opponent | | |
| --- | --- | --- | --- |
| | ND3QN | DQN | PER-DQN |
| Composite $(c = 0.05, \delta = 20, \zeta = 3)$ | **52.60/−0.20** | 19.41/116.19 | 21.69/113.11 |
| Composite $(c = 0.01, \delta = 10, \zeta = 4)$ | 3.62/−31.82 | **65.05/15.60** | 24.68/73.58 |
| Composite $(c = 0.04, \lambda = 0.03)$ | **17.53/−21.23** | 15.85/−37.35 | 11.56/79.39 |

The performance of ND3QN is more stable and effective in the face of opponents with composite strategies, and it can maintain the advantage of defeating opponents. However, the effect of DQN is unstable, which is caused by its overfitting and insufficient exploration.

From the above experiments, the winning rates of the three algorithms are shown in the Table 6. The winning rate of ND3QN is over 95%, the winning rate of DQN is 78.26%, and PER-DQN is only 4.35%. Note that the winning rate is calculated from the above opponent strategies, which does not mean that it can be applied to all situations. Genarally, when the opponent's strategy is more random, it is more difficult to beat it. ND3QN has a high winning rate, regardless of the opponent adopting the traditional, random or composite strategies.

**Table 6.** Comparison of the winning rates against the opponent.

| Opponent strategy | ND3QN | DQN | PER-DQN |
|---|---|---|---|
| Period ($\delta = 10$) | ✓ | ✓ | ✗ |
| Period ($\delta = 15$) | ✓ | ✓ | ✗ |
| Period ($\delta = 20$) | ✓ | ✓ | ✗ |
| Period ($\delta = 25$) | ✓ | ✓ | ✗ |
| Period ($\delta = 30$) | ✓ | ✓ | ✗ |
| Exponential ($\lambda = 0.02$) | ✓ | ✓ | ✗ |
| Exponential ($\lambda = 0.03$) | ✓ | ✓ | ✗ |
| Exponential ($\lambda = 0.04$) | ✓ | ✗ | ✗ |
| Exponential ($\lambda = 0.05$) | ✓ | ✗ | ✗ |
| Exponential ($\lambda = 0.06$) | ✓ | ✓ | ✓ |
| Random Period ($\delta = 10, \zeta = 3$) | ✓ | ✗ | ✗ |
| Random Period ($\delta = 15, \zeta = 4$) | ✓ | ✓ | ✗ |
| Random Period ($\delta = 20, \zeta = 5$) | ✓ | ✓ | ✗ |
| Random Period ($\delta = 25, \zeta = 7$) | ✓ | ✓ | ✗ |
| Random Period ($\delta = 30, \zeta = 8$) | ✓ | ✓ | ✗ |
| Random ($c = 0.04$) | ✓ | ✗ | ✗ |
| Random ($c = 0.06$) | ✓ | ✓ | ✗ |
| Random ($c = 0.08$) | ✓ | ✓ | ✗ |
| Random ($c = 0.10$) | ✓ | ✓ | ✗ |
| Random ($c = 0.12$) | ✓ | ✓ | ✗ |
| Composite($c = 0.05, \delta = 20, \zeta = 3$) | ✓ | ✗ | ✗ |
| Composite($c = 0.01, \delta = 10, \zeta = 4$) | ✓ | ✓ | ✗ |
| Composite($c = 0.04, \lambda = 0.03$) | ✓ | ✓ | ✗ |

✓ represents winning; ✗ represents losing.

**Ablation Experiments of ND3QN.** The ablation experimental results of ND3QN agent vs. opponent is shown in Table 7.

It can be seen that each component has a certain positive impact. The random strategy of the opponent makes the observation space of ND3QN non-stationary. The optimization effect of dropout is relatively obvious for the reason that it can alleviate the over-fitting problem. NoisyNet and Dueling Q-Network are both improve the performance of ND3QN. When the opponent adopts the traditional strategy, Cons-QL doesn't work. While when the opponent adopts the random strategy, Cons-QL takes effect. This is because the traditional attack strategy is relatively fixed and has certain rules, and the estimation of Q value is relatively accurate. Instead, when the opponent's strategy is random, the over-estimation of Q value is more obvious.

Table 7. Ablation results of ND3QN agent vs. opponent.

| Ablation components | Opponent strategy | Last score of ND3QN vs. opponent | |
|---|---|---|---|
| | | Original results | Ablation results |
| NoisyNet | Period ($\delta = 10$) | 80.38/−73.48 | 89.58/−23.36↑ |
| | Exponential ($\lambda = 0.02$) | 19.30/−16.55 | **15.79/−25.94↓** |
| | Random ($c = 0.04$) | 82.78/13.82 | 83.34/14.71↑ |
| | Ran_Period ($\delta = 10, \zeta = 3$) | 41.72/−74.72 | **36.86/−65.36↓** |
| Dropout | Period ($\delta = 10$) | 80.38/−73.48 | 83.59/−72.19↑ |
| | Exponential ($\lambda = 0.02$) | 19.30/−16.55 | **16.46/−23.36↓** |
| | Random ($c = 0.04$) | 82.78/13.82 | **80.49/0.71↓** |
| | Ran_Period ($\delta = 10, \zeta = 3$) | 41.72/−74.72 | **37.05/−78.15↓** |
| Dueling Q-Network | Period ($\delta = 10$) | 80.38/−73.48 | 86.98/−82.43↑ |
| | Exponential ($\lambda = 0.02$) | 19.30/−16.55 | **11.62/73.83↓** |
| | Random ($c = 0.04$) | 82.78/13.82 | 83.34/14.71↑ |
| | Ran_Period ($\delta = 10, \zeta = 3$) | 41.72/−74.72 | **40.10/−75.25↓** |
| Cons-QL | Period ($\delta = 10$) | 80.38/−73.48 | 80.38/−73.48 |
| | Exponential ($\lambda = 0.02$) | 19.30/−16.55 | 19.30/−16.55 |
| | Random ($c = 0.04$) | 82.78/13.82 | 88.17/10.33↑ |
| | Ran_Period ($\delta = 10, \zeta = 3$) | 41.72/−74.72 | **37.24/−77.90↓** |

# 6    Conclusion and Future Work

In this work, we incorporate random factors and propose random strategies of
FlipIt game. We construct a FlipIt-OM model using opponent modeling and deep
reinforcement learning. And we propose ND3QN to perceive the non-stationary
opponent in a FlipIt-OM game to simulate an APT-like scenario. ND3QN solves
the over-estimation, over-fitting and insufficient exploration problems by combining NoisyNet, Dueling Q-Network, Dropout and Cons-QL. Due to the stealth
interaction characteristics of the APT attack, ND3QN can only observe the opponent's last move actions, then stores it into its knowledge. ND3QN perceives
the opponent's strategy accurately, and eventually defeating its opponent. We
demonstrate the efficiency and effectiveness of ND3QN in a FlipIt-OM game
environment against opponents with traditional, non-stationary, and composite
strategies. From the above experiments, the winning rate of ND3QN is over 95%,
and the winning rate of DQN is 78.26%. ND3QN can adapt to more opponent
strategies. And the convergence of ND3QN is more stable.

The FlipIt-OM model and the ND3QN approach proposed in this paper can
be widely used in non-stationary cyberspace game scenarios. In addition, a real
attacker can cheat or launch a feint to hide its real attack ability. Future work
will further examine a deceptive opponent modeling and infer the opponent's
real strategy to suppress the opponent immediately.

# References

1. Baillie, C., Standen, M., Schwartz, J., Docking, M., Bowman, D., Kim, J.: Cyborg: an autonomous cyber operations research gym. arXiv preprint arXiv:2002.10667 (2020)
2. Everett, R., Roberts, S.J.: Learning against non-stationary agents with opponent modelling and deep reinforcement learning. In: AAAI Spring Symposia (2018)
3. Foerster, J.N., Chen, R.Y., Al-Shedivat, M., Whiteson, S., Abbeel, P., Mordatch, I.: Learning with opponent-learning awareness. arXiv preprint arXiv:1709.04326 (2017)
4. Fortunato, M., et al.: Noisy networks for exploration. arXiv preprint arXiv:1706.10295 (2017)
5. Greige, L., Chin, P.: Deep reinforcement learning for flipit security game. In: Benito, R.M., et al. (eds.) COMPLEX NETWORKS 2021, pp. 831–843. Springer, Cham (2022). https://doi.org/10.1007/978-3-030-93409-5_68
6. He, H., Boyd-Graber, J., Kwok, K., Daumé III, H.: Opponent modeling in deep reinforcement learning. In: International Conference on Machine Learning, pp. 1804–1813. PMLR (2016)
7. Hernandez-Leal, P., Zhan, Y., Taylor, M.E., Sucar, L.E., Munoz de Cote, E.: An exploration strategy for non-stationary opponents. Auton. Agent. Multi-Agent Syst. **31**, 971–1002 (2017)
8. Hong, Z.W., Su, S.Y., Shann, T.Y., Chang, Y.H., Lee, C.Y.: A deep policy inference q-network for multi-agent systems. arXiv preprint arXiv:1712.07893 (2017)
9. Kumar, A., Zhou, A., Tucker, G., Levine, S.: Conservative q-learning for offline reinforcement learning. Adv. Neural. Inf. Process. Syst. **33**, 1179–1191 (2020)
10. Laszka, A., Horvath, G., Felegyhazi, M., Buttyán, L.: Flipthem: modeling targeted attacks with flipt, for multiple resources. In: Poovendran, R., Saad, W. (eds.) GameSec 2014. LNCS, vol. 8840, pp. 175–194. Springer, Cham (2014). https://doi.org/10.1007/978-3-319-12601-2_10
11. Li, L., Fayad, R., Taylor, A.: Cygil: a cyber gym for training autonomous agents over emulated network systems. arXiv preprint arXiv:2109.03331 (2021)
12. Liu, Z., Wang, L.: Flipit game model-based defense strategy against cyberattacks on SCADA systems considering insider assistance. IEEE Trans. Inf. Forensics Secur. **16**, 2791–2804 (2021)
13. Ma, Y., et al.: Opponent portrait for multiagent reinforcement learning in competitive environment. Int. J. Intell. Syst. **36**(12), 7461–7474 (2021)
14. Mnih, V., et al.: Human-level control through deep reinforcement learning. Nature **518**(7540), 529–533 (2015)
15. Oakley, L., Oprea, A.: QFlip: an adaptive reinforcement learning strategy for the FlipIt security game. In: Alpcan, T., Vorobeychik, Y., Baras, J.S., Dán, G. (eds.) GameSec 2019. LNCS, vol. 11836, pp. 364–384. Springer, Cham (2019). https://doi.org/10.1007/978-3-030-32430-8_22
16. Raileanu, R., Denton, E., Szlam, A., Fergus, R.: Modeling others using oneself in multi-agent reinforcement learning. In: International Conference on Machine Learning, pp. 4257–4266. PMLR (2018)
17. Schaul, T., Quan, J., Antonoglou, I., Silver, D.: Prioritized experience replay. arXiv preprint arXiv:1511.05952 (2015)
18. Silver, D., et al.: Mastering the game of go without human knowledge. Nature **550**(7676), 354–359 (2017)

19. Srivastava, N., Hinton, G., Krizhevsky, A., Sutskever, I., Salakhutdinov, R.: Dropout: a simple way to prevent neural networks from overfitting. J. Mach. Learn. Res. **15**(1), 1929–1958 (2014)
20. Tang, Z., Zhu, Y., Zhao, D., Lucas, S.M.: Enhanced rolling horizon evolution algorithm with opponent model learning. IEEE Transactions on Games (2020)
21. Tankard, C.: Advanced persistent threats and how to monitor and deter them. Netw. Secur. **2011**(8), 16–19 (2011)
22. Team, M.D.: CyberBattleSim (2021). https://github.com/microsoft/cyberbattlesim
23. Van Dijk, M., Juels, A., Oprea, A., Rivest, R.L.: Flipit: the game of "stealthy takeover.". J. Cryptol. **26**, 655–713 (2013)
24. Van Hasselt, H., Guez, A., Silver, D.: Deep reinforcement learning with double q-learning. In: Proceedings of the AAAI Conference on Artificial Intelligence, vol. 30 (2016)
25. Wang, Z., Schaul, T., Hessel, M., Hasselt, H., Lanctot, M., Freitas, N.: Dueling network architectures for deep reinforcement learning. In: International Conference on Machine Learning, pp. 1995–2003. PMLR (2016)
26. Wu, Z., Li, K., Xu, H., Zang, Y., An, B., Xing, J.: L2e: learning to exploit your opponent. In: 2022 International Joint Conference on Neural Networks (IJCNN), pp. 1–8. IEEE (2022)
27. Zhang, R., Zhu, Q.: Flipin: a game-theoretic cyber insurance framework for incentive-compatible cyber risk management of internet of things. IEEE Trans. Inf. Forensics Secur. **15**, 2026–2041 (2019)
28. Zhu, J., Wei, Y., Kang, Y., Jiang, X., Dullerud, G.E.: Adaptive deep reinforcement learning for non-stationary environments. Sci. Chin. Inf. Sci. **65**(10), 202204 (2022)

# A Multi-Agent Deep Reinforcement Learning-Based Approach to Mobility-Aware Caching

Han Zhao[1]🆔, Shiyun Shao[2]🆔, Yong Ma[3]🆔, Yunni Xia[4(✉)]🆔, Jiajun Su[1]🆔,
Lingmeng Liu[1]🆔, Kaiwei Chen[1]🆔, and Qinglan Peng[5]🆔

[1] School of Digital Industry, Jiangxi Normal University, Shangrao 334000, China
{zhaohan,sujiajun,202241600165,20214160016}@jxnu.edu.cn
[2] Département d'informatique et recherche opérationnelle, Université de Montréa,
Montréal H3T 1N8, Canada
[3] School of Computer and Information Engineering, Jiangxi Normal University,
Nanchang 330000, China
may@jxnu.edu.cn
[4] School of Computer Science, Chongqing University, Chongqing 400030, China
xiayunni@hotmail.com
[5] School of Artificial Intelligence, Henan University, Zhengzhou, China
qinglan.peng@henu.edu.cn

**Abstract.** Mobile Edge Computing (MEC) is a technology that enables on-demand the provision of computing and storage services as close to the user as possible. In an MEC environment, frequently visited content can be deployed and cached upon edge servers to boost the efficiency of content delivery and thus improving user-perceived experience. However, due to the dynamic nature of MEC, it remains a great challenge how to fully exploit mobility information in yielding high-quality content caching decisions for delay-sensitive real-time mobile applications. To address this challenge, this paper proposes a novel mobility-aware caching method by leveraging a Multi-Agent Deep Reinforcement Learning-Based (MAACC) Approach model. The proposed method synthesizes a content fitness algorithm for estimating the priority of caching content with high user fitness and a collaborative caching strategy built upon a multi-agent deep reinforcement learning model. Empirical results clearly show that MAACC outperforms its peers regarding cache hit rate and transfer delay time.

**Keywords:** Mobile Edge Networks · Cooperative Caching · Content Fit · Multi-agent Deep Reinforcement Learning · Mobility

## 1 Introduction

The exponential growth of data traffic generated by Internet of Things (IoT) devices, coupled with the increasing number of resource requests from users using

H. Gao et al. (Eds.): CollaborateCom 2023, LNICST 562, pp. 79–95, 2024.
https://doi.org/10.1007/978-3-031-54528-3_5

smart mobile devices (SMD), has posed new challenges to the traditional cloud center model [1]. In the conventional cloud center model, when users request resources from the cloud center, the data needs to be transmitted to the users via backhaul links, resulting in significant content transmission delays that negatively impact the quality of user experience (QoE) [2]. MEC is a technology that extends computing and storage resources to the network edge [3]. It deploys these resources as close to the user's request as possible, typically on edge servers or base stations owned by network operators. As a result, when users initiate requests, the required computing and storage services can be responded to from a location closer to the users, rather than from traditional cloud centers, reducing the distance and time for data transmission.

Despite the advantages of MEC, its highly distributed and dynamic nature, coupled with heterogeneous preferences, service requests, and mobility, presents a challenge in simultaneously ensuring high cache utilization and high user satisfaction. As a result, using reinforcement learning to determine cache strategies has become a popular approach [4]. Reinforcement learning continuously adjusts cache decisions and gradually optimizes cache strategies through interactions with the environment and real-time feedback. It allows for trial-and-error learning during practical execution, identifying effective cache decisions based on received reward signals, and continually refining the strategy to enhance performance. However, in real-world scenarios involving complex interactions among multiple edge servers and mobile users, single-agent reinforcement learning may not effectively capture all variations and interactions, leading to performance limitations [5]. On the other hand, multi-agent reinforcement learning allows each edge server and mobile user to be treated as an independent agent, capable of collaborating or competing [6]. Through interactions with other agents, each individual agent can perceive more environmental information and actions taken by other agents, enabling more accurate decision-making.

Taking all these factors into account, we introduce a new mobile-aware caching approach utilizing multi-agent deep reinforcement learning. This method combines a content fitness algorithm to predict the priority of caching content that suits the user's preferences and a collaborative caching strategy built upon a reinforcement learning model. We conducted extensive simulations to demonstrate its capabilities and advantages over traditional methods.

## 2   Related Work

In recent years, content caching in the MEC environment has received significant attention as a critical research field both domestically and internationally. This technology is widely recognized as a potential solution for reducing data traffic by deploying popular content locally and thus enabling the server to deliver the content directly to users upon request with greatly reduced latency and network congestion. A series of various MEC caching strategies have been proposed.

Xia et al. [7] investigated collaborative caching in edge computing environments, formulated it as a constrained optimization problem, and proposed an online algorithm for caching decisions. Zhao *et al.* [8] considered MEC caching mechanisms over vehicular networks and aimed at improving the cache hit rate. Recently, personalized caching has also gained considerable attention. Zeng *et al.* [9] proposed a heuristic intelligent caching algorithm that prioritizes content according to user behavioral preferences, based on the historical request count of the corresponding content. Shu *et al.* [10] formulated the decision problem into a collaborative cache optimization model by a collaborative caching (GPCC) method considering group preference and popularity. Then a heuristic algorithm is employed to yield high-quality content placement schedules. Recently, mobility-aware MEC caching drew considerable research interest as well. Musa SS *et al.* [11] provided a mobility-aware active caching solution for an Information Center Network (ICN) generating caching decisions for the maximization of network performance and the reduction of transmission latency. Wei *et al.* [12] predicted the target locations of users and fed predicted trajectories into a caching decision algorithm for yielding cache placement schedules with low response times. Due to the model scale and complexity of the MEC caching problems, deep reinforcement learning algorithms such as Q-learning [13], are recently used and have shown high potency in dealing with related optimization problems. Jiang *et al.* [14] introduced a multi-agent reinforcement learning (MARL) algorithm to address the collaborative content caching problem. The approach is built upon a multi-agent multi-armed bandit model. While the utilization of multi-agent deep reinforcement learning enables experience sharing among agents to enhance learning efficiency, it does not fully take into account the mobility patterns of users, which represents a limitation of the method. Zhong *et al.* [15] presents system models for both centralized caching system and decentralized caching system. They proposed a deep learning-based actor-critic learning framework to optimize content delivery latency. However, unlike this paper, their system models are static in nature. Song *et al.* [16] proposed a single-agent learning mechanism to optimize the cooperative shared caching model for static users in the MEC environment. Compared to single-agent deep reinforcement learning, which often focuses on the learning of a single agent in an isolated environment, multi-agent deep reinforcement learning has the advantage of better leveraging the potential for cooperation among multiple agents. This paper proposes a collaborative caching strategy based on a multi-agent deep reinforcement learning model, which leverages the benefits of collaboration, division of labor, and learning efficiency.

## 3    System Models

### 3.1    System Model

In this paper, we configured an MEC environment where one mobile user is connected to one MEC server. The edge computing system models contain caching and mobility two parts. The architecture describes the process of reducing user request latency and optimization to improve cache hit rates in scenarios where users are moving at high speeds.

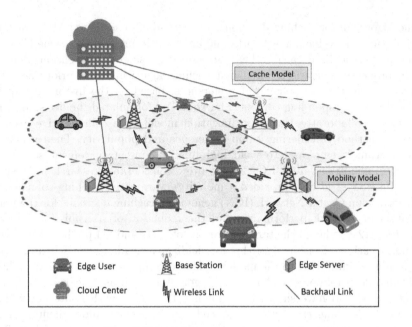

**Fig. 1.** Edge computing system model.

Each base station in the system (as shown in Fig. 1) is equipped with an edge server that performs computing and caching tasks. The cache size is $D$ and the computing capacity is $F$ (in CPU cycles per second). Edge servers are inter-connected through a wireless network with a bandwidth of $\omega$. Base stations connect to the cloud via a backhaul link. A mobile user first sends a request to the base station, which performs a search in the local cache. If the content is locally available, it is directly sent to the mobile user; otherwise, the base station requests the content from neighboring base stations. If there is still no data, it sends a request to the cloud center.

### 3.2 Cache Model

In an MEC environment, when users send computation requests, local nodes, edge nodes or cloud servers can all respond and provide required computation services. If a local computation fails to meet the resource request, this request will be forwarded to the nearest server. When both local and edge computations fail to meet, the request is forwarded to the cloud. Handling times of these occasions differs and can be calculated as follows:

– Local calculation:

$$T_{local} = \sum_{i=1}^{m} \sum_{j=1}^{n} \frac{W_{bs_i,u_j}^{t} \cdot S_f}{C_{bs_i}} \tag{1}$$

where $W_{bs_i,u_j}^t$ denotes the requests generated from the $i_{th}$ base station to the $j_{th}$ user at $t$ time, $S_f$ the size of its request content and $C_{bs_i}$ the processing capacity of the $i_{th}$ base station.

- Edge server calculation:

$$T_{neighbor} = \sum_{i=1}^{m} \sum_{j=1}^{n} \frac{W_{bs_i,u_j}^t \cdot S_f \cdot d_{bs_i,u_j}}{C_{bs_i}} \tag{2}$$

where $d_{bs_i,u_j}$ denotes the distance of communication between the base station and the $j_{th}$ user.

- Cloud server calculation:

$$T_{cloud} = \sum_{i=1}^{m} \sum_{j=1}^{n} \frac{W_{bs_i,u_j}^t \cdot S_f \cdot d_{cloud,u_j}}{C_{bs_i}} \tag{3}$$

where $d_{cloud,u_j}$ represents the distance between the cloud and the $u_{th}$ user.

In an MEC environment, the mobile devices connect to the edge server through a wireless channel. We define the mobile user $u_j$ to transmit data at a rate of $R_{bs_i,u_j}^t$, to the base station $bs_i$ in time slot $t$, denoted as:

$$R_{bs_i,u_j}^t = v log_2(1 + \frac{G_{bs_i,u_j} \cdot P_{bs_i,u_j}}{\sigma^2}), \ 0 < P_{bs_i,u_j} \leq P_{bs_i,u_j}^{max} \tag{4}$$

where, $G_{bs_i,u_j}$ represents the channel gain from mobile user $u_j$ to base station $bsi$, measured in dB. $\sigma^2$ denotes Gaussian white noise. $Rbs_i, u_j{}^t$ represents the transmission power between mobile user $u_j$ and base station $bs_i$. The maximum transmission power between mobile user $u_j$ and base station $bsi$ is defined as $Pbs_i, u_j{}^{max}$. These parameters play a crucial role in the communication process.

Therefore, the communication time between mobile user $u_j$ to base station $bs_i$ is expressed as:

$$T_{comm} = R_{bs_i,u_j}^t \cdot d_{bs_i,u_j}, 0 < d_{bs_i,u_j} \leq d_{max} \tag{5}$$

The time delay incurred by the mobile user when requesting content depends on the location of the requested content, local base station, nearby base station or appearance time in the cloud. The delay time is as follows:

- Local Caching: The time delay is considered to be 0 when the cached content is available to be requested at the local base station.

$$T\_dy_{local} = 0 \tag{6}$$

- Edge Cooperation: When the cached content does not exist at the local base station but can be requested at the neighboring base station, the transmission delay time can be expressed as follows, assuming the base station has the same transmit power:

$$T\_dy_{neighbor} = \sum_{i=1}^{m} \sum_{j=1}^{n} \frac{W_{bs_i,u_j}^t \cdot S_f \cdot \theta_w}{R_{bs_i,u_j}^t} \tag{7}$$

where $\theta_w$ represents the ratio between the amount of data contained in the request $W_{bs_i,u_j}$ sent by the user $u_j$ to the base station $bs_i$ at time slot $t$ and the amount of data returned by the base station in response to the request.

– Cloud Fetching: When a user requests resources cached in the cloud, the content must be transmitted to the user through a backhaul link, leading to an increase in time delay.

$$T\_dy_{cloud} = \sum_{i=1}^{m} \sum_{j=1}^{n} \frac{W_{bs_i,u_j}^t \cdot S_f \cdot \theta_w}{R_{cloud}} \tag{8}$$

where $R_{cloud}$ represents the transmission rate of the backhaul link between the cloud and the base station.

### 3.3   Mobility Model

Assume that the mobility of a mobile user follows an arbitrary pattern, where the direction and angle of movement are time-varying. Thus the user's path is expressed in terms of latitude and longitude as follows:

$$L_{u_i}^t = \{lon_{u_i}(t), lat_{u_i}(t)\} \tag{9}$$

$L_{u_i}^t$ denotes the moving trajectory of the $i_{th}$ user in time slot $t$. Where $lat_{u_i}(t)$ denotes the longitude point of the mobile trajectory of the $i_{th}$ user in time slot $t$, and $lon_{u_i}(t)$ denotes the latitude point of the mobile trajectory of the $i_{th}$ user in time slot $t$.

## 4   Cache Scheme

### 4.1   Problem Formulation

In MEC-based network architectures, where users are moving at high speed and placed in the cache using various policies, our objective is to minimize the content delivery latency. Therefore, the caching problem can be formulated as an optimization process with the following goal:

$$\textbf{F1}: T_{\min} = \min_s \frac{1}{m} \frac{1}{n} \sum_{i=1}^{m} \sum_{j=1}^{n} \alpha_1 \left( \lambda_1 T_{\text{local}} + \lambda_2 T_{\text{neighbor}} + \lambda_3 T_{\text{cloud}} \right) + \alpha_2 T_{\text{comm}}$$

$$+ \alpha_3 \left( \eta_1 T\_dy_{\text{local}} + \eta_2 \, T\_dy_{\text{neighbor}} + \eta_3 T\_dy_{\text{cloud}} \right) \tag{10}$$

$$s.t. \quad \textbf{C1.} \; \sum_{j=1}^{n} W_{u_j}^t \cdot S_f \leq D \quad \forall j \in [1, n]$$
$$\textbf{C2.} \; T\_dy \leq T\_dy_{max}$$
$$\textbf{C3.} \; 0 < d_{u_j} \leq d_{max} \quad \forall j \in [1, n]$$

where, $\lambda_1, \lambda_2, \lambda_3$ denote the weight respectively in the local base station, proximity base station, and computation time delay of cloud generation; $\eta_1, \eta_2, \eta_3$ denote the weight when the local base station, proximity base station, and transmission time delay of content generation in the cloud; $\alpha_1, \alpha_2, \alpha_3$ denote the weight when the computation model generates time delay and the weight when the content transmission generates time delay. The weight value constraints are

(a) $\lambda_1 + \lambda_2 + \lambda_3 = 1 \quad \lambda_1, \lambda_2, \lambda_3 \in (0, 1)$
(b) $\eta_1 + \eta_2 + \eta_3 = 1 \quad \eta_1, \eta_2, \eta_3 \in (0, 1)$
(c) $\alpha_1 + \alpha_2 + \alpha_3 = 1 \quad \alpha_1, \alpha_2, \alpha_3 \in (0, 1)$

The set $s$ represents all rational caching strategies. Constraint C1 ensures that the size of the content requested by the user cannot exceed the capacity size of the edge server. Constraint C2 represents a delay time duration constraint that ensures that the upper limit of requested time is the maximum allowable delay time. Constraint C3 indicates the maximum distance of the user request content.

## 4.2    Multiple DRL Agents

The idea behind reinforcement learning is based on mutual learning between an intelligent agent and its environment. Through continuous attempts, the agent learns to determine the best behavior. In this paper, we use a multi-intelligent deep reinforcement learning framework, and partially incomplete observable reinforcement learning problems can be modeled as Partially Observable Markov Decision Processes (POMDP) [18] modeled as a six-tuple $\{S, A, R, P, \zeta, \delta\}$. $S$ represents the set of states, $A$ denotes the set of actions, $R$ represents the reward function, and $P$ corresponds to the state transition probability matrix.

$$P = \begin{bmatrix} P_{11} & \cdots & P_{1n} \\ \vdots & \ddots & \vdots \\ P_{n1} & \cdots & P_{nn} \end{bmatrix}$$

In this context, $\zeta$ refers to the set of observations, while $\delta$ represents the set of observation probabilities. The state, action, and reward can be defined as follows:

1) State: The state space reflects the state of the mobile user's environment. In multi-agent systems, the set of the proxy is defined as $Ag = \{ag_1, ag_2, ....., ag_n\}$, $ag_i = \{info_i, neighbor_i, CN_i\}$, $info_i$ refers to the content caching status of agent $i$, $neighbor_i$ signifies the content storage status of neighboring nodes for agent $i$, $CN_i$ represents the predicted content for the next moment, acquired using **Algorithm 1**. Each agent determines its own independent caching decisions through actions and global state $\Pi_{ag_i}$ and estimate the strategy of other agents $\Pi_{ag_j}$, the global optimal strategy $\Pi$ is finally determined.

2) Action: The action set represents the current edge server's decision on whether to cache the content fitness resources or not. Since the number of users served by each base station is variable, the number of resources arriving at the base

station in the same time slot varies, and consequently, the action space size of each agent also varies. Notation of the action set as $AC = \{Ac_c^t, Ac_r^t\}$, where $Ac_c^t$ represents the caching action, $Ac_c^t = \{Ac_{c1}^t, Ac_{c2}^t, ..., Ac_{cr}^t\}$, $Ac_{ci}^t$ represents whether the current base station caches the $i_{th}$ content in $CN$; $Ac_r^t$ represents the replacement action, the content should be replaced with the content of the resource with lower content fitness.

*3)* Reward: The reward function is primarily designed to minimize content delivery latency $T_{min}$, and the reward value increases when the action satisfies the request.

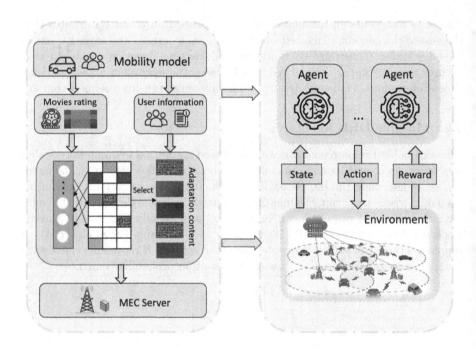

**Fig. 2.** Caching behavior of edge servers when users move.

### 4.3   Adaptation Resource Forecast

Content fit is defined as the degree to which content is suitable for the user, serving as a metric to assess the alignment between content and user demands. A higher content fit indicates that the cached content better matches the user's requests, thus enhancing user experience and system performance. Based on the characteristics of user requests, we outline the features of user-requested content and propose a predictive method for content fit. The detailed algorithm is presented in Algorithm 1.

---

**Algorithm 1.** Content fit algorithm

---

1: $K$ : Content type
2: $T = \{t_0, t_1, ..., t_n\}$: Time period $T$ is then divided into n time slots
3: $f_k(t)$: Access content
4: $R_{f_k}(t_m)$: Number of requests for the corresponding content
5: $P_{f_k}^{t_m}$: Content fitness
6: $Cha_k(t_m)$: Retrieve the relevant attributes of the content
7: $S_k$: Content feature adaptation degree
8: Collect historical request data from users during time period T, including user IDs, timestamps, and requested content information.
9: **for each** $u_i \in$ Users **do**
10:    $P_{f_k}^{t_m} = \frac{R_{f_k}(t_m)}{\sum_k R_{f_k}(t_m)}$
11:    Predict $\hat{P}_{f_k}^{t_m+1}$ from $\left\{ P_{f_k}^{t_0}, \quad P_{f_k}^{t_1}, ..., P_{f_k}^{t_m} \right\}$
12:    $\hat{P}_{f_k}^{t_m+1}$ for $f_k(t_m + 1)$
13:    Predict $\widehat{f_k}(t_m + 1)$
14:    Predict $\widehat{Cha_k}(t + 1)$ from $\widehat{f_k}(t_m + 1)$
15:    Calculate $S_k = \sqrt{\sum_k \theta_k (\widehat{Cha_k}(t_m + 1) - Cha_k(t_m))^2}$
16:    Calculate $P_{f_k}(t_m + 1) = \frac{\sum_{i=0}^{N} S_{k,i}, P_{f_{k,i}}^{t_m}}{N}$
17:    Uploads $P_{f_k}^{t_m}$ to the local BS
18: **end for**
19: Content suitability assessment and selection for inclusion in $CN$.
20: **return** $CN$

---

The content fitness $P_{f_k}^{t_m}$ is defined as the proportion of requests for a specific content at time slot $t_m$ to the total number of user requests. It reflects the proportion of this content in user requests, and a higher content fitness value indicates that the content is more popular among users, as it occupies a larger proportion in user requests. Useful content features are extracted from historical request data and cache content properties, denoted as $Cha_k(t_m)$. These features mainly include content characteristics preferred by users, such as content type and size. $S_k$ represents the predicted similarity of content features, helping to predict the similarity between different content features by calculating a similarity score between them. The relevant formulas are shown in Algorithm 1.

The entire process can be summarized as follows: By predicting the content suitability value for the next moment. $\hat{P}_{f_k}^{t+1}$, predicting the characteristics of the next moment of content $\widehat{Cha_k}(t + 1)$, the predicted content for the next moment is obtained by calculation $\widehat{f_k}(t + 1)$ and the fitness of the content $f_k(t)$ content suitability for the next moment can be determined $P_{f_k}^{t+1}$, from there, the corresponding content can be determined $f_k(t + 1)$.

## 4.4    Multi-Agent Actor-Critic Algorithm for Content Caching

Algorithm 2 is known as MAAC-based Cooperative Cache Algorithm (MAACC). When mobile users send requests, the MEC node simultaneously receives the requests and their features. It then provides the current cache status to the actor network, allowing cache operations to be obtained within the current time slot. After executing actions based on the policy, each agent receives rewards and the next state, and the information received from the environment is stored as a history for future reference. The decision process of the caching policy is shown in Fig. 2: 1) Users move according to the model and send requests and interested content to the MEC node, where the interested content is predicted by Algorithm 1; 2) The system state is observed, and actions are guided according to the corresponding rewards; 3) Based on reward signals and the current system state, the algorithm generates the final collaborative caching decision, guiding cache operations on edge servers to maximize cache hit rate and user satisfaction.

---

**Algorithm 2.** MAACC algorithm

---

**Input:** Number of iterative rounds $T, t = 1$, number of steps per turn, learning rate $\delta$, discount Factor $\gamma$, actor-critic network structure.

1: Initialization: Initialize system parameters, hyper parameters, edge server cache space, mobile user cache space, and initialize a random process for action exploration.
2: **for** each episode **do**
3:     **for** each $t < T$ **do**
4:         MEC receives user requests
5:         Observe the state of this cache for each agent
6:         Input all the states into the actor network to get action
7:         Choose the right action for each agent
8:         Execute the action to store the received reward value and the new status information in the history
9:         $t = t + 1$
10:     **end for**
11:     Store the event set for each agent
12:     update the target network using the formula
13:     Update content properties and cache state
14:     Update network parameters
15: **end for**
**Output:** Optimal strategy $\Pi$

---

# 5    Performance Evaluation

## 5.1    Parameters Setting

We perform simulations and compare the proposed approach with other existing solutions. The simulation configuration utilized the *Shanghai Telecom* dataset [19], which comprises more than 7.2 million records of content access events recorded from 3,233 edge stations and 9,481 mobile users over a span of six months, along with corresponding mobile traces. *Movielens 1M* [20] dataset simulates the content requests from different mobile users. Randomly match a user trajectory from the Shanghai Telecom dataset to each user in the Movielens 1M dataset. Figure 3 shows the distribution location of edge nodes in Shanghai. Figure 4 is an example recording the trajectory of a taxi in the city heart of Shanghai. We use Python to implement the proposed MAACC method. The relevant parameters are shown in Table 1.

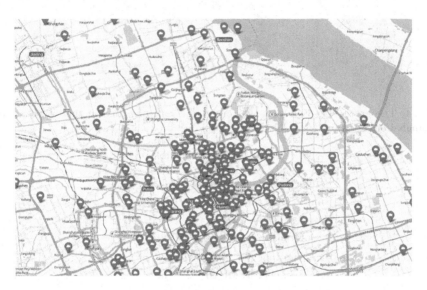

**Fig. 3.** Blue coordinate icons represent each edge node in Shanghai's downtown area showing the general distribution of the whole network. (Color figure online)

### 5.2   Comparison Algorithms

MAACC is compared against the following benchmark algorithms: Thompson sampling (TS) [21], Random Selection Algorithm (RSA) [22], Greedy Algorithm (GA) [23], and the Multi-Agent caching strategy MARL [14].

### 5.3   Performance Analysis

For performance analysis, we set up an environment where each base station was equipped with an edge server. Different base stations cached corresponding contents according to corresponding caching strategies to test the resource requests of mobile vehicles.

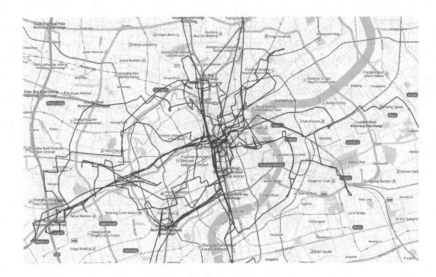

**Fig. 4.** The green lines represent the route trajectory of a taxi in the city heart of Shanghai on a certain day. (Color figure online)

**Table 1.** Parameter table

| Parameter | Value |
|---|---|
| Number of users | 30 |
| Coverage radius (m) | 100–200 |
| Basic Transfer Data Size (KB) | 8 |
| Basic run time per task (ms) | 20 |
| Total bandwidth (Mbps) | 50 |
| Number of rounds of training | 30 |
| Size of cache | 0–500 |
| The number of local epochs | 10 |
| Local batch size | 50 |
| Actor and critic learning rate | 0.001, 0.0005 |
| Network update rate | 0.01 |
| Discount | 0.9 |

As shown in Fig. 5, different kinds of applications are represented by different shapes, such as triangles, prototypes and squares. Different colors indicate the resources cached by different edge servers. When the vehicle moves, the resource hit rates of MAACC and MARL cache are higher than others, which means the vehicle can obtain resources from the nearest base station. On the contrary, TS/RSA/GA request resources from adjacent edge servers resulting in increased latency.

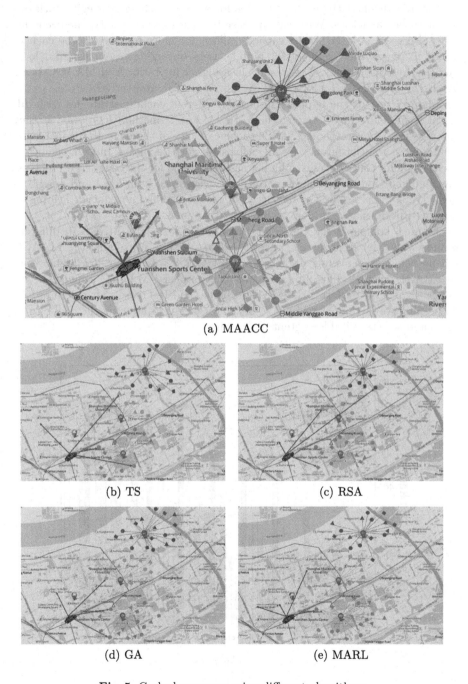

(a) MAACC

(b) TS

(c) RSA

(d) GA

(e) MARL

**Fig. 5.** Cached resources using different algorithms.

Figure 6 displays the cache hit rates for various caching strategies with different cache capacities. With the increase in edge server capacity, the cache hit ratio also rises. A larger cache capacity allows for more resources to be cached, which increases the likelihood of mobile users obtaining resources from local and nearby edge servers. This results in a higher hit ratio. And MAACC beats TS/RSA/GA/MARL by 22.2%/37.6%/15.2%/12.8%, respectively.

Figure 7 reveals the request latency for different caching strategies with different cache capacities. Among them, the MAACC method has lower latency compared to other methods. As the cache capacity of the edge server increases, the resource transfer latency for all cache strategies decreases. Indeed, the larger cache capacity contributes to a higher cache hit ratio for the edge server, increasing the likelihood of mobile users obtaining resources from local and neighboring servers. As a result, the resource transmission delay is reduced, leading to improved performance in delivering content to users.

Figure 8 compares the cache hit rates of MAACC and MARL in different rounds when the edge server capacity is 300. Within 30 rounds, the MAACC scheme achieves an average cache hit rate of 54.02%, which is 22.85% higher than the MARL scheme. This indicates that the proposed MAACC scheme in this paper slightly outperforms the MARL scheme, and the reason for the improved cache hit rate is that the MAACC scheme takes into account the mobility of users and selects suitable content for caching.

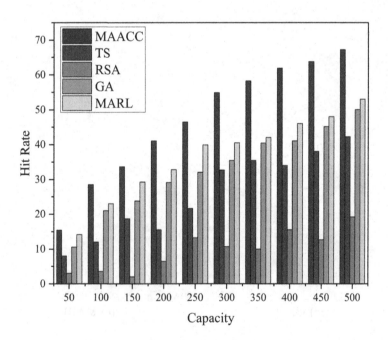

**Fig. 6.** Cache hit rates of MAACC/TS/RSA/GA/MARL under different cache capacities.

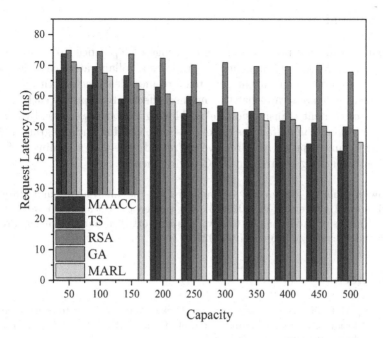

**Fig. 7.** Request latency of MAACC/TS/RSA/GA/MARL under different cache capacities.

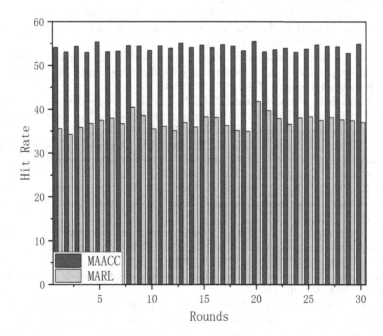

**Fig. 8.** Hit rate of MAACC and MARL under identical capacities but different rounds.

## 6  Conclusion

This paper primarily investigates the challenge of high-speed moving resource caching in the MEC environment and proposes a collaborative caching scheme MAACC based on a multi-agent deep reinforcement learning algorithm. Experimental results demonstrate that this method effectively improves cache hit rate and reduces content transmission delay. Moving forward, we intend to explore the impact of edge node failures during resource caching and integrate a checkpoint algorithm to proactively remove untrusted edge nodes, aiming to further optimize the caching strategy in MEC environments.

**Acknowledgment.** This article is supported by the Innovation Fund Project of Jiangxi Normal University(YJS2022065) and Domestic Visiting Program of Jiangxi Normal University. Additionally, this work is supported in part by Henan Province Science and Technology Projects (232102210024).

## References

1. Farooq, M.J., Zhu, Q.: A multi-layer feedback system approach to resilient connectivity of remotely deployed mobile internet of things. IEEE Trans. Cogn. Commun. Networking **4**(2), 422–432 (2018)
2. Cao, K., Liu, Y., Meng, G., Sun, Q.: An overview on edge computing research. IEEE Access **8**, 85714–85728 (2020)
3. Chen, Z., Chen, Z., Ren, Z., Liang, L., Wen, W., Jia, Y.: Joint optimization of task caching, computation offloading and resource allocation for mobile edge computing. China Commun. **19**, 142–159 (2022)
4. Qiao, G., Leng, S., Maharjan, S., Zhang, Y., Ansari, N.: Deep reinforcement learning for cooperative content caching in vehicular edge computing and networks. IEEE Internet Things J. **7**(1), 247–257 (2020)
5. He, Y., Yu, F.R., Zhao, N., Leung, V.C.M., Yin, H.: Software-defined networks with mobile edge computing and caching for smart cities: a big data deep reinforcement learning approach. IEEE Commun. Mag. **55**(12), 31–37 (2017)
6. Wang, R., Li, M., Peng, L., Hu, Y., Hassan, M.M., Alelaiwi, A.: Cognitive multi-agent empowering mobile edge computing for resource caching and collaboration. Future Gener. Comput. Syst. **102**, 66–74 (2020)
7. Xia, X., Chen, F., He, Q., Grundy, J., Abdelrazek, M., Jin, H.: Online collaborative data caching in edge computing. IEEE Trans. Parallel Distrib. Syst. **32**(2), 281–294 (2021)
8. Zhao, J., Sun, X., Li, Q., Ma, X.: Edge caching and computation management for real-time internet of vehicles: an online and distributed approach. IEEE Trans. Intell. Transp. Syst. **22**(4), 2183–2197 (2021)
9. Zeng, Y., et al.: Smart caching based on user behavior for mobile edge computing. Inf. Sci. **503**, 444–468 (2019)
10. Yao, T., Chai, Y., Wang, S., Miao, X., Bu, X.: Radio signal automatic modulation classification based on deep learning and expert features. IEEE Xplore (2020)
11. Musa, S.S., Zennaro, M., Libsie, M., Pietrosemoli, E.: Mobility-aware proactive edge caching optimization scheme in information-centric IoV networks. Sensors **22**(4), 1387 (2022)

12. Wei, H., Luo, H., Sun, Y.: Mobility-aware service caching in mobile edge computing for internet of things. Sensors **20**(3), 610 (2020)
13. Sadeghi, A., Sheikholeslami, F., Giannakis, G.B.: Optimal and scalable caching for 5g using reinforcement learning of space-time popularities. IEEE J. Sel. Topics Signal Process. **12**(1), 180–190 (2018)
14. Jiang, W., Feng, G., Qin, S., Liang, Y.-C.: Learning-based cooperative content caching policy for mobile edge computing. In: ICC 2019–2019 IEEE International Conference on Communications (ICC). IEEE (2019)
15. Zhong, C., Gursoy, M.C., Velipasalar, S.: Deep reinforcement learning-based edge caching in wireless networks. IEEE Trans. Cogn. Commun. Networki. **6**(1), 48–61 (2020)
16. Song, J., Sheng, M., Quek, T.Q.S., Xu, C., Wang, X.: Learning-based content caching and sharing for wireless networks. IEEE Trans. Commun. **65**(10), 4309–4324 (2017)
17. Jeong, S., Simeone, O., Kang, J.: Mobile edge computing via a UAV-mounted cloudlet: optimization of bit allocation and path planning. IEEE Trans. Veh. Technol. **67**(3), 2049–2063 (2018)
18. Cassandra, A.R., Littman, M.L., Zhang, N.L.: Incremental pruning: a simple, fast, exact method for partially observable Markov decision processes. arXiv:1302.1525 cs (2013)
19. Li, Y., Zhou, A., Ma, X., Wang, S.: Profit-aware edge server placement. IEEE Internet Things J. **9**(1), 55–67 (2022)
20. Harper, F.M., Konstan, J.A.: The MovieLens datasets. ACM Trans. Interact. Intell. Syst. **5**(4), 1–19 (2015)
21. Cui, L., et al.: CREAT: blockchain-assisted compression algorithm of federated learning for content caching in edge computing. IEEE Internet Things J. **9**(16), 14151–14161 (2022)
22. Xiao, H., Zhao, J., Pei, Q., Feng, J., Liu, L., Shi, W.: Vehicle selection and resource optimization for federated learning in vehicular edge computing. IEEE Trans. Intell. Transp. Syst. **28**, 11073–11087 (2021)
23. Banerjee, B., Kulkarni, A., Seetharam, A.: Greedy Caching: an optimized content placement strategy for information-centric networks. Comput. Networks **140**, 78–91 (2018)

# D-AE: A Discriminant Encode-Decode Nets for Data Generation

Gongju Wang, Yulun Song, Yang Li$^{(\boxtimes)}$, Mingjian Ni, Long Yan, Bowen Hu, Quanda Wang, Yixuan Li, and Xingru Huang

China Unicom Digital Technology Co., Ltd., Data Intelligence Division, Technology R&D Department, Beijing 100166, China
liy550@chinaunicom.cn

**Abstract.** Imbalanced datasets often result in poor predictive model performance. To address this, minority class sample expansion is used, but two challenges remain. The first is to use algorithms to learn the main features of minority class samples, and the second is to differentiate the generated data from the majority class samples. To tackle these challenges in binary classification, we propose the Discriminant-Autoencoder (D-AE) algorithm. It has two mechanisms based on our insights. Firstly, an autoencoder is used to learn the main features of minority class samples by reconstructing the data with added noise. Secondly, a discriminator is trained on the raw data to distinguish the generated data from the majority class samples. Our proposed loss function, Discriminant-$L_\theta$, balances the discriminant and reconstruction losses. Results from experiments on three datasets show that D-AE outperforms baseline algorithms and improves dataset applicability.

**Keywords:** Imbalanced datasets · Discriminant-Autoencoder (D-AE) · Discriminant-$L_\theta$ loss function

## 1 Introduction

Machine learning excels in prediction tasks. It aids investors in stock forecasting [29], enhances China's booming online retail through product recommendations [35], and identifies risks in the intricate global financial landscape [4]. Model performance often hinges on training data distribution. While models on balanced datasets perform well and avoid "Label Bias" [36], real-world applications, like anomaly detection [32] and ad clicks [14], typically deal with imbalanced data. This imbalance skews predictions towards the majority class, diminishing model effectiveness. Addressing this challenge involves techniques like data upsampling [7] and downsampling [13].

The idea of data upsampling is to expand the number of minority class samples to balance with the majority class samples through methods such as replication, interpolation [28], and simulation [7]. The Synthetic Minority Oversampling Technique (SMOTE) [7] is a commonly used upsampling algorithm.

© ICST Institute for Computer Sciences, Social Informatics and Telecommunications Engineering 2024
Published by Springer Nature Switzerland AG 2024. All Rights Reserved
H. Gao et al. (Eds.): CollaborateCom 2023, LNICST 562, pp. 96–114, 2024.
https://doi.org/10.1007/978-3-031-54528-3_6

The generation strategy is to randomly select a minority class sample $x_j$ from the nearest neighbors of each minority class sample $x_i$, and then randomly select a point on the connection line between the two samples as the newly generated minority class sample $g_{i,j}$. Borderline Synthetic Minority Over-sampling Technique (Borderline-SMOTE) [17] is a refined version of SMOTE, which only uses the minority class samples on the boundary to generate new samples. Adaptive Synthetic Sampling (ADASYN) [18] is similar to Borderline-SMOTE, assigning different weights to different minority class samples to generate new samples.

Similar to data upsampling, data downsampling is to select part of the majority class samples to balance with the minority class samples. NearMiss [26] algorithm is a downsampling algorithm, which selects the most representative samples from the majority class samples.

The upsampling methods mentioned above generally generate data based on the linear relationship between sampling points, but the samples can also be generated based on the nonlinear relationship. The deep learning based upsampling algorithm uses the nonlinear relationship between samples to generate data. Autoencoder (AE) [30] and its variant Denoising-Autoencoder (Denoising-AE) [23] has been widely used in image reconstruction [24], clustering algorithm [5], etc. However, data generated by AE has the disadvantage of lacking diversity. Generative Adversarial Networks (GAN) [10] overcomes the shortcoming by producing varied output through mutual game learning of at least two modules in the framework: the generating module and the discriminant module. Nevertheless, GAN has the problem of unstable training.

In light of these challenges and existing solutions, this paper introduces the Discriminant-Autoencoder (D-AE), an innovative algorithm designed to address the data imbalance challenge. The D-AE combines the strengths of AE and GAN, and the algorithm is underpinned by two key mechanisms that we've innovatively proposed:

- We employ an autoencoder structure that accepts raw minority class samples and introduces added noise. This not only learns the primary features of the raw minority class samples but also ensures the generated data is diversified.
- A discriminator is introduced, trained using raw data. This ensures that the generated samples are distinguishable from the raw majority class samples, enhancing the robustness of our approach.

Moreover, a unique loss function, termed Discriminant-$L_\theta$ (D-$L_\theta$), forms the backbone of our model. It integrates the discriminator's accuracy and the AE's reconstruction ability, providing a holistic optimization objective.

The structure of the rest parts of the paper is arranged as follows: Sect. 2 introduces traditional sampling algorithms and deep learning based upsampling algorithms. Section 3 describes D-AE with the two mechanisms mentioned above. Section 4 introduces experiments, including datasets, evaluation metrics, and the experimental setup. In Sect. 5, we compare the performance of D-AE with other baseline algorithms and making analysis and discussion on D-AE. Section 6 is the conclusion of this paper.

## 2  Related Work

### 2.1  Traditional Upsampling and Downsampling

In recent years, upsampling technology has achieved significant development and progress. The SMOTE algorithm has been applied to the prediction research of lung cancer [27], network intrusion detection [31], financial risk early warning [34], etc. Researchers use the Borderline-SMOTE method to upsample the non-small cell lung cancer (NSCLC) [37] data, improving the efficiency and accuracy of the prediction of the 5-year survival status of NSCLC patients. ADASYN algorithm has been applied to intrusion detection [8] and telecom fraud identification [22]. Downsampling has also been well developed. The NearMiss algorithm has been applied to solve the problem of misclassification due to imbalanced data of credit card [26].

We symbolize the sampling problem as below. If $S$ is the complete set of the data, $X$ is the set of minority class samples, $Z$ is the set of majority class samples, then $S = X \cup Z$. The set of all features of the data is defined as $C$, the features of minority and majority samples, whose missing rate are higher than 30%, are defined as $C^X$ and $C^Z$ separately, so $C^X \subseteq C, C^Z \subseteq C$. $S$ is divided into training set $S^{train}$, test set $S^{test}$ and validation set $S^{valid}$, where $C^{fin} = (C - (C^Z \cap C^X))$ is the set of features used for prediction. When data upsampling is performed, the generated minority class samples set is defined as $G$.

**SMOTE** [7]: For each minority class sample $x_i \in X$, find its nearest $k$ neighbors $X_i^k = \{x_{i,0}^k, x_{i,1}^k, ..., x_{i,k-1}^k\} \subseteq X, x_i \notin X_i^k$ in $X$, randomly select a minority class sample $x_{i,j}$ from $X_i^k$, and generate a random number $a$ from a value range of $[0, 1]$, so the generated sample $g_{i,j}$ can be expressed as for (1).

$$g_{i,j} = x_i + a \times (x_{i,j} - x_i) \tag{1}$$

**Borderline-SMOTE** [17]: The minority class is divided into three types of samples, namely Safe, Danger and Noise, which are defined correspondingly based on the number of the k-neighbors of the majority class samples. Safe is defined as the samples in which the number of the majority class samples among the nearest k-neighbors is $[0, \frac{k}{2})$. Danger is defined by the number of the majority class samples in $[\frac{k}{2}, k)$. Noise is defined as the samples whose nearest k-neighbors are all majority class samples. The algorithm only upsamples minority class samples in Danger, and the algorithm for generating samples refers to (1). Borderline-SMOTE algorithms can be divided into Borderline-SMOTE1 and Borderline-SMOTE2. Borderline-SMOTE1 randomly selects minority class samples from the nearest k-neighbors for generation. Borderline-SMOTE2 selects any sample from the nearest k-neighbors for generation, regardless of the class of the samples. Compared with the SMOTE method, the Borderline-SMOTE algorithms only perform nearest neighbor linear interpolation for boundary samples, which makes the distribution of the generated minority class samples more reasonable.

**ADASYN** [18]: Denote the number of minority class samples as $n^X$ and the number of majority class samples as $n^Z$. Then calculate the number of minority class samples to be generated as $n = (n^Z - n^X) \times b, b \in [0, 1]$, where $b$ is a parameter used to specify the desired balance level after generation of the generated data. For each minority class sample $x_i$, use Euclidean distance to find its nearest k-neighbors $S_i^k = \{s_{i,0}^k, s_{i,1}^k, ..., s_{i,k-1}^k\} \subseteq S, x_i \notin S_i^k$. Denote $\tau_i$ as the number of samples that belong to the majority class in the nearest k-neighbors of $x_i$ and denote the ratio as $r_i = \tau_i/k, r_i \in [0, 1]$. With the ratio $r_i$ calculated by each minority class sample $x_i$, use (2) to calculate the density distribution $\hat{r}_i$. Therefore, $m_i = \hat{r}_i \times n$ represents the number of the samples that need to be generated for each minority class sample $x_i$. Randomly select a minority class sample $x_{i,j}$ from $S_i^k$ and generate a random number $a$ whose value range is $[0, 1]$, so sample $g_{i,j}$ is generated as shown in (1).

$$\hat{r}_i = r_i / \sum_{j=1}^{n^X} r_j \tag{2}$$

Downsampling aims to balance the sample distribution by randomly eliminating majority class samples. To prevent the information loss problem in most downsampling algorithms, NearMiss [26] extensively uses the nearest neighbor method to select samples for keeping among all the majority class samples.

**NearMiss1**: For each majority class sample $z_i$, find the nearest $k$ minority class samples $X_i^k = \{x_{i,0}^k, x_{i,1}^k, ..., x_{i,k-1}^k\} \in X$, calculate the distance $D_i^k = \{d_{i,0}^k, d_{i,1}^k, ..., d_{i,k-1}^k\}$ from $z_i$ to all minority class samples in $X_i^k$, and then calculate the average distance of all elements in $D_i^k$ as $\overline{d_i^k}$. Sort $\overline{D^k} = \{\overline{d_0^k}, \overline{d_1^k}, ..., \overline{d_{n^Z}^k}\}$ in ascending order and keep the first $n^X$ majority class samples as the result.

**NearMiss2**: For each majority class sample $z_i$, find the furthest $k$ minority class samples $X_i^k = \{x_{i,0}^k, x_{i,1}^k, ..., x_{i,k-1}^k\} \in X$, calculate the distance $D_i^k = \{d_{i,0}^k, d_{i,1}^k, ..., d_{i,k-1}^k\}$ from $z_i$ to all minority class samples in $X_i^k$, and then calculate the average distance of all elements in $D_i^k$ as $\overline{d_i^k}$. Sort $\overline{D^k} = \{\overline{d_0^k}, \overline{d_1^k}, ..., \overline{d_{n^Z}^k}\}$ in ascending order and keep the first $n^X$ majority class samples as the result.

## 2.2 Deep Learning Based Upsampling

The main idea of upsampling algorithms such as SMOTE, Borderline-SMOTE, and ADASYN to solve this problem is to randomly generate minority class samples with adjacent samples according to certain rules. Although such methods greatly increase the number of majority class samples, the distribution of the generated data lacks diversity, which makes the universality of the expanded datasets unsatisfactory in prediction tasks.

In addition to traditional sampling methods, the upsampling methods based on deep learning are also applied to solve the problem of unbalanced datasets. AE is a kind of deep learning methods commonly used in solving the unbalanced datasets problem. The function of AE is to perform representation learning on the input data, that is, AE can learn the data distribution and the main features of the data. Researchers used AE [1] to upsample the unbalanced breast cancer dataset to improve the prediction accuracy, which helped in cancer diagnosis and treatment. Han et al. [16] used the AE for data enhancement by generating data to solve the problem of insufficient fault classification of machinery. The Denoising-AE [9] is a variant of AE, which adds noise to the input data and reconstructs the input data, so that the encoder can learn the main features of the data and represent the data more robustly. Denoising-AE can be used to detect defects in industrial products [20] and fabric products [25]. GAN is also a popular method for upsamling tasks, which has been applied in medical image field, including augmentation, detection, classification, and reconstruction [2].

**AE**: Using AE to process data is divided into two steps. Firstly, the encoder accepts data $x$ as input and encodes the data into low-dimensional representation $v$, as shown in (3). Next, the decoder takes the input $v$ and attempts to reconstruct $x$ as $\hat{x}$, as shown in (4).

$$v = f(x) \tag{3}$$

$$\hat{x} = h(v) \tag{4}$$

**Denoising Auto-Encoder**: Denoising-AE accepts data with noise $x^{noise}$ as input and is trained to reconstruct the raw data as the output. The encoding part is shown as (5) and the decoding part is the same as AE, as shown in (4).

$$v = f(x^{noise}) \tag{5}$$

**GAN**: GAN is divided into two modules: generator $G$ and discriminator $D$. The generator generally accepts noise as the input and generates samples as output. During the training, the generator confronts the discriminator, which aims to ultimately make the discriminator unable to distinguish the generated data from the real data. The training objective of the discriminator is to distinguish the generated data from the real data. The optimization objective of GAN can be expressed as 6, where $\mu$ is the standard normal distribution-based noise.

$$\min_{G} \max_{D} E_{x \sim p_x}[\log D(x)] + E_{\mu \sim p_\mu}[\log(1 - D(G(\mu)))] \tag{6}$$

## 3   Discriminant-Autoencoder

Inspired by the ideas of AE and GAN, we propose an algorithm called Discriminant-Autoencoder (D-AE). The data generation process of D-AE is shown in Fig. 1. The data generation process can be divided into a data general preprocessing module, a D-AE data generation module, and a predictive model processing module. The D-AE data generation module is the core

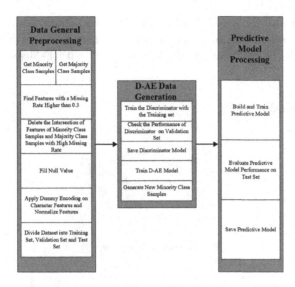

**Fig. 1.** D-AE Based Data Generation Process

innovation of this paper, which includes a set of AE neural network with discriminator and a loss function called Discriminant-$L_\theta$ (D-$L_\theta$) as the optimization object.

### 3.1 D-AE Based Data Generation Process

**Data General Preprocessing Module**: Firstly, the module accepts the input of minority class samples and majority class samples. Next, it gets $C^P$ from features in minority class samples with a missing rate higher than 0.3 and $C^N$ from features in majority class samples with a missing rate higher than 0.3. $C^{fin} = (C - (C^X \cap C^Z))$ is defined as the set of features to preserve. Then, for each feature $c_i \in C^{fin}$, the null values in character types are filled with the mode of the training set, and the null values in numeric types are filled with the mean of the training set. Afterwards, the module uses dummy encoding for the character type data, and keeps the dummy dictionary of the encodings. Finally, the training set $S^{train}$, the validation set $S^{valid}$, and the test set $S^{test}$ are randomly divided according to the ratio of 8:1:1.

**D-AE Data Generation Module**: Firstly, the module accepts the training set $S^{train}$ as input to train the discriminator $D$, and uses the validation set $S^{valid}$ to evaluate the performance of $D$. Next, it normalizes each feature $c_i^{fin}$ of the $S^{train}$ using the maximum and minimum normalization method [12]. Then, the D-AE structure is established and the optimization objectives for model training is set. Finally, when D-AE model has complete the training, the model generates new minority class sample set $G$ from the training set $S^{train}$. The new training set for the following module is defined as $\hat{S}^{train}$, where $\hat{S}^{train} = G \cup S^{train}$.

**Predictive Model Processing Module**: The new training set $\hat{S}^{train}$ with the feature $C^{fin}$ is sent to train the predictive model, and the performance of the predictive model is evaluated on the test set $S^{test}$ with F-Measure, AUC and other metrics.

## 3.2   D-AE Model

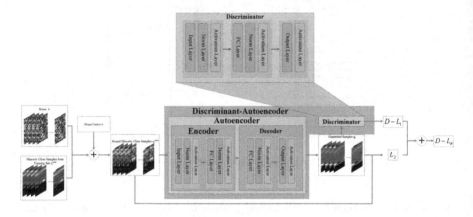

**Fig. 2.** D-AE Model Training Process

The D-AE training process is shown in Fig. 2, which consists of an encoder $f$, a decoder $h$, and a discriminator $D$. In the encoder part, a noise generator is introduced, which adds a standard normal distribution based noise $\mu$ to the input data, and the encoder network accepts the noisy input data. The encoding process is shown in (7) where $\theta^{enc}$ represents the network parameters of the encoder. $v$ represents the low-dimensional vector encoded by the encoder, and $\alpha \in [0,1]$ is the noise factor.

$$v = f_{\theta^{enc}}(x^{noise}), x^{noise} = x + \alpha\mu \tag{7}$$

For the decoder $h$, its role is to reconstruct the input data from the low-dimensional vector $v$ based on the main features of the input data. The decoding process is shown in (8), where $\theta^{dec}$ represents the network parameters of the decoder, and the output $g$ is the generated data.

$$g = h_{\theta^{dec}}(v) \tag{8}$$

The general process of data generation is expressed as (9), and $\theta = (\theta^{enc}, \theta^{dec})$ represents the network parameters of the structure of the AE. The discriminator assists the training of $\theta$ by judging the generation result $g$ to calculate the $D-L2$ loss.

$$g = h_{\theta^{dec}}(f_{\theta^{enc}}(x^{noise})) \tag{9}$$

### 3.3    D-AE Optimization Objectives

In D-AE model, an external discriminator $D$ is introduced and trained based on $S^{train}$. The structure of $D$ is shown in Fig. 2. We define $\theta^{dis}$ as the parameters of $D$. When training $D$, the optimization objective is as shown in (10), where $n^{S^{train}}$ is the number of elements in $S^{train}$, the true label value $y_i$ corresponds to $s_i \in S^{train}$, and $\hat{y}_i$ represents the predicted label value of $s_i$ from the discriminator, as shown in (11). In this paper, we specify that the label value of minority class samples is 1, and the label value of majority class samples is 0.

$$L_{\theta^{dis}} = -\frac{1}{n^{S^{train}}} \sum_{i=1}^{n^{S^{train}}} (y_i \times \ln(\hat{y}_i) + (1 - y_i)\ln(1 - \hat{y}_i)) \tag{10}$$

$$\hat{y}_i = D_{\theta^{dis}}(s_i) \tag{11}$$

The discriminator loss $D$-$L_1$ is designed to measure the difference between the generated samples with the minority class samples in $S^{train}$ according to $D$, as shown in (12), where $m$ is the number of minority class samples in the training set.

$$D\text{-}L_1 = \frac{1}{m} \sum_{i=1}^{m} (1 - D_{\theta^{dis}}(g_i))^2 \tag{12}$$

Secondly, the reconstruction loss $L_2$ is designed as (13), which measures the difference between the generated samples with the minority class samples in $S^{train}$ according to the AE networks.

$$L_2 = \frac{1}{m} \sum_{i=1}^{m} (g_i - x_i^{noise})^2 \tag{13}$$

In this paper, a Discriminant-$L_\theta$ ($D$-$L_\theta$) is proposed by combining discriminator loss and reconstruction loss, as shown in (14). By reducing $D$-$L_\theta$ in the training, the generated samples $G$ are able to gradually approximate the distribution of minority class samples in $X^{train} \subset S^{train}$ .

$$D\text{-}L_\theta = D\text{-}L_1 + L_2 = \frac{1}{m} \sum_{i=1}^{m} ((g_i - x_i^{noise})^2 + (1 - D_{\theta^{dis}}(g_i))^2) \tag{14}$$

This paper summarizes the data generation process as Algorithm 1. The overall process of the algorithm is shown in Fig. 2. To train the discriminator, we initialize the discriminator parameters $\theta^{dis}$ and the AE parameters $\theta$ (Algorithm 1 line 1 and line 2). At first training the discriminator $D$, set $E_1$ and $n_1$ as epochs and batch size for training the discriminator. Therefore an epoch needs $\frac{n^{S^{train}}}{n_1}$ loops to complete. During an epoch, the discriminator $D$ makes a prediction $\hat{y}_i$ for sample $s$ from training set (Algorithm 1 Line 6), and optimizes the parameters $\theta^{dis}$ by using the cross entropy loss between the predicted label $\hat{y}_i$ and the true label $y_i$ (Algorithm 1 line 8). When the discriminator $D$ is well trained, the parameters $\theta^{dis}$ is fixed.

The parameters for training the encode net and the decode net are set as $\theta = (\theta^{enc}, \theta^{dec})$. $E_2$ is the number of epochs for training encode net and decode net. To train $f$ and $h$, combine minority class sample $x$ and noise $\mu$ to obtain input data $x^{noise}$ (Algorithm 1 Line 15). Then get generated data $g$ through $f$ and the $h$ (lines 16 and 17 of Algorithm 1). Finally, get the discriminator loss $D\text{-}L_1$ through $g$ (line 18 of Algorithm 1) and the reconstruction loss $L_2$ through $g$ and $x^{noise}$ (line 19 of Algorithm 1), so as to get the final optimization objective $L_2$ loss $L_\theta$ (Line 21 of Algorithm 1).

---

**Algorithm 1.** Discriminant-Autoencoder for Data Generation

---

1: Initialize discriminator $Ds$ parameters with $\theta^{dis}$
2: Initialize encoder parameters with $\theta^{enc}$ and decoder parameters with $\theta^{dec}$ then $\theta = (\theta^{enc}, \theta^{dec})$
3: **for** $epoch = 1, 2, 3...E_1$ **do**
4:     **for** $k = 1, 2, 3...\frac{n^{S^{train}}}{n_1}$ **do**
5:         Sample a random minibatch of $n_1$ samples from $S^{train}$
6:         Discriminator makes predictions for minibatch data classification $\hat{y}_i = D_{\theta^{dis}}(s_i)$
7:         Update the $\theta^{dis}$ by minimizing the loss
8:         $L_{\theta^{dis}}(s) = -\frac{1}{n_1} \sum_{i=1}^{n_1} y_i \times \ln(\hat{y}_i) + (1 - y_i)\ln(1 - \hat{y}_i)$
9:     **end for**
10: **end for**
11: **for** $epoch = 1, 2, 3...E_2$ **do**
12:     Initialize the standard normal distribution for noise $\mu$
13:     **for** $k = 1, 2, 3...\frac{m}{n_2}$ **do**
14:         Sample a random minibatch of $n_2$ samples from $X^{train}$
15:         Data with noise is $x^{noise} = x + \alpha\mu$
16:         Low-dimensional vector after encoding is $v_i = f_{\theta^{enc}}(x_i^{noise})$
17:         Reconstruct data (generated data) $g_i = h_{\theta^{dec}}(v_i)$
18:         Discriminator loss is $D\text{-}L_1 = \frac{1}{n_2} \sum_{i=1}^{n_2} (1 - D_{\theta^{dis}}(g_i))^2$
19:         Reconstruct loss is $L_2 = \frac{1}{n_2} \sum_{i=1}^{n_2} (g_i - x_i^{noise})^2$
20:         Update $\theta$ by minimizing the loss
21:         $D\text{-}L_\theta = D\text{-}L_1 + L_2 = \frac{1}{n_2} \sum_{i=1}^{n_2} ((g_i - x_i^{noise})^2 + (1 - D_{\theta^{dis}}(g_i))^2)$
22:     **end for**
23: **end for**

---

# 4    Experiment

This section will introduce the datasets involved in evaluating the D-AE algorithm, evaluation metrics, and the experimental setup.

## 4.1    Datasets

The experiments are based on 3 datasets, each of which consist of a sufficient number of features, as shown in Table 1.

**Human Activity Recognition with Smartphones Dataset** [3]: The data for this dataset was collected from 30 volunteers aged 19 to 48 years old. Each volunteer performed six actions (walking, going upstairs, going downstairs, sitting, standing, and lying down) while wearing a smartphone around their waist as the data collection source. The phone's accelerometer and gyroscope captured 3-axis linear acceleration and 3-axis angular velocity. The dataset was preprocessed by applying a noise filter to the sensor signal, resulting in 561 features. The samples labeled as "standing" are considered minority, and the rest are considered majority.

**PTB Diagnostic ECG Dataset** [19]: This electrocardiogram (ECG) dataset contains data for heartbeats in both normal and abnormal cases, such as those affected by different arrhythmias and myocardial infarction. The signals were preprocessed and segmented, with each segment corresponding to a feature. The dataset consists of 14,552 instances and 188 features. The samples labeled as "abnormal" are considered minority, and the rest are considered majority.

**China Unicom Gender Prediction Dataset**: This dataset includes gender data for 99,021 users, along with 343 features, available in the China Unicom database. The user features are sourced from the label system built by China Unicom and include user basic attribute features, interest preference features, and traveling features. The samples labeled as "female" are considered minority, and the samples labeled as "male" are considered majority.

**Table 1.** Overview of Datasets

| Datasets | Positive Sample | Negative Sample | Total |
|---|---|---|---|
| PTB | 4046 | 10506 | 14552 |
| Human | 1906 | 8393 | 9489 |
| Gender | 37527 | 61494 | 99021 |

### 4.2   Evaluation Metrics

This paper uses a set of metrics related to the Receiver Operating Characteristic (ROC) curve [11] to evaluate the performance of the D-AE algorithm. The minority class samples are designated as positive samples and the majority class samples as negative samples. The algorithm performance can be measured using the confusion matrix, as shown in Table 2. The metrics used for evaluation are Precision [6], Recall [15], F-Measure [33], and AUC [33].

**Table 2.** Confusion Matrix

| True Value | Predictive Value | |
|---|---|---|
| | Positive Sample | Negative Sample |
| Positive Sample | True Positives, TP | False Negatives, FN |
| Negative sample | False Positives, FP | True Negatives, TN |

## 4.3  Experiment Setup

The experiments in this paper are conducted based on the algorithm in Fig. 1. The ratio of samples in the training set, test set, and validation set is 8:1:1. The training data goes through the data general preprocessing module to complete the cleaning of missing data features, encoding of character-type features, and the division of training sets, validation sets and test sets. Since there are character features in the gender prediction dataset, a dummy encoder is designated to encode the character features in the training set, and an encoding dictionary is recorded at the same time. Afterwards, the encoding dictionary is used to encode the character data of the validation set and test set.

When training external discriminator $D$, we specify the batch size as 128, the learning rate as 0.001, the training set as $S^{train}$, the validation set as $S^{valid}$, and the epoches as 150. The parameters $\theta^{dis}$ should be saved after the training process of the external discriminator $D$, because parameters $\theta^{dis}$ would be fixed in the learning of subsequent steps.

When training the encoder and decoder, the input data is from the positive sample set $T^P$ of training set $S^{train}$, the specified batch size is 64, the learning rate is 0.0001, the influence factor of noise $\alpha$ is 0.1, and the epoches are 32000.

The next part is using D-AE for data generation. Firstly, calculate the difference $n^{upsample} = n^{trian\_neg} - n^{trian\_pos}$ between the positive samples and the negative samples, and randomly sample $n^{upsample}$ positive samples from $S^{train}$ with replacement as the input data for data generation. Next, the generated positive sample data $\hat{X}$ and $S^{train}$ are combined to form a new training set $\hat{S}^{train}$ after data generation, that is, $\hat{S}^{train} = \hat{X} \cup S^{train}$. When $\hat{S}^{train}$ is input into the predictive model for training, the predictive model is selected as xgboost, the number of training iterations is set to 50. The last but not the least, evaluation metrics such as AUC values are calculated as the degree of improvement of the predictive model using the generated data.

In order to evaluate the performance of the algorithm more objectively, we run the process that is shown in Fig. 1 for 100 times, and each time the process follows the rule of random division to generate $S^{train}$, $S^{valid}$ and $S^{test}$ from the dataset $S$. When training the discriminator $D$, the average value of the AUC in the 100 loops is recorded. Then the generation algorithm is used to generate 100 different $\hat{S}^{train}$. Also, we train the predictive model with the same method each time, calculate and record the evaluation metrics (Precision, Recall, F -Measure, AUC) of the predictive model on the test set $S^{test}$. Finally, the average evaluation metrics of the 100 loops is taken as the final algorithm performance.

# 5   Results and Discussion

Following the experimental steps described in Section IV-C, the training results are shown in Table 3. On the PTB diagnostic electrocardiogram dataset, the number of minority class samples in the training set is 3237, and the number of majority class samples is 8405. The average AUC values of the discriminator $D$ in the 100 loops on the training set is 99.9%. The validation set consists of 404 minority class samples and 1050 majority class samples, and the average AUC values on the validation set is 99.6%. On the human activity recognition with smartphones dataset, the number of minority class samples in the training set is 1525, the number of majority class samples is 6714, and the average AUC values of the discriminator in the 100 loops on the training set is 100%. The validation set consists of 190 minority class samples and 840 majority class samples, and the average value AUC values on the validation set is 99.9%. On the China Unicom gender prediction dataset, the number of minority class samples in the training set is 30,022, and the number of majority class samples is 49,195. The average value AUC values of the discriminator in the 100 loops on the training set is 98.3%. The validation set consists of 3,753 minority class samples and 6,150 majority class samples, and the average AUC values on the validation set is 97.4%. In summary, the discriminator $D$ achieved the best performance on the PTB diagnostic ECG dataset, followed by the human activity recognition with smartphones dataset, and the lowest performance on the China Unicom gender prediction dataset. Further more, the AUC values on all three datasets exceeded 95% [21]. Therefore, the discriminator $D$ is proved to be able to classify the minority and majority class samples well, which meets the requirements of the experiments.

In addition to directly using the training set from the raw dataset, we also select D-AE, SMOTE, Borderline-SMOTE-1, Borderline-SMOTE-2, ADASYN, NearMiss1, NearMiss2, GAN, Denoising AE, and AE to upsample or downsample the data in this paper. The generated dataset is used to train the predictive model, and the results of experiments are shown in Table 4.

On the PTB diagnostic ECG dataset, when the predictive model is trained based on the training set generated by the D-AE algorithm, its Precision, F-Measure and AUC reach the best, which are 96.6%, 96.4% and 98.1% respectively. In terms of recall performance, D-AE is 1.9% lower than the algorithm NearMiss2, which performs best among all the algorithms. In general, D-AE achieves the best in three metrics, and the second in one metric.

**Table 3.** Performance of Discriminator $D$

| Datasets | Pos. Samples | | | | Neg. Samples | | | | Train AUC | Val. AUC |
|---|---|---|---|---|---|---|---|---|---|---|
| | Tot. | Train | Test | Val. | Tot. | Train | Test | Val. | | |
| PTB | 4046 | 3237 | 405 | 404 | 10506 | 8405 | 1051 | 1050 | 99.9% | 99.6% |
| Human | 1906 | 1525 | 191 | 190 | 8393 | 6714 | 839 | 840 | 99.9% | 99.9% |
| Gender | 37527 | 30022 | 3753 | 3753 | 61494 | 49195 | 6149 | 6150 | 98.3% | 97.4% |

On human activity recognition with smartphones dataset, when the predictive model is trained based on the training set generated by the AE algorithm, its Precision, Recall and F-Measure both reach the best, which are 98.9%, 99.9% and 99.4% respectively. On the "Human Activity Recognition with Smartphones" dataset, Borderline-SMOTE-2 algorithm achieves the best performance in terms of Recall with a score of 99.9%. In general, AE performs better than all algorithms.

On the China Unicom gender prediction dataset, the D-AE algorithm outperforms other baseline algorithms in terms of F-Measure and AUC. When the predictive model is trained using the training set generated by D-AE, its F-Measure and AUC reach the best results, with scores of 96.4% and 97.3% respectively. Compared to Borderline-SMOTE-1 and ADASYN, D-AE's precision is improved by 0.3%. Compared to Denoising AE, D-AE's F-Measure is improved by 0.5%. Compared to AE, D-AE's AUC is improved by 1.3%. Overall, D-AE has a better performance than other baseline algorithms.

### 5.1 Visualization

As an example, the PTB diagnostic ECG dataset was used. After analyzing the importance of the features, we selected features 8 and 32 to visually display the results of the oversampling algorithms, thereby directly perceiving the data generation features of each generation algorithm.

As shown in Fig. 3, the display order is based on the algorithm order recorded in Table 1, where '-' represents the effect of no oversampling, i.e. raw data. In these graphs, the red dots are majority class samples (label = 0), the blue dots are minority class samples (label=1), and the green dots are the possible positions of the oversampled samples (label = 2), and the deeper the green dot color, the higher the sampling probability. On the whole, the results of the traditional oversampling algorithms represented by SMOTE have a clear linear feature, while the results of the deep learning-based oversampling algorithms represented by D-AE have a smoother distribution.

**Table 4.** Generating Dataset Universality Validation Results on Test set

| Datasets | Algorithm | Precision | Recall | F-Measure | AUC |
|----------|-----------|-----------|--------|-----------|-----|
| PTB | D-AE | **96.6%** | 96.3% | **96.4%** | **97.5%** |
|  | - | 96.2% | 94.1% | 95.2% | 96.4% |
|  | SMOTE | 93.4% | 96.4% | 94.9% | 96.9% |
|  | Borderline-SMOTE-1 | 92.2% | 96.7% | 94.4% | 96.8% |
|  | Borderline-SMOTE-2 | 87.8% | 96.8% | 92.0% | 95.8% |
|  | ADASYN | 92.1% | 96.7% | 94.4% | 96.8% |
|  | NearMiss1 | 58.5% | 96.4% | 72.8% | 85.0% |
|  | NearMiss2 | 51.6% | **98.2%** | 67.6% | 81.3% |
|  | GAN | 96.1% | 95.7% | 95.9% | 97.1% |
|  | Denoising AE | 96.1% | 96.2% | 96.2% | 97.4% |
|  | AE | **96.0%** | 96.4% | 96.2% | 97.4% |
| Human | D-AE | 98.1% | 99.6% | 98.9% | 99.6% |
|  | - | 97.3% | 97.9% | 97.6% | 98.6% |
|  | SMOTE | 96.8% | 98.4% | 97.6% | 98.8% |
|  | Borderline-SMOTE-1 | 95.5% | 98.3% | 96.9% | 98.6% |
|  | Borderline-SMOTE-2 | 95.8% | **99.9%** | 97.8% | 99.5% |
|  | ADASYN | 95.1% | 98.4% | 96.8% | 98.6% |
|  | NearMiss1 | 34.3% | 99.0% | 51.0% | 77.9% |
|  | NearMiss2 | 29.2% | 98.0% | 45.0% | 72.0% |
|  | GAN | 98.3% | 99.6% | 99.0% | 99.6% |
|  | Denoising AE | 98.8% | 99.7% | 99.2% | **99.9%** |
|  | AE | **98.9%** | **99.9%** | **99.4%** | 99.8% |
| Gender | D-AE | 95.3% | 97.5% | **96.4%** | **97.3%** |
|  | - | 94.8% | 97.3% | 96.1% | 97.0% |
|  | SMOTE | 93.5% | 97.6% | 95.5% | 96.7% |
|  | Borderline-SMOTE-1 | 92.2% | 97.7% | 94.9% | 96.3% |
|  | Borderline-SMOTE-2 | 93.2% | 97.4% | 95.3% | 96.5% |
|  | ADASYN | 93.2% | 97.4% | 95.2% | 96.5% |
|  | NearMiss1 | 88.4% | **98.7%** | 93.2% | 95.4% |
|  | NearMiss2 | 89.6% | 98.4% | 93.8% | 95.7% |
|  | GAN | 82.3% | 93.3% | 87.5% | 90.5% |
|  | Denoising AE | **97.5%** | 94.5% | 95.9% | 96.5% |
|  | AE | 97.0% | 93.7% | 95.3% | 96.0% |

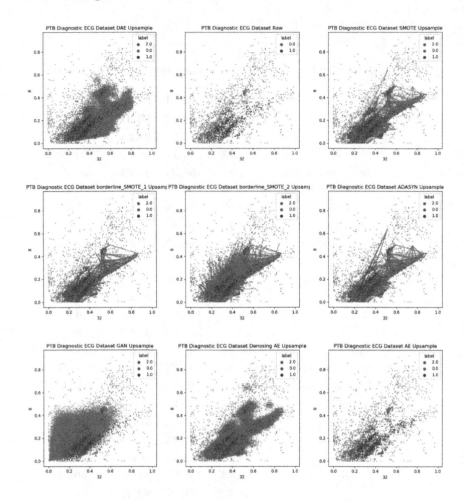

**Fig. 3.** Upsample Data Visualization (Important Feature)

**Table 5.** Ablation Result

| Datasets | ABE_Option | Precision | Recall | F-Measure | AUC |
|---|---|---|---|---|---|
| PTB | - | 96.6% | **96.3%** | **96.4%** | **97.5%** |
| | $D$-$L_1$ | 96.8% | 93.4% | 95.1% | 95.8% |
| | $L_2$ | **97.5%** | 94.5% | 95.9% | 96.5% |
| | noise | 95.7% | 94.6% | 95.1% | 96.5% |
| Human | - | 98.1% | 99.6% | 98.9% | 99.6% |
| | $D$-$L_1$ | 97.6% | 98.6% | 98.1% | 99.0% |
| | $L_2$ | **98.8%** | **99.7%** | **99.2%** | **99.9%** |
| | noise | 97.6% | 98.6% | 98.1% | 99.0% |
| Gender | - | 95.3% | **97.5%** | **96.4%** | **97.3%** |
| | $D$-$L_1$ | 96.8% | 93.4% | 95.1% | 95.8% |
| | $L_2$ | **97.5%** | 94.5% | 95.9% | 96.5% |
| | noise | 97.1% | 93.0% | 95.0% | 95.7% |

## 5.2  Ablation Experiment

We conducted an ablation study under various conditions to evaluate the impact of key components such as the discriminator loss $D$-$L_1$, reconstruction loss $L_2$, and noise. The results are shown in Table 5 in ascending order of accuracy from top to bottom.

On the PTB Diagnostic ECG Dataset, the ablation of noise and $D$-$L_1$ resulted in the greatest decrease in F-Measure value, dropping from 96.4% to 95.1%, a decrease of 1.3%. And the ablation of $D$-$L_1$ resulted in the greatest decrease in AUC value, dropping from 97.5% to 95.8%, a decrease of 1.7%. After removing $D$-$L_1$, the D-AE model closely resembles the Denoising AE. Yet, a key differentiation emerges in their respective loss designs. While the Denoising AE aims to reconstruct the original, noise-free input $x$, D-AE's design entails accepting a noisy input $x^{noise}$ and reconstructing a similar noisy output $g$, akin to the mechanism of a traditional AE. This distinction was evident in our experiments where the baseline AE was fed a noise-free input $x$. This design in D-AE serves to amplify randomness in outputs, enhancing the richness of data representation.

On the Human Activity Recognition with Smartphones dataset, the removal of $L_2$ led to an improvement in performance. This indicates that for datasets with clear boundaries, enhancing randomness can disrupt the inherent features of the dataset, even in the context of data imbalance. 'Clear boundaries' means that there are distinct and easily distinguishable limits between categories or groups within the dataset, ensuring that data points from one category rarely mix or overlap with those from other categories. In such scenarios, increasing randomness might adversely impact the learning efficiency of the classifier.

On the China Unicom Gender Prediction Dataset, the removal of noise had the greatest impact on the values of F-Measure and AUC, decreasing by 1.4% from 96.4% to 95.0% and 1.6% from 97.3% to 95.7%, respectively.

Overall, our studies and observations suggest that $D$-$L_1$ and noise play pivotal roles in determining the performance trajectory of D-AE.

## 5.3  Failure Cases and Limitations

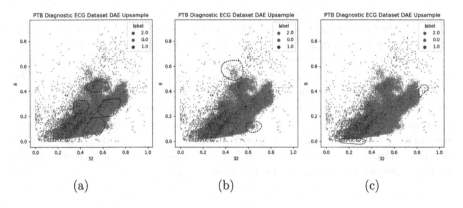

**Fig. 4.** Failure Cases

The D-AE upsampling algorithm still has the situation of poor sample generation. Here, we still take PTB heart disease data set as an example to analyze the causes of badcases.

**Failure Case 1:** As shown by the black dotted circle in Fig. 4(a), the range of values for generated samples that are far from the center of the category tends to be biased towards the distribution of the minority class. Some minority samples have poor distinguishability from majority samples, leading to generated samples based on that minority sample also having poor distinguishability from majority samples.

**Failure Case 2:** As shown by the black dotted circle in Fig. 4(b), some minority class samples are affected by noise, and since the noise has an isolated characteristic, the generated samples based on the noise lack generality and are not distinguishable from the majority class samples, while there is still a certain probability of generating samples around the noise as shown in the figure

**Failure Case 3:** As shown in the black dotted circle in Fig. 4(c), the model refuses to generate samples around the shown minority class samples. There are two possible reasons for this: (1) The sample generation based on D-AE is insensitive to the input value boundary points (the output activation function of the AE part is sigmoid), as shown in the figure the input features are close to 0 or 1; (2) There are also minority class outliers (points away from the principle class center) in the test set. The generated data based on the test set outliers is more inclined to the distribution of the minority class samples in the training set, so there is no probability of sample generation around the test set outliers.

The results of this paper show that the D-AE algorithm effectively solved datasets with unbalance degrees ranging from 1:1.6 to 1:4.4, where the data volume was between 1900 to 37000 and the number of features was below 561.

# 6    Conclusion

In this study, we present the Discriminant-Autoencoder (D-AE) algorithm. This algorithm leverages a pre-trained external discriminator to generate synthetic data that resembles the minority class samples in the original dataset. The D-AE algorithm also adds Gaussian noise to increase the diversity of the generated data. By considering the nonlinear distribution of minority samples in the raw data and generating new samples, the D-AE addresses the issue of class imbalance and improves the performance of subsequent predictive models. The PTB diagnostic ECG dataset, human activity recognition with smartphones, and China Unicom gender prediction dataset were used for training the discriminator, encoder, and decoder, generating minority class samples, training predictive models, and evaluating performance. The results demonstrate that the predictive model trained on the D-AE generated data outperforms other baseline algorithms in terms of performance metrics.

# References

1. Akkalakshmi, M., Riyazuddin, Y.M., Revathi, V., Pal, A.: Autoencoder-based feature learning and up-sampling to enhance cancer prediction. Int. J. Future Gener. Commun. Netw. **13**(1), 1453–1459 (2020)
2. AlAmir, M., AlGhamdi, M.: The role of generative adversarial network in medical image analysis: an in-depth survey. ACM Comput. Surv. (CSUR) **55**(5), 1–36 (2022)
3. Anguita, D., Ghio, A., Oneto, L., Parra Perez, X., Reyes Ortiz, J.L.: A public domain dataset for human activity recognition using smartphones. In: Proceedings of the 21th International European Symposium on Artificial Neural Networks, Computational Intelligence and Machine Learning, pp. 437–442 (2013)
4. Back, K., Crotty, K., Kazempour, S.M., Schwert, G.W.: Validity, tightness, and forecasting power of risk premium bounds. J. Financ. Econ. **144**, 732–760 (2022)
5. Baldi, P.: Boolean autoencoders and hypercube clustering complexity. Des. Codes Crypt. **65**(3), 383–403 (2012)
6. Cetinkunt, S., Donmez, A.: CMAC learning controller for servo control of high precision machine tools. In: 1993 American Control Conference (1993)
7. Chawla, N.V., Bowyer, K.W., Hall, L.O., Kegelmeyer, W.P.: Smote: synthetic minority over-sampling technique. AI Access Found. (1) (2002)
8. Chen, Z., Zhou, L., Yu, W.: Adasyn-random forest based intrusion detection model (2021)
9. Cho, K.: Simple sparsification improves sparse denoising autoencoders in denoising highly corrupted images. In: International Conference on Machine Learning (2013)
10. Creswell, A., White, T., Dumoulin, V., Arulkumaran, K., Sengupta, B., Bharath, A.A.: Generative adversarial networks: an overview. IEEE Signal Process. Mag. **35**(1), 53–65 (2018)
11. Egan, J.P.: Signal detection theory and roc analysis. In: Series in Cognition and Perception. Academic Press, New York (1975)
12. Gajera, V., Shubham, Gupta, R., Jana, P.K.: An effective multi-objective task scheduling algorithm using min-max normalization in cloud computing. In: 2016 2nd International Conference on Applied and Theoretical Computing and Communication Technology (iCATccT) (2016)
13. Garcia, S., Derrac, J., Cano, J., Herrera, F.: Prototype selection for nearest neighbor classification: taxonomy and empirical study. IEEE Trans. Pattern Anal. Mach. Intell. **34**(3), 417 (2012)
14. Gu, S., Yan, J., Xiao, Z., Ning, L., Tech, V.: What are driving users to click ads? User habit, attitude, and commercial intention (2010)
15. Gupta, A., Anand, A., Hasija, Y.: Recall-based machine learning approach for early detection of cervical cancer. In: 2021 6th International Conference for Convergence in Technology (I2CT) (2021)
16. Han, B., Wang, X., Ji, S., Zhang, G., He, J.: Data-enhanced stacked autoencoders for insufficient fault classification of machinery and its understanding via visualization. IEEE Access **8**(99), 67790–67798 (2020)
17. Han, H., Wang, W.Y., Mao, B.H.: Borderline-smote: a new over-sampling method in imbalanced data sets learning. In: Proceedings of the 2005 international conference on Advances in Intelligent Computing - Volume Part I (2005)
18. He, H., Yang, B., Garcia, E.A., Li, S.: Adasyn: adaptive synthetic sampling approach for imbalanced learning. In: IEEE International Joint Conference on Neural Networks, IJCNN 2008 (IEEE World Congress on Computational Intelligence) (2008)

19. Kachuee, M., Fazeli, S., Sarrafzadeh, M.: ECG heartbeat classification: a deep transferable representation. In: 2018 IEEE International Conference on Healthcare Informatics (ICHI), pp. 443–444. IEEE (2018)
20. Komoto, K., Nakatsuka, S., Aizawa, H., Kato, K., Kobayashi, H., Banno, K.: A performance evaluation of defect detection by using denoising autoencoder generative adversarial networks. In: 2018 International Workshop on Advanced Image Technology (IWAIT), pp. 1–4. IEEE (2018)
21. Lobo, J.M., Jiménez-Valverde, A., Real, R.: AUC: a misleading measure of the performance of predictive distribution models. Glob. Ecol. Biogeogr. **17**(2), 145–151 (2008)
22. Lu, C., Lin, S., Liu, X., Shi, H.: Telecom fraud identification based on adasyn and random forest. In: 2020 5th International Conference on Computer and Communication Systems (ICCCS) (2020)
23. Lu, X., Tsao, Y., Matsuda, S., Hori, C.: Speech enhancement based on deep denoising autoencoder. In: Interspeech, vol. 2013, pp. 436–440 (2013)
24. Mehta, J., Majumdar, A.: Rodeo: robust de-aliasing autoencoder for real-time medical image reconstruction. Pattern Recognit. J. Pattern Recognit. Soc. **63**, 499–510 (2017)
25. Mei, S., Wang, Y., Wen, G.: Automatic fabric defect detection with a multi-scale convolutional denoising autoencoder network model. Sensors **18**(4), 1064 (2018)
26. Mqadi, N.M., Naicker, N., Adeliyi, T.: Solving misclassification of the credit card imbalance problem using near miss. Math. Probl. Eng. Theory Methods Appl. (2021-Pt.32) (2021)
27. Naseriparsa, M., Kashani, M.: Combination of PCA with smote resampling to boost the prediction rate in lung cancer dataset. Found. Comput. Sci. (FCS) (3) (2013)
28. Perri, S.: Design of flexible hardware accelerators for image convolutions and transposed convolutions. J. Imaging **7**, 210 (2021)
29. Prabakaran, N., Dudi, S.V., Palaniappan, R., Kannadasan, R., Sasidhar, V.: Forecasting the momentum using customised loss function for financial series. Int. J. Intell. Comput. Cybern. **14**(4), 702–713 (2021)
30. Pu, Y., Zhe, G., Henao, R., Xin, Y., Carin, L.: Variational autoencoder for deep learning of images, labels and captions. In: NIPS 2016 (2016)
31. Seo, J.H., Kim, Y.H.: Machine-learning approach to optimize smote ratio in class imbalance dataset for intrusion detection. Hindawi Limited (2018)
32. Shon, T., Moon, J.: A hybrid machine learning approach to network anomaly detection. Inf. Sci. **177**(18), 3799–3821 (2007)
33. Sokolova, M., Japkowicz, N., Szpakowicz, S.: Beyond accuracy, F-score and ROC: a family of discriminant measures for performance evaluation. In: Sattar, A., Kang, B. (eds.) Australasian Joint Conference on Artificial Intelligence. LNCS, vol. 4304, pp. 1015–1021. Springer, Heidelberg (2006). https://doi.org/10.1007/11941439_114
34. Song, Y., Peng, Y.: A MCDM-based evaluation approach for imbalanced classification methods in financial risk prediction. IEEE Access **7**, 84897–84906 (2019)
35. Wang, L.J., Jiang, Y.: Collocating recommendation method for E-commerce based on fuzzy C-means clustering algorithm. J. Math. **2022** (2022)
36. Yang, Y., Xu, Z.: Rethinking the value of labels for improving class-imbalanced learning (2020)
37. Zhao, Y., et al.: Constructing non-small cell lung cancer survival prediction model based on borderline-smote and PFS. Int. J. Biomed. Eng. 336–341 (2019)

# ECCRG: A Emotion- and Content-Controllable Response Generation Model

Hui Chen[1], Bo Wang[2(✉)], Ke Yang[1], and Yi Song[2]

[1] Hunan Seefore Information Technology Co., Ltd., Yueyang, China
yk@singhand.com
[2] College of Intelligence and Computing, Tianjin University, Tianjin, China
bo_wang@tju.edu.cn

**Abstract.** Most methods of emotional dialogue generation focus on how to make the generated replies express the set emotion categories, while ignoring the control over the semantic content of the replies. To this end, in this paper, we propose a emotion- and content-controllable response generation model, ECCRG. ECCRG allows for text-controlled conditions and integration into the decoding process of the language model through a self-attention layer, enabling more precise control over the content of the generated responses. We use a variety of optimization objectives including self-reconfiguration loss and adversarial learning loss to jointly train the model. Experimental results show that ECCRG can embody the set target content in the generated responses, allowing us to achieve controllability on both emotion and textual content.

**Keywords:** Dialogue systems · Emotional response generation · Controllable text generation

## 1 Introduction

Early research Partala and Surakka (2004) showed that dialogue systems capable of appropriate emotional expressions in replies can directly improve user satisfaction and make users feel more engaged. Ideally, a dialogue system with emotional intelligence can make the user experience more comfortable by means of emotional interaction, and even have the effect of psychological comfort and treatment. Some researchers have tried to make dialogue systems appear more human-like by making the system mimic human emotional expressions. Early representative work (Polzin and Waibel (2000); Skowron (2010)) used human-written rules to select responses related to specific emotions from a dialogue corpus. These rules usually need to be written by experienced experts, so such methods are difficult to scale to scenes and larger corpora containing complex, subtle emotions.

In the era of deep learning, sequence-to-sequence (Seq2seq) models have gradually been widely used in dialogue generation tasks. In early attempts to develop

H. Gao et al. (Eds.): CollaborateCom 2023, LNICST 562, pp. 115–130, 2024.
https://doi.org/10.1007/978-3-031-54528-3_7

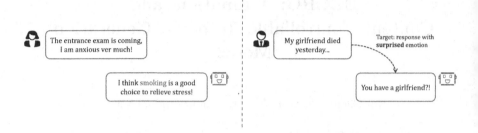

**Fig. 1.** A case of uncontrolled reply generation

chatbots through the Seq2seq framework, many efforts (Li et al. (2015); Gao et al. (2019)) were made to avoid boring words (like "I'm fine" and "go on") in responses, and works to make the responses more informative. But only a few works focus on the emotional expression problem in dialogue generation. Incorporating emotional expressions in a dialogue system mainly faces several challenges:

(1) Dialogue data with sufficient scale and marked emotion categories are difficult to obtain. Some work in recent years has contributed many high-quality dialogue datasets to the academic community, which are mostly manually written and annotated and limited in size. Because the task of emotion recognition in dialogue is also quite challenging, accurate emotion annotation is difficult to scale to large-scale datasets.
(2) It is difficult for us to consider emotions in a natural and coherent way. Emotional factors are only expressed on the surface of the text by emotional words in a few cases, but are often implied under the semantics of the text. Both abstraction and incorporating emotional information present difficulties.
(3) The experiments of Zhou et al. (2018) show that simply embedding emotional information into a neural network model cannot generate ideal emotional responses.

To address these challenges, Zhou et al. (2018) successfully constructed an emotion chat machine (ECM) based on the Seq2seq model, which is able to generate responses expressing that emotion based on pre-defined emotion categories. After this, there have been some studies with similar goals (Song et al. (2019); Huang et al. (2018); Asghar et al. (2018)). Zhou and Wang (2018) proposed MojiTalk, which uses a series of emoji "emoji" in the conditional variational The process of generating emotional responses is controlled within an encoder (CVAE) framework. Some studies have proposed ways to motivate models to express emotion more explicitly, for example, assigning additional probability distribution weights to related emotion words under a given emotion during decoding, or incorporating the use of emotion words into the loss function.

All of the methods mentioned above are effective in generating responses that express specific emotions. From the emotional level, most of them represent emotional categories as independent labels, such as "<happy>" or the corresponding "emoji", and convert them into the form of embedding vectors and then integrate them into the basic generative model, or It is to integrate the emotion vector into the hidden state of the decoder to affect the decoding result, or use it as a conditional latent variable in the CVAE framework, and then splicing emotion words and general words in the decoding process to achieve the purpose of expressing emotion. This control method with emotion as a high-level attribute makes it difficult for the model to learn the specific way to express emotion from semantics. Meanwhile, the methods that try to express emotions explicitly by using a large number of emotional words are difficult to balance emotional words and other words, resulting in less fluent responses, and explicit expressions appear unnatural in many cases.

From the semantic level, related research work only focuses on the control of emotional expression, but ignores the quality of the generated content. Dialogue generation technology is widely used in more rigorous application scenarios including legal and political court trials, and medical dialogue for mental health. Taking counseling conversations in health care as an example, users may be troubled by various psychological barriers and frustrations, such as listening to the user's conversation about test anxiety, inappropriate counseling and guidance shown in the left part in Fig. 1 is likely to have serious consequences. For open-domain dialogue systems, most of the corpus comes from chats crawled by social media platforms. Chatbots trained by such data are likely to generate "toxic" sentences. For example, in the case shown on the right part in Fig. 1, even if the emotion type "surprise" that should be expressed in the reply is specified, such a reply will obviously reduce the user's experience.

To address the above problems, we attempts to jointly constrain response generation from both the emotional level and semantic level, and control the generated text content at a finer granularity. We propose an Emotion- and Content-Controllable Response Generation model (ECCRG). ECCRG is built on a large-scale pre-trained language model, which guarantees the basic fluency of the text it generates. We add an intermediate layer into the multi-layer Transformer structure of the language model, which can incorporate control conditions in the form of text into the downstream language model through a self-attention mechanism, and thereby guide the subsequent generated content.

## 2  Related Work

Humans have the unique ability to perceive complex, subtle emotions and to communicate their experiences and feelings with each other through language. Existing research Partala and Surakka (2004) suggested that dialogue systems with appropriate emotional expressions in responses can directly improve user satisfaction and help increase user engagement. However, making dialogue systems more "emotional" remains a huge challenge.

In early representative work, researchers used some hand-crafted rules to select sentences associated with specific emotions from a dialogue corpus. These rules need to be written by trained experts and are difficult to scale to handle more complex and subtle emotions in large-scale corpora. In 2014, Microsoft launched Xiaoice (Zhou et al. (2020)), a social chatbot that recognizes users' emotional needs and has empathy. It was not until Zhou et al. (2018) proposed the Emotional Chatting Machine (ECM), which used deep learning methods to build an emotion-aware dialogue system on large-scale corpus, research related to emotional dialogue generation became popular.

After this, Colombo et al. (2019) improved ECM, they used VAD lexicons to represent emotion, and improved the decoding process and loss function for the emotion factor. Song et al. (2019) pointed out that the more general way to express emotions is to express them implicitly through semantics. They used a emotion classifier co-trained with the model to guide the process of response generation to ensure the appropriate expression of specific emotions in the responses. Asghar et al. (2018) proposed an emotion-diverse beam search algorithm for decoding, and employed reinforcement learning to encourage the model to present the specified emotion at generation time. Zhong et al. (2020a) constructed an emotion-aware commonsense concept graph based on Concept-Net using emotion-annotated corpus, and then they captured the most relevant knowledge tuples under different expected emotions through mechanisms such as graph attention, and fused into the Transformer model.

In the trend of pre-trained language models (Devlin et al. (2018); Liu et al. (2019); Radford et al. (2019)) sweeping the NLP field, the research on controllable dialogue generation has also made breakthroughs. Some studies reconstruct and retrain the pre-trained model so that the generated results meet certain preset conditions. Lin et al. (2021) built a series of lightweight adaptive models for various dialogue generation needs based on the pre-trained model DialoGPT(Zhang et al. (2019)), these models allow various control for different conversational needs Conditions (including emotion, language style, etc.) for advanced control and integration.

Most of the above-mentioned methods rely on specific emotion labels to express emotions, but do not explicitly model the emotional information in the context, so that the models does not really understand the current emotional state of the dialogue and the user's intents. Meanwhile, most approaches of emotional dialogue generation focus on how to make the model more accurately express the specified emotion type, while ignoring the control over the semantic content of the responses.

## 3    Methodology

### 3.1    Problem Setup

In this paper, our task is to generate response sentences that are coherent with the dialogue history and user input and satisfy the controlled conditions, given the dialogue context and the control conditions of the emotion or content that needs to be expressed in the responses to be generated. The specific formulation of the task is as follows: Given a dialogue context $X = \{x_1, ..., x_N\}$ that may contain $N$ utterances, where $x_i = \{w_{i,1}, w_{i,2}, ..., w_{i,l_i}\}$, $x_N$ is the user's last input, and a control conditional text $c$, The model needs to generate corresponding response $Y = \{y_1, y_2, ..., y_{l_y}\}$ based on these conditions. The goal of the generation is to keep $Y$ semantically coherent with the dialogue history and user input, and meet the requirements of controlled conditions. Where $l_i$, $l_y$, $l_c$ are the lengths of $x_i$, $Y$, $c$ respectively.

In the response generation model proposed in this paper, the control condition $c$ includes target emotion type or textual content. For the former, we input the emotion label into the control condition, then the corresponding emotional expression should be made in $Y$. In the latter case, the generated response $Y$ should contain semantics consistent with the target content.

### 3.2 Model Architecture

ECCRG is built on a large-scale pre-trained language model. This kind of language model has comprehensively learned language knowledge (such as semantics, syntax, grammar, etc.), commonsense knowledge, and specialized knowledge from a large-scale corpus in the pre-training stage. Specifically in the experiments of ECCRG, we use the pre-trained parameters of GPT-2 (Radford et al. (2019)) to initialize the language model, denoted as LM, which ensures that the text generated by ECCRG has basic fluency and diversity sex. GPT-2 generates text in an auto-regressive manner, which can be expressed as:

$$p(x_t, ..., x_l | x_1, ..., x_{t-1}) = \prod_{i=t}^{l} p(x_i | x_1, ..., x_{i-1}), \qquad (1)$$

where $t - 1$ is the length of the input sequence, and $l$ is the maximum length of the sequence generated by the language model. Due to the auto-regressive generation manner of GPT-2, the words generated in the current step will be added to the end of the original input sequence to form a new sequence as the input sequence generated in the next step. For step $t$, that is, the first word $x_t$ generated in the GPT-2 generation process, it is sampled from the probability distribution of the output of the language model $o_t = \text{LM}(x_{:t-1})$. For the reply generation task, we take user utterances as the raw input sequence for GPT-2.

Figure 2 shows the overall architecture of ECCRG. The GPT-2 language model is composed of stacked multiple layers, each layer is a Transformer block. We add an intermediate layer based on the self-attention mechanism in the middle of the multi-layer structure, which separates the language model into two parts. We call the middle layer ECC-layer, the upstream language model is denoted as $\text{LM}_A$, and the downstream part is denoted as $\text{LM}_B$. $\text{LM}_A$ extracts features from the embedded representation of the input sequence and outputs its current hidden state $h_{:t-1}$:

$$h_{:t-1} = \text{LM}_A(x_{:t-1}). \qquad (2)$$

$\text{LM}_B$ takes $h_{:t-1}$ as input and outputs the predicted probability distribution $o_t$ of the language model:

$$o_t = \text{LM}_B(h_{:t-1}). \qquad (3)$$

Equations (2) and (3) can be combined as:

$$o_t = \text{LM}(x_{:t-1}) = \text{LM}_B(\text{LM}_A(x_{:t-1})) = \text{LM}_B(h_{:t-1}). \qquad (4)$$

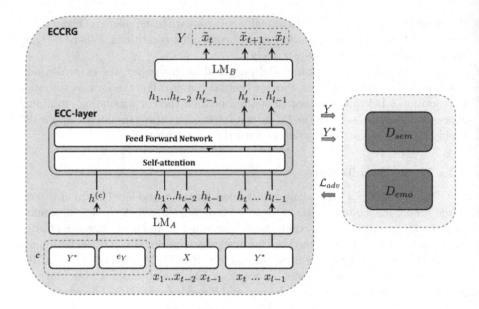

**Fig. 2.** Model structure of ECCRG

It can be seen from (4) that the probability distribution $o$ of the next word generated by $\text{LM}_B$ is affected by the hidden state $h$ of $\text{LM}_A$. Using this effect, we integrate the controlled condition sequence $c$ with the original hidden state $h$ in ECC-layer to obtain a new hidden state $h'$:

$$h'_{:t-1} = \text{ECC}(h^{(c)}, h_{:t-1}), \tag{5}$$

where $h^{(c)}$ is the hidden state obtained by $\text{LM}_A$ with the embedded representation of the control condition sequence as input, that is, $h^{(c)} = \text{LM}_A(c)$.

Specifically, ECC-layer integrates $h^{(c)}$ and $h$ through self-attention, first from $h_{:t-1}$ obtains $Q \in \mathbb{R}^{(t-1)\times d}$, $K \in \mathbb{R}^{(t-1)\times d}$ and $V \in \mathbb{R}^{(t-1)\times d}$ of the original hidden state through linear transformation, where $d$ is the dimension of the hidden state. Similarly, from $h^{(c)}$ we can obtain $K^{(c)}, V^{(c)} \in \mathbb{R}^{l_c \times d}$, where $l_c$ is the length of the control condition sequence, then calculate the output of self-attention $A \in \mathbb{R}^{(t-1)\times d}$:

$$K' = [K^{(c)}; K] \in \mathbb{R}^{(l_c + t - 1)\times d},$$
$$V' = [V^{(c)}; V] \in \mathbb{R}^{(l_c + t - 1)\times d}, \tag{6}$$
$$A = \text{softmax}(QK'^{\text{T}})V' \in \mathbb{R}^{(t-1)\times d},$$

where $A = \{a_1, a_2, ..., a_{t-1}\}$, $a_{t-1}$ is converted by a fully connected layer to get $h'_{t-1} = \mathrm{FFN}(a_{t-1})$, which is the new hidden state integrating control condition information obtained through ECC-layer at the current step. By concatenating $h'_{t-1}$ with the original hidden state of the previous step and sending them to $LM_B$, new probability distribution $\tilde{o}_t$ is conditioned on $c$:

$$\tilde{o}_t = LM_B([h_{:t-2}; h'_{t-1}]), \tag{7}$$

The $\tilde{x}_t$ sampled by $\tilde{o}_t$ is the controlled generation result affected by the control condition $c$.

We fine-tune the pre-trained GPT-2 on the Reddit dataset. In the subsequent training process of ECC-layer, we fixed the parameters of the language model and only updated the parameters of ECC-layer.

## 3.3   Training of ECC-Layer

The training goal of ECCRG is to make the responses it generates controllable both at emotional level and content level.

At emotional level, although we incorporate emotion information into the input embedding of each token, it is difficult for the model to learn the difference in sampling space under different emotion types. Therefore, like other work on emotional response generation, we need to inject the target emotion label into the control condition of ECC-layer to explicitly guide the emotional expression in response generation.

At content level, due to the diversity of natural language and the randomness of sampling in the decoding process of auto-regressive models, even given sufficient dialogue context information, there may be a huge number of candidate responses that can maintain semantic coherence with the context. In other words, the probability of the model generating ground-truth is very low given only the dialogue history and no target response.

For these two problems, we design multiple loss functions as optimization targets for ECC-layer training.

**Self-reconstruction Loss.** In order to make the responses generated by the model close to the text content in the controlled condition, inspired by Chan et al. (2020), we adopt their proposed self-reconstruction loss to concatenate the context and the ground-truth response as the input sequence, and with the ground-truth response as the control condition.

Specifically, we concatenate the dialogue context $X$ and the ground-truth response $Y^*$ into a new input sequence $X' = [X; Y^*]$ and denote it as $X' = \{x_1, ..., x_{t-1}, x_t, , ..., x_l\}$, where $l$ is the total length of the sequence, $x_{:t-1}$ is the original context, $x_{t:l}$ is the original response. Meanwhile, we use $Y^*$ as control condition, denoted as $c = Y^*$. Same as Eq. (2), we first get the intermediate hidden states of $X'$ and $c$ from $LM_A$:

$$h_{:l} = LM_A(x_{:l}), \ h^{(c)}_{l_c} = LM_A(c) = LM_A(x_{t:l}), \tag{8}$$

where $l_c = l - t + 1$ is the sequence length of $c$. Similar to Eq. (5), ECC-layer fuses $h^{(c)}_{l_c}$ with the original hidden state $h_{t:l}$ of the reply generation stage to obtain the conditioned hidden state:

$$h'_i = ECC(h^{(c)}_{:l_c}; h_i), \text{ where } i \in [t-1, l]. \tag{9}$$

Similar to Eq. (7), the original hidden states of the context is concatenated with the conditioned hidden states of the response transformed by ECC-layer, and passed into $LM_B$ to produce the LM logits:

$$\tilde{o}_{i+1} = LM_B([h_{:t-2}; h'_{t-1:i}]), p(\tilde{x}_{i+1}|x_{:i}, c) = \text{softmax}(\tilde{o}_{i+1}), \quad \text{where } i \in [t-1, l]. \tag{10}$$

The self-reconstruction loss $\mathcal{L}_{recon}$ is defined as the cross-entropy loss between the generated and the ground-truth response:

$$\mathcal{L}_{recon} = -\sum_{i=t}^{l} \log p(x_i|\{x_1, x_2, ..., x_{i-1}\}, (c = x_{t:l})). \tag{11}$$

**Emotion Controlled Loss.** In order to make the decoding process adapted by the model under the condition of the specified emotion type still generate syntactically and syntactically fluent responses, we inject the emotion type corresponding to the real response into the ECC layer as a controlled condition. For the emotion category $e_{Y^*}$ marked by the real reply $Y^*$, we refer to the conceptual interpretation in English and simply convert it into a short sentence describing the emotion, for example, for the emotion type "admiration", describe it as "I feel a state of admiration and pride.", still denoted as $c = e_{Y^*}$. Similar to the self-reconstruction loss, we define the emotion controlled loss $\mathcal{L}_{emo}$ as:

$$\mathcal{L}_{recon} = -\sum_{i=t}^{l} \log p(x_i|\{x_1, x_2, ..., x_{i-1}\}, (c = e_{Y^*})). \tag{12}$$

It should be noted that in the training and testing stages, when the self-reconstruction loss and the emotion controlled loss are activated at the same time, we concatenate the corresponding control conditions to the self-reconstruction loss and the emotion-controlled loss and inject it into ECC-layer, namely $c = [Y^*; e_{Y^*}]$, to evaluate the performance of ECCRG under the condition on emotion and content variables.

**Adversarial Loss.** In order to motivate the model to generate emotional expressions in replies and make replies closer to real text, we introduce two discriminator models to provide additional signals for the training of ECC-layers, namely the semantic discriminator $D_{sem}$ and the emotion discriminator $D_{emo}$. Both discriminators are classifier structures constructed based on convolutional neural networks.

The semantic discriminator measures the semantic distance between the generated responses $Y$ and the ground-truth $Y^*$. In order to avoid the discriminator loss cannot be back-propagated to ECC-layer caused by discrete sampling in the decoding process, We do not use the sampled token id sequence, instead send the probability distribution obtained from $LM_B$ to $LM_A$ to obtain the embedded representation of the hidden layer. Based on this we define the semantic adversarial loss $\mathcal{L}_{adv}^{sem}$:

$$\mathcal{L}_{adv}^{sem} = \log D_{sem}(LM_A(Y^*)) + \log(1 - D_{sem}(LM_A(Y))). \tag{13}$$

The emotion discriminator determines whether the generated response expresses the specified emotion type. We also define the emotion-based adversarial loss $\mathcal{L}_{adv}^{emo}$:

$$\mathcal{L}_{adv}^{emo} = \log p_{\theta_{D_{emo}}}(e_{Y^*}|\text{LM}_A(Y^*)) - \log p_{\theta_{D_{emo}}}(e_{Y^*}|\text{LM}_A(Y))), \quad (14)$$

Table 1. Statistics for the Reddit dataset

| Dataset | #Dial. | Emotion label Statistics of Responses | | | | | | |
|---|---|---|---|---|---|---|---|---|
| | | Admiration | Approval | Caring | Joy | Sadness | Surprise | Neutral |
| Train | 146,451 | 67,738 | 10,166 | 7544 | 18,919 | 6887 | 21,033 | 14,164 |
| Valid | 18,961 | 8904 | 1347 | 993 | 2321 | 886 | 2654 | 1856 |
| Test | 20,137 | 9606 | 1320 | 1056 | 2540 | 815 | 2898 | 1902 |

where $\theta_{D_{emo}}$ is the parameter of $D_{emo}$.

In adversarial learning, the training objective of ECC-layer is to minimize the adversarial losses $\mathcal{L}_{adv}^{sem}$ and $\mathcal{L}_{adv}^{emo}$, while the training objectives of the semantic discriminator and the emotion discriminator are to maximize $\mathcal{L}_{adv}^{sem}$ and $\mathcal{L}_{adv}^{emo}$ respectively. ECCRG is trained in an end-to-end manner with two discriminators.

**Training.** ECCRG still needs to perform basic auto-regressive generation without setting any control variables. We define the auto-regressive loss $\mathcal{L}_{ar}$:

$$\mathcal{L}_{ar} = -\sum_{i=t}^{l} \log p(x_i|\{x_1, ..., x_{i-1}\}). \quad (15)$$

The total optimization objective of training is to minimize the sum of all the above loss functions:

$$\mathcal{L} = \lambda_{ar}\mathcal{L}_{ar} + \lambda_{recon}\mathcal{L}_{recon} + \lambda_{emo}\mathcal{L}_{emo} + \lambda_{adv}^{sem}\mathcal{L}_{adv}^{sem} + \lambda_{adv}^{emo}\mathcal{L}_{adv}^{emo}, \quad (16)$$

where $\lambda$ is the weight factor that balances the influence of each part of the losses.

## 4 Experimental Setup

### 4.1 Dataset

Zhong et al. (2020b) proposed a large-scale dialogue dataset scraped from the social forum Reddit. The dialogues in this dataset come from two partitions Happy and Offmychest where users communicate emotionally. This chapter uses the Reddit dataset to train and evaluate ECCRG, mainly considering that the response sentences in this dataset are shown to contain distinct emotional expressions and empathy. In addition, we use the emotion annotation on the dataset by Zheng et al. (2021), they use a BERT-based classifier to label 8 emotion types and neutral for each utterance. The accuracy on the testset is 65.8%. To alleviate the problem of unbalance distribution of emotion types, we filter out dialogues containing utterances labeld as "anger" or "fear". The statistics of the dataset are shown in Table 1. For each dialogue, we keep the last two sentences as context and response, respectively. We set the maximum number of token per utterance to 30.

## 4.2   Experimental Settings

We initialize the language model in ECCRG using the model configuration and parameters of GPT2-medium. We take the first 6 layers of the language model as $LM_A$, and the last 18 layers as $LM_B$.

During training, we first fine-tune the GPT-2 on the trainset for 10 epochs. Then, the parameters of the language model are fixed, ECC-layer and the two discriminators are updated for 10 epochs with a batch size of 4. We use the Adam optimizer for the above training process, with the learning rate set to $5e-5$. For each part of the weight factor $\lambda$ in the loss function, we set all of them to 1.0. To obtain the generated samples for ECCRG, we sample the next word from the probability distribution obtained by the downstream language model using kernel sampling algorithm with p set to 0.9.

## 4.3   Baselines

We compare ECCRG with the following methods in our experiments:

**Seq2seq-emo.** On the basis of the Seq2seq model, the emotion label of the target reply is encoded into an embedding vector, which is used as an additional input to the decoder.

**ECM** (Zhou et al. (2018)) is the first model to generate emotional responses on large-scale dialogue datasets. We implemented it based on code published by the open source community.

**DialoGPT** (Zhang et al. (2019)) is a large-scale dialogue generation model based on GPT-2, trained on more than 147M dialogues captured from Reddit. We fine-tune DialoGPT for 5 epochs with the Reddit dataset.

## 4.4   Automatic Metrics

(1) **Perplexity** is a gram-based method to measure the strengths and weaknesses of language probability models.
(2) **BLEU** (Papineni et al. (2002)) measures how close the model-generated text is to the ground-truth by how much the n-gram phrases overlap. Some studies have pointed out that BLEU is not suitable for evaluating dialogue generation tasks because its results are less correlated with human evaluations. In this paper, we evaluate the effect of controllable generation by calculating the distance between the generated responses and the ground-truths by BLEU-1 and BLEU-2.

(3) **Distinct** (Li et al. (2015)) evaluate the diversity of generated responses based on n-gram counts. We use Distinct metrics under uni-gram and bi-gram, denoted as Dist-1 and Dist-2, respectively.

(4) **Emotion Accuracy Rate (Emo-acc):** We use a emotion classifier based on RoBERTa (Liu et al. (2019)) to evaluate the emotion accuracy the generated responses.

**Table 2.** Experiment results on Reddit dataset

| Model | Content Similarity | | Fluency | Diversity | | Emotion |
|---|---|---|---|---|---|---|
| | BLEU-2 ↑ | BLEU-4 ↑ | PPL ↓ | Dist-1 ↑ | Dist-2 ↑ | Emo-acc ↑ |
| Seq2seq-emo | 6.86 | 1.95 | **55.7** | 0.038 | 0.142 | 60.4 |
| ECM | 7.33 | 1.97 | 63.8 | 0.042 | 0.172 | 63.5 |
| DialoGPT | 12.73 | 3.23 | 58.7 | **0.065** | **0.247** | 54.1 |
| ECCRG | 19.26 | 6.44 | 65.8 | 0.053 | 0.216 | **69.7** |
| w/o $\mathcal{L}_{recon}$ | 14.67 | 3.82 | 65.2 | 0.059 | 0.233 | 67.2 |
| w/o $\mathcal{L}_{emo}$ | 16.44 | 5.72 | 68.6 | 0.052 | 0.210 | 64.1 |
| w/o $\mathcal{L}_{adv}^{emo}$ | 19.53 | 6.61 | 64.9 | 0.049 | 0.208 | 65.9 |
| w/o $\mathcal{L}_{adv}^{sem}$ | **19.77** | **6.80** | 64.4 | 0.050 | 0.210 | 68.6 |

## 4.5   Human Evaluation Metrics

We recruited 5 volunteers with good English language skill to manually evaluate the dialogues generated by the model. We sampled 20 dialogues for each emotion type from dialogues generated by ECCRG and two other baseline models for emotion controllable response generation, and also sampled 120 dialogues from DialoGPT-generated dialogues, with volunteers from three Dimensions score the quality of model generation. These three dimensions are: (1) **fluency** measures whether the response is natural and fluent; (2) **relevance** measures whether the response is semantically coherent with the context; (3) **emotion quality** measures whether the response accurately expressed the specified emotion type. Volunteers were asked to rate 1 to 5 on each of the three dimensions according to which responses were made: 1-unacceptable, 3-moderate, 5-very excellent, and 2 and 4 for transitions of uncertainty.

# 5   Results and Analysis

## 5.1   Automatic Evaluation

**Comparison with Baselines.** The upper part of Table 2 shows the experimental results of ECCRG with baseline methods on automatic evaluation metrics. BLEU-1 and BLEU-2 represent the similarity of the generated response to the ground-truth, and also reflect the impact of ECC-layer fused with control

**Table 3.** Manual evaluation results

| Model | Fluency | Relevance | Emotion Quality |
|---|---|---|---|
| Seq2seq-emo | 3.47 | 2.93 | 2.79 |
| ECM | 3.17 | 3.38 | 2.98 |
| DialoGPT | **3.68** | 3.53 | – |
| ECCRG | 3.45 | **3.82** | **3.36** |

conditions; PPL represents the fluency of the generated utterances. From the comparative experimental results, it can be seen that ECCRG is significantly outperform than other baselines on BLEU and emotion accuracy. In terms of distinct indicators, the score of ECCRG is lower compared with the advanced model DialoGPT, but it still shows advantages in comparison with Seq2seq-emo and ECM. In general, ECCRG generates responses under the influence of control conditions, which reduces the search space during the decoding process to a certain extent, the generated responses are significantly closer to the ground-truth, and can express the specified emotions more accurately. Considering our motivation to generate models in a controlled range, it should be explainable at the expense of some fluency and variety, a problem that also arises in other controllable text generation methods.

**Ablation Study.** The lower part of Table 2 shows the comparative experimental results of ECCRG after ablation of partially optimization targets. From the comparison results with the full model, we make the following analysis:

(1) Without using the self-reconstruction loss $\mathcal{L}_{recon}$, the most significant change that can be observed is the reduction of the BLEU value, and the emotional accuracy rate is also reduced to a certain extent, which indicates that the self-reconstruction Loss is a key part of the controlled generation of the model, which can significantly improve the similarity between the response generated by the model and the specified text content, and it is also helpful for emotion expression when the text content and target emotion in the control conditions are consistent.

(2) Without using the emotion controlled loss $\mathcal{L}_{emo}$, we find that the performance of the model on all metrics is getting worse. Different from $\mathcal{L}_{recon}$, $\mathcal{L}_{emo}$ fuses emotion labels with language models. In this case, the generation of the model needs to consider the fluency of the text content, meanwhile, the emotion information is used as additional knowledge to enrich the diversity of the generated responses.

(3) Without using the adversarial learning loss, the performance of the model on BLEU is improved, which may be because the model is affected by more $\mathcal{L}_{recon}$. Except that $\mathcal{L}_{adv}^{emo}$ is helpful for emotion accuracy, the overall adversarial loss did not bring about the impact we expected. Without using the semantic adversarial loss $WhenL_{adv}^{sem}$, the model achieves the best performance on fluency. This shows that it is difficult for the model to process the adversarial loss signal returned by the discriminator. In order to weigh the adversarial loss, the quality of the generated text is reduced.

## 5.2   Manual Evaluation

Table 3 shows the results of manual evaluation. We used the Fleiss' Kappa score to measure the consistency of ratings among 5 volunteers, in which the Fleiss' Kappa scores for fluency, relevance, and emotion quality were 0.51, 0.46, and 0.57, respectively, indicating that the three evaluation dimensions of human evaluation results Both achieved "moderate consistency".

The results of manual evaluation show that, compared with the baseline method, ECCRG shows the best effect in both relevancy and sentiment quality, especially in relevancy, which shows the controllability of ECCRG in content An advantageous effect is provided. In terms of fluency, both ECCRG and another emotion-controllable response generation model, ECM, are lower than GPT-2 and Seq2seq-emo, and our model favors the target emotion in generating results at the expense of fluency. Another possible reason for the lower fluency than the Seq2seq model is that our model generates longer replies, and the semantic inconsistency in responses is caused by the instability of multiple optimization objectives during training.

**Table 4.** Samples of emotion-controllable response generated by ECM and ECCRG

| | What do you think of Starbucks? | |
|---|---|---|
| ECM | Admiration | It's a nice **place**! |
| | Approval | It is _cool to be kind! |
| | Caring | I think it's good for you. |
| | Joy | Big smiles, good for you! |
| | Sadness | I'm sorry to hear that. |
| | Surprise | I'm _not sure_ why it's not being done. |
| ECCRG | Admiration | I'm not a _fan_ of Starbucks, but I do love their **coffee**. |
| | Approval | I'm _with you_. I'm going to try and get a cup of **coffee** every day. |
| | Caring | I don't know, but I' m sure it's good for your **wallet**. |
| | Joy | It's the best. I'm a **coffee** drinker, and I love it! |
| | Sadness | I don 't hate Starbucks. I just don't like the way they **serve coffee**. |
| | Surprise | I'm _not sure_, but it's just a **coffee place** , _isn't it?_ |
| | Rock music always makes me feel alive. | |
| ECM | Admiration | Wow, you look great! |
| | Approval | I _hope you enjoy it. |
| | Caring | Good for you man! |
| | Joy | So happy for you man! |
| | Sadness | This music makes me crying. |
| | Surprise | What music is this? |
| ECCRG | Admiration | Awesome! I'm a _big fan_ of **the Beatles**. |
| | Approval | Good luck dude, I'm pretty sure that's a quote from the **movie**! |
| | Caring | I wish you guys are doing well! |
| | Joy | I'm glad I'm not the only one who _feels this way_. |
| | Sadness | I'm not sure if you're serious or not, but I _don't really listen_ to it. |
| | Surprise | Because it's so **metal**? |

## 5.3   Case Study

For emotion control, we convert the specified emotion labels into text adding to the control condition in the manner described in Sect. 3.3. For content control, we add the target text directly to the control condition.

**Table 5.** Emotion- and content-controllable response samples generated by ECCRG

| Do you like cats or dogs? | |
| --- | --- |
| Content: I like dogs | I like dogs, but I'm not a fan of cats |
| Content: I like cats | I like cats because they're cute and they're not that bad |
| Content: I like cats Emotion: Joy | I <u>love</u> cats so much! I've had a few cats that were very <u>comfortable</u> |
| Content: I like cats Emotion: Sadness | I like cats but they 're <u>loud</u> and annoying |

Table 4 presents two set of cases where ECM and ECCRG generate responses under emotion control conditions. From the comparison of the generation results of ECCRG and ECM in the table, we can first intuitively observe that the utterances generated by ECCRG are longer, which makes the responses contain richer information and reflects better diversity. More emotional words (underlined words in the table) are used in the responses generated by ECM to express emotions explicitly, but too much reliance on emotional words makes the semantic content of the sentence relatively simple, and it's also difficult to capture the subtle differences between positive emotions like "joy" and "admiration". In addition to a small amount of emotional words, the responses generated by ECCRG can also express the specified emotions through combinations of general words (words in italics in the table), for example, "approval" is expressed by "I'm with you". Since ECCRG is built based on pre-trained language model, which makes the quality of its generation benefit from the linguistic and commonsense knowledge accumulated by the pre-trained model, additional concept words are used in the responses (bold in the table) such as "coffee" in relation to "Starbucks" and "the Beatles" in relation to "rock music".

Table 5 presents a case where ECCRG generates responses given specified emotion and content. Overall, ECCRG is able to well reflect the content conditions in the generated responses, which means that we can adjust the semantics of the responses generated by the dialogue system by modifying the textual content. But we can also see from the table that when the given emotion and content control conditions are inconsistent, for example, when the emotion condition is specified as "sadness" and the target content is specified as "I like cats" at the same time, the response semantics generated by ECCRG are not coherence, which is a problem that should be further solved in practical applications.

# 6 Conclusion

In this paper, we propose a emotion- and content-controlled response generation model ECCRG, which integrates a text-type control condition into the language model's intermediate hidden state by adding a self-attention layer to the pre-trained language model, to achieve the purpose of making the language model generation results controllable at a fine-grained level. We separately write emotion type and textual content into the control condition text, enabling the responses generated by ECCRG to express specific emotions, or to include semantic conditioned on content. We fine-tune the pre-trained language model and train ECC-layer on the Reddit dataset. The experimental results compared with multiple baseline methods show that ECCRG, given both emotion and content conditions, generates responses that are closer to the ground-truths and have better emotion accuracy. However, the experimental results also show that ECCRG is insufficient in balancing the natural expressions of emotion and semantics, which will also be a worthwhile research direction in our future work.

# References

Asghar, N., Poupart, P., Hoey, J., Jiang, X., Mou, L.: Affective neural response generation. In: Pasi, G., Piwowarski, B., Azzopardi, L., Hanbury, A. (eds.) ECIR 2018. LNCS, vol. 10772, pp. 154–166. Springer, Cham (2018). https://doi.org/10.1007/978-3-319-76941-7_12

Chan, A., Ong, Y.-S., Pung, B., Zhang, A., Fu, J.: CoCon: a self-supervised approach for controlled text generation. In: International Conference on Learning Representations (2020)

Colombo, P., Witon, W., Modi, A., Kennedy, J., Kapadia, M.: Affect-driven dialog generation. arXiv preprint arXiv:1904.02793 (2019)

Devlin, J., Chang, M.-W., Lee, K., Toutanova, K.: Bert: pre-training of deep bidirectional transformers for language understanding. arXiv preprint arXiv:1810.04805 (2018)

Gao, J., Bi, W., Liu, X., Li, J., Shi, S.: Generating multiple diverse responses for short-text conversation. In: Proceedings of the AAAI Conference on Artificial Intelligence, vol. 33, pp. 6383–6390 (2019)

Huang, C., Zaiane, O.R., Trabelsi, A., Dziri, N.: Automatic dialogue generation with expressed emotions. In: Proceedings of the 2018 Conference of the North American Chapter of the Association for Computational Linguistics: Human Language Technologies, Volume 2 (Short Papers), pp. 49–54 (2018)

Li, J., Galley, M., Brockett, C., Gao, J., Dolan, B.: A diversity-promoting objective function for neural conversation models. arXiv preprint arXiv:1510.03055 (2015)

Lin, Z., Madotto, A., Bang, Y., Fung, P.: The adapter-bot: all-in-one controllable conversational model. In: Proceedings of the AAAI Conference on Artificial Intelligence, vol. 35, pp. 16081–16083 (2021)

Liu, Y., et al.: Roberta: a robustly optimized bert pretraining approach. arXiv preprint arXiv:1907.11692 (2019)

Papineni, K., Roukos, S., Ward, T., Zhu, W.-J.: Bleu: a method for automatic evaluation of machine translation. In: Proceedings of the 40th Annual Meeting of the Association for Computational Linguistics, pp. 311–318 (2002)

Partala, T., Surakka, V.: The effects of affective interventions in human-computer interaction. Interact. Comput. **16**(2), 295–309 (2004)

Polzin, T.S., Waibel, A.: Emotion-sensitive human-computer interfaces. In: ISCA Tutorial and Research Workshop (ITRW) on Speech and Emotion (2000)

Radford, A., et al.: Language models are unsupervised multitask learners. OpenAI Blog **1**(8), 9 (2019)

Skowron, M.: Affect listeners: acquisition of affective states by means of conversational systems. In: Esposito, A., Campbell, N., Vogel, C., Hussain, A., Nijholt, A. (eds.) Development of Multimodal Interfaces: Active Listening and Synchrony. LNCS, vol. 5967, pp. 169–181. Springer, Heidelberg (2010). https://doi.org/10.1007/978-3-642-12397-9_14

Song, Z., Zheng, X., Liu, L., Xu, M., Huang, X.-J.: Generating responses with a specific emotion in dialog. In: Proceedings of the 57th Annual Meeting of the Association for Computational Linguistics, pp. 3685–3695 (2019)

Zhang, Y., et al.: Dialogpt: large-scale generative pre-training for conversational response generation. arXiv preprint arXiv:1911.00536 (2019)

Zheng, C., Liu, Y., Chen, W., Leng, Y., Huang, M.: Comae: a multi-factor hierarchical framework for empathetic response generation. In: Findings of the Association for Computational Linguistics: ACL-IJCNLP 2021, pp. 813–824 (2021)

Zhong, P., Wang, D., Li, P., Zhang, C., Wang, H., Miao, C.: Care: commonsense-aware emotional response generation with latent concepts. arXiv preprint arXiv:2012.08377 (2020a)

Zhong, P., Zhang, C., Wang, H., Liu, Y., Miao, C.: Towards persona-based empathetic conversational models. In: Proceedings of the 2020 Conference on Empirical Methods in Natural Language Processing (EMNLP), pp. 6556–6566 (2020b)

Zhou, H., Huang, M., Zhang, T., Zhu, X., Liu, B.: Emotional chatting machine: Emotional conversation generation with internal and external memory. In: Proceedings of the AAAI Conference on Artificial Intelligence, vol. 32 (2018)

Zhou, L., Gao, J., Li, D., Shum, H.-Y.: The design and implementation of xiaoice, an empathetic social chatbot. Comput. Linguist. **46**(1), 53–93 (2020)

Zhou, X., Wang, W.Y.: Mojitalk: generating emotional responses at scale. In: Proceedings of the 56th Annual Meeting of the Association for Computational Linguistics (Volume 1: Long Papers), pp. 1128–1137 (2018)

# Origin-Destination Convolution Recurrent Network: A Novel OD Matrix Prediction Framework

Jiayu Chang, Tian Liang, Wanzhi Xiao, and Li Kuang[(✉)]

Central South University, South Lushan Road 932, Changsha 410083, Hunan, China
{8209200123,leungtien,wanzhixiao,kuangli}@csu.edu.cn

**Abstract.** Origin-Destination (OD) Matrix Prediction is an important part of public transportation service which aims to predict the number of passenger demands from one region to another and capture the passengers' mobility patterns. This problem is challenging because it requires forecasting not only the number of demands within a region, but the origin and destination of each trip as well. To address this challenge, we propose an effective model, ODCRN (Origin-Destination Convolution Recurrent Network) which incorporates traffic context and bi-directional semantic information. First, we obtain the semantic embedded features of the region as the static traffic context by the Node2vec algorithm, and the traffic flow of the region is counted as the dynamic traffic context. Second, we construct two adjacency matrices which represent *origin-destination* and *destination-origin* travel demands within urban areas respectively based on the OD matrices of each time slot, and use the graph convolutional network to aggregate traffic context information of the semantic neighbors in both directions. Then, we use a unit constructed by GRU and the graph convolution network to capture the spatial-temporal correlations of the input data. Finally, we use those correlations and traffic contexts to predict the OD matrix for the next time slot. Our model is evaluated on *TaxiNYC* and *TaxiCD* datasets, and experimental results demonstrate the superiority of our ODCRN model against the state-of-the-art approaches.

**Keywords:** OD matrix prediction · Graph diffusion convolution · Spatial-temporal data

## 1 Introduction

Recently, ride-hailing applications are becoming prevalent choices for daily commutes, such as Didi, UCAR, and Uber, which aim to provide passengers with convenient ride services and improve the efficiency of public transportation. To provide high-quality services and achieve company profits, ride-hailing platforms need to fully understand the passenger demands in real-time, which helps avoid

© ICST Institute for Computer Sciences, Social Informatics and Telecommunications Engineering 2024
Published by Springer Nature Switzerland AG 2024. All Rights Reserved
H. Gao et al. (Eds.): CollaborateCom 2023, LNICST 562, pp. 131–150, 2024.
https://doi.org/10.1007/978-3-031-54528-3_8

empty drives (i.e., driving without passengers). Therefore, instead of merely forecasting the possible number of passenger demands within a region, it is rather important to gain knowledge of passenger demands in terms of the origin and destination of each trip. Because the demand quantity between two regions at different time slots also takes mining useful mobility patterns into consideration. If Origin-Destination (OD) travel demand can be found earlier, popular destinations and travel routes can be provided for travel service providers, and vehicles can be scheduled in advance.

OD matrix prediction has received increasing attention because of its importance. Existing studies [1,14,21] predict the OD travel demand between all regions of the city by constructing an OD matrix. As shown in Fig. 1, we regard the urban region as a large rectangle, and then divide it into $m \times n$ regions, making the dimension of the OD matrix in each time slot reach $N \times N(N = m \times n)$. And then form an OD matrix sequence according to a temporal order, where $M_{i,j}^{(t)}$ in the OD matrix represents the number of trips from region $r_i$ to region $r_j$ from time $t - 1$ to time $t$. OD matrix prediction aims to predict the OD matrix of a future moment based on the OD matrix of multiple historical moments.

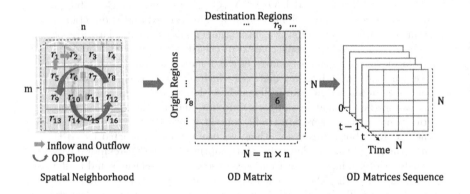

**Fig. 1.** Spatial neighborhood and OD matrix.

Although recent works consider combining traffic flows to utilize mobility patterns into OD matrix prediction, it is still a challenging problem, affected by the following aspects:

**(1) Directed semantics of travel demand.** There is a directed semantic relationship between OD travel demands among urban regions. In the left diagram of Fig. 2, *A, B, and C* represent the *office region, residential region, and residential region*, respectively. During the morning rush hour, there are similar travel demands from *B to A* and *C to A*. There are more travel demands with *A as the destination*, but less travel demand with *A as the origin*, which indicates that the semantic neighbors in the two directions between departure and arrival of *A* is different in the same period. The right diagram of Fig. 2 shows the *10-day OD demand curves between A and B* revealing a large number of taxi demands *from B to A*. At the same time, due to the marginality of region *B*, the demand for taxis *from A to B* appears to be random. This non-periodic and non-stationary curve increases the difficulty of forecasting.

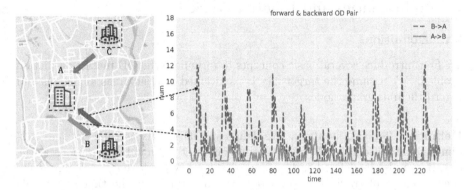

**Fig. 2.** OD spatial correlation (left) and OD flow time series (right) among different urban regions

**(2) Various Traffic Context.** In the existing OD matrix prediction studies, in addition to the number of travel demands between regions, other information, such as the traffic context of the origin and destination regions, has not been fully considered. Traffic context includes *static traffic context information* and *dynamic traffic context information*. Different traffic contexts contain different contextual information. For example, static POI information reflects the function of the region while the dynamic traffic context of the region, such as inflow and outflow traffic, reflects the dynamic traffic conditions of the region.

To tackle these challenges, we propose an effective model named ODCRN, to collectively predict the OD matrix in the following time slot more accurately and more efficiently. The primary contributions of this paper can be summarized as follows:

(1) In order to capture the directional information of travel demand, we construct two OD matrices from the origin to the destination(*forward*) and from the destination to the origin(*backward*) to capture the forward and backward information by *bi-directional graph diffusion convolution network*. Then we combine them together to integrate the bi-directional semantic information.

(2) We comprehensively consider static and dynamic context information by taking POI information which reflects regional functions as static traffic context information by establishing a bootstrap to better represent origins and destinations, and traffic flow information between regions as dynamic traffic context information. Then we capture the features through dynamic

and static traffic context learning networks to collaborate with OD matrix prediction.

(3) Extensive experiments on two open datasets, *TaxiNYC* and *TaxiCD*, demonstrate the proposed ODCRN model outperforms baselines.

# 2 Preliminaries and Related Work

## 2.1 Definitions

We first introduce several basic concepts to formulate the OD matrix prediction problem. We assume the target city is partitioned into subareas as regions and regard them as graph nodes.

**Definition 2-1 OD Matrix.** We define an OD matrix at time slot t as a 2-dimensional tensor $M_t \in \mathbb{R}^{N_l \times N_l}$, where $N_l$ is the total number of regions in the city. It can also be defined as $M_t = \{m_{i,j}, 1 \le i, j \le N_l\}$, where $m_{i,j} \in \mathbb{R}$ represents specific figure of traffic flow from region $i$ to region $j$ at the time slot t. OD Matrices Sequence is defined as a 3-dimensional tensor $M = [M_1, \cdots, M_{N_t}] \in \mathbb{R}^{N_t \times N_l \times N_l}$, where $N_t$ is the total number of slots of historical traffic data.

**Definition 2-2 Semantic Neighbors.** $m_{i,j}$ represents the number of travels from region $v_i$ to region $v_j$. $v_i$ and $v_j$ are the OD semantic neighbors in this particular travel demand. $v_i$ and $v_j$ needn't be geographically adjacent.

**Definition 2-3 Static Traffic Context.** We define the traffic graph of city as $G = \{V, A\}$ where $V = [v_1, \cdots, v_{N_l}]$ and $|V| = N_l$. $v_i \in V$ is a node on the traffic graph which represents a region in the city. 2-dimensional tensor $S \in \mathbb{R}^{N_l \times F}$ represents the static traffic context on all regions, such as POIs and embedding features.

**Definition 2-4 Dynamic Traffic Context.** We define the dynamic traffic context in regions as a 3-dimensional tensor $X = [X_1, \cdots, X_{N_t}] \in \mathbb{R}^{N_t \times N_l \times D_t}$, where the $D_t$ represents the features' dimension of dynamic traffic context. For example, when we use inflow and outflow as features of context, features' dimension $D_t = 2$.

## 2.2 Origin-Destination Matrix Prediction

For a given time slot t, using OD matrices for the past p time slots $[M_{t-p+1}, \cdots, M_t] \in \mathbb{R}^{P \times N_l \times N_l}$, dynamic traffic contexts of every region for the past p time slots $[X_{t-P+1}, \cdots, X_t] \in \mathbb{R}^{P \times N_l \times D_t}$, static traffic context of every region $S \in \mathbb{R}^{N_l \times F}$ and adjacent matrix which represents the region's geographic proximity $A \in \mathbb{R}^{N_l \times N_l}$ as inputs, to predict OD matrix $M_{t+1} \in \mathbb{R}^{N_l \times N_l}$ of one-time slot in the future.

Generally, OD Matrix prediction task [2–4] can be divided into two categories, static approaches and dynamic approaches. Static approaches [5,6] consider the traffic flow as independent time slots and ignore the spatial-temporal information by calculating the average traveling demand to predict the OD matrix over a long period of time. Dynamic approaches [7] take the time-variant traffichttps://www.overleaf.com/project/6424167639f3dccab22016fa flow information under consideration so they can be used for the management of the traffic flow and the dynamic path induction.

In recent years, an increasing number of neural network approaches, especially Graph Neural Networks (GNN) [9] have been applied to OD matrix prediction tasks. Since urban transportation networks can be seen as graph structures, GNN can naturally deal with the spatial relation of traffic flows in non-Euclidean city traffic networks. Those approaches consider sensors as graph nodes [12], the data at fixed time intervals as node features and the geographical proximity, distance, traffic similarity or road connectivity between sensors or regions as edges between two nodes. Researchers such as Wang and Ke [1,14] proposed graph embedding methods to embed the grid and combine it with LSTM to predict the OD matrix. Multi-task learning traffic prediction approaches [15–18] were proposed for both regional traffic flow and OD matrix prediction tasks. Liu et al. [19] constructed station distance and similarity in traffic patterns for predicting subway OD trip traffic based on a combination of physical and virtual approaches. Zheng et al. [1] proposed a method to predict the OD matrix via graph convolution and Liu et al. [8] combine the spatial-temporal context to predict taxi OD demand.

We found that they rely heavily on the construction of traffic graphs to capture the spatial correlation of flows between geo-locations. Moreover, due to the functional differences between locations and the real-time mobility and variability of traffic flows, most graph neural networks fail to capture the dynamic spatial correlations between urban locations, as well as the hierarchical spatial correlations of both local traffic correlations and global traffic similarities.

## 3   The ODCRN Framework

In this section, we present the detailed architecture of the proposed model ODCRN. As the Fig. 3 shows, the model consists of three parts. The first part is the spatial-temporal information capture model, which is constructed by the Bi-GDC-GRU unit based on the architecture of RNN. As Fig. 4(a) shows, each GRU unit integrates the bi-direction diffusion graph convolution (in Fig. 4(b)) to capture the temporal and spatial correlations of the OD matrices. The other two components are dynamic and static traffic context learning networks, which are used to capture the traffic context features associated with each time slot and input them as node features $TC_t$ into the Bi-GDC-GRU unit. We use CNN with the kernel size of $1 \times 1$ to predict the OD matrix of the next time slot $M_{t+1}$ by using the last hidden state $h_t$ in the prediction phase.

The inputs to the model include the OD matrix of the historical $p$ time segments $[M_{t-p+1}, \cdots, M_t]$ and traffic context information for historical $p$ time slot

$[TC_{t-p+1}, \cdots, TC_t]$. As Fig. 3 shows, the traffic context learning network module learns regionally relevant traffic contextual information and consists of two sub-networks, including a static context learning network and a dynamic context learning network. We use Node2vec [20] embedding features which illustrate the regional structural features as input of the static traffic context learning network. To predict the number of passengers from one region to another region, we use the inflows and outflows of all regions in each time slot as inputs of the dynamic traffic context learning network.

### 3.1   Constructing Traffic Context from Historical Data

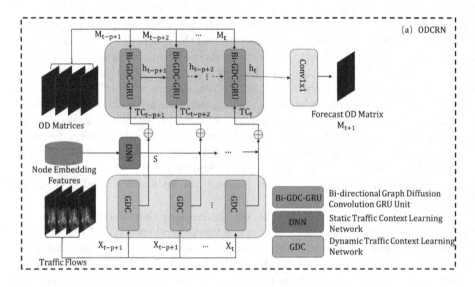

**Fig. 3.** ODCRN architecture

**Static Traffic Context Learning Network Module.** The attributes of the region itself, such as POI, population and other information, affect its traffic flow and influence its fluency as the origin or destination for commutes. We pretrain the embedding features of each node with Node2vec algorithm as the static traffic contexts for each node. Node embedding features represent the structural properties of the nodes on the graph and the similarity between nodes.

After constructing the static traffic context, we use a deep neural network DNN as a Static Context Learner (SCL) to map the static traffic context into node hidden states as follows:

$$h_1 = SCL(S) = DNN(S) \tag{1}$$

In Eq. 1, $h_1 \in \mathbb{R}^{N_I \times F_1}$ is the output of the static traffic context learning network SCL and the DNN is a multi-layers deep neural network.

**Dynamic Traffic Context Learning Network Module.** We count the inflow and outflow traffic in each subarea of the city for each time segment from the historical travel records. We use $X = [X_1, \cdots, X_{Nt}] \in \mathbb{R}^{N_t N_l D_t}$ as regional dynamic traffic context. Since the inflow and outflow traffic of a region are affected by adjacent regions, we use a graph convolution network as a Dynamic Context Learner (DCL) network to capture spatial correlations. DCL maps the dynamic traffic context of all nodes in each time slot into hidden state representations:

$$h_2 = DCL(X_t) = GDC(A, X_t, W) = \sum_{k=0}^{K} A^k X_t W_k \tag{2}$$

In Eq. 2, GDC denotes the graph diffusion convolution [13] operation, which will be introduced in the following Sect. 3.2. $X_t \in \mathbb{R}^{N_l \times D_t}$ is the dynamic traffic context at time slot t of the input, and W is the graph convolution parameters.

For each time slot t, we combine those two types of traffic context as shown in the Eq. 3:

$$TC_t = SCL(S) \;\|\; DCL(X_t) = h_1 \;\|\; h_2 \tag{3}$$

## 3.2 Capturing Spatial-Temporal Correlations by Bi-GDC-GRU Unit

We propose Bi-directional Graph Diffusion Convolution GRU (Bi-GDC-GRU) unit to capture correlations of spatial-temporal information. Demands of different OD travel directions might be different at the same time. For example, office regions have more arrival demand in the morning and less departure demand. Figure 5(a) and Fig. 5(b) show that the OD semantic neighbors departing from and arriving at region r2 at the same time are different. Therefore, in order to partially solve the sparsity problem of the OD matrix, we construct the semantically adjacent edges of $r_i$ in two directions(both in and out), which can aggregate more OD semantic neighbor node information.

Specifically, for each input time t, we use the OD matrix $M_t$ to construct two directed weighted adjacency matrices as shown in Fig. 4(b) and Fig. 4(c) as graphs to aggregate neighbor node information. The forward adjacency matrix is expressed as $A_f^{(t)} \in \mathbb{R}^{N_l \times N_l}$ and the backward adjacency matrix is expressed as $A_b^{(t)} \in \mathbb{R}^{N_l \times N_l}$:

$$A_f^{(t)} = Norm(M_t) \tag{4}$$

$$A_b^{(t)} = A_f^{(t)}.T \tag{5}$$

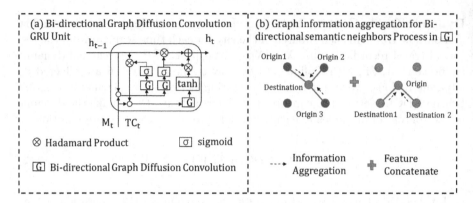

**Fig. 4.** Details of Bi-GDC-GRU unit (in Fig. 4(a)) and an example of graph information aggregation process in Bi-GDC-GRU (in Fig. 4(b))

In Eq. 4, *Norm* is to normalize the OD matrix $M_t$ to prevent the gradient explosion problem after the graph convolution operation. In Eq. 5, *.T* is the transpose operation. Since there is some correlations between the region set as the origin and set as the destination, using the forward and backward adjacency matrix to simultaneously aggregate the semantic neighbor node features on the OD pair starting from node $v_i$ and arriving at node $v_j$.

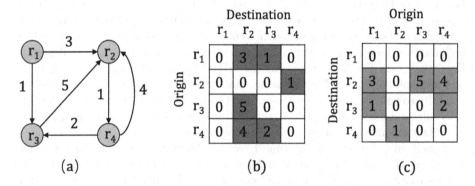

**Fig. 5.** An example of forward and backward OD matrix. Figure 5(a) shows the trip times and directions of the four nodes. Figure 5(b) and Fig. 5(c) show the corresponding OD matrix. The travel demand relationship from r2 to r1, r2, r3, and r4 represents as [0,0,0,1], and the number of trips arriving at r2 is [3,0,5,4].

After constructing the forward and backward adjacency matrices, we use bi-directional diffusion graph convolution to capture the spatial correlation between OD pairs, as shown in Eq. 6:

$$h^{(t)} = \sum_{k=0}^{K} \left(A_f^{(t)}\right)^k \mathrm{TC}_t W_{k1} + \left(A_b^{(t)}\right)^k \mathrm{TC}_t W_{k2} \tag{6}$$

$TC_t$ represents the traffic context at time $t$, and W is the graph convolution kernel parameter. For time t, the diffusion graph convolution of Eq. 6 is defined as a finite number of directed diffusion processes on the graph, k is the number of diffusions, and $(A_f^{(t)})^k$ represents the diffusion probability to the $k - th$ hop neighbor. Figure 4, 5 and 6 shows the convolution process of the forward diffusion graph. The central node is represented by the aggregation and summation of the information of neighboring nodes of different hops. The diffusion probability $A_f^{(t)}$ indicates the strength of the edge connection between nodes. The OD traffic of nodes is bi-directional, and the forward and backward diffusion graph convolution in Eq. 6 can aggregate the region as the information of multi-hop semantic neighbor nodes in the two directions of the origin and the destination.

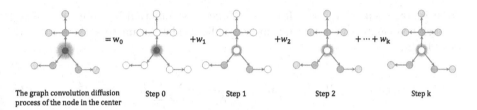

The graph convolution diffusion process of the node in the center    Step 0    Step 1    Step 2    Step k

**Fig. 6.** An schematic of k-steps forward graph diffusion convolution

Then, the time correlations of the OD matrix at different moments are captured by the GRU units based on the recurrent neural network. Specifically, we use GRU to capture the temporal correlation between OD matrices, and replace the matrix multiplication operation in GRU with the bi-directional diffusion graph convolution operation in Eq. 6.

$$r^{(t)} = \sigma(\Theta_r *_G \left[TC_t, H^{(t-1)}\right] + b_r) \tag{7}$$

$$u^{(t)} = \sigma \left(\Theta_u *_G \left[TC_t, H^{(t-1)}\right] + b_u\right) \tag{8}$$

$$c^{(t)} = tanh(\Theta_c *_G [TC_t, r^{(t)} \odot H^{(t-1)}] + b_c) \tag{9}$$

$$H^{(t)} = u^{(t)} \odot H^{(t-1)} + (1 - u^{(t)}) \odot c^{(t)} \tag{10}$$

In Eq. 10, $H^{(t)}$ is the output of the GRU unit at time $t$. $*_G$ is the diffusion map convolution operation represented by Eqs. (4–6). In Eq. 7, 8, and 9, $\Theta$ is the graph convolution kernel parameter, $\sigma$ is the Sigmoid activation function, and $\odot$ is the Hadamard product. The reset gate $r^{(t)}$ and the update gate $u^{(t)}$ of the GRU unit at time $t$ are used to control the forgetting information and control output respectively, and the input is the traffic context $TC_t$ at the current time t and the previous time. The hidden state $H^{(t-1)}$ output by the GRU unit is concatenated and used as node features to input into the diffusion graph convolution represented by Eq. 6. Diffusion Graph Convolution GRU units can capture both temporal and spatial correlations.

In the model prediction stage, we regard the hidden state output by the last GRU unit as the input of the prediction network. Since we need to predict the OD matrix next moment, we adopt a single-layer convolutional neural network with a $1 \times 1$ convolution kernel as the prediction network, which is shown in Eq. 11:

$$\hat{M}_{t+1} = \Theta *_C \left( H^{(t)} \right) \tag{11}$$

where $H^{(t)} \in \mathbb{R}^{N \times F}$ is the hidden state output by the last GRU unit, $*_C$ is the convolution operation, $\Theta$ is the convolution kernel parameter, $\hat{M}_{t+1} \in \mathbb{R}^{N_l \times N_l}$ is the predicted OD matrix at the next moment.

### 3.3    Loss Function of OD Matrix Prediction

We use Mean Square Error (MSE), a common loss function in regression tasks, to back-propagate the error and optimize the model parameters. As shown in Eq. (4–12):

$$L(W_\theta) = MSE\left( M_{t+1}, \hat{M}_{t+1} \right) = \frac{1}{N_l * N_l} \sum_{i=1}^{N_l} \sum_{j=1}^{N_l} \left( m_{i,j} - \hat{m}_{i,j} \right)^2 \tag{12}$$

$W_\theta$ are the parameters of the whole model. $M_{t+1}, \hat{M}_{t+1} \in \mathbb{R}^{N_l \times N_l}$ are the true and predicted values of the OD matrix at the next moment, respectively. $N_l$ is the total number of nodes, namely the number of regions in the city.

## 4    Experiment

### 4.1    Datasets and Evaluation Metrics

We use taxi order data from New York City and Chengdu for the experiments. The raw data information includes boarding time, alighting time, boarding longitude, boarding latitude, alighting longitude and alighting latitude.

We divide the whole city into $m \times n$ regions. New York City is divided into $256(16 \times 16)$ regions while Chengdu City is divided into $256(16 \times 16)$ regions as well. Firstly, based on the data of orders, the number of orders corresponding to the boarding and alighting regions per hour is counted and used to construct an OD Matrix, which is arranged in chronological order to form a sequence of OD Matrices with a dimension of $T * N * N$, where the $T$ is the total number of time periods and $N = m \times n$ is the total number of regions. Specific information on the dataset is shown in Table 1:

**Table 1.** Description of Dataset

| Dataset Name | TaxiNYC[a] | TaxiCD[b] |
|---|---|---|
| Data Type | Taxi Order | Taxi Order |
| City | New York | ChengDu |
| Longitude range | −74.02–73.95 | 104.02–104.12 |
| Latitude range | 40.67–40.77 | 30.62-30.70 |
| Time range | 2015/1/1–2015/4/30 | 2016/11/1–2016/11/30 |
| Total number of time slots | 2880 | 720 |
| Length of unit time period | 1 h | 1 h |
| Number of grids | 16 × 16 | 16 × 16 |
| Static Traffic Context Information | Node2vec Node Embedding | Node2vec Node Embedding |
| Dynamic Traffic Context Information | Regional inflow/outflow | Regional inflow/outflow |

[a] https://www.nyc.gov/site/tlc/about/tlc-trip-record-data.page
[b] https://outreach.didichuxing.com/research/opendata/

At the same time, we construct two kinds of traffic context information:

(1) Static Traffic Context Information. Using the data of orders within two weeks, we construct the graph by using the starting grid and the ending grid as two nodes on an edge. The number of orders is the weight of the edge. The embedding vector for each grid was pre-trained with Node2vec.

(2) Dynamic Traffic Context Information. The number of boardings and alightings corresponding to each zone per hour is counted as the inflow and outflow of the zone.

The OD matrix prediction task uses historical data from the past 8 h (8 unit time slots) to predict the future OD matrix of 1 h (1 time slot). The dataset is divided in chronological order with training, validation and test set at the ratio of 8:1:1. We evaluate the performance by two commonly used regression task evaluation indicators, root mean square error(RMSE) and mean absolute error(MAE).

## 4.2   Parameter Setting

The hyperparameters of our model are set as follows:

(1) Dimension of the Node2vec nodes embedding feature is 10. The static context learning network consists of 2 layers neural network where the number of hidden layer units in each layer is 32. The dynamic context learning network is a 3 layers GDC network, and the number of units in each layer is 32.

(2) The ODCRN has a total of two layers of recurrent networks, where each recursive cell contains two layers of diffusion map convolutional networks. The number of hidden layer cells is 32, and the number of GDC diffusion steps is set to 2.

(3) We use Adam optimizer to train the model. The learning rate during the training stage is 0.01 with a batch size of 128. In addition, to prevent overfitting, the regularization parameter is set to 0.0001 and an early stop mechanism is used.

### 4.3    Spatial-Temporal Data Preprocess

For OD matrix prediction, we use historical data from the traffic flows' dataset to generate static and dynamic traffic contexts as the input of traffic context, and generate the OD matrices for the past 8 h as input of the historical OD matrices sequence.

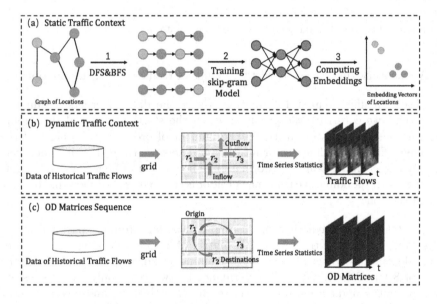

**Fig. 7.** Traffic context and OD matrix construction process

**Static Traffic Context Data.** According to the statistics of the start point, end point and traveling counts between them, we use Node2vec to train the embedding features of each region as our static traffic context, including graph structural characteristics and node similarity.

**Dynamic Traffic Context Data.** As shown in Fig. 7(b), we count the inflow and outflow of each region in hourly intervals as our dynamic traffic context data. regions with high inflow flows tend to be the end of the commute, while those with high outflow flows tend to be the origin of the commute.

**OD Matrices Sequence.** Since inter-regional commuting takes time, the OD matrices are also counted in hours. We first grid the data to find the semantic neighbors of each region. Then we perform temporal statistics on the order start and end points of each region to determine the weights of the adjacency matrix. We regard the OD matrix as the adjacency matrix and use it as our input of the Bi-GDC-GRU cell to capture the spatial association of OD semantic neighbors.

### 4.4  Comparison and Analysis of Model Prediction Accuracy

Table 2 shows the prediction results of each method on the TaxiNYC and TaxiCD datasets. It is clear that the traditional models HA and ARIMA have poor prediction results, due to the randomness of OD travel demand between some regions. ARIMA and the historical averaging method (HA) are simple but less effective. The deep learning method ST-ResNet, which considers the trend, period, proximity, and other temporally more relevant historical data, and deposits a residual network to enhance the network depth, improves the prediction effect. In contrast, as an improved version of ST-ResNet [11], MDL [15] model designs node network and edge network branches to extract edge flow (OD) and node flow (inflow and outflow) features respectively, and uses a multi-task learning approach to predict both flows. But its performance is inferior to that of the single-task ST-ResNet. MDL and ST-ResNet use three segments of historical data as input. GEML [1] is a GNN-based OD matrix prediction model that uses a grid embedding approach and graph convolution to aggregate information about the semantic and geographic neighbors of OD pairs to pre-weight the importance of neighbor nodes in the OD matrices, and adapts LSTM to capture temporal correlations. But the model neither considers the matrix prediction in terms of dynamic and static contextual information of the starting and ending points, nor does it explicitly distinguish the direction of the edges of the adjacency matrix.

**Table 2.** Comparison Results of TaxiNYC and TaxiCD

| Models | RMSE(NYC) | MAE(NYC) | RMSE(CD) | MAE(CD) |
|---|---|---|---|---|
| HA | 1.085 | 0.163 | 0.440 | 0.114 |
| ARIMA | 4.027 | 2.713 | 0.813 | 0.328 |
| ST-ResNet | 0.647 | 0.195 | 0.325 | 0.146 |
| MDL | 1.081 | 0.993 | 0.413 | 0.319 |
| GEML | 0.865 | 0.156 | 0.332 | 0.090 |
| **ODCRN(ours)** | **0.622** | **0.153** | **0.322** | **0.116** |

Among all models, ODCRN has the lowest error on the OD matrix prediction task. The prediction performance is improved because ODCRN uses the time-varying OD matrix as the adjacency matrix, the values of the OD matrix as the weights of edges, and considers both forward and backward-directed edges to aggregate neighbor node features more effectively. In addition, ODCRN incorporates both static and dynamic traffic context information of each region, which enables the traffic conditions in the region to be captured to further improve the prediction.

## 4.5   Comparison of Model Complexity and Speed

We compare the number of parameters (complexity), training speed and inference speed (testing speed) of ODCRN and several deep learning-based baseline models, where model complexity and speed are important reference metrics for model deployment. In the OD matrix prediction task, we define the OD matrix of the first 8 time slots with the OD matrix of the next 1 time slot representing the labeled data as one sample. Define the speed as the number of samples that can be processed per unit of time (samples/s).

**Table 3.** Comparison of the number of Parameters on the Model and Speed

| Model | The Number of Trainable Parameters | Training Speed | Reasoning Speed |
|-------|-----------------------------------|----------------|-----------------|
| MDL | 7,694,106 | 81 | 238 |
| ST-ResNet | 7,202,579 | 93 | 323 |
| GEML | 395,264 | 53 | 138 |
| **ODCRN(ours)** | 108,640 | 108 | 324 |

As shown in Table 3, the MDL model uses multi-task learning to extract both regional traffic flow features and OD matrix features, and each task uses three deep convolutional networks with residual connections to extract spatial-temporal features from three highly correlated historical data, respectively, with the highest complexity. ST-ResNet only performs feature extraction on the OD matrix, and the single task makes the model parametric number and speed better.

Our ODCRN model, compared with the GEML model, is an OD matrix prediction model with an LSTM networkwhich has a much smaller number of parameters. For inputs at different time steps, the parameters in the LSTM units are shared, greatly reducing the number of parameters. In contrast, since the ODCRN model integrates both GRU and GCN, the number of parameters in the whole model is mainly the convolutional kernel parameters in the bi-direction diffusion graph convolution in the GRU units, which further reduces the number of parameters compared with the serial structure of GCN and LSTM in GEML. The design of the recurrent unit in ODCRN can capture both temporal and spatial correlations, which improves the training and inference speed while reducing the parameters.

## 4.6    Hyperparameter Experiments

In this section, we adjust the hyperparameters in the ODCRN model and compare the prediction errors of the model under different parameters. This experiment adjusts the hidden status dimension of the bi-directional diffusion graph convolution in GRU, the hidden state dimension of the static traffic context learning network DNN, and the hidden state dimension of the dynamic traffic context learning network GDC. The experiments are conducted by using the control variates, where one of the parameters is adjusted to observe the prediction accuracy of the model while the other parameters remain unchanged.

In Fig. 8a(b) and Fig. 8b(b), a hidden state of 32 in the static context network provides a better representation of spatially static information, while smaller hidden state dimensions (16 dimensions) and larger hidden state dimensions (128 dimensions) suffer from underfitting and overfitting problems. Finally, the dynamic traffic context, i.e. the GDC with input features of regional inflow and outflow traffic (2 dimensions), was adjusted for different hidden states. As shown in Fig. 8a(c) and Fig. 8b(c), the model over-fits as the dimensionality of the GDC hidden layer increases, indicating that the dynamic traffic context features can be better extracted by using GDCs with low-dimensional (16-dimensional) hidden layers at lower input feature dimensions.

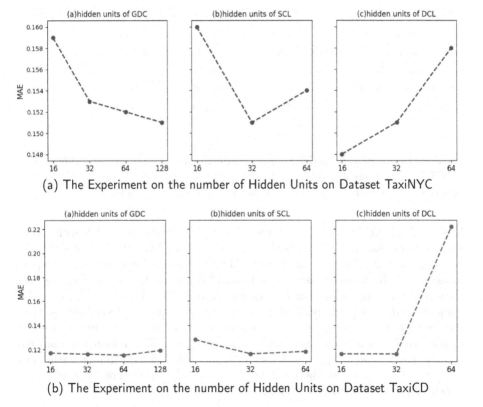

(a) The Experiment on the number of Hidden Units on Dataset TaxiNYC

(b) The Experiment on the number of Hidden Units on Dataset TaxiCD

**Fig. 8.** The Influence of the Number of Hidden Units on Model Performance

## 4.7    Ablation Experiment

We conduct extensive ablation studies to quantify the performance benefit of each component in our model. Four variants of the ODCRN-based model are constructed and tested as follows:

(1) W/O Static Context Learner: without inputting the static traffic context information, i.e., Node2vec node embedding features.
(2) W/O Dynamic Context Learner: without inputting the dynamic traffic context information, i.e., The inflow and outflow for each region at each moment.
(3) W/O Forward GDC: removing the graph aggregation from the central node, the forward adjacency matrix is an $N \times N(N = m \times n)$ matrix from Origin to Destination.
(4) W/O Backward GDC: removing the graph aggregation to the central node, the backward adjacency matrix is an $N \times N(N = m \times n)$ matrix from Destination to Origin.

**Table 4.** Results of Ablation Experiments on Dataset TaxiNYC and TaxiCD

| Model Variant | RMSE(NYC) | MAE(NYC) | RMSE(CD) | MAE(CD) |
|---|---|---|---|---|
| w/o static context learner | 0.628 | 0.157 | 0.322 | 0.118 |
| w/o dynamic context learner | 0.687 | 0.204 | 0.327 | 0.123 |
| w/o forward GDC | 0.663 | 0.161 | 0.328 | 0.121 |
| w/o backward GDC | 0.631 | 0.159 | 0.322 | 0.119 |
| **ODCRN** | 0.622 | 0.153 | 0.322 | 0.116 |

The results of the model ablation experiments are shown in Table 4. The ODCRN model has the best prediction with all components retained, and the effectiveness of each component will be described in turn as follow.

**Static Context Learning Network.** When the static context learning network is removed, RMSE and MAE increase compared to ODCRN, which indicates that adding Node2vec node embedding features helps to improve the performance of the model. Since there is no POI information of the regions, we count the starting region, the ending region, and the number of orders as the connected edges between regions (nodes) from one month of taxi orders, so that the constructed graph structure can reflect the community structure, and other characteristics of a region as a popular starting or ending region has multiple connected edges on the graph. Node2vec trains the node embedding features to allow the OD matrix prediction model to learn the prior knowledge of nodes which helps improve the prediction.

**Dynamic Context Learning Network.** Regions with high inflow traffic tend to be set as the endpoint in OD travel demand, while regions with high outflow traffic tend to be set as the starting point in OD travel demand. Using the dynamic traffic contexts of regions as the dynamic characteristics of nodes can improve the OD matrix prediction.

**Forward and Backward Diffusion Graph Convolution.** Due to the regularity of commuting activities, the OD travel demand has different directions at different moments, and departure and arrival are correlated. Therefore, using the OD matrix with directions (forward) and its transposed DO matrix (backward) to construct bidirectional edges from the target region to other regions, and from other regions to the target region, the graph convolution learns more effective node representations than one-way edges and is aggregated with more information about neighbor nodes.

### 4.8 Comparison Experiment of Predicted Value and Actual Value

For a more intuitive view of the model predictions, we selected Region 113 and Region 198 in the TaxiNYC dataset and plotted the predicted versus actual value curves of OD travel demand between the two regions for a total of 10 days from April 21, 2015 to April 30, 2015, respectively.

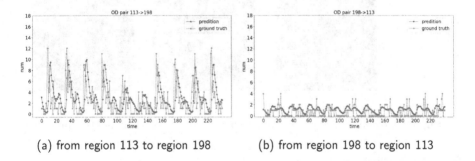

(a) from region 113 to region 198         (b) from region 198 to region 113

**Fig. 9.** Comparison between Predicted and Actual value between regions

From Fig. 9, we can see that the true values of the OD curves change irregularly with time, which shows an overall cyclical nature and a more obvious morning and evening peak. The trend of the curve and the range of values are different, and the demand for taxis from *region 113* to *region 198* is more than the demand for taxis from *region 198* to *region 113*, which indicates that the travel demand between regions is asymmetric, and the forward OD matrix and backward OD matrix we constructed aggregates the characteristics of neighbor nodes with OD semantic relationship through a directed and weighted adjacency matrix. The ODCRN fits the real data well and is generally consistent with the real values in terms of trend and numerical magnitude. Secondly, we can also find from Figs. 9 that the OD curves show dramatic local fluctuations due to the dynamic changes in taxi demand between regions. And this acyclic, randomly changing curve increases the difficulty of prediction, so the model fails to give a more accurate prediction in detail.

Figure 10 shows the predicted values of the OD matrix $(N \times N, N = 256)$ compared to the true values at three different moments on April 30, 2015 at 8 am, 2 pm and 10 pm. It can be seen that the smaller number suburban regions keep the values of the corresponding locations of the OD matrix silent due to the sparse number of taking taxis. The OD matrix predicted by our model is close to the real OD matrix in terms of spatial distribution and temporal variation of ride-hirings, and can better predict the OD travel demand among urban regions.

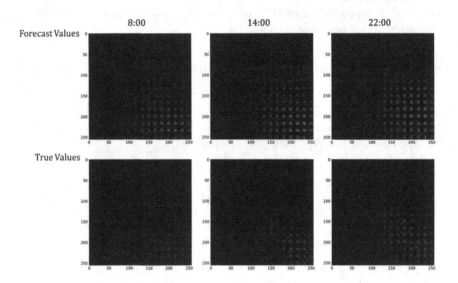

**Fig. 10.** Comparison of the Predicted Value and Actual Value of OD Matrix

# 5 Limitation Analysis

Although the method proposed in this paper is better than the existing traffic prediction model in terms of prediction effect, there still exist some aspects which can be further improved.

**Prediction of Non-stationary and Non-strictly Periodic Traffic Time Series.** Due to the uneven development of urban regions, differences in travel demand, or uneven distribution of data collection devices, there are non-stationary and non-periodic trends in the time series of some nodes, and the prediction of such time series is more difficult than that of regular and periodically varying time series. So, a more robust and better prediction model for the input time series is needed.

**Traffic Flow Prediction Under Abnormal Conditions.** By visualizing the prediction results, we find that the model has difficulty in achieving accurate prediction for traffic flow surges or sudden decreases caused by peak hours, holidays, extreme weather, social events, traffic accidents, etc. We consider increasing the amount of training data, which can add external features containing the above events, or time series anomaly detection methods to achieve more accurate prediction.

# 6  Conclusion

In this paper we propose ODCRN, a novel model that integrates traffic context and spatial-temporal information of OD matrices. We take advantage of the bi-directional semantic information of each travel demand's semantic neighbors to capture both the inflow and outflow of one region. Then we construct traffic context information by static and dynamic traffic contexts to coordinate with OD matrices in the prediction task. We conduct extensive experiments in two datasets and the results demonstrate that our method outperforms baseline methods in terms of prediction accuracy and model complexity.

In future work, we will explore predicting traffic spikes or dips caused by rush hours in the day, holidays, extreme weathers and social events more accurately. Also, we will consider integrating more traffic features into the model elegantly, which requires more experiments on model design and data mining.

**Acknowledgements.** This work was supported in part by the High Performance Computing Center of Central South University.

# References

1. Wang, Y., Yin, H., Chen, H., Wo, T., Xu, J., Zheng, K.: Origin-destination matrix prediction via graph convolution: a new perspective of passenger demand modeling. In: Proceedings of the 25th ACM SIGKDD International Conference on Knowledge Discovery & Data Mining (KDD 2019), pp. 1227–1235. Association for Computing Machinery, New York (2019). https://doi.org/10.1145/3292500.3330877
2. Tamin, O., Willumsen, L.: Transport demand model estimation from traffic counts. Transportation 16(1), 3–26 (1989)
3. Cascetta, E., Nguyen, S.: A unified framework for estimating or updating origin/destination matrices from traffic counts. Transp. Res. Part B Methodol. 22(6), 437–455 (1988)
4. Zhou, X., Mahmassani, H.S.: Dynamic origin-destination demand estimation using automatic vehicle identification data. TITS 7(1), 105–114 (2006)
5. Tamin, O.Z., Hidayat, H., Indriastuti, A.K.: The development of maximum-entropy (ME) and Bayesian-inference (BI) estimation methods for calibrating transport demand models based on link volume information. In: EASTS, vol. 4, pp. 630–647 (2003)
6. Hazelton, M.L.: Some comments on origin-destination matrix estimation. Transp. Res. Part A Policy Pract. 37(10), 811–822 (2003)

7. Zhou, X., Qin, X., Mahmassani, H.: Dynamic origin-destination demand estimation with multiday link traffic counts for planning applications. Transp. Res. Rec. J. Transp. Res. Board **1831**, 30–38 (2003)
8. Liu, L., Qiu, Z., Li, G., Wang, Q., Ouyang, W., Lin, L.: Contextualized spatial-temporal network for taxi origin-destination demand prediction. IEEE Trans. Intell. Transp. Syst. **20**(10), 3875–3887 (2019). https://doi.org/10.1109/TITS.2019.2915525
9. Scarselli, F., Gori, M., Tsoi, A.C., Hagenbuchner, M., Monfardini, G.: The graph neural network model. IEEE Trans. Neural Networks **20**(1), 61–80 (2009). https://doi.org/10.1109/TNN.2008.2005605
10. Xia, J., Zhu, Y., Du, Y., Li, S.: A Survey of Pretraining on Graphs: Taxonomy, Methods, and Applications (2022)
11. Zhang, J., Zheng, Y., Qi, D.: Deep spatio-temporal residual networks for city-wide crowd flows prediction. In: Proceedings of the AAAI Conference on Artificial Intelligence, vol. 31, p. 1 (2017). https://doi.org/10.1609/aaai.v31i1.10735
12. Li, Z., Li, L., Peng, Y., Tao, X.: A two-stream graph convolutional neural network for dynamic traffic flow forecasting. In: 2020 IEEE 32nd International Conference on Tools with Artificial Intelligence (ICTAI), Baltimore, MD, USA, pp. 355–362 (2020). https://doi.org/10.1109/ICTAI50040.2020.00063
13. Li, Y., et al.: Diffusion convolutional recurrent neural network: data-driven traffic forecasting. arXiv preprint arXiv:1707.01926 (2017)
14. Ke, J., et al.: Predicting origin-destination ride-sourcing demand with a spatial-temporal encoder-decoder residual multi-graph convolutional network. Transp. Res. Part C Emerg. Technol. **122**, 102858 (2021)
15. Zhang, J., et al.: Flow prediction in spatial-temporal networks based on multitask deep learning. IEEE Trans. Knowl. Data Eng. **32**(3), 468–478 (2019)
16. Wang, S., et al.: Multi-task adversarial spatial-temporal networks for crowd flow prediction. In: Proceedings of the 29th ACM International Conference on Information & Knowledge Management (2020)
17. Zhang, K., et al.: A deep learning based multitask model for network-wide traffic speed prediction. Neurocomputing **396**, 438–450 (2020)
18. Ke, J., et al.: Joint predictions of multi-modal ride-hailing demands: a deep multi-task multi-graph learning-based approach. Transp. Res. Part C Emerg. Technol. **127**, 103063 (2021)
19. Liu, L., et al.: Physical-virtual collaboration modeling for intra-and inter-station metro ridership prediction. IEEE Trans. Intell. Transp. Syst. **23**(4), 3377–3391 (2020)
20. Grover, A., Leskovec, J.: node2vec: scalable feature learning for networks. In: Proceedings of the 22nd ACM SIGKDD International Conference on Knowledge Discovery and Data Mining (2016)
21. Cheng, Y., Ye, X., Zhou, L.: Forecasting the peak-period station-to-station origin-destination matrix in urban rail transit system: case study of Chongqing, China. In: Transportation Research Board 97th Annual Meeting. National Academy of Sciences (2018)
22. Yuan, Q., et al.: Time-aware point-of-interest recommendation. In: Proceedings of the 36th International ACM SIGIR Conference on Research and Development in Information Retrieval (2013)

# MD-TransUNet: TransUNet with Multi-attention and Dilated Convolution for Brain Stroke Lesion Segmentation

Jie Xu[1,2], Jian Wan[1,3], and Xin Zhang[1,2,4(✉)]

[1] School of Computer Science and Technology, Hangzhou Dianzi University,
310018 Zhejiang, China
{211050059,zhangxin}@hdu.edu.cn, wanjian@zust.edu.cn
[2] Key Laboratory of Complex Systems Modeling and Simulation Ministry of
Education, Ministry of Education, Beijing, China
[3] School of Information and Electronic Engineering, Zhejiang University of Science
and Technology, Zhejiang, China
[4] Key Laboratory of Marine Ecosystem Dynamics, Second Institute of
Oceanography, Ministry of Natural Resources, Hangzhou, China

**Abstract.** The accurate segmentation of stroke lesion regions holds immense significance in shaping treatment strategies and rehabilitation protocols. Due to the large difference in the volume of stroke lesion areas and the great similarity between lesion areas and normal tissues, most of the existing methods for lesion segmentation cannot deal with these problems well. This paper proposes a novel network named MD-TransUNet for the segmentation of stroke lesions, whose framework is based on the UNet architecture. To fully obtain deep image features, it uses ResNet50 for downsampling. MD (multi-dilated) module is employed as the skip connection to gain more receptive fields. Different receptive fields can adapt to varying volumes of lesion areas. Then, a feature extraction module with multi-level attention mechanism is designed using ConvLSTM, non-local spatial attention, and channel attention modules to suppress useless information expression in skip connections and upsampling processes while focusing more on effective spatial and channel information in features. The experiments show that our proposed network gets superior performance than benchmark methods and indicates the generalization and effectiveness of the proposed model.

**Keywords:** Brain Stroke Lesion · Attention · Dilated Convolution

## 1 Introduction

According to recent global statistics, stroke is ranked second as a cause of mortality and third as a cause of both mortality and disability in 2019. In fact, the

H. Gao et al. (Eds.): CollaborateCom 2023, LNICST 562, pp. 151–170, 2024.
https://doi.org/10.1007/978-3-031-54528-3_9

total number of stroke cases recorded that year was 12.2 million, contributing to a massive 6.55 million deaths worldwide [1]. MRI (Magnetic Resonance Imaging) scans are useful in detecting ischemic strokes in the early stage. Additionally, MRI provides essential functional information, including cerebral blood flow and tissue metabolism, which is beneficial in the early diagnosis and differential diagnosis of strokes. Therefore, segmentation of the lesion areas from the MR images is particularly important.

Initially, before the rise of deep learning technology, Montiel et al. [2] calculated the edge confidence on DWI images and assigned each observation value to the point closest to the gradient direction along the observation point, grouping a set of observation values into different classes. Subsequently, all voxels that had converged to the same point were used to merge and mark the tissue region. Ozertem et al. [3] used kernel annealing to automatically segment brain lesion regions.

In recent years, with the development of deep learning methods, the architectures such as UNet [4], DeepLab3+ [5] and CLCI-Net [6] have been widely used in the field of image segmentation and have achieved great success. UNet uses an encoder-decoder symmetric architecture. This structure facilitates the extraction of more accurate information by fusing high-resolution features with their corresponding upsampled counterparts via skip connections. In the upsampling process, the network has more channels due to the combination of downsampling features, allowing the network to capture more feature information and achieve greater accuracy with less training data. DeepLab3+ incorporates a substantial ensemble of dilated convolution layers within its encoder module to augment the receptive field without compromising information loss. The utilization of dilated convolutions enables each convolutional layer to accumulate information across a wider spatial extent. By applying a specific dilation rate to each convolutional layer, the receptive field expands progressively, facilitating the integration of contextual information from a larger region. Consequently, this design empowers DeepLab3+ to capture long-range dependencies and exploit global contextual cues, leading to a more comprehensive understanding of the input data. Although UNet is efficient, easy to build, and has strong scalability, it has fewer layers in the encoder and cannot obtain deeper features. The deficiency in obtaining deeper features restricts the network's capability to comprehend intricate visual contexts and nuances present within the input data. Pure attention mechanisms and dilated convolution cannot compensate for this deficiency when applied to brain lesion segmentation.

In this paper, our model uses the TransUNet architecture [7] as the backbone. The model combines UNet and vision transformer, integrating both their advantages to extract improved global and local information that includes shallow and deep features. This fusion of methods allows for comprehensive analysis of the input data, empowering the model to effectively extract and incorporate both local and global visual cues. However, brain lesion segmentation is significantly different from brain structure segmentation. There are two key differences. One is that the size of brain lesions is difficult to predict and tends to vary widely. The other is that the proportion of positive and negative samples in the dataset is extremely unbalanced. In order to enhance the receptive field and facilitate the integration of a greater volume of information into the upsampling process, we introduce the MD (multi-dilated) module within the skip connection pathway. By incorporating the MD module, we address the limitations of conventional skip connections, which may not adequately capture and incorporate expansive contextual information. Through the utilization of dilated convolutions within the MD module, we enable an increased receptive field, allowing for a more comprehensive understanding of the input data. As a result, the expanded receptive field enables the model to effectively exploit long-range dependencies and capture important contextual cues, enriching the feature representation and improving the accuracy of the upsampling process. Then, we integrate a FEM (Feature Extraction Module) in the upsampling process, which consists of two parts: GCCA (Global Context Channel Attention) and ConvLSTM (Long short-term memory). Given that each convolutional layer in the upsampling process combines downsampling features, resulting in an increased number of channels, we employ the GCCA to effectively mitigate redundant channels and prioritize the expression of pertinent spatial information. By leveraging the GCCA, we can enhance the discriminative power of feature representations by selectively attending to informative channels and suppressing irrelevant ones. By using ConvLSTM to learn long-term dependent information, it reduces the negative impact of excessive useless information generated during the encoder-to-decoder process on the prediction results. Our main contributions are summarized as follows:

- In this study, we introduce the MD-TransUNet model, which addresses the challenge of the network's tendency to overlook small lesion features caused by the significant difference in lesion region sizes, and the problem of the abundance of irrelevant information due to reuse features.
- We use the convolutional MD module to expand the receptive field so that the upsampling process can obtain as much downsampled feature information as possible.
- We propose a Feature Extraction module, which makes the feature restoration of the upsampling process more efficient, suppresses useless channels and increases the weight of useful information.
- We evaluate our network on an open-source dataset of stroke lesions. Extensive experiments are conducted to demonstrate the superiority of our method.

## 2    Related Work

Medical image segmentation can separate the pathological tissue structures or specific human organs that need special attention in an image, which can help doctors make more accurate diagnoses and reduce the proportion of misdiagnoses or missed diagnoses. In recent years, with the development of intelligent diagnosis and online medical technologies, medical image segmentation plays an extremely important role. In general, image segmentation can be divided into semantic segmentation and instance segmentation. Semantic segmentation is usually used to classify each pixel in an image, resulting in a pixelated set. Instance segmentation is more detailed than semantic segmentation and can distinguish objects of the same category but not belonging to the same entity. Due to the unique characteristics of medical images, it is only necessary to know whether it's tissue that needs attention. Therefore, medical image segmentation belongs to semantic segmentation. Currently, popular medical image segmentation tasks include liver and liver tumor segmentation, brain and brain tumor segmentation, optic disc segmentation, cell segmentation, lung segmentation, and lung nodule segmentation [8].

## 2.1    Traditional Methods

Early medical image segmentation relies on methods such as edge detection, template matching, and statistical shape models.

- Threshold-based segmentation method [9] divides the greyscale histogram of a medical image into multiple classes by setting one or multiple thresholds to achieve segmentation. The threshold can be set manually or calculated by specific algorithms, such as fixed threshold segmentation, histogram bimodal method, iterative threshold image segmentation, adaptive threshold image segmentation, Otsu's method, mean method, and optimal threshold method. Because of the simplicity of the algorithm, it has been widely used.
- The basic idea of the edge detection segmentation method [10] is to first identify the edge pixels in the image and then connect them to form the target area. Edge pixels refer to the set of pixels where the greyscale of the image undergoes a spatial variation. Conventionally, first-order and second-order derivatives are employed to depict and detect these edges. First-order differential operators, such as the Roberts, Prewitt, and Sobel operators are commonly utilized to capture the primary characteristics of edges. On the other hand, second-order differential operators, such as the Laplace and Kirsh operators are frequently employed to uncover more intricate edge features.
- Clustering-based segmentation method [11] belongs to unsupervised segmentation. It divides the samples in the dataset into several disjoint subsets, each subset is called a "cluster". Specifically, Similar pixels in the dataset are grouped into the same cluster, while dissimilar pixels are assigned to different clusters. By employing this pixel classification technique, the objective is to unveil the intrinsic characteristics and underlying patterns inherent in the image.
- The method based on deformable model is an improvement of edge detection algorithms [12]. The method is based on the boundaries of the object is considering the shape, smoothness, and external forces that act on the segmented object, which are all factors that positively influence the results of the segmentation. Then, closed curves and shapes in the image are used to determine the boundary of the segmented object, which can be continuously segmented through different sections.

- Region-based segmentation method [13] includes threshold method, region growing method, region separation and merging method, and clustering segmentation method, which mainly uses the local spatial information of the image to connect and combine pixels with similar properties to obtain the final target area.
- The registration-based segmentation method [14] is mainly divided into the atlas-based segmentation algorithm and the joint segmentation and registration algorithm. The atlas-based algorithm is to align a pre-segmented image with a target image and utilizes spatial transformation parameters to deform the pre-segmented image to match the target image. Joint segmentation is to incorporate image-related structural information on the basis of registration, constructs a joint energy function, and obtains the segmentation result by minimizing the function.

These methods are basically applied directly to the information from the pixel images and to the structural similarity to achieve segmentation. Traditional segmentation methods are often susceptible to various factors, including image clarity and variations in the size of the lesion areas. With the development of deep learning in recent years, medical images no longer require manually crafted features, and convolutional neural networks can achieve hierarchical feature representation of images well and are less sensitive to factors such as clarity.

## 2.2 Deep Learning-Based Methods

There are two directions, supervised learning and weak supervised learning, for deep learning based medical image segmentation.

The primary motivation behind adopting weakly supervised learning for segmentation tasks in medical imaging stems from the inherent challenges associated with the manual labeling process. Labeling medical images requires the expertise and involvement of qualified professionals, which can be both time-consuming and resource-intensive. Generative confrontation networks have good applications in many fields such as image restoration, which has attracted the attention of researchers. Guibas et al. [15] proposed a pipeline that composed of GAN and cGAN for a segmentation task. They input random variables into the GAN to generate labeled images of retinal blood vessels and then put the generated image into a conditional GAN to generate real retinal fundus images. Finally, the discriminator judges the similarity between the generated image and the real image. Through continuous iteration, segmentation results are achieved. The model proposed by Chen et al. [16] is adapted to CT and MRI images. They use GAN to transform the labeled original image into the required image, which combines the features of CT and MRI and enables the network to have a good performance on images from both modalities. Then, the transformed image and the original image share the same segmentation network, and the loss function generated by both modalities is used to update the segmentation model. As a result, only CT labels are needed to train a network for MRI segmentation.

Supervised learning is a more mainstream direction. Supervised learning is to use labeled training data to learn a model, and then use this model to predict new samples. In essence, the goal of supervised learning is to construct a mapping from input to output, which is represented by a model. The current mainstream segmentation model usually adopts the encoder-decoder structure. The encoder extracts the features in the image, and the decoder restores the extracted features to the original image size and classifies the output results, typically U-Net, FCN, DeepLab etc.

In 2015, Long et al. proposed methods that can classify images at the pixel level [17]. FCN is a classification of image pixel level. It is different from CNN. CNN is fixed by using a fully connected layer in the convolutional layer. The length of the feature vector is classified and the FCN can accept images of any resolution. After downsampling, the deconvolution layer is used to restore the low-resolution features to the original resolution. In this way, each Pixel classification, while preserving the spatial information. In 2017, Yang et al. [6] proposed a segmentation method that fully exploits cross-scale information, which uses UNet as a framework and reuses features in the encoder process. The subsequent convolution layers include the features of the previous layer, and an improved ASPP is used to expand the receptive field.

In 2021, Gu et al. [18] proposed to utilize multiple attentionas to boost the feature representation in CNN, which is also a modification of the UNet framework. They use ratio attention modules and channel attention modules to suppress the expression of irrelevant information and focus more on useful information. Bao et al. [19] proposed a segmentation method based on mirror difference perception. They used the differential feature augmentation (DFA) module and the mirror position-based difference augmentation (MDA) module to compare and enhance the differences between the original image and the horizontally flipped image. The segmentation accuracy is improved by learning the feature differences between normal and diseased regions. Yu et al. [20] proposed a Fourier-based adaptive normalisation (FAN) and a domain classifier with a gradient reversal layer to reduce the domain shifting problem caused by the different sites where the MR images were acquired. This approach can improve the robustness and prediction accuracy of the model.

However, the existing relatively lightweight models have shortcomings in feature acquisition and cannot extract deeper features. In addition, when using residual connections, a lot of useless information is often added due to the superposition of a large number of channels. Furthermore, they ignore the negative impact on the network caused by the large difference in the area of lesion regions. Using a small convolution kernel for small volume images can only capture local features, so some information may be lost when processing global features. Using a large convolution kernel will ignore the feature information of small area lesions because it will capture broader features such as noise and background. Some models rely on the symmetry of the brain to discriminate the lesion area without considering into account the non-pathological asymmetry, which can lead to misclassification of the lesion area [21–27]. The model we proposed solves

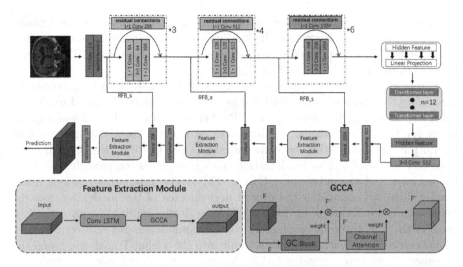

**Fig. 1.** Overview of our model framework (top). The data flow of the attention module of each layer of the decoder (bottom left). The detailed data flow of GCCA (bottom right). The network captures deep feature maps from the input data by ResNet50. Subsequently, these deep feature maps are fed into a transformer module, where self-attention weights are learned. Following the transformer module, the obtained feature maps undergo decoding through four decoder blocks. Black arrows indicate the direction of data flow.

the above problems through the MD module and feature refinement modules. Through sufficient experiments, the effectiveness of the two modules has been proved and better accuracy has been achieved.

Since there are relatively many labeled images in the ATLAS2.0 dataset (Anatomical Tracings of Lesions After Stroke), our model belongs to the branch of supervised learning. Using the encoder-decoder architecture idea, combined with the advantages of transformer and ResNet50, compared with recent models, the effect significantly increased.

## 3    Methods

In this section, we first introduce the overall architecture of the model in Sect. 3.1. Then, we introduce the implementation details of the vision transformer in Sect. 3.2. Next, we introduce the implementation details of MD module in Sect. 3.3 and the details of the FEM (feature extraction module) in Sect. 3.4.

### 3.1    Network Architecture

The network consists of four parts, including downsampling, vision transformer, upsampling and skip connection. We extract deep features from images by downsampling. Then the vision transformer effectively captures global contextual information and establishes dependencies between various image regions. Upsampling decodes deep features into the final image. And skip connection combines both shallow and deep features to enhance feature information. The general framework of our model is illustrated in Fig. 1.

We adopt a strategy to improve the input representation for the network by expanding the single-channel MRI image to a three-channel input. First is the Encoder, using the first four layers of ResNet50 as our model's downsampling layers for feature extraction. Additionally, we make necessary adjustments to the output channels of the first convolution block to facilitate the integration of ConvLSTM modules. This modification enables seamless compatibility between the encoder and the subsequent ConvLSTM layers, promoting efficient information flow and enhancing the overall performance of the model, so that the final feature dimension is 14*14*1024. During downsampling, we save the features of the first three downsampling convolutional layers for skip connections. The obtained deep features are then input into the Vision Transformer, and the sequence outputs are reconstructed in dimension after the encoder and reshaped to the original input size. Finally, the decoder uses the MD module to process the downsampling features and concatenate them with each layer.

The process of concatenation facilitates the integration of multiscale information, enhancing the model's ability to capture fine-grained details and contextual cues. The output of the FEM is used as the input to the next layer of the decoder. The prediction result is obtained using softmax.

## 3.2   Vision Transformer

Through analysis of the dataset, we find that stroke lesion areas are generally located in three areas of the brain, namely gray matter, white matter, and lateral ventricles. However, there is a lack of labels for segmenting these three areas, so we need to use self-attention mechanism to focus on the recognition of these three locations. Therefore, we utilize the self-attention feature of the Vision Transformer to learn self-attention on the deep features extracted by ResNet50. In the original vision transformer network [28], the input is a three-channel image, which is segmented into patches of a certain size and flattened. Taking ViT-H/14 as an example, the 224*224*3 input image is convolved with a kernel to obtain a 14*14*768 feature map, which then is flattened into a 196*768 matrix. In this paper, we only use the linear projection layer and the Transformer encoder layer of ViT, which consists of four encoder blocks. The 14*14*1024 deep features extracted by ResNet50 are used as input for patch embedding. Then, a class token and learnable position embedding are added, and the input is passed to the transformer encoder. Finally, the class token is removed and the flattened two-dimensional matrix is reshaped back to a 14*14*1024 feature matrix for the upsampling stage.

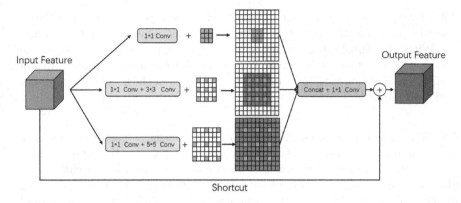

**Fig. 2.** The structure of MD module. The input is fed into 4 branches. The original input is added to the three branches to obtain the data after expanding the receptive field.

### 3.3 MD Skip Connection

One of the advantages of the UNet framework is the use of the skip structure which fuses downsampled deep features into upsampled shallow features. This structure can provide the basis for object category recognition and accurate segmentation and positioning. ResNet50 can obtain the deep features of the picture. But the deepness of the network, information will be lost and lesions in the small area cannot be accurately segmented.

In our approach, we incorporate dilated convolutions in the skip structure to expand the receptive field. This method makes up for the loss of information to a certain extent. However, a significant challenge arises in accurately segmenting stroke lesion areas due to the substantial variation of their sizes. When employing a single dilated convolution kernel, smaller lesions often go unnoticed and are consequently ignored, leading to inadequate extraction of crucial information. Taking these issues and inspired by RFBNet [29], we design a multi-dilated skip connection. As shown in Fig. 2, this module is a multi-branched convolutional layer, which comprises three individual branches with dilation rates 1, 3, and 5. Respectively, the MD module effectively combines and fuses diverse features. Incorporating dilated convolutions with varying dilation rates enables the model to capture a broader range of contextual information and significantly expand the receptive field. This strategy effectively mitigates the limitations imposed by a single dilation rate, allowing for a more comprehensive extraction of relevant features and contextual cues.

### 3.4 Feature Extraction Module

During the upsampling process, since each layer needs to concatenate the features from the downsampling, it doubles the number of channels, resulting in a doubling of irrelevant information in the feature matrix, and increasing the difficulty of lesion segmentation. The overall framework of the Feature Extraction Module is illustrated in Fig. 3. To address this issue, we use GCCA module. With its channel attention and spatial attention to emphasize channels and regions which contain useful information, while ignoring irrelevant areas. In addition, we employ ConvLSTM to retain essential data in the sequence and discard irrelevant data.

**GCCA.** In neural networks, the attention mechanism is usually an additional neural network that can selectively choose certain parts of the input or assign different weights to different parts of the input. The attention mechanism can filter out important information from a large amount of information. We design the GCCA module which incorporate both spatial and channel attention mechanisms. The input features undergo spatial attention processing to capture their relative importance, followed by channel attention processing to learn the importance of each channel. We implement the simplified non-local attention mechanism (GC: Global Context block) [30] for the spatial attention component:

$$F'' = M_c\left(M_n(F) \otimes F\right) \otimes M_n(F) \otimes F,$$

where the $F$ and $F''$ respectively represent the input and output of the module. They have the same dimension. $M_n(F) \otimes F$ represents the operation in the first half, which is the GC block. And $M_c\left(M_n(F) \otimes F\right)$ represents the channel attention.

Compared with non-local attention module, GC block eliminates unnecessary calculation and greatly reduces the calculation cost of parameters. At the same time they are almost identical in their ability to obtain a position-independent global context. GC block performs global attention pooling on the input, uses 1*1 convolution and softmax functions to obtain attention weights, and multiplies them with the flattened features to obtain global contextual features. Then the 1*1 convolution is deployed to integrate the extracted features with the original ones, thereby acquiring comprehensive global contextual information:

$$M_n(F) = F + W_2 * W_1 * \sum_{n=1}^{N_p} \frac{\exp\left(W_c * F_n\right)}{\sum_{j=1}^{N_p} \exp\left(W_c * F_j\right)} * F_n,$$

where F represents the C*H*W input. $\frac{\exp(W_c * F_n)}{\sum_{j=1}^{N_p} \exp(W_c * F_j)}$ represents the weight of global attention pooling. $N_p$ represents the number of positions in the F. $n$ and $j$ respectively represent the index of the position, enumerating all possible positions. $W_2$ and $W_1$ represent the linear transformation matrix respectively.

Then the channel attention is performed by using both max pooling and average pooling on the input. The average pooling and max pooling are used to aggregate the spatial information of the feature map. And we do not perform spatial compression when aggregating spatial information to avoid losing some spatial information during compression and restoration. Then, the module uses share MLP module to integrate information from both feature maps. After the sigmoid activation function, the weights of channel attention are obtained by addition:

$$M_C(F) = \sigma\left(W_1 * W_0 * (F_{avg}) + W_1 * W_0 * (F_{\max})\right),$$

where $F_{avg}$ represents the average pooling. $F_{\max}$ represents the maximum pooling. $W_1$ and $W_0$ represent the linear transformation matrix (1*1 Conv). $\sigma$ represents the activation function of the sigmoid.

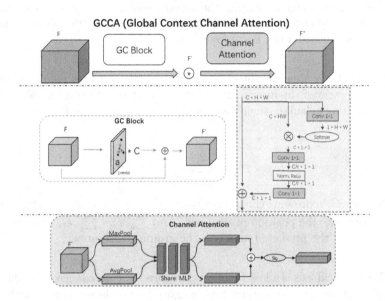

**Fig. 3.** The structure of GCCA. On the top is an overview of GCCA, which is composed of simplified non-local attention and channel attention. In the middle is the detailed data flow of the GC block, and it represents the detailed implementation process of the GC (Global Context) block. The bottom one shows the detailed data flow of channel attention.

**ConvLSTM.** LSTM is good at handling temporal information and can also handle spatial information. However, for three-dimensional images, each pixel in the image has strong correlations with the surroundings and contains extremely rich spatial information, which cannot be captured by traditional LSTM. Therefore, we use ConvLSTM [31], which differs from traditional LSTM by using 3D tensors instead of 2D inputs. The difference between traditional LSTM is that it changes from 2D input to 3D tensor.

ConvLSTM is implemented using four components. One is the forget gate, which reads the previous input and current input, applies a sigmoid nonlinearity, outputs a vector used to decide what to forget from the cell state, and finally multiplies with the cell state. The second component is the input gate, which determines the new information to be stored in the cell state. The third component is the cell state, which is the result of adding the output of the forget and input gates, equivalent to filtering and storing spatial information. The final output gate controls the visibility of the state value at time t.

### 3.5 Loss Function

During the training process, our model takes in a pair of brain MRI images and a black-and-white image indicating the lesion region, which is used to compare with the predicted lesion region by the model. Our loss function consists of the Dice coefficient loss and the Focal loss.

**Dice Loss.** This is a measurement function that calculates the similarity of two sets. It is the ratio of the intersection of the two sets to the total number of the two sets. Here we calculate their ratio by the number of pixels. It can be defined as:

$$L_{\text{dice}} = 1 - \frac{2 * \sum_i^N P_i * G_i}{\sum_i^N P_i + \sum_i^N G_i},$$

where $\sum_i^N P_i * G_i$ represents the intersection of the predicted area and the ground truth. $i$ represents the position of the pixel. And $\sum_i^N P_i + \sum_i^N G_i$ represents the sum of pixels in the predicted area and the ground truth area.

**Focal Loss.** Focal loss is a loss function that solves the unbalanced classification of samples. It focuses on adding loss weights to the losses corresponding to samples according to the difficulty of sample resolution, adding smaller weights to samples that are easy to distinguish, and adding greater weight to samples that are not easy to distinguish. Samples add larger weights, defined as:

$$L_{\text{focal loss}} = -\gamma_t * (1 - P_t)^\alpha * \log(p_t),$$

where $\alpha = 2$. $P_t$ is the probability of making a correct prediction for the class t. Our goal is to segment the lesion area. This is a dichotomous task. Therefore $t \in (0, 1)$. $\gamma_{t=0} = 1$ and $\gamma_{t=1} = 50$.

## 4    Experimental Results

In this section, we first introduce the dataset and evaluation metrics for stroke lesion segmentation. Then we perform qualitative and quantitative experiments on the effectiveness of our proposed model.

## 4.1 Dataset and Experiment Settings

We evaluate our model on the ATLAS-V2.0 dataset [32]. The dataset has 401 MRI case images, which contain a large number of images of non-lesional areas. In order to reduce the number of images of non-lesional areas, we select the MRI slices in the middle part and finally obtain more than 70,000 pairs of images. We select more than 40,000 images as training sets, and about 15,000 images are used as test sets and verification sets. We crop these data to a uniform size of 224*224.

We implement our proposed method and comparison methods with CUDA 11.1 and train them on a single NVIDIA RTX 3090 GPU. We train our model using Adam optimizer with batch size 8 and weight decay $10^-8$. The learning rate for our approach is set as 0.0001.

## 4.2 Evaluation Metrics

Dice score is one of the commonly used indicators for image segmentation. It is a set similarity measurement function that is used to calculate the similarity between two samples. It is defined as follows:

$$Dice = \frac{2|X \cap Y|}{|X| + |Y|} = \frac{2 * TP}{2 * TP + FN + FP},$$

where TP represents the number of pixels that are themselves positive samples and are predicted to be positive samples. FN represents the number of pixels whose label is a negative sample and is correctly predicted as a negative sample. FP represents that the label itself is a negative sample but is predicted to be a positive sample The number of pixels. FP represents the number of pixels whose label itself is a positive sample but is predicted to be a negative sample.

Precision is also a commonly used image segmentation index. It considers how many of the predicted positive samples are positive samples themselves. The larger the value, the higher the accuracy of the prediction. It is defined as follows:

$$Precision = \frac{TP}{TP + FP}.$$

Recall is similar to Precision. It considers how many positive samples on the label are correctly predicted. The larger the value, the more comprehensive the prediction. It is defined as follows:

$$Recall = \frac{TP}{TP + FN}.$$

IOU calculates the overlap ratio of the intersection of two sets and their union, and the larger the value, the more consistent the predicted lesion area with the location of the label. It is defined as:

$$IOU = \frac{TP}{TP + FN + FP}.$$

**Table 1.** Quantitative comparison results on the ATLAS-V2 Dataset of our network compared to the state-of-the-art methods for brain stroke lesion segmentation in terms of Dice, IOU, Precision, RVD, VOE, and Recall. The best result is in bold.

| Methods | Dice | Precision | Recall | VOE | RVD | IOU |
|---------|------|-----------|--------|-----|-----|-----|
| U-Net | 0.7604 | 0.8743 | 0.8318 | 0.6198 | −0.7946 | 0.7490 |
| CA Net | 0.6558 | 0.7929 | 0.8080 | 0.6721 | **−0.6634** | 0.6511 |
| DeepLab3+ | 0.8152 | **0.9793** | 0.8179 | 0.5924 | −0.9681 | 0.8069 |
| TransUnet | 0.8581 | 0.9602 | 0.8516 | 0.5709 | −0.9000 | 0.8404 |
| CLCI-Net | 0.8062 | 0.9300 | 0.8394 | 0.5969 | −0.9102 | 0.7909 |
| Our model | **0.8681** | 0.9692 | **0.8669** | **0.5660** | −0.8921 | **0.8494** |

RVD represents the difference between the volume of the predicted region and the region in the label, which can be defined as:

$$RVD = \frac{V_{seg}}{V_{gt}} - 1.$$

VOE can be called the volume overlap error, which represents the error rate. It can be said to be the opposite of the definition of Dice, which can be defined as:

$$VOE = 1 - \frac{|X \cap Y|}{|X \cup Y|} = 1 - \frac{TP}{TP + FN + FP}.$$

### 4.3 Comparison with Baselines

We compare our model to five models, including UNet [4] and DeepLab3+ [5], which are classic medical image segmentation models. CA-Net [18], TransUnet [7], and CLCI-Net [6] are proposed in recent years and have relatively good performance in ATLAS segmentation. We demonstrate the superiority of our model by observing several evaluation metrics, including Dice, IOU, RVD, VOR, Recall, and Precision. As shown in Table 1, our proposed model achieves 0.8681, 0.9692, 0.8669, 0.5660, −0.8921, and 0.8494 for Dice, precision, recall, VOE, RVD, and IOU, respectively.

Compare with the compared models, our model's Dice score improves by 0.01 to 0.1, indicating a higher similarity between the predicted labels and Ground Truth. Our model's precision score is 0.01 lower than DeepLab3+ but improves by 0.08 to 0.15 compared to other models. This is mainly due to the inclusion of the FE module, which uses spatial attention to represent channels carrying useless information during the upsampling process with the help of spatial attention. Non-local and ConvLSTM help the network to focus more on the feature representation of the target area, while retaining more effective feature information and avoiding the influence of too many background features on the prediction. Next is the recall metric, which measures how many true positives are predicted as positives. Our model's recall score improves by 0.03 to 0.07

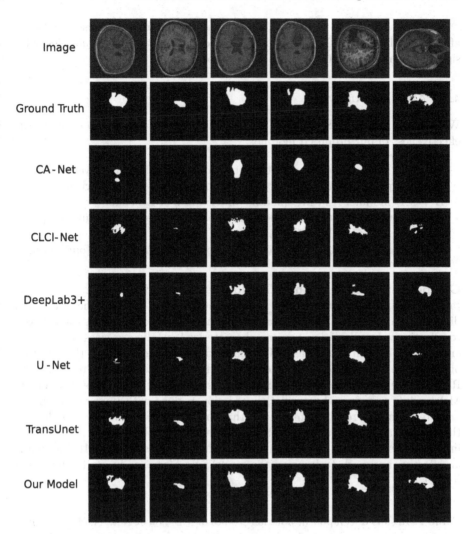

**Fig. 4.** Comparisons of our method, U-Net, DeepLabv3+, CLCI-Net, CA-Net and Trans-Unet on six different patients.

compared to other models, indicating more accurate predictions of lesion areas. The VOE metric measures the opposite effect of Dice, and our model is 0.02 to 0.11 lower than other models, indicating a lower error rate. RVD and IOU are metrics that measure the difference in volume between the predicted region and the Ground Truth. The improvement in these metrics is mainly due to the fact that the MD module expands the sensory field to adequately extract feature information through multi-scale cavity convolution.

In general, our model achieves higher accuracy in stroke lesion segmentation after using dilated pooling convolution and feature enhancement modules, with significant improvements in region size and overlap.

## 4.4 Ablation Analysis

We conduct ablation experiments on the ATLAS-V2.0 dataset to evaluate the effectiveness of our proposed module:

- Baseline: Change the convolution output channel of the first layer of ResNet downsampling in TransUNet to 128 as a benchmark for comparison.
- B + MD module: Add MD module on the basis of Baseline.
- B + Feature Extraction Module: Add a feature extraction module composed of GCCA and ConvLSTM on the basis of Baseline.
- B + Feature Extraction Module + MD module: Filling module (our module).

**Component Analysis of the MD Module.** As Shown in Table 2, we incorporate an MD module that combines features with different receptive fields through dilated convolutions at different rates. This novel approach enables the network to effectively handle lesion regions characterized by diverse sizes and shapes encountered within the dataset. Compare to the baseline model, the addition of the MD module lead to an increase in the Dice coefficient, Precision, and Recall, indicating improved performance. As a result, the incorporation of the MD module enhances the prediction of lesion regions with improved accuracy and precision. The results demonstrate that this dynamic fusion process enhances the model's ability to capture both local details and global context, resulting in improved performance for the semantic segmentation task. The MD module is an effective approach to improve the model's performance in predicting lesion regions.

**Table 2.** Results of component ablation studies of MD-TransUNet. The best result is in bold.

| Methods | Dice | Precision | Recall | VOE | RVD | IOU |
|---|---|---|---|---|---|---|
| Base-model | 0.8529 | 0.9681 | 0.8575 | **0.5736** | −0.8978 | 0.8347 |
| B + FEM | 0.8621 | 0.9640 | **0.8683** | 0.5689 | **−0.8774** | 0.8441 |
| B + MD | 0.8554 | 0.9560 | 0.8659 | 0.5723 | −0.8803 | 0.8369 |
| B + FEM + MD(our model) | **0.8681** | **0.9692** | 0.8669 | 0.5660 | −0.8921 | **0.8494** |

**Component Analysis of the FE Module.** To address the loss of features associated with the downsampling process, we incorporate a feature extraction module into our model to repair and compensate for the lost features. Our model showed improvements in various evaluation metrics compared to the baseline model and achieved comparable results to models that contained only the MD module. Our model exhibits superior performance across all evaluation metrics compared to models that featured only a single module. This indicates that the MD module improves the network's ability to integrate complete feature information, and the feature extraction module retains more useful features. These modules complement each other effectively. Consequently, our model exhibits a considerable advantage over other models.

### 4.5  Visual Comparison

To further validate the effectiveness of our MD-TransUnet network, we select six groups of stroke MRI images and their predicted results from various models in Fig. 4. It is clear from the images that our model's predictions are superior to those of other models. As shown in the evaluation metrics such as the Dice coefficient in the table above, our model can achieve more accurate predictions in small lesion areas compared to U-Net, CLCI-Net, and other models, demonstrating the effectiveness of incorporating the MD module. In predicting large lesion areas, our model's predictions are more detailed, and the predicted shapes are extremely similar to the Ground Truth, indicating that the GCCA module can indeed enrich the details of the predicted results. These prove the effectiveness of our model.

## 5  Conclusions

This paper proposes a novel deep neural network based on UNet, which is specifically designed to segment brain hemorrhages in stroke patients. To enhance the performance of the model, we introduce the MD module into the skip-connection part, which provides a connection between deep down-sampling and up-sampling features. This approach preserves more information about the texture and edge pertinent to the hemorrhagic region during the convolution process. To mitigate the information loss that arises from the depth of the network during the downsampling process, we employ a feature extraction module consisting of ConvLSTM and GCCA. This module learns long-term dependency information and retains additional information. The GCCA specifically learns multilevel attention weights that help eliminate useless channels and retain more useful information on high channel features in each layer of the up-sampling process. GCCA also reduces the impact of background noise and counteracts other negative factors that could undermine the validity of the spatial dimension information. We further perform comparative experiments with other models in the same field and ablation experiments to test the model's effectiveness.

Our future goal is to adopt more advanced techniques, such as clinician evaluations comparing regions of the left and right brain regions, to achieve greater precision in the segmentation of stroke lesions.

**Acknowledgements.** This research was supported by "Pioneer" and "Leading Goose" R&D Program of Zhejiang Province under No. 2022C03043, Natural Science

Foundation of Zhejiang Province under No. LQ21F020015, and the Open Research Project Fund of Key Laboratory of Marine Ecosystem Dynamics, Ministry of Natural Resources under Grants MED202202.

# References

1. Feigin, V.L., et al.: Global, regional, and national burden of stroke and its risk factors, 1990–2019: a systematic analysis for the global burden of disease study 2019. The Lancet Neurol. **20**(10), 795–820 (2021)
2. Hevia-Montiel, N., et al.: Robust nonparametric segmentation of infarct lesion from diffusion-weighted MR images. In: 2007 29th Annual International Conference of the IEEE Engineering in Medicine and Biology Society, pp. 2102–2105. IEEE (2007)
3. Ozertem, U., Gruber, A., Erdogmus, D.: Automatic brain image segmentation for evaluation of experimental ischemic stroke using gradient vector flow and kernel annealing. In: 2007 International Joint Conference on Neural Networks, pp. 1397–1400. IEEE (2007)
4. Ronneberger, O., Fischer, P., Brox, T.: U-Net: convolutional networks for biomedical image segmentation. In: Navab, N., Hornegger, J., Wells, W.M., Frangi, A.F. (eds.) MICCAI 2015. LNCS, vol. 9351, pp. 234–241. Springer, Cham (2015). https://doi.org/10.1007/978-3-319-24574-4_28
5. Chen, L.-C., Zhu, Y., Papandreou, G., Schroff, F., Adam, H.: Encoder-decoder with Atrous separable convolution for semantic image segmentation. In: Proceedings of the European Conference on Computer Vision (ECCV), pp. 801–818 (2018)
6. Yang, H., et al.: CLCI-Net: cross-level fusion and context inference networks for lesion segmentation of chronic stroke. In: Shen, D., et al. (eds.) MICCAI 2019. LNCS, vol. 11766, pp. 266–274. Springer, Cham (2019). https://doi.org/10.1007/978-3-030-32248-9_30
7. Chen, J., et al.: TransUNet: transformers make strong encoders for medical image segmentation. arXiv preprint arXiv:2102.04306 (2021)
8. Wang, R., Lei, T., Cui, R., Zhang, B., Meng, H., Nandi, A.K.: Medical image segmentation using deep learning: a survey. IET Image Process. **16**(5), 1243–1267 (2022)
9. Johnson, L.A., Pearlman, J.D., Miller, C.A., Young, T.I., Thulborn, K.R.: MR quantification of cerebral ventricular volume using a semiautomated algorithm. Am. J. Neuroradiol. **14**(6), 1373–1378 (1993)
10. Pujar, J.H., Gurjal, P.S., Kunnur, K.S., et al.: Medical image segmentation based on vigorous smoothing and edge detection ideology. Int. J. Electr. Comput. Eng. **4**(8), 1143–1149 (2010)
11. Li, B.N., Chui, C.K., Chang, S., Ong, S.H.: Integrating spatial fuzzy clustering with level set methods for automated medical image segmentation. Comput. Biol. Med. **41**(1), 1–10 (2011)
12. Jayadevappa, D., Srinivas Kumar, S., Murty, D.S.: Medical image segmentation algorithms using deformable models: a review. IETE Tech. Rev. **28**(3), 248–255 (2011)
13. Patil, D.D., Deore, S.G.: Medical image segmentation: a review. Int. J. Comput. Sci. Mobile Comput. **2**(1), 22–27 (2013)
14. Hao, L.: Registration-based Segmentation of Medical Images. School of Computing National University of Singapore, Singapore (2006)

15. Guibas, J.T., Virdi, T.S., Li, P.S.: Synthetic medical images from dual generative adversarial networks. arXiv preprint arXiv:1709.01872 (2017)
16. Chen, C., Dou, Q., Chen, H., Qin, J., Heng, P.A.: Unsupervised bidirectional cross-modality adaptation via deeply synergistic image and feature alignment for medical image segmentation. IEEE Trans. Med. Imaging **39**(7), 2494–2505 (2020)
17. Long, J., Shelhamer, E., Darrell, T.: Fully convolutional networks for semantic segmentation. In Proceedings of the IEEE Conference on Computer Vision and Pattern Recognition, pp. 3431–3440 (2015)
18. Ran, G., et al.: CA-Net: comprehensive attention convolutional neural networks for explainable medical image segmentation. IEEE Trans. Med. Imaging **40**(2), 699–711 (2020)
19. Bao, Q., Mi, S., Gang, B., Yang, W., Chen, J., Liao, Q.: MDAN: mirror difference aware network for brain stroke lesion segmentation. IEEE J. Biomed. Health Inform. **26**(4), 1628–1639 (2021)
20. Yu, W., Lei, Y., Shan, H.: FAN-Net: fourier-based adaptive normalization for cross-domain stroke lesion segmentation. In: ICASSP 2023–2023 IEEE International Conference on Acoustics, Speech and Signal Processing (ICASSP), pp. 1–5. IEEE (2023)
21. He, X., Chen, K., Yang, M.: Semi-automatic segmentation of tissue regions in digital histopathological image. In: Gao, H., Wang, X. (eds.) CollaborateCom 2021. LNICST, vol. 406, pp. 678–696. Springer, Cham (2021). https://doi.org/10.1007/978-3-030-92635-9_39
22. Lin, B., Deng, S., Yin, J., Zhang, J., Li, Y., Gao, H.: FocAnnot: patch-wise active learning for intensive cell image segmentation. In: Gao, H., Wang, X., Iqbal, M., Yin, Y., Yin, J., Gu, N. (eds.) CollaborateCom 2020. LNICST, vol. 350, pp. 355–371. Springer, Cham (2021). https://doi.org/10.1007/978-3-030-67540-0_21
23. Abdmouleh, N., Echtioui, A., Kallel, F., Hamida, A.B.: Modified u-net architecture based ischemic stroke lesions segmentation. In: 2022 IEEE 21st international ccnference on Sciences and Techniques of Automatic Control and Computer Engineering (STA), pp. 361–365. IEEE (2022)
24. Chaitanya, K., Erdil, E., Karani, N., Konukoglu, E.: Local contrastive loss with pseudo-label based self-training for semi-supervised medical image segmentation. Med. Image Anal. **87**, 102792 (2023)
25. Liu, L., Huang, C., Cai, C., Zhang, X., Hu, Q.: Multi-task learning improves the brain stoke lesion segmentation. In: ICASSP 2022–2022 IEEE International Conference on Acoustics, Speech and Signal Processing (ICASSP), pp. 2385–2389. IEEE (2022)
26. Thiyagarajan, S.K., Murugan, K.: Performance analysis of ischemic stroke lesion segmentation in brain MR images using histogram based filter enhanced FCM. In: 2023 5th International Conference on Smart Systems and Inventive Technology (ICSSIT), pp. 1343–1348. IEEE (2023)
27. Aboudi, F., Drissi, C., Kraiem, T.: Efficient u-net CNN with data augmentation for MRI ischemic stroke brain segmentation. In: 2022 8th International Conference on Control, Decision and Information Technologies (CoDIT), vol. 1, pp. 724–728. IEEE (2022)
28. Dosovitskiy, A., et al.: An image is worth 16 × 16 words: transformers for image recognition at scale. arXiv preprint arXiv:2010.11929 (2020)
29. Liu, S., Huang, D., et al.: Receptive field block net for accurate and fast object detection. In: Proceedings of the European Conference on Computer Vision (ECCV), pp. 385–400 (2018)

30. Cao, Y., Xu, J., Lin, S., Wei, F., Hu, H.: GCNet: non-local networks meet squeeze-excitation networks and beyond. In: Proceedings of the IEEE/CVF International Conference on Computer Vision Workshops (2019)
31. Shi, X., Chen, Z., Wang, H., Yeung, D.-Y., Wong, W.-K., Woo, W.-C.: Convolutional LSTM network: a machine learning approach for precipitation nowcasting. In: Advances in Neural Information Processing Systems, vol. 28 (2015)
32. Liew, S.-L., et al.: A large, open source dataset of stroke anatomical brain images and manual lesion segmentations. Sci. Data 5(1), 1–11 (2018)

# Graph Computing

# DGFormer: An Effective Dynamic Graph Transformer Based Anomaly Detection Model for IoT Time Series

Hongxia He, Xi Li$^{(\boxtimes)}$, Peng Chen$^{(\boxtimes)}$, Juan Chen, Weijian Song, and Qinghui Xi

School of Computer and Software Engineering, Xihua University, Chengdu, China
lixi13@gmail.com, chenpeng@mail.xhu.edu.cn

**Abstract.** Internet of Things (IoT) is network based on information carriers such as the Internet and traditional telecommunications networks, so that all ordinary physical objects that can be independently addressed can be interconnected. In the face of the IoT produces a large of time series data, which is very necessary to detect anomaly data. Transformer has proven to be a powerful tool in several areas, but still has some limitations, such as the prediction accuracy is not high enough. As the dominant trend of multivariate time series in different scenarios becomes increasingly evident, it is particularly important to accurately capture the spatio-temporal features between them. To address these issues, we propose Dynamic Graph transFormer (DGFormer), an effective Dynamic Graph Transformer based Anomaly Detection Model for IoT Time Series. We first use Transformer with anomaly attention mechanism to extract time features. Then, a dynamic relationship embedding strategy is proposed to capture spatio-temporal features dynamically and learn the adjacency matrix adaptively. Besides, each layer of GNN is soft clustered by Diffpooling. Finally, in order to further improve the detection performance of model, we integrate the traditional autoregressive linear model with the nonlinear neural network in parallel. The experimental results show that the proposed model achieves the highest F1-score on three public IoT datasets, and the F1-score is improved by 19.3% on average.

**Keywords:** Internet of Things · Anomaly detection · Time series · Transformer · Graph neural network

## 1 Introduction

With the rapid growth of interconnecting devices and sensors in information physical systems such as autonomous vehicle, intelligent buildings, water treatment and distribution plants [1], the emergence of the IoT further promotes the application of network physical systems to various tasks, and it is increasingly necessary to monitor these devices from attacks, which is particularly important for key infrastructure such as power grids and communication networks [2]. The IoT can use blockchain, edge computing, deep learning and other methods to achieve target monitoring, positioning, recognition, user

© ICST Institute for Computer Sciences, Social Informatics and Telecommunications Engineering 2024
Published by Springer Nature Switzerland AG 2024. All Rights Reserved
H. Gao et al. (Eds.): CollaborateCom 2023, LNICST 562, pp. 173–188, 2024.
https://doi.org/10.1007/978-3-031-54528-3_10

privacy safe storage and other functions [3]. Nowadays, the amount of data is increasing exponentially. Faced with these massive amounts of data, the improvement of the IoT can greatly promote the future application and development of wireless sensor networks [4]. Therefore, it is very necessary to perform anomaly detection on the data in monitoring, that is, by analyzing the anomaly patterns of the target monitoring data to detect the anomaly behavior of the monitoring object. How to accurately and efficiently perform anomaly detection has also become a hot issue in the field of IoT security [5].

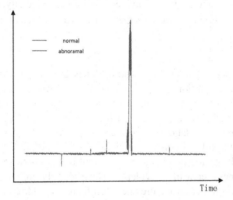

**Fig. 1.** Typical IoT anomaly detection, with red representing anomaly data and blue representing normal data.

Anomaly detection, a.k.a. outlier detection, has a wide range of applications in many fields, including network security, medicine, machine vision, statistics, credit card theft, and large expenditures [6]. The anomaly detection algorithm mainly learns to detect anomalies or emit danger signals when anomaly events occur by observing unlabeled datasets of normal events. As shown in Fig. 1, in real-world IoT environment, detecting anomalies from IoT sensors is essentially multivariate time series anomaly detection, as real-time IoT data collected from various sensors are processed and stored in multivariate time series. Due to the lack of anomaly labels in the data collected by sensors, and the unpredictable and diverse nature of anomalies, anomaly detection is often seen as an unsupervised learning problem. Based on above, we will focus on time series anomaly detection in an unsupervised environment.

Before machine learning, classic time series algorithms are generally used to statistical model. However, nowadays, the multivariate time series generated by cyber physics systems are highly complex and inherently nonlinear. These methods only model the relationships between sensors and can only capture linear relationships [7]. Therefore, in recent years, researchers have utilized deep learning-based techniques for anomaly detection in high-dimensional data, thereby to develop more intelligent and cost-effective methods to identify anomalies. For example, unsupervised anomaly detection algorithms such as OCSVM [34], ridge regression [8], RNN [9] and LSTM [37] are used to build models. These deep learning methods can capture long-term dependencies in time series data and are suitable for processing time series anomaly data. However, due to the relatively complex internal structure of these models, the training efficiency is very low, and the calculation amount is also large and time-consuming. Moreover, they have weak distribution assumptions about anomaly data and easy to be affected by normal data, which may lead to the problem of false detection and missing detection. In particular, the training accuracy of these models is not high enough, and the optimization of model performance needs to be strengthened. With the further development of deep learning technology in recent years, Transformer and GNN have achieved a series of important results in many areas.

Nowadays, New applications of the Transformer self-attention network have been recognized, published, and successfully used in research areas such as computer vision, image processing, and natural language processing. Its structure includes self-attention mechanism, location coding, Add&Normalize, fully connected layer Feed Forward and other modules. These modules cooperate with each other, can achieve fast parallel operation by using self-attention mechanism, and can better process time series data and extract time features. By learning the spatio-temporal representation of graph structure, GNN can consider both spatial and temporal dimensions of data. Based on above, we consider combining Transformer with GNN for time series anomaly detection. GNN have been extensively studied in recent years and have successfully completed difficult machine learning tasks such as node classification, link prediction, and graph classification, due to high expressiveness through message passing in effective learning graph representation [10]. GNN can learn both temporal and spatial dependencies and display high-dimensional data with complex relationships, and can be widely used in the modeling of complex systems. Based on this, GNN can be a promising way to model multivariate time series data. It takes graph structure data as input. If it is applied to anomaly detection of multivariate time series, the complex relationships in time series need to be converted into graphs and learned together with the model.

We propose Dynamic Graph transFormer (DGFormer), an effective Dynamic Graph Transformer based Anomaly Detection Model for IoT Time Series. First, we design a novel anomaly attention mechanism and construct an effective Transform model to extract time features of time series data. To compute the association discrepancy, we renovate the self-attention mechanism to anomaly attention, which contains a two-branch structure to model the prior association and series association for each time point respectively. The prior association employs a learnable Gaussian kernel to present the adjacent concentration inductive bias at each time point, while a series association corresponds to the self-attention weights learned from the original sequence. The distance between the two associations at each time point is then calculated to quantify the anomaly criteria. Besides, a dynamic relational embedding strategy is proposed to capture the spatio-temporal features of the sequences to improve the timeliness of the model. And then, GNN model is used to realize the spatio-temporal dependence relationship of time series and make spatio-temporal prediction better. Finally, in order to further improve the detection performance of model, and our data have both linear and nonlinear feature parts, we consider adding an autoregressive linear model AR to extract its linear part to supplement the overall performance other than nonlinear. Experiments on real time series datasets have been proved the accuracy and effectiveness of the proposed method. These contributions are summarized as follows:

- In order to learn the spatio-temporal dependence of time series data, we propose a Transformer integrated with GNN model to dynamically capture spatio-temporal features to improve the timeliness of the model.
- We propose a dynamic relationship embedding strategy based on graph structure learning to adaptively learn the adjacency matrix to simulate potential relationships in a given time series sample.
- In order to extract the linear feature part of the time series data, we integrate the traditional autoregressive linear model AR with the nonlinear neural network in parallel, which further improves the robustness of the model.
- We demonstrate that DGFormer outperforms eight state-of-art baseline methods on three public IoT time series datasets, with a 19.3% improvement in the model's average F1-score.

The related work is introduced in Sect. 2. Section 3 introduces the proposed DGFormer model. Section 4 evaluates the methodology on real time series datasets. Section 5 summarizes the work.

## 2 Related Work

The study of anomaly detection in time series has been carried out for several decades and is an active research area that is gaining increasing attention in machine learning and data mining. At the same time, many models for time series anomaly detection are proposed. Here we mainly introduce our work from two aspects: the statistics-based method and the deep learning-based method.

### 2.1 Statistics-Based Method

Traditional statistical methods are mainly used on single-feature time series data, and most of them are linear methods. Kahya et al. used the statistical methods of Cumulative Sum (CUSUM) [11] to build the correlation model of time series data to strengthen the forecasting ability of the US stock exchange and retail industry. Janacek et al. use Autoregressive Integrated Moving Average (ARIMA) [12] model to predict time series data. And Chen et al. propose to use isolated forest and elliptical envelope to detect geochemical anomalies [13]. These methods are good for short-term linear time series data prediction, but not so good for long-term time series data prediction. As time series data become more and more multi-dimensional and complex, these methods can no longer meet the current needs, and deep learning methods have received widespread attention due to the powerful representation ability of deep neural networks.

### 2.2 Deep Learning-Based Method

Currently, two popular deep learning models, CNN and RNN, are widely used for anomaly detection. These models typically use LSTM layers and stacked CNN layers to extract features from time series, and then apply softmax layers to predict labels. For more accurate prediction, complex structures such as the recursive skip layer (LSTNet-S), the temporal attention layer (LSTNet-A) [14], and the new temporal pattern attention mechanism have been proposed [15]. Park et al. propose the LSTM-VAE model [16], which adopts the LSTM backbone for time modeling and adopts Variational Auto Encoder (VAE) for reconstruction. MLSTM-FCN [17] uses LSTM layers and stacked CNN layers along extruding and exciting blocks to generate potential features. TapNet [18] also builds the LSTM layer and the stacked CNN layer. Bidirectional Recurrent Neural Network (BiRNN) models [19] improve the prediction accuracy of the model by adding a direction to the general RNN. Compared with LSTM, Gate Recurrent Unit (GRU) [20] has only update gates and reset gates, which greatly simplifies the running time of the model and reduces the complexity of the model, but its prediction accuracy is close to that of LSTM. In addition, some deep learning models, including THOC [21] uses recurrent neural networks (RNN) with jump connections to effectively extract multi-scale time features from time series, integrate multi-scale time features through hierarchical clustering mechanism, and then detect anomalies through multi-layer distance. GANs [22] detects anomalies by modeling nonlinear correlations between multiple time series and performing adversarial regularization. However, the limitations of the above models are obvious: they assume the same effects between time series variables, so they cannot model pairwise dependencies between variables explicitly, and the model accuracy is not high enough [23]. Recent studies show that GNN combined with Transformer can be an effective method for anomaly detection.

In traditional anomaly detection, Transformer can be used to capture global dependencies and context information of data. By introducing self-attention mechanism in Transformer, models can focus more on important nodes and edges to capture unusual patterns and features. While GNN can be used to model relationships and dependencies between data. Both have their advantages. Graph Transformer [24] provides an example of how to generalize the Transformer architecture to graphs by introducing the topological structure properties of graphs in Transformer, so that the model has prior of structural positions in a high-dimensional space. Use Laplacian eigenvectors as absolute encoding and calculate attention on the immediate region of each node, rather than on the entire graph [25]. It combines the core of Transformer (global focus) with the core of GNN (considering the topological properties of graphs). SAN [26] is similar but computes attention on the full picture, distinguishing between real edges and created edges. Mialon et al. [27] propose a way to bias self-attention calculations by relative coding via a kernel on the graph, and then incorporate the location information into Transformer by selecting a kernel function. Other recent work has attempted to incorporate structural information into graph Transformer by using GNN to integrate graph structures [28, 29]. All of them explicitly incorporate graph structures to design graph Transformer architectures that take into account both local and global information.

However, the past methods have always mined the features in time series statically, ignoring the dynamic evolution of time series. Therefore, we first use Transformer with anomaly attention to extract time features [39], and then use graph structure learning to propose a dynamic relationship embedding strategy to dynamically capture spatio-temporal features, adaptively learn the adjacency matrix, and finally improve the timeliness of the entire model.

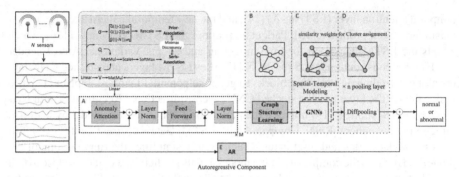

**Fig. 2.** DGFormer Framework.

# 3 Method

We'll look at the DGFormer model in detail. A diagram of DGFormer is shown in Fig. 2. The first input is a set of time series $X = \{x_1, x_2, ..., x_n\}$, which is a sequence of measurements in chronological order observed by $N$ sensors working with each other, usually the time interval between two consecutive measurements is constant, where $x_t \in R^N$ represents the observation at time t. The whole model is a parallel structure, that is, the model is processed by nonlinear module and linear module in parallel. In the nonlinear module, we propose to use an effective Anomaly Transformer model with anomaly attention module (see Fig. 2(A)) to embed each univariate sequence in $X$ into the representation vector of time information, and extract the time features. Then the adjacency matrix is generated adaptively by learning the spatio-temporal features of dynamically captured sequences through the graph structure (see Fig. 2(B)). Besides, soft clustering is carried out on each layer of GNN (see Fig. 2(C)) based on the node Embedding vector by Diffpooling module (see Fig. 2(D)), and deep GNN are established by Stacking repeatedly. After that, anomaly detection results of nonlinear modules are output. The linear module consists of an autoregressive model AR (see Fig. 2(E)). Finally, the results of these two parts are weighted and summed, and the result output $x_t$ is normal or abnormal.

## 3.1 Transformer with Anomaly Attention Mechanism

As shown in Fig. 2(A), considering the limitations of traditional Transformer in anomaly detection, we design an effective Transformer with anomaly attention mechanism [39]. It has the anomaly attention of two branch structures (the upper part of Fig. 2(A)), and for the prior association, a learnable Gaussian kernel is used to calculate the prior with respect to the relative time distance. A learnable scaling parameter $\sigma$ is also used for Gaussian kernels to adapt prior correlations to various time series patterns. The sequence association branch learns the association relationship from the original sequence, and it can adaptively find the most effective association relationship. (1) The module has shown effective results in practice. The Transformer itself consists of two main modules: anomaly attention block and fully connected layer Feed Forward, which together make up the Transformer layer. (2) Stack multiple layers to form Transformer model. The purpose of this stage is to extract the time features and construct the feature matrix $X^{(i)}$ as well as to get anomaly attention. The feature matrix for each sequence is as follows:

$$X^{(i)} = Embed_1(x_t) \in R^{n \times N} \tag{1}$$

In the anomaly attention module, a learnable Gaussian kernel is first used to calculate the prior relative to the relative time distance, and then the input node feature $X$ is projected onto the query $(Q)$, key $(K)$ and value $(V)$ matrix by linear projection. Assume that the model contains $M$ layers with length $n$ and input time series $X \in R^{n \times N}$. The anomaly attention in layer m is:

$$P^m = \text{Rescale}\left( \left[ \frac{1}{\sqrt{2\pi}\sigma_i} \exp\left( -\frac{|j-i|^2}{2\sigma_i^2} \right) \right]_{i,j \in \{1,\dots,n\}} \right) \tag{2}$$

$$Z^m = Softmax(\frac{QK^T}{\sqrt{d}}) \cdot V \tag{3}$$

wherel $m \in \{1, \dots, M\}$ denotes the output of the $m^{th}$ layer with $N_{\text{mod } el}$ channels, $Q, K, V \in R^{n \times N_{\text{mod } el}}$, generates a prior association $P^m \in R^{n \times n}$ based on the learning scale $\sigma \in R^{n \times 1}$, and the $i^{th}$ element $\sigma_i$ corresponds to the $i^{th}$ point in time. Its associated weight with the $j^{th}$ point is calculated by the Gaussian kernel $G(|j-i|; \sigma_i) = \frac{1}{\sqrt{2\pi}\sigma_i} \exp\left( -\frac{|j-i|^2}{2\sigma_i^2} \right)$ w.r.t. the distance $|j-i|$. In addition, $\text{Rescale}(\cdot)$ is used to transform the associated weights into discrete distributions $P^m$ by partitioning rows. $Z^m \in R^{n \times n}$ represents sequence association, and $Soft \max(\cdot)$ represents normalization of the attention force along the last dimension. In order to better control associative learning, a minimax strategy is proposed. Specifically, the minimization phase is one that drives a prior association to approximate the sequence association learned from the original sequence. This process will adapt the prior associations to various time patterns. In the maximization phase the sequence association is optimized to enlarge the association difference.

The module also uses a multi-head attention mechanism, and for K heads, the learning scale is $\sigma \in R^{n \times K}$. $Q_k, K_k, V_k \in R^{n \times \frac{N_{\text{mod } el}}{K}}$ represents the query, key, and value of the $k^{th}$ head respectively. The outputs $\left\{ \hat{Z}_k^m \in R^{n \times \frac{N_{\text{mod } el}}{K}}_{1 \le k \le K} \right\}$ from the multiple heads is then connected and the final result $\hat{Z}^m \in R^{n \times N_{\text{mod } el}}$ is obtained.and the symmetric KL difference between prior association and sequence association is used for anomaly differences, which represents the information gain between these two distributions [30]. Its formula is as follows:

$$Dis(P, Z; X) = \left[ \frac{1}{M} \sum_{m=1}^{M} \left( KL\left(P_i^m, : \| Z_i^m, :\right) + KL\left(Z_i^m, : \| P_i^m, :\right) \right) \right]_{i=1,\dots N} \tag{4}$$

where KL $(\cdot \| \cdot)$ is the KL divergence calculated between two discrete distributions corresponding to each row of $P^m$ and $Z^m$. $Dis(P, Z; X) \in R^{n \times 1}$ is the point-by-point association difference of $X$ with respect to a prior association $P$ and sequence association $Z$ from multiple layers.

## 3.2 Dynamic Graph Learning

The main feature of the latter part is to dynamically capture spatio-temporal features of time series to generate the adjacency matrix, and then transfer it to the GNN to extract the attribute information and structure information of the nodes.

In the dynamic graph learning part, a dynamic relationship embedding strategy is proposed, which considers the dynamic modeling of the spatio-temporal features information of datasets. As shown in Fig. 2(B), the time window is mainly used to deal with data that is continuous in time, and GNN model is applied to it for feature learning within each time window. Then the data of the whole time series is processed by sliding the time window to capture its dynamic evolution process. Associations between sensors have been learned through graph structures. Because undirected graphs are symmetric, they cannot represent asymmetric dependencies and causality between sensors. Therefore, this paper will use the directed graph connection feature to show the dependencies between different sensors, use the nodes of the graph to represent the sensors, and use the edges between the nodes to represent their dependencies. The layer adaptively learns the adjacency matrix $A^{(i)} \in R^{N \times N}$ for sequences passing through the Transformer module to simulate potential relationships in a given time series sample $x_t$. The learned graph structure (adjacency matrix) $A^{(i)}$ is defined as:

$$A^{(i)} = Embed_2(x_t) \tag{5}$$

We first calculate the similarity matrix between the sample time series, the formula is as follows:

$$C_{ij}^{(i)} = \frac{\exp(-\sigma(distance(x_i, x_j)))}{\sum_{p=0}^{n} \exp(-\sigma(distance(x_i, x_p)))} \tag{6}$$

where distance represents distance measurements, such as Euclidean distance, absolute distance, dynamic time warping, etc. The dynamic adjacency matrix $A^{(i)}$ can then be calculated as:

$$A^{(i)} = \sigma\left(C^{(i)} W_1\right) \tag{7}$$

where $W_1$ is the learnable model parameter and $\sigma$ is the activation function. In addition, in order to improve training efficiency, reduce noise effects, and make the model more robust, set the threshold value $c_1$ to make the adjacency matrix sparse:

$$A^{(i)} = \begin{cases} A_{ij}^{(i)} A_{ij}^{(i)} \geq c_1 \\ 0 A_{ij}^{(i)} \leq c_1 \end{cases} \tag{8}$$

Finally, normalization is applied to $A^{(i)}$.

## 3.3 Graph Neural Network

As shown in Fig. 2(C), the module uses 3 GNN layers ($G_1$, $G_2$, $G_3$) on the input graph (expressed as $X^{(i)}$, $A^{(i)}$) to model the spatio-temporal relationship. The GNN layer can integrate spatial dependence and time patterns to embed the features of nodes, and transform the feature dimensions of nodes into decoding, The formula is as follows:

$$X_{encode}^{(i)}, A_{encode}^{(i)} = G_3(G_2(G_1(X^{(i)}, A^{(i)}))) \tag{9}$$

where $i = 1, 2, ..., n, X_{encode}^{(i)} \in R^{n \times N_{mod\,el}}, A_{encode}^{(i)} \in R^{n \times n}$ is composed of graph neural network layer GNN and batch normalization layer. GNN can be such as GCN, GAT and GIN, etc. Then, during the pooling phase, GNN is trained using classical Diffpool and the soft cluster allocation of nodes at each layer of deep GNN is learned. As shown in Fig. 2(D), the overall transformation of a pooling layer is shown in Eq. (9) and the following two equations show the process in the Diffpool layer, where $W_2 \in R^{N_{mod\,el} \times N_{Diffpool}}$ is the trainable parameter matrix representing the linear transformation and $S^{(i)} \in R^{n_{Diffpool} \times n}$ is the distribution matrix representing the projection from the original node to the pooled node (cluster). $X_{Diffpool}^{(i)} \in R^{n_{Diffpool} \times N_{Diffpool}}$ and $A_{Diffpool}^{(i)} \in R^{n_{Diffpool} \times n_{Diffpool}}$ which has less nodes than the input graph, the parameter T represents inverting the matrix $S^{(i)}$.

$$X_{Diffpool}^{(i)} = \sigma\left(S^{(i)} X_{encode}^{(i)} W_2\right) \tag{10}$$

$$A_{Diffpool}^{(i)} = \sigma\left(S^{(i)} A_{encode}^{(i)} \left(S^{(i)}\right)^T\right) \tag{11}$$

We generate centroids $K^{(i)} \in R^{N \times n_{Diffpool} \times N_{mod\,el}}$ based on the input graph and then compute and aggregate the relationship between every batch of centroids and the encoded graph for assignment matrix $S^{(i)}$. We can compute the relationship $S_p^{(i)} \in R^{n_{Diffpool} \times n}(p = 1, 2, ..., N)$ and $K_p^{(i)} \in R^{n_{Diffpool} \times N_{model}}(p = 1, 2, ..., N)$. We use cosine similarity to evaluate the relationship between input node embeddings and centroids, followed by a row normalization deployed in the resulting assignment matrix.

$$S_p^{(i)} = \cos ine\left(K_p^{(i)}, X_{encode}^{(i)}\right) \tag{12}$$

$$S_p^{(i)} = normalize\left(S_p^{(i)}\right) \tag{13}$$

Then we concatenate $S_p^{(i)}(p = 1, 2, ..., N)$ and perform a trainable weighted sum $\Gamma_\varphi$ to the concatenated matrix, leading to the final assignment matrix $S^{(i)}$.

$$S^{(i)} = \Gamma_\varphi\left(\overset{|N|}{\underset{p=1}{||}} S_p^{(i)}\right) \tag{14}$$

After stacking several Diffpool, we can pool the original graph to a single node and get its graph-level representation vector $x_{final}$, as follows:

$$x_{final}^{(i)} = P_3\left(P_2\left(P_1\left(X_{encode}^{(i)}\right)\right)\right) \tag{15}$$

## 3.4 Autoregressive Model

As shown in Fig. 2(E), AR model is widely used in time series analysis. As a linear model, it is easy to understand and implement. It describes the relationship between the current value and the historical value, and uses the historical time data of the variable to predict itself. It provides a simple and efficient way to model and predict time series data using only past observations as independent variables, with no other complex factors to consider. The four parts of Fig. 2(A,B,C,D), together form a nonlinear module, which mainly extracts the nonlinear feature part of the data. It makes the output scale of the neural network insensitive to the input scale, because our data set has both linear feature parts and nonlinear feature parts. A mixture of linear and nonlinear modules is used as the final result of DGFormer to enhance the recognition ability of linear features. We first use the output of the nonlinear module to get the result $x_{final} \in R^{n \times N_{mod\,el}}$, while the result obtained by the AR part of the linear module is expressed as $x_{AR} \in R^{n \times N_{mod\,el}}$. Finally, the weighted sum of the two is used to get the final result $\hat{X}_t$ of DGFormer.

The final anomaly score is as follows:

$$Score(X) = soft \max(-Dis(P, Z; X))\Theta[\|x_t - \hat{x}_t\|_2^2]_{t=1,...,n} \qquad (16)$$

where $\Theta$ is element-by-element multiplication.

# 4  Experiment

The three main points we try to verify in our experimental study are as follows:

(1) Does the DGFormer framework allow us to find anomaly more efficientlythan we would otherwise? Yes.
(2) What is the influence of dynamic graph structure learning on anomaly detection? The dynamic adjacency matrix used in our model finally achieves the best result compared to other adjacency matrices.
(3) Does a hybrid anomaly score provide more information than an anomaly score using Transformer or GNN alone? Yes.

**Table 1.** Details of the experimental baseline datasets. #App represents the application of the data set, #AR represents the proportion of truth value anomalies in the entire data set, and d represents the dimension.

| Datasets | #App | #Train | #Test | #AR | d |
|---|---|---|---|---|---|
| MSL | Space | 58317 | 73729 | 0.105 | 55 |
| SMAP | Space | 135183 | 427617 | 0.128 | 25 |
| PSM | Server | 132481 | 87841 | 0.278 | 25 |

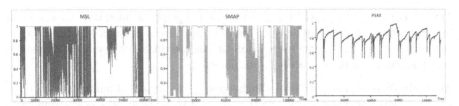

**Fig. 3.** The feature representation for one dimension of MSL, SMAP and PSM datasets.

### 4.1 Datasets and Experimental Setup

**Datasets.** Since this paper is based on time series data in IoT, we mainly choose the practical datasets related to IoT to evaluate our propose DGFormer model: The first is the two public datasets on the IoT, MSL (Mars Science Laboratory Rover) and SMAP (Soil Moisture Active and Passive Satellite) [31], contain remote sensing anomaly data obtained in the Spacecraft Monitoring System Event Surprise Anomaly Emergency Anomaly (ISA) report. And the dataset PSM(Pool Server Metrics) [32] collected within multiple application server nodes is also used as a supplementary dataset. Table 1 reports the statistics for these datasets. Figure 3 describes the one-dimensional feature representation of the three datasets. It can be seen that there are significant differences in feature distribution among them, and also shows that datasets we select have diversity distribution.

**Baseline Model.** To fully demonstrate the strength of our model, we compare DGFormer to the following eight baselines, these include several classic models such as ALAD, OC-SVM, LSTM, SO_GAAL and USAD, several recent new models such as TRANAD, Anomaly Transformer and MTAD_GAT.

**ALAD:** Adversarially Learned Anomaly Detection [33], is implemented using the PYOD[1] library, with hyperparameters set to batch_size $= 32$, dec_layers $= 10$, and dropout_size $= 0.2$ as a rule of experience.

**OC-SVM:** One-Class Support Vector Machines [34], is implemented using PYOD[1] library, and the hyperparameter is set to kernel $=$ 'rbf', degree $= 3$, coef $= 0.0$.

**SO_GAAL:** Single-Objective Generative Adversarial Active Learning [35], uses a mini-max game between a generator and a discriminator that generates adversarial learning to directly generate information-rich potential outliers.

**USAD:** UnSupervised Anomaly Detection on Multivariate Time Series [36], Combine autoencoder and adversarial training, the ordinary autoencoder is divided into one encoder and two decoders. One decoder produces fake data and trains the other decoder against it to improve its ability to recognize fake data.

**LSTM:** Long short-term memory [37], is a neural network model used to process sequence data. It captures long-term dependencies in sequence through gating mechanism and memory unit, and can solve problems such as gradient disappearance and gradient explosion.

---

[1] http://github.com/yzhao062/pyod.

**MTAD_GAT:** MTAD_GAT [38], uses two parallel graph attention layers to learn timing and feature dependencies between multiple time series, and a reconstruction-based approach to learn normal data from historical data, in which (VAE) models are used to detect anomalies by reconstructing probabilities.

**Anomaly Transformer:** Anomaly Transformer [39], consists of multiple layers overlapping anomaly attention modules and Feed Forward neural networks, in which anomaly attention has two branches: a prior association branch and a sequence association branch. Their correlation differences are then calculated to create the final outlier score.

**TRANAD:** TRANAD [40], consist of Transformer and GAN, uses score based adaptation to achieve multi-modal feature extraction and stability through adversarial training, and introduces the idea of adversarial training.

**Experimental Setup.** Experimental details follow Shen et al. [21]. All neural network models are optimized by using the Adam optimizer, with the initial learning rate set to $10^{-4}$. If the anomaly scores of a point in time (Eq. (13)) are greater than some threshold $\delta$, then we mark the point in time as an anomaly. A threshold of $\delta$ is determined so that r proportion of the data in validation datasets are marked as anomaly. Specifically, non-overlapping sliding Windows are mainly used to obtain a set of subsequences, and the size of sliding Windows is fixed at 100. The Transformer with the anomaly attention have 3 layers, 512 channels to set hidden state, and 8 digits of h. GNN have three layers with an output dimension of 128, and the number of nodes in the pooling layer is 1. For the experiment, set r to equal 1%. The hyperparameter $\lambda$ is set to 3 to weigh the two parts of the loss function, and the training process is stopped early in 10 periods with a batch size of 32. All experiments were implemented in Pytorch3.8 using a single NVIDIA GeForce 930MX GPU.

### 4.2 Main Result

**DGFormer Achieves a Consistent Up-to-Date Level Across All Baseline Model Tests.** In order to measure the effectiveness of various anomaly detection methods, we use Precision, Recall and the harmonic average of precision and recall (F1-score) as evaluation indicators. As shown in Table 2, DGFormer achieve 94.92%、98.11% and 96.53% F1-scores on datasets MSL, PSM and SMAP, respectively, which are 20.34%, 18.2% and 19.48% higher on average than other methods. Precision and Recall are consistently up to date across all benchmark models, and we observe that it is compelling to consider the advantages of transformer's integration with GNN in time series anomaly detection. In addition, we plot the F1-score bar chart in Fig. 4 for a complete comparison. DGFormer has the highest F1-score on all three datasets. This means that is important for real-world applications.

### 4.3 Ablation Study

To demonstrate the efficiency of our architecture design, careful ablation studies are conducted, and the test results measured using F1-score(%) are shown in Table 3.

**Table 2.** DGFormer's quantitative results across three real world datasets. P, R and F1 indicate Precision, Recall, and F1-score (expressed in %), respectively. The F1-score is a harmonic average of precision and recall. For these three metrics, a higher value indicates better performance, where the highest score is highlighted in bold.

| Datasets | MSL | | | SMAP | | | PSM | | |
|---|---|---|---|---|---|---|---|---|---|
| Metric | P | R | F1 | P | R | F1 | P | R | F1 |
| ALAD | 52.58 | 95.31 | 68.06 | 53.34 | 59.07 | 56.17 | 61.15 | 93.95 | 74.08 |
| OCSVM | 59.96 | 90.11 | 65.41 | 53.91 | 59.07 | 56.37 | 78.52 | 90.21 | 83.96 |
| SO_GAAL | 89.94 | 90.34 | 61.78 | 67.28 | 53.30 | 59.48 | 46.25 | 49.59 | 47.86 |
| LSTM | 85.45 | 82.50 | 83.95 | 89.41 | 78.13 | 83.39 | 76.93 | 89.64 | 82.80 |
| USAD | 97.95 | 99.12 | 88.57 | 81.39 | 96.27 | 89.74 | 79.62 | 97.29 | 76.53 |
| TRANAD | 96.15 | 99.99 | 94.64 | 80.43 | 98.72 | 89.15 | 81.50 | 98.99 | 95.97 |
| MTAD_GAT | 76.23 | 98.24 | 86.78 | 75.16 | 99.91 | 85.83 | 76.28 | 98.33 | 81.09 |
| Anomaly Transformer | 98.46 | 98.33 | 94.19 | 93.54 | 98.18 | 96.27 | 95.20 | 96.89 | 97.01 |
| **DGFormer** | 98.85 | 97.59 | **94.92** | 94.32 | 98.89 | **96.53** | 97.64 | 98.58 | **98.11** |

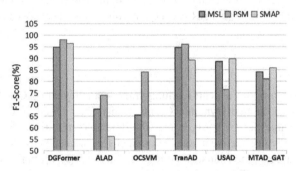

**Fig. 4.** Comparison of F1-score (%) results between DGFormer and partial baseline models on three datasets using bar charts. The MSL, SMPA and PSM datasets are represented in blue, gray, and pink columns, respectively. (Color figure online)

**The Impact of Embedding Strategies on Anomaly Detection Using Dynamic Graph.** In Table 3, DGFormer-one is a DGFormer framework with an all-in-one adjacency matrix. DGFormer-corr is a DGFormer framework with adjacency matrix of correlation coefficients. DGFormer framework has the dynamic adjacency matrix proposed by us. You can see that different adjacency matrices can be used in our DGFormer framework. However, the performance of the all-one matrix is slightly worse than that of the correlation coefficient matrix, and our dynamic matrix achieves the best.

**Hybrid Transformer and GNN Have a Higher Average F1-Score Than Other Combinations.** In Table 3, DGFormer-woAR means that the AR component is removed

**Table 3.** Ablation results of DGFormer (F1-score (%)). Where, DGFormer-one, DGFormer-corr, DGFormer-woAR and DGFormer-woDG represent neural network modules with full adjacency matrix, adjacency matrix with correlation coefficient, no autoregressive module and no dynamic embedded graph, highest scores are highlighted in bold.

| Methods | MSL | SMAP | PSM | Avg F1(as %) |
| --- | --- | --- | --- | --- |
| DGFormer-one | 92.40 | 96.19 | 97.68 | 95.42 |
| DGFormer-corr | 92.69 | 96.50 | 97.65 | 95.61 |
| DGFormer-woAR | 92.35 | 95.48 | 97.29 | 95.04 |
| DGFormer-woDG | 92.82 | 96.47 | 97.33 | 95.54 |
| **DGFormer** | **94.92** | **96.53** | **98.11** | **96.52** |

from the DGFormer model, and DGFormer-woDG means that the dynamic graph embedding and graph neural network segments are removed from the DGFormer model. The complete DGFormer obtains the best results in different batchsizes. It shows that all components contribute to detection performance of the overall model. The performance of DGFormer-woDG has decreased, which indicates that adding GNN to dynamically capture temporal features can improve the timeliness of the model. DGFormer-woAR's performance degradation is even more pronounced, indicating that AR components play a crucial role. The reason is that AR is generally robust to scale changes in the data [32].

## 5   Summary

In this paper, we propose a deep learning framework, Dynamic Graph transFormer (DGFormer), An Effective Dynamic Graph Transformer based Anomaly Detection Model for IoT Time Series. It overcomes the defects of traditional Transformer and GNN, and proposes an effective model to obtain GNN parameters by using Transformer with anomaly attention mechanism, and dynamically capture timing features by learning the graph structure. Finally, by parallelizing an autoregressive model AR, a model with strong interpretability was obtained. DGFormer has achieved state-of-art results on a detailed set of empirical studies. For future research, there is hope to explore and design more powerful graph Transformer that can be incorporated into our DGFormer framework to obtain more expressive performance and further improve the usefulness of our method.

## References

1. Renjie, W., Eamonn, J.K.: Current time series anomaly detection benchmarks are flawed and are creating the illusion of progress. IEEE Trans. Knowl. Data Eng. **35**(3), 2421–2429 (2021)
2. Liang, W., Huang, W., Long, J., et al.: Deep reinforcement learning for resource protection and real-time detection in IoT environment. IEEE Internet Things J. **7**(7), 6392–6401 (2020)
3. Muhammad, S.: Fog computing and its role in the internet of things: concept, security and privacy issues. Int. J. Comput. Appl. **180**(32), 7–9 (2018)

4. Xin, R., Chen, P., Zhao, Z.: CausalRCA: causal inference based precise fine-grained root cause localization for microservice applications. J. Syst. Softw. **203**, 111724 (2023). https://doi.org/10.1016/j.jss.2023.111724

5. Peng, C., et al.: Effectively detecting operational anomalies in large-scale IoT data infrastructures by using a GAN-based predictive model. Comput. J. **65**(11), 2909–2925 (2022)

6. Chandola, V., Banerjee, A., Kumar, V.: Anomaly detection: a survey. ACM Comput. Surv. (CSUR) **41**(3), 1–58 (2009)

7. Zhang, R., Chen, J., Song, Y., Shan, W., Chen, P., Xia, Y.: An effective transformation-encoding-attention framework for multivariate time series anomaly detection in IoT environment. Mob. Netw. Appl. 1–13 (2023). https://doi.org/10.1007/s11036-023-02204-9

8. Tang, M., Fu, X., Wu, H., Huang, Q., Zhao, Q.: Traffic flow anomaly detection based on robust ridge regression with particle swarm optimization algorithm. Math. Prob. Eng. **2020**, 1–10 (2020)

9. Venkatesan, R., et al.: Hyperspectral image features classification using deep learning recurrent neural networks. J. Med. Syst. (2019). https://doi.org/10.1007/s10916-019-1347-9

10. Wu, Y., Dai, H.N., Tang, H.: Graph neural networks for anomaly detection in industrial internet of things. IEEE Internet Things J. **9**(12), 9214–9231 (2021). https://doi.org/10.1109/JIOT.2021.3094295

11. Kahya, E., Theodossiou, P.: Predicting corporate finacial distress: a time-series CUSUM methodology'. Rev. Quant. Finan. Account. **13**(4), 323–345 (1996)

12. Janacek, G.: Time series analysis forecasting and control. J. Time **31**(4), 303 (2010)

13. Chen, Y., Wang, S., Zhao, Q., Sun, G.: Detection of multivariate geochemical anomalies using the bat-optimized isolation forest and bat-optimized elliptic envelope models. J. Earth Sci. **32**(2), 415–426 (2021)

14. Lai, G., Chang, W.C., Yang, Y., Liu, H.: Modeling long-and short-term temporal patterns with deep neural networks. In: International ACM SIGIR Conference on Research and Development in Information Retrieval, pp. 95–104. ACM (2018)

15. Song, Y., Xin, R., Chen, P., Zhang, R., Chen, J., Zhao, Z.: Identifying performance anomalies in fluctuating cloud environments: a robust correlative-GNN-based explainable approach. Future Gener. Comput. Syst. **145**, 77–86 (2023)

16. Park, D., Hoshi, Y., Kemp, C.C.: A multimodal anomaly detector for robot-assisted feeding using an lstm-based variational autoencoder. IEEE Rob. Autom. Lett. **3**(3), 1544–1551 (2018)

17. Fazle, K., Somshubra, M., Houshang, D.: Insights into lstm fully convolutional networks for time series classification. IEEE Access **7**, 67718–67725 (2019)

18. Zhang, X., Gao, Y., Lin, J., et al.: TapNet: multivariate time series classification with attentional prototypical network. In: Proceedings of the AAAI Conference on Artificial Intelligence, vol. 34, pp. 6845–6852 (2020)

19. Schuster, M., Paliwal, K.K.: Bidirectional recurrent neural networks. IEEE Trans. Signal Process. **45**(11), 2673–2681 (1997)

20. Cho, K., et al.: Learning phrase representations using RNN encoder-decoder for statistical machine translation (2014). https://doi.org/10.3115/v1/D14-1179

21. Shen, L., Li, Z., Kwok, J.: Timeseries anomaly detection using temporal hierarchical one-class network. Adv. Neural Inf. Process. Syst. **33**, 13016–13026 (2020)

22. Mehdi, M., Bing, X., et al.: Generative adversarial networks. Commun. ACM **63**, 139–144 (2020)

23. Qi, S., Chen, J., Chen, P., Wen, P., Niu, X., Xu, L.: An efficient GAN-based predictive framework for multivariate time series anomaly prediction in cloud data centers. J. Supercomput. 1–26 (2023). https://doi.org/10.1007/s11227-023-05534-3

24. Xavier, B., et al.: A generalization of Transformer networks to graphs. DLG-AAAI (2020). https://doi.org/10.48550/arXiv.2012.09699

25. Shao, P., He, J., Li, G., Zhang, D., Tao, J.: Hierarchical graph attention network for temporal knowledge graph reasoning. Neurocomputing **550**, 126390 (2023)
26. Devin, K., et al.: Rethinking graph transformers with spectral attention. In: NeurIPS (2021). https://doi.org/10.48550/arXiv.2106.03893
27. Chen, D., et al.: A trainable optimal transport embedding for feature aggregation and its relationship to attention. In: ICLR (2021). https://doi.org/10.48550/arXiv.2006.12065
28. Pan, Y., et al.: A novel approach to scheduling workflows upon cloud resources with fluctuating performance. MONET **25**(2), 690–700 (2020)
29. Chen, P., Xia, Y., Pang, S., Li, J.: A probabilistic model for performance analysis of cloud infrastructures. Concurr. Comput. Pract. Exp. **27**(17), 4784–4796 (2015)
30. Christopher, M.B., et al.: Pattern Recognition and Machine Learning. Springer, New York (2006)
31. Ahmed, A., Zhuanghua, L., Tomer, L.: Practical approach to asynchronous multivariate time series anomaly detection and localization. In: KDD, pp. 2485–2494 (2021)
32. Ya, S., Wei, S., et al.: Robust anomaly detection for multivariate time series through stochastic recurrent neural network. In: SIGKDD Explorations, pp. 2828–2837 (2019)
33. Houssam, Z., Manon, R., Bruno, L., et al.: Adversarially learned anomaly detection. In: IEEE International Conference on Data Mining (ICDM) (2018). https://doi.org/10.1109/ICDM.2018.00088
34. Bernhard, S., et al.: Support vector method for novelty detection. Adv. Neural Inf. Process. Syst. (1999)
35. Liu, Y., Li, Z., Zhou, C., et al.: Generative adversarial active learning for unsupervised outlier detection. IEEE Trans. Knowl. Data Eng. **32**(8), 1517–1528 (2019). https://doi.org/10.1109/TKDE.2019.2905606
36. Julien, A., Pietro, M., Frédéric, G., Sébastien, M., Maria A.Z.: USAD: unsupervised anomaly detection on multivariate time series. In: Proceedings of the 26th ACM SIGKDD International Conference on Knowledge Discovery & Data Mining, pp. 3395–3404 (2020)
37. Martin, S., Ralf, S., Hermann, N.: LSTM neural networks for language modeling. In: Interspeech (2012). https://doi.org/10.1016/0165-6074(89)90269-X
38. Zhao, H., Wang, Y., Duan, J., et al.: Multivariate time-series anomaly detection via graph attention network. In: ICDM (2020). https://doi.org/10.1109/ICDM50108.2020.00093
39. Xu, J., Wu, H., Wang, J., Long, M.: Anomaly transformer: time series anomaly detection with association discrepancy. In: ICLR (2021). arXiv preprint arXiv:2110.02642
40. Giuliano, C.: TranAD: deep Transformer networks for anomaly detection in multivariate time series data. In: Proceedings of the VLDB Endowment (2022). https://doi.org/10.48550/arXiv.2201.07284

# STAPointGNN: Spatial-Temporal Attention Graph Neural Network for Gesture Recognition Using Millimeter-Wave Radar

Jun Zhang[1,3], Chunyu Wang[1], Shunli Wang[1], and Lihua Zhang[1,2,3,4(✉)]

[1] Academy for Engineering and Technology, Fudan University, Shanghai, China
junzhang22@m.fudan.edu.cn, {wangcy20,slwang19,lihuazhang}@fudan.edu.cn
[2] Jilin Provincial Key Laboratory of Intelligence Science and Engineering,
Changchun, China
[3] Engineering Research Center of AI and Robotics, Ministry of Education,
Shanghai, China
[4] Engineering Research Center of AI and Unmanned Vehicle Systems of Jilin
Province, Changchun, China

**Abstract.** Gesture recognition plays a pivotal role in enabling natural and intuitive human-computer interaction (HCI), finding applications in diverse domains such as smart homes, robot control, and virtual reality. Thanks to advances in computer vision, the most popular method currently is to use the camera for gesture recognition. However, the camera struggles to function properly in poor lighting and inclement weather, and risks invading privacy. Due to the robust and non-invasive features of millimeter-wave radar, gesture recognition based on millimeter-wave radar has received extensive attention from researchers in recent years. In this paper, we propose a novel graph neural network named STA-PointGNN for gesture recognition using millimeter-wave radar. In order to better extract features in the spatial and temporal dimensions of point clouds collected by millimeter-wave radar, we designed a spatial-temporal attention mechanism based on graph neural network. We also propose a novel point flow embedding method to capture the motion features of the point clouds in adjacent frames. To verify the superiority of our method, we conduct experiments on two public millimeter-wave radar gesture recognition datasets. The results show that our model outperforms existing mainstream algorithms.

**Keywords:** Human-computer interaction · Millimeter-wave radar · Gesture recognition · Graph neural network · Attention mechanism

## 1 Introduction

Gesture recognition is the key to human-computer interaction (HCI) and has a wide range of applications, such as smart home [6], robot control [3] and virtual

H. Gao et al. (Eds.): CollaborateCom 2023, LNICST 562, pp. 189–204, 2024.
https://doi.org/10.1007/978-3-031-54528-3_11

reality [27], etc. Traditional work uses wearable devices [4,22] for gesture recognition, but it has the obvious disadvantages of not being readily available and uncomfortable to wear. Camera-based approaches [26,28] can avoid the above disadvantages, but the fatal drawback is the risk of privacy leakage, which will not be used in some scenarios with high privacy requirements. To realize natural HCI, researchers turn their attention to wireless sensing devices, such as Wi-Fi signals [10,40]. However, this solution is unable to recognize fine-grained gestures and is susceptible to interference from the surrounding environment. Beyond Wi-Fi signals, millimeter-wave radar as another wireless sensing device is gradually attracting extensive attention from researchers due to its unique advantages. Compared to other wireless sensors, millimeter-wave radar has better fine resolution of range and velocity, and has a certain penetration. Millimeter-wave radar can work in all-weather conditions, including rain, fog and low-light environments. Moreover, millimeter-wave signals, as the main venue of 5G technology, will be deployed on a huge number of IoT devices and smart home appliances, promising to become a ubiquitous sensing device.

There have been some studies on gesture recognition using millimeter-wave radar. MHomeGes [18] customizes a lightweight convolution neural network for millimeter-wave gesture recognition in smart homes. M-Gesture [19] proposes a person-independent real-time millimeter-wave gesture recognition solution and releases the MMGesture dataset. MTransSee [17] proposes a novel transfer-learning approach that can achieve decent recognition accuracy for new users using fewer training samples. However, all of the above tasks require manually designing the inputs to the network and ignore the 3D coordinate information, and more importantly they do not consider the connection between adjacent frames.

Compared with existing methods [17–19] that manually design network input and use convolutional neural network (CNN) processing, we retain the 3D coordinate of the original point and process data from the perspective of point cloud, which can make full use of spatial information. Unlike LiDAR, the point clouds captured by millimeter-wave radar in each frame are sparse and uneven, which increases the complexity of neural network structure design [8]. We use graph neural network (GNN) to extract point cloud features because graph constitutes a succinct, abstractive, and intuitively apprehensible mathematical representation delineating entities and their interconnections. Several studies [8,34] have demonstrated the effectiveness of adopting GNN to process sparse point clouds collected by millimeter-wave radar.

In this work, we propose a novel graph neural network named STAPointGNN for gesture recognition using millimeter-wave radar. Inspired by the success of attention mechanism in natural language processing [33] and image processing [21], we designed a spatial-temporal attention mechanism based on graph neural network, which better extracts features in the spatial and temporal dimensions of sparse point clouds collected by millimeter-wave radar. Moreover, since gesture movements are continuous, the information between adjacent frames has great potential for capturing motion features. Motivated by [12], we propose a novel point flow embedding method designed for millimeter-wave radar point clouds, which can efficiently capture the motion features of the point clouds in adjacent frames. The proposed method is evaluated on the MMGesture dataset [19] and the MTransSee dataset [17], achieving the state-of-the-art accuracy.

In summary, the main contributions of this work are as follows:

- We propose a spatial-temporal attention graph neural network (STAPoint-GNN) for point cloud processing.
- We propose a novel point flow embedding method designed for millimeter-wave radar point clouds, which can efficiently capture the motion features of the point clouds in adjacent frames.
- We propose an end-to-end model for gesture recognition using millimeter-wave radar.

## 2    Related Work

### 2.1    MmWave and Wireless Sensing

With the rapid development of 5G, non-contact wireless sensing devices have gradually become a research hotspot. WiFall [37] implements a device-free fall detection system using WiFi signals to detect the fall of the elderly. WiTrack [1] is a WiFi-based system that enables precise 3D motion tracking through reflected radio signals. Chen et al. [5] uses FM broadcast radio signals for robust indoor localization.

Compared with other wireless sensing devices, millimeter-wave radar has attracted much attention due to its advantages of higher range and velocity resolution, penetrating capability, fine-grained and robust sensing ability. Millimeter-wave radar can be used for simultaneous localization and environment mapping, due to its high localization accuracy and obstacle detection capability [39]. MBeats [42] is a robot-mounted millimeter wave radar system for dynamic heart rate monitoring during diverse user activities. In addition, there are many other research areas of millimeter-wave radar such as human activity recognition [8,31], gesture recognition [17–19] and gait recognition [12,34].

### 2.2    Gesture Recognition

Gestures are a form of non-verbal communication that can be used in a variety of areas such as robot control, human-computer interaction and home automation. There are many sensing technologies used for gesture recognition. Data gloves as a wearable device are a common form of implementing gesture recognition [7,14]. Vision-based gesture recognition is a relatively mature technique that utilizes a camera to capture a scene containing a gesture, and then uses computer vision algorithms to recognize, extract, and classify the image [13,16,32]. WiG [10] utilizes WiFi signals for gesture recognition. In addition, there are researchers using surface electromyography [15] and ultrasound [11] for gesture recognition.

Gesture recognition through millimeter-wave radar has garnered noteworthy academic attention. Due to the diversity of data captured by millimeter-wave radar, current research can be broadly categorized into three categories. The first way uses range doppler images, range angle image or doppler angle image [2,35,38]. However, this approach does not fully utilize the three-dimensional coordinate information. The second approach is to manually design the inputs to the model [18,19]. Nevertheless, hand-designed features need to be carefully designed by experienced domain experts, and the quality of the design features directly determines the model accuracy. The third method is to utilize point cloud data [20], which can fully leverage spatial information. The method proposed in this paper deals directly with point clouds and belongs to the third.

### 2.3   Graph Neural Network

CNN is suitable for processing images, recurrent neural network is suitable for processing sequential data. However, these two networks are not suitable for directly processing point clouds. Point clouds can be naturally viewed as graph structures and thus processed using graph neural networks. Point-GNN [29] is the first work to use graph neural networks to process point clouds. In millimeter-wave radar-based human activity recognition, RADHAR [31] uses CNN to process voxelized representations of point clouds, however, this is computationally prohibitive, and MMPoint-GNN [8] uses graphs to represent point clouds and achieves better results on the same dataset. In millimeter-wave radar-based gait recognition, STPointGCN [34] uses graph convolutional networks to extract features from point clouds superior to mmGait [23] using CNN. The temporal edges in STPointGCN are similar to the temporal attention module of our proposed method. A certain point in STPointGCN is only connected to the closest point in the adjacent frames. However, in our proposed method, a certain point is connected to all points in the adjacent frames and the connection is learned through the attention mechanism.

In this work, we propose a new graph neural network which is suitable for extracting spatial-temporal features of sparse point clouds collected by millimeter-wave radar. Specially, we designed a spatial-temporal attention mechanism based on graph neural network, which effectively integrates the attention mechanism into graph neural network. Moreover, we propose a novel point flow embedding method designed for millimeter-wave radar point clouds, which can efficiently capture the motion features of the point clouds in adjacent frames.

## 3   Method

### 3.1   Point Flow Embedding

The data generated by millimeter-wave radar is usually returned in the form of frames, with each frame containing several points and each point containing several features. Formally, we define a frame containing $N$ points as a set $P = \{p_1, p_2, \ldots, p_N\}$, where $p_i = (x_i, s_i)$ denotes a point with 3D coordinates $x_i \in \mathbb{R}^3$ and state features $s_i \in \mathbb{R}^k$. In this work, $s_i$ contains two properties, the doppler velocity $v_i$ and the reflection intensity $\epsilon_i$. So $p_i$ can be represented as $p_i = (x_i, v_i, \epsilon_i)$.

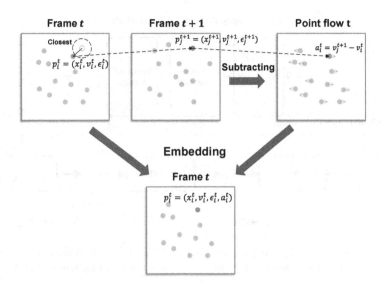

**Fig. 1.** Point flow embedding method.

Optical flow has been shown to be effective in the field of video based human action recognition [30]. It can effectively capture the features of motion. Gesture recognition as a subtask of human action recognition also has the above properties. Video based and millimeter-wave radar based gesture recognition are very similar, both consisting of many frames of data. The difference is that the former frame is an image, while the latter frame is a point cloud. On the other hand, millimeter wave radar senses the target at a certain sampling rate and therefore loses the information between two adjacent frames. Inspired by [12], We use point flow to capture motion information between adjacent frames.

Here is the specific description of point flow embedding method. As shown in Fig. 1, take two adjacent frames $P^t$ and $P^{t+1}$ as examples. For a certain point in the frame $P^t$, denoted as $p_i^t$, to find the motion relationship between adjacent frames, we find the point with the closest spatial distance to it in the frame $P^{t+1}$, denoted as $p_j^{t+1}$. Subtracting the doppler velocity of these two points, we obtain the characteristic of acceleration $a_i^t = v_j^{t+1} - v_i^t$. Then add acceleration as an additional property to the state features of the point cloud, so now the point $p_i^t$ can be represented as $p_i^t = (x_i^t, v_i^t, \epsilon_i^t, a_i^t)$. Then we take the point clouds through point flow embedding method as the input of model.

## 3.2  STAPointGNN

The overall architecture of the proposed STAPointGNN is illustrated in Fig. 2. The whole network consists of three components: (a) spatial-temporal feature extraction, (b) temporal aggregation and (c) classification. Given several frames of raw point clouds, a module composed of PointGNN, spatial attention, and

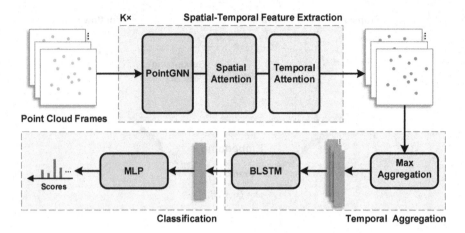

**Fig. 2.** The overall architecture of proposed STAPointGNN. It consists of three components: (a) spatial-temporal feature extraction, (b) temporal aggregation and (c) classification.

temporal attention extracts spatial-temporal features. After $K$ iterations, we use max aggregation with each frame to obtain feature vectors representing each frame, then use bidirectional LSTM to further extract features from the time dimension. Finally, the output of bidirectional LSTM is processed through multi-layer perceptron (MLP) to obtain the prediction probabilities of different gestures. Next, we will introduce PointGNN and spatial-temporal attention in detail.

### 3.3    PointGNN

Unlike LiDAR, the points collected by millimeter-wave radar are sparse. We don't need to use voxel downsampling like [29] for the graph construction. The proposed method directly construct each point in the point cloud as each vertex in the graph. We use state features $s_i$ as the initial vertex features. Then, we construct a fully connected graph $G(P, E)$ using $P$ as vertices and define edges as:

$$E = \{(p_i, p_j) \mid i, j \in N\} \tag{1}$$

In an image, the convolution operation updates the current pixel value through adjacent pixel values. Similarly, message passing in a graph structure can be achieved by aggregating features along the edges [29]. Figure 3 takes the central vertex as an example to show the process of one iteration of PointGNN. In the $(k + 1)^{th}$ iteration, the features of vertex are represented as follows:

$$\begin{aligned} v_i^{k+1} &= g^k(\rho(\{e_{ji}^k \mid (j, i) \in E\}), v_i^k) \\ e_{ji}^k &= f^k(v_i^k, v_j^k) \end{aligned} \tag{2}$$

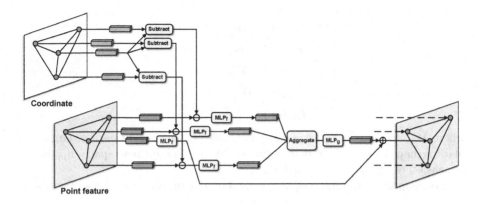

**Fig. 3.** Architecture of the proposed PointGNN. It takes the central vertex as an example to show the process of one iteration of PointGNN.

where $v_i^k$ represents the vertex features of vertex $i$ in the $k^{th}$ iteration, $e_{ji}^k$ represents the features of the directed edge from vertex $j$ to vertex $i$ in the $k^{th}$ iteration. $f^k(\cdot)$ calculates the edge features between two vertices. $\rho(\cdot)$ is a permutation invariant function, which can be $Max$, $Mean$ or $Sum$ operations, used to aggregate the features of edges for each vertex. $g^k(\cdot)$ updates vertex features using aggregated edge features.

We use relative coordinates to extract edge features and model $f^k(\cdot)$ using MLP. Specifically, the difference between vertex $i$ coordinates $x_i$ and vertex $j$ coordinates $x_j$ is concatenated onto vertex $j$ features $v_j$, and then MLP is used to update the edge features:

$$e_{ji}^k = MLP_f^k(cat(x_i - x_j, v_j^k)) \tag{3}$$

We use the $Max$ operation as $\rho(\cdot)$ to aggregate edge features, model $g^k(\cdot)$ using MLP to update vertex features, and add a residual connection in $g^k(\cdot)$:

$$v_i^{k+1} = MLP_g^k(Max(\{e_{ji}^k \mid (j,i) \in E\})) + v_i^k \tag{4}$$

### 3.4 Spatial-Temporal Attention

After PointGNN, the vertex features are further extracted through the spatial-temporal attention module. The spatial attention module is shown in Fig. 4.

Similar to natural language processing tasks, we treat a frame of point cloud as a sentence and each point as a token. For the spatial attention, we adopt the self-attention introduced in Transformer [33], as shown in Fig. 4. We define the dimension of the input feature and the dimension of the output feature as $d_i$ and $d_o$, respectively. Let $\boldsymbol{Q}$, $\boldsymbol{K}$, and $\boldsymbol{V}$ represent *query*, *key*, and *value* respectively. They are respectively passed through a linear transformation by the input feature $\boldsymbol{F}_{in} \in \mathbb{R}^{N \times d_i}$ as follows:

$$Q = F_{in} \cdot W_q$$
$$K = F_{in} \cdot W_k$$
$$V = F_{in} \cdot W_v \quad (5)$$
$$W_q, W_k, W_v \in \mathbb{R}^{d_i \times d_m}$$
$$Q, K, V \in \mathbb{R}^{N \times d_m}$$

where $W_q$, $W_k$, and $W_v$ are shared learnable linear transformation, aiming to place semantically similar points closer together in the new space. $d_m$ is the dimension of the query, key, and value.

We compute attention weights via matrix dot product using query and key:

$$\tilde{A} = Q \cdot K^T, \quad \tilde{A} \in \mathbb{R}^{N \times N} \quad (6)$$

Divide $\tilde{A}$ by $d_m$, and apply softmax function for normalization:

$$A = softmax(\frac{\tilde{A}}{\sqrt{d_m}}), \quad A \in \mathbb{R}^{N \times N} \quad (7)$$

We use the attention score and value to do dot product to get the attention output feature. In order to meet the requirements of the output dimension, we add MLP transformation with residual connection:

$$F_{out} = MLP(A \cdot V) + MLP(F_{in}), \quad F_{out} \in \mathbb{R}^{N \times d_o} \quad (8)$$

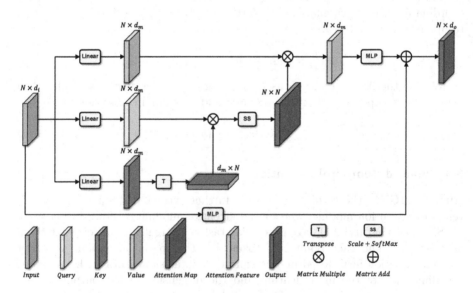

**Fig. 4.** Architecture of the proposed spatial attention module.

For the temporal attention module, the input is two adjacent frames, as shown in Fig. 5. For a certain point $p_j^{t+1}$ in the frame $P^{t+1}$, all points features in the frame $P^t$ are weighted and summed to update $p_j^{t+1}$.

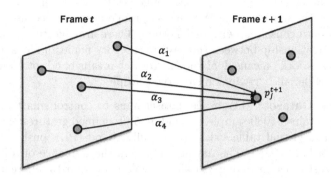

**Fig. 5.** Illustration of temporal attention module. For a certain point $p_j^{t+1}$ in the frame $P^{t+1}$, all points features in the frame $P^t$ are weighted and summed to update $p_j^{t+1}$.

In terms of specific implementation, we still use the spatial attention module, just set point features in frame $P^{t+1}$ as *query*, point features in the frame $P^t$ as *key* and *value*.

### 3.5  Loss Function

Gesture recognition is a multi-class classification task, softmax and cross entropy are adopted as the loss function:

$$loss(y, c) = -\log(\frac{\exp{(y[c])}}{\sum_{i=0}^{C-1} \exp{(y[i])}})$$
$$= -y[c] + \log(\sum_{i=0}^{C-1} \exp{(y[i])}) \tag{9}$$

where $C$ is the number of gesture categories, $c$ is the ground truth label, $y = [y_0, y_1, \ldots, y_{n-1}]$ is the confidence vector predicted by the model.

## 4  Experiments

### 4.1  Datasets

We use two public gesture datasets MMGesture dataset [19] and MTransSee dataset [17] to evaluate our proposed STAPointGNN method.

**MMGesture Dataset**[1] MMGesture dataset is the first gesture dataset collected with millimeter-wave radar. It has 56420 gesture sample instances with a total duration of 1357 min involving 144 volunteers (64 men and 80 women). The dataset contains two scenarios, short range gesture (less than 0.5m) for interacting with accessory devices and long range gesture (between 2m and 5m) for interacting with smart homes. We use long range gestures because it provides point cloud data consistent with our method. There are 4 gestures, and the corresponding relationship between the gesture category name and its actual action is as follows: "knock" means dual knock, "rotate" means hand rotation, "lswipe" means left swipe, and "rswipe" means right swipe.

**MTransSee Dataset**[2] MTransSee dataset aims to control smart home appliances and contains 54080 samples, including 5 predefined gestures: draw a circle (CR), knock a virtual table twice (KO), pull a hand (PL), push a hand (PS) and lift up a hand (UP). The dataset considers the influence of different user habits and distances, involving 32 different volunteers and 13 different distances between 1.2m and 4.8m. In addition, the influence of the reflection of uneven objects on the data collected by the millimeter-wave radar is also considered. Volunteers perform gestures near different objects: such as chair, metal table, metal oven, TV, etc.

## 4.2 Implementation Details

We divide the dataset into training and testing set in proportion 80% and 20%. We use a sliding window with length $T = 20$ and moving step s $= 20$ to generate the data to fit the model input. Since the point flow is only calculated in adjacent frames, one input sample contains 19 frames.

Spatial-temporal feature extraction module repeats for 3 iterations, where the feature dimensions for each iteration are [16, 64, 128]. In the temporal aggregation module, the LSTM used is a bidirectional LSTM with 1 layer and 16 hidden units. The optimizer is Adam and the initial learning rate is 0.001. We implement the model in PyTorch.

## 4.3 Experimental Results

We evaluated different benchmark algorithms on two datasets including PointNet [24] combined with LSTM, PointNet++ [25] combined with LSTM, Point cloud transformer [9] combined with LSTM, Point Transformer [41] combined with LSTM and DGCNN [36] combined with LSTM. In Table 1, the results of methods [1–3] are baselines from [8], including PointNet combined with LSTM, Point-GNN combined with LSTM and MMPoint-GNN combined with LSTM.

Table 1 reports the accuracy of different algorithms on MMGesture dataset. The best baseline on MMGesture dataset is MMPoint-GNN + LSTM, achieving 92.67% accuracy. MMPoint-GNN has strong spatial feature extraction ability

---

[1] https://github.com/fengxudi/mmWave-gesture-dataset.
[2] https://github.com/mmTransGes/mTransSee_Dataset.

**Table 1.** Test accuracy of different algorithms on MMGesture dataset.

| S. No | Method | Accuracy (%) |
|---|---|---|
| 1 | PointNet + LSTM | 61.51 |
| 2 | Point-GNN + LSTM | 92.10 |
| 3 | MMPoint-GNN + LSTM | 92.67 |
| 4 | PointNet++ + LSTM | 89.62 |
| 5 | Point cloud transformer + LSTM | 87.09 |
| 6 | Point Transformer + LSTM | 91.66 |
| 7 | DGCNN + LSTM | 88.03 |
| 8 | **STAPointGNN (Ours)** | **94.61** |

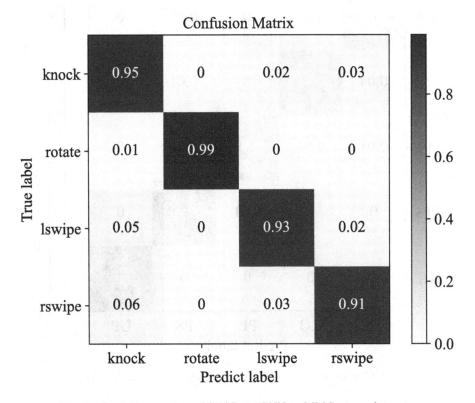

**Fig. 6.** Confusion matrix of STAPointGNN in MMGesture dataset.

**Table 2.** Test accuracy of different algorithms on MTransSee dataset.

| S. No | Method | Accuracy (%) |
|---|---|---|
| 1 | PointNet + LSTM | 95.45 |
| 2 | PointNet++ + LSTM | 95.96 |
| 3 | Point cloud transformer + LSTM | 93.57 |
| 4 | Point Transformer + LSTM | 96.67 |
| 5 | DGCNN + LSTM | 96.11 |
| 6 | **STAPointGNN (Ours)** | **97.56** |

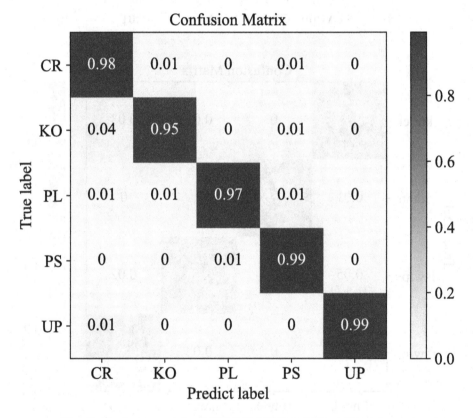

**Fig. 7.** Confusion matrix of STAPointGNN in MTransSee dataset.

due to its dynamic edge design [8]. Among other comparative algorithms such as PointNet++ + LSTM, Point cloud transformer + LSTM, Point Transformer + LSTM and DGCNN + LSTM, only Point Transformer + LSTM has an accuracy rate exceeding 90%, reaching 91.66%, but it is still inferior to MMPoint-GNN + LSTM. However, our method STAPointGNN achieves an accuracy of 94.61%, surpassing MMPoint-GNN + LSTM by about 2%, which is currently the state-of-the-art method on MMGesture dataset. Figure 6 shows the confusion matrix of STAPointGNN in MMGesture dataset. It can be seen that our method can accurately distinguish various gestures. Rotate is the easiest action to distinguish because it is distinctly different from the other gestures. Left swipe and right swipe gestures are difficult to distinguish because they are similar except that they move in opposite directions. Moreover, left swipe and right swipe are easily recognized as dual knock.

Table 2 reports the accuracy of different algorithms on MTransSee dataset. The different algorithms perform well on this dataset compared to the previous dataset, all exceeding 93% accuracy. Mainly because the dataset has more samples and considers the influence of distance. The method PointNet + LSTM based on the set representation reached 95.45%, and the improved PointNet++ + LSTM based on PointNet + LSTM reached 95.96%. The method based on graph representation DGCNN + LSTM reached 96.11%, which shows that GNN is more suitable for the extraction of millimeter-wave radar point cloud features. The Point Transformer + LSTM of the attention-based method reaches 96.67%, which shows that the attention mechanism is effective. Our method STAPoint-GNN achieves 97.56%, surpassing the best baseline by about 1%. The confusion matrix of STAPointGNN in MTransSee dataset is shown in Fig. 7. Overall, although the number of gesture categories increases, the classification accuracy of gestures generally improves. PS and UP gestures are the most easily recognized gestures, while KO is easily recognized as CR.

Compared to existing methods, STAPointGNN incorporates graph neural networks and attention mechanisms to establish associations between adjacent frames, which can extract spatial and temporal features more efficiently. As a result, STAPointGNN excels in the field of millimeter-wave radar gesture recognition.

## 5   Conclusion

In this paper, we propose a novel graph neural network named STAPointGNN for gesture recognition using millimeter-wave radar. Our method based on spatial-temporal attention mechanism of graph neural network can extract spatial and temporal features of point clouds generated by millimeter-wave radar more efficiently. In addition, we propose a novel point flow embedding method to capture the motion features of the point clouds in adjacent frames. In the public datasets MMGesture and MTransSee, our method achieves leading accuracy compared to existing methods. In the future, we will consider real-time and multi-person gesture recognition issues to get closer to real scenarios.

**Acknowledgement.** This work was supported by National Key R&D Program of China (2021ZD0113502) and Shanghai Municipal Science and Technology Major Project (2021SHZDZX0103).

# References

1. Adib, F., Kabelac, Z., Katabi, D., Miller, R.C.: 3D tracking via body radio reflections. In: 11th USENIX Symposium on Networked Systems Design and Implementation (NSDI 14), pp. 317–329 (2014)
2. Ali, A., et al.: End-to-end dynamic gesture recognition using mmWave radar. IEEE Access 10, 88692–88706 (2022)
3. Van den Bergh, M., et al.: Real-time 3D hand gesture interaction with a robot for understanding directions from humans. In: 2011 Ro-Man, pp. 357–362. IEEE (2011)
4. Chen, L., Zhang, Y., Peng, L.: METIER: a deep multi-task learning based activity and user recognition model using wearable sensors. Proceedings of the ACM on Interactive, Mobile, Wearable and Ubiquitous Technologies 4(1), 1–18 (2020)
5. Chen, Y., Lymberopoulos, D., Liu, J., Priyantha, B.: FM-based indoor localization. In: Proceedings of the 10th International Conference on Mobile Systems, Applications, and Services, pp. 169–182 (2012)
6. Desai, S., Desai, A.: Human computer interaction through hand gestures for home automation using microsoft kinect. In: Modi, N., Verma, P., Trivedi, B. (eds.) Human computer interaction through hand gestures for home automation using microsoft kinect. AISC, vol. 508, pp. 19–29. Springer, Singapore (2017). https://doi.org/10.1007/978-981-10-2750-5_3
7. Fang, B., Sun, F., Liu, H., Liu, C.: 3D human gesture capturing and recognition by the IMMU-based data glove. Neurocomputing 277, 198–207 (2018)
8. Gong, P., Wang, C., Zhang, L.: MMPoint-GNN: graph neural network with dynamic edges for human activity recognition through a millimeter-wave radar. In: 2021 International Joint Conference on Neural Networks (IJCNN), pp. 1–7. IEEE (2021)
9. Guo, M.H., Cai, J.X., Liu, Z.N., Mu, T.J., Martin, R.R., Hu, S.M.: PCT: Point cloud transformer. Comput. Vis. Media 7, 187–199 (2021)
10. He, W., Wu, K., Zou, Y., Ming, Z.: WiG: WiFi-based gesture recognition system. In: 2015 24th International Conference on Computer Communication and Networks (ICCCN), pp. 1–7. IEEE (2015)
11. Hettiarachchi, N., Ju, Z., Liu, H.: A new wearable ultrasound muscle activity sensing system for dexterous prosthetic control. In: 2015 IEEE International Conference on Systems, Man, and Cybernetics, pp. 1415–1420. IEEE (2015)
12. Huang, Y., Wang, Y., Shi, K., Gu, C., Fu, Y., Zhuo, C., Shi, Z.: HDNet: hierarchical dynamic network for gait recognition using millimeter-wave radar. In: ICASSP 2023–2023 IEEE International Conference on Acoustics, Speech and Signal Processing (ICASSP), pp. 1–5. IEEE (2023)
13. Indra, D., Madenda, S., Wibowo, E.P., et al.: Indonesian sign language recognition based on shape of hand gesture. Procedia Comput. Sci. 161, 74–81 (2019)
14. Kakoty, N.M., Sharma, M.D.: Recognition of sign language alphabets and numbers based on hand kinematics using a data glove. Procedia Comput. Sci. 133, 55–62 (2018)
15. Ketykó, I., Kovács, F., Varga, K.Z.: Domain adaptation for semg-based gesture recognition with recurrent neural networks. In: 2019 International Joint Conference on Neural Networks (IJCNN), pp. 1–7. IEEE (2019)
16. Lin, J., Ding, Y.: A temporal hand gesture recognition system based on hog and motion trajectory. Optik 124(24), 6795–6798 (2013)

17. Liu, H., et al.: mTranssee: enabling environment-independent mmWave sensing based gesture recognition via transfer learning. Proc. ACM Interact. Mobile, Wearable Ubiquitous Technol. **6**(1), 1–28 (2022)
18. Liu, H., et al.: Real-time arm gesture recognition in smart home scenarios via millimeter wave sensing. Proc. ACM Interact. Mobile, Wearable and Ubiquitous Technol. **4**(4), 1–28 (2020)
19. Liu, H., et al.: M-gesture: Person-independent real-time in-air gesture recognition using commodity millimeter wave radar. IEEE Internet Things J. **9**(5), 3397–3415 (2021)
20. Liu, Yu., Wang, Y., Liu, H., Zhou, A., Liu, J., Yang, N.: Long-range gesture recognition using millimeter wave radar. In: Yu, Z., Becker, C., Xing, G. (eds.) GPC 2020. LNCS, vol. 12398, pp. 30–44. Springer, Cham (2020). https://doi.org/10.1007/978-3-030-64243-3_3
21. Liu, Z., et al.: Video swin transformer. In: Proceedings of the IEEE/CVF Conference on Computer Vision and Pattern Recognition, pp. 3202–3211 (2022)
22. Lu, Y., Huang, B., Yu, C., Liu, G., Shi, Y.: Designing and evaluating hand-to-hand gestures with dual commodity wrist-worn devices. Proc. ACM Interact., Mobile, Wearable Ubiquitous Technol. **4**(1), 1–27 (2020)
23. Meng, Z., et al.: Gait recognition for co-existing multiple people using millimeter wave sensing. In: Proceedings of the AAAI Conference on Artificial Intelligence, vol. 34, pp. 849–856 (2020)
24. Qi, C.R., Su, H., Mo, K., Guibas, L.J.: PointNet: deep learning on point sets for 3D classification and segmentation. In: Proceedings of the IEEE Conference on Computer Vision and Pattern Recognition (CVPR), pp. 652–660 (2017)
25. Qi, C.R., Yi, L., Su, H., Guibas, L.J.: PointNet++: deep hierarchical feature learning on point sets in a metric space. In: Advances in Neural Information Processing Systems, vol. 30 (2017)
26. Radu, V., Henne, M.: Vision2Sensor: knowledge transfer across sensing modalities for human activity recognition. Proc. ACM Interact., Mobile, Wearable Ubiquitous Technol. **3**(3), 1–21 (2019)
27. Sagayam, K.M., Hemanth, D.J.: Hand posture and gesture recognition techniques for virtual reality applications: a survey. Virtual Reality **21**, 91–107 (2017)
28. Sharp, T., et al.: Accurate, robust, and flexible real-time hand tracking. In: Proceedings of the 33rd Annual ACM Conference on Human Factors in Computing Systems, pp. 3633–3642 (2015)
29. Shi, W., Rajkumar, R.: Point-GNN: graph neural network for 3D object detection in a point cloud. In: Proceedings of the IEEE/CVF Conference on Computer Vision and Pattern Recognition, pp. 1711–1719 (2020)
30. Simonyan, K., Zisserman, A.: Two-stream convolutional networks for action recognition in videos. In: Ghahramani, Z., Welling, M., Cortes, C., Lawrence, N., Weinberger, K. (eds.) Advances in Neural Information Processing Systems, vol. 27. Curran Associates, Inc. (2014)
31. Singh, A.D., Sandha, S.S., Garcia, L., Srivastava, M.: RadHAR: human activity recognition from point clouds generated through a millimeter-wave radar. In: Proceedings of the 3rd ACM Workshop on Millimeter-wave Networks and Sensing Systems, pp. 51–56 (2019)
32. Sun, J.H., Ji, T.T., Zhang, S.B., Yang, J.K., Ji, G.R.: Research on the hand gesture recognition based on deep learning. In: 2018 12th International Symposium on Antennas, Propagation and EM Theory (ISAPE), pp. 1–4. IEEE (2018)
33. Vaswani, A., et al.: Attention is all you need. In: Advances in Neural Information Processing Systems, vol. 30 (2017)

34. Wang, C., Gong, P., Zhang, L.: Stpointgcn: spatial temporal graph convolutional network for multiple people recognition using millimeter-wave radar. In: ICASSP 2022–2022 IEEE International Conference on Acoustics, Speech and Signal Processing (ICASSP), pp. 3433–3437. IEEE (2022)
35. Wang, S., Song, J., Lien, J., Poupyrev, I., Hilliges, O.: Interacting with soli: exploring fine-grained dynamic gesture recognition in the radio-frequency spectrum. In: Proceedings of the 29th Annual Symposium on User Interface Software and Technology, pp. 851–860 (2016)
36. Wang, Y., Sun, Y., Liu, Z., Sarma, S.E., Bronstein, M.M., Solomon, J.M.: Dynamic graph CNN for learning on point clouds. ACM Trans. Graph. (tog) **38**(5), 1–12 (2019)
37. Wang, Y., Wu, K., Ni, L.M.: WiFall: device-free fall detection by wireless networks. IEEE Trans. Mob. Comput. **16**(2), 581–594 (2016)
38. Yan, B., Wang, P., Du, L., Chen, X., Fang, Z., Wu, Y.: mmGesture: semi-supervised gesture recognition system using mmWave radar. Expert Syst. Appl. **213**, 119042 (2023)
39. Yassin, A., Nasser, Y., Al-Dubai, A.Y., Awad, M.: MOSAIC: simultaneous localization and environment mapping using mmWave without a-priori knowledge. IEEE Access **6**, 68932–68947 (2018)
40. Yu, N., Wang, W., Liu, A.X., Kong, L.: QGesture: quantifying gesture distance and direction with WiFi signals. Proc. ACM Interact. Mobile, Wearable Ubiquitous Technol. **2**(1), 1–23 (2018)
41. Zhao, H., Jiang, L., Jia, J., Torr, P.H., Koltun, V.: Point transformer. In: Proceedings of the IEEE/CVF International Conference on Computer Vision, pp. 16259–16268 (2021)
42. Zhao, P., et al.: Heart rate sensing with a robot mounted mmWave radar. In: 2020 IEEE International Conference on Robotics and Automation (ICRA), pp. 2812–2818. IEEE (2020)

# NPGraph: An Efficient Graph Computing Model in NUMA-Based Persistent Memory Systems

Baoke Li[1,2], Cong Cao[1], Fangfang Yuan[1], Yuling Yang[1,2], Majing Su[3], Yanbing Liu[1(✉)], and Jianhui Fu[4]

[1] Institute of Information Engineering, Chinese Academy of Sciences, Beijing 100085, China
{libaoke,caocong,yangyuling,yuanfangfang,liuyanbing}@iie.ac.cn
[2] School of Cyber Security, University of Chinese Academy of Sciences, Beijing 100085, China
[3] The 6th Research Institute of China Electronic Corporations, Beijing, China
sumj@ncse.com.cn
[4] Shandong Institutes of Industrial Technology, Jinan, China

**Abstract.** The massive volume and the inherent imbalance of graphs are inevitable challenges for efficient graph computing, primarily due to the limited capacity of main memory (DRAM). Fortunately, a promising solution has emerged in the form of hybrid memory systems (HMS) which combine DRAM and persistent memory (PMEM) to enable data-centric graph computing. However, directly transitioning existing DRAM-based models to HMS can lead to inefficiency issues, especially when crossing Non-Uniform Memory Access (NUMA) nodes. In this paper, we present NPGraph, a novel approach that fully exploits the advantages of HMS for in-memory graph computing models. The main contributions of NPGraph lie in three aspects. Firstly, a dual-block graph representation strategy is devised to accelerate the process of subgraph construction. By utilizing data layering, it fully utilizes the storage architecture of HMS and optimizes the data access process. Secondly, an adaptive push-pull update strategy is proposed to optimize the message-updating process. With data-driven algorithms, it dynamically migrates subgraphs which are used in future iterations. Thirdly, the effectiveness of NPGraph is evaluated on five public graph data sets. Our model can improve the temporal locality and the spatial locality of graph computing concurrently. Extensive evaluation results show that NPGraph outperforms state-of-the-art graph computing models by 21.67%–32.03%.

**Keywords:** Graph computing · Adaptive updating strategy · Data-driven algorithms · Hybrid memory · NUMA

## 1 Introduction

In recent years, with the rapid development of artificial intelligence, graph computing has received wide attention. It plays significant roles in a spectrum of

H. Gao et al. (Eds.): CollaborateCom 2023, LNICST 562, pp. 205–222, 2024.
https://doi.org/10.1007/978-3-031-54528-3_12

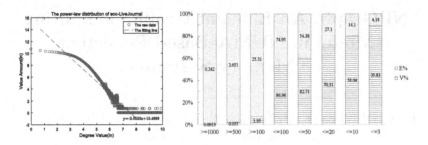

**Fig. 1.** The power-law analysis and degree distribution in soc-LiveJournal.

fields, ranging from relationship analysis and product recommendation to fraud detection. All these applications benefit from the advantages of graph computing: the flexibility of data modeling, the feasibility of pattern mining, and the visibility of association analysis.

However, with the rapid development of the internet and digital technology, the volume of graph data has grown exponentially which leads to an enormous memory footprint. For example, the foundation model GPT-3 has more than 175 billion parameters in deep learning networks. In addition to the enormous volume, graphs frequently display imbalanced distribution. In most cases, the degree distribution and vertex count satisfy the linear fitting relationship: $ln(Vertex) = ln(c) - rln(Degree)$. When $r$ approaches 2, the graph displays a power-law characteristic. Figure 1 illustrates that in soc-LiveJournal, $r = 2.05$. In particular, 25% of the edges are connected to the top 2% of vertices. However, just 4% of the edges are connected to the bottom 36% of vertices. The inherent imbalanced characteristic can lead to load imbalance and parallel inefficiency.

To process the inherent challenges, many in-memory systems (e.g., Pregel [4], GraphLab [5] and HyVE [16]) provide large aggregated memory to avoid the overhead of disk I/O [2,19,28]. Some distributed in-memory systems like GraphX [6], Gemini [8,10] parallel process subgraphs to improve the scalability of the single-machine systems. As a kind of precious storage resource, DRAM is very expensive. Thus, its high price and low cost performance have seriously hampered the use of in-memory systems. NUMA-based systems such as Ligra [7] and GraphOne [9] are promising solutions for developing parallel graph computing on multi-core systems. Although the performance of these models can meet some basic demands, DRAM also must be large enough to accommodate all the graph data, which severely restricts the use of models for in-memory graph computation.

Recently, with the release of Intel Optane Persistent Memory, the research on persistent memory (PMEM) has made significant progress [11,20,21]. The new memory devices and traditional DRAM compose the hybrid memory systems (HMS) which are feasible solutions for large-scale data-centric applications [30]. Therefore, PMEM can be used in NUMA-based graph computing models to reduce the amount of DRAM and improve the scalability of in-memory graph computing systems.

However, the phenomenon of incommensurate scaling has always existed in computer systems. That is to say, there are definitely performance gaps between DRAM and PMEM. Compared to DRAM, PMEM shows low bandwidth and high read/write latency, as shown in Table 1. These performance gaps mean that the DRAM-based graph computing models might not be optimized in HMS [16, 17, 29]. As a result, properly using the benefits of NUMA-based graph computing models in HMS becomes critical.

Table 1. The features of PMEM compared to DRAM and SATA SSD.

| Device | Operation | Bandwidth | Latency | Standby Power |
|--------|-----------|-----------|---------|---------------|
| DRAM | Read | 14.5 GB/s | 81 ns | Fresh Power |
| | Write | 14.5 GB/s | 86 ns | |
| PMEM | Read | 7.45 GB/s | 170 ns | Zero Power |
| | Write | 2.25 GB/s | 320 ns | |
| SATA SSD | Read | 560 MB/s | 10–100 μs | Zero Power |
| | Write | 510 MB/s | 10–100 μs | |

In this paper, we propose NPGraph which is a novel and effective NUMA-based graph computing model specially developed in HMS. It utilizes a dual-block graph representation strategy to support the adaptive push-pull strategy. During the iteration process, it designs data-driven algorithms and a dynamic data migration strategy to optimize the overall performance. To the best of our knowledge, this is the first work to optimize the process of subgraph construction and the message updating model simultaneously. To summarize, the following are the primary contributions of our work:

- NPGraph adopts a lightweight compressed dual-block graph representation strategy to optimize the process of subgraph construction. Specifically, it separately stores the out-blocks and in-blocks of subgraphs in two NUMA nodes. By utilizing data layering in HMS, it restricts data access to specific out-blocks or in-blocks for different updating models.
- NPGraph provides an adaptive push-pull updating strategy to accommodate different data-driven algorithms. According to the activity of subgraphs, it adaptively selects the optimal updating strategy. Then, it dynamically migrates subgraphs which are used in future iterations.
- The effectiveness of NPGraph is thoroughly evaluated on 5 real-world graphs. It can improve the temporal locality and the spatial locality of graph computing at the same time. Extensive experimental results show that NPGraph outperforms state-of-the-art graph computing models by 21.67%–32.03%.

## 2    Background and Motivation

In this section, we first introduce the performance gaps between PMEM and traditional DRAM. Then, inspired by GraphChi [1], we obtain the optimization process of subgraph construction. Finally, we present prominent features of the adaptive push-pull model and the data-driven algorithms. All of these motivate us to propose an efficient graph computing model: NPGraph.

## 2.1    Incommensurate Scaling in HMS

Most real-world graphs tend to show skewed distributions. As shown in Fig. 1, the degree distribution of vertices differs significantly. A little number of hub-vertices connect more than millions of edges. In order to simplify the processing of complicated graphs, many models(e.g., XPGraph [12], NVMGraph [13] and EPGraph [30]) separate the entire graph into numerous subgraphs and load these subgraphs into DRAM and PMEM.

However, the performance gaps between DRAM and PMEM in terms of bandwidth and latency are quite significant, as shown in Table 1. DRAM is more than 3 times faster than PMEM in random reading and writing. In contrast to that, PMEM has a latency that is more than 3 times that of DRAM. Significantly, between NUMA nodes, remote DRAM access is faster than local PMEM access [12]. Therefore, the efficiency of graph data access is concentrated during the iterative graph processing in HMS.

Evidently, the performance differences between DRAM and PMEM might cause the overall performance of typical in-memory systems to deteriorate. [30]. Thus, an effective storage strategy should thus be taken into account in HMS. Furthermore, graph algorithm execution time is related to the access efficiency of active vertices. However, the number of active vertices of different subgraphs in different iterations may vary greatly [30] which could result in the asymmetric convergence phenomena. It inspires us to design an efficient graph representation strategy and the data layering strategy in NUMA-based HMS.

## 2.2    Analysis of Subgraph Construction

Subgraph construction is an important process in graph computing. Such as GraphChi [1], it divides the vertices into disjoint intervals and breaks the edge list into tiny blocks. For a given vertex interval, it exploits the parallel sliding windows (PSW) to process all intervals and blocks. As shown in Fig. 2, during interval $i$, PSW loads the i-th in-block and traverses the i-th segments of all the other in-block to construct subgraph $i$. Obviously, the subgraph construction phase significantly degrades the overall performance.

If storing both in-blocks and out-blocks, there is no need to traverse all the in-blocks during the subgraph construction phase. That is to say, the construction subgraph $i$ only needs the in-block $i$ and the out-block $i$, which is undoubtedly efficient. Although this format increases storage space, it is common to trade space consumption for time efficiency, especially for PMEM.

In view of the fact that remote memory access is faster than local PMEM access when crossing NUMA nodes, it's wise to translate local PMEM data access to remote memory access. Therefore, separately storing the out-blocks and in-blocks of subgraphs between different NUMA nodes may be beneficial to subgraph construction.

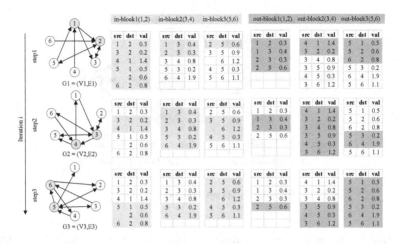

**Fig. 2.** Subgraph construction of PSW in GraphChi.

## 2.3 Push-Pull Model and Data-Driven Algorithms

The push and pull updating models are widely employed by large-scale graph processing systems, such as GraphLab [5], Ligra [7] and Gemini [8]. As shown in Fig. 3, in the push model, each vertex scatters (writes) the changes to its neighbors through its outgoing edges. Conversely, in the pull model, each vertex gathers (reads) information from its incoming neighbors and then updates its own value with the gathered information. Obviously, the number of active vertices and edges determines which scenarios the push and pull updating models are appropriate for. The push model, in particular, is appropriate for sparse active edge sets since it only traverses the outgoing edges of active vertices that have modified their values. The pull model, on the reverse hand, supports dense active edge sets since it eliminates data races during the message passing process.

However, many existing graph computing systems either use the push model or the pull model in HMS [9,12,16]. Furthermore, the push model for these systems is based on all vertices rather than the active vertices, as they put a higher priority on graph storage than graph computing efficiency.

Actually, the adaptive push-pull model works well in HMS. When running algorithms with sparse active edge sets, the push model enables selective data access that only traverses the active edges. It fully avoids the access of useless data. When running algorithms with dense active edge sets, the pull model sequentially accesses the edges of all vertices. It overcomes the challenges of random accesses and enables efficient parallelism.

In addition, based on work activation, graph algorithms can be classified into two categories: topology-driven and data-driven. For a topology-driven algorithm, all the vertices need to be processed in each iteration. In contrast, vertices in a data-driven algorithm are dynamically activated by their neighbors, meaning that user-defined functions determine whether a vertice is active or inactive. Data-driven algorithms enables developers to focus more on "hot vertices" in a

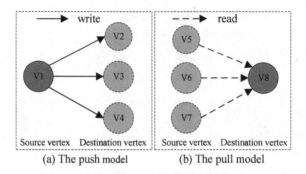

(a) The push model          (b) The pull model

**Fig. 3.** The push and pull models.

graph that require more frequent updates. As a result, in many cases, data-driven algorithms can outperform topology-driven algorithms. To provide a comprehensive analysis of the data-driven push and pull models, let's take the PageRank algorithm as an example.

| **Algorithm 1** Push-based PageRank | **Algorithm 2** Pull-based PageRank |
|---|---|
| **Input:** $G = (V, E)$, $\alpha$, $\epsilon$. | **Input:** $G = (V, E)$, $\alpha$, $\epsilon$. |
| **Output:** PageRank $PR$. | **Output:** PageRank $PR$. |
| 1: Initialize $PR = (1 - \alpha)\mathbf{e}$, $\mathbf{r} = 0$; | 1: Initialize $PR = (1 - \alpha)\mathbf{e}$; |
| 2: **for** (each $v \in V$) **do** | 2: //All the vertices are active; |
| 3:    **for** (each $w \in S_v$) **do** | 3: **for** (each $v \in V$) **do** |
| 4:       $r_v = r_v + 1/|D_w|$; | 4:    $worklist.push(v)$; |
| 5:    **end for** | 5: **end for** |
| 6:    $r_v = (1 - \alpha) + \alpha \times r_v$; | 6: **while** (!$worklist.isEmpty()$) **do** |
| 7:    $worklist.push(v)$; | 7:    $v = worklist.pop()$; |
| 8: **end for** | 8:    $pr_v^{next} = \alpha \times \Sigma_{w \in S_v} \frac{pr_w}{|D_w|} + (1 - \alpha)$; |
| 9: **while** (!$worklist.isEmpty()$) **do** | 9:    //update $pr_v$; |
| 10:    $v = worklist.pop()$; | 10:    **if** ($|pr_v^{next} - pr_v| \geq \epsilon$) **then** |
| 11:    $pr_v^{next} = pr_v + r_v$; | 11:       $pr_v = pr_v^{next}$; |
| 12:    **for** (each $w \in D_v$) **do** | 12:       **for** (each $w \in D_v$) **do** |
| 13:       $r_w^{old} = r_w$; | 13:       //Add destination vertices; |
| 14:       $r_w = r_w + \alpha \times r_v/|D_v|$; | 14:       **if** ($|pr_v^{next} - pr_v| \geq \epsilon$) **then** |
| 15:       **if** ($r_w > \epsilon$)&($r_w^{old} < \epsilon$) **then** | 15:          $w \notin worklist$; |
| 16:          $worklist.push(w)$; | 16:          $worklist.push(w)$; |
| 17:       **end if** | 17:       **end if** |
| 18:    **end for** | 18:    **end for** |
| 19:    $r_w = 0$; | 19:    **end if** |
| 20: **end while** | 20: **end while** |

Algorithm 1 shows the push-based data-driven PageRank. Given a graph $G = (V, E)$, with vertex set $V$ and edge set $E$, let $\alpha$ denote the damping ratio and $\epsilon$ denote the residual. Also, let us define $S_v$ to be the set of incoming vertices of $v$ and $D_v$ to be the set of destination vertices of $v$. Initially, the worklist is set to be the entire vertex set $V$. An active vertex $v$ updates its own value $pr_v$ and only pushes $r_v$ to destination vertices $D_v$. That is to say, the $pr_v^{next}$ of vertex $v$ is equivalent to the $pr_v$ and its $r_v$, as seen in lines 9 through 20. Push-based algorithms invoke more frequent updates, which might be helpful to

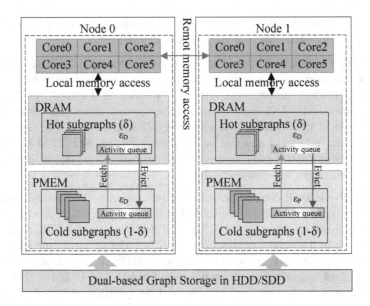

**Fig. 4.** The architecture of NPGraph.

achieve faster information propagation over the network. However, compared to pull-based algorithms, push-based algorithms can be more costly in the sense that they require more write operations.

Algorithm 2 shows the pull-based data-driven PageRank. The algorithm proceeds by picking a vertex $v$ from the worklist, computing the $v$'s PageRank value $pr_v^{next}$, and adding its destination vertices to the worklist. Indeed, when $pr_v^{next}$ is updated, each of its outgoing vertex' residual $r_v$ is added $\alpha \times r_v / |D_v|$, as shown between lines 6 and 20. Thus, it guarantees work efficiency by concentrating on a more active list of vertices.

In many cases, the benefit of filtering active vertices outweighs the overhead of residual computations. For graph algorithms, the execution order of active vertices is crucial [30]. For example, in push-based PageRank, whenever a vertex $v$ has a new residual $r_v$, and then its $pr_v$ is updated. The overall residual $r_v$ is reduced by $(1 - \alpha) \times r_v$. This suggests that if the large residual vertices are processed first, the algorithm might converge faster.

## 3   Model Design

As shown in Fig. 4, NPGraph is a novel and effective graph computing model specially developed in NUMA-based HMS. The specific implementation of NPGraph is introduced in this section.

### 3.1   Overview of NPGraph

NPGraph aims to improve the efficiency of large-scale graph processing in HMS. It adopts a lightweight compressed dual-block representation to organize graphs.

What's more, it provides an adaptive push-pull updating strategy across NUMA nodes to accommodate different data-driven algorithms.

**Dual-Block Graph Representation.** Like GraphChi [1], NPGraph divides graph vertices and corresponding edges into tiny intervals and blocks. But it adopts a dual-block graph representation strategy in forward and backward manner, respectively. Although the storage space has increased, it can support push-pull hybrid updating models effectively. It fully utilizes the random data access function of DRAM and the large capacity feature of PMEM in HMS. By translating local PMEM data access to remote memory access, it improves the data access efficiency to a certain extent.

**Adaptive Push-Pull Strategy.** As mentioned above, the forward manner of in-memory graph structures is suitable for the push updating model, and the backward manner is instrumental in the pull updating model. NPGraph adopts a hybrid push-pull strategy to dynamically adjust the updating model. Inspired by EPGraph [30], it fetches and evicts blocks in HMS. What's more, it proposes a dynamic data migration strategy between DRAM and PMEM. To a certain extent, it improves the temporal locality and the spatial locality of graph computing in HMS.

### 3.2 Dual-Block Graph Representation

Like some existing systems (e.g., GraphChi [1], Ligra [7] and Gemini [8]), NPGraph partitions graph $G = (V, E)$ into $P$ subgraphs: $G_1 \sim G_p$. That is, the vertex set $V$ and edge set $E$ are split into $P$ disjoint intervals and blocks: $V_1 \sim V_p$ and $E_1 \sim E_p$. Each subgraph $G_i = (V_i, E_i)$ is associated with both the forward and backward manners, as shown in Fig. 5. The two manners store the out-edges and in-edges of vertex sets in each subgraph, respectively.

In-memory graph structure data includes graph structure data, attribute data and status data. Specifically, graph structure data includes vertices and corresponding out-edges or in-edges. Graph attribute data is the value of vertices. Graph status data indicates which vertices have been accessed or the values have been updated. During the implementation of dual-block graph representation, *Row* and *Col* represent the vertices and connected edges, as shown in Fig. 5. In order to reduce data storage space, graph structure data are generally based on CSR compression format. In addition, to facilitate the execution of graph algorithms, the in-memory status data and attribute data have to be built. They are separately marked as $S_{curr}$, $S_{next}$, $D_{curr}$ and $D_{next}$.

As shown in Fig. 5(a), the graph $G$ with six vertices and thirteen edges is partitioned into $G_0 = (V_0, E_0)$ and $G_1 = (V_1, E_1)$. $V_0 = \{0, 1, 2\}$ and $V_1 = \{3, 4, 5\}$. Its forward manner and backward manner are organized as Fig. 5(b) and (c). Execution flows start with active vertices to travel and update their outgoing neighbors or themselves. In the forward manner, there are two execution flows indicated by orange and blue arrows, separately. Specifically, during one iterative processing, due to $S_{curr}[0]=1$ and $S_{curr}[5]=1$, $v_0$ and $v_5$ are active vertices. The vertex $v_0$ has out-edges $E_0 = Col[Row[0], Row[1]) = \{(0, 1), (0, 2)\}$. Another

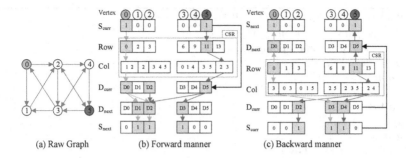

(a) Raw Graph            (b) Forward manner            (c) Backward manner

**Fig. 5.** Forward and backward manners of in-memory graph structures.

vertex $v_5$ has out-edges $E_5 = Col[Row[5], sizeof(Row)) = \{(5,2),(5,3)\}$. In the push model, the corresponding $D_{next}[1,2,3]$ and $S_{next}[1,2,3]$ of $v_1$, $v_2$ and $v_3$ are updated during the subsequent execution flows.

However, in the backward manner, execution flows need to update vertices $v_0$ and $v_5$ by gathering the information of their in-edge neighbors. $v_0$ needs to gather information from $v_3$. According to $D_{curr}[3]$ and $S_{curr}[3]$, $v_3$ updates its $D_{next}[0]$ and $S_{next}[0]$. Similarly, to $v_5$, it needs to gather information from $v_2$ and $v_4$, then update its $D_{next}[5]$ and $S_{next}[5]$.

Inspired by the incommensurate scaling of HMS, we analyze the data access rate of DRAM in HMS [30]. According to the execution flow of the in-memory graph structures mentioned in Fig. 5, graph status data and attribute data ($S_{curr}$, $S_{next}$, $D_{curr}$ and $D_{next}$) should be placed in DRAM. Based on sparsity and density, graph structure data ($Row$ and $Col$) are placed in DRAM and PMEM selectively. Based on the dual-block representation and layered placement, NPGraph may get better performance in HMS. In addition, due to the fact that the remote memory access is faster than local PMEM access, NPGraph converts local PMEM data access to remote memory access when crossing NUMA nodes. During the programming process, two NUMA nodes respectively store the forward and backward manners graph data. We will evaluate the efficiency of NPGraph in Sect. 4.

### 3.3 Adaptive Push-Pull Strategy

Due to the unequal distribution of graph data [5], the phenomenon of asymmetric convergence is common in graph computing. That is the reason sparse subgraphs usually converge rapidly and dense subgraphs converge gradually [15]. As mentioned in Sect. 2, sparse and dense subgraphs should be handled by push and pull models individually. In addition, graph algorithms' execution time is proportional to the memory access of active edges and vertices [30]. As a result, the run-time data migration strategy in HMS should be taken into account.

Algorithm 3 shows the computation procedure of the adaptive push-pull update strategy during one iteration. As mentioned in Algorithm 1 and 2, we

**Algorithm 3.** Adaptive Push-Pull Update Strategy

1: Initialize parameter: $sum$, $\varepsilon$, $D_v$, $S_v$, $k$;
2: /*Choose the optimal update model*/
3: **for** (each $v \in V_i$) **do**
4:     $sum[i] = sum[i] + d_v$;
5:     $\varepsilon[i] = \varepsilon[i] + S_{curr}[v] \times d_v$;
6: **end for**
7: $\varepsilon[i] = \varepsilon[i]/sum[i]$;
8: $model = selectModel(\varepsilon[i], \theta)$;
9: **if** ($model = Push$) **then**
10:     $PushModel(V_i, E_i)$;//Algorithm 4;
11: **else**
12:     $wardPullModel(V_i, E_i)$;//Algorithm 5;
13: **end if**
14: / $*$ $DataMigrate$ $*$ /
15: **for** ($i = 1 : P$) **do**
16:     **if** ($G_i \in PMEM$) **then**
17:         Descending $\varepsilon_{PMEM}[i]$;
18:     **else**
19:         Ascending $\varepsilon_{DRAM}[i]$;
20:     **end if**
21: **end for**
22: **for** ($i = 1 : k$) **do**
23:     /*use memcpy();*/
24:     $MigrateData(G_{DRAM}[i], G_{PMEM}[i])$;
25: **end for**

also maintain two copies of vertex values for each subgraph $G_i$: the source vertex set $S_v$ and the destination vertex set $D_v$. $S_v$ stores the vertex values of the previous iteration, serving as the source vertices. Similarly, $D_v$ stores the vertex values of the current iteration, serving as the destination vertices. $selectModel()$ is a threshold function which is based on $\varepsilon[i]$ selecting $\theta$. When $\varepsilon[i]$ is less than $\theta$, it returns $Push$. Contrary, it returns $Pull$. For each subgraph, NPGraph adaptively selects the push or pull model to accommodate different graph computing tasks. The selection between the push and pull models is based on the number of active vertices and the data access performance prediction method.

Algorithm 4 shows the execution of the data-driven push model. It utilizes the corresponding out-index of the forward manner to process the out-edges of a vertex interval $V_i$. As soon as vertex $v$ is in $worklist()$, it traverses the out-going edges and pushes the updates to their out-neighbors $D_v$ with a update function defined by the researchers. In this process, it reads vertex values from $D_{curr}$ and writes updates to $D_{next}$. If its destination vertices are activated, they are added to the $worklist$ and will be scheduled in the next iteration, such as the push-based PageRank in Algorithm 1. Algorithm 5 shows the execution of the data-driven pull model. Similarly, it processes the in-edges of a vertex interval $V_i$ by the corresponding in-index of the backward manner.

| **Algorithm 4** Push Model | **Algorithm 5** Pull Model |
|---|---|
| 1: /* for each active vertex $v$;*/ | 1: **for** $(v \in V_i)$ **do** |
| 2: **for** $(v \in$ worklist $\& V_i)$ **do** | 2:    **for** (each edge $e \in E_i$) **do** |
| 3:    **for** (each edge $e \in E_i$) **do** | 3:      $S_v = e.src$; |
| 4:      $D_v = e.dst$; | 4:    **end for** |
| 5:    **end for** | 5:    **if** $(S_{curr}v == 1)$ **then** |
| 6:    /*run user defined algorithm;*/ | 6:      **if** $(Function(v, S_v)$ **then** |
| 7:    **if** $(Function(v, D_v)$ **then** | 7:        $worklist.add(S_v)$ |
| 8:      $worklist.add(D_v)$ | 8:      **end if** |
| 9:    **end if** | 9:    **end if** |
| 10: **end for** | 10: **end for** |

As mentioned in Sect. 2.2, $S_{curr}[v]$, $D_v$ and $S_v$ represent the activities of different subgraphs. So, based on the relative activities, NPGraph executes evicting and fetching operations in HMS. Lines 14 to 23 of Algorithm 3 present the procedure of the dynamic data migration strategy. During the iterative process of graph algorithms like PageRank and WCC, the migration strategy calculates the relative activity $\varepsilon$ of each subgraph in DRAM and PMEM separately. $\varepsilon_{PMEM}[i]$ represents the subgraph with the maximum $\varepsilon$ in PMEM, and $\varepsilon_{DRAM}[i]$ represents the minimum $\varepsilon$ in DRAM. Making use of the $memcpy()$ function, it fetches and evicts $G_{PMEM}[i]$ and $G_{DRAM}[i]$, simultaneously.

Naturally, there is a certain of time cost for data migration [30]. But, based on the difference of reading and writing performance between DRAM and PMEM, reasonable $\varepsilon$ and $k$ can improve the data access efficiency. Due to the adaptive push-pull updating strategy and the dynamic data migration strategy, NPGraph maximizes the rate of cache hit in DRAM. Binding the process to a given processor and turning off the automatic NUMA balancing has benefits for improving graph computing performance between different NUMA nodes. We will evaluate the efficiency of the dynamic migration mechanism in Sect. 4.

## 4 Evaluation

In this section, we first introduce the evaluation environment, graph data sets and graph algorithms. Secondly, we conduct experiments to assess the efficiency of the dual-block graph representation strategy. Thirdly, we evaluate the influence of the adaptive push-pull updating strategy. At last, we evaluate the effectiveness of NPGraph by comparing it with state-of-the-art systems.

### 4.1 Experiment Setup

All experiments are conducted on 2 NUMA nodes. Each node includes an Intel Xeon Gold 5218R CPU which is equipped with twenty cores, forty threads. L2 and L3 cache are 32 KB and 27.5 MB respectively. To emulate the experimental setup with limited DRAM resources, each NUMA node is equiped with 16 GB of DRAM and 256 GB of Optane DC persistent memory modules. The experimental

**Table 2.** Five public graph data sets.

| Dataset | Vertices | Edges | Type |
|---|---|---|---|
| Facebook [22] | 4,039 | 88,234 | Social Graphs |
| Soc-LiveJournal [23] | 4,847,571 | 68,993,773 | Social Graphs |
| Twitter-2010 [24] | 61,578,416 | 246,313,664 | Social Graphs |
| Friendster [25] | 65,608,366 | 1,806,067,135 | Game Graphs |
| Yahoo Web [26] | 1,413,511,424 | 5,654,045,696 | Web Graphs |

platform runs on Ubuntu 18.04 LTS system and works for large-scale graph processing.

As stated in Table 2, all graph data sets utilized in the studies are actual graphs. Social networks Facebook and soc-LiveJournal are chosen to evaluate NPGraph. Twitter-2010, Friendster, and Yahoo Web are all social networks, gaming sites, and web sites in their own right. They include trillions of edges and vertices. With dual-block format, the last 3 graphs are 1.56x, 1.94x, and 6.81x bigger than the available DRAM, respectively.

In the evaluations we performed, we utilized the representative PageRank and the traversal-based WCC. PageRank is set to run for 10 iterations in experiments. WCC continues to run until it converges. These algorithms give a thorough examination and have various calculation properties. Finally, NPGraph is compared with state-of-the-art systems: GraphOne [9] and XPGraph [12].

### 4.2   Effect of Adaptive Push-Pull Strategy

We make a full comparison of the forward-push model, the backward-pull model and the dual-adaptive push-pull model. We conduct single-threaded experiments with WCC and PageRank on the above five public graph data sets. The execution time of the above three update models are shown in Fig. 6. Obviously, the overall performance of the adaptive push-pull strategy outperforms push-based implementations. To be more precise, for WCC, the adaptive strategy performs 15.3%–27.6% better than the push model. For PageRank, the performance of adaptive strategy is 14.7%–28.9% higher than push model.

In this experiment, one surprising result is that the push-based implementation outperforms the pull-based model. In general, the read-mostly nature of the pull-based model is more cache-friendly. However, due to the six degrees of separation, there is a lot of random data access during graph computing iteratively. It is interesting to see that optimizing for cache behavior (pull-based model) may not necessarily be as successful as optimizing for transferring the most information rapidly (push-based model). That is to say, for updating propagation, the push-based model has more advantages than the pull-based model. The extra write operations in the push-based model are not just an alternate implementation of the vertex update but rather influence the scheduling of tasks. They convert states of vertices, allowing vertices to only be processed when they are profitable. This improved scheduling makes up for the increased write load.

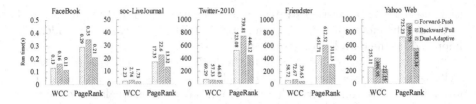

**Fig. 6.** Execution time of different update strategies.

## 4.3  Effect of Data Layering Strategy

To evaluate the efficacy of the data layering method in HMS, we conduct comparative experiments with a multi-threaded configuration (from 1 to 64 threads) on Friendster. As mentioned in Sect. 3.2, a graph $G$ is partitioned into $P$ subgraphs. By the offset of $Row$ and the size of $Col$, it's easy to determine the sparsity or density of subgraphs. Therefore, it's a natural approach to load dense subgraphs into DRAM, preferentially. One situation is that all the structure data of subgraphs is loaded in PMEM. Under this condition, as shown in Fig. 7, PageRank and WCC are labeled as PR and WCC. As a comparison, depending on the DRAM size and the size of the data sets, we set the top 20% of subgraphs to be loaded into memory. In this case, PageRank and WCC are labeled as PR-L and WCC-L respectively.

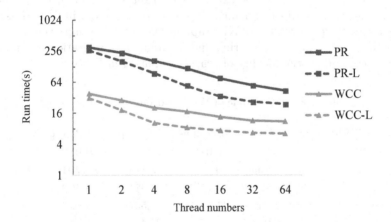

**Fig. 7.** Multi-thread execution time for PageRank and WCC on Friendster.

More importantly, we adopt an adaptive push-pull strategy to obtain optimal performance. Meanwhile, exchange primitives are used in code programs such as *atomic_compare_exchange*(). All the execution time decreases as the number of threads increases. As we can see in Fig. 7, the performance of PR-L and WCC-L are 1.51–1.83 times that of PR and WCC. Similarly, this trend demonstrates that the graph data-layering strategy can take advantage of DRAM and PMEM in HMS. Therefore, the overall performance of NPGraph can be considerably improved by the data layering strategy.

We may make two inferences from the findings above: (1) Due to its sensitivity to heterogeneous memory, PageRank outperforms WCC in terms of performance. (2) We can observe that NPGraph has excellent scalability from the trend of the multi-threaded execution times.

### 4.4  Effect of Dynamic Data Migration Strategy

In order to evaluate the effectiveness of the data migration strategy, we run WCC and PageRank on the above 5 graphs. NPGraph is organized by the adaptive push-pull format, the layered format and data migration format respectively. Uniformly, they are marked as NPGraph-A, NPGraph-L and NPGraph-LM respectively. It is generally acknowledged that parallel computing can entirely employ graph computing systems. Thus, we evaluate their effectiveness with 64 threads.

As shown in Table 3, NPGraph-M outperforms NPGraph-L which exceeds a pure NPGraph-A version. More specifically, the performance of NPGraph-M is 14.3%–34.6% higher than that of NPGraph-A. It also confirms the experimental results in Sect. 4.3. More than that, the performance of NPGraph-M is 14.1%–23.5% higher than that of NPGraph-L in WCC. Meanwhile, the performance of NPGraph-M is 12.9%–18.5% higher than that of NPGraph-L in PageRank.

By thoroughly analyzing the experimental results of Table 3, we can determine the effectiveness of the dynamic data migration strategy in HMS. Based on this strategy, the performance of NPGraph has been further improved. It further proves that combining data layering and dynamic data migration can improve the temporal and spatial locality of graph computing in HMS.

**Table 3.** Execution time of WCC and PageRank(in seconds)

| Algorithm | Dataset | NPGraph-A | NPGraph-L | NPGraph-M |
|-----------|---------|-----------|-----------|-----------|
| WCC | Facebook | 0.021 | 0.018 | **0.019** |
| | LiveJournal | 0.216 | 0.176 | **0.201** |
| | Twitter-2010 | 5.755 | 4.374 | **3.409** |
| | Friendster | 11.21 | 6.537 | **5.613** |
| | Yahoo Web | 31.43 | 22.41 | **17.14** |
| PageRank | Facebook | 0.026 | 0.017 | **0.019** |
| | LiveJournal | 0.716 | 0.531 | **0.601** |
| | Twitter-2010 | 33.12 | 24.31 | **21.16** |
| | Friendster | 40.67 | 32.08 | **26.13** |
| | Yahoo Web | 102.29 | 83.11 | **69.73** |

**Fig. 8.** Compare with state-of-the-art graph computing models.

### 4.5 Comparison with Other Systems

We compare NPGraph with state-of-the-art in-memory systems: GraphOne [9] and XPGraph [12]. They are all capable of parallel graph processing. To get the optimal performance, we provide two NUMA-nodes. Each node has 16 GB DRAM and 256 GB PMEM. To make it fair, GraphOne, XPGraph and NPGraph are executed in the same environment and the number of threads is set to 64. In Fig. 8, we display the execution time for each of the five different graphs.

It is obviously that NPGraph outperforms GraphOne and XPGraph in terms of the overall efficiency. Specifically, it outperforms GraphOne by 27.36% to 43.8% on Pagerank and WCC. Moreover, it outperforms XPGraph by 21.67% to 32.03% on Pagerank and WCC. The combination of the graph data layering approach with the dynamic data migration mechanism enhances the performance of NPGraph.

In order to store scale-free graphs, edge list and adjacency list, two of the most popular in-memory graph storage formats, are combined to create a hybrid storage format in GraphOne [9]. The vertex-centric random access pattern is used to navigate the data of graph structures. However, since it ignores the dynamic properties of graph computing, it must traverse all in-memory graph data, which is time-consuming. Furthermore, it generates a significant number of writing operations of intermediate results, resulting in a massive amount of I/O overhead. Based on NUMA, XPGraph [12] develops an XPLine-friendly graph access model with vertex-centric graph buffering. However, its main solution is large-scale evolving graphs. It overlooks the issue of load imbalance across numerous threads in each iteration. That is NPGraph's most powerful feature. Based on the adaptive push-pull strategy and the predictive data migration strategy, NPGraph brings lower memory access costs and better utilization of parallelism in the NUMA-based hybrid memory system.

## 5   Related Work

Current single-machine graph computing models enable clients to store, analyze and mine large-scale graph data sets [17,18,27,30]. These systems can be divided into traditional in-memory models and emerging hybrid memory models.

**Traditional In-memory Models.** To load the entire graph data, they normally use a the highest level machine, such as [3,7,14]. The underlying properties such as NUMA, memory locality, and multi-cores are utilized. Specifically,

GraphIt [3] has able to run on varying sizes of graphs, even though they have different structures. It separates computation and scheduling through its graph calculation programs. Ligra [7] is an easy-to-use platform for different graph algorithms that enhances single-machine parallel graph computing. At the same time, it takes advantage of the hybrid push-pull model. Thus, graph algorithms are simple to implement in Ligra. By utilizing NUMA characteristics, Polymer [14] creates a hierarchical barrier to increase parallelism. It suggests a differential data placement method to decrease random remote accesses, based on the observation that the bandwidth of sequential remote access is larger than that of random remote access. Additionally, it changes random remote access into sequential remote access by utilizing vertex replications.

Due to the huge capacity of DRAM, these above models avoid the overhead of disk I/O. However, their implementation is challenging when big graphs cannot fit in main memory. Thus, the hybrid memory system must be considered in single-machine graph computing models.

**Emerging Hybrid-Memory Models.** With the unprecedented development of persistent memory (PMEM), a few research on graph computing in persistent memory have been conducted. For example, Huang *et al.* [16] places all the edges in PMEM and all the vertices in DRAM. They make use of SRAM as a form of data buffer to decrease the random access to vertices. Based on the interval-block graph partition approach, it increases the effectiveness of data access. However, rather than emphasizing the overall performance of graph computing systems, it concentrates on lowering the amount of energy they consume. GraphOne [9] uses a hybrid storage format by combining the edge list and the adjacency list to process evolving graphs. Specifically, it first uses a circular edge log in DRAM to store the latest graph updates in the edge list format. Besides, it also uses many adjacency lists to store the older data, i.e., edges that are archived periodically from the edge log, thus supporting efficient graph queries. XPGraph [12] first introduces a PMEM-based graph store model. It proposes a PMEM-friendly graph access model to support high-performance dynamic graph stores for large-scale graphs. By using NUMA-friendly graph access, XPGraph manages the process of flushing graph data to PMEM. Based on the above systems, XPGraph realizes performance optimization in HMS.

However, they only focus on how to efficiently store graph data. As we all know, efficiently utilizing graph data is more important in graph computing. Inspired by the above works, our goal is to design an efficient graph computing model in the NUMA-based HMS. It is worth optimizing the process of subgraph construction and the adaptive push-pull model.

# 6 Conclusion

In this paper, we propose NPGraph which is an efficient graph computing model specially designed in NUMA-based hybrid memory systems. Simultaneously, it focuses on data storage optimization and model calculation optimization. With the graph data layering strategy, it utilizes the dual-block graph representation strategy to support the adaptive push-pull strategy. To improve the data access efficiency, it simultaneously stores the forward and backward manners of graph data in two different NUMA nodes. What's more, during the adaptive updating process, it adopts data-driven algorithms and the dynamic data migration strategy to optimize the overall performance of graph computing.

Although it consumes twice the space to store the dual-block graph, it improves the temporal locality and the spatial locality. Moreover, it fully utilizes multi-threaded parallel technology to enhance overall performance between two NUMA nodes. Based on the above three portions, NPGraph is capable of calculating large-scale graphs effectively on a single machine. The experimental evaluation shows that NPGraph outperforms the other state-of-the-art models by 21.67% to 32.03%.

With a small amount of DRAM, NPGraph is designed as an efficient graph computing model in NUMA-based persistent memory systems. Although this model can automatically allocate graph data and adaptively update subgraphs, it needs to be extended. We plan to increase the model's scalability and multitasking capacity in the future.

# References

1. Kyrola, A., Blelloch, G., Guestrin, C.: GraphChi: large-scale graph computation on just a PC. In: OSDI'12, pp. 31–46 (2012)
2. Sun, P., Wen, Y., Ta, D., Xiao, X.: GraphMP: I/O-efficient big graph analytics on a single commodity machine. IEEE Trans. Big Data, 2908384 (2019, to be published). https://doi.org/10.1109/TBDATA
3. Zhang, Y., Yang, M., Baghdadi, R., et al.: Graphit: a high-performance graph DSL, In: Proceedings of the ACM on Programming Languages, vol. 2, no. OOPSLA, p. 121 (2018)
4. Malewicz, G., et al.: Pregel: a system for large-scale graph computing. In: SIGMOD'10, pp. 135–146 (2010)
5. Low, Y., et al.: Distributed GraphLab: a framework for machine learning in the cloud. Proc. VLDB Endow. 5(8) (2012)
6. Gonzalez, J.E., Xin, R.S., et al.: GraphX: graph computing in a distributed dataflow system. In: OSDI'14, pp. 599–613 (2014)
7. Shun, J., Blelloch, G.E.: Ligra: a lightweight graph computing system for shared memory. ACM SIGPLAN Not. 48(8), 135–146 (2013). ACM
8. Zhou, S.: Gemini: graph estimation with matrix variate normal instances. Ann. Stat. 42(2), 532–562 (2014)
9. Kumar, P., Huang, H.H.: Graphone: a data store for real-time analytics on evolving graphs. ACM Trans. Storage (TOS) 15(4), 1–40 (2020)
10. Gonzalez, J.E., et al.: PowerGraph: distributed graph-parallel computation on natural graphs. In: Usenix Conference on Operating Systems Design Implementation USENIX Association (2012)
11. https://www.intel.com/content/www/us/en/architecture-and-technology/optane-dc-persistent-memory.html
12. Wang, R., et al.: XPGraph: XPline-friendly persistent memory graph stores for large-scale evolving graphs. In: 2022 55th IEEE/ACM International Symposium on Microarchitecture (MICRO). IEEE (2022)

13. Liu, W., Liu, H., Liao, X., Jin, H., Zhang, Y.: Straggler-aware parallel graph processing in hybrid memory systems. In: IEEE/ACM 21st International Symposium on Cluster, Cloud and Internet Computing (CCGrid). Melbourne, Australia, 2021, pp. 217–226 (2021). https://doi.org/10.1109/CCGrid51090.2021.00031

14. Zhang, K., Chen, R., Chen, H.: Numa-aware graph-structured analytics. ACM SIGPLAN Not. **50**(8), 183–193 (2015)

15. Tian, Y., Balmin, A., Corsten, S.A., Tatikonda, S., McPherson, J.: From think like a vertex to think like a graph. Proc. VLDB Endow. **7**(3), 193–204 (2013)

16. Huang, T., et al.: HyVE: hybrid vertex-edge memory hierarchy for energy-efficient graph processing. In: 2018 Design, Automation Test in Europe Conference Exhibition (DATE). IEEE (2018)

17. Gill, G., Dathathri, R., Hoang, L., et al.: Single machine graph analytics on massive datasets using Intel Optane DC persistent memory. Proc. VLDB Endow. **13**(8), 1304–1318 (2020)

18. Liu, H., Liu, R., Liao, X., Jin, H., He, B., Zhang, Y.: Object-level memory allocation and migration in hybrid memory systems. IEEE Trans. Comput. **69**(9), 1401–1413 (2020). https://doi.org/10.1109/TC.2020.2973134

19. Vora, K.: Lumos: dependency-driven disk-based graph processing. In: USENIX ATC, pp. 429–442 (2019)

20. Dang, Z., et al.: Nvalloc: rethinking heap metadata management in persistent memory allocators. In: ACM ASPLOS, pp. 115–127 (2022)

21. Wang, Q., Lu, Y., Li, J., Shu, J.: Nap: a black-box approach to NUMA-aware persistent memory indexes. In: USENIX OSDI, pp. 93–111 (2021)

22. http://snap.stanford.edu/data/ego-Facebook.html

23. Backstrom, L., Huttenlocher, D., Kleinberg, J., Lan, X.: Group formation in large social networks: membership, growth, and evolution. In: KDD'06, pp. 44–54 (2006)

24. Kwak, H., Lee, C., Park, H., Moon, S.: What is Twitter, a social network or a news media. In: WWW'10, pp. 591–600 (2010)

25. Boldi, P., Vigna, S.: The webgraph system I: compression techniques. In: WWW'04, pp. 595–602 (2004)

26. http://developer.yahoo.com/blogs/616566076523839488/

27. Li, B., et al.: $D^2$Graph: an efficient and unified out-of-core graph computing model. In: 2021 IEEE ISPA, pp. 193–201 (2021). https://doi.org/10.1109/ISPA-BDCloud-SocialCom-SustainCom52081.2021.00038

28. Yu, J., et al.: DFOGraph: An I/O and Communication-Efficient System for Distributed Fully-out-of-Core Graph Processing (2021)

29. Liu, W., Liu, H., Liao, X., Jin, H., Zhang, Y: Straggler-aware parallel graph processing in hybrid memory systems. In: IEEE/ACM 21st International Symposium on Cluster. Cloud and Internet Computing (CCGrid) 2021, pp. 217–226 (2021). https://doi.org/10.1109/CCGrid51090.2021.00031

30. Li, B., et al.: EPGraph: an efficient graph computing model in persistent memory system. In: 2022 IEEE ISPA, pp. 9–17 (2022). https://doi.org/10.1109/ISPA-BDCloud-SocialCom-SustainCom57177.2022.00009

# tHR-Net: A Hybrid Reasoning Framework for Temporal Knowledge Graph

Yijing Zhao[1,2], Yumeng Liu[1,2(✉)], Zihang Wan[1], and Hongan Wang[1,2]

[1] Institute of Software Chinese Academy of Sciences, Beijing, China
{yijing,yumeng,hongan}@iscas.ac.cn
[2] University of Chinese Academy of Sciences, Beijing, China

**Abstract.** Entity prediction and relation prediction are the two major tasks of temporal knowledge graph (TKG) reasoning. The key to answering queries about future events is to understand historical trends and extract the information most likely to affect the future, i.e., the TKG reasoning task is both influenced by the trends of time-evolving graphs and directly driven by the facts relevant to a specific query. Existing methods mostly build models separately for these two characteristics, namely evolution representation learning and query-specific methods, failing to integrate these two crucial factors that determine reasoning results into a single framework. In this paper, we propose a novel temporal hybrid reasoning network (tHR-NET), simultaneously considering the modeling of graph feature space evolution and the enhancement of query-related feature representations in TKG. Specifically, we introduce a global graph space evolution module to extract graph trends, which influence entity/relation representations at each timestamp through a temporal view projection. Additionally, we propose a query-specific increment module for targeted enhancement of entity and relation representations, capturing query-related factors over extended durations. Through extensive experiments on real datasets, tHR-NET demonstrates distinct advantages in parallel entity and relation prediction.

**Keywords:** Temporal Knowledge Graph Reasoning · Event Prediction · Evolutional Representation Learning · Graph Neural Network

## 1 Introduction

The temporal knowledge graph (TKG) has been widely employed to model temporal data in various fields such as event reasoning [2,3], resource scheduling [21], and commodity recommendation [19], which brought simplification and efficiency to problem description and solution. On the basis of static KG [1], TKG is composed of a sequence of quadruples, i.e., (subject, relation, object, timestamp), which consists of a complete set of entities and relations existing at one time, organized in chronological order [8]. Due to the incompleteness and dynamic change of graph structure, TKG reasoning is a complex task that worth

© ICST Institute for Computer Sciences, Social Informatics and Telecommunications Engineering 2024
Published by Springer Nature Switzerland AG 2024. All Rights Reserved
H. Gao et al. (Eds.): CollaborateCom 2023, LNICST 562, pp. 223–241, 2024.
https://doi.org/10.1007/978-3-031-54528-3_13

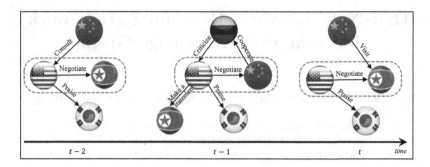

(a) Different timestamps *(t-2, t-1, t)* yield varying inference results for the same query *(the United States, Negotiate, ?)* as the TKG evolves.

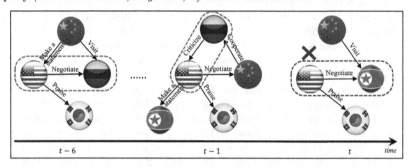

(b) The events leading to *(the United States, Negotiate, Russia)* at timestamp *t+1* are neither recent nor temporally continuous.

**Fig. 1.** Two examples of reasoning over TKG.

study. Two kinds of typical issues in TKG reasoning are entity prediction and relation prediction [31], i.e., inferring the entities or relations that will exist in future facts using historical knowledge graph sequences.

Deep learning methods have been developed as one of the main research directions to solve TKG reasoning problems due to its powerful data mining and intelligent computing ability. Formally, this type of methods involves two processes: one is the encoding process, which accurately models and represents input data as low dimensional vectors; the other is the decoding process, which generates problem outputs for downstream tasks based on the represented data. To achieve accurate TKG reasoning for downstream application tasks, there is an increasing need to research representation learning methods to optimize the utilization of historical knowledge graph sequences. Two categories are primarily covered by their optimization directions [1]. One is structural feature extraction, which involves optimizing the fusion and aggregation of entity and relation features within a time snapshot and typically makes use of graph neural networks and their variants [6,12,18]. Another is temporal pattern mining, in which models like recurrent neural networks [3,12,18] or transformers [6] recognize and combine the feature information under various time slices. The combination of these two categories enables the identification of trends in entity and relation evolution.

The key to answering queries about future events lies in a thorough understanding of history and the ability to extract information most likely to influence the future. Consequently, two principles that need to be adhered to become critical for TKG reasoning: (1) Temporal Variability - graph evolution exhibits continuous variability over time [16]; (2) Causal Discontinuity - A substantial number of events rely on discontinuous histories [6]. In TKG reasoning, the former provides an overall context characterizing the evolution of the knowledge graph, uncovering the variations of the graph over time, and thus influencing local entities and relations. The latter can selectively capture evidence related to specific queries from historical events, thereby reducing the interference from non-causal events in continuous time. Figure 1 illustrates these two phenomena, respectively. In Fig. 1a, as the graph evolves, the same prediction task under different timestamps *(t-2, t-1, t)*-for example, the query *(the United States, Negotiate, ?)*-yields different inference results. In Fig. 1b, the events causing the occurrence of the event *(the United States, Negotiate, Russia)* at timestamp $t+1$ are neither the most recent nor temporally continuous.

Existing models have often unilaterally focused on one of these two kinds of problems, and can thus be categorized into: evolution representation learning methods and query-specific methods [15]. Evolution representation learning methods [15,18,27,29] are based on updating the embeddings of each entity and relation at each timestamp within historical KGs, learning the trends of feature evolution. Query-specific methods [6,12] retrieve context information from historical KGs for a query, such as entities and relations. These kinds of methods possess advantages such as low space occupancy and rapid convergence, but they overlook the impact of global graph feature space evolution on entity and relation representation. HisMatch [16] considers both candidate and query histories, but its use of recurrent neural networks in extracting features from query-related historical events leads to struggles with temporal forgetting, thereby hindering the extraction of relevant events.

In this paper, we propose a novel temporal hybrid reasoning network, called thR-NET, that simultaneously considers the aforementioned two issues by unifying the modeling of graph feature space evolution and the enhancement of query-relevant feature representations in TKG. Specifically, we propose a global graph space evolution module in order to effectively extract graph evolution trends which will influence the entity/relation representations at every timestamp. Meanwhile, we design a local feature aggregation module to acquire entity/relation representations. Following that, we apply a computation with temporal view projection to align the aggregated local entities/relations features with the current graph evolution features, ensuring adherence to the temporal variability inherent in graph evolution. Then, we propose the query-specific increment module to enhance the entity/relation representations based on specific queries, enabling the capture of factors most relevant to the queries over a long duration. Finally, the entity representations and relation representations are obtained in parallel, enabling entity and relation prediction tasks by connecting any downstream application task model. Our contributions can be summarized as follows:

- We designed a novel temporal hybrid reasoning network framework. To the best of our knowledge, this is the first study that simultaneously models both the continuous variability of graph evolution over time and the non-continuous features of query-related history in TKG reasoning.
- We propose a new temporal projection technique to align the aggregated local features of entities/relations with the current graph evolution feature, which ensures entity/relation representations adherence to the continuous variability inherent in graph evolution.
- We have developed a query-specific increment module, capable of caching and extracting features from the representations output by entity/relation evolution learning based on specific queries, which can break the temporal forgetfulness in evolution representation learning.
- Extensive experiments demonstrate that tHR-NET achieves significantly better performance over both entity and relation prediction tasks on four benchmarks by modeling the hybrid reasoning framework comprehensively.

## 2   Related Work

Temporal knowledge graph (TKG) reasoning settings encompass both interpolation and extrapolation [12]. Interpolation approaches predominantly focus on inferring and completing absent information within historical time points. Typical techniques such as HyTE [4], TTransE [13], and TA-DistMult [7] have been employed, while their capacity to foresee future occurrences remains limited. Extrapolation methodologies deduce novel facts, encompassing subjects, objects, and relations, that may transpire in the future by relying on a chronologically arranged series of historical facts. By capturing historical event information, these methods seek to make a reasonable prediction of the future, which has recently become a research hotspot. They can be divided into two classes based on how they use the events historical information: evolution representation learning and query-specific methods [27].

**Evolution Representation Learning Methods.** These methods are based on encoding each entity and relation at each timestamp within historical KGs, learning the trends of feature evolution, and considering the query only at the decoding stage. For example, RE-GCN [12] encodes fixed-length historical facts into the entity and relation evolutionary representation for future fact prediction. CEN [15] models variable-length facts sequences. TANGO [10] employs neural ordinary differential equations to model the structural information for each candidate entity. CRNet [27] effectively models the mutual influence of events that occur concurrently in the future.

**Query-Specific Methods.** These methods retrieve context information related to the query from historical KGs. RE-NET [12] employs both GCN and GRU to model the sequence of 1-hop subgraphs associated with the given subject entity.

xERTE [9] learns a dynamic pruning process to identify subgraphs related to the query. Both CluSteR [17] and TITer [25] utilize reinforcement learning to discover paths relevant to the query in history. rGalt [6] augments the capacity to extract features of interest over extended periods by embedding graphs at distinct time points into parallel input transformer structures.

The recent method HiSMatch [16] considers the query-related histories and evolution histories of all the candidate entities under the matching framework. But its use of recurrent neural networks in extracting features from query-related historical events leads to struggles with temporal forgetting.

## 3  Preliminaries

A TKG $\mathcal{G}$ can be formalized as a sequence of KGs with timestamps, i.e., $\mathcal{G} = \{\mathcal{G}_1, \mathcal{G}_2, ..., \mathcal{G}_t, ...\}$. Let $\mathcal{E}$ be a finite set of entities and $\mathcal{R}$ be a finite set of relations belong to $\mathcal{G}$. The KG of each time $t$ can be represented as a directed multi-relational graph $\mathcal{G}_t = (\mathcal{E}_t, \mathcal{R}_t)$, where $\mathcal{E}_t \in \mathcal{E}$ is the set of entities and $\mathcal{R}_t \in \mathcal{R}$ is the set of relations at timestamp $t$. Any fact in $\mathcal{G}_t$ can be denoted as a triplet, $(s_t, r_t, o_t)$, which represents a fact of relation $r_t \in \mathcal{R}_t$ that occurs with $s_t \in \mathcal{E}_t$ as its subject entity and $o_t \in \mathcal{E}_t$ as its object entity at timestamp $t$. Under the assumption that the facts predictions at a future timestamp $t+1$ depends on the KGs at the latest $k$ timestamps (i.e., $\{\mathcal{G}_{t-k+1}, ..., \mathcal{G}_{t-1}, \mathcal{G}_t\}$), the two temporal prediction problems can be formulated as follows:

**Problem 1. Entity Prediction.** The entity prediction task aims to predict the missing object entity of a query $(s_{t+1}, r_{t+1}, ?_{t+1})$ and the missing subject entity of a query $(?_{t+1}, r_{t+1}, o_{t+1})$ which can be converted to $(s_{t+1}, r_{t+1}^{-1}, ?_{t+1})$. We model the conditional probability vector of all object entities with the subject entity $s$, the relation $r$ and the historical KG sequence $\mathcal{G}_{t-k+1:t}$:

$$\mathbb{P}(o|s, r, \mathcal{G}_{t-k+1:t}) \tag{1}$$

**Problem 2. Relation Prediction.** The relation prediction task attempts to predict the missing relation of a query $(s_{t+1}, ?_{t+1}, o_{t+1})$. We model the conditional probability vector of all relations with the subject entity $s$, the object entity $o$ and the historical KG sequence $\mathcal{G}_{t-k+1:t}$:

$$\mathbb{P}(r|s, o, \mathcal{G}_{t-k+1:t}) \tag{2}$$

## 4  Methodology

We introduce a novel temporal Hybrid Reasoning Networks (tHR-NET) that unifies the concepts of evolution representation learning and query-specific methods to perform reasoning over the TKG. Figure 2 illustrates the working flow of tHR-NET, which comprises four key modules: 1) Global Graph Space Evolution - This module performs global graph features vectorization at each time and

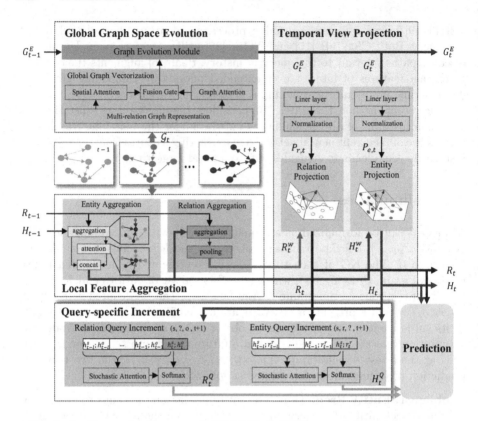

**Fig. 2.** An illustrative diagram of tHR-NET for TKG reasoning at timestamp t.

then obtains the global graph evolution representation. 2) Local Feature Aggregation - It aggregates entity and relation features through the known structural information and uncertain attention information from the micro-level perspective. 3) Temporal View Projection - It aligns the aggregated local features of entity/relation representations to the current graph evolution space through the projection technique. 4) Query-specific Increment - This module enhances the entity/relation representations based on specific queries, enabling the capture of factors most relevant to the query over a long duration. In the following sections, we provide detailed explanations of each of the four modules.

## 4.1  Global Graph Space Evolution

This module focuses on the representation of global graph feature evolution trends over time, which provides a macro-level alignment and adjustment background for entity and relation evolution.

**Global Graph Vectorization.** To form complete graph feature vectorization at each time, tHR-NET extracts the interactions between entities from different relational perspectives. We utilize matrix $G_{r_i}^M(t) \in \mathbb{R}^{N \times N}$ as one relation graph and each element represents whether exists a relation $r_i$ between entities in $\mathcal{G}_t$. Then we employ a fully-connected neural network to transform the matrix into a multidimensional vector $G_{r_i,e_j}^M(t) \in \mathbb{R}^H$, where $r_i, e_j$ is an arbitrary relation and entity at any time.

In order to acquire inner and outer correlations of multi-relation graphs, we design a multi-layer spatial-graph attention fusion component. The $l$-th layer input is denoted as $G^{(l-1)}$, and the hidden state of entity $e_j$ on relation graph $r_i$ is denoted as $g_{r_i,e_j}^{(l-1)}$. The 1-th layer input is initialized as $g_{r_i,e_j}^{(0)} = G_{r_i,e_j}^M$. Then, spatial attention and graph attention calculations are performed at each layer.

As an illustration, consider the graph attention mechanism, which captures the correlations between the same entities in multi-relation graphs. The $h$-th head graph attention coefficient $\beta_{r_i,r_m}^{(h)}$ is calculated as follows:

$$\beta_{r_i,r_m}^{(h)} = \frac{exp\left(< f_g^{(h)}\left(g_{r_i,e_j}^{(l-1)}\right), f_g^{(h)}\left(g_{r_m,e_j}^{(l-1)}\right) >\right)}{\sum_{m \in M} exp\left(< f_g^{(h)}\left(g_{r_i,e_j}^{(l-1)}\right), f_g^{(h)}\left(g_{r_m,e_j}^{(l-1)}\right) >\right)} \tag{3}$$

where $f_g^{(h)}$ is ReLU function, and $r_m$ can be an arbitrary relation graph. Then we obtain the next layer state from graph attention for $e_j$ in relation $r_i$ as follows:

$$g_{r_i,e_j}^{g,(l)} = \sum_{h=1}^{H} \left( \sum_{m=1}^{M} \beta_{r_i,r_m}^{(h)} \cdot f_g^{(h)}\left(g_{r_m,e_j}^{(l-1)}\right) \right) \tag{4}$$

The spatial attention mechanism mainly captures the correlations of different entities in the same relation graph. Similarly, we can calculate the spatial attention coefficient $\alpha_{e_j,e_n}^{(h)}$ and the next layer state $g_{r_i,e_j}^{s,(l)}$.

To further combine correlations on different spatial and graphs, outputs from spatial attention $G^{s,(l)}$ and graph attention $G^{g,(l)}$ in the l-th block are fused:

$$G^{(l)} = \omega \otimes G^{s,(l)} + (1 - \omega) \otimes G^{g,(l)} \tag{5}$$

where $\omega$ is a gate inspired by [30] and $\otimes$ indicates a Hadamard product operation.

**Graph Evolution Module.** We update the global graph evolution embedding matrix $G_{t-1}^E$ to $G_t^E$ via the GRU with the fusion feature $G_t$ obtained before:

$$G_t^E = GRU\left(G_{t-1}^E, G_t\right) \tag{6}$$

where $G_t^E$ are randomly initialized at the time of $t = 0$.

### 4.2   Local Feature Aggregation

This module focuses on micro-level entity and relation feature extraction, which utilizes local structure information and mines hidden information via the attention mechanism.

**Entity Feature Aggregation.** In order to acquire complete and accuracy entity feature representations, tHR-NET considers the impacts of both known local structure and uncertain attention on entities. To this end, we utilize a multi-layer GCN for entity feature aggregation and obtain the local information in the $l$-th layer as follows:

$$h_{o,t}^{(l),loc} = f \left( \sum_{(s,r),\exists(s,r,o)\in\mathcal{G}_t} W_l^1 \left( h_{s,t}^{w,(l-1)} + r_{t-1} \right) + W_l^2 h_{o,t}^{w,(l-1)} \right) \quad (7)$$

where $h_{s,t}^{w,(l-1)}, h_{o,t}^{w,(l-1)}$ are the elements in $H_t^{w,(l-1)}$, $r_{t-1}$ is the element in $R_{t-1}$. $W_l^1$ and $W_l^2$ are the learnable parameters, and $f(\cdot)$ is ReLU function. The 1-th layer input $H_t^{w,(0)} = H_{t-1}$. Inspired by [2], a structure-aware Transformer can be constructed to consolidate the attention information concerning the entities.

$$h_{v,t}^{(l),nloc} = h_{v,t}^{(l),loc} + 1/\sqrt{d_v} \cdot \sum_{u,w\in\mathcal{N}_k(v)} \frac{exp(< h_{v,t}^{(l),loc}, h_{u,t}^{(l),loc} >)}{\sum exp(< h_{v,t}^{(l),loc}, h_{w,t}^{(l),loc} >)} h_{u,t}^{(l),loc} \quad (8)$$

where $d_v$ denotes the number of the $k$-hop neighborhood $\mathcal{N}_k(v)$ of entity $v$, and $u, w$ are the entities within $\mathcal{N}_k(v)$. $k$ is an adjustable hyperparameter and the larger $k$ is, the more uncertain information is concerned. Especially, to combine the known structural information with the uncertain attention information of entities, we utilize the residual technique by concatenating both types of information and passing through a linear layer to produce the output $h_t^{w,(l)}$. The final embedding matrix $H_t^w$ can be obtained after several aggregations.

**Relation Feature Aggregation.** Similar to entity aggregation, the calculation of relation aggregation is also directional. For each relation $r \in \mathcal{R}$ existing in $\mathcal{G}_t$ at time $t$, the update is calculated as follows:

$$r_t^w = f \left( \sum_{(s,o),\exists(s,r,o)\in\mathcal{G}_t} W_r^1 \left( h_{o,t}^w - h_{s,t}^w \right) + W_r^2 r_{t-1} \right) \quad (9)$$

where $W_r^1$ and $W_r^2$ are the learnable parameters, and $f(\cdot)$ is ReLU function. Then we can acquire relation embedding matrix $R_t^w$.

### 4.3 Temporal View Projection

We apply a temporal space projection computation to align the aggregated local features of entity/relation representations with the current graph evolution space. This ensures that the entities/relations representations after local feature aggregation also adhere to the continuous variability inherent in the graph evolution.

To capture projection space, graph evolution embedding $G_{t-1}^E$ and $G_t^E$ are used calculating the evolution dynamics of the entity and relation $P_{e,t}$ and $P_{r,t}$:

$$P_{e,t} = W_p^1 (G_{t-1}^E)^{-1} G_t^E + b_p^1 \tag{10}$$

$$P_{r,t} = W_p^2 (G_{t-1}^E)^{-1} G_t^E + b_p^2 \tag{11}$$

where $W_p^1$, $W_p^2$, and $b_p^1$, $b_p^2$ are learnable parameters, which represent entities and relations will be projected into different parameter spaces. Then we restrict $||P_{e,t}||_2 = 1$ and $||P_{r,t}||_2 = 1$ by normalization. After that, we use the entity embedding $H_t^w$ and relation embedding $R_t^w$ calculating the projection [4] to transform their feature space into current feature space. Each entity and relation evolution embedding $h_t$ and $r_t$ are calculated by different learnable weights as follows:

$$h_t = h_t^w + (W_p^3 P_{e,t})^T h_t^w (W_p^3 P_{e,t}) \tag{12}$$

$$r_t = r_t^w + (W_p^4 P_{r,t})^T r_t^w (W_p^4 P_{r,t}) \tag{13}$$

Finally, we acquire entity and relation evolution embedding matrices $H_t$ and $R_t$.

### 4.4 Query-Specific Increment

This module aims to break the temporal forgetfulness in the evolution representation of entities and relations, thereby reducing or eliminating the reliance on recent non-causal related events in inference. It enhances the entity/relation representations based on specific queries, enabling the capture of aspects most relevant to the query over a long duration.

We designed a query-based buffer pool that can retain information related to queries over an extended time period $l$. Taking the entity prediction query $(s, r, ?, t+1)$ as an example, the information in the query buffer pool can be represented as:

$$X_{(s,r),t} = \{(h_{t-l}^s; r_{t-l}^r), ..., (h_{t-1}^s; r_{t-1}^r), (h_t^s; r_t^r)\} \tag{14}$$

where $h_k^s, r_k^r$, $k \in [t-l, ..., t-1, t]$ are the vector representations of entity $s$ and relation $r$ from $H_t$ and $R_t$ respectively. Similarly, for the relation prediction query $(s, ?, o, t+1)$, the result is $X_{(s,o),t}$.

To minimize the noise impact of non-causal factors and retain only the most relevant historical aspects, we make improvements to a type of random attention mechanism [22]. For each timestamp information in the query buffer pool $(h_k^s; r_k^r)$, we map it to $p_{(s,r),k} \in [0, 1]$ through an MLP layer followed by a sigmoid activation function. Then, for each forward training, we draw random attention from the Bernoulli distribution $\alpha_{(s,r),k} \sim Bern(p_{(s,r),k})$. To ensure that the gradient is computable, we apply the gumbel-softmax reparameterization trick [11]. Subsequently, we obtain the information increment corresponding to the entity prediction query as follows:

$$(h_t^{Q,s}, r_t^{Q,r}) = \sum_{k=t-l}^{l} \alpha_{(s,r),k} \cdot X_{(s,r),k} \tag{15}$$

Similarly, for relation prediction queries, the information increment can be obtained as $(h_t^{Q,s}, h_t^{Q,o})$. To facilitate a unified representation, we denote the collection of the above entity and relation enhanced representations as $H_t^Q$ and $R_t^Q$, respectively.

### 4.5   Prediction and Loss Function

This model is to solve the entity and relation prediction problems in TKG reasoning. We choose ConvTransE [24] as the downstream task decoder and acquire the probability vector of all entities and relations:

$$p\left(o|s,r,H_t,R_t\right) = \sigma\left(H_t ConvTransE\left(s_t + s_t^Q, r_t + r_t^Q\right)\right) \tag{16}$$

$$p\left(r|s,o,H_t,R_t\right) = \sigma\left(R_t ConvTransE\left(s_t + s_t^Q, o_t + o_t^Q\right)\right) \tag{17}$$

where $\sigma\left(\cdot\right)$ is the sigmoid function, $s_t, r_t, o_t, s_t^Q, r_t^Q, o_t^Q$ are the embeddings of $s, r$ and $o$ at timestamp $t$ in $H_t, R_t, H_t^Q$ and $R_t^Q$ respectively.

We construct the objective function to guide both the evolution learning of entities/relations and the query increment to produce the desired effects during training our model. Formally, we use a binary crossentropy loss to optimize the model parameters as follows:

$$L_e = \sum_{t=0}^{T-1} \sum_{(s,r,o)\in\ G_{t+1}} \left(-log\ p\left(o\,|s,r,H_t,R_t\right) - \beta \cdot log\ \left(1 - p\left(o\,|s,r,H_t^w,R_t^w\right)\right)\right) \tag{18}$$

$$L_r = \sum_{t=0}^{T-1} \sum_{(s,r,o)\in\ G_{t+1}} \left(-log\ p\left(r\,|s,o,H_t,R_t\right) - \beta \cdot log\ \left(1 - p\left(r\,|s,o,H_t^w,R_t^w\right)\right)\right) \tag{19}$$

where $T$ is the number of timestamps in the training set. While $p\left(o|s,r,H_t^w,R_t^w\right)$ and $p\left(r|s,o,H_t^w,R_t^w\right)$ without projection are regarded as negative samples to accelerate convergence process. $\beta$ is the hyper-parameter to balance positive and negative samples.

In order to combined different prediction task loss, we minimize the following objective function to learn the model parameter:

$$L = \alpha L_e + (1 - \alpha) L_r \tag{20}$$

where $\alpha$ is the hyper-parameter to balance the weight of the multi-task learning problem.

## 5   Experiment

In this section, we perform experiments to validate the effectiveness of our proposed tHR-NET model by investigating the research questions as follows:

**RQ1:** How does our proposed thR-NET method perform compared with state-of-the-art TKG facts prediction methods?

**RQ2:** How do the different components of thR-NET contribute to the model performance?

**RQ3:** How do the configurations of model hyperparameters affect the prediction performance?

**RQ4:** Can the proposed thR-NET model show interpretability, through the effective modeling of TKGs evolution trends and the enhancement of query-related features?

### 5.1 Experimental Settings

**Datasets.** The experimental evaluation was executed on four different event datasets with three different lengths of time intervals. Table 1 provides a summary of the dataset statistics. The **ICEWS14** and **ICEWS05-15** datasets [7] originate from the Integrated Crisis Early Warning System (ICEWS), a repository containing political events, which occurred within a time interval of 24 h. **YAGO** [20], is a comprehensive semantic knowledge base from wiki resources, and our experiments are taken from a subset of it with a 1-year time interval. **GDELT** [14] is drawn from the Global Database of Events, Language, and Tone with a 15-minute time interval. Each of these aforementioned datasets was partitioned into training, validation, and test sets, approximately maintaining a proportion of 8:1:1 respectively.

**Table 1.** Dataset Statistics. $|\mathcal{S}_{train}|$, $|\mathcal{S}_{valid}|$, $|\mathcal{S}_{test}|$ are the numbers of facts in training, validation, and test sets. The time interval donates time granularity between temporally adjacent facts.

| Datasets | $|\mathcal{E}|$ | $|\mathcal{R}|$ | $|\mathcal{S}_{train}|$ | $|\mathcal{S}_{valid}|$ | $|\mathcal{S}_{test}|$ | time interval |
|---|---|---|---|---|---|---|
| ICEWS14 | 6869 | 230 | 74,845 | 8,514 | 7,371 | 24 h |
| ICEWS05-15 | 10,094 | 251 | 368,868 | 46,302 | 46,159 | 24 h |
| YAGO | 10,623 | 10 | 161,540 | 19,523 | 20,026 | 1 year |
| GDELT | 7,691 | 240 | 1,734,399 | 238,765 | 305,241 | 15 min |

**Baselines.** To fully evaluate the performance of our method, we compare thR-NET with static KG embedding models and TKG embedding models as well as state-of-the-art methods. For **entity prediction**, we opt for DistMult [28], ComplEx [26], R-GCN [23], ConvE [5], and ConvTransE [24] as static models, disregarding temporal data to facilitate the completion of absent entities within knowledge graphs. We employ HyTE [4], TTransE [13], TA-DistMult [7], RE-NET [12], RE-GCN [18], rGalT [6], CEN [15], HisMatch [16] and CRNet [27] as TKG embedding models. For **relation prediction**, we choose from the aforementioned models that are directly applicable to address relation completion or prediction challenges including ConvE [5] and ConvTransE [24] for static models, and RE-GCN [18] for temporal models.

**Evaluation Metrics.** To evaluate our method quantitatively, we adopt two widely used metrics for entity prediction and relation prediction [6,12,18]: *MRR* denotes the Mean Reciprocal Ranks which is a more stable evaluation metric compared with MR [12]. *Hits@k* denotes the percentage that the top-$k$ recommended list contains at least one ground truth item. In our experiments, $k$ is set to 1, 3 and 10. Specifically, for the entity prediction task on YAGO, since the previous works RE-NET and RE-GCN did not report the results of *Hits@1*, we then only report the results of *MRR* and *Hits@{3, 10}*. Following previous work [6], during evaluations, We compare the experimental results under the raw setting rather than the filtered setting utilized in [12].

**Implementation Details.** We implement our model using Pytorch and adopt Adam optimizer for model optimization. During the training phase, the model inference process is conducted with a learning rate of 0.001 configured with a 0.99 decay rate. The default setting for hidden state dimensionality is 100 and the dropout rate is 0.5. The length of historical sequences in the Global Graph Space Evolution module is chosen from the range [1, 2, 3, 4, 5, 6] with the best setting of 4 for ICEWS14 and ICEWS05-15 dataset, 3 for YAGO dataset and 5 for GDELT dataset. The number of entity and relation aggregation layers is set to 2 and 1 for all datasets respectively. The length of the extended time period in the Query-specific Increment module is set to 20 for all datasets. For the downstream ConvTransE model, we refer to the settings of RE-GCN [18]. The hyperparameter $\alpha$ for balancing the multi-task learning problem, and the hyperparameter $\beta$ for balancing the two representation learning process, are optimized according to grid search in different datasets.

**Table 2.** Performance results of the proposed method vs. baselines for the entity prediction task over all datasets (%).

| Model | ICEWS14 | | | | ICEWS05-15 | | | | YAGO | | | GDELT | | | |
|---|---|---|---|---|---|---|---|---|---|---|---|---|---|---|---|
| | MRR | H@1 | H@3 | H@10 | MRR | H@1 | H@3 | H@10 | MRR | H@3 | H@10 | MRR | H@1 | H@3 | H@10 |
| DistMult | 20.32 | 6.13 | 27.59 | 46.61 | 19.91 | 5.63 | 27.22 | 47.33 | 44.05 | 49.70 | 59.94 | 8.61 | 3.91 | 8.27 | 17.04 |
| ComplEx | 22.61 | 9.88 | 28.93 | 47.57 | 20.26 | 6.67 | 26.43 | 47.31 | 44.09 | 49.57 | 59.64 | 9.84 | 5.17 | 9.58 | 18.23 |
| R-GCN | 28.03 | 19.42 | 31.95 | 44.83 | 27.13 | 18.83 | 30.41 | 43.16 | 20.25 | 24.01 | 37.30 | 12.17 | 7.40 | 12.37 | 20.63 |
| ConvE | 30.30 | 21.30 | 34.42 | 47.89 | 31.40 | 21.56 | 35.70 | 50.96 | 41.22 | 47.03 | 59.90 | 18.37 | 11.29 | 19.36 | 32.13 |
| ConvTransE | 31.50 | 22.46 | 34.98 | 50.03 | 30.28 | 20.79 | 33.80 | 49.95 | 46.67 | 52.22 | 62.52 | 19.07 | 11.85 | 20.32 | 33.14 |
| HyTE | 16.78 | 2.13 | 24.84 | 43.94 | 16.05 | 6.53 | 20.20 | 34.72 | 14.42 | 39.73 | 46.98 | 6.69 | 0.01 | 7.57 | 19.06 |
| TTransE | 12.86 | 3.14 | 15.72 | 33.65 | 16.53 | 5.51 | 20.77 | 39.26 | 26.10 | 36.28 | 47.73 | 5.53 | 0.46 | 4.97 | 15.37 |
| TA-DistMult | 26.22 | 16.83 | 29.72 | 45.23 | 27.51 | 17.57 | 31.46 | 47.32 | 44.98 | 50.64 | 61.11 | 10.34 | 4.44 | 10.44 | 21.63 |
| RE-NET | 35.77 | 25.99 | 40.10 | 54.87 | 36.86 | 26.24 | 41.85 | 57.60 | 46.81 | 52.71 | 61.93 | 19.60 | 12.03 | 20.56 | 33.89 |
| RE-GCN | 40.39 | 30.66 | 44.96 | 59.21 | 48.03 | 37.33 | 53.85 | 68.27 | 58.27 | 65.62 | 75.94 | 19.64 | 12.42 | 20.90 | 33.69 |
| rGalT | 38.33 | 28.57 | 42.86 | 58.13 | 38.89 | 27.58 | 44.19 | 59.10 | 51.54 | 54.76 | 68.31 | 19.56 | 12.11 | 20.89 | 34.15 |
| CEN | 42.20 | 30.08 | 47.46 | 61.31 | 43.76 | 31.58 | 50.10 | 63.77 | 54.92 | 55.77 | 71.04 | 21.16 | 13.43 | 22.71 | 36.38 |
| CRNet | 48.37 | 38.21 | 53.79 | 67.79 | 48.90 | 39.14 | 54.93 | 69.18 | 60.65 | 63.98 | 74.62 | 25.32 | 15.39 | 27.82 | 44.07 |
| HisMatch | 46.42 | 35.91 | 51.63 | 66.84 | 52.85 | 42.01 | 59.05 | 73.28 | 59.97 | 64.08 | 74.35 | 22.01 | 14.45 | 23.80 | 36.61 |
| tHR-Net | 51.74 | 39.52 | 55.08 | 70.53 | 52.97 | 43.12 | 58.84 | 72.97 | 69.54 | 71.54 | 88.78 | 23.00 | 15.19 | 26.84 | 40.03 |

**Table 3.** Performance results of the proposed method vs. baselines for the relation prediction task over all datasets (%).

| Model | ICEWS14 | ICEWS05-15 | YAGO | GDELT |
|---|---|---|---|---|
| ConvE | 38.80 | 37.89 | 91.33 | 18.84 |
| ConvTransE | 38.40 | 38.26 | 90.98 | 18.97 |
| RE-GCN | 39.73 | 38.56 | 95.18 | 19.17 |
| tHR-NET | **50.78** | **51.05** | **97.87** | **22.39** |

## 5.2  Performance Results (RQ1)

**Results on Entity Prediction.** Table 2 presents a comprehensive comparison between our proposed method and baseline approaches for entity prediction tasks on four TKG datasets: ICEWS14, ICEWS05-15, YAGO, and GDELT. tHR-NET consistently achieves the best or near-best results on the aforementioned datasets. Specifically, tHR-NET performs much better than all static methods (the first block) and temporal models under interpolation settings (the second block) primarily due to our model considers temporal factors and has abilities to predict.

Concerning temporal models based on extrapolation settings (the third block), tHR-NET outperforms query-specific methods RE-NET and rGalT on all datasets. Unlike those methods, which focus solely on historical facts related to entities, tHR-NET also considers the possibility of future events that have not yet occurred. This makes tHR-NET more adept at mining and exploring events, leading to its superior performance. Compared to query-specific methods, evolution representation learning methods such as RE-GCN, CEN, and CRNet more rationally model the continuous process of TKG evolving over time, achieving superior results. Specifically, CRNet, through a post-processing module predicting interactions of concurrent related events, obtains the best results on the GDELT dataset, where numerous concurrent events exist. HisMatch considers both evolution and query-related histories, but its reliance on recurrent neural networks for extracting features from query-related historical events results in challenges with temporal forgetting. In contrast, our tHR-NET's query-specific increment module has the ability to capture the most relevant information to a query over extended periods, achieving better results in most cases.

**Results on Relation Prediction.** In Table 3, we present the experimental results of the MRR metric comparison, which show evidence that tHR-NET surpasses all other baselines in all the datasets. This superior performance can probably be attributed to our model's ability to catch both the global evolution trends and the query-related information, which provides accurate modeling for relation representation and reasoning.

**Table 4.** Ablation studies on entity prediction.

| Model | ICEWS14 | ICEWS05-15 | YAGO | GDELT |
|---|---|---|---|---|
| tHR-Net | **51.74** | **52.97** | **69.54** | **23.00** |
| - GGSE | 37.16 | 39.21 | 45.74 | 16.16 |
| + FCN | 42.89 | 44.78 | 51.34 | 19.27 |
| - local agg. | 45.08 | 47.12 | 58.57 | 19.97 |
| - nlocal agg. | 47.31 | 47.04 | 60.01 | 20.64 |
| - PW | 43.17 | 46.57 | 60.22 | 21.01 |
| - Lw loss | 48.53 | 44.60 | 59.19 | 21.76 |
| - query inc. | 39.55 | 39.88 | 64.39 | 19.94 |

**Table 5.** Ablation studies on relation prediction.

| Model | ICEWS14 | ICEWS05-15 | YAGO | GDELT |
|---|---|---|---|---|
| tHR-NET | **50.78** | **51.05** | **97.87** | **22.39** |
| - GGSE | 40.09 | 40.78 | 94.00 | 18.29 |
| + FCN | 45.92 | 45.30 | 95.32 | 19.07 |
| - local agg. | 47.03 | 48.03 | 96.19 | 19.39 |
| - nlocal agg. | 46.58 | 47.91 | 96.99 | 19.16 |
| - PW | 48.12 | 46.58 | 96.04 | 19.88 |
| - Lw loss | 47.65 | 47.42 | 96.72 | 20.75 |
| - query inc. | 41.97 | 42.08 | 97.85 | 19.76 |

### 5.3  Ablation Study (RQ2)

To verify the effects of the designed different components in our model, we conduct ablation experiments on the above datasets. We discuss the effects of each component as follows:

**Effect of Global Graph Space Evolution.** As demonstrated in Tables 4 and 5, we removed the Global Graph Space Evolution module, denoted as "-GGSE". The term "+FCN" indicates the replacement of the Spatial-Graph Attention Fusion method with a simple single-layer fully connected network. A notable impact on the results for all datasets can be observed, signifying that this module enables the model to capture the evolutionary trends and preferences in the global feature space of graphs.

**Effect of Local Feature Aggregation.** The "-local agg." scenario represents the removal of the local structure aggregation layer based on GCN from the Local Feature Aggregation module. Only the attention mechanism based on Transformers is retained. Conversely, the "-nlocal agg." scenario is the exact opposite. The results reveal that both two feature aggregation mechanisms effectively impact the model's performance.

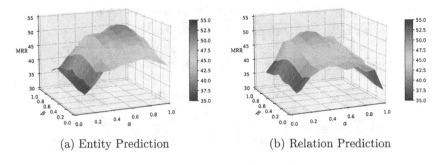

(a) Entity Prediction                    (b) Relation Prediction

**Fig. 3.** Parameter sensitivity analysis on ICEWS14 dataset.

**Effect of Temporal Evolution Learning.** We modified Eq. (8) and investigated the use of the same projection matrix for entity and relation calculation in the Temporal View Projection module over time, denoted as "-$PW$". It was observed that the performance of the "-$PW$" scenario slightly declined across all four datasets. Additionally, the "-$Lw$ loss" scenario retains only the loss functions for entity and relation prediction tasks. The performance demonstrated the important role of evolution negative samples in facilitating model convergence.

**Effect of Query-Specific Increment.** By removing the Query-specific Increment module, denoted as "-$query$ inc.", we observed a notable impact on the results across all datasets. This phenomenon indicates that selectively relying on query-related history, rather than strictly depending on recent history, can lead to more accurate representations of entities and relations.

### 5.4 Parameter Sensitive (RQ3)

Figure 3 displays the influence of the hyperparameters $\alpha$ and $\beta$ on entity prediction and relation prediction performance on the ICEWS14 dataset. $\alpha$ balances the entity prediction with the relation prediction results, while $\beta$ balances downstream tasks with evolution trends. As observed, within the $\alpha$ range of 0.5 to 0.9, there is an inverse relation between the entity and relation predictions changes trends consistent with intuitive expectations. At approximately 0.8, $\beta$ yields relatively better results for both tasks.

### 5.5 Case Study (RQ4)

This section provides an explanation for the model's predictions by examining the trends in the changes of inter-entity correlations during the graph evolution process. We investigated a selected query *(Catherine Ashton, Express intent to meet or negotiate, ?, 339)* from the ICEWS14 test set. Figuer 4 shows how tHR-NET infers the prediction result for this query by mining the trend of correlation changes between entities throughout the evolution process of relevant facts. Here,

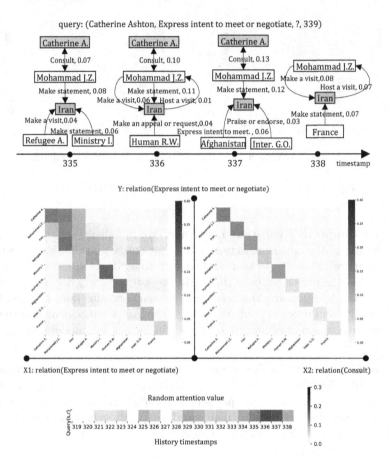

**Fig. 4.** An example to illustrate how tHR-NET identifies the evolution trend of facts. The upper part displays the subgraphs of facts related to the query *(Catherine Ashton, Express intent to meet or negotiate, ?, 339)* at different timestamps. The middle part presents the two types of attention coefficients of the global graph evolution module for relevant entities at timestamp 339. The lower part presents the random attention value for the recent 20 timestamps.

the historical time refers to timestamps from 335 to 338. The upper part of Fig. 4 displays the subgraphs consisting of partially relevant facts at different timestamps. We model the attention scores for associated entities of a given entity type using Eq. (8) to quantify the relevance between entities. It can be observed that the correlation between the same two entities changes according to a certain trend as time progresses. For instance, as *(Catherine Ashton, Consult, Mohammad Javad Zarif)* repeatedly appears at timestamps 335, 336, and 337, the correlation between the two entities gradually strengthens, resulting in a higher attention coefficient, which is consistent with human reasoning intuition. The middle part of Fig. 4 shows the two types of attention coefficients in the global graph evolution module for relevant entities at timestamp 339. The left graph displays the spatial attention coefficients calculated by Eq. (3) for entities in the subgraph of the relation *Express intent to meet or negotiate*. The right graph presents the graph attention coefficients between the same entities in the subgraphs of relations *Express intent to meet or negotiate* and *Consult*. We can observe that the entities *Catherine Ashton, Mohammad Javad Zarif* and *Iran* demonstrate notable associations in both perspectives, which can be regarded as the inference evolution trend for this query. The lower part of Fig. 4 shows the random attention values in the query-specific increment module for the recent 20 timestamps. We can observe that event reasoning can be influenced by features over an extended period without apparent temporal forgetfulness. At timestamps 336 and 337, higher values indicate the capture of influential factors related to the query, reflecting the model's ability to retain relevant historical information.

# 6 Conclusion

We proposed a novel temporal hybrid reasoning network for TKG reasoning, referred to as thR-NET, which simultaneously considers the continuous variability of graph evolution and the causal discontinuity of query-related histories for the first time. Our proposed temporal projection technique aligns local entities/relations representations with graph evolution dynamics, maintaining consistency with temporal continuous variability. Additionally, the query-specific increment module addresses the issue of temporal forgetfulness in evolution representation learning, leading to improved reasoning performance. Experimental results on four commonly used datasets demonstrate that our model exhibits excellent performance in both entity prediction and relation prediction tasks. Our future work aims to introduce the idea of the information bottleneck to further refine the representation of query-related histories.

**Acknowledgements.** The authors would like to thank the anonymous reviewers for their valuable comments. This work is supported by National Key Research and Development Program of China No. 2022-JCJQ-JJ-0587.

# References

1. Barros, C.D.T., Mendonça, M.R.F., Vieira, A.B., Ziviani, A.: A survey on embedding dynamic graphs. ACM Comput. Surv. **55**(1), 1–37 (2023)
2. Chen, D., O'Bray, L., Borgwardt, K.: Structure-aware transformer for graph representation learning. In: Proceedings of the 39th International Conference on Machine Learning, vol. 162, pp. 3469–3489 (2022)
3. Chen, J., Wang, X., Xu, X.: GC-LSTM: graph convolution embedded LSTM for dynamic network link prediction. Appl. Intell. **52**(7), 7513–7528 (2022)
4. Dasgupta, S.S., Ray, S.N., Talukdar, P.: HyTE: hyperplane-based Temporally aware knowledge graph embedding. In: Proceedings of the 2018 Conference on Empirical Methods in Natural Language Processing, pp. 2001–2011 (2018)

5. Dettmers, T., Minervini, P., Stenetorp, P., Riedel, S.: Convolutional 2D knowledge graph embeddings. In: Proceedings of the AAAI Conference on Artificial Intelligence, vol. 32, no. 1 (2018)
6. Gao, Y., Feng, L., Kan, Z., Han, Y., Qiao, L., Li, D.: Modeling precursors for temporal knowledge graph reasoning via auto-encoder structure. In: Proceedings of the Thirty-First International Joint Conference on Artificial Intelligence, pp. 2044–2051 (2022)
7. Garcia-Duran, A., Dumančić, S., Niepert, M.: Learning sequence encoders for temporal knowledge graph completion. In: Proceedings of the 2018 Conference on Empirical Methods in Natural Language Processing, pp. 4816–4821 (2018)
8. Goyal, P., Kamra, N., He, X., Liu, Y.: Dyngem: deep embedding method for dynamic graphs (2018)
9. Han, Z., Chen, P., Ma, Y., Tresp, V.: Explainable subgraph reasoning for forecasting on temporal knowledge graphs. In: International Conference on Learning Representations (2021)
10. Han, Z., Ding, Z., Ma, Y., Gu, Y., Tresp, V.: Learning neural ordinary equations for forecasting future links on temporal knowledge graphs. In: Proceedings of the 2021 Conference on Empirical Methods in Natural Language Processing (2021)
11. Jang, E., Gu, S., Poole, B.: Categorical reparameterization with gumbel-softmax. In: International Conference on Learning Representations (2017)
12. Jin, W., et al.: Recurrent event network: global structure inference over temporal knowledge graph (2019)
13. Leblay, J., Chekol, M.W.: Deriving validity time in knowledge graph. In: Companion Proceedings of the the Web Conference 2018, pp. 1771–1776 (2018)
14. Leetaru, K., Schrodt, P.A.: Gdelt: global data on events, location, and tone. ISA Annual Convention (2013)
15. Li, Z., et al.: Complex evolutional pattern learning for temporal knowledge graph reasoning. In: Proceedings of the 60th Annual Meeting of the Association for Computational Linguistics, pp. 290–296 (2022)
16. Li, Z., et al.: HiSMatch: historical structure matching based temporal knowledge graph reasoning. In: Findings of the Association for Computational Linguistics: EMNLP 2022, pp. 7328–7338 (2022)
17. Li, Z., et al.: Search from history and reason for future: two-stage reasoning on temporal knowledge graphs. In: Proceedings of the 59th Annual Meeting of the Association for Computational Linguistics and the 11th International Joint Conference on Natural Language Processing (2021)
18. Li, Z., et al.: Temporal knowledge graph reasoning based on evolutional representation learning. In: Proceedings of the 44th International ACM SIGIR Conference on Research and Development in Information Retrieval, pp. 408–417 (2021)
19. Liu, D., et al.: User-event graph embedding learning for context-aware recommendation. In: Proceedings of the 28th ACM SIGKDD Conference on Knowledge Discovery and Data Mining, pp. 1051–1059 (2022)
20. Mahdisoltani, F., Biega, J.A., Suchanek, F.M.: Yago3: a knowledge base from multilingual Wikipedias. In: Conference on Innovative Data Systems Research (2015)
21. Mao, H., Schwarzkopf, M., Venkatakrishnan, S.B., Meng, Z., Alizadeh, M.: Learning scheduling algorithms for data processing clusters. In: Proceedings of the ACM Special Interest Group on Data Communication, pp. 270–288. Beijing China (2019)
22. Miao, S., Liu, M., Li, P.: Interpretable and generalizable graph learning via stochastic attention mechanism. In: Proceedings of the 39th International Conference on Machine Learning, vol. 162, pp. 15524–15543 (2022)

23. Schlichtkrull, M., Kipf, T.N., Bloem, P., van den Berg, R., Titov, I., Welling, M.: Modeling relational data with graph convolutional networks. In: Gangemi, A., et al. (eds.) ESWC 2018. LNCS, vol. 10843, pp. 593–607. Springer, Cham (2018). https://doi.org/10.1007/978-3-319-93417-4_38
24. Shang, C., Tang, Y., Huang, J., Bi, J., He, X., Zhou, B.: End-to-end structure-aware convolutional networks for knowledge base completion. In: Proceedings of the AAAI Conference on Artificial Intelligence, vol. 33, no. 01, pp. 3060–3067 (2019)
25. Sun, H., Zhong, J., Ma, Y., Han, Z., He, K.: TimeTraveler: reinforcement learning for temporal knowledge graph forecasting. In: Proceedings of the 2021 Conference on Empirical Methods in Natural Language Processing (2021)
26. Trouillon, T., Welbl, J., Riedel, S., Gaussier, E., Bouchard, G.: Complex embeddings for simple link prediction. In: Proceedings of The 33rd International Conference on Machine Learning, pp. 2071–2080 (2016)
27. Wang, S., Cai, X., Zhang, Y., Yuan, X.: CRnet: modeling concurrent events over temporal knowledge graph. In: Sattler, U., et al. (eds.) ISWC 2022. LNCS, vol. 13489, pp. 516–533. Springer, Cham (2022). https://doi.org/10.1007/978-3-031-19433-7_30
28. Yang, B., Yih, W.T., He, X., Gao, J., Deng, L.: Embedding entities and relations for learning and inference in knowledge bases (2014)
29. Zhang, M., Xia, Y., Liu, Q., Wu, S., Wang, L.: Learning latent relations for temporal knowledge graph reasoning. In: Proceedings of the 61st Annual Meeting of the Association for Computational Linguistics, pp. 12617–12631 (2023)
30. Zheng, C., Fan, X., Wang, C., Qi, J.: Gman: a graph multi-attention network for traffic prediction. In: Proceedings of the AAAI Conference on Artificial Intelligence, vol. 34, pp. 1234–1241 (2020)
31. Zhu, C., Chen, M., Fan, C., Cheng, G.: Learning from history: modeling temporal knowledge graphs with sequential copy-generation networks. In: Proceedings of the AAAI Conference on Artificial Intelligence, vol. 35, no. 5, pp. 4732–4740 (2021)

# Improving Code Representation Learning via Multi-view Contrastive Graph Pooling for Abstract Syntax Tree

Ruoting Wu⬥, Yuxin Zhang⬥, and Liang Chen[✉]⬥

School of Computer Science, Sun Yat-sen University, Guangzhou, China
{wurt8,zhangyx355}@mail2.sysu.edu.cn, chenliang6@mail.sysu.edu.cn

**Abstract.** As the field of code intelligence continues to grow, Code representation learning has emerged as a research hot spot. Given that code structure can be naturally represented as graphs, Graph Neural Networks (GNNs) have proven highly effective for learning graph representations of source code. Pooling, as an essential operation for GNN-based models, is limited in its ability to leverage the rich hierarchical information presented in tree-like graph, especially Abstract Syntax Trees. In order to learn the graph representation of code more effectively, we propose a novel pooling method called TreePool. TreePool directly splits tree-like graphs using depth filtering based on the tree structure to form a sequence of pooled graphs sorted by descending size of subgraphs. Then local-local contrastive learning between these neighboring subgraphs is conducted to preserve the information of the graph before pooling. Through TreePool, multiple views of representation are learned and fused to obtain the final code graph representation. We conduct TreePool on a supervised framework and experimental results demonstrate that the average improvements on two real-world datasets in terms of accuracy are 1.1% and 3.3%. It also exhibits excellent performance in an unsupervised framework. Our results show that TreePool can effectively learn meaningful Abstract Syntax Tree representation of code and exhibit good performance in code classification tasks.

**Keywords:** Code Representation Learning · Graph Pooling · Graph Neural Networks

## 1 Introduction

As an essential application in the context of collaborative computing, intelligent software engineering provides intelligent solutions to the software development domain. With the successful application of deep learning, there is a growing trend in intelligent code-related tasks which will further enable multiple collaborative computing scenarios, e.g., collaborative code development, automated code analysis, or code project management. The performance of code-related tasks, method name prediction [2], code completion [5], or code classification [36]

© ICST Institute for Computer Sciences, Social Informatics and Telecommunications Engineering 2024
Published by Springer Nature Switzerland AG 2024. All Rights Reserved
H. Gao et al. (Eds.): CollaborateCom 2023, LNICST 562, pp. 242–261, 2024.
https://doi.org/10.1007/978-3-031-54528-3_14

etc., are relied on the precisely generation of the representation of code snippets. To further improve the code representation learning in these tasks, researchers exploit deep learning methods to extract deep features not only from the original sequence of code but also the structures generated from the compiler, such as Abstract Syntax Tree (AST), Control Flow Graph, etc. While sequential models [7,13] are generally used due to the similarity between code sequence and natural language, the study treating code as graph is still in its infancy. There is a challenge in developing graph-based code representation learning techniques.

Illustrated in Fig. 1, as Graph Neural Networks (GNNs) have widely applied to the non-Euclidean structure (e.g., graph) in multiple fields [18–20,33], methods on code representation learning exploit GNNs to [5,16] encode nodes in an AST or an enhanced code graph with the return of a final representation of code for downstream tasks. GNNs, which apply a message-passing mechanism to aggregate the neighborhood information, show powerful expressiveness on encode node and graph representation. However, existing GNN-based methods have some flaws: (1) Recent methods [5,32] designed for code datasets consider enhancing the AST by adding different types of edges but ignore the original tree structure of AST. (2) Typically graph learning methods with GNNs, from simple readout functions [28] to complex pooling methods [9,17,31] are mostly designed for traditional graphs and cannot easily be transferred to code area.

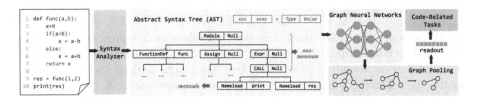

**Fig. 1.** The utilization of Abstract Syntax Tree for code representation learning

To obtain reasonable and effective graph-level representation, graph pooling methods are essential in GNN-based models for code representation learning. Trees have sequential layers, which indicates that the spatial information between nodes can be considered in pooling methods like the field of image, in which models such as Convolutional Neural Networks can easily select a small part based on the spatial proximity to generate max-pooling or mean-pooling [15]. Meanwhile, most of the information is in the leaf nodes of AST, while nodes in the upper layers contain little information in semantics. Simply adding more views may introduce more noise into the final graph representation.

In this work, we propose TreePool, a multi-view contrastive graph pooling method for Abstract Syntax Tree. The contributions of this work are:

- We propose a simple node selection strategy for pooling the tree-like graph, which creates views based on the spatial proximity of the tree structure. It reduces the calculation of the assignment matrix.

- We conduct a simplified local-local contrastive learning between graphs before and after pooling to preserve information.
- TreePool works on both supervised and unsupervised architecture. The results demonstrate the effectiveness of the code classification task.

The structure of the remaining sections in this paper is outlined as follows. Section 2 discusses the preliminaries and presents the problem definition. Section 3 introduces the detailed design of TreePool. The experimental setting and results are reported in Sects. 4 and 5, respectively. We provide a comprehensive discussion of the model in Sect. 6. The related works are presented in Sect. 7. Lastly, Sect. 8 concludes the paper.

## 2    Preliminaries

### 2.1    Abstract Syntax Tree

Abstract Syntax Tree (AST) of code is a tree structure generated by Syntax Analyzer with a typical unambiguous context-free language grammar [1]. AST reflects the structural and syntax information of code. In a syntax tree, the top node represents the beginning symbol, the middle nodes denote the non-terminals, and the bottom nodes indicate the terminals, usually consisting of the variables and identifiers from the original code sequence.

AST can be seen as a tree-like graph denoted as $G = (V, E)$, where $V$ and $E$ are the sets of nodes and edges. The directed edges in $E$ represent the parent-child node relationships, with each edge $e = (u, v) \in E$ indicating that node $u$ is the parent of node $v$. To represent the tree-like graphs in deep learning models, we use the adjacency matrix $A \in \mathbb{R}^{n \times n}$ and the feature matrix $X \in \mathbb{R}^{n \times d}$, where $n$ is the number of nodes and $d$ is the number of features per node.

### 2.2    Code Representation Learning

The goal of code representation learning is to generate a useful representation of the code snippet (i.e., code files, functions) which captures the semantic and syntactic information of code and further improve various downstream tasks. In the context of graph representation learning, the goal is to learn a compact and low-dimensional global graph-level embedding $Z_g \in \mathbb{R}^{1 \times k}$, where $k \ll d$, using $A \in \mathbb{R}^{n \times n}$ and $X \in \mathbb{R}^{n \times d}$ to represent graph structure such as AST.

### 2.3    Graph Pooling for Graph Learning

Graph pooling is a critical component in graph representation learning. As a down-sample operation, graph pooling refers to the process of aggregating information from a graph and creating a new coarsened graph with a smaller size or fewer nodes, while preserving the most important structural information.

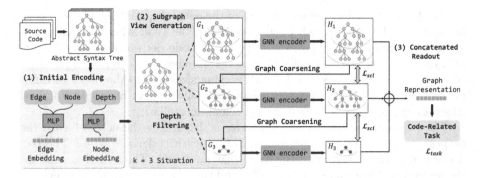

**Fig. 2.** The overview of TreePool in code representation learning architecture.

Formally, graph pooling process is shown as Eq. (1), which coarsen the $i$-th view $G_i$ into a smaller subgraph view $G_{i+1}$, where $X_i$ and $A_i$ denote the node features and adjacency matrix of the original view respectively. $G_i$ is first encoded by GNN layer, followed by the coarsening operation to obtain new adjacency matrix $A_{i+1}$ and feature matrix $X_{i+1}$ with new node indexes $idx$.

$$Z_i = \sigma(GNN(X_i, A_i)); \; X_{i+1} = Z_i(idx, :); \; A_{i+1} = A_i(idx, idx) \qquad (1)$$

Typically, some standard readout functions [28], such as mean, max, or sum, take the updated node representations and aggregate them to produce the graph-level representation.

# 3   Present Work: TreePool

Illustrated in Fig. 2, TreePool can incorporate Graph Neural Networks for graph learning. (1) The initial Encoding module first models the information from AST, then (2) Subgraph View Generation module utilizes depth filtering to determine the subgraphs that will be coarsened. In pooling process, the GNN encoder and the coarsening operation based on the views previously decided upon alternates. Finally, all subgraph representations used (3) Concatenated Readout to combine as a graph-level representation for downstream tasks. In the following section, we will describe each part separately.

## 3.1   Subgraph View Generation

The key step in graph pooling is simplifying graphs to new small graph views by reducing the number of nodes and edges, i.e., the assignment from the original view to the new view. In TreePool, the procedure is succinct which requires no further calculation for the assignment matrix compared to typical graph pooling methods. The nodes and edges are decided only by the depth of the nodes through the subgraph view generation module.

TreePool emphasizes the significance of the natural spatial neighbors in tree-like graphs. Throughout each pooling iteration, the generation of smaller subgraph views is the opposite of the direction of node derivation in an Abstract Syntax Tree using semantic rules. Each subgraph view can be regarded as a subtree encompassing the root node, with varying sizes due to the depth of information. Since each subgraph view can be perceived as an incomplete derived Abstract Syntax Tree, all views share a semantic similarity.

The depth of the Abstract Syntax Tree is decided by the node which is the deepest in the graph. For each graph $G$, the depth is denoted as $d_g$. The tree depth is divided average with the fixed view number $k$. The $i$-th view contains the nodes with depth $d_v \in [0, (k - i)\frac{d_g}{k})$ and the edges between these nodes.

The number of views $k$, which can be customized, defines the time that coarsening procedure is utilized. As the module generates a sequence of subgraph views length of $k$, the graph coarsening procedure is conducted $k - 1$ times.

## 3.2  Mutual Information Maximization

TreePool introduces contrastive learning to maximize the mutual information between the subgraph views to let the coarsened graph reflects the previous graph maximally. It promotes alignment and semantic consistency between different views while avoiding the problem of information redundancy that may arise from simply combining multiple views. Therefore, the node features in the coarsened graph preserve the information of the original graph before pooling.

Maximizing the mutual information between each of the graph pairs is a local-local mutual contrastive learning problem. Mathematically, the mutual information between the graph before and after pooling (i.e., graph $G_i$ and $G_{i+1}$) can be defined as $I(G_i, G_{i+1})$.

However, the input graphs have different scales, which are unable to use the common paradigm of local-local contrastive learning, such as [37]. To address this issue, we first simplify it into a local-global contrastive learning problem. Inspired by previous work on contrastive learning [27,35], we later maximize $I(G_i, G_{i+1})$ by using a binary cross entropy (BCE) loss between the node and graph representations of these views, as shown in Fig. 3.

**Neural Estimation.** The mutual information $I(\cdot, \cdot)$ between the views before and after pooling is defined as the KL-divergence between the joint distribution $P(G_i, G_{i+1})$ and the product of their marginal distributions $P(G_i) \otimes P(G_{i+1})$:

$$I(G_i, G_{i+1}) = D_{KL}(P(G_i, G_{i+1}) \| P(G_i \otimes G_{i+1})). \tag{2}$$

The KL-divergence can be effectively estimated by the f-divergence representation [3]. The lower bound $I_\theta(G_i, G_{i+1})$ defines as Eq. (3), where $\sigma$ represents the activation function, $L(\cdot, \cdot)$ represents the projection function from node space to the real domain. In practice, we can maximize the mutual information by optimizing the lower bound. We use neural network $L_\theta$ to replace the $L(\cdot, \cdot)$ to estimate the mutual information of the inputs $G_i$ and $G_{i+1}$.

$$I_\theta(G_i, G_{i+1}) \geq \mathbb{E}_{G_i, G_{i+1}} log(\sigma(L(G_i, G_{i+1}))) +$$
$$\mathbb{E}_{G_i, G_{i+1}} log(1 - \sigma(L(G_i, G_{i+1}))). \tag{3}$$

**Simplified Contrastive Learning.** To transform the local-local contrastive learning into a simpler local-global problem, TreePool encode the graph before pooling as a graph-level representation. We use a standard readout operation (max, mean or sum) and a single-layer MLP to encode and project the graph representation. As Eq. (4), the output is a summary vector $s_i$.

$$s_i = W_s readout(X_i) + b_s, \tag{4}$$

where $X_i$ represents the total node embedding in graph $G_i$, $W_s$ and $b_s$ represent the learnable weight and bias from the projection layer for $G_i$.

For the local representation of the new graph $G_{i+1}$, we followed the previous design for $G_i$, with a single-layer MLP for graph after pooling to make sure that hidden dimensions are the same as the summary vector $s_i$.

We first employ negative sampling to create a corrupted graph $\tilde{G}_{i+1}$ after pooling the new graph $G_{i+1}$. It is commonly used in creating negative sampling to randomly permute the embedding of nodes within a view [27]. However, it not only fails to truly separate the positive and negative local nodes from one another when projected into a new dimension, but also does not capture the information between different features within each node.

Therefore, TreePool generates negative samples by permuting the feature dimensions of each node. Specifically, we randomly select a feature index and permute the feature values of all nodes up to that index, resulting in a randomized feature matrix $X_{i+1}^{neg} = X_{i+1}[: random(feature)]$ for $\tilde{G}_{i+1}$.

The projection layer takes both the original and corrupted nodes as input. Equation (5) shows the result for the original graph as input, while the corrupted graph receives $\tilde{l}_{i+1}$ as the output, where $W_l$ and $b_l$ represent the learnable weight and bias from the projection layer for both $G_i$ and $\tilde{G}_{i+1}$.

$$l_{i+1} = W_l X_{i+1} + b_l. \tag{5}$$

In a typical graph contrastive learning framework, the discriminator scores the local-global pairs using a bilinear scoring function, which indicates the function $L_\theta$. It can be formulated as follows:

$$D(l_{i+1}, s_i) = \sigma(l_{i+1}^T W s_i), \tag{6}$$

where $W$ is a learnable scoring matrix, $\sigma$ is the logistic Sigmoid nonlineaity.

To reduce the calculation of the bilinear layer, we follow the simplification of Group Discrimination [35], combine the projected positive and negative node representation (after pooling)with the projected graph embedding (before pooling). After adding $s_i$ and $l_{i+1}(\tilde{l}_{i+1})$, we use sum operation feature-wise to get the final score as the input of the discriminator, to further predict the result of positive and negative samples, as shown in Eq. (7), where $\boldsymbol{combine}(\cdot, \cdot)$ contains the add and sum operation conducted on the $s_i$ and $l_{i+1}$ ($\tilde{l}_{i+1}$).

$$D(l_{i+1}, s_i) = \boldsymbol{combine}(l_{i+1}, s_i), \tag{7}$$

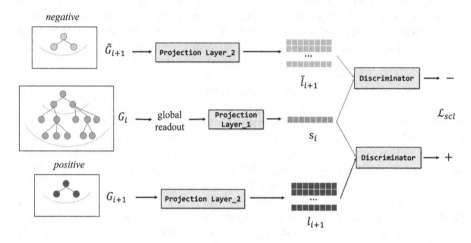

**Fig. 3.** The computation of the simplified contrastive loss.

**Objective Function.** The objective function of the simplified contrastive learning on the adjacent subgraph views can be formulated as Eq. (8).

$$L_{scl} = \frac{1}{2N}(\Sigma_{i=1}^{N} log D(l_{i+1}, s_i) + log(1 - D(\tilde{l}_{i+1}, s_i))), \tag{8}$$

where $N$ represents the node num after pooling. Following Group Discrimination, we can rewrite the loss as a simple BCE loss, where $y_i' = combine(l_{i+1}, s_i)$.

$$L_{scl} = -\frac{1}{2N}(\Sigma_{i=1}^{N} y_i(log(y_i')) + (1 - y_i)(log(1 - y_i'))). \tag{9}$$

As shown in Eq. (9), we give a simplified contrastive loss $L_{scl}$ for the adjacent views during graph coarsening.

### 3.3 Graph Encoder

For the node encoder, we choose Graph Convolutional Network (GCN) [14]. The type of GNN encoder is easily replaced by other types, and we provide a detailed discussion on the GNN encoder type in Sect. 5.5. The GCN encoder processes the nodes in the view to generate node embeddings, propagating information via the input graph's structure using the propagation rule:

$$X^{(m+1)} = \sigma(\tilde{D}^{-\frac{1}{2}} A \tilde{D}^{-\frac{1}{2}} X^{(m)} W^{(m)}), \tag{10}$$

where $X^{(m)}$ is the input feature matrix at network layer $m$, $W^{(m)}$ is the trainable weight matrix, $\tilde{D}$ is the diagonal degree matrix of adjacency matrix $A$, and $\sigma$ is an activation function.

To incorporate edge information, we extend the standard GCN by adding edge embeddings. Specifically, as shown in Eq. (11), where $X_n^{(m)}$ and $X_e^{(m)}$ are the node and edge embedding at layer $m$. Other symbols are the same as Eq. (10). The GCN layer takes both node and edge embeddings generated by the initial encoding module as illustrated in Fig. 2.

$$X_n^{(m+1)} = \sigma(\tilde{D}^{-\frac{1}{2}} A \tilde{D}^{-\frac{1}{2}} (X_n^{(m)} + X_e^{(m)}) W^{(m)}).  \tag{11}$$

### 3.4 Final Readout

The final multi-view representations $Z_g$ will be obtained by aggregating the view-level representations $Z_i$ across all views. Each view-level representation are generated by element-wise readout function across all node embedding. Equation (12) show the concatenated mean readout, where $n$ represents the number of nodes in the $i$-th view, $k$ represents the view number.

$$Z_i = \frac{1}{n} \Sigma_{i=1}^{n} h_i; \ Z_g = \Sigma_{i=1}^{k} Z_i.  \tag{12}$$

### 3.5 Architecture

TreePool is mainly used in supervised framework as depicted in Fig. 2. Nonetheless, it can be conveniently adapted to an unsupervised model as well, and we have conducted experiments on both architectures. In this section, we aim to clarify the supervised and unsupervised architectures and provide details on how the objective function is computed.

**Supervised Architecture.** In supervised model architecture, we follow the previous works, which mainly have two basic architectures [17]. One architecture is global, in which coarsening operations are performed after multiple GNN layers pass messages through the graph. The other architecture is hierarchical, in which the single GNN layer and coarsening layer are arranged alternately. We represent the global one and the hierarchical one as $TreePool_g$ and $TreePool_h$.

For each framework, we combined the simplified contrastive loss, (i.e., $L_{scl}$) and task-related loss as the final loss can be calculated as followed:

$$L = \alpha L_{scl} + \beta L_{task},  \tag{13}$$

where $\alpha$ and $\beta$ are weight parameters that control the contribution of two losses. It is noted that $L_{scl}$ may represents the sum of multiple contrastive loss if the subgraphs sequence length is at least 2. The process of supervised learning is shown in Algorithm 1.

**Unsupervised Architecture.** In the unsupervised learning model, TreePool serves as a pre-training stage and learns the program representations by the task of local-local contrastive learning between the adjacent subgraph views.

---

**Algorithm 1:** Supervised Representation Learning

---

**Input:** the training set $v_{train}$ and the number of pooling layers $N$
**Output:** The classified result

1 Initialize supervised model $M$'s parameters $\theta$ ;
2 **while** $M$ *not converged* **do**
3     $L_{scl} \leftarrow 0$ ;
4     Sample a mini-batch of graphs and get the total adjacent matrix of graph $A_0$, the encoded node feature $X_n^0$, and edge feature $X_e^0$ ;
5     **for** $i \in \{0, 1, ...N - 2\}$ **do**
        // compute with GNN layer
6         $X_n^i \leftarrow GNN(A_i, X_n^i, X_e^i)$;
        // filter new subgraph
7         $A_{i+1}, X_n^{i+1} \leftarrow filter(A_i, X_n^i)$;
8         Calculate $L_{scl}^i$ for this layer;
9         $L_{scl} \leftarrow L_{scl} + L_{scl}^i$;
10     **end**
11     Calculate task-related loss $L_{task}$ ;
12     Update $\theta$ by minimizing $\alpha L_{scl} + \beta L_{task}$ ;
13 **end**
14 **return** *the classified result using trained M*

---

Unlike Algorithm 1, the graph pooling stage acts as a pre-training step in which the graph embedding is trained unsupervised only based on the simplified contrastive loss $L_{scl}$. Then the encoder's parameters are frozen for downstream tasks and train the new supervised model using only the task loss $L_{task}$. The final graph readout are the same as supervised architecture.

## 4    Experimental Setting

### 4.1    Research Questions

In order to evaluate TreePool, we design and answer the following research questions with the experimental results:

RQ1: **Comparison of Pooling baselines** How does TreePool perform compared to recent pooling methods on the benchmark datasets?

RQ2: **Ablation Study** How effective are the components of TreePool, such as the projection layer and simplified process?

RQ3: **Unsupervised Scene** Can the mutual information loss be transferred to an unsupervised learning framework?

RQ4: **Study of Views** How the number and generation of view affect the final result? Which view affects the final result most?

RQ5:**Model Analysis** What is the impact of hyper-parameters on the performance of TreePool?

## 4.2   Datasets

In experiments, we evaluate TreePool on graph classification task with OJ-104 dataset [23]. The dataset contains C/C++ code collected from Online Judge system in 104 classes. Programs with the same target label have the same functionality. We also created a new dataset named OJ-DEEP which includes the top 20% deepest graphs (no less than 15) in order to more accurately evaluate the effectiveness of TreePool on large AST representation. OJ-DEEP contains only the large graphs on the origin dataset. The statistical information of the two datasets is summarized in Table 1.

## 4.3   Baselines

**Table 1.** Summary of the datasets

| Dataset | Graph | Node | | | Depth | | |
|---------|-------|------|-----|-----|-------|-----|-----|
|         |       | avg  | min | max | avg   | min | max |
| OJ-104  | 51,976 | 189.56 | 29 | 7,027 | 13.31 | 6 | 76 |
| OJDEEP  | 13,371 | 259.25 | 42 | 7,027 | 17.92 | 15 | 76 |

Since TreePool is designed initially for the supervised framework, we report the performance between TreePool and the supervised graph pooling methods in the study of RQ1, while also reporting TreePool with the unsupervised learning framework in the study of RQ4. We select the following methods as baselines, which could be divided into two groups: (1) supervised graph pooling approaches SAGPool [17], DiffPool [31], and Graph U-net [9], and (2) unsupervised graph contrastive learning methods DGI [27], GRACE [37].

**SAGPool** [17] use the graph convolution layer to calculate the self-attention score in each pooling stage, which indicates the selection of the next-level nodes with the pooling ratio. The SAGPool has two architectures: the hierarchical architecture $SAGPool_h$ and the global architecture $SAGPool_g$.

**DiffPool** [31] learns differentiable soft cluster assignments, which indicates the relation between the node of the origin and the coarsened graph, to coarsen graph. The new adjacency matrix and feature matrix are the aggregation of the original graph generated with the assignment matrix.

**Graph U-net** [9] has an encoder-decoder architecture with gPool and gUnpool operations. gPool operation pools the graph into top-k nodes subgraphs based on the value produced from the trained projection vector. gUnpool recovers the node embedding from the coarsened graph to the original graph.

**DGI** [27] relies on maximizing mutual information between patch representations and corresponding high-level summaries of graphs, which are derived using graph convolutional network architectures.

**GRACE** [37] generates two correlated graph views by randomly performing corruption, specifically, removing edges and masking node features. the model maximizes the mutual information between the two views.

### 4.4  Implementation Details

Following the AST extraction and the dataset splitting step of TBCNN [23], for both datasets, we randomly split them with the train/validation/test ratio of 3.2:0.8:1. We use the same data splitting for all methods and each experiment is run 5 times to calculate the average performance for fairness. We report the mean accuracy along with the standard deviation of five runs for each model and dataset. The standard deviation is represented in percentages while the accuracy is in decimals. We train all the models on a maximum of 100 epochs with 10-epoch patience for early stopping. We used the Adam optimizer and hyperparameter selection strategy. The learning rate is selected from the range [0.01,0.05,0.005,0.0001,0.0005]. All the baseline models are reproduced with Pytorch 1.8 on two parallel GPUs and adjust the parameters to get a better result.

We set the subgraph view number 3, indicating that the original graph will be separated into three subgraphs and pooled twice. The hyperparameter of the subgraph view number is studied in the Sect. 5.4. For the supervised framework, we set the parameter $\alpha$ and $\beta$ in the loss function as 0.5 and 0.5.

The depth and type of a node in an AST are initially encoded using two one-hot vectors, which are then compressed into a 300-dimensional vector via a single-layer MLP. To ensure the same level of expressiveness across different graph learning model architectures, equal numbers of layers ($n = 3$) are used, and the hidden dimensions are set equal to the embedding dimension. Following the GNN layer, a ReLU layer and dropout layer are applied[1].

### 4.5  Evaluation Metric

As defined in Eq. (14), we use accuracy for evaluation, which measures the proportion of correctly predicted labels out of the total number of instances.

$$Acc = \frac{\sum_{i=1}^{|\mathcal{D}|} \mathcal{I}(\hat{y}, y)}{|\mathcal{D}|} \tag{14}$$

where $\hat{y}$ is the model's prediction, $y$ is the ground truth label, $|\mathcal{D}|$ is the total number of samples, $\mathcal{I}(\cdot, \cdot)$ the indicator function which returns 1 if the predicted label is the same as the true label, and 0 otherwise.

## 5  Results

### 5.1  RQ1: Comparison of Pooling Baselines

To answer the first question, we compare TreePool with 4 baseline graph pooling methods on the supervised learning framework on OJ-104 and OJ-DEEP. Based on the results in Table 2, we have the following observations.

---

[1] Our implementation is available at: https://github.com/codingClaire/TreePool.

**Deeper Graphs are Harder to Learn the Graph Representation.** We observe that the performance of most methods is higher on the OJ-104 compared to OJ-DEEP, indicating that the former is an easier dataset for graph classification. The result indicates that graph-based models may perform badly as the code snippets become longer and complicated.

**Original Node Information is Essential for Code Representation.** Among the baseline methods, we note that Graph U-net achieves the highest accuracy on both datasets. In contrast, DiffPool achieves the lowest. We found out that DiffPool requires multiple loss functions, which makes the model difficult to converge. Although SAGPool or DiffPool works well on small graph classification, the result in Table 2 shows that when the scale of the graph dataset increases, they are more likely to lose information and be unable to fit this situation. For example, DiffPool generates new virtual nodes for the views after the original graph as the first view, which may be the reason of its results.

**TreePool Outperforms All Baseline Methods.** We observe that TreePool outperforms all the baseline methods on the two datasets in terms of accuracy. In particular, in OJ-104 and OJ-DEEP datasets, $TreePool_g$ achieves better performance compared to the best baseline methods with an improvement of 0.2% and 2.9% respectively. The corresponding relative improvements are 1.1% and 3.3% in $TreePool_g$. The results show that TreePool is a promising method for code classification, with comparable performance to SAGPool and Graph U-net.

**Global Framework is Better than Hierarchical Framework.** Compare to the result of the hierarchical and global framework of SAGPool and TreePool, we found out that the global framework works better. Compare to the hierarchical framework, the global framework of SAGPool relatively improves by 1.1% and 1.8% in OJ-104 and OJ-DEEP. For TreePool, we observe similar results in which the improvements are 1.2% and 0.8% respectively. The results indicate that a simple framework can make the result of graph representation learning

**Table 2.** Comparison of graph pooling methods (Accuracy)

| Method | OJ-104 | OJ-DEEP |
|---|---|---|
| $SAGPool_h$ | $0.9070 \pm 3.15$ | $0.8927 \pm 2.87$ |
| $SAGPool_g$ | $0.9169 \pm 3.28$ | $0.9091 \pm 2.73$ |
| $DiffPool$ | $0.7148 \pm 0.90$ | $0.7362 \pm 1.68$ |
| $Graph\ U-net$ | $0.9430 \pm 0.28$ | $0.9024 \pm 0.58$ |
| $TreePool_h$ | $0.9453 \pm 0.18$ | $0.9287 \pm 0.32$ |
| $TreePool_g$ | $0.9563 \pm 0.12$ | $0.9323 \pm 0.32$ |
| w/o GNN encoder | $0.8943 \pm 0.08$ | $0.8734 \pm 0.40$ |
| w/o projection layer | $0.9451 \pm 0.06$ | $0.9175 \pm 0.42$ |
| w/o simplified process | $0.9527 \pm 0.07$ | $0.9257 \pm 0.71$ |

effective. One hypothesis to explain is that when multiple losses are added to the downstream loss, the hierarchical model may be more complicated to optimize.

> **Answer of RQ1:** Our experiments demonstrate that TreePool outperforms all the baselines in terms of accuracy. In particular, TreePool achieves better performance with 1.1% and 3.3% improvements on both datasets, respectively.

## 5.2  RQ2: Ablation Study

To further explore the effectiveness of different components in TreePool and answer RQ2, we conduct multiple ablation experiments using the OJ-DEEP dataset and evaluate the effectiveness of the TreePool model on the following models. Besides the original architectures, we report the best results with the hierarchical and global architectures. The results are shown in Table 2.

- w/o GNN encoder: The model is trained without GNN, which means that the node and edge embeddings are directly fed into the pooling layer.
- w/o projection layer: The model is trained without the projection layers for the graphs before and after pooling.
- w/o simplified process: The model is trained without simplified loss, which means trains by the original contrastive learning loss proposed by DGI.

Our ablation studies demonstrate the importance of each component in the TreePool model. The GNN component helps capture the relationships between nodes and edges in the graph, while the projection layer helps to align the representations between the global and local levels. Although the result of model without simplified calculation is close to the original results, the simplified calculation still works with less calculation as previous analysis.

> **Answer of RQ2:** We observe a consistent performance improvement on different modifications of original contrastive loss and framework, confirming their benefits on the pooling methods.

## 5.3  RQ3: Unsupervised Scene

We aim to explore whether simplified contrastive loss can transfer to the unsupervised learning scene. We conduct experiments on 2 view layers of $TreePool_g$ in unsupervised learning framework and compare the model with our unsupervised baselines. The detailed results are shown in Table 3.

In general, compared to a supervised learning framework, the performance of the unsupervised learning framework is worse due to the absence of labels. In both the DGI and GRACE methods, DGI outperformed GRACE significantly in both datasets. When compared to DGI, TreePool, which utilizes an unsupervised framework, performed slightly worse on the OJ-104 dataset with a decrease of approximately 0.4%. However, on the OJ-DEEP dataset, TreePool's performance showed a remarkable improvement, surpassing DGI by 3.0% and even outperforming its performance on the OJ-104 dataset.

**Table 3.** Comparison of graph contrastive methods (Accuracy)

| Method | OJ-104 | OJ-DEEP |
|---|---|---|
| $DGI$ | $0.9191 \pm 0.59$ | $0.9001 \pm 0.54$ |
| $GRACE$ | $0.8761 \pm 0.54$ | $0.8204 \pm 0.68$ |
| $URL + TreePool$ | $0.9154 \pm 0.24$ | $0.9270 \pm 0.35$ |

**Answer of RQ3:** Our experiments demonstrate that TreePool is effective in both supervised and unsupervised learning tasks. TreePool in unsupervised representation learning obtains significant improvements on the OJ-DEEP dataset.

### 5.4   RQ4: Study of Views

To answer the fourth question, we explore the impact of views during pooling, including the way of view generation, the number of views, and the impact of multiple views on performance.

**View Generation.** TreePool generates multiple subgraph views based on the hierarchical relation of tree architecture. Based on the hierarchical form of TreePool, we change the way of generating views to study whether this way of view generation is reasonable. With these views, the model will calculate simplified contrastive loss and further predict the result as the original model.

$TreePool_A$: Randomly select the nodes with the same amount in the subgraph view generation module instead of selecting hierarchically.

$TreePool_B$: Randomly select half of amount of nodes from hierarchical views.

The best result of all architectures is shown in Table 4. When the nodes are randomly chosen, the accuracy of $TreePool_A$ will decrease by 0.2% and 1.4% in OJ-104 and OJ-DEEP, indicating the importance of hierarchical view generation. In $TreePool_B$, the model only chooses half of the nodes from each hierarchical view, which influence the process of calculating the simplified contrastive loss. The accuracy of $TreePool_B$ decreases by 0.4% and 1.0%. The result of $TreePool_A$ shows that it is meaningful to generate views hierarchically. Furthermore, the experiments of $TreePool_B$ prove the effectiveness of preserving the information from all nodes of views.

**View Numbers.** Another factor that may affect the pooling effect is the number of subgraph view numbers. More views leads to more pooling times and calculation. We conducted experiments to investigate the impact of view numbers. Specifically, we explored the effects of 2 to 6 views on supervised $TreePool_h$.

As shown in Table 5, the best result is 1.7% higher than the worst result, while only 0.9% for OJ-104. We expected that when the number of view layers becomes higher, even OJ-DEEP, which contains larger depth data, may have a minimal difference in using contrastive learning before and after pooling due to the small space size. Therefore, in this situation, employing TreePool may lead to a decrease in performance and is not cost-effective in terms of efficiency. However, selecting a smaller number of views, such as 2, may cause the model to lose some hierarchical information by comparing two graphs with significant differences. Therefore, determining a suitable number of views is crucial for the results and is one of the future works that deserves investigation.

**Table 4.** Result of view generation study (Accuracy)

| Number | OJ-104 | OJ-DEEP |
|---|---|---|
| $TreePool_A$ | $0.9540 \pm 0.12$ | $0.9161 \pm 0.38$ |
| $TreePool_B$ | $0.9523 \pm 0.02$ | $0.9193 \pm 0.24$ |
| $TreePool$ | $0.9563 \pm 0.12$ | $0.9323 \pm 0.32$ |

**Table 5.** Result of View Number Study (Accuracy)

| View | OJ-104 | OJ-DEEP |
|---|---|---|
| 2 | $0.9491 \pm 0.18$ | $0.9127 \pm 0.38$ |
| 3 | $0.9453 \pm 0.18$ | $0.9287 \pm 0.32$ |
| 4 | $0.9535 \pm 0.14$ | $0.9248 \pm 0.30$ |
| 5 | $0.9540 \pm 0.07$ | $0.9283 \pm 0.34$ |
| 6 | $0.9523 \pm 0.20$ | $0.9248 \pm 0.27$ |

**View Importance.** To study which readout of view contribute more to the final result, we conduct experiments on $TreePool_g$ with total view numbers of 2,3,4 on OJ-DEEP to check which view matters more on the performance of the model. For each model, we maintain the consistency with the calculation of loss function but used every single view's readout generated through pooling to get the final graph representation. All results are presented in Fig. 4, where last data point of the line represents the final result of the concatenated mean readout.

We observed that when view number is 3 and 4, both single-view and multi-view models exhibited a similar trend in which an decreased number of nodes

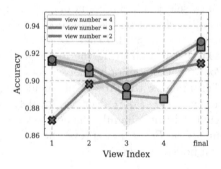

**Fig. 4.** The result of the experiment of view importance study on OJ-DEEP.

led to worse classification performance. Overall, the results obtained using single views were inferior to those achieved with multi-view models. These findings demonstrate that the multi-view approach introduced more information into the model, resulting in more comprehensive representations being learned.

> **Answer of RQ4:** We examine the impact of views on model performance and demonstrate the effectiveness of hierarchically generating the views, as well as the importance of properly selecting view numbers and employing multi-view training methods.

### 5.5   RQ5: Model Analysis

To answer RQ5, we analyzed two hyperparameters that affect model performance: the layer number and type of GNN encoder.

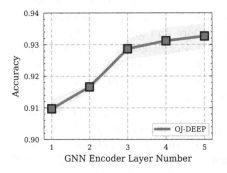

**Fig. 5.** The effect of the number of GNN encoder layers on performance.

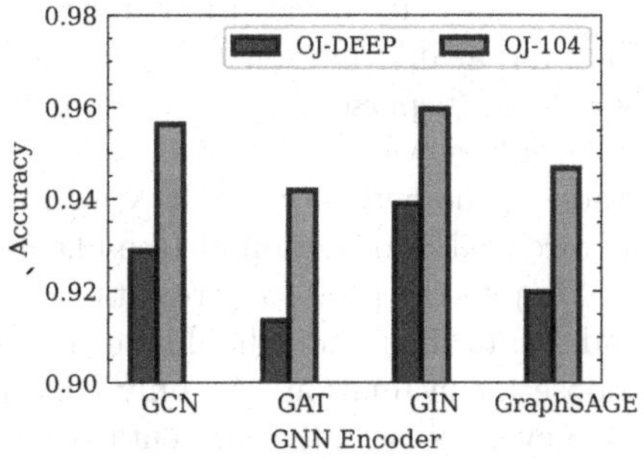

**Fig. 6.** The result of different GNN types.

**Layer Number.** We investigate the impact of the number of layers in GNN encoder on the performance of our proposed method. By varying the number of layers, we aim to find the optimal depth of the GNN model for our task.

The result in Fig. 5 indicate that the model perform best when the GNN encoder has three layers, which is also slightly improved with four or more layers. However, this leads to an increase in model parameters and training time. We speculate that increasing the number of layers in the GNN encoder could result in over-smoothing, as commonly observed. Due to the high depth of the overall OJ-DEEP dataset, no such issue is observed within the five layers.

**Type of GNN Encoder.** We analyze the impact of different GNN encoders on the performance of our proposed method. Specifically, we evaluate three popular GNN-based models as encoders, including GAT [26], GIN [30], and GraphSAGE [10], on the code classification task.

The results in Fig. 6 show that GIN outperforms all other GNN encoders followed by GCN and GraphSAGE. GAT has inferior performance compared to the other models, indicating its limitation in capturing global-level graph structures. Although GIN performs better than GCN, it is computationally expensive, as it requires multiple layers of MLPs to aggregate the node features. Therefore, the respective strengths of GNN models must be considered along with their limitations for specific datasets and tasks.

> **Answer of RQ5:** Our experiments provide a thorough evaluation of how the number and type of GNN layers can influence the performance, and we analyze their respective strengths and limitations.

## 6    Discussion

The effectiveness of TreePool can be attributed to its ability to capture the information flow within the graph and coarsen it in a hierarchical way. By maximizing the mutual information between the graph before and after pooling, TreePool is able to disperse the information from leaf nodes of lower layers to multiple subgraph views based on semantic relationships. By conducting a concatenated readout, the generated multi-view representation of the graph can capture the hierarchical information of tree-like graphs.

Despite the promising results of TreePool, there are several potential threats and limitations that should be addressed. One limitation is the datasets we choose for evaluation. We only conduct our experiments in C/C++ language, so they may be not representative of other languages. In the future, we will evaluate more datasets in other programming languages. Another limitation is that TreePool is compared solely with graph representation methods due to the method being designed for tree-like graphs in GNN-based models. As the large language models have taken great advantages in the code intelligence area, we will extend our approach combined with other sequential models.

## 7    Related Work

### 7.1    AST-Based Code Representation Learning

Abstract Syntax Trees are widely used for encoding program representations on code-related tasks, which can be categorized into tree-based and graph-based approaches. Graph Neural Networks are less commonly used in tree-structured AST approaches, where Basic Recursive Neural Networks [6] and Convolutional Neural Networks [22] are more prevalent. On the other hand, some works focus on the graph perspective and employ modified GGNN [8], combinations with RNN or sequential models [25], convolutional GNN [16], Graph Attention Network [29] for encoding AST nodes and edges. To fully taking into account the topology differences between Abstract Syntax Tree and other typical graphs, certain existing methods add edges to enhance the AST [5,32]. Compared to these methods, our approach introduces the graph pooling module to directly extract more effective graph representations from the original AST.

### 7.2    Graph Pooling

Based on the differences in the coarsening process, the pooling methods can be classified into two categories: node clustering pooling and node drop pooling. Node clustering pooling [4,21] aims to partition nodes into clusters and subsequently treat these clusters as new nodes in a coarsened graph. However, these approaches are subject to a drawback regarding time and storage complexity, which arises from the computation of the dense cluster assignment matrix. Node drop pooling [9,34] utilizes learnable scoring functions to keep nodes with higher significant scores. These methods are prone to losing a significant amount of nodes, resulting in inevitable information loss.

### 7.3    Neural Estimation of Mutual Information Maximization

The goal of contrastive learning is to improve the agreement between positively paired samples, which are jointly sampled, while contrasting them with negatively paired samples that are independently sampled. Estimating Mutual Information (MI) is a commonly used technique but difficult to calculate. Neural estimation of mutual information is extensively studied in unsupervised and self-supervised learning. Previous works have used it to learn graph representations, including DGI [27] between patch representations of subgraphs and global high-level summaries of the graph, Deep InfoMax [12] between input data and learned high-level representations and InfoGraph [24] between the graph-level representation and the representations of substructures of different scales. Some works also leverage a contrastive object between views, such as GRACE [37] and MVGRL [11]. The former method contrasts between two correlated graph views by randomly performing corruption, while the latter between views from first-order neighbors and a graph diffusion.

## 8    Conclusion

In this paper, we propose a novel graph pooling method named TreePool, which aims to address the challenge of generating an informative graph representation for Abstract Syntax Trees, a kind of tree-like code graph. TreePool incorporates spatial proximity of nodes and local-local contrastive learning to preserve leaf information and hierarchical information. With TreePool, code representation learning with Abstract Syntax Trees can be accomplished more effectively by leveraging the hierarchical structure of code graphs. The improved code representation can be used in multiple code tasks for collaborative computing. Our experiments demonstrate the effectiveness of TreePool in both supervised and unsupervised frameworks for the code classification task. In the future, we plan to explore the potential of TreePool in other code languages and tasks, as well as investigate its scalability to sequential language models.

**Acknowledgement.** The research is supported by the National Key R&D Program of China under grant No. 2022YFF0902500, the Guangdong Basic and Applied Basic Research Foundation, China (No. 2023A1515011050). Liang Chen is the corresponding author.

# References

1. Aho, A.V., Lam, M.S., Sethi, R., Ullman, J.D.: Compilers: principles, techniques and tools (2020)
2. Alon, U., Zilberstein, M., Levy, O., Yahav, E.: code2vec: Learning distributed representations of code (2019)
3. Belghazi, M.I., et al.: Mutual information neural estimation. In: International Conference on Machine Learning, pp. 531–540. PMLR (2018)
4. Bianchi, F.M., Grattarola, D., Alippi, C.: Spectral clustering with graph neural networks for graph pooling. In: International Conference on Machine Learning, pp. 874–883. PMLR (2020)
5. Brockschmidt, M., Allamanis, M., Gaunt, A.L., Polozov, O.: Generative code modeling with graphs. In: International Conference on Learning Representations (2018)
6. Chakraborty, S., Ding, Y., Allamanis, M., Ray, B.: Codit: code editing with tree-based neural models. IEEE Trans. Softw. Eng. **48**(4), 1385–1399 (2020)
7. Feng, Z., et al.: CodeBERT: a pre-trained model for programming and natural languages. arXiv Computation and Language (2020)
8. Fernandes, P., Allamanis, M., Brockschmidt, M.: Structured neural summarization. In: International Conference on Learning Representations (2018)
9. Gao, H., Ji, S.: Graph u-nets. In: international Conference on Machine Learning, pp. 2083–2092. PMLR (2019)
10. Hamilton, W., Ying, Z., Leskovec, J.: Inductive representation learning on large graphs. In: Advances in Neural Information Processing Systems, vol. 30 (2017)
11. Hassani, K., Khasahmadi, A.H.: Contrastive multi-view representation learning on graphs. In: International Conference on Machine Learning, pp. 4116–4126 (2020)
12. Hjelm, R.D., et al.: Learning deep representations by mutual information estimation and maximization. arXiv preprint arXiv:1808.06670 (2018)
13. Hussain, Y., Huang, Z., Zhou, Y., Wang, S.: CodeGRU: context-aware deep learning with gated recurrent unit for source code modeling. Inf. Softw. Technol. **125**, 106309 (2020)
14. Kipf, T.N., Welling, M.: Semi-supervised classification with graph convolutional networks. arXiv preprint arXiv:1609.02907 (2016)
15. Krizhevsky, A., Sutskever, I., Hinton, G.E.: Imagenet classification with deep convolutional neural networks. Commun. ACM **60**(6), 84–90 (2017)
16. LeClair, A., Haque, S., Wu, L., McMillan, C.: Improved code summarization via a graph neural network. In: Proceedings of the 28th International Conference on Program Comprehension, pp. 184–195 (2020)
17. Lee, J., Lee, I., Kang, J.: Self-attention graph pooling. In: International Conference on Machine Learning, pp. 3734–3743. PMLR (2019)
18. Li, J., Peng, J., Chen, L., Zheng, Z., Liang, T., Ling, Q.: Spectral adversarial training for robust graph neural network. IEEE TKDE (2022)

19. Li, J., Xie, T., Chen, L., Xie, F., He, X., Zheng, Z.: Adversarial attack on large scale graph. IEEE TKDE **35**(1), 82–95 (2021)
20. Liu, Y., Chen, L., He, X., Peng, J., Zheng, Z., Tang, J.: Modelling high-order social relations for item recommendation. IEEE TKDE **34**(9), 4385–4397 (2020)
21. Ma, Y., Wang, S., Aggarwal, C.C., Tang, J.: Graph convolutional networks with eigenpooling. In: Proceedings of the 25th ACM SIGKDD International Conference on Knowledge Discovery and Data Mining, pp. 723–731 (2019)
22. Mou, L., Li, G., Jin, Z., Zhang, L., Wang, T.: TBCNN: a tree-based convolutional neural network for programming language processing. arXiv preprint arXiv:1409.5718 (2014)
23. Mou, L., Li, G., Zhang, L., Wang, T., Jin, Z.: Convolutional neural networks over tree structures for programming language processing. In: Proceedings of the AAAI Conference on Artificial Intelligence, vol. 30 (2016)
24. Sun, F.Y., Hoffmann, J., Verma, V., Tang, J.: Infograph: unsupervised and semi-supervised graph-level representation learning via mutual information maximization. arXiv preprint arXiv:1908.01000 (2019)
25. Tarlow, D., et al.: Learning to fix build errors with graph2diff neural networks. arXiv preprint arXiv:1911.01205 (2019)
26. Veličković, P., Cucurull, G., Casanova, A., Romero, A., Lio, P., Bengio, Y.: Graph attention networks. arXiv preprint arXiv:1710.10903 (2017)
27. Veličković, P., Fedus, W., Hamilton, W.L., Liò, P., Bengio, Y., Hjelm, R.D.: Deep graph infomax. arXiv preprint arXiv:1809.10341 (2018)
28. Wagstaff, E., Fuchs, F., Engelcke, M., Posner, I., Osborne, M.A.: On the limitations of representing functions on sets. In: International Conference on Machine Learning, pp. 6487–6494. PMLR (2019)
29. Wang, Y., Li, H.: Code completion by modeling flattened abstract syntax trees as graphs. In: Proceedings of the AAAI Conference on Artificial Intelligence, vol. 35, pp. 14015–14023 (2021)
30. Xu, K., Hu, W., Leskovec, J., Jegelka, S.: How powerful are graph neural networks? arXiv preprint arXiv:1810.00826 (2018)
31. Ying, Z., You, J., Morris, C., Ren, X., Hamilton, W., Leskovec, J.: Hierarchical graph representation learning with differentiable pooling. In: Advances in Neural Information Processing Systems, vol. 31 (2018)
32. Zhang, K., Wang, W., Zhang, H., Li, G., Jin, Z.: Learning to represent programs with heterogeneous graphs. In: Proceedings of the 30th IEEE/ACM International Conference on Program Comprehension, pp. 378–389 (2022)
33. Zhang, Z., Zhuang, F., Zhu, H., Shi, Z., Xiong, H., He, Q.: Relational graph neural network with hierarchical attention for knowledge graph completion. In: Proceedings of the AAAI Conference on Artificial Intelligence, vol. 34, pp. 9612–9619 (2020)
34. Zhang, Z., et al.: Hierarchical graph pooling with structure learning. arXiv preprint arXiv:1911.05954 (2019)
35. Zheng, Y., Pan, S., Lee, V., Zheng, Y., Yu, P.S.: Rethinking and scaling up graph contrastive learning: an extremely efficient approach with group discrimination. In: Advances in Neural Information Processing Systems, vol. 35, pp. 10809–10820 (2022)
36. Zhou, Y., Liu, S., Siow, J., Du, X., Liu, Y.: DevIGN: effective vulnerability identification by learning comprehensive program semantics via graph neural networks. In: Advances in Neural Information Processing Systems, vol. 32 (2019)
37. Zhu, Y., Xu, Y., Yu, F., Liu, Q., Wu, S., Wang, L.: Deep graph contrastive representation learning. arXiv preprint arXiv:2006.04131 (2020)

# Security and Privacy Protection

# Protect Applications and Data in Use in IoT Environment Using Collaborative Computing

Xincai Peng[1], Li Shan Cang[1(✉)], Shuai Zhang[1], and Muddesar Iqbal[2]

[1] University of Electronic Science and Technology of China, Chengdu, China
shancang.li@outlook.com
[2] College of Engineering, Prince Sultan University, Riyadh, Saudi Arabia

**Abstract.** In IoT systems, traditional encryption can be used to protect IoT applications and data at rest or in transit that transforms data in to ciphertext making it unreadable. However, it is very challenging to protect IoT systems against attacks targeting data and applications in use. Using homomorphic encryption, this work proposed a lightweight collaborative computing scheme to protect both applications and data in IoT environment that includes IoT devices, mobile apps, and cloud server. A novel key management system scheme proposed as a trusted third party to collaboratively generate and distribute keys by cloud servers and IoT devices, in which data is only visible to the data owner but keep encrypted to other parties. A SEAL-CKKS scheme and a K-means clustering algorithms were validated, and the experimental results demonstrated the effectiveness of proposed schemes, in which the K-means clustering algorithm in the plaintext state, the proposed scheme still maintains an accuracy up to 84.1%.

**Keywords:** Collaborative computing · IoT · Data Privacy · Data Security

## 1 Introduction

The Internet of Things (IoT) has been one of the fastest developing techniques in recent years and significantly increasing number of IoT devices are interconnected in Internet of Things (IoT) systems. According to [6,11], there will be more than 27 billion IoT devices will be connected to Internet by 2025. This makes it is very challenging to protect sensitive information and privacy in IoT environment due to increasing security concerns [1,7], such as *software vulnerabilities, enlarged attack surface, limited resources, lack of standardisation, data diversity, etc.*

Data collected by IoT devices is usually transmitted to IoT applications or cloud server for analysis. Any vulnerability can lead sensitive data disclosure or system failure, which can affect the IoT users, applications, third-parties and even can cause security issues [4]. In IoT applications, smart sensors, devices, and

H. Gao et al. (Eds.): CollaborateCom 2023, LNICST 562, pp. 265–280, 2024.
https://doi.org/10.1007/978-3-031-54528-3_15

IoT systems can collaboratively collect, process, and share data in an efficient way. In IoT collaborative computing, following main features need to be considered [14]: (1) data sharing and fusion; (2) interoperability; (3) collaborative analytics; (4) security and privacy [17].

The IoT data lifecycle includes *data generation, data transmission, data storage, data in use, data processing, data analytics, etc.* Data in use security is a critical stage in IoT data lifecycle, which focus the security of a specific state of data within the overall data lifecycle [9,16]. Ensuring the security of data in use is crucial for safeguarding IoT systems from different IoT threats and vulnerabilities, key security measurements include [20]: *data encryption, communication security, access control, authentication and authorisation, data anonymisation and masking, real-time threat detection, etc.* [18].

The homomorphic encryption (HE) shows great potential to encrypt the data in use, and IoT applications or cloud sever could then perform computations on encrypted data, such that statistical analysis or machine learning (ML), without decryption the data [2,8,12]. The HE can significantly enhance data privacy in IoT applications where user data is collected and analyzed [5]. For example, in a healthcare IoT system, HE could be used to encrypt patient health data before transmission to a cloud server for analysis [10]. This would ensure that the patient's sensitive health data remains private and secure, even during the analysis process.

Using HE and smart IoT devices, this work developed a lightweight privacy enhancing solution for IoT applications that can enhance privacy protection in IoT systems by allowing data to be encrypted before transmission, while still allowing computations to be performed on the encrypted data. This can help to protect sensitive data and maintain user privacy in IoT applications. The main contribution of this work are summarised as:

1) Aiming at deploying HE over IoT devices, a four phase scheme: *data encoding, encryption, decryption, and decoding* was introduced to enhance the efficiency of HE;
2) A lightweight secure collaborative computing scheme was proposed for IoT devices using the homomorphic encryption to conduct secret computing without concerning data disclosure concerns;
3) A robust key management scheme (KM was proposed for the HE enabled lightweight secure collaborative computing protocol over resource constrained IoT scenarios;
4) To validate the proposed solution in cloud scenarios, this work re-implemented the $k$-means scheme proposed in [21], the experimental results demonstrate affordable performance can be achieved.

## 2    Related Works

The amount of sensitive data being collected and transmitted has increased significantly in IoT systems. This data may involve personal individual information (PII), sensitive information such as *financial data, healthcare recordes, confidential business information, etc.* that make privacy a critical concern for IoT systems. In the past decade, the HE based solutions have been developed to enhance privacy [8]. In our previous works [15], we proposed a privacy-preserving IoT data analysis system that uses HE to protect sensitive data. The proposed system uses the Paillier homomorphic encryption (PHE) algorithm to encrypt the data before transmitting it to the cloud server for analysis.

Shrestha *et al.* proposed a secure computing system for IoT using the Fan-Vercauteren (FV) HE algorithm to enable computations to be performed on encrypted data [19]. The system was evaluated using a synthetic IoT dataset and was found to be effective in protecting the privacy of the data while still allowing computations to be performed on it. Halder *et al.* proposed a secure data storage system for IoT using the Brakerski-Gentry-Vaikuntanathan (BGV) HE algorithm to encrypt the data before storing it on the cloud server [4].

Louki *et al.* provided an overview of the use of HE for IoT data security in [10] that reviewed various HE schemes that can be used for IoT security, as well as the challenges and limitations of using homomorphic encryption in IoT. Overall, HE has been shown to be an effective solution to several IoT security challenges. However, there are still challenges to be addressed, such as the high computational overhead of homomorphic encryption and the need for standardized homomorphic encryption algorithms for IoT [6].

Some other approaches have also been developed to implement HE over IoT and cloud scenarios to protect the confidentiality of data stored on IoT devices. For example, HE can be used to encrypt sensor data before it is stored on the device, thereby preventing unauthorized access to the data. HE can also be used to perform analytics on encrypted data, enabling privacy-preserving machine learning algorithms to be used in IoT systems.

Marcolla *et al.* detailed the implementation of HE on FPGA for IoT applications [13], in which the benefits of implementing HE on FPGA were highlighted, such as the ability to perform high-speed computations with low latency and power consumption. This work also discussed the challenges of implementing HE on FPGA, such as the need for efficient hardware design and optimization techniques.

While the HE has the potential to enhance IoT privacy, there are several challenges that need to be addressed, including the high computational overhead of HE, key management scheme, and the lack of standardization. In the following works, we focus on developing more efficient HE algorithms, improving key management for HE in IoT systems.

## 3   Methodology

This work focuses on an 'IoT Device' - 'Cloud Server' scenario to achieve outsourced secure computing of individual IoT device data. In this scenario, both IoT device and cloud server do not support multi-party collaborative computing between multiple devices, so data between multiple devices of the same type cannot be merged for more efficient utilization. Therefore, we first propose an improved model with a key management system (KMS) to address the issues of the above model. KMS is used to generate keys for collaborative computing, publish the public key to IoT devices in need and the cloud server, and send the private key to the data owner to protect data while ensuring that the cloud server can merge and calculate data from different devices.

In recent, researchers proposed the "multi-key" model to solve the problem of data collaborative computing [3,11]. One drawback of this "multi-key" scheme is that the upper limit of the number of participants must be known when generating keys, as the parameters increase with the increase of the number of participants. However, the number of IoT devices is often dynamic and growing rapidly in the real IoT environment, using a "multi-key" solution is not suitable for IoT environments.

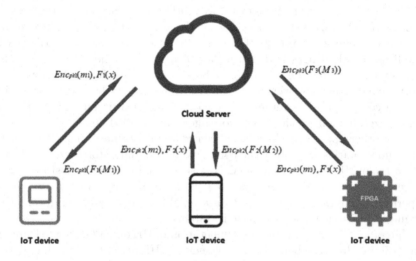

**Fig. 1.** Lightweight HE in IoT scenario

### 3.1    Key Management Scheme

To address above concern, we re-designed the KMS to form a trusted IoT systems, in which IoT devices are in a mutually trusted system, they can directly use the same key pair inside the system to encrypt data with homomorphic encryption and send those encrypted data to the Cloud Sever(CS). IoT devices in the same system trust each other and can share plaintext data. Therefore, data within the system does not need to be shared through encryption.

In multiple independent IoT systems, as shown in the Fig. 1, data owners (DOs) directly interact with the CS, transmit encrypted data through communication channels, and store it on the cloud server. The DOs can read and use this batch of data encrypted by their own. If there is no prior agreement, each system will use different homomorphic encryption keys, which hinders the collaborative computing of data in different systems on the CS.

To enhance the trustworthiness, a reliable KMS can be introduced as a trusted third party for generating and publishing keys. With the help of KMS, the IoT devices in different systems could obtain the same key pairs of HE. This means that IoT devices can use the same public key to encrypt their data and send it to CS for data sharing, without exposing the content of the data. On the other hand, the CS is responsible for responding to user requests, integrating data with the same features but different ones, which can be seen as a horizontal federated learning model, and providing computing services, without sharing the ciphertext data of DOs with other users. Figure 2 shows the structure of privacy protection scheme with KMS.

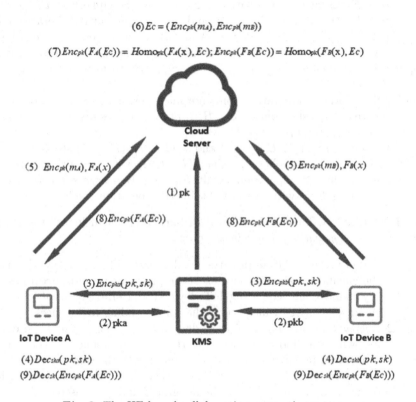

$$(6) Ec = (Enc_{pk}(m_A), Enc_{pk}(m_B))$$

$$(7) Enc_{pk}(F_A(Ec)) = Homo_{pk}(F_A(x), Ec); Enc_{pk}(F_B(Ec)) = Homo_{pk}(F_B(x), Ec)$$

**Fig. 2.** The HE-based collaboration computing system

**System Initialisation and Keys Generation.** In Fig. 2, the KMS can help CS to collect ciphertext from different IoT systems and integrate them for collaborative computing over devices do not trust each other (e.g., IoT device $A$ and $B$), which includes following nine steps:

Step 1 KMS generates a pair of homomorphic encryption keys, including public key $pk$ and private key $sk$, $(pk, sk)$, and then sends the collaborative homomorphic public key $pk$ to CS;

Step 2 Device $A$ generates a pair of keys $(pka, ska)$ for communication and sends the public key $pka$ to KMS; Device $B$ generates a pair of keys $(pkb, skb)$ for communication and sends the public key $pkb$ to KMS;

Step 3 KMS encrypts homomorphic keys $(pk, sk)$ used for collaborative operations using $pka$ and $pkb$ and returns the encryption result $Enc_{pka(pk,sk)}$ to $A$, $Enc_{pkb(pk,sk)}$ to $B$;

Step 4 To obtain the collaborative homomorphic public key $pk$, device $A$ decrypts $Enc_{pka}(pk)$ through $ska$, device $B$ decrypts $Enc_{pkb}(pk)$ through $skb$;

Step 5 Using the collaborative homomorphic public key $pk$, device $A$ encrypts its own data $mA$, device $B$ encrypts its own $mB$, and then $A$ send the ciphertext $Enc_{pk}(mA)$ to CS with $F_A(x)$, $B$ send the ciphertext $Enc_{pk}(mB)$ to CS with $F_B(x)$, while $F_A(x)$ and $F_B(x)$ represent collaborative computing requests sent by devices A and B to the server, which can be an arithmetic function or a complex model, such as the Kmeans algorithm;

Step 6 CS consolidates $Enc_{pk}(mA)$ and $Enc_{pk}(mB)$ to form a larger dataset $E_c$;

Step 7 CS perform collaborative homomorphic operations on $E_c$ according to different requests from $A$ and $B$ to obtain the results $Enc_{pk}(F_A(E_C))$ and $Enc_{pk}(F_B(E_C))$

Step 8 CS send $Enc_{pk}(F_A(E_C))$ to $A$ and send $Enc_{pk}(F_B(E_C))$ to $B$.

Step 9 A decrypts the ciphertext $Enc_{pk}(F_A(E_C))$ with the private key $sk$, and obtains the operation result $F_A(E_C)$. B decrypts the ciphertext $Enc_{pk}(F_B(E_C))$ with $sk$, and obtains the operation result $F_B(E_C)$.

**Key Distribution.** The proposed key distribution scheme includes three stages: *Initialization, aggregation, and collaboration:*

Stage 1 *Initialization*: KMS **generates** a collaborative key pair $(pk, sk)$ ($pk$ is the collaborative public key, $sk$ is the private key), **synchronizes** the key pair to the requesting IoT devices, and **shares** the $pk$ with the cloud server (CS) which serves the corresponding IoT devices;

Stage 2 *Aggregation*: IoT device $I$ use collaborative public key $pk$ to **encrypt** its own data, and **send** the ciphertext and its requests $F_I(x)$ to the cloud, who integrates the data encrypted with the same key.

Stage 3 *Collaboration*: CS firstly consolidates encrypted data from different IoT devices, and then calculates the integrated data $E_C$ based on functions $F_I(x)$ and $pk$, and returns the results to the corresponding IoT device.

## 3.2 Implementation of Collaborative Computing Services

As mentioned above, the collaborative computing can be delivered over ciphertext as a service. In this sub section, we will introduce a collaborative $k$-means clustering algorithm over ciphertext as a use case of collaborative computing application.

**Use case: Collaborative $k$-Means Clustering Algorithm.** The data in IoT needs to be well protected using collaborative computing services, which could be an algorithm, a function, or a complex task in IoT scenarios. In this work, we will implement the $k$-means algorithms as an example to demonstrate the proposed collaborative computing scheme. The $k$-means algorithm is widely used in many IoT applications, such as *healthcare data analysis, finace analysis, etc.*, in which key information is often used for analysis but can only be shared in a trusted way.

In implementing collaborative $k$-means algorithm, following four components were introduced: *K-means clustering under ciphertext, homomorphic squared Euclidean distance calculation, homomorphic comparison, and homomorphic minization*, to achieve clustering analysis of multi-party data in the constructed privacy protection architecture.

**$K$-Means Algorithm.** As shown in Algorithm 1, in the $k$-means clustering algorithm the data $X = \{\mathbf{x_0}, \mathbf{x_1}, \dots, \mathbf{x_{N-1}}\}$ has $M$ attributes, namely $0 \leq i \leq N - 1$, the number of clusters is $k$, and the maximum number of iterations $\epsilon$. The output is clustering result $C^{(\epsilon)}$.

During the initialization process, $t = 0$ and randomly select $k$ sample points as the cluster center as $\mathbf{m}^{(0)} = (\mathbf{m}_1^{(0)}, \dots, \mathbf{m}_k^{(0)})$.

At $t$-th iteration of the clustering process, for $\mathbf{x}_i \notin \mathbf{m}^{(t)}$, the square Euclidean distance from $\mathbf{x_i}$ to cluster center $\mathbf{m}_l^{(t)}$, $d_{il}^2$, can be achieved by

$$d_{il}^2 = \sum_{j=0}^{M-1} (x_i[j] - m_l[j])^2 \tag{1}$$

where $l = 1, \dots, k$, and merge them into the cluster where the nearest sample center is located. Then we can obtain the clustering results of this round of iteration $t$.

For clustering result $C^t$ obtained at $t$-$th$ iteration, we can iteratively calculate the mean of all samples in each cluster to obtain a new sample center point $\mathbf{m}^{(t)}$. Until the termination condition is reached when the number of iterations is greater than or equal to $\epsilon$.

**Homomorphic Squared Euclidean Distance.** The general definition of Euclidean distance for any two given sample points $\mathbf{x_i}, \mathbf{y_i}$ is

$$d_{ij}^2(x_i, x_j) = \sum_{j=0}^{M-1} \sqrt{(x_i[j] - y_i[j])^2} \tag{2}$$

where $M$ is the dimension of vector $\mathbf{x}$.

In the operation of homomorphic scheme, in order to avoid the calculation of roots, we use the form of squared Euclidean distance, and define the loss function as

---

**Algorithm 1.** K-means algorithm

---

**Input:** $X = (\mathbf{x}_0, \mathbf{x}_1, \ldots, \mathbf{x}_{N-1})$, $k$, $\epsilon$
**Output:** Clustering of $k$ sample sets $C^{(\epsilon)}$

1: **Initialization.** Let $t = 0$, randomly select $K$ sample points as the initial clustering center $\mathbf{m}^{(0)} = (\mathbf{m}_1^{(0)}, \ldots, \mathbf{m}_k^{(0)})$.
2: **Clustering.** For a fixed sample center $\mathbf{m}^{(t)}$, in which $m_l^{(t)}$ is the center of class $G_l$, calculate the square Euclidean distance $d_{it}$ from each sample $(\mathbf{x}_i) \notin \mathbf{m}^{(t)}$ to the center of the class, assign each sample to the class closest to it, and form the clustering result $C^{(t)} = (C_1^{(t)}, \ldots, C_k^{(t)})$.
3: **Update Class Centers.** For clustering result $C^{(t)}$, calculate the mean $(\overline{x_l}, \overline{y_l})$ of all samples in different clusters $C_l^{(t)}$ as the new class center $\mathbf{m}^{(t+1)} = (\mathbf{m}_1^{(t+1)}$.
4: **if** $t \geq \epsilon$ **then**
5:     $C^* = C^{(t)}$
6: **else**
7:     $t = t + 1$ goto step 2.
8: **end if**

---

$$L(C) = \sum_{l=1}^{k} \sum_{i=0}^{M-1} ||x_i - m_l||^2 \tag{3}$$

Then, the square Euclidean distance can be obtained by

$$d_{ij}^2(x_i, x_j) = \sum_{j=0}^{M-1} (x_i[j] -_h m_l[j]) \times_h (x_i[j] -_h m_l[j]) \tag{4}$$

**Homomorphic Comparison.** In clustering algorithms, the main goal is to minimize the loss function $L$. It is an critical process to compare the distance between sample point and the sample center in each iteration, this can be can be implemented via the *homomorphic comparison algorithm*, as shown in Algorithm 2, in which the input parameters include a plaintext space modulus $p$, and two distances $d_{C_i}, d_{C_j}$, obtained by Eq. (4).

The goal is to obtain ciphertext with lower plaintext values. For scheme's security, we add a random number $b \in \{0, 1\}$ to avoid the IoT devices learning the order of ciphertexts. According to the value of $b$, the CS can perform corresponding homomorphic operation. $Cq$ is the operated result of CS, and be sent to the IoT devices. The IoT devices can decrypt the $Cq$ to get plaintext $q$.

The $\lfloor log_2q \rfloor$-th bit of $q$ determines the return value $\omega$ from IoT devices to cloud server. Then, the Cloud Server judges the size of $d_{C_i}$, $d_{C_j}$ based on the values of $b$ and $\omega$. The important steps of the Algorithm 2 are explained as follows:

**In Stage 1-CS:**

Input $d_{C_i}, d_{C_j}$, and $C_p$. $p$ is plaintext modulus of homomorphic parameters and $C_p$ is the ciphertext of $p$ under the same $pk$ with $d_{C_i}, d_{C_j}$.

**Line 1: Generate a random number** $b$. It can be implemented using a simple random number generator.

**Line 2 to 5: Compute to get** $C_q$. According to $b$, the algorithm will choose Line 3 or 5 as the next step.

**In Stage 2-IoT devices:**

**Line 1: Decrypt** $C_q$ **to obtain** $q$. $C_q$ is the ciphertext of $p$ under the same $pk$ with $d_{C_i}, d_{C_j}$ and can be decrypt with $sk$ owned by IoT devices.

**Line 2 to 5: Get** $\omega$, **the** $\lfloor log_2 q \rfloor$-**th bit of** $q$. IoT devices do not know how CS compares $d_{C_i}$ and $d_{C_j}$ without knowing the value of the random number $b$ selected by CS, so they cannot determine the meaning of $\omega$. Meanwhile, CS does not have $sk$, it needs this $\omega$ to confirm the next step of operation.

**In Stage 3-CS:**

**Line 1: Make a Judgement.** According to the value of $b$ and $\omega$, CS could determine the return value. For example, if $b = 0$, it means that $C_q = C_p +_h d_{C_i} -_h d_{C_j}$, i.e. finding the difference between $d_{C_i}$ and $d_{C_j}$ in plaintext. At this time, if $\omega = 0$, it means that the difference between $d_{C_i}$ and $d_{C_j}$ in plaintext is less than 0, which means $d_{C_i} < d_{C_j}$, so we return the smaller one, $d_{C_i}$.

---

**Algorithm 2.** Homomorphic Comparison Algorithm

---

**Function: Comp($d_{C_i}, d_{C_j}$)**
**Input:**$d_{C_i}, d_{C_j}$, and $C_p$
**Output:**The comparison result.

**Stage 1-CS:**

1: Choose a random bit $b \in \{0, 1\}$
2: **if** b=0 **then**
3:    Compute $C_q = C_p +_h d_{C_i} -_h d_{C_j}$
4: **else**
5:    Compute $C_q = C_p +_h d_{C_j} -_h d_{C_i}$
6:    send $Cq$ to IoT devices;
7: **end if**

**Stage 2-IoT devices:**

1: Decrypt $C_q$ to obtain $q$ with secret key $sk$;
2: **if** the $\lfloor log_2 q \rfloor$-$th$ bit of $q$ is 0 **then**
3:    send $\omega = 0$ to cloud server
4: **else**
5:    send $\omega = 1$ to cloud server
6: **end if**

**Stage 3-CS:**

1: **if** $b = 0, \omega = 0$  $or$  $b = 1, \omega = 1$ **then**
2:    **return** $d_{C_i}$
3: **else**
4:    **return** $d_{C_j}$
5: **end if**

---

**Homomorphic Minimisation.** For every sample in each iteration, there will be $k$ distances, $d_{C_i}, i = 1, \ldots, k$. Initially we set $d_{C_{min}} = INF$ to as the minimum value, where $INF$ is a ciphertext with plaintext value that larger than all possible plaintext value of $d_{C_i}$. By iterating through all the elements in $d_{C_i}$, we can obtain the minimum distance $d_{C_{min}}$ using Algorithm 3.

---

**Algorithm 3.** Homomorphic Minimization Algorithm

---

**Function: Min($d_{C_1}, ..., d_{C_k}$)**
**Input:** $d_{C_i}, i = 1, ..., k$, and $d_{C_{min}} = INF$.
**Output:** The minimum distance $d_{C_{min}}$. CS:
  1: **for** $i = 1$ to $k$ **do**
  2:    $d_{C_{min}} = Comp(d_{C_{min}}, d_{C_i})$
  3: **end for**
  4: **return** $d_{C_{min}}$

---

## 4  Validation

To validate the proposed solution, we introduced a practical cloud scenario with *IoT device, IoT app, edge device, and cloud server* to conduct tests. In order to eliminate interference, the experiment is only used to verify the functionality and efficiency of each part, ignoring the time consumed by data transmission in the communication channel.

A Raspberry *pi* is used as typical IoT devices, an Android mobile *app* was developed on *IQOO Z5* as typical IoT applications, and the Altera Cyclone *DE0* platform as an *Edgedevices* with ARM + FPGA architecture. We have built a local server for low latency communication on a desktop (Intel i7 2.5GHz, 32GB). A cloud server (CS) was set up at the *Alibaba Cloud* platform to meet more realistic scenario requirements.

We use physiological information about heart disease patients dataset (301 records each with 11 features) for an unsupervised clustering analysis, which can category similar treatment methods to patients[1].

**Evaluation Criteria.** In this work, we introduce *time efficiency, space efficiency, accuracy*, and *energy efficiency* to evaluate the proposed solution. The key generation and distribution speed are used to evaluate the efficiency of KMS systems. The efficiency and accuracy of the $K$-means algorithm based on homomorphic encryption were used to evaluate the proposed scheme in executing the function $F(x)$ on the CS. The pace of *encoding, decoding, encryption, and decryption* is used to evaluate the efficiency of IoT devices in the entire environment. The spatial and energy efficiency of IoT devices have also been included in the evaluation criteria.

---

[1] https://www.kaggle.com/datasets/kingabzpro/heart-disease-patients.

**Time Efficiency.** Regarding the time efficiency of our proposed scheme, (1) the IoT devices first submit an encryption request to KMS; (2) After receiving the request, KMS generates key pairs for collaborative computing and encrypts the collaborative key pair $(pk, sk)$ using the IoT device's public key; (3) Then, the encryption result is packaged and sent to the IoT device.

We compared the performance with the widely used CKKS scheme [11]. There are two main parameters in CKKS scheme: *polynomial modulus degree* and *coefficient modulus*: (1) the polynomial modulus degree is a power of 2 whose value will affect the calculation speed. A large polynomial modulus degree will cause a low calculation pace, while it can support more complex encryption operations; (2) The length of the coefficient modulus is the sum of its prime factor lengths.

In order to conduct control experiments, in the following analysis, we will uniformly set the polynomial modulus degree value of 8192, and set the coefficient modulus value of 200. The time consumption for initializing homomorphic encryption all related variables with the above parameters is 0.131 s.

Table 1. Time consumption of proposed scheme for *encoding & encrypting* batch data vs the SEAL-CKKS scheme(ms).

|                 | encoding | encryption | decryption | decoding |
|-----------------|----------|------------|------------|----------|
| SEAL-CKKS       | 2.407    | 3.381      | 0.194      | 2.504    |
| Proposed scheme | 0.1125   | 3.1488     | 0.1347     | 1.8486   |

Table 1 shows the performance of proposed scheme compared with *SEAL-CKKS* scheme, it can be seen that the average times of SEAL-CKKS scheme for *encoding, encryption, decryption, and decoding* are 2.407, 3.381, 0.1940, and 2.500 respectively, while the consumed time in proposed scheme were 0.1125, 3.1488, 0.1347, 1.8486, respectively. The performance of encoding in the proposed scheme can significantly reduce the time than that of SEAL-CKKS based scheme and the performance of *encryption, decryption,* and *decoding* are slightly less than in SEAL-CKKS scheme.

Table 2 shows the performance of proposed scheme over IoT devices. The average times for *encoding, encryption, decryption, decoding* on IoT devices are 0.3749, 10.4948, 0.4491, 6.1614 respectively.

Figure 3 presents the time consumed by different IoT devices are very similar, and the time consumed for subtraction and addition operation is pretty low and the time for square operation is about 200 us. Actually, the operation relinearize costs the main time, average 1.19 ms. Figure 4 shows the execution efficiency of proposed scheme on a dataset of heart disease patients. We conducted 40, 60, and 80 rounds of iterations for clusters value of 2, 4, and 6, respectively. It can be seen in Fig. 4 that under the same number of iterations, the algorithm's time varies with the number of clusters.

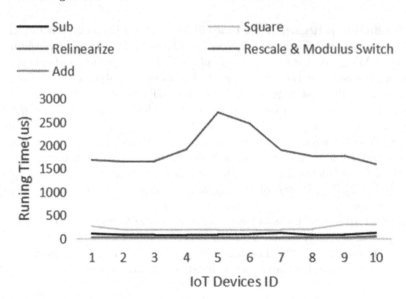

**Fig. 3.** Time consumption of steps of get Euclid distances

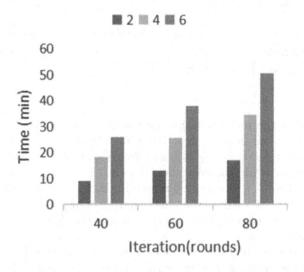

**Fig. 4.** The efficiency of our collaboration k-means clustering scheme.

**Table 2.** Encoding, encryption, decryption, and decoding of IoT devices(ms).

| Device ID | Encoding | Encryption | Decryption | Decoding |
|---|---|---|---|---|
| 1 | 0.3721 | 10.4739 | 0.4699 | 6.2976 |
| 2 | 0.3686 | 10.2436 | 0.4716 | 6.1405 |
| 3 | 0.3872 | 10.5427 | 0.4369 | 6.1829 |
| 4 | 0.3670 | 10.5438 | 0.4477 | 6.3591 |
| 5 | 0.3753 | 10.4750 | 0.4518 | 6.0873 |
| 6 | 0.3757 | 10.5477 | 0.4316 | 6.0702 |
| 7 | 0.3831 | 10.5776 | 0.4571 | 6.3392 |
| 8 | 0.3585 | 10.4122 | 0.4429 | 6.0313 |
| 9 | 0.3912 | 10.6525 | 0.4405 | 6.1123 |
| 10 | 0.3699 | 10.4791 | 0.4409 | 5.9939 |
| Average | 0.3749 | 10.4948 | 0.4491 | 6.1614 |

**Space Efficiency.** We tested the resident memory size consumed when encrypting data of different sizes on IoT devices. When the polynomial modulus is 8192 and the coefficient modulus is 200, the double precision floating point numbers with the size of 100, 1000, 2000, 3000 are encrypted, and the memory consumed is shown in the Fig. 6. Adopting the single instruction multiple data (SIMD) mode for batch processing of data can greatly save memory space and is friendly to the IoT environment.

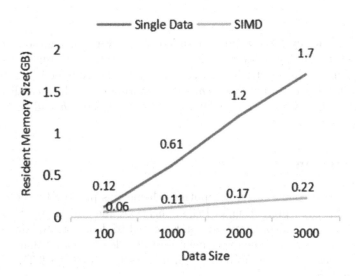

**Fig. 5.** Resident Memory Size by encrypting different sizes of Data.

**Accuracy.** Here we will compare and analyze the accuracy of the proposed k-means clustering algorithm for ciphertext and plaintext. The number of experiments increased from 40 to 80, and the accuracy of ciphertext increased from 58.2% to 84.1%. As the number of experiments increased from 40 to 80, the performance of ciphertext gradually approached that of plaintext (Fig. 5).

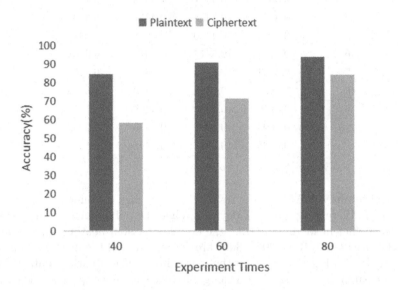

**Fig. 6.** The accuracy of k-means clustering on ciphertext compared with on plaintext.

**Energy Efficiency.** We mainly measured the power consumption of $pi$ and DE10-nano in standby mode and continuously operating in proposed solution. In standby mode, the electricity consumption of the DE10-nano is $0.1216\,kW \cdot h$ and the $pi$ is $0.065\,kW \cdot h$ within 24 h. Under continuous working conditions, the electrical energy consumption of DE10-nano is $0.144\,kW \cdot h$ and that of $pi$ is $0.099\,kW \cdot h$ within 24 h.

## 5    Conclusion

Using the HE, a collaborative computing scheme was proposed to enhance the security and privacy protection for IoT applications and data in use. Specifically, a $k$-mean clustering algorithm were implemented to demonstrate how to secure IoT applications in use. The experimental results demonstrated that the developed scheme can provide affordable secure protection for both IoT application and data in use.

# References

1. Asare, B.T., Quist-Aphetsi, K., Nana, L., Simpson, G.: A nodal authentication iot data model for heterogeneous connected sensor nodes within a blockchain network. In: 2021 International Conference on Cyber Security and Internet of Things (ICSIoT), pp. 65–71 (2021). https://doi.org/10.1109/ICSIoT55070.2021.00021
2. Chaudhary, P., Gupta, R., Singh, A., Majumder, P.: Analysis and comparison of various fully homomorphic encryption techniques. In: 2019 International Conference on Computing, Power and Communication Technologies (GUCON), pp. 58–62 (2019)
3. Chen, H., Chillotti, I., Song, Y.: Multi-key homomorphic encryption from tfhe. In: Advances in Cryptology-ASIACRYPT 2019: 25th International Conference on the Theory and Application of Cryptology and Information Security, Kobe, Japan, December 8–12, 2019, Proceedings, Part II 25, pp. 446–472. Springer (2019)
4. Halder, S., Newe, T.: Enabling secure time-series data sharing via homomorphic encryption in cloud-assisted iiot. Futur. Gener. Comput. Syst. **133**, 351–363 (2022)
5. Joshua, W.X.K., Justin, X.W.T., Yap, C.N.: Arithmetic circuit homomorphic encryption key pairing comparisons and analysis between elliptic curve Diffie Hellman and supersingular isogeny Diffie Hellman. In: 2021 2nd Asia Conference on Computers and Communications (ACCC), pp. 138–142 (2021). https://doi.org/10.1109/ACCC54619.2021.00030
6. Li, S.: Zero trust based internet of things. EAI Endorsed Trans. Internet Things **5**(20), e1–e1 (2019)
7. Li, S., Zhao, S., Min, G., Qi, L., Liu, G.: Lightweight privacy-preserving scheme using homomorphic encryption in industrial internet of things. IEEE Internet Things J. **9**(16), 14542–14550 (2022). https://doi.org/10.1109/JIOT.2021.3066427
8. Li, X., et al.: Design and verification of the arm confidential compute architecture. In: 16th USENIX Symposium on Operating Systems Design and Implementation (OSDI 22), pp. 465–484 (2022)
9. Liu, X.K., Wang, S.Q., Chi, M., Liu, Z.W., Wang, Y.W.: Resilient secondary control and stability analysis for dc microgrids under mixed cyber attacks. IEEE Trans. Industr. Electron. **71**(2), 1938–1947 (2024). https://doi.org/10.1109/TIE.2023.3262893
10. Loukil, F., Ghedira-Guegan, C., Boukadi, K., Benharkat, A.N.: Privacy-preserving iot data aggregation based on blockchain and homomorphic encryption. Sensors **21**(7), 2452 (2021)
11. Ma, J., Naas, S.A., Sigg, S., Lyu, X.: Privacy-preserving federated learning based on multi-key homomorphic encryption. Int. J. Intell. Syst. **37**(9), 5880–5901 (2022)
12. Mahmood, Z.H., Ibrahem, M.K.: New fully homomorphic encryption scheme based on multistage partial homomorphic encryption applied in cloud computing. In: 2018 1st Annual International Conference on Information and Sciences (AiCIS), pp. 182–186 (2018). https://doi.org/10.1109/AiCIS.2018.00043
13. Marcolla, C., Sucasas, V., Manzano, M., Bassoli, R., Fitzek, F.H., Aaraj, N.: Survey on fully homomorphic encryption, theory, and applications. Proc. IEEE **110**(10), 1572–1609 (2022)
14. Ni, C., Cang, L.S., Gope, P., Min, G.: Data anonymization evaluation for big data and iot environment. Inf. Sci. **605**, 381–392 (2022)
15. Ren, W., et al.: Privacy-preserving using homomorphic encryption in mobile iot systems. Comput. Commun. **165**, 105–111 (2021)

16. Sandomirskii, M., et al.: Femtosecond direct laser writing on bi-layer gold-silicon films for hidden data storage and random key generation. In: 2023 IEEE 23rd International Conference on Nanotechnology (NANO), pp. 1090–1094 (2023). https://doi.org/10.1109/NANO58406.2023.10231269

17. Sharbaf, M.S.: Iot driving new business model, and iot security, privacy, and awareness challenges. In: 2022 IEEE 8th World Forum on Internet of Things (WF-IoT), pp. 1–4 (2022). https://doi.org/10.1109/WF-IoT54382.2022.10152044

18. Shoji, Y., Nakauchi, K., Liu, W., Watanabe, Y., Maruyama, K., Okamoto, K.: A community-based iot service platform to locally disseminate socially-valuable data : Best effort local data sharing network with no conscious effort? In: 2019 IEEE 5th World Forum on Internet of Things (WF-IoT), pp. 724–728 (2019). https://doi.org/10.1109/WF-IoT.2019.8767237

19. Shrestha, R., Kim, S.: Integration of iot with blockchain and homomorphic encryption: challenging issues and opportunities. In: Advances in Computers, vol. 115, pp. 293–331. Elsevier (2019)

20. Wang, G., Huang, X., Zhang, X., Liu, G., Zuo, F.: Design and analysis of secure localization against vulnerability-induced attack for internet of things. In: 2023 IEEE/CIC International Conference on Communications in China (ICCC Workshops), pp. 1–6 (2023). https://doi.org/10.1109/ICCCWorkshops57813.2023.10233751

21. Zhang, P., et al.: Privacy-preserving and outsourced multi-party k-means clustering based on multi-key fully homomorphic encryption. IEEE Trans. Dependable Secure Comput. (2022)

# Robustness-Enhanced Assertion Generation Method Based on Code Mutation and Attack Defense

Min Li, Shizhan Chen, Guodong Fan, Lu Zhang, Hongyue Wu$^{(\boxtimes)}$, Xiao Xue, and Zhiyong Feng

Tianjin University, Tianjin, China
{plainminbao,shizhan,guodongfan,zlu_4435,jzxuexiao,
hongyue.wu,zyfeng}@tju.edu.cn

**Abstract.** Writing high-quality unit tests plays a crucial role in discovering and diagnosing early-stage errors and preventing their further propagation throughout the development cycle. However, the low readability of existing automated test case tools hinders developers from directly using them. In addition, current approaches exhibit sensitivity to individual words in the input code, often producing completely different results for minor changes in the input code. To tackle these problems, we propose AssertGen, a powerful Java assertion generation model that maintains consistent output for minor variations in code snippets. Inspired by software mutation testing, we propose 11 heuristic strategies for code mutation, aiming to generate variant code that is human-readable but misleading to the model, by making minor changes to code text or structural information. Then, we use the variant code to attack the model to test the model's robustness. We observe that the variant based on variable names (VM), the mutation based on method names (FM), and the mutation method False_Control_Flow, which adds additional control flow, have the greatest impact on the quality of generated assertions by the model. To enhance the robustness of AssertGen, we use multiple mutations to expand the original dataset, allowing the model to learn how to counter the instability caused by mutations during the training process. Experiment results show our assertion generation model achieves a BLEU score of 60.08 and a perfect prediction rate of 47.91%, surpassing previous work significantly.

**Keywords:** Unit Tests · Model Robustness · Code Mutation · Attack Defense

## 1 Introduction

Unit testing is a testing method in software development that involves checking and validating the smallest testable software units that are isolated from other parts of the program [1–4]. While unit testing can quickly identify issues within

H. Gao et al. (Eds.): CollaborateCom 2023, LNICST 562, pp. 281–300, 2024.
https://doi.org/10.1007/978-3-031-54528-3_16

the tested modules, previous work [5] has shown that as the scale and complexity of software products increase, merging unit tests incurs significant costs in terms of traceability [6]. This reduces the feasibility of adding unit tests to software, making legacy code difficult to maintain and evolve. Adding unit tests to previously written code has become a challenge in the software development lifecycle. The software development research community has conducted extensive research [7,8] to assist developers by generating automated testing methods. However, some work points out limitations of current automated test generation tools and questions their ability to generate high-quality unit tests [9,10].

The application of pre-trained models in code-related tasks includes code autocompletion [11,12], code defect repair [13–15], code refactoring [16], code comment generation [17,18], and more. Among them, code autocompletion is one of the most common tasks. Currently, some large pre-trained models have made significant breakthroughs in code-related tasks, such as Codet5 [19], Code-BERT [21], CodeGPT [20], etc. These models have achieved good performance in code completion, code defect detection, and code search tasks. Among them, the CodeT5 model launched by the Salesforce research team has been proven to excel in various works related to code-related tasks [22,23].

While pre-trained models have greatly enhanced the software development process, according to our observations, these models are not omnipotent or perfect. Sometimes, they can produce sequences that are highly problematic or even incorrect. We do not expect the models to generate 100% accurate sentences, but such suboptimal or erroneous results are not desirable. They diminish the performance and effectiveness of code generation by the models, indicating a lack of robustness. So far, research on the issues with pre-trained models has primarily focused on their widespread use in various domains, model security, and reducing training time [24–28]. The problem of inconsistency in model-generated outputs has only been recognized in a few works [29], and these works have merely designed a pipeline for selecting the optimal output, rather than directly enhancing the consistency of model outputs. This issue has not been addressed at all in the context of automated test case generation.

In Fig. 1(left), we can see that after providing the test method code before the tested method and the assertion, the T5-based model generates 'perfect' assertion statements. However, when the variable name 'list' is changed to 'l', the model outputs different assertion statements. The assertions generated on the left are completely correct and comprehensive, while the assertions obtained from fine-tuned input have some errors because 'list.size()' should clearly be 3. This example illustrates the issue of input sensitivity in pre-trained models leading to inconsistent outputs. Figure 1(right) is an incorrect generation that cannot run correctly. In summary, the model's inconsistency in outputting results is due to its sensitivity to certain flags in the input, indicating that when the model learns on a large-scale dataset, it overly focuses on variable names, leading to a lack of robustness. Unlike traditional code generation, during the process of generating test cases, only the code's flow needs to be known, without requiring details such as variable names. The goal is to verify the correctness of program execution results, and the model only needs to generate a set of test cases that cover all program branches. In other words, the variable name being 'list' or 'l' should not affect the generated assertion content; the same assertions should be generated. We can unify the variable names in the tested function to make the model more focused on learning the program flow.

```
class ListFactory {
    public List<Integer> createList() {
        List<Integer> list = new ArrayList<>();
        list.add(1);
        list.add(2);                      class ListFactory {
        list.add(3);                          public List<Integer> createList() {
        return list;                              List<Integer> l = new ArrayList<>();
    }                                             l.add(1);
}                                                 l.add(2);
                                                  l.add(3);
public class ListFactoryTest {                    return l;
                                              }
    @Test                                 }
    public void testCreateList() {
        ListFactory listFactory = new ListFactory();   public class ListFactoryTest {
        List<Integer> list = listFactory.createList();
        assertEquals(3, list.size());          @Test
        assertEquals(Integer.valueOf(1), list.get(0));   public void testCreateList() {
        assertEquals(Integer.valueOf(2), list.get(1));       ListFactory listFactory = new ListFactory();
        assertEquals(Integer.valueOf(3), list.get(2));       List<Integer> list = listFactory.createList();
    }                                                  assertEquals ( 4, list. size ( ) ) ;
}                                                      assertEquals ( Integer. valueOf ( 1 ), list. get ( 0 ) ) ;
                                                       assertEquals ( Integer. valueOf ( 2 ), list. get ( 1 ) ) ;
                                                       assertEquals ( Integer. valueOf ( 3 ), list. get ( 2 ) ) ;
                                                   }
                                               }
```

**Fig. 1.** Inconsistency in the output of pre-trained models with slightly modified inputs.

Inspired by the mutation testing technique [30], we propose 11 code mutation strategies based on code text information and structural information. Then, using mutations of different tested functions to attack the model. We explore the robustness of the model under different variant influences and quantitatively evaluate the quality of the generated assertions, quantifying the model's sensitivity to the training data. Finally, the enhanced data is used to augment the original data for fine-tuning large pre-trained models, enabling the model to learn how to counter uncertainties and enhance its sensitivity resistance during the training process.

In summary, this paper offers the following contributions:

1. We propose 11 code mutation rules, where four code mutation strategies are introduced starting from the perspective of variable names in obfuscated code. Additionally, we propose 7 control flow mutations from the angle of code control flow.
2. We employ code attack models generated from the tested function under different mutation rules. Through this process, we identify three mutations that have the most significant impact on the quality of assertions generated by pre-trained models. Furthermore, we use multiple mutations to augment the training data, enabling the model to learn how to counteract unstable factors during the training process.
3. Experiment results show our assertion generation model achieves a BLEU score of 60.08 and a perfect prediction rate of 47.91%.
4. We provide an open source implementation of AssertGen at https://github. com/Bossism/test_gen.

**Paper Organization.** Section 1 describes the motivation of the problem. Section 2 presents the problem background and limitations of existing methods. Section 3 provides a detailed description of our method, AssertGen. Sections 4 introduce the experimental setup and results. Section 5 discusses threats to validity. Section 6 concludes the paper.

## 2    Background and Related Work

Traditional unit test generation techniques utilize search-based [31–33], constraint-based [34–36], or random-based strategies [37, 38] to generate a set of unit tests with the main goal of maximizing the coverage of the tested software. Although these automatically generated tests achieve reasonable coverage, they often lack readability and meaningfulness compared to manually written tests, which is why developers are reluctant to adopt them directly in practice [9].

The two most widely used tools in this field are Randoop [8] and EvoSuite [7]. Previous work [39] compared the effectiveness of Randoop, EvoSuite, and Agitar, three automatic unit test generation tools, in detecting 357 real defects in the Defects4J dataset. The results showed that while the generated test suites overall detected 55.7% of the defects, only 19.9% of individual test suites detected defects. There is still significant room for improvement in automatically generated test cases for defect detection.

In recent years, there have been some approaches that leverage knowledge from the NLP field to address automated test case generation. TESTNMT [40] demonstrated the feasibility of using neural machine translation models for automated testing. It used a modified neural machine translation model to generate test cases for Java methods. However, the effect of generating test cases across projects is not satisfactory. ATLAS [5] also applies DL methods to the generation of automated test cases. Unlike TESTNMT, it focuses on generating meaningful assertion statements rather than the entire test. It takes the tested function and the test method after removing the assertion as input to the model and outputs predicted assertion statements. However, to simplify the problem, this model can only generate a single assertion statement. Michele Tufano [41] achieved good results by pre-training a BART-based model called ATHENATEST on a large-scale English and source code corpus, followed by fine-tuning on an assertion generation dataset. White R [42] proposed the ReAssert model, which is based on the Reformer model, to address the limitation of ATLAS in generating only a single assertion statement. ReAssert can generate multiple consecutive assertion statements, but the evaluation metrics such as BLEU and ROUGE indicate suboptimal performance. CONTEST [43], for the first time, leverages the structural information of the code and creatively utilizes the functions called in the test method and focal method to generate different content AST trees, which are combined as inputs to the model. However, a drawback is that the model serializes the entire combined AST tree and inputs it into a Transformer-based model. This may lead to truncation of excessively long sequences, resulting in information loss, incomplete context, and high computational complexity. TOGA [49] is a neural methodology based on a unified Transformer architecture that employs a focus-based approach for context-based inference of anomalies and assertion test oracles. Its primary emphasis lies in identifying exceptions within methods. However, our model places a greater emphasis on generating assertions of high quality and strong consistency.

While traditional testing tools such as Evosuit have achieved commendable coverage, they suffer from limited readability and demand a comprehensive code execution environment. Furthermore, source code analysis necessitates compilation. In contrast, our methodology eliminates the requirement for executable code environments. It merely entails declaring the targeted functions and variables within the testing functions, rendering it markedly pragmatic. This approach effectively assists developers in composing test cases in real-time. In contrast to models based on RNN that are plagued by gradient vanishing, and LSTM models that suffer from extended training times and gradient explosion, Assert-Gen employs relative positional encoding to ensure the model's stability when processing lengthy sequences, thereby mitigating the risks of gradient explosion or vanishing. Additionally, we incorporate layer normalization during the training process to enhance the model's robustness. In comparison to ATLAS, our approach generates multiple consecutive assertion statements, as opposed to singular assertion statements, rendering it more versatile and impactful.

## 3  Approach

This chapter mainly describes the heuristic rules for generating different mutations and the use of these mutations to attack the model, exploring the parts of the tested code that have a significant impact on the model's robustness. The selected mutations are used to augment the training dataset, enabling the model to learn how to handle the instability caused by these mutations during training.

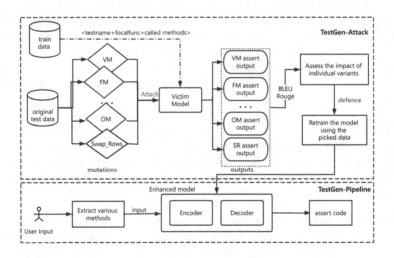

**Fig. 2.** Structure diagram of AssertGen.

## 3.1   Overview

AssertGen is an assertion generation model based on the T5 architecture. The structure diagram is shown in Fig. 2. For a given method under test, in Step 1, we apply heuristic mutation rules to generate mutations at both the code text and structural levels. We first use these mutations individually to attack the model and investigate which mutations have the greatest impact on the quality of generated assertions. These mutated mutations are then processed in Step 2 using BPE tokenization to obtain subword tokenization. Position vectors are added to the embedded input code, and the new embeddings go through N encoder blocks to obtain hidden layer outputs. The decoder maps the hidden layer outputs from the encoder to code sequences and consists of N decoder blocks. The generated code sequences are then passed through a linear layer with softmax activation to obtain a probability distribution over the vocabulary. AssertGen uses beam search on the probability distribution to generate the final candidate words as the predicted results. The following sections will provide detailed explanations of the mutation rules and the attack and adversarial steps.

## 3.2   Mutation Rules

The quality of model results is greatly influenced by the quality of the training data. Code blocks with the same structural and functional information may have different variable names across different projects. This "uncertainty" poses challenges for the model to learn the semantic information of code blocks with the same functionality. To address this issue, we propose heuristic mutation rules for variable names and expressions, incorporating control flow information for variable names.

**VM(Variable Mutation).** The VM technique replaces variable names with special characters. It's important to note that variable names referred to here are the ones defined by developers, such as *res* in the statement *boolean res = a >b;*. We use $\langle extra\_id\_ID \rangle$ to represent *res*. The reason for this approach is that a method may contain multiple variables, and we replace instances of the same variable with the same identifier $\langle extra\_id\_ID \rangle$. Here, *ID* represents the order of the variable's first appearance in the method.

**PM(Param Mutation).** The VM mutation rule is designed to handle variable names defined by developers. However, parameter names in method signatures are also commonly used custom variable names. Therefore, we have devised the PM mutation rule. The PM rule primarily focuses on parameter names within methods, replacing them with the identifier *param_id*.

**FM(Function Name Mutation).** Previous research [48] has found that when using natural language descriptions and method signatures as input to generate code examples using pre-trained models, the method name in the input has a significant impact on the model's output. Replacing the method name in the method signature leads to the generation of different and partially incorrect code by the model. This finding demonstrates that even minor modifications to the method name can deceive the model and result in erroneous outputs.

In our approach, we modify the method names in the tested code. Prior to this, we trained a Word2Vec model using all the method names in the dataset. For each tested method, we split its method name into individual words using camel case notation. For each word, we select the top k similar words as candidates and introduce three additional candidates for each word: randomly swapping two characters, randomly deleting one character, and replacing a character with a similar one. This process results in combinations of candidate words for each original word. By replacing the method name in the original method with these combinations of candidates, we input the modified method into the model to obtain the output. We calculate the BLEU score between the current output and the ground truth and select the method name with the lowest BLEU score. This means that we have identified the method name that has the greatest impact on the model. By using this method name, we launch an attack on the model to maximize its performance degradation.

**OM(Operator Mutation).** OM is a mutation rule specifically designed for assignment expressions. We have observed that the presence of compound assignment operators in expressions can affect the model's judgment of the output. To address this, we decompose expressions containing assignment operators into simpler patterns. For example, the expression $a \mathrel{+}= b$, we represent it as $a = a + b$. By using simpler expressions, we can increase the frequency of variable occurrences and enhance the model's understanding.

In the mutation of structural information in code, the objective is to obtain mutated code that does not change the semantics and can execute correctly by introducing specific control flows or altering the code's execution flow. Different mutations of structural information are used to attack the model and observe its recognition capability regarding specific control flows.

**Add_Print.** We randomly insert print statements into method code, including both developer-defined variable names and parameter names from the method's parameter list. Although this type of mutation may not have a direct purpose, it simulates the coding habits of developers during the code-writing process. Developers often like to print important variables for code debugging. By simulating this process, we observe whether the randomly inserted print statements affect the model's learning of the source code.

**False_Control_Flow.** False_Control_Flow introduces random control flow statements such as if(false) into method code. Although these statements will never be executed, our aim is to observe the impact of randomly added control flow information on the model. By observing the model's performance in generating high-quality assertion statements under the attack of randomly added control flow, we can determine whether the model can still generate accurate assertions.

In addition to simulating the impact of programming habits in actual development, inspired by data augmentation techniques, we also made some "semantic consistency" changes to the tested code. These changes preserve syntactic naturalness and semantic invariance from a human perspective but introduce noticeable differences for pre-trained models. By attacking the model with these semantically equivalent but structurally different mutations, we can observe their impact on the model's robustness.

**While2For & For2While.** For the While2For variant, we employed the SPAT [45] tool to identify the while statement blocks in the tested method and applied specific rules to transform them into syntactically equivalent for loops that are compilable. Conversely, for the For2While variant, we performed the opposite transformation by converting for loops into while loops using similar rules.

**Switch2If.** Similar to the previous two mutations, the Switch2If variant involves transforming switch statement blocks in the code into *if-elif-...-else* statements. This allows us to observe the impact of different code structures on the model.

**Swap_If_Else.** In this set of mutations, the if and else parts are swapped by exchanging the code within them while negating the if condition. This variant aims to investigate whether the model tends to excessively focus on a particular branch.

**Swap_Rows.** If there are no shared variables between two lines of code, the Swap_Rows variant swaps these two lines. Similar to the previous mutations, using the Swap_Rows variant to attack the model allows us to determine whether the model is sensitive to the order of certain lines of code.

### 3.3  Model

Our AssertGen model is based on the T5 model [19]. As shown in Fig. 3, we briefly introduce the model structure.

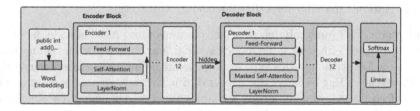

**Fig. 3.** Structural diagram of the AssertGen model.

**Encoder Block.** The encoder consists of $N$ encoder blocks, which aim to transform the input code sequence into hidden states. Here, $N$ is 12. We use relative positional encoding to effectively represent the relative positional information of each token in the input sequence, employing self-attention mechanisms with relative positional encoding.

We utilize a multi-head attention mechanism to force the model to jointly attend to different subspaces of code token representations from different positions in the input sequence. Specifically, we define multiple sets of queries ($Q$), keys $(K)$, and values $(V)$ that focus on different contexts. For an input matrix $X$, each set of $Q$, $K$, and $V$ produces an output matrix $Z_i$. We concatenate the $Z_i$ matrices generated by multiple attention heads and feed them into a fully connected layer.

$$MultiHead(Q, K, V) = Concat(head_1, head_2, ..., head_n)W \tag{1}$$

$$head_i = Attention(QW_i^Q, KW_i^K, VW_i^V) \tag{2}$$

During the calculation of attention, we perform padding and masking operations on the remaining sentences based on the maximum sentence length within each batch.

Each encoder block consists of two parts: a multi-head self-attention mechanism with relative positional encoding and a feed-forward neural network. Both parts include residual connections and layer normalization.

$$X_{attention} = LayerNorm(X + X_{attention}) \tag{3}$$

$$X_{hidden} = Linear(ReLU(Linear(X_{attention}))) \tag{4}$$

$$X_{hidden} = LayerNorm(X_{attention} + X_{hidden}) \tag{5}$$

**Decoder Block.** The decoder block mainly consists of three parts: Masked Multi-Head Self-Attention, Multi-Head Encoder-Decoder Attention, and a Feed-Forward Network. Similar to the encoder block, all three parts include residual connections and layer normalization. The Masked Multi-Head Self-Attention layer in the decoder is used to compute attention representations specific to the decoder itself. In this layer, each input sequence of the decoder undergoes self-attention calculations, resulting in an attention representation tailored to the current decoder input. This representation takes into account the relationships between all words in the input sequence, excluding the current token's context. It allows for better predictions in the next step. Therefore, during each time step of generating predictions, the model can only focus on the current token and the preceding context, while the sequence following the current token remains invisible to the model.

**Linear & Softmax.** The linear layer takes the output of the decoder as input and projects it into a vector of dimensionality equal to the size of the vocabulary. The softmax layer converts the vector values into a probability distribution that sums to 1. This produces the final output of the entire model.

### 3.4  Attacks and Adversarial Training

**Attacks.** It is well-known that deep neural networks often lack robustness. Specifically, deep neural models are easily fooled by adversarial examples, which are generated by introducing slight perturbations to the original samples. To explore the perturbations that have the greatest impact on the quality of assertion generation, we first fine-tune the T5 model on a training dataset to obtain the base assertion generation model. Then, we generate 11 code mutations as adversarial attacks for each input code in the test set, with each variant corresponding to a generated assertion. By comparing the quality of generated assertions (mainly evaluated using BLEU and ROUGE metrics) between the model under different attack mutations and the original test set, we observe which mutations have the strongest ability to fool the model.

**Adversarial Training.** We select three mutations, namely VM, FM, and False_Control_Flow, which have the greatest impact on the quality of assertion generation. For each input code in the training set, we combine these three mutations $(M)$ with the original input code $(O)$ to form a new training set $T = M \cup O$. The assertion generation model is fine-tuned on this new dataset. During the model's learning process on the new dataset, it learns to generate correct assertion statements even when the input is a variant with slight perturbations. This enhances the model's ability to withstand minor perturbations and improves its robustness.

## 4   Experiments

### 4.1   Experimental Design

**Dataset.** For our research questions, we utilize the CONTEST dataset, which is an open-source dataset provided in prior work [43]. This dataset consists of test methods collected from projects on GitHub that utilize Junit as the testing framework. Focusing on the Java programming language, the dataset includes 365,450 pairs of test methods. Each test method pair consists of an input code block and an assertion code block. As shown in Fig. 4, the input code block is divided into three parts: the tested method, the test method declaration and some precode, and other methods called within the two blocks.

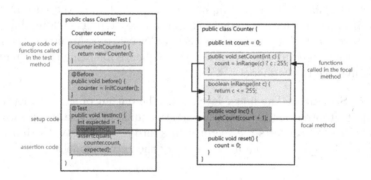

**Fig. 4.** Dataset composition.

In the first phase, we employ different mutations of input code to attack the model and investigate which parts of the input code have a significant impact on the model's robustness. By analyzing the effects of different mutations on the model's assertion generation quality, we identify the influential parts.

**Adversarial Training and Parameter Study.** In the second phase, we use the identified influential mutations to augment the training data and study the effect on the adversarial learning of the assertion generation model. We also examine different pre-trained models and parameters to assess their impact on generating assertions.

**Research Questions (RQs).** To evaluate the effectiveness of our approach, we address the following research questions:

- RQ1: Which parts of the tested code have a significant impact on the robustness of pre-trained models?
- RQ2: How does the assertion generation model perform after data augmentation using the influential mutations identified in RQ1? How does it compare to the baseline model?
- RQ3: How does AssertGen perform on the testing data containing a single variant?
- RQ4: What is the quality of the generated assertions?

**Baselines.** For our baseline models, we adopt the Contest model [43] proposed in the open-source CONTEST dataset work, as it is highly relevant to our research. Additionally, we include two other classical code pre-training models: CodeGPT [20] and CodeBERT [21]. These models share the same input format as our model, which consists of code blocks containing the tested method, with the output being the generated assertion statements.

**Evaluation Metrics.** BLEU [46] and ROUGE [47] are commonly used evaluation metrics in the field of machine translation. BLEU assesses translation quality based on precision, while ROUGE evaluates translation quality based on recall. Additionally, precision in assertion generation is of utmost significance, with accuracy equaling 1 only when the predicted assertion statements match the ground truth exactly; otherwise, it remains 0.

When extracting different tokens from the input code blocks, we employ the javalang[1] module for abstract syntax tree analysis. The T5 model serves as the foundational framework for our assertion generation model, implemented using Transformer[2] and PyTorch[3]. The hyperparameters of the model have been optimized based on empirical performance.

By answering these research questions, we aim to gain insights into the impact of different code mutations, data augmentation, and pre-trained models on the effectiveness of the assertion generation process.

**Experimental Platform.** All experiments were conducted on a Linux server equipped with an AMD EPYC 7371 CPU and an RTX A5000 GPU.

---

[1] https://github.com/c2nes/javalang.
[2] https://github.com/huggingface/transformers.
[3] https://pytorch.org/.

## 4.2    Experimental Results

**RQ1: Which parts of the tested code have a significant impact on the robustness of the pre-trained model?**

**Table 1.** Output assertion quality under 11 variant attacks.

| mutation | BLEU | BLEU-1 | BLEU-2 | BLEU-3 | BLEU-4 | ROUGE-1 | ROUGE-2 | ROUGE-L | Acc(%) |
|---|---|---|---|---|---|---|---|---|---|
| AssertGen | 55.23 | 64.84 | 55.95 | 56.73 | 53.23 | 81.57 | 73.07 | 80.54 | 45.44 |
| VM | **12.07** | **23.09** | **14.52** | **14.99** | **12.07** | **62.00** | **39.98** | **60.78** | **3.90** |
| PM | 51.28 | 63.11 | 54.06 | 54.85 | 51.28 | 80.78 | 71.62 | 79.79 | 41.46 |
| FM | **44.04** | **56.42** | **46.88** | **47.72** | **44.04** | **78.36** | **67.50** | **77.25** | **36.20** |
| OM | 53.78 | 65.61 | 56.46 | 57.31 | 53.78 | 81.66 | 73.14 | 80.62 | 45.33 |
| Add_Print | 51.58 | 63.14 | 54.20 | 55.05 | 51.58 | 81.19 | 72.40 | 80.12 | 44.86 |
| False_Control_Flow | **50.26** | **62.64** | **53.07** | **53.90** | **50.26** | **78.15** | **68.30** | **77.04** | **38.98** |
| While2For | 53.25 | 64.86 | 55.97 | 56.74 | 53.25 | 81.57 | 73.07 | 80.54 | 45.41 |
| For2While | 52.80 | 64.54 | 55.54 | 56.33 | 52.80 | 81.43 | 72.86 | 80.40 | 45.35 |
| Switch2If | 53.20 | 64.81 | 55.92 | 56.70 | 53.20 | 81.56 | 73.06 | 80.54 | 45.39 |
| Swap_If_Else | 53.11 | 64.73 | 55.84 | 56.61 | 53.11 | 81.51 | 72.99 | 80.49 | 45.28 |
| Swap_Rows | 53.40 | 65.07 | 56.14 | 56.91 | 53.40 | 81.28 | 72.75 | 80.29 | 45.02 |

Firstly, we fine-tuned our assertion generation model using the training set. Then, we attacked the model using 11 variations of code methods, and the results of the assertion generation model on the test set under different variant attacks are presented in Table 1. Compared to the original model's performance on the test set, the model performed the worst under the VM attack, with BLEU and ROUGE-L scores dropping from 55.23 and 80.54 to 12.07 and 60.78, respectively. The perfect prediction rate also decreased from 45.44% to 3.9%. This reveals the significant impact of variable names in the input code block on the model's robustness. When the encoder learns the semantics of the source code, it focuses too much on user-defined variable names, resulting in the model providing completely different predicted assertions when faced with test code written in different developer styles. Moreover, the model's excessive attention to variable names makes its prediction quality highly dependent on the quality of the training set, thereby severely reducing the model's robustness and assertion consistency. Furthermore, the FM attack had the greatest impact on the generation performance, with the perfect prediction rate decreasing by 9.24%. The BLEU and ROUGE scores also dropped by 11.19 and 3.29 compared to the original model's performance. This validates our hypothesis that well-named tested code methods directly reveal the purpose of the methods. Learning the semantics of method names enhances the model's ability to generate accurate assertions by correctly invoking methods, thereby improving the quality of generated assertions. The FM variant constructs mutated attacks on the assertion generation model by selecting candidate method names that have the greatest impact on the model's predicted results and replacing the original method names in the code block. As a result, the model fails to extract meaningful information from method names, leading to a deterioration in the quality of generated assertions. Overall, the method names in the code block also significantly influence the generation quality of the model.

The addition of random "garbage" code statements also leads to a decrease in assertion generation quality. This is evident in the model's performance under the False_Control_Flow attack, where the perfect prediction rate is only 38.98%. The reason for this is that unnecessary control flow statements increase the difficulty for the model to comprehend the semantics of the source code, resulting in less accurate outputs. Under the Add_Print mutation attack, which adds print statements, the model's BLEU and ROUGE-L scores slightly decrease, and the perfect prediction rate also decreases by 0.58%, further supporting our observation.

Another interesting finding is that our assertion generation model remains robust in the face of certain control flow-related variations in the input code. For example, the Operator_Simple, While2For, For2While, Switch2If, Swap_If_Else, and Swap_Rows mutations. Under these attack variations, the generated assertions only experience a slight decrease in quality, with the perfect prediction rate dropping within a range of 0.6%. This indicates that different branch categories have a minimal impact on assertion generation quality, and our model has the ability to recognize different branch types and learn code structure and semantic information from them. Additionally, the model is almost unaffected when two lines of code are swapped without any shared variables. This can be attributed to the T5 model's pre-training on a large-scale code corpus, which provides strong robustness against small perturbations introduced by attackers targeting different branches.

**RQ2: How does the assertion generation model perform after data augmentation using some of the variations identified in Question 1? How does it compare to the baseline model?**

In RQ1, we found that the model's assertion generation quality was most affected by the variable name variation (VM), method name variation (FM), and "garbage" control flow variation (False_Control_Flow) attacks. Inspired by these findings, we incorporated these three variations into the model's training process, enabling the model to develop the ability to counteract these unstable factors and improve its robustness and assertion generation quality.

To address RQ2, we conducted experiments to evaluate the performance of the assertion generation model after data augmentation with the identified variations. We compared the augmented model's performance against the baseline model. Specifically, we examined how the model's generated assertions differ in terms of quality, robustness, and consistency.

By integrating the VM, FM, and False_Control_Flow variations into the training process, we aimed to enhance the model's ability to handle code blocks with different variable names, method names, and control flow patterns. The augmented model was expected to generate more accurate and reliable assertions, even when faced with variations and adversarial attacks.

Our experimental results demonstrate that the augmented model outperforms the baseline model in terms of assertion generation quality, robustness, and resilience to attacks. The augmentation process helps the model generalize better and improve its ability to handle different coding styles, variable and method name variations, and control flow structures.

In Table 2, the AssertGen_O model represents the assertion generation model trained on the original training set, while the AssertGen_M model represents the model trained using the three variations and the original training set through adversarial learning. It can be observed that the model trained through adversarial learning with the variations outperforms the AssertGen_O model in terms of metrics measuring the quality of generated assertions. Specifically, the perfect prediction rate increases from 45.44% to 47.91%. This indicates that the model has learned how to generate correct assertions even in the presence of different variations in the augmented data. The model has acquired the ability to counteract minor perturbations in the input, demonstrating stronger robustness.

**Table 2.** Comparison of the AssertGen_M model after defensive learning with the original AssertGen and other baselines.

| model | BLEU | BLEU-1 | BLEU-2 | BLEU-3 | BLEU-4 | ROUGE-1 | ROUGE-2 | ROUGE-L | Acc(%) |
|---|---|---|---|---|---|---|---|---|---|
| Contest | 38.19 | 56.31 | 42.35 | 32.85 | 27.15 | 68.61 | 70.04 | 55.04 | - |
| codeBERT | 30.41 | 43.69 | 33.36 | 34.21 | 30.41 | 73.44 | 60.17 | 72.43 | 27.45 |
| codeGPT | 32.62 | 46.60 | 35.76 | 36.61 | 32.62 | 72.84 | 59.72 | 71.82 | 27.42 |
| AssertGen_O | 55.23 | 64.84 | 55.95 | 56.73 | 53.23 | 81.57 | 73.07 | 80.54 | 45.44 |
| AssertGen_M | **60.08** | **71.22** | **62.66** | **63.43** | **60.08** | **81.83** | **74.11** | **80.94** | **47.91** |

Compared to the baseline model Contest, our model performs significantly better. AssertGen_O achieves a notable improvement in BLEU score and ROUGE-L score by 17.04 and 25.5, respectively, compared to Contest. In comparison to the code pre-training models CodeBERT and CodeGPT, AssertGen_O trained on the original dataset demonstrates better performance. CodeBERT and Code-GPT achieve a BLEU score of only 30.41 and 32.62, respectively, while AssertGen_O achieves a BLEU score of 55.23. Furthermore, AssertGen_M, which is trained through adversarial learning, achieves a BLEU score of 60.08. Our model significantly outperforms CodeBERT and CodeGPT in terms of generating high-quality assertions.

These findings highlight the superiority of our model in generating high-quality assertions compared to the baseline model and code pre-training models. The performance improvements can be attributed to the model's ability to effectively handle variations and adversarial attacks, as well as its robustness in the face of input perturbations. The results underscore the significance of our approach in enhancing assertion generation models for improved software development and testing practices.

**RQ3: How does AssertGen perform on individual variations of the test data?**

The experimental results of RQ2 demonstrated that AssertGen_M, after adversarial training against multiple attacks, learned how to generate high-quality assertions accurately. We further tested the enhanced AssertGen_M against individual variations to assess the quality of generated assertions and determine if it exhibits stronger robustness compared to AssertGen. As shown in Table 3, AssertGen_M outperforms the original AssertGen_O in the case of VM attack. Specifically, the original AssertGen_O achieved BLEU and ROUGE-L scores of 12.07 and 60.78, respectively, while AssertGen_M achieved scores of 51.21 and 77.09, showing significant improvements. Moreover, the perfect prediction rate increased from 3.9% to 42.28%. This indicates that the model, after adversarial learning to defend against variations, has acquired the ability to identify subtle changes and generate correct assertions, thus enhancing its robustness.

**Table 3.** Performance of AssertGen_O and AssertGen_M under VM attack.

| model | BLEU | BLEU-1 | BLEU-2 | BLEU-3 | BLEU-4 | ROUGE-1 | ROUGE-2 | ROUGE-L | Acc(%) |
|---|---|---|---|---|---|---|---|---|---|
| codeT5 | 12.07 | 23.09 | 14.52 | 14.99 | 12.07 | 62.00 | 39.98 | 60.78 | 3.90 |
| AssertGen_O | 46.18 | 59.51 | 49.00 | 49.92 | 46.18 | 72.53 | 62.37 | 71.49 | 39.70 |
| AssertGen_M | **51.21** | **63.88** | **54.33** | **55.03** | **51.21** | **78.13** | **69.02** | **77.09** | **42.28** |

Furthermore, we compared the performance of the models subjected to only VM attack and those subjected to VM, FM, and False_Control_Flow attacks on generating assertions. It can be observed that the model subjected to only VM attack shows significant improvements in BLEU and ROUGE-L compared to the original model, with the BLEU score increasing from 12.07 to 46.18 and the ROUGE-L score increasing from 60.78 to 77.09. This suggests that the model has learned how to counteract VM attacks through single-variation attacks. However, compared to the model subjected to attacks from all three variations, the performance of the model under single-variation attacks is relatively inferior. This can be attributed to the fact that multi-variation attacks and adversarial training enable the model to acquire more comprehensive knowledge of code, leading to better performance.

**RQ4: How is the quality of the generated assertions?**

To substantiate the quality of assertions generated by the model, we conducted a comparative analysis of the test coverage outcomes pertaining to the assertions produced by EvoSuite and AssertGen on the public methods of the NumberUtils class within the context of Lang-1-f[4]. Line coverage and branch coverage are two metrics for measuring code coverage, which describe the extent to which the source code of a program has been tested. These metrics aid in assessing the efficiency of test execution.

Table 4 presents the class-level line coverage and condition coverage for each individual public method in the class. From the results provided in Table 4, the following observations can be made: (i) Both EvoSuite and AssertGen have effectively tested all methods. (ii) ATHENATEST has generated accurate test cases for all methods, thereby achieving optimal coverage in the majority of scenarios.

---

[4] https://github.com/rjust/defects4j.

**Table 4.** Compare condition coverage and line coverage of test cases generated by EvoSuite and AssertGen in class NumberUtils for each public method.

| Focal Method | EvoSuite | | AssertGen | |
|---|---|---|---|---|
| | Lines | Conditions | Lines | Conditions |
| toInt(String, int) | 25 (5.7%) | 1(0.2% ) | **26(5.9%)** | **2(0.5%)** |
| toLong(String, long) | 25(5.7%) | 1(0.2%) | **31(7.0%)** | **2(0.5%)** |
| toFloat(String, float) | 27(6.1%) | 1(0.2%) | **28(6.3%)** | 1(0.2%) |
| toDouble(String, double) | 24(5.4%) | 1(0.2%) | **25(5.7%)** | 1(0.2%) |
| toByte(String, byte) | 25(5.7%) | 1(0.2%) | **26(5.9%)** | **2(0.5%)** |
| toShort(String, short) | 25(5.7%) | 1(0.2%) | **26(5.9%)** | **2(0.5%)** |
| createFloat(String) | 23(5.2%) | 1(0.2%) | **24(5.4%)** | **2(0.5%)** |
| createDouble(String) | 23(5.2%) | 1(0.2%) | **24(5.4%)** | **2(0.5%)** |
| createInteger(String) | 23(5.2%) | 1(0.2%) | **24(5.4%)** | **2(0.5%)** |
| createLong(String) | 23(5.2%) | 1(0.2%) | **24(5.4%)** | **2(0.5%)** |
| createBigInteger(String) | 33(7.5%) | 6(1.4%) | **36(8.1%)** | **13(3.1%)** |
| createBigDecimal(String) | 24(5.4%) | 2(0.5%) | **25(5.7%)** | **3(0.7%)** |
| min(long[]) | 30(6.8%) | 4(1.0%) | 30(6.8%) | 4(1.0%) |
| min(int, int, int) | 24(5.4%) | 2(0.5%) | **26(5.9%)** | **4(1.0%)** |
| max(long[]) | 24(5.4%) | 1(0.2%) | **29(6.6%)** | **5(1.2%)** |
| max(byte, byte, byte) | 25(5.7%) | 2(0.5%) | **26(5.9%)** | **4(1.0%)** |
| isDigits(String) | 22(5.0%) | 1(0.2%) | 22(5.0%) | 1(0.2%) |
| isNumber(String) | 37(8.4%) | 10(2.4%) | **45(10.2%)** | **20(4.8%)** |

Subsequently, a qualitative analysis of the quality of assertions generated by AssertGen was performed. Simulating an authentic development process, as depicted in Figure xx, the code sections comprising the method "elementMult" and the pre-test code were utilized as model inputs. The objective was to observe the assertions predicted by codeGPT, codeBERT, and AssertGen (highlighted in red in Fig. 5).

As illustrated in Fig. 5, the assertions generated by AssertGen exhibit the highest quality, aligning with the ground truth. The assertions generated by codeGPT exhibit proximity to the ground truth; however, an error arises during the prediction of the computation method for "expected" within the code, where the Math.pow() function is erroneously employed. Conversely, the results generated by codeBERT are notably unsatisfactory, attributed to its inability to predict the extensive variables "i" and "j" within A.get(i, j), and its failure to generate assertions for the focal method elementMult(). In this instance, both codeBERT and codeGPT have produced assertions of subpar quality. In contrast, our model, AssertGen, emerges as the superior performer in terms of assertion quality.

# 5    Threats to Validity

**Internal Threats.** Internal threats refer to potential flaws in our use of baseline methods and implementation. To mitigate internal threats, we employed publicly available replicable packages of the baseline methods and strictly followed their original implementations. Additionally, to ensure the fairness of the results, we conducted double-checking of the code and peer reviews.

**External Threats.** The selection of pretrained models and datasets contributes to external threats. To address this, we manually examined the validity of the dataset and removed any data that failed compilation to ensure the authenticity and validity of the data. For pretrained models, we chose three of the most popular models currently available, namely CodeT5, CodeGPT, and CodeBERT.

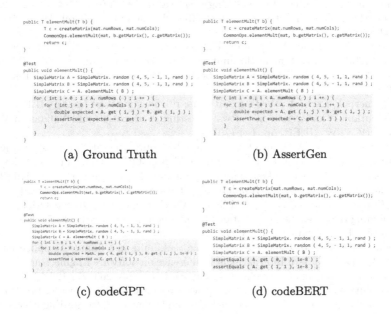

(a) Ground Truth                    (b) AssertGen

(c) codeGPT                         (d) codeBERT

**Fig. 5.** Assertions generated by codeBERT, codeGPT, and AssertGen models under a specific function.

# 6    Conclusion

From the perspective of robustness, we employed heuristic rules to create various input mutations to attack the T5 model, aiming to explore the factors that have the greatest impact on the model's robustness. The experimental results demonstrate that variable names, method names, and randomly inserted erroneous control flow statements in the input are the factors that have the most significant influence on the model's robustness. We augmented the training data with these three types of mutations to enable the model to learn how to counter-act these unstable factors and generate high-quality assertions. In future work, we plan to investigate the performance and interpretability of pretrained models in addressing other tasks in the field of software engineering.

**Acknowledgments.** This project was funded by the National Natural Science Foundation of China (62032016, 61832014).

# References

1. Zhu, H., Hall, P.A., May, J.H.: Software unit test coverage and adequacy. ACM Comput. Surv. (CSUR) **29**(4), 366–427 (1997)
2. Cohn, M.: Succeeding with agile: software development using Scrum. Pearson Education (2010)
3. Runeson, P.: A survey of unit testing practices. IEEE Softw. **23**(4), 22–29 (2006)
4. Olan, M.: Unit testing: test early, test often. J. Comput. Sci. Coll. **19**(2), 319–328 (2003)
5. Watson, C., Tufano, M., Moran, K., Bavota, G., Poshyvanyk, D.: On learning meaningful assert statements for unit test cases. In: Proceedings of the ACM/IEEE 42nd International Conference on Software Engineering, 2020, pp. 1398–1409 (2020)
6. Klammer, C., Kern, A.: Writing unit tests: It's now or never! In: 2015 IEEE Eighth International Conference on Software Testing, Verification and Validation Workshops (ICSTW). IEEE, pp. 1–4 (2015)
7. Fraser, G., Arcuri, A.: Evosuite: automatic test suite generation for object-oriented software. In: Proceedings of the 19th ACM SIGSOFT Symposium and the 13th European Conference on Foundations of Software Engineering, pp. 416–419 (2011)
8. Pacheco, C., Ernst, M.D.: Randoop: feedback-directed random testing for Java. In: Companion to the 22nd ACM SIGPLAN Conference on Object- Oriented Programming Systems and Applications Companion, pp. 815–816 (2007)
9. Almasi, M.M., Hemmati, H., Fraser, G., Arcuri, A., Benefelds, J.: An industrial evaluation of unit test generation: finding real faults in a financial application. In: 2017 IEEE/ACM 39th International Conference on Software Engineering: Software Engineering in Practice Track (ICSE-SEIP). IEEE, pp. 263–272 (2017)
10. Shamshiri, S.: Automated unit test generation for evolving software. In: Proceedings of the 2015 10th Joint Meeting on Foundations of Software Engineering, pp. 1038–1041 (2015)
11. Zhang, J., Panthaplackel, S., Nie, P., Li, J.J., Gligoric, M.: Coditt5: pretraining for source code and natural language editing. In: 37th IEEE/ACM International Conference on Automated Software Engineering, pp. 1–12 (2022)
12. Fukumoto, D., Kashiwa, Y., Hirao, T., Fujiwara, K., Iida, H.: An empirical investigation on the performance of domain adaptation for t5 code completion. In: 2023 IEEE International Conference on Software Analysis, Evolution and Reengineering (SANER), pp. 693–697. IEEE (2023)
13. Xia, C.S., Wei, Y., Zhang, L.: Automated program repair in the era of large pretrained language models. In: Proceedings of the 45th International Conference on Software Engineering (ICSE 2023). Association for Computing Machinery (2023)
14. Kolak, S.D., Martins, R., Le Goues, C., Hellendoorn, V.J.: Patch generation with language models: Feasibility and scaling behavior. In: Deep Learning for Code Workshop (2022)

15. Prenner, J.A., Babii, H., Robbes, R.: Can openai's codex fix bugs? an evaluation on quixbugs. In: Proceedings of the Third International Workshop on Automated Program Repair, pp. 69–75 (2022)
16. White, J., Hays, S., Fu, Q., Spencer-Smith, J., Schmidt, D.C.: Chatgpt prompt patterns for improving code quality, refactoring, requirements elicitation, and software design, arXiv preprint arXiv:2303.07839 (2023)
17. Jiang, X., Zheng, Z., Lyu, C., Li, L., Lyu, L.: Treebert: a tree-based pre-trained model for programming language. In: Uncertainty in Artificial Intelligence. PMLR, pp. 54–63 (2021)
18. Wan, Y., Zhao, W., Zhang, H., Sui, Y., Xu, G., Jin, H.: What do they capture? a structural analysis of pre-trained language models for source code. In: Proceedings of the 44th International Conference on Software Engineering, pp. 2377–2388 (2022)
19. Wang, Y., Wang, W., Joty, S., Hoi, S.C.: Codet5: identifier-aware unified pre-trained encoder-decoder models for code understanding and generation. arXiv preprint arXiv:2109.00859 (2021)
20. Lu, S., et al.: Codexglue: a machine learning benchmark dataset for code understanding and generation. arXiv preprint arXiv:2102.04664 (2021)
21. Feng, Z., et al.: Codebert: a pre-trained model for programming and natural languages. arXiv preprint arXiv:2002.08155 (2020)
22. Fu, M., Tantithamthavorn, C., Le, T., Nguyen, V., Phung, D.: Vulrepair: a t5-based automated software vulnerability repair. In: Proceedings of the 30th ACM Joint European Software Engineering Conference and Symposium on the Foundations of Software Engineering, pp. 935–947 (2022)
23. Fan, G., et al.: Dialog summarization for software collaborative platform via tuning pre-trained models. J. Syst. Softw., 111763 (2023)
24. Imai, S.: Is github copilot a substitute for human pair-programming? an empirical study. In: Proceedings of the ACM/IEEE 44th International Conference on Software Engineering: Companion Proceedings, pp. 319–321 (2022)
25. Pearce, H., Tan, B., Ahmad, B., Karri, R., Dolan-Gavitt, B.: Can openai codex and other large language models help us fix security bugs? arXiv preprint arXiv:2112.02125 (2021)
26. Pearce, H., Tan, B., Krishnamurthy, P., Khorrami, F., Karri, R., Dolan Gavitt, B.: Pop quiz! can a large language model help with reverse engineering? arXiv preprint arXiv:2202.01142 (2022)
27. Sarsa, S., Denny, P., Hellas, A., Leinonen, J.: Automatic generation of programming exercises and code explanations using large language models. In: Proceedings of the 2022 ACM Conference on International Computing Education Research-Volume 1, pp. 27–43 (2022)
28. Zhang, Z., Zhang, H., Shen, B., Gu, X.: Diet code is healthy: simplifying programs for pre-trained models of code. In: Proceedings of the 30th ACM Joint European Software Engineering Conference and Symposium on the Foundations of Software Engineering, pp. 1073–1084 (2022)
29. Li, Z., Wang, C., Liu, Z., Wang, H., Wang, S., Gao, C.: Cctest: testing and repairing code completion systems. arXiv preprint arXiv:2208.08289 (2022)
30. Ojdanic, M., Soremekun, E., Degiovanni, R., Papadakis, M., Le Traon, Y.: Mutation testing in evolving systems: studying the relevance of mutants to code evolution. ACM Trans. Softw. Eng. Methodol. **32**(1), 1–39 (2023)
31. Harman, M., McMinn, P.: A theoretical and empirical study of search-based testing: Local, global, and hybrid search. IEEE Trans. Software Eng. **36**(2), 226–247 (2009)

32. Blasi, A., Gorla, A., Ernst, M.D., Pezz'e, M.: Call me maybe: using nlp to automatically generate unit test cases respecting temporal constraints. In: 37th IEEE/ACM International Conference on Automated Software Engineering, pp. 1–11 (2022)
33. Delgado-Perez, A., Ramirez, A., Valle-Gomez, K.J., Medina-Bulo, I., Romero, J.R.: Interevo-tr: Interactive evolutionary test generation with readability assessment. IEEE Trans. Softw. Eng. (2022)
34. Ernst, M.D., et al.: The daikon system for dynamic detection of likely invariants. Sci. Comput. Program. **69**(1–3), 35–45 (2007)
35. Csallner, C., Tillmann, N., Smaragdakis, Y.: Dysy: dynamic symbolic execution for invariant inference. In: Proceedings of the 30th International Conference on Software Engineering, pp. 281–290 (2008)
36. Xiao, X., Li, S., Xie, T., Tillmann, N.: Characteristic studies of loop problems for structural test generation via symbolic execution. In: 2013 28th IEEE/ACM International Conference on Automated Software Engineering (ASE). IEEE, pp. 246–256 (2013)
37. Zeller, A., Gopinath, R., Bohme, M., Fraser, G., Holler, C.: The fuzzing book (2019)
38. Pacheco, C., Lahiri, S.K., Ernst, M.D., Ball, T.: Feedback-directed random test generation. In: 29th International Conference on Software Engineering (ICSE'07), pp. 75–84. IEEE (2007)
39. Shamshiri, S., Just, R., Rojas, J.M., Fraser, G., McMinn, P., Arcuri, A.: Do automatically generated unit tests find real faults? an empirical study of effectiveness and challenges (t). In: 2015 30th IEEE/ACM International Conference on Automated Software Engineering (ASE). IEEE, pp. 201–211 (2015)
40. White, R., Krinke, J.: Testnmt: function-to-test neural machine translation. In: Proceedings of the 4th ACM SIGSOFT International Workshop on NLP for Software Engineering, pp. 30–33 (2018)
41. Tufano, M., Drain, D., Svyatkovskiy, A., Deng, S.K., Sundaresan, N.: Unit test case generation with transformers and focal context
42. White, R., Krinke, J: Reassert: deep learning for assert generation. arXiv preprint arXiv:2011.09784 (2020)
43. Villmow, J., Depoix, J., Ulges, A.: Contest: a unit test completion benchmark featuring context. In: Proceedings of the 1st Workshop on Natural Language Processing for Programming (NLP4Prog 2021), pp. 17–25 (2021)
44. Pascanu, R., Mikolov, T., Bengio, Y.: On the difficulty of training recurrent neural networks. In: International conference on machine learning. Pmlr, pp. 1310–1318 (2013)
45. Yu, S., Wang, T., Wang, J.: Data augmentation by program transformation. J. Syst. Softw. **190**, 111304 (2022)
46. Papineni, K., Roukos, S., Ward, T., Zhu, W.-J.: Bleu: a method for automatic evaluation of machine translation. In: Proceedings of the 40th Annual Meeting of the Association for Computational Linguistics, pp. 311–318 (2002)
47. Lin, C.-Y.: Rouge: a package for automatic evaluation of summaries. In: Text Summarization Branches Out, pp. 74–81 (2004)
48. Yang, G., Zhou, Y., Yang, W., Yue, T., Chen, X., Chen, T.: How important are good method names in neural code generation? a model robustness perspective. arXiv preprint arXiv:2211.15844 (2022)
49. Dinella, E., Ryan, G., Mytkowicz, T., Lahiri, S.K.: Toga: a neural method for test oracle generation. In: Proceedings of the 44th International Conference on Software Engineering, pp. 2130–2141 (2022)

# Secure Traffic Data Sharing in UAV-Assisted VANETs

Yilin Liu[1], Yujue Wang[2], Chen Yi[4(✉)], Yong Ding[3,4], Changsong Yang[3], and Huiyong Wang[1]

[1] School of Mathematics and Computing Science,
Guilin University of Electronic Technology, Guilin 541004, China
[2] Hangzhou Innovation Institute of Beihang University, Hangzhou 310000, China
[3] Laboratory of Cryptography and Information Security,
School of Computer Science and Information Security,
Guilin University of Electronic Technology, Guilin 541004, China
[4] Institute of Cyberspace Technology, HKCT Institute for Higher Education, Hong Kong 999077, China
alexyi@ctihe.edu.hk

**Abstract.** Aiming at the issues of low comprehensiveness and timeliness of data, difficulty in balancing data anonymity and traceability, and challenges of securely storing massive data in traditional traffic data sharing systems, this paper proposes a UAV-VANET integrated system (UVIS) based on consortium blockchain. The UAV integrated into the VANET can promptly provide drivers and traffic managers with comprehensive traffic information and images for traffic planning, thus enhancing transportation efficiency and safety. To achieve traceability of anonymous data sharing, we introduce a proxy re-encryption mechanism to realize precise data access control, which can not only protect data and identity privacy but also trace the true identity of malicious users. Additionally, it effectively prevents the collusion between proxies and data requesters from stealing unauthorized confidential information. To alleviate the pressure of traffic data storage, we adopt a storage method that combines blockchain and IPFS, ensuring secure storage of massive data. Security analysis shows that the UVIS has achieved secure sharing of traffic data. We analyze its efficiency theoretically, and demonstrate the practicality through experiments.

**Keywords:** UAV-VANET integrated system · data sharing · blockchain · privacy preservation · proxy re-encryption

## 1 Introduction

With the acceleration of urbanization, traditional traffic data sharing systems are confronted with many challenges. Limited access to timely, comprehensive, and multi-perspective traffic data hinders drivers from fully comprehending the increasingly complex traffic conditions, thus impeding effective traffic management and planning. At the same time, during traffic data sharing, it is difficult

H. Gao et al. (Eds.): CollaborateCom 2023, LNICST 562, pp. 301–320, 2024.
https://doi.org/10.1007/978-3-031-54528-3_17

to trace real identities under the premise of protecting data and identity privacy, making it impossible to effectively supervise and penalize malicious users, thus affecting the data quality and development of data sharing. In addition, the secure storage of massive traffic data requires substantial storage resources, so a suitable secure storage method is needed to ensure the integrity and reliability of data. This makes us continuously explore traffic data sharing systems that are more suitable for modern smart cities. In the future development of smart traffic, the collection, privacy protection, secure sharing, and secure storage of traffic data are important components of an intelligent traffic data sharing system.

The Vehicular Ad Hoc Network (VANET) has emerged as a crucial component of smart traffic and intelligent travel, making it one of the fastest developing technologies in Intelligent Transportation Systems (ITS) [2]. Its wide applications in intelligent navigation, vehicle positioning, and traffic information collection have significantly contributed to transportation intelligence, reducing traffic accidents and improving road safety [20,23]. The Unmanned Aerial Vehicle (UAV), characterized by its small size, easy deployment, and high flexibility [3], can conveniently capture real-time traffic data and images from an aerial perspective, conduct road patrols, and monitor traffic [13]. Their applications in traffic management are gradually maturing. Integrating the UAV into VANET will conduce to a more accurate and comprehensive understanding of vehicle and traffic conditions. This enables more efficient traffic flow management, alleviation of urban traffic congestion, reduction of traffic accidents, and enhancement of transportation safety. The UAV-VANET integrated system can support decision-making in vehicle navigation, traffic flow control, and road safety, thus facilitating various application scenarios of UVIS such as traffic monitoring, intelligent navigation, environmental monitoring, and emergency response.

In the UVIS that we construct, the data collected by the UAV comes from two primary sources. First, vehicle-related data, which often has a certain degree of privacy, should not involve other vehicles. Second, external environmental data, such as terrain, traffic flow, and traffic condition, is generally public information. The UAV implements access control on different types of traffic data it collects. First, the on-board unit (OBU) of the vehicle applies to the UAV for its own vehicle-related data and external environmental data to control the real-time traffic situation in an all-round way, reducing the burden of the vehicle networking communication base station GS. Second, the GS applies to the UAV for external environmental data and carries out high-level data processing and analysis of road traffic data from a macro perspective. Subsequently, the GS sends traffic instructions to communication devices such as the OBU and RSU, to achieve control of the whole road and traffic management. The two data-sharing patterns are designed from the micro and macro perspectives respectively, and the synergistic operation can achieve better traffic control effects.

## 1.1 Related Techniques

In the process of traffic data sharing, message accuracy, user privacy, and access control are critical factors that impact VANET service provision [9]. Due to the sensitivity of certain data, such as vehicle location, vehicle sensor data, vehicle images, and vehicle videos, unauthorized access may lead to data leakage, data tampering, or data loss. These security breaches will have detrimental effects on VANET decision-making and operations, thus endangering the safety of vehicles and traffic. Failure to guarantee data accuracy and user privacy not only jeopardizes lives and property but diminishes user engagement [22]. However, a reliable data sharing scheme for VANET is always a great challenge.

In recent years, several solutions have been proposed to address the issue of secure data sharing in VANET. Li et al. [11] proposed the FADB scheme, which combines blockchain and CP-ABE algorithms to enable fine-grained access control and distributed storage in VANET. However, schemes based on attribute encryption always have high computational costs. Liu et al. [15] introduced a security-aware information propagation model based on attribute encryption and proxy re-encryption (PRE) for access control in VANET. Han et al. [7] protected vehicle identity privacy through a broadcast proxy re-encryption scheme with cubic spline interpolation. Wang et al. [21] designed a public key re-encryption scheme based on ciphertext delegation equality testing (PRE-DET), allowing users to share outsourced data. Eltayieb et al. [4] proposed a certificateless proxy re-encryption access mechanism for data outsourcing computation. Noh et al. [16] presented a secure data sharing system based on blockchain. But their proxy re-encryption scheme poses the risk of collusion between the cloud server and data requester to obtain the data owner's private key. The above proxy re-encryption-based data sharing schemes provide inspiration for data sharing in VANET, but do not maintain the balance between user identity privacy and traceability well and prevent collusion attacks. A secure VANET system should ensure user identity privacy protection and traceability [24].

Blockchain is an innovative technology that utilizes a chained data structure composed of chronologically connected data blocks. It employs distributed ledger and cryptographic techniques to ensure data immutability and prevent forgery [12]. Through distributed networks and consensus mechanisms, it achieves decentralized data verification, ensuring that all participating nodes can verify data authenticity [14]. The typical features of blockchain technology include decentralization, collective maintenance, resistance to single-point attacks, and immutability, which can effectively solve the problems of centralization, mutual distrust among entities, and privacy leakage in traditional VANET [1]. Therefore, blockchain establishes a trustworthy foundation for participants in untrusted environments, promoting safer, more reliable, and efficient collaborations [14].

However, the data generated by vehicles is becoming increasingly fine-grained and complex [8], leading to a sharp increase in the amount of traffic data, which causes a storage bottleneck for blockchain. Whether storage resources can meet the actual demand will be a challenge [5]. To address the issue of limited storage capacity, it is feasible to combine blockchain with IPFS (InterPlanetary File System). This combination allows for secure storage of traffic data through a collaborative on-chain and off-chain storage model. The IPFS provides a peer-to-peer (P2P) distributed storage structure [10], which can effectively avoid single-point failures of centralized cloud servers [19]. Moreover, it can easily store large amounts of data, overcoming limitations of traditional traffic data storage systems, such as high deployment costs and insufficient storage resources. Simply storing the IPFS hash of the data rather than the complete traffic data in the block, the pressure on blockchain data storage can be relieved [26].

### 1.2 Our Contributions

To address the aforementioned shortcomings of traditional data sharing systems, we design a UAV-VANET integrated system and propose a consortium blockchain-based anonymous conditionally traceable data secure sharing scheme suitable for this system. The proposed scheme provides more reliable data support for the decision-making and operation of the vehicular network system, realizing the secure sharing and circulation protection of traffic data. The main contributions of this paper can be summarized as follows:

1. According to the characteristics of different types of data collected by UAV, UVIS utilizes an integrated approach of macro management and micro control strategies to cooperatively operate the different data sharing patterns, achieving the full use of data and more effective traffic control.
2. The UVIS adopts an anonymized identity and traceable authentication protocol, which not only protects user identity with pseudonyms but also reveals the identity of malicious nodes under certain conditions. It improves the efficiency of authentication by using batch authentication. Moreover, based on this protocol, this scheme allows for the easy implementation of key recovery.
3. The UVIS constructs a decentralized architecture based on the transportation consortium blockchain (TCB), creating a trusted environment for traffic data sharing and collaboration. To enhance storage capacity, UVIS combines blockchain technology with the IPFS distributed file system. Only the IPFS hash of the data is stored on the blockchain, while the complete data is transferred to IPFS, effectively alleviating the storage pressure on the blockchain.
4. The UVIS utilizes Proxy Re-Encryption for access control of data, which effectively protects data privacy and security, preventing data leakage and abuse. We use the random number generated by the Verifiable Random Function (VRF) to elect a leader (proxy node) and design for encryption and data access applications. This can prevent the proxy and data requester from conspiring to steal confidential information without authorization.

## 2  System Architecture and Security Requirements

### 2.1  UVIS Architecture

As shown in Fig. 1, the UAV-VANET integrated system (UVIS) consists of three main components: UAV, TCB, and IPFS.

1. UAV: The UAV transmits the collected traffic data to the vehicle networking communication base station (GS) and On-Board Unit (OBU) through wireless communication technology. It provides real-time data to the VANET, which can be used for traffic condition monitoring, road condition prediction, and traffic management.
2. TCB: The transportation consortium blockchain network comprises three types of nodes:

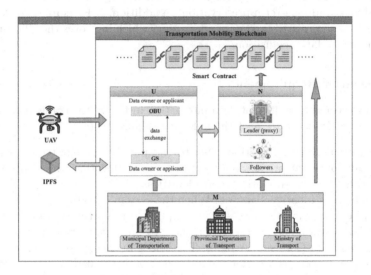

**Fig. 1.** System architecture of UVIS

(1) User nodes $\mathcal{U}$: $\mathcal{U}$ are composed of data owners and data requesters. In UVIS, OBU and GS are both data owners and data requesters, interacting with each other for data access. On the one hand, the OBU and GS are respectively responsible for receiving vehicle-related information and external environmental data shared by UAVs. On the other hand, the GS needs to request certain vehicle-related information from the OBU for better traffic control, and the OBU also needs to apply to the GS for specific traffic indication data after its analysis and processing to assist drivers and facilitate road traffic management.
(2) Consensus nodes $\mathcal{N}$: $\mathcal{N}$ represent the nodes participating in the consensus process. They are responsible for generating and verifying data and blocks, as well as tracing the identities of $\mathcal{U}$. They are usually authoritative institutions such as regional traffic police teams and traffic management bureaus. In the consensus mechanism, the nodes are categorized into two roles: leader and follower, and the leader performs the proxy re-encryption process acting as a proxy.

(3) Management node $\mathcal{M}$: $\mathcal{M}$ is typically controlled by the municipal transportation bureau, provincial transportation department, or national transportation department, whose duty is to manage the identity information of users $\mathcal{U}$ and play a supervisory role.

3. IPFS: IPFS adopts a decentralized storage approach to distribute data across multiple nodes in the network, which can avoid single points of failure, enhancing data storage reliability and stability. In UVIS, vehicles and GS can securely store the collected data on IPFS network nodes, ensuring data safety, reliability, and long-term preservation. In addition, IPFS employs distributed hash tables for distributed data addressing, which improves the efficiency and accuracy of data acquisition.

## 2.2   Security Requirements

To achieve secure and efficient data interaction in UVIS, the traffic data sharing scheme of UVIS needs to meet the following requirements:

1. Identity Privacy Protection: Due to the possibility that traffic data may contain personal privacy data such as vehicle location, many driviers are concerned about disclosing their identities.
2. Conditional Identity Tracking: When the system detects any security event, such as unauthorized access or attempts to invade the system, it needs to track the real identity of malicious user to prevent further security threats.
3. Resistance to Collusion Attacks: The leader in the consensus group, acting as a proxy node, is a curious semi-trusted entity that may collude with the data applicant to steal unauthorized traffic data.
4. User Key Recovery: In traffic data sharing, users, such as OBU and GS, may experience private keys loss owing to various factors, such as equipment failure, virus attacks, human errors, and natural disasters. The loss of private keys will disrupt the secure transmission of traffic information, thus impacting traffic efficiency and safety.
5. Secure Storage of Traffic Data: The storage capacity of the blockchain system is limited. With the increase of mass traffic data, there will be problems of insufficient storage capacity, which may bring about incomplete data storage or inability to store, affecting the security of traffic data storage.

## 3   The Proposed Scheme

### 3.1   System Initialization

Given a security parameter $\kappa$, the management node $\mathcal{M}$ generates a bilinear map $e : G_1 \times G_1 \rightarrow G_T$, where $G_1$ and $G_T$ are cyclic groups of prime order $q$, and $g_1, g_2$ are two distinct generators of $G_1$. Then, $\mathcal{M}$ picks eight collision-resistant hash functions: $H_1 : G_1 \rightarrow \{0,1\}^*, H_2 : \{0,1\}^* \rightarrow Z_q^*, H_3 : G_1 \rightarrow Z_q^*, H_4 : G_1 \rightarrow G_1, H_5 : Z_q^* \rightarrow G_1, H_6 : G_1 \times G_1 \rightarrow Z_q^*, H_7 : G_T \times \{0,1\}^* \times Z_q^* \rightarrow$

$Z_q^*, H_8 : G_1 \times G_1 \times G_1 \times G_1 \times G_1 \times G_1 \to Z_q^*$, randomly selects the private key $sk_{mn} \in Z_q^*$, and computes the corresponding public key $pk_{mn} = g_1^{sk_{mn}}$. The consensus node $\mathcal{N}_c$ randomly selects a private key $sk_c \in Z_q^*$, and computes the public key $pk_c = g_1^{sk_c}$, $1 \leqslant c \leqslant n$. Let the leader in the consensus group be $\mathcal{N}_{\mathscr{L}}$, whose private key is $sk_{\mathscr{L}}$ and public key is $pk_{\mathscr{L}}$. The users $\mathcal{U}$ choose a secure signature scheme $\mathcal{F} = (SigGen, SigVerif)$ [17]. Finally, $\mathcal{M}$ publishes the public system parameters $params = \{\kappa, G_1, G_2, g_1, g_2, q, e, H_1, \ldots, H_8, pk_{mn}, n\}$.

## 3.2   User Registration

**Pseudo-Identity Generation.** First, $\mathcal{M}$ constructs real identity information $Info_i$ for a user $\mathcal{U}_i$. Then, $\mathcal{M}$ randomly selects $s_{1,i} \in Z_q^*$, calculates $S_{1,i} = g_1^{s_{1,i}}$, and generates identity-protected information $\pi_i = H_1(S_{1,i}) \oplus Info_i$ for $\mathcal{U}_i$.

Next, $\mathcal{M}$ selects two random numbers $\alpha_i, \beta_i \in Z_q^*$, and calculates the pseudo-identity $PID_i$ and signature $\sigma_i$ of $\mathcal{U}_i$ through the following equations:

$$z_i = \alpha_i(\beta_i + H_2(\pi_i)) \bmod q, PID_i = g_1^{z_i}$$
$$\delta_i = H_3(PID_i), \sigma_i = (z_i + \delta_i sk_{mn}) \bmod q$$

Finally, $\mathcal{M}$ sends the identity information $\{PID_i, \sigma_i\}$ to the user $\mathcal{U}_i$.

**Key Generation.** After receiving the identity information $\{PID_i, \sigma_i\}$ from $\mathcal{M}$, $\mathcal{U}_i$ computes $\delta^* = H_3(PID_i)$, and verifies:

$$g_1^{\sigma_i} = (pk_{mn})^{\delta^*} \times PID_i \tag{1}$$

If the authentication condition is satisfied, $\mathcal{U}_i$ takes $PID_i$ as his pseudo-identity.

The user $\mathcal{U}_i$ chooses a random number $a_i \in Z_q^*$, computes $s_{2,i} = s_{1,i} - a_i$, $S_{2,i} = g_1^{s_{2,i}}$, and generates his own private key $sk_i = H_3(S_{2,i})$ and public key $pk_i = H_4(PID_i)^{sk_i}$. Then, $\mathcal{U}_i$ computes $A_i = g_1^{a_i}$, generates the signature $sig_{A,i}$ though the $F.Sign$ signature algorithm, and saves $\{a_i, A_i, sig_{A,i}\}$.

Then, $\mathcal{U}_i$ acquires the public random number $u \in Z_q^*$ locally generated by the current leader using the VRF function, picks a random number $k_i \in Z_q^*$, and computes:

$$K_i = g_1^{k_i}, u_i = H_5(u)^{sk_i}$$
$$\delta_{u,i} = H_2(PID_i \parallel K_i \parallel u_i)$$
$$\sigma_{u,i} = (u + \delta_{u,i} sk_i) \bmod q$$

Finally, $\mathcal{U}_i$ generates his own basic information $\{PID_i, \sigma_i, K_i, u_i, \sigma_{u,i}\}$.

## 3.3   Encryption

The user $\mathcal{U}_i$ chooses a random number $\omega \in \{0, 1\}^*$ and encrypts traffic data $m$ as follows:

$$D = e(H_4(PID_i), H_5(u)^{a_i})$$
$$C_1 = (m \parallel \omega) \oplus D^{H_6(PID_i \parallel pk_i)}$$
$$C_2 = H_4(PID_i)^u$$
$$C_3 = (u + sk_i H_7(D \parallel C_1 \parallel C_2)) \bmod q$$

Finally, $\mathcal{U}_i$ sends the ciphertext $\{D, C_1, C_2, C_3\}$ to $IPFS$.

## 3.4 Data Storage

When receiving $\{D, C_1, C_2, C_3\}$ from $\mathcal{U}_i$, $IPFS$ verifies the following equation:

$$H_4(PID_i)^{C_3} = C_2 \times pk_i^{H_7(D\|C_1\|C_2)} \tag{2}$$

If the verification condition is satisfied, $IPFS$ stores $\{D, C_1, C_2, C_3\}$ and generates the corresponding download address $url$ of the ciphertext for $\mathcal{U}_i$.

## 3.5 Data Upchain

To alleviate the storage burden of blockchain, $\mathcal{U}_i$ initiates an on-chain request to record his metadata, which only includes the download address $url$, the hash value $h_m$ of the traffic data $m$, and the pseudo-identity $PID_i$ of $\mathcal{U}_i$.

After the successful block upload, the consensus group determines the leader of the next round is $\mathcal{N}_{\mathscr{L}}$ through the verifiable random number $num$ generated by the VRF function and the formula $\mathscr{L} = (num \mod n) + 1$. The detailed process is as follows:

The current leader takes his private key $sk$ and current timestamp $x$ as inputs to generate a random number $num$ and proof $p$. The leader publicly broadcasts the parameters $\{num, p\}$, and other follower nodes can verify whether the random number $num$ generated by the leader is effective through the leader's public key $pk_{\mathscr{L}}$, current timestamp $x$, and proof $p$.

After all nodes pass the verification, the consensus group calculates $\mathscr{L} = (num \mod n) + 1$ and elects $\mathcal{N}_{\mathscr{L}}$ as the leader. Applying the randomized output value of the VRF function to determine the leader can ensure the fairness and unpredictability of the election.

## 3.6 Application, Authorization and Access

If a data applicant $\mathcal{U}_j$ wants to access $m$ of $\mathcal{U}_i$, $\mathcal{U}_j$ needs to be authorized by $\mathcal{U}_i$.

**Application and Authorization.** The data applicant $\mathcal{U}_j$ requests data access from $\mathcal{U}_i$ and sends his basic information $\{PID_j, \sigma_j, K_j, u_j, \sigma_{u,j}\}$. Then, $\mathcal{U}_i$ verifies the identity of $\mathcal{U}_j$ by Eq. (1), and verifies the parameter $u_j$:

$$H_4(PID_j)^{\sigma_{u,j}} = (pk_j)^{H_2(PID_j\|K_j\|u_j)} \times H_4(PID_j)^u$$

If the above equation holds, the verification is successful. Then $\mathcal{U}_i$ grants permission to $\mathcal{U}_j$ to access the requested data.

**Re-encryption Key Generation.** The user $\mathcal{U}_i$ computes:

$$d_j = PID_j \times (pk_{mn})^{H_3(PID_j)}$$
$$rk_1 = H_8(d_j^{k_i} \parallel K_j^{\sigma_i} \parallel PID_i \parallel PID_j \parallel pk_i \parallel pk_j)$$
$$rk_2 = (u_j)^{\frac{a_i}{sk_i}}$$

Then, $\mathcal{U}_i$ generates the re-encryption key $r_{i \to j} = \{rk_1, rk_2\}$, uses $\mathcal{F}.Sign$ to generate signature $sig_r$ on $r_{i \to j}$, and sends $\{r_{i \to j}, sig_r\}$ to the proxy node.

## 3.7   Proxy Re-encryption

Because the leader is the proxy node, the proxy node's private key is $sk_{\mathscr{L}}$ and public key is $pk_{\mathscr{L}}$. The proxy node receives $\{r_{i \to j}, sig_r\}$ and executes the $\mathcal{F}.SignVerif$ algorithm to verify the signature. Upon successful verification, it obtains the ciphertext $\{D, C_1, C_2, C_3\}$ from $IPFS$ and verifies it by equation (2). If the verification is successful, the proxy node re-encrypts the ciphertext by the following equations:

$$D' = e(pk_i, rk_2)$$
$$C_1' = C_1^{rk_1}$$
$$C_2' = g_1^{u}$$
$$C_3' = (u + sk_{\mathscr{L}} H_7(D' \parallel C_1' \parallel C_2')) \bmod q$$

then generates the re-encrypted ciphertext $\{D', C_1', C_2', C_3'\}$, which is transmitted to $\mathcal{U}_j$.

## 3.8   Ciphertext Decryption

**Self-decryption.** The user $\mathcal{U}_i$ derives the ciphertext $\{D, C_1, C_2, C_3\}$ from $IPFS$, and verifies it with equation (2). After successful verification, the ciphertext is decrypted by the following equations:

$$D = e(H_4(PID_i), H_5(u)^{a_i})$$
$$m \parallel \omega = C_1 \oplus D^{H_6(PID_i \parallel pk_i)}$$

**Re-decryption.** After receiving the re-encrypted ciphertext $\{D', C_1', C_2', C_3'\}$, $\mathcal{U}_j$ then verifies it through the following equation:

$$g_1^{C_3'} = C_2' \times pk_{\mathscr{L}}^{H_7(D' \parallel C_1' \parallel C_2')}$$

After successful verification, $\mathcal{U}_j$ decrypts the re-encrypted ciphertext using the following formulas:

$$d_i = PID_i \times (pk_{mn})^{H_3(PID_i)}$$
$$rk_1 = H_8(K_i^{\sigma_j} \parallel d_i^{k_j} \parallel PID_i \parallel PID_j \parallel pk_i \parallel pk_j) \tag{3}$$

$$C_1 = (C_1')^{\frac{1}{rk_1}} = (m \parallel \omega) \oplus D^{H_6(PID_i \parallel pk_i)}$$

$$D = (D')^{\frac{1}{sk_j}}$$

$$m \parallel \omega = C_1 \oplus D^{H_6(PID_i \parallel pk_i)}$$

### 3.9    Traceability of Pseudo-identities

In this paper, a secret sharing method is employed to achieve the traceability of pseudo-identities. To share $s_{1,i}$, $\mathcal{M}$ selects $t-1$ random numbers $a_{1,i}, \ldots, a_{t-1,i} \in Z_q^*$, constructs a $(t-1)$-degree polynomial:

$$f_i(x) = a_{0,i} + a_{1,i}x + a_{2,i}x^2 + \cdots + a_{t-1,i}x^{t-1} \bmod q$$

where $a_{0,i} = s_{1,i}$, computes the polynomial shares $\{f_i(1), f_i(2), \cdots, f_i(n)\}$, and generates the commitments of polynomial shares $\langle Y_c \rangle_{c=1 \sim n}$:

$$Y_c = pk_c{}^{f_i(c)}, 1 \leqslant c \leqslant n$$

For subsequent verifications of the polynomial shares, $\mathcal{M}$ also needs to compute the commitments of the polynomial parameters $\langle C_l \rangle_{l=0 \sim t-1}$:

$$C_l = g_2{}^{a_{l,i}}, 0 \leqslant l < t-1$$

commitments of all polynomial shares $\langle X_c \rangle_{c=1 \sim n}$:

$$X_c = g_2{}^{f_i(c)}, 1 \leqslant c \leqslant n$$

Then, $\mathcal{M}$ broadcasts $\{\pi_i, \langle C_l \rangle_{l=0 \sim t-1}, \langle X_c \rangle_{c=1 \sim n}, \langle Y_c \rangle_{c=1 \sim n}\}$ to the entire TCB network.

With the public information $\{\pi_i, \langle C_l \rangle_{l=0 \sim t-1}, \langle X_c \rangle_{c=1 \sim n}, \langle Y_c \rangle_{c=1 \sim n}\}$, each $\mathcal{N}_c$ can not only verify the correctness of the received polynomial commitment $Y_c$ but also check the consistency of all polynomial commitments $\langle Y_c \rangle_{c=1 \sim n}$, ensuring that $\mathcal{M}$ is honest during the distribution process of $\langle Y_c \rangle_{c=1 \sim n}$. The specific verification steps are as follows:

First, to check whether $f_i(c)$ in the commitment $X_c$ is generated by the polynomial $f_i(x)$ constructed by $\mathcal{M}$, $\mathcal{N}_c$ verifies the following equation:

$$X_c = \prod_{l=0}^{t-1} (C_l)^{c^l} \tag{4}$$

Then, $\mathcal{N}_c$ computes :

$$R_c = e(X_c, pk_c), 1 \leqslant c \leqslant n$$

and employs the following approach for batch verification:

$$\prod_{c=1}^{n} R_c = e(g_2, \prod_{c=1}^{n} Y_c) \tag{5}$$

If the above equation holds, $\mathcal{N}_c$ acknowledges that all the received polynomial commitments $\langle Y_c \rangle_{c=1\sim n}$ are correct and stores the corresponding $\{\pi_i, Y_c\}$.

Each $\mathcal{N}_c$ further uses its own private key $sk_c$ to recover $share_c$ from $Y_c$.

$$share_c = (Y_c)^{\frac{1}{sk_c}}$$

In the subsequent transmission of $share_c$ by $\mathcal{N}_c$, to ensure that the recipients indeed receive $share_c$ from the corresponding $Y_c$, $\mathcal{N}_c$ needs to provide relevant proof information. First, $\mathcal{N}_c$ selects a random number $r_c \in Z_q^*$ and calculates $B_{c,1} = (share_c)^{r_c}, B_{c,2} = (g_1)^{r_c}$. Then, $\mathcal{N}_c$ calculates:

$$e_c = H_2(share_c \parallel g_1 \parallel Y_c \parallel pk_c \parallel B_{1,c} \parallel B_{2,c}), b_c = r_c + e_c sk_c$$

and finally generates share information $\{share_c, e_c, b_c\}$ that can be used to trace identities and recover keys.

### 3.10  Traceability of Malicious Nodes

The $\mathcal{M}$ initiates an on-chain request to record user's traceability information $\{\pi_i, PID_i\}$, and the consensus group can search for this information to trace the identity of any malicious user. The smart contract is used to automatically trace the malicious node. if a user has malicious behavior, once the number of $\mathcal{N}_c$ that considers the user to be malicious exceeds the threshold $t$, the tracing process will be automatically triggered. The specific tracking steps are as follows:

---

**Algorithm 1.** Tracking of Malicious Nodes

---

**Require:** $\pi_i, [share_1, share_2, \ldots, share_t], [e_1, e_2, \ldots, e_t], [b_1, b_2, \ldots, b_t]$
**Ensure:** $\pi_i \oplus H_1(S_{1,i})$
 1: **for** $c \leftarrow 1$ **to** $t$ **do**
 2:     Compute:
 3:         $temp \leftarrow share_c \parallel g_1 \parallel Y_c \parallel pk_c \parallel (share_c)^{b_c} (Y_c)^{-e_c} \parallel g_1^{b_c} (Y_c)^{-e_c}$
 4:         $e_c^* \leftarrow H_2(temp)$
 5:         **if** $e_c^* \neq e_c$ **then**
 6:             fail
 7:         **end if**
 8: **end for**
 9: $S_{1,c} \leftarrow 1$
10: **for** $c \leftarrow 1$ **to** $t$ **do**
11:     $L_c \leftarrow 1$
12:     **for** $j \in [1, t]$ **do**
13:         **if** $j \neq c$ **then**
14:             $L_c \leftarrow L_c \times \frac{j}{j-c}$
15:         **end if**
16:     **end for**
17:     $S_{1,c} \leftarrow S_{1,c} \times pow(share_c, L_c)$
18: **end for**

---

Each $\mathcal{N}_c$ submits its tracing shares $\{share_c, e_c, b_c\}$ to the smart contract. When the number of tracing shares inputted into the smart contract reaches $t$, the smart contract automatically executes the tracing algorithm as shown in Algorithm 1 to recover the user's $S_{1,i}$. Eventually, the consensus group will reveal the real identity information $Info_i$ of user $\mathcal{U}_i$ by the following formula:

$$Info_i = \pi_i \oplus H_1(S_{1,i})$$

### 3.11  Key Recovery

The smart contract is used to automatically recover a user's lost private key. When a user $\mathcal{U}_i$ loses his private key $sk_i$, the user immediately broadcasts a message indicating the key loss along with important parameter information $\{PID_i, \sigma_i\}$ to the TCB. Each $\mathcal{N}_c$ verifies his identity by the formula (1). If the identity verification of $\mathcal{U}_i$ passes, $\mathcal{N}_c$ can confirm that $PID_i$ represents the user $\mathcal{U}_i$. Then, $\mathcal{N}_c$ responds to the user by submitting $\{share_c, e_c, b_c\}$ to the smart contract. In the same way as the verification process of tracing the identities of malicious nodes, the smart contract automatically performs information verification to ensure that the received $share_c$ comes from the original $Y_c$. Simultaneously, $\mathcal{U}_i$ submits $\{A_i, sig_{A,i}\}$ to the smart contract, which automatically performs the $\mathcal{F}.SignVerif$ algorithm to verify $A_i$.

When the identity verification of $\mathcal{U}_i$ and the verification of $A_i$ have both passed, and the number of $\mathcal{N}_c$ responding to $\mathcal{U}_i$ has reached the threshold $t$, the key recovery procedure of the smart contract will be executed as follows:

$$L_c = \prod_{j=1, j \neq c}^{t} \frac{j}{j-c}, S_{1,i} = \prod_{c=1}^{t} (share_c)^{L_c}, S_{2,i} = \frac{S_{1,i}}{g_1^{a_i}} \tag{6}$$

Subsequently, the smart contract only sends $S_{2,i}$ to $\mathcal{U}_i$, and $\mathcal{U}_i$ can finally recover his private key $sk_i = H_3(S_{2,i})$. Any consensus node cannot have access to the related information of $A_i$, the polynomial commitments of other consensus nodes, and $S_{2,i}$.

## 4  Scheme Analysis

### 4.1  Correctness Analysis

**Theorem 1.** *The UVIS scheme proposed in this paper is correct.*

*Proof.* To prove the correctness of the proposed UVIS scheme, it only needs to demonstrate equations in (1)–(6) hold.

(1) For the identity information $\{PID_i, \sigma_i\}$, if the computed $\delta^*$ is equal to $\delta_i$, then we have:

$$g_1^{\sigma_i} = g_1^{(z_i + \delta_i sk_{mn})} = (pk_{mn})^{\delta^*} \times PID_i$$

Therefore, the Eq. (1) holds.

(2) The ciphertext $\{D, C_1, C_2, C_3\}$ satisfies the Eq. (2).

$$H_4(PID_i)^{C_3} = H_4(PID_i)^{(u+sk_iH_7(D,C_1,C_2))} = C_2 \times pk_i^{H_7(D,C_1,C_2)}$$

(3) The $rk_1 = H_8(d_j^{k_i} \parallel K_j^{\sigma_i} \parallel PID_i \parallel PID_j \parallel pk_i \parallel pk_j)$ used by $\mathcal{U}_i$ for encryption satisfies the Eq. (3).

$$\begin{aligned}
rk_1 &= H_8(d_j^{k_i} \parallel K_j^{\sigma_i} \parallel PID_i \parallel PID_j \parallel pk_i \parallel pk_j) \\
&= H_8((PID_j \times (pk_{mn})^{H_3(PID_j)})^{k_i} \parallel (g_1^{k_j})^{\sigma_i} \parallel PID_i \parallel PID_j \parallel pk_i \parallel pk_j) \\
&= H_8(K_i^{z_j+sk_{mn}H_3(PID_j)} \parallel g_1^{k_j(z_i+sk_{mn}H_3(PID_i))} \parallel PID_i \parallel PID_j \parallel pk_i \parallel pk_j) \\
&= H_8(K_i^{\sigma_j} \parallel d_i^{k_j} \parallel PID_i \parallel PID_j \parallel pk_i \parallel pk_j)
\end{aligned}$$

(4) For the commitments $\langle C_l \rangle_{l=0 \sim t-1}$ published by $\mathcal{U}_i$, if the $f_i(c)$ hidden in $X_c$ is generated by the polynomial $f_i(x)$, then we have:

$$\prod_{l=0}^{t-1} (C_l)^{c^l} = \prod_{l=0}^{t-1} (g_2)^{a_{l,i}c^l} = g_2^{\sum_{j=0}^{t-1} a_{l,i}c^l} = g_2^{f_i(c)} = X_c$$

Therefore, the Eq. (4) holds.

(5) For the public information $\{\langle X_c \rangle_{c=1 \sim n}, \langle R_c \rangle_{c=1 \sim n}\}$, if $\langle Y_c \rangle_{c=1 \sim n}$ are correct, then we have:

$$\prod_{c=1}^{n} R_c = \prod_{c=1}^{n} e(X_c, pk_c) = \prod_{c=1}^{n} e(g_2^{f_i(c)}, pk_c) = \prod_{c=1}^{n} e(g_2, Y_i)$$

$$= e(g_2, Y_1 \cdot Y_2 \cdots Y_n) = e(g_2, \prod_{c=1}^{n} Y_c)$$

Therefore, the Eq. (5) holds.

(6) The $t$ or more correct copies of $share_c$ and $S_{1,i}$ satisfy the Eq. (6).

$$\prod_{c=1}^{t} (share_c)^{L_c} = \prod_{c=1}^{t} ((Y_c)^{\frac{1}{sk_c}})^{L_c} = \prod_{c=1}^{t} (g_1^{f_i(c)})^{L_c} = g_1^{\sum_{c=1}^{t} (f_i(c) \prod_{j=1,j\neq c}^{t} \frac{j}{j-c})}$$

$$= g_1^{f_i(0)} = S_{1,i}$$

## 4.2   Security Analysis

**Theorem 2.** *If the DL and CDH assumptions hold, identity privacy-preserving mechanism with anonymity and traceability is secure in the distributed environment.*

*Proof.* In this identity privacy protection mechanism, there are three ways in which an attacker can obtain the user's real identity information:

1. The adversary manages to reveal $share_c$ by exploiting the public information $\{g_1, g_2, X_c, Y_c, pk_c\}$. Once obtaining $t$ copies of $share_c$, the adversary proceeds to recover $S_{1,i}$ and compute $Info_i$ by $\pi_i$.

To simplify the proof, let $g_1 = g_2{}^\alpha$, $X_c = g_2{}^{f_i(c)} = g_2{}^\beta$, $pk_c = g_1{}^{sk_c} = g_2{}^{\alpha sk_c} = g_2{}^\gamma$, and then we have $Y_c = pk_c{}^{f_i(c)} = g_2{}^{\beta\gamma}$. The adversary tries to obtain $share_c = g_1{}^{f_i(c)} = g_2{}^{\alpha f_i(c)} = g_2{}^{\alpha\beta}$. Therefore, the problem can be transformed into calculating $g_2{}^{\alpha\beta}$, given $g_2{}^\beta$, $g_2{}^\gamma$ and $g_2{}^{\beta\gamma}$, for any $\alpha, \beta, \gamma \in Z_q^*$. An adversary, with all publicly available information, might try to calculate $g_2{}^{\alpha\beta}$ from two perspectives:

(1) The adversary may attempt to compute $g_2{}^{\alpha\beta}$ directly from $g_2{}^\alpha$ and $g_2{}^\beta$. However, according to the $CDH$ assumption, given $g_2, g_2{}^\alpha$ and $g_2{}^\beta$, for any $\alpha, \beta \in Z_q^*$, there does not exist a probabilistic polynomial-time adversary that can compute $g_2{}^{\alpha\beta}$ with non-negligible advantage. Therefore, this approach contradicts the $CDH$ assumption.

(2) The adversary may consider deriving $\beta$ from $g_2{}^\gamma$ and $g_2{}^{\beta\gamma}$. However, under the $DL$ assumption, given $g_2{}^\gamma$ and $g_2{}^{\beta\gamma}$, for any $\gamma \in Z_q^*$, there does not exist a probabilistic polynomial-time adversary that can compute $\beta$ with non-negligible advantage. Therefore, unless the adversary can obtain $\beta$, it is not possible to further compute $g_2{}^{\alpha\beta}$.

In summary, under the $DL$ and $CDH$ assumptions, the adversary is unable to obtain $share_c$ simply by the public information. As a result, the adversary cannot collect enough shares to recover $S_{1,i}$ and further compute $Info_i$.

2. The adversary can destroy up to $t - 1$ $N_c$, then obtain their $\langle sk_c \rangle_{c=1\sim t-1}$ and $\langle share_c \rangle_{c=1\sim t-1}$. The adversary may attempt to recover $S_{1,i}$ and $Info_i$ of $U_i$ through $\{\langle sk_c \rangle_{c=1\sim t-1}, \langle share_c \rangle_{c=1\sim t-1}\}$ and other public information $\{\langle X_c \rangle_{c=1\sim n}, \langle Y_c \rangle_{c=1\sim n}, \langle pk_c \rangle_{c=1\sim n}, \langle C_l \rangle_{l=0\sim t-1}\}$.

Let $g_1 = g_2{}^\alpha$ and $C_0 = g_2{}^{a_{0,i}} = g_2{}^{s_{1,i}} = g_2{}^\beta$, then the adversary's target is to compute $\beta$ or $g_2{}^{\alpha\beta}$. Given the information available, the adversary may try to compute $\beta$ or $g_2{}^{\alpha\beta}$ from the following three perspectives:

(1) The adversary may consider computing $\beta$ from $C_0 = g_2{}^\beta$, which is equivalent to solving the $DL$ problem. Hence, this contradicts the DL assumption.
(2) The adversary may consider computing $g_2{}^{\alpha\beta}$ from $g_2{}^\alpha$ and $C_0 = g_2{}^\beta$. However, this is equivalent to solving the $CDH$ problem, which contradicts the $CDH$ assumption.
(3) The adversary may consider recovering $g_2{}^{\alpha\beta}$ by $\langle share_c \rangle_{c=1\sim t-1}$. However, according to the Lagrange interpolation theorem, the adversary can recover $g_2{}^{\alpha\beta}$ only if $t$ or more copies of $share_c$ are collected.

$$\prod_{c=1}^{t} (share_c)^{L_c} = \prod_{c=1}^{t} (g_1{}^{f_i(c)})^{L_c} = g_1{}^{\sum_{c=1}^{t} f_i(c)L_c} = g_1{}^{f_i(0)} = g_2{}^{s_{1,i}} = g_2{}^{\alpha\beta}$$

$$L_c = \prod_{j=1, j\neq c}^{t} \frac{j}{j - c}$$

But the adversary possesses at most $t - 1$ copies of $share_c$, from which he cannot recover $s_{1,i}$ or $S_{1,i}$. Furthermore, the adversary and the corrupted $N_c$ may try to use the information they possess to break the remaining $\langle share_c \rangle_{c=t\sim n}$ in order to meet the threshold $t$. However, under the $DL$ and $CDH$ assumptions, we have proved that an adversary cannot obtain shares of the uncorrupted $N_c$ through the public information.

In conclusion, if the $DL$ and $CDH$ assumptions hold, the adversary cannot reconstruct $S_{1,i}$ and $Info_i$ by corrupting $t - 1$ or less $N_c$.

3. The attacker attempts to violently crack the hidde $Info_i$ by exploiting the public identity protection information $\pi_i$.

$$\prod_{c=1}^{t} (share_c)^{L_c} = S_{1,i}, Info_i = \pi_i \oplus H_1(S_{1,i})$$

To protect the real identity of $U_i$, $\mathcal{M}$ generates the identity protection information $\pi_i = H_1(S_{1,i}) \oplus Info_i$ for $U_i$. According to the previous text, no adversary can recover $S_{1,i}$. At the same time, as long as the security parameter $\kappa$ is strong enough, it is difficult to violently crack the real identity information $Info_i$ from the protection information $\pi_i$. Therefore, under reasonable security intensity, the adversary cannot disclose $Info_i$ from $\pi_i$.

All in all, the proposed identity privacy protection mechanism with anonymity and traceability is secure. The user's identity will be revealed only if there are $t$ or more consensus nodes that perceive the user's malicious behavior.

**Theorem 3.** *This scheme ensures the confidentiality of data.*

*Proof.* The proposed proxy re-encryption algorithm serves as the core component of data sharing in UVIS, ensuring the confidentiality of traffic data transmission. When a data owner grants access to a data requester, a re-encryption key is generated for the requester and sent to the proxy node $N_{\mathscr{L}}$. Then, $N_{\mathscr{L}}$ uses the re-encryption key to re-encrypt the data ciphertext so that the data requester can decrypt re-encrypted ciphertext to obtain target data by his private key. Throughout this process, the proxy node is only responsible for receiving the re-encryption key from $U_i$ and re-encrypting the ciphertext, and unable to obtain any useful information from the original or re-encrypted ciphertext. Hence, this scheme achieves data confidentiality.

**Theorem 4.** *This scheme is capable of resisting collusion attacks.*

*Proof.* In this scheme, the consensus mechanism selects the leader $N_{\mathscr{L}}$ from $N_c$ based on the formula $\mathscr{L} = (num \bmod n) + 1$. The leader publishes a random number $u$ for data encryption. Suppose that $Leader_1$ records the random number $u^{(1)}$ generated in this phase in a block with a height of $H_1$, and also records the metadata containing data information $m_1$ in the same block. If a data requester $U_j$ wants to retrieve the data associated with that block, he needs to use $u^{(1)}$ and his private key $sk_j$ to compute $u_j = H_5(u)^{sk_j}$, then initiate an access request to $\mathcal{U}_i$ with the information $u_j$. If $\mathcal{U}_i$ allows $\mathcal{U}_j$ to access $m_1$, $\mathcal{U}_i$ will generate a re-encryption key $rk_{i \to j} = (u_j^{(1)})^{a_i/sk_i}$ using $u_j$ and his private key $sk_i$, and send it to the proxy node.

After the current consensus ends, the consensus group will elect the next leader $Leader_2$ according to the rules. Similarly, the new random number $u^{(2)}$ published by $Leader_2$ and the metadata of $m_2$ are recorded in a block with a height of $H_2$. In the encryption phase, $\mathcal{U}_i$ encrypts $m_2$ by the following formulas:

$$D^{(2)} = e(H_4(PID_i), (u_i^{(2)})^{a_i})$$

$$C_1^{(2)} = (m_2 \parallel \omega) \oplus (D^{(2)})^{H_6(PID_i \parallel pk_i)}$$

$$C_2^{(2)} = H_4(PID_i)^{(u^{(2)})}$$

$$C_3^{(2)} = (u^{(2)} + sk_i H_7(D^{(2)} \parallel C_1^{(2)} \parallel C_2^{(2)})) \bmod q$$

If $\mathcal{U}_j$ colludes with the proxy node to access unauthorized $m_2$, they can only obtain $(H_5(u^{(1)}))^{a_i/sk_i}$ about the previous random number $u^{(1)}$ and further calculate $e(pk_i, (H_5(u^{(1)}))^{a_i/sk_i}) = e(H_4(PID_i), H_5(u^{(1)}))^{a_i}$. However, it differs from $D^{(2)} = e(H_4(PID_i), H_5(u^{(2)}))^{a_i}$, making it ineffective for obtaining $m_2$. So is the case for other data. Therefore, this scheme effectively resists the collusion attacks between the proxy node and data requesters.

**Theorem 5.** *This scheme can securely reconstruct the user's original private key in case a user loses his private key.*

*Proof.* On the basis of achieving identity privacy protection and traceability, this scheme adds the functionality of key recovery. When a user $\mathcal{U}_i$ loses his private key $sk_i$, the user only needs to submit $A_i$ and his signature $Sig_{A,i}$ to the smart contract, and the smart contract can automatically execute the key recovery procedure to help $\mathcal{U}_i$ recover his private key $sk_i$. According to the previous text, we have proved that an adversary cannot steal user's $S_{1,i}$ and further obtain $S_{2,i}$, the adversary cannot obtain critical information $A_i$ for key recovery during this process either. Consequently, even if the number of colluding consensus nodes reaches the threshold $t$, the private key $sk_i$ of $\mathcal{U}_i$ cannot be recovered.

## 5   Analysis and Comparison

### 5.1   Functional Analysis

We compared our scheme with the following proxy re-encryption-based data sharing schemes in terms of functionality and security features (see Table 1). Eltayieb et al. [4] proposed a certificateless proxy re-encryption scheme based on cloud blockchain (CPRCB), providing complete data transparency and auditability in cloud servers. Zeng et al. [25] introduced SS-PRE, a conditional proxy re-encryption technique (C-PRE) for fine-grained access control.

**Table 1.** Comparison of functional features

| Scheme | Confidentiality | Integrity | Identity privacy | Identity tracking | Anti-collusion security | Single point of failure prevention | Decentralized storage | Key recovery |
|---|---|---|---|---|---|---|---|---|
| Zeng et al. [25] | ✓ | ✓ | × | × | ✓ | × | × | × |
| Ge et al. [6] | ✓ | ✓ | × | ✓ | ✓ | × | × | × |
| Su et al. [18] | ✓ | ✓ | × | × | ✓ | × | × | × |
| Eltayieb et al. [4] | ✓ | ✓ | × | × | × | ✓ | ✓ | × |
| Ours | ✓ | ✓ | ✓ | ✓ | ✓ | ✓ | ✓ | ✓ |

Ge et al. [6] proposed an identity-based broadcast proxy re-encryption mechanism for secure data sharing and revocation of access permissions. Su et al. [18] proposed a trusted authorization scheme based on proxy re-encryption for nodes on CloudIoT (PRTA), which can update trusted authorization in CloudIoT.

All the above schemes can realize data confidentiality and integrity. However, they all fail to satisfy the user's desire for protecting identity privacy in data sharing. Our scheme not only protects identity privacy, but also allows for identity tracking when necessary. Furthermore, due to the inherent characteristics of the blockchain, the proposed scheme in [4] can prevent single-point failures and the data stored on the blockchain is traceable, but it cannot ensure the traceability of malicious users while protecting users' identity privacy in data sharing, which is a key security feature of data sharing scenario in UVIS. The schemes in [6,18,25] have risks of single-point failures and data loss but we do not, and they can resist collusion attacks. To ensure safe data sharing, the risk of malicious collusion between a proxy and data applicants needs to be considered. We incorporate appropriate defensive measures into the proxy re-encryption, making the scheme resistant to collusion attacks. Moreover, our scheme has a key recovery function for users who lost their private keys.

### 5.2 Theoretical Analysis

Table 2 compares the computational complexities of the encryption, re-encryption key generation, re-encryption, self-decryption, and re-decryption of proxy re-encryption in our scheme with those in the comparative literature. We focus on analyzing the most time-consuming operations in these phases, such as exponentiations in the $G_1$ group and bilinear pairing $e$. Exp and Pair denote

**Table 2.** Comparison of Computation Complexity

| Scheme | Zeng et al. [25] | Ge et al. [6] | Su et al. [18] | Eltayieb et al. [4] | Ours |
|---|---|---|---|---|---|
| Encrypt | 2Exp+2Pair | 8Exp | 4Exp | 3Exp+1Pair | 3Exp+1Pair |
| ReKeyGen | 2Exp | 2Exp | 2Exp | 5Exp | 4Exp |
| ReEncrypt | Exp+1Pair | 2Exp+5Pair | 1Exp+2Pair | 2Exp+4Pair | 4Exp+1Pair |
| Self-Decrypt | 1Pair | 3Exp+3Pair | – | – | 4Exp+1Pair |
| ReDecrypt | 1Exp+2Pair | 2Exp+2Pair | 1Exp+3Pair | 2Exp+4Pair | 8Exp |

the time of an exponentiation operation in $G_1$ and a bilinear pairing operation, respectively.

From the computational complexity results of different stages in Table 2, our scheme has considerable computational performance in the re-encryption and re-decryption. The computational efficiency in the encryption and self-decryption stages is moderate. As for re-encryption key generation, it is not advantageous, but the gap is not large.

### 5.3  Experimental Analysis

This section presents a comprehensive performance simulation and quantitative analysis of the UVIS. We tested the average time consumption of fifteen experiments for each of the six stages of initialization, encryption, re-encryption key generation, re-encryption, self-decryption, and re-decryption in proxy re-encryption. According to practical application scenarios, we simulated the proposed scheme using the PBC library (https://pkg.go.dev/github.com/Nik-U/pbc) based on the go language. The experiment ran on a Linux operating system, with a quad-core Xeon processor and 16GB memory.

According to Fig. 2, the average time spent on the initialization, encryption, re-encryption key generation, re-encryption, self-decryption, and re-decryption is 11.248 ms, 4.035 ms, 6.026 ms, 5.516 ms, 5.729 ms, and 8.018 ms, respectively. From the average time consumed in each stage, the performance of encryption, re-encryption, and self-decryption in the proxy re-encryption scheme is relatively good. The overhead of the re-encryption key generation and re-decryption is slightly higher, mainly due to the exponentiation operations whose execution time is affected by the size and complexity of the input data, as well as the optimization of the functions in the PBC library. These two stages involve more complex exponentiation operations and more variables to be processed, resulting in the time of execution longer. Overall, the computational cost of this scheme is within a reasonable and manageable range.

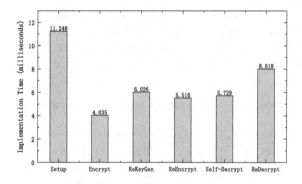

**Fig. 2.** Time consumed at each stage

# 6  Conclusion

This paper proposes a UAV-VANET integrated system that leverages UAV to equip VANET with more comprehensive and timely data support. To create a secure and efficient environment for VANET data sharing, UVIS employs a proxy re-encryption data sharing scheme based on the transportation consortium blockchain to achieve precise access control over data. It enables traceability of malicious users while protecting data and identity privacy, effectively resisting collusion attacks caused by proxies and data requesters. Furthermore, UVIS establishes a secure data storage model though the combination of blockchain and IPFS, which effectively solves the issue of secure storage of massive data. Through security analysis, experimental evaluation, and comparison of relevant technologies, UVIS is proved effective and secure as a practical data sharing system.

**Acknowledgments.** This article is supported in part by the Guangxi Natural Science Foundation under grants AA22068067 and 2023GXNSFAA026236, the National Natural Science Foundation of China under projects 62162017 and 61962012, and the special fund of the High-level Innovation Team and Outstanding Scholar Program for universities of Guangxi.

# References

1. Chen, L., Liang, H., Li, X., Ding, Y., Huang, W., Wang, Y., Zhou, X.: Blockchain-based uav-assisted forest supervision and data sharing. In: International Conference on Blockchain and Trustworthy Systems, pp. 251–264. Springer (2022)
2. Da, L., Wang, Y., Ding, Y., Qin, B., Zhou, X., Liang, H., Wang, H.: Cloud-assisted road condition monitoring with privacy protection in vanets. In: 2022 18th International Conference on Mobility, Sensing and Networking (MSN). pp. 304–311 (2022)
3. Da, L., Wang, Y., Ding, Y., Xiong, W., Wang, H., Liang, H.: An efficient certificateless signcryption scheme for secure communication in uav cluster network. In: 2021 IEEE Intl Conf on Parallel & Distributed Processing with Applications, Big Data & Cloud Computing, Sustainable Computing & Communications, Social Computing & Networking (ISPA/BDCloud/SocialCom/SustainCom), pp. 884–891. IEEE (2021)
4. Eltayieb, N., Sun, L., Wang, K., Li, F.: A certificateless proxy re-encryption scheme for cloud-based blockchain. In: Frontiers in Cyber Security: Second International Conference, FCS 2019, Xi'an, China, November 15–17, 2019, Proceedings 2, pp. 293–307. Springer (2019)
5. Fan, K., Li, F., Yu, H., Yang, Z.: A blockchain-based flexible data auditing scheme for the cloud service. Chin. J. Electron. **30**(6), 1159–1166 (2021)
6. Ge, C., Liu, Z., Xia, J., Fang, L.: Revocable identity-based broadcast proxy re-encryption for data sharing in clouds. IEEE Trans. Dependable Secure Comput. **18**(3), 1214–1226 (2021)
7. Han, X., Tian, D., Zhou, J., Duan, X., Sheng, Z., Leung, V.C.: Privacy-preserving proxy re-encryption with decentralized trust management for mec-empowered vanets. IEEE Trans. Intell. Vehicles, 1–15 (2023)

8. He, J., Ni, Y., Cai, L., Pan, J., Chen, C.: Optimal dropbox deployment algorithm for data dissemination in vehicular networks. IEEE Trans. Mob. Comput. **17**(3), 632–645 (2017)
9. Horng, S.J., Lu, C.C., Zhou, W.: An identity-based and revocable data-sharing scheme in vanets. IEEE Trans. Veh. Technol. **69**(12), 15933–15946 (2020)
10. Kumar, R., Marchang, N., Tripathi, R.: Distributed off-chain storage of patient diagnostic reports in healthcare system using ipfs and blockchain. In: 2020 International Conference on COMmunication Systems & NETworkS (COMSNETS). pp. 1–5 (2020)
11. Li, H., Pei, L., Liao, D., Chen, S., Zhang, M., Xu, D.: Fadb: a fine-grained access control scheme for vanet data based on blockchain. IEEE Access **8**, 85190–85203 (2020)
12. Li, H., Pei, L., Liao, D., Sun, G., Xu, D.: Blockchain meets vanet: an architecture for identity and location privacy protection in vanet. Peer-to-Peer Networking Appl. **12**, 1178–1193 (2019)
13. Li, J., Wang, Y., Ding, Y., Wu, W., Li, C., Wang, H.: A certificateless pairing-free authentication scheme for unmanned aerial vehicle networks. Secur. Commun. Networks **2021**, 9463606 (2021)
14. Liu, J., Jiang, W., Sun, R., Bashir, A.K., Alshehri, M.D., Hua, Q., Yu, K.: Conditional anonymous remote healthcare data sharing over blockchain. IEEE J. Biomed. Health Inform. **27**(5), 2231–2242 (2023)
15. Liu, X., Chen, W., Xia, Y.: Security-aware information dissemination with fine-grained access control in cooperative multi-rsu of vanets. IEEE Trans. Intell. Transp. Syst. **23**(3), 2170–2179 (2020)
16. Noh, S.W., Park, Y., Sur, C., Shin, S.U., Rhee, K.H.: Blockchain-based user-centric records management system. Int. J. Control Autom. **10**(11), 133–144 (2017)
17. Schnorr, C.P.: Efficient identification and signatures for smart cards. In: Advances in Cryptology-CRYPTO 1989 Proceedings 9, pp. 239–252. Springer (1990)
18. Su, M., Zhou, B., Fu, A., Yu, Y., Zhang, G.: Prta: a proxy re-encryption based trusted authorization scheme for nodes on cloudiot. Inf. Sci. **527**, 533–547 (2020)
19. Sun, J., Yao, X., Wang, S., Wu, Y.: Blockchain-based secure storage and access scheme for electronic medical records in ipfs. IEEE Access **8**, 59389–59401 (2020)
20. Wang, Y., Ding, Y., Wu, Q., Wei, Y., Qin, B., Wang, H.: Privacy-preserving cloud-based road condition monitoring with source authentication in vanets. IEEE Trans. Inf. Forensics Secur. **14**(7), 1779–1790 (2019)
21. Wang, Y., Pang, H., Deng, R.H., Ding, Y., Wu, Q., Qin, B., Fan, K.: Secure server-aided data sharing clique with attestation. Inf. Sci. **522**, 80–98 (2020)
22. Wang, Z., Xu, Y., Liu, J., Li, Z., Li, Z., Jia, H., Wang, D.: An efficient data sharing scheme for privacy protection based on blockchain and edge intelligence in 6g-vanet. Wirel. Commun. Mob. Comput. **2022**, 1–18 (2022)
23. Xiong, W., Wang, R., Wang, Y., Wei, Y., Zhou, F., Luo, X.: Improved certificateless aggregate signature scheme against collusion attacks for vanets. IEEE Syst. J. **17**(1), 1098–1109 (2023)
24. Xiong, W., Wang, R., Wang, Y., Zhou, F., Luo, X.: Cppa-d: efficient conditional privacy-preserving authentication scheme with double-insurance in vanets. IEEE Trans. Veh. Technol. **70**(4), 3456–3468 (2021)
25. Zeng, P., Choo, K.K.R.: A new kind of conditional proxy re-encryption for secure cloud storage. IEEE Access **6**, 70017–70024 (2018)
26. Zheng, Q., Li, Y., Chen, P., Dong, X.: An innovative ipfs-based storage model for blockchain. In: 2018 IEEE/WIC/ACM International Conference on Web Intelligence (WI), pp. 704–708 (2018)

# A Lightweight PUF-Based Group Authentication Scheme for Privacy-Preserving Metering Data Collection in Smart Grid

Ya-Nan Cao[1], Yujue Wang[2], Yong Ding[3,4], Zhenwei Guo[2], Changsong Yang[3], and Hai Liang[3(✉)]

[1] Guangdong University of Science and Technology, Dongguan, China
[2] Hangzhou Innovation Institute of Beihang University, Hangzhou, China
[3] Guangxi Key Laboratory of Cryptography and Information Security, School of Computer Science and Information Security, Guilin University of Electronic Technology, Guilin, China
lianghai@guet.edu.cn
[4] Institute of Cyberspace Technology, HKCT Institute for Higher Education, Hong Kong SAR, China

**Abstract.** With the development of information and communication technologies, the services provided by smart grid attract more users to join smart grid. However, with the explosive growth of the number of smart meters, the transmission between the control center and smart meters has brought huge data transmission and computing costs to the smart grid, which is prone to network congestion, untimely power service supply and other network conditions. This paper proposes a Physically Unclonable Function (PUF)-based lightweight group authenticated metering data collection scheme with privacy protection in smart grid (PGAC). The PGAC scheme is designed with lightweight cryptographic primitives, which is suitable for resource-constrained devices. In addition, the PGAC scheme divides the users into groups and uses the gateway as the repeater and aggregator of the communication data of each group, which reduces signaling and communication costs for activating additional request messages from a large number of devices. Security analysis shows that the PGAC scheme maintains the security and privacy of the data collection process for large-scale smart meters. Functional analysis, theoretical analysis and performance analysis show that PGAC scheme has better authentication function and low communication cost.

**Keywords:** Physically unclonable function · Security · Privacy · Authentication · Aggregation · Encryption · Smart grid

## 1 Introduction

Smart grid is a new type of intelligent network that optimizes power service and facilitates the user's participation in the operation and management of the power

H. Gao et al. (Eds.): CollaborateCom 2023, LNICST 562, pp. 321–340, 2024.
https://doi.org/10.1007/978-3-031-54528-3_18

system [22]. At present, electricity mainly comes from large power companies [20]. The control center, as the management organization of the power company, makes two-way communication with the power grid equipments, collects the electricity consumption information of users in real time, and provides timely and accurate electricity demand data for the implementation of smart grid pricing and power supply. Therefore, smart grid has achieved efficient and reliable power management [19,26], achieved dynamic balance of power supply, and simplified the cumbersome traditional electricity information collection method.

The metering data collection process of the control center (CC) for smart meters (SMs) is carried out in the public network, and the integrity and confidentiality of the metering data may be threatened [1,10]. The adversary may affect the user's billing bill or even disrupt the supply and demand balance of the grid by tampering with the metering data transmitted in the communication [14]. The adversary may be able to infer the daily behavior of users by analyzing their power consumption information over time. Smart meters are installed on the external grid equipment, users may change the configuration of the smart meter to reduce billing. In addition, the control center needs to communicate with a large number of smart meters at the same time, and a large number of messages are transmitted within the network at the same time may cause network congestion and other situations.

## 1.1 Related Works

Many solutions have been proposed to solve the problem of identity authentication and key agreement. Kumar et al. [18] proposed an identity authentication scheme based on elliptic curve cryptosystem, which establishes secret session keys through mutual authentication between power grid equipment and control center, so as to securely exchange electricity demand information. Khan et al. [17] established a lightweight smart grid authentication and key negotiation protocol between users and servers based on elliptic curve encryption mechanism and biometrics technology, which does not have key escrow problems and improves the security and confidentiality of the protocol. Zhang et al. [27] designed a lightweight anonymous authentication and key protocol scheme for smart grid, which not only ensures the anonymity and non-traceability of smart meters, but also realizes the rapid mutual authentication between smart meters and service providers.

There are a large number of users and data in smart grid, and efficient data aggregation solutions for privacy protection has become a hot research direction in recent years. Lu et al. [21] discussed the edge layer data security and privacy issues faced by data aggregation schemes, and designed a three-layer privacy protection data aggregation scheme combining edge computing and blockchain architecture. This scheme combines Paillier homomorphic encryption and one-way hash chain technology, and uses edge servers to aggregate data from the same region, and can filter false data in advance. Fan, Liu and Zeng [9] proposed a privacy-protecting data aggregation scheme based on blockchain, which adopted the leader election algorithm and Paillier encryption algorithm to ensure that data privacy would not be disclosed in the process of metering data collection. In order to solve the problem of communication security, Guan et al. [12] proposed a smart grid privacy protection aggregation authentication scheme, which realizes data source authentication and data aggregation efficiently and flexibly.

Many PUF-based secure authentication and communication schemes have been proposed. Gope and Sikdar [11] introduced an identity authentication key protocol scheme based on PUF to protect privacy and ensure the physical security of smart meters. Cao et al. [2] proposed a PUF-based lightweight identity authentication and privacy protection data collection scheme in smart grid, which can simultaneously solve the security and privacy problems faced in the process of smart grid metering data collection. Ren et al. [24] proposed an Internet of Things (IoT) packet authentication and data transmission scheme based on PUFs. This scheme generates session keys based on the output of PUFs, and sets group leaders to aggregate and forward authentication information, thus reducing the communication cost of activating additional request messages from a large number of devices.

## 1.2   Our Contributions

In order to solve the security, privacy and efficiency problems of smart grid data collection for multiple users at the same time, a lightweight PUF-based privacy-preserving group authentication metering data collection scheme (PGAC) is proposed. In the PGAC scheme, gateway is introduced as a repeater and aggregator, and PUF is used to realize group authentication. Compared with the public key cryptosystem, the computing cost, communication cost and storage cost of the PGAC scheme are significantly reduced, and can better meet the requirements of resource-constrained devices. The security analysis shows that the scheme can not only guarantee the unforgetability of the identity of the control center, gateway and smart meters, but also protect the physical security of smart meters. Experimental analysis show that the scheme is efficient and can be widely used in multi-user data acquisition scenarios.

## 1.3   Paper Organization

The rest of this article is organized as follows. Section 2 briefly introduces the knowledge of PUF and fuzzy extractor. In Sect. 3, the system model and system requirements of PGAC are presented. Section 4 presents a concrete PGAC construction in detail. Section 5 includes security analysis, theoretical comparision, and experimental performance analysis. In Sect. 6, the paper is concluded.

## 2   Preliminaries

This section summarizes some basic knowledge of PUF and fuzzy extractor.

## 2.1  Physical Unclonable Function

PUF is first proposed by Pappu [23] in 2002. A PUF is a physical entity that is hard to clone based on random physical factors introduced during its production [5]. With a specific challenge $Chal$, the PUF can generate a random, unique and unclonable response $R$ according to its production variability, i.e. $R = PUF(Chal)$. PUF can be used for privacy protection, identity authentication and key generation for resource-constrained devices because it is unique, non-clonable, lightweight and resistant to physical attacks. It should also be noted that PUF has a drawback in that it is difficult to reproduce the original response for the same input due to bit errors caused by factors such as temperature or aging effects [4].

## 2.2  Fuzzy Extractor

Fuzzy extractor allows input data with a certain amount of noise (or error), as long as the inputs are close enough to extract the same uniform random string. Therefore, fuzzy extractor is able to convert unevenly distributed data such as biometrics that have bias at the time of input into uniformly distributed random numbers required by the cryptosystem. Fuzzy extractor consists of two algorithms: $FE.Gen$ and $FE.Rec$ [8,16]. $FE.Gen$ is the key generation algorithm, which takes as input a random string $R$, and outputs a key $K$ and a help string $hd$, i.e., $(K, hd) = FE.Gen(R)$. $FE.Rec$ is the key recovery algorithm, which takes as input a random string $R$ containing noise and a help string $hd$, and outputs the key $K$, i.e., $K = FE.Rec(R, hd)$.

# 3   System Model and Requirements

This section defines the architecture of PGAC and formalizes the system requirements.

## 3.1  System Model

The PGAC system structure is shown in Fig. 1, which consists of three types of entities, including smart meters (SMs), gateway (GW) and control center (CC), and the communication between different entities is through a public network. During the metering data collection process, CC generates a set of data collection request information and sends it to the target GW. The GW forwards the set of information to the group of SMs after verifying the source of the message. Then each smart meter verifies the source of the request information, encrypts the collected metering data and sends it to the GW. After that, the GW verifies the source of these responses, aggregates the authentication code of the SMs into one aggregated authentication code, and aggregates the response and the authentication code into one aggregated response. Finally, the CC verifies the source of the aggregated response and the authenticity of the aggregated authentication code, decrypts the encrypted metering data, and obtains the metering data collected by the SMs.

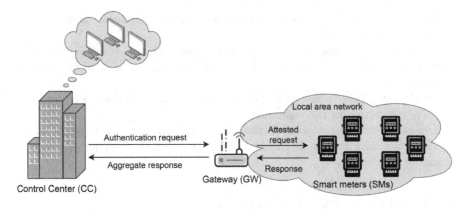

**Fig. 1.** PGAC system model in smart grid.

- SM is installed on the user side and embedded with a PUF component, which is responsible for collecting the user's power consumption information. After receiving the collection request from CC, the SM transmits the encrypted metering data to CC through the GW, which has the functions of data collection, authentication and encryption in the PGAC system.
- CC is the largest power center of the PGAC system, which is responsible for regulating the balance of power supply and demand and power billing. It has the functions of initiating communication, authentication, encryption and decryption and devices registration in the PGAC system.
- GW is also embedded with a PUF, and is installed by CC between the CC and the SMs based on the geographical range and number of nearby users, which is responsible for forwarding messages to users of its group and aggregating data. It has the functions of authentication, encryption and aggregation in the PGAC system.

### 3.2 System Requirements

In the PGAC system, a large number of smart meters communicate with the control center through the public network. Besides the security of communication, privacy and physical security of smart meters are vulnerable to threats, the power system often faces high computing overhead and bandwidth occupation due to the massive data transmission at the same time. Therefore, the PGAC system needs to meet the following requirements.

*Confidentiality of metering data*: Only CC can obtain the real information related to the metering data sent by smart meters, and the regional GW cannot effectively analyze the data sent by smart meters.

*Resistance to man-in-the-middle attacks*: In the whole communication process, no malicious entity can tamper with or replace the transmitted data without being discovered by the receiver.

*Resistance to impersonation attacks*: Any entity posing as the identity of CC, GW and smart meter will be detected by the receiver.

*Resistance to replay attacks*: Any entity sending duplicate tuples can be detected by the receiver.

*Resistance to physical attacks*: Any tampering with the smart meter configuration can be detected by GW and CC, and any tampering with GW can be detected by CC.

*Lightweight*: There is not a lot of complex computing and there is no resource-intensive computing at the smart meter side.

*Low bandwidth consumption*: In the process of collecting massive users' metering data, the data length should be compressed and the number of messages should be reduced.

## 4  A Concrete PGAC Construction

This section describes the proposed PGAC construction.

### 4.1  PGAC Construction

**System Setup.** With the security parameter $\gamma$, CC randomly selects a large prime $q$, chooses a collision-resistant hash function $H : \{0,1\}^* \rightarrow \{0,1\}^\delta$ and a secure symmetric AES encryption scheme $\Pi$ with encryption algorithm $ENC$ and decryption algorithm $DEC$, where $\delta$ is determined by $\gamma$. CC publishes the parameters $pubparam = \{q, H, ENC, DEC\}$.

After that, CC divides the power consumption range into multiple areas according to the information such as geographical location and number of users, and assigns a GW to each area. All smart meters in this area communicate with CC through the gateway they have. Then CC generates a unique identity $GID$ and a challenge $C_{GW,CC}$ for the GW, and sends $GID$ and $C_{GW,CC}$ to the GW through a secure channel.

With the challenge $C_{GW,CC}$, the GW computes the PUF response $R_{GW,CC}$

$$R_{GW,CC} = PUF_{GW,CC}(C_{GW,CC}) \tag{1}$$

and sends $R_{GW,CC}$ to CC over a secure channel.

Then, CC calculates the shared key $K_{GW,CC}$ with the GW and the help string $hd_{GW,CC}$

$$(K_{GW,CC}, hd_{GW,CC}) = FE.Gen(R_{GW,CC}) \tag{2}$$

CC stores $\{C_{GW,CC}, K_{GW,CC}, GID\}$ in the database and sends $hd_{GW,CC}$ to the GW through a secure channel.

At last, the GW stores $\{C_{GW,CC}, hd_{GW,CC}, GID\}$ securely at local.

**Registration.** When the smart meter $SM_i$ newly connected to the smart grid, it should perform the registration process with CC and the GW. Above all, CC randomly generates a unique identity $ID_i$ and a set of challenges $C_i =$

$\{C_{i,1}, C_{i,2}, ..., C_{i,s}\}$ for $SM_i$. CC also assigns a GW as its group leader for $SM_i$ based on its area. Then CC sends $\{ID_i, C_i, GID\}$ to $SM_i$ and $ID_i$ to GW through secure channels.

With the challenges $C_i$, $SM_i$ computes the PUF responses $R_i = \{R_{i,1}, R_{i,2}, ..., R_{i,s}\}$ as follows

$$R_{i,j} = PUF_i(C_{i,j}), j = 1, 2, ..., s \tag{3}$$

and sends these PUF responses to CC through a secure channel.

Then, CC calculates a set of shared keys $K_i = \{K_{i,1}, K_{i,2}, ..., K_{i,s}\}$ with $SM_i$ and help strings $hd_i = \{hd_{i,1}, hd_{i,2}, ..., hd_{i,s}\}$ as follows

$$(K_{i,j}, hd_{i,j}) = FE.Gen(R_{i,j}), j = 1, 2, ..., s \tag{4}$$

CC stores $\{C_i, K_i, ID_i, GID\}$ in the database and sends $hd_i$ to $SM_i$ through a secure channel.

After receiving $ID_i$ sent by CC, the GW generates a challenge $C_{i,GW}$ and sends it to $SM_i$ through a secure channel.

Then $SM_i$ computes the PUF responses $R_{i,GW}$ as follows

$$R_{i,GW} = PUF_i(C_{i,GW}) \tag{5}$$

and sends $R_{i,GW}$ to the GW through a secure channel.

Next, the GW calculates the shared keys $K_{i,GW}$ with $SM_i$ and help strings $hd_{i,GW}$ as follows

$$(K_{i,GW}, hd_{i,GW}) = FE.Gen(R_{i,GW}) \tag{6}$$

The GW stores $\{C_{i,GW}, K_{GW,CC}, ID_i\}$ securely at local and sends $hd_{i,GW}$ to $SM_i$ through a secure channel.

At last, $SM_i$ stores $\{hd_i, ID_i, GID, hd_{i,GW}\}$ securely at local.

**Request.** CC retrieves the information $\{C_{GW,CC}, K_{GW,CC}, ID_{GW,CC}, GID\}$ for the GW with the identity $GID$ and the group members $SM_i$ $(i = 1, 2, ..., n)$ information $\{(C_{i,j}, K_{i,j}, ID_i) : i = 1, 2, ..., n\}$. Then CC generates a request information $Req$, a timestamp $t$ and a random number $r \in Z_q^*$. Then CC calculates

$$r_i^* = H(K_{i,j} \| t) \oplus r, i = 1, 2, ..., n \tag{7}$$

Also, CC calculates the authentication codes for $SM_i$ $(i = 1, 2, ..., n)$

$$AUTH_{CC-i} = H(Request \| C_{i,j} \| ID_i \| GID \| t \| r_i^* \| K_{i,j}) \tag{8}$$

and the authentication code for the GW

$$AUTH_{CC-GW} = H(ID_{GW} \| GID \| t \| Req \| K_{GW,CC} \| C_{GW,CC} \| IDEN_{CC-SMs}) \tag{9}$$

where $IDEN_{CC-SMs} = \{(ID_i, C_{i,j}, r_i^*, AUTH_{CC-i} : i = 1, 2, ..., n\}$. At last, CC sends the request data tuple $DT_1 = (ID_{GW}, t, AUTH_{CC-GW}, IDEN_{CC-SMs}, Req)$ to the GW.

**Forwarding.** After receiving the request data tuple $DT_1$, the GW retrieves $(C_{GW,CC}, hd_{GW,CC})$ from its memory, then generates the PUF response

$$R'_{GW} = PUF_{GW}(C_{GW,CC}) \tag{10}$$

and recovers the shared key with $CC$ by invoking $FE.Rec$ algorithm

$$K_{GW,CC} = FE.Rec(R'_{GW}, hd_{GW,CC}) \tag{11}$$

Next, the GW verifies the authentication code of CC as follows

$$H(ID_{GW}\|GID\|t\|Req\|K_{GW,CC}\|C_{GW,CC}\|IDEN_{CC-SMs}) \overset{?}{=} AUTH_{CC-GW} \tag{12}$$

If it holds, the GW broadcasts the forwarding data tuple $DT_2 = (IDEN_{CC-SMs}, t, Req)$ to $SM_i$ ($i = 1, 2, ..., n$), otherwise the protocol terminates.

**Encryption.** After receiving the request information broadcast by the GW, $SM_i$ generates the PUF response as follows

$$R'_{i,j} = PUF_i(C_{i,j}) \tag{13}$$

Next, $SM_i$ retrieves $hd_{i,j}$ from its memory and invokes $Fe.Rec$ to recover the key

$$K_{i,j} = FE.Rec(R'_{i,j}, hd_{i,j}) \tag{14}$$

Then $SM_i$ retrieves $GID$ and verifies the correctness of CC's authentication code $AUTH_{CC-i}$ as follows

$$H(Req\|C_{i,j}\|ID_i\|GID\|t\|r_i^*\|K_{i,j}) \overset{?}{=} AUTH_{CC-i} \tag{15}$$

If it holds, $SM_i$ calculates

$$r = H(K_{i,j}\|t) \oplus r_i^* \tag{16}$$

$$SK_{i,j} = H(r\|K_{i,j}\|ID_i\|GID\|t) \tag{17}$$

$SM_i$ encrypts the metering data $M_i$ using the session key $SK_{i,j}$

$$E_i = ENC(SK_{i,j}, M_i) \tag{18}$$

and $SM_i$ calculates the authentication code

$$AUTH_{i-CC} = H(ID_i\|GID\|E_i\|r\|K_{i,j}) \tag{19}$$

Next, $SM_i$ retrives $\{C_{i,GW}, hd_{i,GW}\}$ and calculates

$$R'_{i,GW} = PUF_i(C_{i,GW}) \tag{20}$$

$$K_{i,GW} = FE.Rec(R'_{i,GW}, hd_{i,GW}) \tag{21}$$

Also, $SM_i$ generates a timestamp $t_i$ and calculates

$$AUTH_{i-GW} = H(ID_i\|E_i\|t_i\|GID\|K_{i,GW}\|AUTH_{i-CC}) \tag{22}$$

At last, $SM_i$ sends the response data tuple $DT_3 = (E_i, t_i, ID_i, AUTH_{i-CC}, AUTH_{i-GW})$ to the GW.

**Aggregation.** After receiving the data $DT_{3,i}$ from the group's smart meter $SM_i$, the GW retrieves the stored $K_{i,GW}$, and verifies the authentication code $AUTH_{i-GW}$ as follows

$$H(ID_i\|E_i\|t_i\|GID\|K_{i,GW}\|AUTH_{i-CC}) \overset{?}{=} AUTH_{i-GW} \qquad (23)$$

If authentication codes $AUTH_{i-GW}$ $(i = 1, 2, ..., n)$ are all verified successfully, the GW calculates the aggregated authentication code

$$AUTH = AUTH_{1-CC} \oplus AUTH_{2-CC} \oplus ... \oplus AUTH_{n-CC} \qquad (24)$$

Then the GW generates a timestamp $t_{GW}$ and calculates

$$AUTH_{GW-CC} = H(AUTH\|GID\|t_{GW}\|K_{GW,CC}\|CT_{SMs}) \qquad (25)$$

where $CT_{SMs} = \{(ID_i, E_i) : i = 1, 2, ..., n\}$. In the end, the GW aggregates the messages into one message $MES = (GID, t_{GW}, AUTH_{GW-CC}, AUTH, CT_{SMs})$ and sends it to the CC.

**Decryption.** After receiving the aggregated response $MES$ from the GW, CC verifies the identity authentication code $AUTH_{GW-CC}$

$$H(AUTH\|GID\|t_{GW}\|K_{GW}) \overset{?}{=} AUTH_{GW-CC} \qquad (26)$$

If it holds, CC calculates the identity authentication codes for the group of smart meters $SM_i$ $(i = 1, 2...n)$ as follows

$$AUTH'_{i-CC} = H(ID_i\|GID\|E_i\|r\|K_{i,j}) \qquad (27)$$

and verifies the authenticity of the group authentication code $AUTH$

$$AUTH'_{1-CC} \oplus AUTH'_{2-CC} \oplus ... \oplus AUTH'_{n-CC} \overset{?}{=} AUTH \qquad (28)$$

If it holds, CC calculates the session keys with each $SM_i$ $(i = 1, 2, ..., n)$

$$SK_{i,j} = H(r\|K_{i,j}\|ID_i\|GID\|t) \qquad (29)$$

then uses the session keys $SK_{i,j}$ $(i = 1, 2, ..., n)$ to decrypt the corresponding metering data ciphertext respectively

$$M_i = DEC(SK_{i,j}, E_i) \qquad (30)$$

and stores the metering data $M_i$ $(i = 1, 2, ..., n)$ in the database to provide data support for subsequent power services.

**Theorem 1.** *The proposed PGAC construction is correct.*

*Proof.* To prove the correctness of the proposed PGAC construction, it is only necessary to prove that all equations in Eq. (12), Eq. (15), Eq. (23), Eq. (26), Eq. (28) and Eq. (30) hold.

1) The GW generates the response $R'_{GW}$ through Eq. (10), recovers the key $K_{GW,CC}$ through Eq. (11), and then verifies Eq. (12) according to the data tuple from CC as follows

$$H(ID_{GW}\|GID\|t\|Req\|IDEN_{CC-SMs}) = AUTH_{CC-GW}$$

Therefore, the GW can successfully verify the authenticity of the data tuple$DT_1$ sent by CC.

2) $SM_i$ $(i = 1, 2, ..., n)$ generates the responses $R'_{i,j}$ $(i = 1, 2, ..., n)$ through Eq. (13), recovers the keys $K_{i,j}$ $(i = 1, 2, ..., n)$ through Eq. (14), and then verifies Eq. (15) according to the data tuple $DT_2 = (t, Req, IDEN_{CC-SMs})$ from the GW as follows

$$H(Req\|C_{i,j}\|ID_i\|GID\|t\|r_i^*\|K_{i,j}) = AUTH_{CC-i}$$

Therefore, $SM_i$ $(i = 1, 2, ..., n)$ can successfully verify the authenticity of the request information sent by CC.

3) The GW verifies Eq. (23) based on the data tuple $DT_{3,i} = (E_i, t_i, ID_i, AUTH_{i-CC}, AUTH_{i-GW})$ from $SM_i$ and the key $K_{i,GW}$ as follow

$$H(ID_i\|E_i\|t_i\|GID\|K_{i,GW}\|AUTH_{i-CC}) = AUTH_{i-GW} \tag{31}$$

Therefore, the GW can successfully verify the authenticity of the data tuples $DT_{3,i}$ sent by $SM_i$ $(i = 1, 2, ..., n)$.

4) CC verifies Eq. (26) based on the aggregated response $MES = (GID, t_{GW}, AUTH_{GW-CC}, AUTH, CT_{SMs})$ from the GW and the key $K_{GW,CC}$ as follows

$$H(AUTH\|GID\|t_{GW}\|K_{GW,CC}\|CT_{SMs}) = AUTH_{GW-CC}$$

Therefore, CC can successfully verify the authenticity of the aggregated response $MES$ sent by the GW.

5) CC verifies Eq. (28) based on the aggregated response $MES$, random number $r$, and the keys $K_{i,j}$ $(i = 1, 2, ..., n)$ from the GW as follows

$$AUTH'_{i-CC} = H(ID_i\|GID\|E_i\|r\|K_{i,j}) = AUTH_{i-CC}, i = 1, 2, ..., n$$

$$AUTH'_{1-CC} \oplus AUTH'_{2-CC} \oplus ... \oplus AUTH'_{n-CC} = AUTH$$

Therefore, CC can successfully verify the authenticity of ciphertext $E_i$ $(i = 1, 2, ..., n)$ of the metering data in the aggregate response $MES$.

6) For ciphertext $E_i$ of metering data from $SM_i$ $(i = 1, 2, ..., n)$, CC can calculate the session key $SK_{i,j}$ through Eq. (29), which meets

$$DEC(SK_{i,j}, E_i) = DEC(SK_{i,j}, ENC(SK_{i,j}, M_i)) = M_i$$

Therefore, CC can correctly decrypt ciphertext $E_i$ of the metering data $E_i$ $(i = 1, 2, ..., n)$.

Therefore, the proposed PGAC scheme is correct.

## 4.2   Construction Optimization

Note that if CC fails to verify $AUTH$ during the decryption phase, it needs to find out the source of the error. To this end, the truncation code technology can be adopted to optimize the above PGAC construction. The truncation code enables CC to locate the source of faulty data effectively, and avoids the waste of computing resources, communication cost and time of grid devices caused by the repeated transmission and computation of a large number of data. Furthermore, the truncation code replaces long data transmission with short data, which greatly reduces communication transmission costs and bandwidth consumptions. The optimized PGAC construction has the same system setup, registration, request, forwarding and encryption phases as in Sect. 4.1, thus they are omitted here.

**Aggregation.** This phase is the same as in Sect. 4.1 before aggregating the data into the message $MES$. The GW truncates the first eight bits of $AUTH_{i-CC}$, which is represented as $AUTH_{i-trun}$. Then the GW aggregates the response data tuples from $SM_i$ $(i = 1, 2, ..., n)$ into one message $MES' = (GID, t_{GW}, AUTH_{GW-CC}, AUTH, \{(ID_i, E_i, AUTH_{i-trun}) : i = 1, 2, ...n\})$ and sends it to CC.

**Decryption.** This phase has the same authentication process for $SM_i$ $(i = 1, 2, ..., n)$ and GW as in Sect. 4.1. If Eq. (28) does not hold, CC verifies whether $AUTH'_{i-trun} = AUTH_{i-trun}$ $(i = 1, 2, ..., n)$ holds one by one. If any truncation code is not satisfied, CC re-requests the metering data of the owner of the wrong truncation code. Otherwise, CC starts the metering data collection process for all smart meters $SM_i$ $(i = 1, 2, ..., n)$ in the group again.

## 5   Scheme Analysis

This section analyzes the security and performance of the proposed PGAC construction.

### 5.1   Security Analysis

**Theorem 2.** *Assuming that the symmetric encryption scheme $\Pi$ is secure, the proposed PGAC scheme can protect the privacy of users, that is, other entities cannot infer any metering data information of users from the data transmitted during the communication.*

*Proof.* In the proposed PGAC construction, the confidentiality of metering data depends on the confidentiality of the session key. The legitimate CC has the shared key $K_{i,j}$ and can compute $r_i^* = H(K_{i,j}\|t) \oplus r$ and the session key $SK_{i,j} = H(r\|K_{i,j}\|ID_i\|GID\|t)$. $SM_i$ is able to calculate $R'_{i,j} = PUF_i(C_{i,j})$, thus recovering $K_{i,j} = FE.Rec(R'_{i,j}, hd_{i,j})$, and then calculate $r = r^* \oplus H(K\|t_u)$

and the decryption key $SK_{i,j} = H(r\|K_{i,j}\|ID_i\|GID\|t)$. Because PUF is insep-arable from the microprocessor of the smart meter [13], $K_{i,j}$ and $SK_{i,j}$ cannot be obtained by other entities. In addition, random elements such as the one-time key $K_{i,j}$ and the random number $r$ are used in the generation of session key $SK_{i,j}$, so that the confidentiality of session key is not affected by past or future session key leakage. Therefore, the proposed PGAC scheme can ensure the confidentiality and integrity of the session key, and ensure that the privacy of users is not leaked.

**Theorem 3.** *The proposed PGAC scheme can resist man-in-the middle attacks. That is, any malicious entity cannot deduce any information about metering data by intercepting the communication data transmitted during metering data collection, nor can it make the GW, $SM_i$ ($i = 1, 2, ..., n$) or CC accept tampered or forged communication data.*

*Proof.* According to Theorem 2, entities other than CC and $SM_i$ cannot destroy the confidentiality of metering data $M_i$ through sniffer attacks. When a malicious entity attempts to tamper with the intercepted tuple $DT_1$ or the aggregated response $MES$, a valid authentication code $AUTH_{CC-GW}$ or $AUTH_{GW-CC}$ must be generated. According to Theorem 2, only legitimate CC and GW can obtain the key $K_{GW,CC}$, thus no other entity can generate valid authentication codes $AUTH_{CC-GW}$ or $AUTH_{GW-CC}$. When a malicious entity attempts to tamper with the intercepted data tuple $DT_2 = (t, Req, IDEN_{CC-SMs})$, a valid authentication code $AUTH_{CC-i}$ ($i = 1, 2, ..., n$) must be generated. By the same token, only legitimate CC and $M_i$ ($i = 1, 2, ..., n$) can obtain the key $K_{i,j}$, other entities cannot generate valid authentication code $AUTH_{CC-i}$. When a malicious entity attempts to tamper with the intercepted tuple $DT_{3,i}$, a valid authentication code $AUTH_{i-GW}$ must be generated. Similarly, only $SM_i$ and the legitimate GW can obtain key $K_{i,GW}$, while other entities cannot generate valid $AUTH_{i-GW}$. Therefore, the proposed PGAC scheme can resist man-in-the-middle attacks.

**Theorem 4.** *The proposed PGAC construction is resistant to impersonation attacks. That is, any malicious entity cannot impersonate the identity of $SM_i$ ($i = 1, 2, ..., n$), the GW or CC without being detected.*

*Proof.* To impersonate CC, the malicious entity must compute a valid $AUTH_{CC-GW}$ and a valid $AUTH_{CC-i}$ ($i = 1, 2, ..., n$). In addition, if the adver-sary tries to impersonate the GW, she/he must send a valid $AUTH_{GW-CC}$ to CC. Also, if the malicious entity tries to impersonate $SM_i$, she/he must com-pute a valid $AUTH_{i-GW}$ and $AUTH_{i-CC}$. According to Theorem 2, the mali-cious entity cannot compute valid $AUTH_{CC-GW}$, $AUTH_{CC-i}$, $AUTH_{GW-CC}$, $AUTH_{i-GW}$ and $AUTH_{i-CC}$. Thus, the proposed PGAC construction is resis-tant to impersonation attacks.

**Theorem 5.** *The proposed PGAC construction is resistant to replay attacks, which means any malicious entity cannot make CC, the GW or $SM_i$ accept a data tuple that has been accepted before.*

*Proof.* In the proposed PGAC construction, the timestamp $t$ is employed in generating data tuples $DT_1$ and $DT_2$, the timestamp $t_i$ ($i = 1, 2, ..., n$) are employed in generating data tuples $DT_{3,i}$, the timestamp $t_{GW}$ is employed in generating the data tuple $MES$. Thus, when the data tuple $DT_1$, $DT_2$, $DT_3$ or $MES$ is resent, it would be recognized as invalid according to the freshness of timestamps. Thus, the proposed PGAC construction can resist replay attacks.

**Theorem 6.** *The proposed PGAC construction is resistant to physical attacks. That is, the user cannot modify metering data by changing the configuration of smart meters.*

*Proof.* PUF is unclonable, and no entity can recreate the same PUF [25]. In addition, the PUF will lose its function after being tampered with. When $PUF_{GW}$ and $PUF_i$ are tampered with, the behaviors of the GW and $SM_i$ will be changed [3]. That is, the PUF would not be able to correctly generate $R'_{GW}$, $R'_{i,j}$ and $R'_{i,GW}$, which implies the keys $K_{GW,CC} = FE.Rec(R'_{GW}, hd_{GW,CC})$, $K_{i,j} = FE.Rec(R'_{i,j})$ and $K_{i,GW} = FE.Rec(R'_{i,GW}, hd_{i,GW})$ could not be recovered. This causes $SM_i$ and the GW to be unable to calculate valid authentication codes, which will be detected by the receivers. Thus, the proposed PGAC construction is resistant to physical attacks.

## 5.2  Functional Analysis

This section compares the functions implemented by Ding et al.'s scheme [6], Cao et al.'s scheme [2], Ren et al.'s scheme [24], and our PGAC scheme. Ding et al. [6] proposed an identity-based metering data aggregation scheme for the security of metering data collection in industrial smart grids. In [6], the collector can collect and aggregate metering data of users in their respective management domains, and supports the collector to perform batch verification of user signatures in the management domains, thus maintaining the confidentiality and integrity of metering data. However, the solution does not employ any authentication mechanism to verify the data collection request from the service provider before the smart meter performs the signature process.

Ren et al. [24] proposed a group authentication and data transmission scheme based on PUF to solve the large-scale concurrent access authentication problem in narrowband IoT. In [24], the data management server communicates with all narrowband IoT devices within the group through a specified gateway to perform efficient authentication and data transfer processes. However, the scheme does not use any authentication mechanism to verify the authenticity of the data request from the data management server before the gateway forwards the data request to the narrowband IoT devices in its region. In addition, when the gateway aggregates the responses of all narrowband IoT devices it manages, the scheme similarly does not employ any authentication mechanism to verify the authenticity of those responses.

Cao et al.'s scheme [2] mainly aims at the mutual identity authentication and data privacy protection problems faced by real-time data collection between the control center and a single smart meter, and does not take into account the measurement data collection of large-scale smart meters at the same time. In our PGAC scheme, control center uses the gateway to collect metering data of all smart meters in the area and realize group authentication function. In addition, the PGAC scheme uses the gateway to verify the source of data collection request and ciphertext of metering data respectively in the forwarding phase and the aggregation phase, which improves the security of the system and reduces the waste of computing resources caused by invalid data to the control center and smart meters Table 1.

**Table 1.** Function comparison

| Scheme | Forwarding authentication | Request authentication | Response authentication | Aggregate response | Group authentication | Batch authentication |
|--------|---------------------------|------------------------|-------------------------|--------------------|----------------------|----------------------|
| [6]    | ×  | ×  | √  | √  | ×  | √  |
| [2]    | ×  | √  | √  | ×  | ×  | ×  |
| [24]   | ×  | √  | ×  | √  | √  | ×  |
| PGAC   | √  | √  | √  | √  | √  | ×  |

Notes: √ indicates support, × indicates no support.

## 5.3  Theoretical Comparision

In this section, the proposed PGAC scheme, Ding et al.'s scheme [6], Cao et al.'s scheme [2] and Ren et al.'s scheme [24] are analyzed theoretically and compared in terms of computational cost. Table 2 summarizes in detail the computing costs required by system setup phase, registration phase, request phase, forwarding phase, encryption phase, aggregation phase and decryption phase in these four schemes. Among them, the number of smart meters is $n$, $T_{Mod}$ represents the operation time of a modular exponentiation operation, $T_E$ represents the operation time of a bilinear pair operation, $T_{Mp}$ represents the operation time of a multiplication operation, and $T_{Log}$ represents the operation time of a discrete logarithm operation. $T_H$ indicates the operation time of a hash operation, $T_{Gen}$ indicates the operation time of a $FE.Gen$ algorithm, $T_{Rec}$ represents the run time of a $FE.Rec$ algorithm, $T_{PUF}$ denotes the run time of a PUF operation, and $T_S$ indicates the run time of a encryption or decryption algorithm of symmetric encryption scheme $\Pi$.

Cao et al.'s scheme [2], Ren et al.'s scheme [24] and our PGAC scheme only carry out lightweight operations such as hash operation and PUF operation, while Ding et al.'s scheme [6] has complex bilinear pair operation and a large number of modular exponentiation operation, discrete logarithm operation and multiplication operation, thus it has more computational time costs.

Since Ren et al.'s scheme [24] assumes that PUF is idealized, it is not equipped with a fuzzy extractor, so the following analysis does not take into account the extra time spent on the $FE.Gen$ and $FE.Rec$ algorithms by Cao et al.'s scheme [2] and our PGAC scheme. For the system setup procedure, since

**Table 2.** Computing cost comparison

| Phase | Scheme [6] | Scheme [2] | Scheme [24] | PGAC |
|---|---|---|---|---|
| System setup | $2T_{Mod} + T_H + T_E$ | $\triangle$ | $T_{PUF}$ | $T_{PUF} + T_{Gen}$ |
| Registration | $(n+1)T_H + (n+1)T_{Mod}$ | $nT_{PUF} + nT_{Gen}$ | $nT_{PUF}$ | $2nT_{PUF} + 2nT_{Gen}$ |
| Request | $\triangle$ | $nT_H$ | $T_{PUF} + (4n+2)T_H$ | $2nT_H$ |
| Forwarding | – | – | $\triangle$ | $T_{PUF} + T_{Rec} + T_H$ |
| Encryption | $nT_H + 3nT_{Mod} + 2nT_{Mp}$ | $nT_{PUF} + nT_{Rec} + 4nT_H + nT_s$ | $nT_{PUF} + 5nT_H + nT_s$ | $2nT_{PUF} + 2nT_{Rec} + 5nT_H + nT_s$ |
| Aggregation | $(2n+1)T_H + (2n+2)T_{Mod} + (6n-1)T_{Mp}$ | – | $\triangle$ | $(n+1)T_H$ |
| Decryption | $T_{Mod} + 2T_H + 3T_{Mp} + T_E + nT_{Log}$ | $3nT_H + nT_S$ | $nT_H + nT_S$ | $(2n+1)T_H + nT_S$ |

Notes: $\triangle$ denotes that the execution time of lightweight operations not defined in this phase, such as $\oplus$ and random number generation.

Cao et al.'s scheme [2] does not have an aggregator, the computing time of Cao et al.'s scheme [2] and Ren et al.'s scheme [24] can be regarded as consistent with our PGAC scheme. For the registration procedure, because Cao et al.'s scheme [2] and Ren et al.'s scheme [24] lack the identity authentication mechanism between the gateway and the smart meter, our PGAC scheme costs $nT_{PUF}$ more than Ren et al.'s scheme [24]. For the request procedure, Ren et al.'s scheme [24] costs $T_{PUF} + (2n+2)T_H$ more than our PGAC scheme, and our PGAC scheme costs $nT_H$ more than Cao et al.'s scheme [2].

For the forwarding procedure, our PGAC scheme costs $T_{PUF} + T_{Rec} + T_H$ more than Cao et al.'s scheme [2] and Ren et al.'s scheme [24], but Cao et al.'s scheme [2] does not have an aggregator, and the gateway in Ren et al.'s scheme [24] does not have the function of gateway to verify the identity of the control center. For the encryption procedure, Ren et al.'s scheme [24] costs $nT_H$ more than Cao et al.'s scheme [2], and our PGAC scheme costs $nT_{PUF} + nT_{Rec} + nT_H$ more than Cao et al.'s scheme [2]. However, Cao et al.'s scheme [2] and Ren et al.'s scheme [24] lack the function of gateway to verify the identity of each smart meter. For the aggregation procedure, our PGAC scheme costs $(n+1)T_H$ more than Cao et al.'s scheme [2] and Ren et al.'s scheme [24], but Cao et al.'s scheme [2] does not have the aggregation function and Ren et al.'s scheme [24] does not realize the function of gateway to verify the identity of each smart meter. For the decryption procedure, Cao et al.'s scheme [2] costs $(n-1)T_H$ more than our PGAC scheme, and our PGAC scheme costs $(n+1)T_H$ more than Ren et al.'s scheme [24].

To sum up, compared with Ding et al.'s scheme [6], our PGAC scheme has obvious advantages in computational time cost, but spends more on computational time cost than Cao et al.'s scheme [2] and Ren et al.'s scheme [24]. However, our PGAC scheme implements more comprehensive authentication function and only rely on lightweight operations.

## 5.4    Experimental Performance

In this section, the experimental performance of the proposed PGAC system is compared with Cao et al.'s scheme [2] and Ren et al.'s scheme [24]. This section uses the Python HashLib module to implement the SHA-256 algorithm and the Crypto library to implement the 256-bit AES-CBC encryption algorithm. The simulation experiments are run on Microsoft Windows 11 operating system with Intel(R) Core(TM)i7-11800H CPU@2.30 GHz and 32GB RAM. Moreover, the simulation results of a 128-bit arbiter PUF circuit on an MSP430 microcontroller machine with a CPU of 798MHz in [15] are used to evaluate the performance of PUF operations. The proposed PGAC system uses the BCH code migration mechanism [7] to implement the FE.Gen and FE.Rec operations of fuzzy extractor, where $T_{Gen}$ is 1.17ms and $T_{Rec}$ is 3.28ms. Table 3 shows the parameter length in the simulation.

**Table 3.** Parameter length

| Parameter | Size (bits) |
|---|---|
| Number of user $n$ | 500 |
| Challenge $C$ | 128 |
| Response $R$ | 128 |
| Shared key $K$ | 128 |
| Identity code $ID$ | 128 |
| Random number $r$ | 128 |
| Timestamp $t$ | 64 |
| Request information $Req$ | 512 |
| Metering data $M$ | 2048 |

This section sets up a group of 500 users and uses the same metering data to fairly test the performance of each scheme. Figure 2 shows the computing time of Cao et al.'s scheme [2], Ren et al.'s scheme [24] and our PGAC scheme in the five procedures of request, forwarding, encryption, aggregation and deception. In the request procedure, Cao et al.'s scheme [2] takes about one-third as long as Ren et al.'s scheme [24], and our PGAC scheme takes about half as long as Ren et al.'s scheme [24]. In the forwarding procedure, only the PGAC scheme has the capability of the gateway authentication request and costs 3.402ms. In the encryption and aggregation procedure, Ren et al.'s scheme [24] did not set a fuzzy extractor, so it took about twice as long as Cao et al.'s scheme [2], while our PGAC scheme designed a mutual authentication mechanism with gateway, so it took about twice as long as Cao et al.'s scheme [2] and Ren et al.'s scheme [24]. In the decrption procedure, Ren et al.'s scheme [24] and our PGAC scheme perform group authentication in about half the time of Cao et al.'s scheme [2]. The proposed PGAC scheme takes more total time than the other two ones, but implements a more complete authentication mechanism.

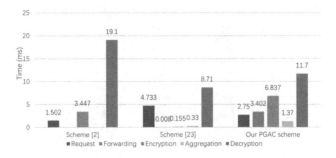

**Fig. 2.** Comparison of execution times for each procedure of the communication process.

Figure 3 shows the total number of messages sent by Cao et al.'s scheme [2], Ren et al.'s scheme [24], and our PGAC scheme in the four procedures of request, forwarding, encryption, and aggregation. In Ren et al.'s scheme [24] and our PGAC scheme, only one message is sent between the control center and a group of smart meters in mutual communication, while 500 messages are sent between smart meters and control center in Cao et al.'s scheme [2].

Figure 4 shows these three schemes to send the ciphertext response to the control center or data management server. Ren et al.'s scheme [24] and our PGAC scheme have basically the same size of data transmitted, while Cao et al.'s scheme [2] has at least 42.41 KB more data than the two schemes. Figure 3 and Fig. 4 show the superiority of group authentication mechanism in the large-scale user data collection scenario of smart grid. This mechanism can effectively reduce the number of message transmission and shorten the total length of transmitted data to a certain extent, thus achieving the design goal of controlling the bandwidth pressure of the main communication network.

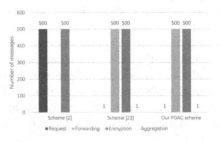

**Fig. 3.** Number of messages sent in the request, forward, encrypt and aggregate phases.

Then, the computing time of control center, gateway and smart meter in PGAC scheme is analyzed when the number of group users is 100 through 1000. Because the calculation of a single smart meter has nothing to do with the number of groups, the smart meter has maintained a time cost of about 6.837ms. Figure 5 shows the time spent by the control center and gateway in different group users. As shown in Fig. 5, the computing time of the control center and gateway increases linearly with the number of group users.

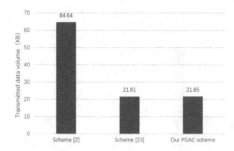

**Fig. 4.** Send data volume to the control center or data management server.

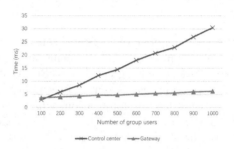

**Fig. 5.** Time overhead of the control center and gateway.

## 6   Conclusion

In order to ensure the confidentiality and integrity of metering data and the high efficiency of communication in the process of data acquisition of a large number of users, a multi-user data acquisition scheme (PGAC) based on PUF is proposed in smart grid. The PGAC scheme realizes the group authentication process of the control center for smart meters and the mutual identity authentication of the communication among the control center, gateway and smart meters. The security analysis shows that the PGAC scheme can resist the traditional attacks and physical attacks, and user privacy can be prevented from disclosure. Based on the results of functional analysis, theoretical analysis and efficiency analysis, the proposed PGAC scheme has more advantages in computing cost and communication overhead compared with other schemes.

**Acknowledgments.** This article is supported in part by the Guangxi Natural Science Foundation under grant 2019GXNSFGA245004 and 2023GXNSFAA026236, the National Natural Science Foundation of China under projects 61962012 and 62303037, the Zhejiang Soft Science Research Program under grant 2023C35081, and the special fund of the High-level Innovation Team and Outstanding Scholar Program for universities of Guangxi.

# References

1. Cao, Y.N., Wang, Y., Ding, Y., Guo, Z., Wu, Q., Liang, H.: Blockchain-empowered security and privacy protection technologies for smart grid. Comput. Stand. Interf. **85**, 103708 (2023)
2. Cao, Y.N., Wang, Y., Ding, Y., Zheng, H., Guan, Z., Wang, H.: A puf-based lightweight authenticated metering data collection scheme with privacy protection in smart grid. In: 2021 IEEE Intl Conf on Parallel & Distributed Processing with Applications, Big Data & Cloud Computing, Sustainable Computing & Communications, Social Computing & Networking (ISPA/BDCloud/SocialCom/SustainCom), New York City, NY, USA, September 30 - Oct. 3, 2021, pp. 876–883. IEEE (2021)
3. Delavar, M., Mirzakuchaki, S., Ameri, M., Mohajeri, J.: Puf-based solutions for secure communications in advanced metering infrastructure (ami): Puf-based solutions for secure communications in ami. Int. J. Commun. Syst. **30**, e3195 (10 2016)
4. Delvaux, J., Peeters, R., Gu, D., Verbauwhede, I.: A survey on lightweight entity authentication with strong pufs. ACM Comput. Surv. **48**(2) (oct 2015)
5. Devadas, S., Suh, E., Paral, S., Sowell, R., Ziola, T., Khandelwal, V.: Design and implementation of puf-based "unclonable" rfid ics for anti-counterfeiting and security applications. In: 2008 IEEE International Conference on RFID, pp. 58–64 (2008)
6. Ding, Y., Wang, B., Wang, Y., Zhang, K., Wang, H.: Secure metering data aggregation with batch verification in industrial smart grid. IEEE Trans. Industr. Inf. **16**(10), 6607–6616 (2020)
7. Dodis, Y., Ostrovsky, R., Reyzin, L., Smith, A.: Fuzzy extractors: How to generate strong keys from biometrics and other noisy data. SIAM J. Comput. 38(1), 97–139 (2008)
8. Dodis, Y., Reyzin, L., Smith, A.: Fuzzy extractors: how to generate strong keys from biometrics and other noisy data. In: Cachin, C., Camenisch, J.L. (eds.) Advances in Cryptology - EUROCRYPT 2004, pp. 523–540. Springer, Berlin Heidelberg, Berlin, Heidelberg (2004)
9. Fan, H., Liu, Y., Zeng, Z.: Decentralizing privacy-preserving data aggregation scheme using blockchain in smart grid. In: Security and Privacy in Digital Economy: First International Conference, SPDE 2020, Quzhou, China, October 30-November 1, 2020, Proceedings 1, pp. 131–142. Springer (2020)
10. Fang, L., Li, M., Liu, Z., Lin, C., Ji, S., Zhou, A., Susilo, W., Ge, C.: A secure and authenticated mobile payment protocol against off-site attack strategy. IEEE Trans. Dependable Secure Comput. **19**(5), 3564–3578 (2022). https://doi.org/10.1109/TDSC.2021.3102099
11. Gope, P., Sikdar, B.: Privacy-aware authenticated key agreement scheme for secure smart grid communication. IEEE Trans. Smart Grid **10**(4), 3953–3962 (2018)
12. Guan, Z., Zhang, Y., Zhu, L., Wu, L., Yu, S.: Effect: an efficient flexible privacy-preserving data aggregation scheme with authentication in smart grid. SCIENCE CHINA Inf. Sci. **62**, 1–14 (2019)
13. Guilley, S., Pacalet, R.: Soc security: a war against side-channels. Annals of Telecommunications-annales des télécommunications (2004)
14. Guo, Z., Qin, B., Guan, Z., Wang, Y., Zheng, H., Wu, Q.: A high-efficiency and incentive-compatible peer-to-peer energy trading mechanism. IEEE Transactions on Smart Grid, pp. 1–1 (2023)

15. Herder, C., Yu, M.D., Koushanfar, F., Devadas, S.: Physical unclonable functions and applications: a tutorial. Proc. IEEE **102**(8), 1126–1141 (2014)
16. Kaur, T., Kaur, M.: Cryptographic key generation from multimodal template using fuzzy extractor. In: 2017 Tenth International Conference on Contemporary Computing (IC3), pp. 1–6 (2017)
17. Khan, A.A., Kumar, V., Ahmad, M., Rana, S.: Lakaf: lightweight authentication and key agreement framework for smart grid network. J. Syst. Architect. **116**, 102053 (2021)
18. Kumar, N., Aujla, G.S., Das, A.K., Conti, M.: Eccauth: a secure authentication protocol for demand response management in a smart grid system. IEEE Trans. Industr. Inf. **15**(12), 6572–6582 (2019)
19. Li, X., et al.: A privacy-preserving lightweight energy data sharing scheme based on blockchain for smart grid. In: Gao, H., Wang, X., Wei, W., Dagiuklas, T. (eds.) Collaborative Computing: Networking, Applications and Worksharing - 18th EAI International Conference, CollaborateCom 2022, Hangzhou, China, October 15–16, 2022, Proceedings, Part II. Lecture Notes of the Institute for Computer Sciences, Social Informatics and Telecommunications Engineering, vol. 461, pp. 91–110. Springer (2022). https://doi.org/10.1007/978-3-031-24386-8_6
20. Liu, S., Zhang, Q., Liu, H.: Privacy protection of the smart grid system based on blockchain. J. Phys.: Conf. Series **1744**(2), 022129 (Feb 2021)
21. Lu, W., Ren, Z., Xu, J., Chen, S.: Edge blockchain assisted lightweight privacy-preserving data aggregation for smart grid. IEEE Trans. Netw. Serv. Manage. **18**(2), 1246–1259 (2021)
22. M, N.B., Pushparajesh, V.: Review of internet of things: distributed power in smart grid. IOP Conf. Series: Mater. Sci. Eng. **1055**(1), 012139 (feb 2021)
23. Pappu, R., Recht, B., Taylor, J., Gershenfeld, N.: Physical one-way functions. Science **297**(5589), 2026–2030 (2002)
24. Ren, X., Cao, J., Ma, M., Li, H., Zhang, Y.: A novel puf-based group authentication and data transmission scheme for nb-iot in 3g pp 5g networks. IEEE Internet Things J. **9**(5), 3642–3656 (2022)
25. Tuyls, P., Batina, L.: Rfid-tags for anti-counterfeiting. In: Topics in Cryptology-CT-RSA 2006: The Cryptographers' Track at the RSA Conference 2006, San Jose, CA, USA, February 13–17, 2005. Proceedings. pp. 115–131. Springer (2006). https://doi.org/10.1007/11605805_8
26. Zeng, X., Liu, Q., Huang, H., Jia, X.: A lightweight privacy-preserving scheme for metering data collection in smart grid. In: 2017 IEEE 18th International Symposium on A World of Wireless, Mobile and Multimedia Networks (WoWMoM), pp. 1–6 (2017)
27. Zhang, L., Zhao, L., Yin, S., Chi, C.H., Liu, R., Zhang, Y.: A lightweight authentication scheme with privacy protection for smart grid communications. Futur. Gener. Comput. Syst. **100**, 770–778 (2019)

# A Semi-supervised Learning Method for Malware Traffic Classification with Raw Bitmaps

Jingrun Ma[1,2], Xiaolin Xu[3], Tianning Zang[1,2], Xi Wang[1(✉)], Beibei Feng[1,2], and Xiang Li[1,2]

[1] Institute of Information Engineering, Chinese Academy of Sciences, Beijing, China
{majingrun,zangtianning,wangxi,fengbeibei,lixiang1}@iie.ac.cn
[2] School of Cyber Security, University of Chinese Academy of Sciences, Beijing, China
[3] National Computer Network Emergency Response Technical Team/Coordination Center of China, Beijing, China

**Abstract.** The rapid growth of malware and its variants has a significant detrimental effect on the security of the Internet infrastructure. In recent years, deep learning-based methods have demonstrated significant success in malware detection. Nonetheless, there are concerns regarding the requirement for substantial labeled data and the feature selection methods used in present approaches. In this paper, we propose a semi-supervised learning-based method for malware traffic classification, which exploits the raw bitmap representation of malware traffic. We employ stacked bi-LSTM to learn the feature representation of malware traffic and adopt semi-supervised learning (SSL) to enhance the model performance by leveraging unlabeled traffic. Pseudo-labeling and consistency regularization are used to produce pseudo-labels, which can compute unsupervised loss. The loss function consists of two terms: a supervised loss applied to labeled data and an unsupervised loss, which are combined together for model training. Experiments indicate that our method is capable of classifying malware traffic with satisfactory accuracy.

**Keywords:** Malware traffic classification · Semi-Supervised Learning

## 1 Introduction

With the proliferation of Internet technology, cyber attacks are becoming more frequent and sophisticated. Malware plays a notorious role in cyber attacks. Adversary among cyber attacks often utilizes malware to achieve their ulterior purpose, which results in extensive damage to individual users, corporations, and governments. According to a report of Statista, the worldwide number of malware attacks has reached 5.5 billion in 2022 [2]. It is important for the cyber security expert to accurately identify malware in the network, while it is not a trivial thing. An automatic identification method is able to facilitate the detection of malware, which would minimize the threat of cyber attacks on enterprise networks to some extent.

© ICST Institute for Computer Sciences, Social Informatics and Telecommunications Engineering 2024
Published by Springer Nature Switzerland AG 2024. All Rights Reserved
H. Gao et al. (Eds.): CollaborateCom 2023, LNICST 562, pp. 341–356, 2024.
https://doi.org/10.1007/978-3-031-54528-3_19

In order to cope with increasingly complex cyber attacks, there is a variety of works on malware classification based on network traffic analysis using machine learning techniques. They establish machine learning frameworks by leveraging various network traffic features to identify malware on a network. Yan et al. [21] propose a two-tier method that utilizes statistical features of network traffic to detect malware. Furthermore, they enhance it with incremental learning, which can update models without retraining from scratch. Chen et al. [6] propose an imbalanced data gravitation-based classification algorithm to classify mobile malware and build a machine learning based model, which leverages 6 statistical features extracted from network traffic. Gezer et al. [7] propose a machine learning based method to detect TrickBot malware by utilizing 37 statistical features. Wang et al. [18] propose an Android malware detection method that utilizes text semantic features of HTTP traffic.

However, these machine learning-based methods conduct the analysis relying on the statistical features of network traffic, which need expert knowledge to carry out feature engineering. Moreover, some methods need to inspect the payload of packets to extract features, which may bring privacy risks and will be useless when encrypted traffic is introduced. Additionally, these supervised learning based methods often require a large labeled dataset to achieve competitive performance, which needs lots of expert manual labeling work.

In this paper, we address the above problem by developing a semi-supervised learning-based method that exploits raw bit features of network traffic to classify malware. Our method can identify malware efficiently as it relies only on the raw binary data of a few packets without any statistical computation or inspecting payloads. A traffic flow refers to a packet sequence that consists of multiple packets. We extract bitmap representation from each packet. Therefore, we represent a flow as a collection of bitmap representation features, which can characterize each malware from the original bits angle. We utilize bi-LSTM to extract temporal features between packets for learning the timing relationship. Moreover, by leveraging unlabeled data, we use semi-supervised learning (SSL) to improve performance and mitigate the reliance on labeled data to some extent. Pseudo-labeling and consistency regularization are used to produce pseudo-labels. Specifically, the pseudo-label is generated based on an original unlabeled flow. When the model is fed an augmented version of the same flow, the pseudo-label is used as a target to compute cross-entropy loss. We leverage mask technology for augmentation, which can produce disturbed versions of a given flow. Additionally, we retain an pseudo-label only if the model assigns a probability exceeding the threshold.

Contributions of this paper are as follows:

- We conduct an analysis of the bitmap representation of various types of malware traffic, which facilitates the characterization of traffic associated with malware.
- We propose a deep learning-based method that exploits the raw bitmap representation features to classify malware traffic. The method employs semi-supervised learning to derive effective features from unlabeled data, which

can mitigate the reliance on labeled data. And stacked bi-LSTM is incorporated to learn temporal features between packets. Our method characterizes the traffic patterns of malware without inspecting packet payloads, which can avoid privacy leakage risks.
- We conduct adequate experimentation to validate our methodology. According to experiment results, our method achieves an average accuracy of 96.41% and an average F1-score of 96.47% across three distinct datasets.

The rest of this paper is organized as follows: Sect. 2 describes relevant prior work. In Sect. 3, we present the data preprocessing of malware traffic and analysis of bitmap representation features. We introduce the methodology detailedly in Sect. 4. Section 5 presents the experiments and results. Finally, Sect. 6 concludes this paper.

## 2 Related Work

**Semi-supervised Learning.** Lee et al. [10] proposed a simple and efficient method of semi-supervised learning by using pseudo-label. They trained the model on labeled and unlabeled data simultaneously. For unlabeled data, they picked up the class which has the maximum predicted probability as pseudo-label. Sajjadi et al. [14] proposed an unsupervised loss function that minimizes the difference of diverse views of the same sample, and these views can be generated by randomized data augmentation, dropout, and random max-pooling. They showed that using the transformation loss function can achieve significant improvements in accuracy. Sohn et al. [16] proposed FixMatch, a simpler semi-supervised learning algorithm that achieves huge improvement across many datasets by using pseudo-labeling and consistency regularization. Aouedi et al. [4] proposed a semi-supervised approach using stacked sparse autoencoder accompanied by denoising and dropout techniques, which can improve the robustness of extracted features and prevent the over-fitting problem during the training process.

**Malware Traffic Classification.** There are a lot of methods relying on building deep learning models using statistical features of malware traffic. These methods usually leverage supervised learning to characterize traffic patterns for each malware. He et al. [8] proposed an anomaly detection method based on CNN and autoencoder, which can utilize only a few abnormal samples to pre-train the model. Rios et al. [13] used SVM and a broad learning system to detect anomalies and intrusions. Shone et al. [15] presented a nonsymmetric deep autoencoder based method for unsupervised feature learning, which can facilitate improving classification performance. Li et al. [11] proposed a machine learning method for detecting organizations of IoT malware in APT attacks, which can better identify APT activity and protect the security of IoT. Bovenzi et al. [5] provided a fair assessment of three models (Decision Tree, Random Forest, and 1-D CNN) to classify Android malware traffic, and the evaluation indicated that the classical machine learning method is still effective in some scenarios.

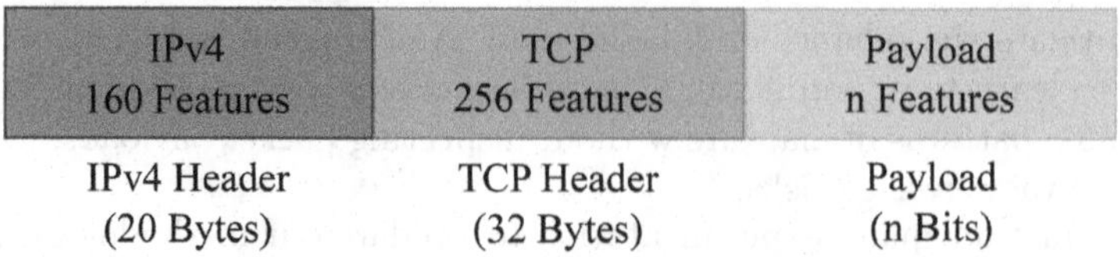

| IPv4<br>160 Features | TCP<br>256 Features | Payload<br>n Features |
|:---:|:---:|:---:|
| IPv4 Header<br>(20 Bytes) | TCP Header<br>(32 Bytes) | Payload<br>(n Bits) |

**Fig. 1.** Bitmap representation of a packet.

## 3  Data Preprocess and Feature Analysis

In this paper, a bidirectional TCP flow is considered as a sample to be classified. A flow is a collection of multiple associated packets between two computer addresses using a particular protocol on a particular pair of ports [20]. Packets with the same quintuple (*source IP, destination IP, source port, destination port, protocol*) belong to the same flow. The flow is bidirectional, including packets from client to server and server to client.

We use the raw bitmap representation of these flows, which can preserve original features and mitigate reliance on manual feature engineering. Figure 1 illustrates the bitmap representation of a packet. We use 160 bits for the IPv4 header, 256 bits for the TCP header (20 bytes fixed part and 12 bytes options), and $n$ bits for payload respectively. TCP option orderings can have improvement on classification performance, and a binary representation of the TCP options can preserve ordering [9]. We examine three datasets (presented in Sect. 5) and find that the TCP header has 20 bytes in 73.67% packets and 21–32 bytes in 25.63% packets respectively. Overall, 99.3% TCP header of packets is less than or equal to 32 bytes. Therefore, we set 256 bits (32 bytes) for the TCP header. The employment of raw bitmap representation leads to a consistent, pre-normalized representation of each packet.

### 3.1  Data Preprocess

We extract raw binary data above the Ethernet layer from PCAP files of malware and reconstruct flows by leveraging 5-tuple information. Each flow consists of multiple packets, from which our sequence model will learn representative features.

Moreover, the number of packets in traffic flows is not always the same, which conflicts with the requirement of our classification model which needs a uniform size of input data. Hence, the flows that we reconstructed before need to be processed into the same format. The following unified preprocessing measures including padding and segmentation are applied to make input flows have a uniform size:

- Initially, if the length of the TCP header exceeds 256 bits, we truncate it. Conversely, we pad the TCP header with zeros.
- If the number of bits in a packet payload exceeds a certain threshold, we select the first $n$ bits. Conversely, we pad the feature sequence with zeros.

– If the number of packets in a flow exceeds a certain threshold, we select the first $M$ packets to represent it as a whole. Conversely, we pad the packet sequence with zeros.

A traffic flow is preprocessed according to the above rules, which allows for reducing the amount of data and unifying the data size.

**Table 1.** The Breakdown of MTA

| ID | Malware | Flow (#) | ID | Malware | Flow (#) |
|----|---------|----------|----|---------|----------|
| 0 | Benign | 1,000 | 17 | Goon | 458 |
| 1 | Hancitor | 1,000 | 19 | Flashpack | 430 |
| 2 | Qakbot | 1,000 | 18 | Styx | 430 |
| 3 | Fiesta | 1,000 | 20 | Bazaloader | 421 |
| 4 | Nuclear | 1,000 | 21 | Zloader | 401 |
| 5 | Trickbot | 1,000 | 22 | Grandsoft | 381 |
| 6 | Angler | 1,000 | 23 | Dridex | 356 |
| 7 | Magnitude | 1,000 | 24 | Mirrorblast | 305 |
| 8 | Icedid | 1,000 | 25 | Gandcrab | 273 |
| 9 | Rig | 971 | 26 | Formbook | 238 |
| 10 | Sweet-orange | 958 | 27 | Zuponcic | 162 |
| 11 | Ursnif | 936 | 28 | Mydoom | 117 |
| 12 | Bumblebee | 882 | 29 | Lokibot | 113 |
| 13 | Neutrino | 591 | 30 | Blackhole | 108 |
| 14 | Svcready | 549 | 31 | Kaixin | 105 |
| 15 | Astaroth | 532 | 32 | Sundown | 104 |
| 16 | Emotet | 495 | 33 | Infinity | 104 |

## 3.2 Bitmap Representation of Packet Analysis

In this paper, we select raw bits sequence to identify the malware traffic correctly, which is unnecessary to compute statistical features of flows. The premise is that bitmap patterns of different malware are distinct, which can be used to characterize the malware [9]. We analyze these bitmaps of different malware on part data from MTA [1] that is also used in the evaluation. The list of malware is shown in Table 1.

We select four types of malware including Sweet-orange, Zloader, Grandsoft, and Zuponcic from Table 1. To conduct an analysis of their bitmap representation, we select $M$ packets of each flow and parse $N$ bits of each packet. By setting $M = 6$, and $N = 1,024$, therefore, a flow can be arranged into a binary matrix of $6 \times 1,024$. Then we reshape it into a matrix of $6 \times 32 \times 32$ to facilitate further analysis. For the convenience of observation, we sum the corresponding bits of each packet, and a visual heatmap (32 × 32) of a flow can be obtained. We group flows by malware class and compute the mean heatmap for each malware. After that, each malware has a corresponding heatmap. An advantage of visual representation is that we can efficiently observe the overall situation corresponding to network traffic. Four types of malware heatmap are shown in Fig. 2, and each heatmap exhibits distinct color distribution patterns. It is observed that some malware displays higher heat in specific regions, while others exhibit higher heat in different areas. By conducting a visual comparison, we observe that the four types of malware have obviously different patterns of bitmaps. These disparities serve as a foundation for purposes of classification.

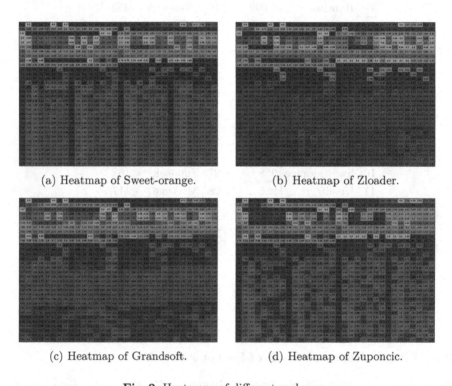

(a) Heatmap of Sweet-orange.                (b) Heatmap of Zloader.

(c) Heatmap of Grandsoft.                (d) Heatmap of Zuponcic.

**Fig. 2.** Heatmaps of different malware.

# 4   Methodology

In this section, we build a semi-supervised learning based neural network model. Afterwards, we provide a comprehensive overview of the model's overall structure and detail each individual component.

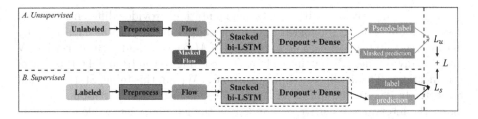

**Fig. 3.** Workflow of the method.

## 4.1 Overview

The proposed semi-supervised learning based neural network model consists of an unsupervised module and a supervised module, as shown in Fig. 3. The raw binary data are extracted from unlabeled and labeled flows during data preprocessing for the unsupervised module and supervised module respectively. Then the unsupervised module computes an pseudo-label for each unlabeled flow that is then used in a standard cross-entropy loss. To obtain an pseudo-label, we first compute the model's predicted class distribution of a given unlabeled flow. If the predicted probability exceeds a given threshold, the predicted class is used as a pseudo-label. Subsequently, we conduct data augmentation within the unsupervised module by randomly masking certain fields of raw binary data. And we leverage the pseudo-label and the model output for the augmented flow to compute loss $L_u$. Then the supervised module computes loss $L_s$ for labeled flows. Finally, the sum of $L_u$ and $L_s$ is used as the overall cross-entropy loss $L$ to train the model.

## 4.2 Semi-supervised

Semi-supervised methods typically generate an pseudo-label for unlabeled data and train the model with a lot of unlabeled data and a small amount of labeled data.

**Unsupervised.** We leverage pseudo-labeling and consistency regularization to complete the unsupervised module, like [16].

Pseudo-labeling leverages the idea of using the model itself to obtain pseudo-labels for unlabeled data. Given a batch of $K$ unlabeled flows $U$, $U = \{u_1, u_2, u_3, ..., u_K\}$, where $u_i$ is an unlabeled flow, the pseudo-label can be generated by:

$$y_u^i = argmax(F(u_i)) \tag{1}$$

where $F(\cdot)$ is the neural network that can extract representation for a given input $x$. In order to make the model have a better predictive effect, we retain the pseudo-labels only when $max(F(u_i)) \geq \theta$, where $\theta$ is a manually set threshold.

Consistency regularization aims to produce consistent predictions for input from different views, which means its prediction should be consistent even if the input is slightly disturbed. Data augmentation provides different views of a single input. For an unlabeled flow $u_i$, we apply an augmentation $Aug(\cdot)$ by masking certain fields of $u_i$. The $u_i$ consists of $M$ packets, and each packet has $N$ bits. We divide these $N$ bits into 24 parts according to the IP and TCP protocol specifications. The details are shown in Table 2. Within this table, Start and End respectively denote the initial and terminal indices of each partition. Furthermore, the interval is inclusively bounded by the left endpoint, while exclusively bounded by the right endpoint $[start, end)$. We randomly select $m$ packets, and for each packet, we randomly select $n$ parts ($n < 24$), and mask them with -1.

Then we compute the cross-entropy loss between pseudo-label $y_u^i$ and the output for an augmented version of $u_i$ as follows:

$$L_u = \frac{1}{K} \sum_{i=0}^{K} \mathbb{1}(max(F(u_i)) \geq \theta) H(y_u^i, F(Aug(u_i))) \tag{2}$$

where $H(\cdot)$ denotes cross-entropy loss function.

**Table 2.** IP and TCP Specification Partition

| Field Name | start | end | Field Name | start | end |
|---|---|---|---|---|---|
| IP version | 0 | 4 | TCP sport | 160 | 176 |
| IP header len | 4 | 8 | TCP dport | 176 | 192 |
| IP service | 8 | 16 | TCP seq | 192 | 224 |
| IP total len | 16 | 32 | TCP ack | 224 | 256 |
| IP identification | 32 | 48 | TCP header len | 256 | 260 |
| IP flags | 48 | 51 | TCP keep | 260 | 266 |
| IP frag offset | 51 | 64 | TCP flags | 266 | 272 |
| IP ttl | 64 | 72 | TCP window size | 272 | 288 |
| IP protocol | 72 | 80 | TCP header check | 288 | 304 |
| IP hdr check | 80 | 96 | TCP urg ptr | 304 | 320 |
| IP src | 96 | 128 | TCP options | 320 | 416 |
| IP dst | 128 | 160 | TCP payload | 416 | N |

**Supervised.** For labeled flows, $L_s$ is the standard cross-entropy loss. Given a batch of $B$ labeled flows $X$, $X = \{x_1, x_2, x_3, ..., x_B\}$, where $x_i$ is labeled flow, the $L_s$ can be computed by:

$$L_s = \frac{1}{B} \sum_{i=0}^{B} H(y^i, F(x_i)) \tag{3}$$

After acquiring the loss of unlabeled flows and labeled flows respectively, the overall loss can be computed as follows:

$$L = L_s + \lambda_u \cdot L_u \tag{4}$$

where $\lambda_u$ is a hyperparameter denoting the weight of the unlabeled loss.

### 4.3   Model Architecture

Network traffic is the conversation between the client and the server, which means that the packet sequence is naturally temporal. LSTM is a special kind of Recurrent Neural Network (RNN) that can process a sequence of inputs. Traditional RNNs have the disadvantage of long-term dependency problem which will result in gradient disappearance or explosion. LSTM uses gate structure to remember or forget information to avoid the long-term dependency problem. Therefore, we use stacked bi-LSTM to extract feature representation and followed by a dropout layer and a fully-connected layer to classify malware traffic.

**Stacked Bi-LSTM.** An LSTM has three gates to control the cell state including forget gate, input gate, and output gate. Before adding new information, The forget gate decides what information to be discarded from the previous sequence. $f_t$ outputs a value between 0 and 1 according to the hidden information $h_{t-1}$ and the input $x_t$. The current cell keeps more information if $f_t$ is close to 1 otherwise less.

$$f_t = \sigma(W_f \cdot [h_{t-1}, x_t] + b_f) \tag{5}$$

After discarding the information, the input gate decides what new information to be stored in the current cell. A *tanh* layer creates new information according to the hidden information $h_{t-1}$ and the input $x_t$.

$$i_t = \sigma(W_i \cdot [h_{t-1}, x_t] + b_i) \tag{6}$$

$$\tilde{C}_t = tanh(W_C \cdot [h_{t-1}, x_t] + b_C) \tag{7}$$

Based on $f_t$, $i_t$ and $\tilde{C}_t$, cell updates $C_{t-1}$ into the new state $C_t$.

$$C_t = f_t \times C_{t-1} + i_t \times \tilde{C}_t \tag{8}$$

After the cell is updated, we need to determine the output $h_t$ of the cell, which is controlled by the output gate $o_t$.

$$o_t = \sigma(W_o \cdot [h_{t-1}, x_t] + b_o) \tag{9}$$

$$h_t = o_t \times tanh(C_t) \tag{10}$$

To learn sequential features from both forward and backward directions, we use bidirectional LSTM (bi-LSTM) to incorporate the contextual features of the packet feature sequence. To improve the representation of the model, we adopt multi-layer bi-LSTM to learn the low-level and high-level features at the same time.

**Dense Layer.** The last part of the model includes a dropout layer and a fully-connected layer followed by a softmax function to obtain a prediction vector.

# 5  Evaluation

In prior sections, we analyze the traffic of malware and preliminarily introduce the architecture of the model. This section sequentially introduces the experiment-used datasets, the evaluation metrics, and the performance comparison between the prior work and ours.

## 5.1  Datasets

We conduct experiments on three public datasets to verify the effectiveness of the method. Next, we give a brief description of these datasets. Table 3 shows the breakdown of these datasets.

**Table 3.** The Breakdown of Datasets

| Dataset | Malware (#) | Flows (#) | Year |
|---|---|---|---|
| MTA [1] | 34 | 19,420 | 2013-2023 |
| Stratosphere [17] | 68 | 13,065 | 2013-2021 |
| USTC-TFC2016 [19] | 9 | 4,236 | 2016 |
| Unlabeled | - | 108,752 | - |

**MTA.** Malware-traffic-analysis.net [1] is a website that provides sources for packet capture (PCAP) files and malware samples. We discard both the PCAPs with multi-class flows and the malware that owns only a few flows here. We also set max flows per malware. Finally, 34 types of malware are left to use in this experiment.

**Stratosphere.** Stratosphere ISP [17] provides a Malware Capture Facility Project that is responsible for making long-term malware captures and continually obtaining malware and normal data. It includes over 400GB PCAPs, and to obtain a balanced dataset, we use a part of them to evaluate our method. Specifically, after discarding extremely large PCAP files, 68 types of malware are used in our evaluation.

**USTC-TFC2016.** Wang et al. [19] publish a dataset consisting of ten types of malware traffic and ten types of normal traffic respectively. After excluding a malware that solely contained UDP flows, we use 9 types of malware traffic in the evaluation.

**Unlabeled.** In order to conduct semi-supervised learning, we selectively utilize a portion of the traffic present in the first three datasets, along with our own laboratory-derived traffic, as the unlabeled dataset. Our own laboratory-derived traffic is incorporated as benign traffic to enhance the diversity. It is pertinent to note that only a designated fraction of the unlabeled traffic was incorporated into the training process, namely, in a 5:1 ratio with labeled traffic.

## 5.2 Metrics

Here, we use precision (P), recall (R), F1-score (F1), and accuracy (ACC) to evaluate the effectiveness of our approach. In our setting, for each malware, a correctly identified flow is treated as a true positive (TP); a flow identified as belonging to this malware but actually not is treated as a false positive (FP); a flow of this malware identified to others is treated as a false negative (FN). Based on these three definitions, above metrics are defined for each device as follows.

$$Precision = \frac{TP}{TP + FP} \tag{11}$$

$$Recall = \frac{TP}{TP + FN} \tag{12}$$

$$F1\text{-}score = \frac{2 * Precision * Recall}{Precision + Recall} \tag{13}$$

We use macro averages of these three metrics and accuracy in evaluation. Accuracy is defined as follows.

$$Accuracy = \frac{\#\ of\ correct\ identification}{\#\ of\ total\ identification} \tag{14}$$

## 5.3 Experimental Setting

We take the raw bits as the input of the model. The packet number is set to 6 and bits number is set to 2,048 (256 bytes). The $\lambda_u$ is set to 1 and $\theta$ is set to 0.95. Besides, we set the dimension of hidden states of each bi-LSTM to 256 and take the 2-layer bi-LSTM in each sequence. The dense layer size is also set to 256. Moreover, we take dropout with a 0.3 ratio to avoid over-fitting, and use 0.001 as the learning rate of the *AdamW* optimizer. We implement our approach with Pytorch 1.13 and deploy it on a server with 20-cores CPU and 64GB memory. The server uses an NVIDIA 2080 for accelerating computing.

## 5.4 Experimental Results

We use three well-known malware traffic datasets to evaluate the performance of our method in terms of precision, recall, F1-score, and accuracy. After extracting features from malware traffic to generate training and testing samples, we have randomly split these instances into three groups, one containing 80% of the instances for training, one containing 10% of the instances for validating, and the other containing 10% of the instances for testing.

**Table 4.** Result on Three Datasets

| Method | MTA [1] | | | | Stratosphere [17] | | | | USTC-TFC2016 [19] | | | |
|---|---|---|---|---|---|---|---|---|---|---|---|---|
| | ACC (%) | P (%) | R (%) | F1 (%) | ACC (%) | P (%) | R (%) | F1 (%) | ACC (%) | P (%) | R (%) | F1 (%) |
| DT | 91.92 | 90.36 | 91.15 | 90.64 | 92.29 | 92.03 | 92.12 | 91.92 | 92.33 | 92.92 | 92.73 | 92.8 |
| RF | 94.44 | 95.65 | 93.38 | 94.23 | 95.96 | 96.01 | 95.7 | 95.74 | 92.1 | 92.37 | 92.59 | 92.36 |
| CNN [19] | 76.93 | 80.48 | 76.61 | 77.49 | 81.76 | 82.84 | 81.59 | 81.47 | 90.33 | 91.0 | 91.38 | 91.14 |
| CNN+LSTM [12] | 81.31 | 79.46 | 79.7 | 79.31 | 84.41 | 84.21 | 84.37 | 84.06 | 86.67 | 88.2 | 87.95 | 88.0 |
| Ours (bytes) | 90.58 | 91.08 | 89.8 | 90.29 | 88.32 | 88.5 | 88.03 | 87.93 | 87.5 | 88.28 | 89.0 | 88.47 |
| Ours (bits) | **97.48** | **97.91** | **97.27** | **97.51** | **97.65** | **97.51** | **97.48** | **97.46** | **94.1** | **94.49** | **94.45** | **94.45** |

Table 4 presents the experiment results on three datasets. Our method reaches the accuracy of 97.48%, 97.65%, and 94.1% on MTA, Stratosphere, and USTC-TFC2016 datasets, respectively. Precision, recall, and F1-score all exceed 94.45%. In order to better analyze the classification result of each type of malware traffic, we generate a confusion matrix for the result on MTA dataset. Figure 4 shows the confusion matrix on MTA dataset, in which rows represent actual labels and columns represent predictions. The diagonal values show the correct classifications. Figure 4 illustrates that our method performs well on most malware and only a few types are not correctly identified. Our method has reached an identifying recall of 100% on 21 types of malware. The Blackhole malware has the lowest recall rate, with only 81.8% of instances, and 18.2% of the Blackhole samples are found to be misidentified as Styx. Figure 5 shows the heatmap of Blackhole and Styx. It is obvious that there is a high level of similarity between their heatmaps, extending from the protocol header to the payload. BlackHole and Styx are two exploit kits that work in the same way: each includes a variety of exploits plus an administrator panel. We speculate that they are based on what is essentially the same implementation, which results in a challenge to differentiate between them. Overall, the experimental results clearly show that our approach has the ability to conduct accurate malware traffic classification.

**Comparison with Other Methods.** To demonstrate the effectiveness of our method, we conduct a comparative analysis with four other methods:

- Decision Tree (DT) and Random Forest (RF), are traditional machine learning methods. We use scikit-learn to perform Decision Tree (DT) and Random Forest (RF) [3]. In order to prove the effectiveness of our model, they also take bitmap representation as input.
- CNN [19], is a deep learning method. Wang et al. [19] propose a malware traffic classification method using a convolutional neural network by taking traffic data as images. The method uses the first 784 bytes of each bidirectional flow, and the bytes can be transformed into images with shape 28×28.

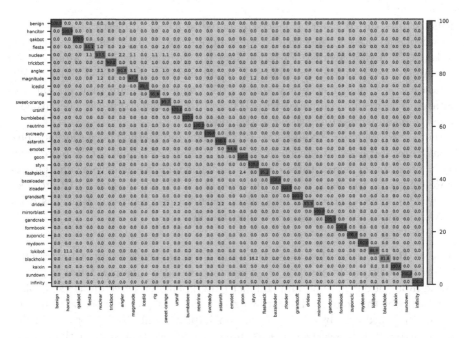

**Fig. 4.** Confusion matrix on MTA dataset.

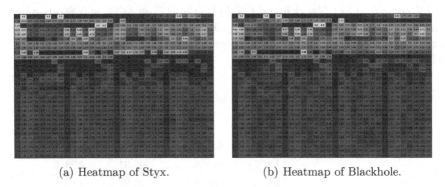

(a) Heatmap of Styx.                    (b) Heatmap of Blackhole.

**Fig. 5.** Heatmaps of Styx and Blackhole.

– CNN+LSTM [12], is a deep learning method. Marín et al. [12] propose a deep learning based method that also uses raw bytes as the input. The method uses CNN to learn spatial features from raw bytes data and uses LSTM to learn temporal features from packet sequences.

Our method achieves a notable margin of improvement compared with other methods on MTA and Stratosphere. On USTC-TFC2016, our method exhibits a less substantial but still noteworthy edge in performance.

For DT and RF methods, RF outperforms the DT on MTA and Stratosphere, while slightly lags behind the DT method on USTC-TFC2016. Our method demonstrates superior performance compared to RF in all metrics for MTA and Stratosphere datasets. Specifically, we achieve a 2.37% higher average accuracy and a 2.5% higher average F1-score than RF on these datasets. Moreover, it exhibits better performance than DT in all metrics on USTC-TFC2016. We obtain a 1.77% higher accuracy and a 1.65% higher F1-score than DT on this dataset. The results compared with DT and RF demonstrate the effectiveness of our semi-supervised neural network model.

For CNN [19] and CNN+LSTM [12] methods, our method outperforms theirs on all three datasets. We reach at least 16.17%, 13.24%, and 3.77% more than theirs on accuracy across three datasets. Additionally, we achieve a superior F1-score compared to theirs, with an increase of 18.2%, 13.4%, and 3.31%, respectively. Our semi-supervised model, along with bitmap representation, has been proven effective when compared to their results.

**Bits vs Bytes.** Several studies utilize raw bytes sequence as input for training neural networks, including [12,19]. Therefore, we also take raw bytes sequence as the input of our method and conduct experiments on three datasets. Table 4 demonstrates that our method utilizing bits as input yields superior results to our method utilizing bytes, exhibiting an improvement in F1-score of 7.22%, 9.53%, and 5.98% respectively across three datasets. Notably, our method utilizing bytes also achieves an improvement in F1-score of no less than 10.98% and 3.87% compared to CNN [19] and CNN+LSTM [12] on MTA and Stratosphere. Although it slightly lags behind CNN [19] on USTC-TFC2016, it is worth noting that the overall superiority of our semi-supervised neural network model is evident.

**Table 5.** Ablation Study of SSL on Three Datasets

| Dataset | Metrics | Without-SSL | With-SSL | Gap |
|---------|---------|-------------|----------|-----|
| MTA [1] | ACC (%) | 95.78 | 97.48 | 1.7 ↑ |
|         | P (%)   | 95.68 | 97.91 | 2.23 ↑ |
|         | R (%)   | 94.14 | 97.27 | 3.13 ↑ |
|         | F1 (%)  | 94.58 | 97.51 | 2.93 ↑ |
| Stratosphere [17] | ACC (%) | 96.89 | 97.65 | 0.76 ↑ |
|         | P (%)   | 96.85 | 97.51 | 0.66 ↑ |
|         | R (%)   | 96.68 | 97.48 | 0.8 ↑ |
|         | F1 (%)  | 96.7 | 97.46 | 0.76 ↑ |
| USTC-TFC2016 [19] | ACC (%) | 92.33 | 94.1 | 1.77 ↑ |
|         | P (%)   | 93.32 | 94.49 | 1.17 ↑ |
|         | R (%)   | 92.91 | 94.45 | 1.54 ↑ |
|         | F1 (%)  | 92.82 | 94.45 | 1.63 ↑ |

**Ablation Study.** We present ablation results in Table 5. Without-SSL denotes training without the unsupervised module, while with-SSL refers to training with all modules. Table 5 indicates that incorporating the unsupervised module leads to an improvement in accuracy, precision, recall, and F1-score on the MTA dataset by 1.7%, 2.23%, 3.13%, and 2.93%, respectively, pointing towards superior results. Similarly, on the USTC-TFC2016 dataset, our proposed method achieves an increase in accuracy, precision, recall, and F1-score by 1.77%, 1.17%, 1.54%, and 1.63%, respectively, validating the effectiveness of our approach. For the Stratosphere dataset, although our method shows only a slight improvement, it still improves on all metrics.

**Discussion.** Our model demonstrates effectiveness in the raw bitmap patterns of malware traffic. Furthermore, semi-supervised learning can effectively improve experimental outcomes by extracting useful features from unlabeled data. We evaluate our model on various datasets, and its performance demonstrates consistent accuracy. However, we have identified a few limitations in our model. For instance, it marginally enhances the Stratosphere dataset when compared to exclusively utilizing supervised learning. Therefore, we intend to enhance this aspect in future research. Moreover, the RF algorithm demonstrates favorable outcomes across various datasets. Notwithstanding the prevalence of deep learning, traditional machine learning approaches, such as random forest, continue to exhibit some competitiveness.

## 6   Conclusion

In this paper, we propose a semi-supervised learning-based method for the purpose of malware traffic classification, which takes raw bit sequences of flow as input and automatically infers the malware class. Our method solely relies on network packet traces and utilizes stacked bi-LSTM to learn representative features of typical malware classes from the network traffic. Additionally, we employ semi-supervised learning to effectively extract features from unlabeled traffic, thereby enhancing its classification capability. Experimental results demonstrate that our proposed method achieves high accuracy in identifying malware traffic.

**Acknowledgements.** We thank the anonymous reviewers for their insightful comments. The corresponding author is Xi Wang.

## References

1. malware-traffic-analysis.net, https://www.malware-traffic-analysis.net/
2. Number of malware attacks per year 2022 — statista. https://www.statista.com/statistics/873097/malware-attacks-per-year-worldwide/
3. scikit-learn: machine learning in python. https://scikit-learn.org/stable/
4. Aouedi, O., Piamrat, K., Bagadthey, D.: A semi-supervised stacked autoencoder approach for network traffic classification. In: 2020 IEEE 28th International Conference on Network Protocols (ICNP), pp. 1–6. IEEE (2020)

5. Bovenzi, G., Cerasuolo, F., Montieri, A., Nascita, A., Persico, V., Pescapé, A.: A comparison of machine and deep learning models for detection and classification of android malware traffic. In: 2022 IEEE Symposium on Computers and Communications (ISCC), pp. 1–6. IEEE (2022)
6. Chen, Z., et al.: Machine learning based mobile malware detection using highly imbalanced network traffic. Inf. Sci. **433**, 346–364 (2018)
7. Gezer, A., Warner, G., Wilson, C., Shrestha, P.: A flow-based approach for trickbot banking trojan detection. Comput. Secur. **84**, 179–192 (2019)
8. He, M., Wang, X., Zhou, J., Xi, Y., Jin, L., Wang, X.: Deep-feature-based autoencoder network for few-shot malicious traffic detection. Secur. Commun. Netw. **2021**, 1–13 (2021)
9. Holland, J., Schmitt, P., Feamster, N., Mittal, P.: New directions in automated traffic analysis. In: Proceedings of the 2021 ACM SIGSAC Conference on Computer and Communications Security, pp. 3366–3383 (2021)
10. Lee, D.H., et al.: Pseudo-label: The simple and efficient semi-supervised learning method for deep neural networks. In: Workshop on challenges in representation learning, ICML. vol. 3, p. 896 (2013)
11. Li, S., Zhang, Q., Wu, X., Han, W., Tian, Z.: Attribution classification method of apt malware in Iot using machine learning techniques. Secur. Commun. Netw. **2021**, 1–12 (2021)
12. Marín, G., Casas, P., Capdehourat, G.: Deep in the dark-deep learning-based malware traffic detection without expert knowledge. In: 2019 IEEE Security and Privacy Workshops (SPW), pp. 36–42. IEEE (2019)
13. Rios, A.L.G., Li, Z., Xu, G., Alonso, A.D., Trajković, L.: Detecting network anomalies and intrusions in communication networks. In: 2019 IEEE 23rd International Conference on Intelligent Engineering Systems (INES), pp. 000029–000034. IEEE (2019)
14. Sajjadi, M., Javanmardi, M., Tasdizen, T.: Regularization with stochastic transformations and perturbations for deep semi-supervised learning. In: Advances in Neural Information Processing Systems 29 (2016)
15. Shone, N., Ngoc, T.N., Phai, V.D., Shi, Q.: A deep learning approach to network intrusion detection. IEEE Trans. Emerg. Topics Comput. Intell. **2**(1), 41–50 (2018)
16. Sohn, K.: Fixmatch: simplifying semi-supervised learning with consistency and confidence. Adv. Neural. Inf. Process. Syst. **33**, 596–608 (2020)
17. Stratosphere: Stratosphere laboratory datasets (2015), retrieved March 13, 2020. https://www.stratosphereips.org/datasets-overview
18. Wang, S., Yan, Q., Chen, Z., Yang, B., Zhao, C., Conti, M.: Detecting android malware leveraging text semantics of network flows. IEEE Trans. Inf. Forensics Secur. **13**(5), 1096–1109 (2017)
19. Wang, W., Zhu, M., Zeng, X., Ye, X., Sheng, Y.: Malware traffic classification using convolutional neural network for representation learning. In: 2017 International Conference On Information Networking (ICOIN), pp. 712–717. IEEE (2017)
20. Xu, C., Shen, J., Du, X.: A method of few-shot network intrusion detection based on meta-learning framework. IEEE Trans. Inf. Forensics Secur. **15**, 3540–3552 (2020)
21. Yan, A., et al.: Network-based malware detection with a two-tier architecture for online incremental update. In: 2020 IEEE/ACM 28th International Symposium on Quality of Service (IWQoS), pp. 1–10. IEEE (2020)

# Secure and Private Approximated Coded Distributed Computing Using Elliptic Curve Cryptography

Houming Qiu[1,2] and Kun Zhu[1,2(✉)]

[1] College of Computer Science and Technology, Nanjing University of Aeronautics and Astronautics, Nanjing 210016, China
{hmqiu56,zhukun}@nuaa.edu.cn
[2] Collaborative Innovation Center of Novel Software Technology and Industrialization, Nanjing, China

**Abstract.** In large-scale distributed computing systems, coded computing has attracted considerable attention since it can effectively mitigate the impact of stragglers. Nonetheless, several emerging issues seriously restrict the performance of coded distributed systems. First, the presence of colluding workers collude results in serious privacy leakage issues. Second, few existing works consider security issues in data transmission. Third, the number of required results to wait for increases with the degree of polynomial functions. In this paper, we propose a secure and private approximated coded distributed computing (SPACDC) scheme that addresses the aforementioned issues simultaneously. The SPACDC scheme ensures data security during the transmission process by leveraging a proposed matrix encryption algorithm based on elliptic curve cryptography. Unlike existing coding schemes, our SPACDC scheme does not impose strict constraints on the minimum number of results required to wait for. Furthermore, the SPACDC scheme provides information-theoretic privacy protection for raw data. Finally, extensive performance analysis is provided to demonstrate the effectiveness of the proposed SPACDC scheme.

**Keywords:** Coded distributed computing · Distributed system · Security · Privacy · Stragglers · Collaborative computing

## 1 Introduction

In recent years, distributed computing has emerged as an effective paradigm widely applied to handle numerous computation tasks involving massive amounts of data in various fields, including big data analysis [1], signal processing [2] and machine learning (ML) [3]. Distributed computing involves dividing a computation task owned by a master into subtasks that are then assigned to multiple workers. The workers utilize their computing resources to perform the subtasks

---

This work was supported by National Natural Science Foundation of China (62071230).

H. Gao et al. (Eds.): CollaborateCom 2023, LNICST 562, pp. 357–374, 2024.
https://doi.org/10.1007/978-3-031-54528-3_20

and subsequently return the subtask results to the master. The waiting time for the master to receive all subtask results is known as computation latency. Leveraging multiple workers to perform the parallel computation of the subtasks significantly reduces the computation latency [4]. Therefore, distributed computing has received growing attention, especially in large-scale computing scenarios [5].

However, a critical performance bottleneck in traditional distributed computing systems is the requirement of waiting for computation results from all workers. Consequently, the extremely-slow or faulty workers become the "stragglers", inevitably leading to unpredictable latency [6]. Coded distributed computing (CDC) is proposed as a solution to alleviate the impact of stragglers by carefully embedding "computation redundancy" into computation tasks through coding techniques. With CDC, the master can recover the final result successfully even in the presence of missing results from some workers. This motivates numerous studies on CDC for large-scale distributed computing systems, which suffers from the effects of stragglers [7–12].

Recently, another emerging issue of data privacy is highlighted by the existence of colluding workers in CDC systems. Colluding workers refer to some curious worker nodes, which collaborate with each other to access information from the assigned data. In [10], the authors considered the data privacy issue on high-dimensional matrix multiplication in CDC systems by adding random matrices. However, the recovery threshold proves to be too large. Moreover, most of the existing works primarily focus on data security at workers, while ignoring the concern of data transmission security. In practical scenarios, data is susceptible to eavesdropping during the transmission process [13]. Therefore, ensuring secure data transmission in CDC systems is imperative.

In this paper, we propose a secure and private approximated coded distributed computing (SPACDC) scheme based on elliptic curve cryptography (ECC) to jointly address the aforementioned issues. To the best of our knowledge, this is the first proposed work that addresses secure data transmission in CDC systems. The main contributions of this paper are listed as follows:

- We design a secure and private approximated coded distributed computing (SPACDC) scheme, which provides resiliency against stragglers, and enables information-theoretic privacy protection. Particularly, the SPACDC scheme imposes no strict constraints on the minimum number of required results returned from workers.
- We propose a matrix encryption algorithm based on ECC for CDC systems, which is able to guarantee data security during the transmission process.
- Then, the theoretical proof for the information-theoretic privacy of input data guaranteed by the SPACDC scheme is demonstrated.
- Finally, extensive performance analysis further demonstrate the low complexity of the SPACDC scheme.

The rest of the paper is organized as follows. Section 2 presents the system model and problem formulation of CDC systems. Then, in Sect. 3, we introduce the proposed matrix encryption algorithm. In Sect. 4, we describe the proposed SPACDC scheme. Finally, we conclude this paper in Sect. 5.

The notations frequently used in this paper are listed in Table 1.

## 2    System Model and Problem Formulation

In this section, we first describe a distributed system model with encrypted communication. Then, we introduce some relevant definitions used in this paper. Finally, we formulate the secure and private large-scale computing problem in CDC systems.

**Table 1.** Main notations in this paper

| Notation | Description |
| --- | --- |
| $\mathbf{C}_i$ | Ciphertext of $\mathbf{X}_i$ |
| $G$ | A generator point |
| $K$ | Number of submatrix blocks |
| $\mathcal{K}$ | set of indexes of the fastest $k^*$ workers |
| $\mathbf{M}_i$ | A confidential matrix of worker $W_i$ |
| $N$ | Number of workers |
| $\mathcal{N}$ | set of indexes of the $N$ workers |
| $\mathcal{P}$ | Set of colluding workers |
| $pk_M$ | Public key of the master |
| $pk_{W_i}$ | Public key of worker $W_i$ |
| $\mathcal{S}$ | Set of stragglers |
| $S$ | Number of stragglers |
| $sk_M$ | Private key of the master |
| $sk_{W_i}$ | Private key of worker $W_i$ |
| $s_{K_i}$ | Share key |
| $T$ | Number of colluding workers |
| $W_i$ | Worker node with index $i$ |
| $\mathbf{X}$ | Input large-scale dataset |
| $\tilde{\mathbf{X}}_i$ | Encoded submatrix of $\mathbf{X}$ assigned to worker $W_i$ |
| $\mathbf{Y}$ | Final result |
| $\tilde{\mathbf{Y}}_i$ | Computed subresult of worker $W_i$ |
| $\mathbf{Z}_i$ | Random matrix |

### 2.1    System Model

We consider a master-worker distributed computing system consisting of a master and $N$ worker nodes $W_i$ for $i \in \mathcal{N}$. We assume that there are $S$ straggling workers and $T$ colluding workers among $N$ worker nodes. Let $\mathcal{P}$ be the set of the indexes of the $T$ colluding workers. The master is interesting in approximately evaluating a multivariate polynomial $f : \mathbb{V} \to \mathbb{U}$ over a large-scale dataset $\mathbf{X}$, i.e., $\mathbf{Y} \approx f(\mathbf{X})$, where $\mathbb{V}$ and $\mathbb{U}$ are two real matrix spaces, $\mathbf{X} \in \mathbb{F}^{m \times d}$, $m$ and $d$ are positive integer. $\mathbb{F}$ denotes a sufficiently large field. Particularly, our system may encounter the presence of eavesdroppers during data transmission. As shown in Fig. 1, we describe the whole computation process by the following steps.

1) **Data Process:** The master receives the input dataset $\mathbf{X}$. Then, the dataset $\mathbf{X}$ is encoded by $N$ encoding functions into $N$ encoded matrices, is given by

$$\tilde{\mathbf{X}}_i = g_i(\mathbf{X}) \text{ for } i \in \mathcal{N}. \tag{1}$$

where $\mathcal{N} \triangleq \{0, 1, \ldots, N-1\}$, $\tilde{\mathbf{X}}_i \in \mathbb{F}^{\frac{m}{K} \times d}$, and $K$ is a positive integer. Encoding function $g_i$ such that $g_i : \mathbb{F}^{m \times d} \to \mathbb{F}^{\frac{m}{K} \times d}$. To protect data security, the master encrypts encoded matrix $\tilde{\mathbf{X}}_i$ into ciphertext $\mathbf{C}_i$ using the proposed encryption Algorithm 1. After that, the master sends $\mathbf{C}_i$ to worker $W_i$ for $i \in \mathcal{N}$.

2) **Task Computing:** Each worker $W_i$ decrypts the received encrypted data $\mathbf{C}_i$ to obtain the original data $\tilde{\mathbf{X}}_i$ by its private key. Then, worker $W_i$ performs the computational task $\hat{\mathbf{Y}}_i = f(\tilde{\mathbf{X}}_i)$. After completing the task, worker $W_i$ encrypts the computed result $\tilde{\mathbf{Y}}_i$ into ciphertext $\tilde{\mathbf{C}}_i$ by Algorithm 1 and then return it back to the master. Note that some workers may fail to complete the task or return $\tilde{\mathbf{Y}}_i$ to the master slower than others.

3) **Result Recovering:** The master collects the encrypted data $\{\tilde{\mathbf{C}}_i\}_{i \in \mathcal{K}}$ returned from the fastest $k^* = |\mathcal{K}|$ $(\mathcal{K} \subseteq \mathcal{N})$ workers. Then, the master decrypts the encrypted data $\{\tilde{\mathbf{C}}_i\}_{i \in \mathcal{K}}$ to obtain original computed results $\{\tilde{\mathbf{Y}}_i\}_{i \in \mathcal{K}}$ by Algorithm 1. After then, the master recovers the final result $\mathbf{Y}$ by using decoding functions $\{\hbar_i\}_{i \in \mathcal{K}}$, is given by

$$\mathbf{Y} = \hbar_{\mathcal{K}}\left(\{\tilde{\mathbf{Y}}_i\}_{i \in \mathcal{K}}\right). \tag{2}$$

## 2.2    Related Definitions

**Definition 1 (Recovery Threshold [8]).** *The recovery threshold is the minimum number of returned results of worker nodes which can be utilized to decode the final desired result. The lower the recovery threshold, the fewer subtask results returned by the worker nodes are required for the master to recover the final desired result.*

**Definition 2 (Straggling Workers [14]).** *The straggling workers are also called stragglers, refer to some worker nodes fail to compute the subtasks or return computed results to the master extremely slowly.*

**Definition 3 (Colluding Workers [15]).** *The colluding workers denote some worker nodes are curious and honest. They collude with each other to obtain information from assigned data from the master.*

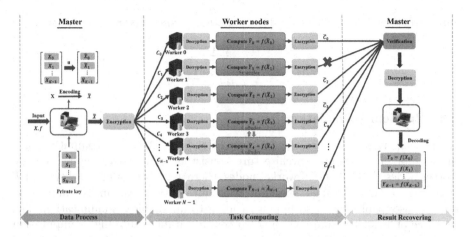

**Fig. 1.** An overview of the coded distributed computing system using elliptic curve cryptography is shown. In the system, the master want to evaluate a multivariate polynomial over a dataset $\mathbf{X} = [\mathbf{X}_0^T, \mathbf{X}_1^T, ..., \mathbf{X}_{K-1}^T]^T$. Firstly, the master encodes the sub-matrices $\{\mathbf{X}_i\}_{i=0}^{K-1}$ into $\{\tilde{\mathbf{X}}_i\}_{i=0}^{N-1}$. To provide secure data transmission, each encoded sub-matrices $\tilde{\mathbf{X}}_i$ is encrypted as $\tilde{\mathbf{C}}_i$ and then sent to worker $W_i$ for $i \in \mathcal{N}$. Each worker $W_i$ computes $\hat{\mathbf{Y}}_i = f(\tilde{\mathbf{X}}_i)$ and encrypts the computed result before sending it back to the master node. The master decrypts the returned result $\tilde{\mathbf{C}}_i$ to obtain the result $\tilde{\mathbf{Y}}_i$. Finally, the master computes $\mathbf{Y} = \hbar_{\mathcal{K}}\big(\{\tilde{\mathbf{Y}}_i\}_{i \in \mathcal{K}}\big)$ to obtain approximated $f(\mathbf{X}_i)$ for $i \in \mathcal{N}$.

**Definition 4 (*Privacy Constraint [10]*).** *The privacy constraint of the CDC system for encoded data $\tilde{\mathbf{X}}_{\mathcal{P}}$ that assigned to colluding worker $W_i$ for $i \in \mathcal{P}$ is specified by:*

$$\mathbf{I}(\tilde{\mathbf{X}}_{\mathcal{P}}; \mathbf{X}) = 0, \tag{3}$$

*where $\mathbf{I}(\bullet; \bullet)$ denotes mutual information.*

**Definition 5 (*Elliptic Curve [16]*).** *The elliptic curve over finite field $\mathbb{F}_q$ is the set of solutions of the following on-singular Weierstrass equation:*

$$y^2 = x^3 + ax + b, \tag{4}$$

*where $a$ and $b \in \mathbb{F}$ are the coefficients of the elliptic curve, and satisfies:*

$$4a^3 + 27b^2 \neq 0. \tag{5}$$

**Definition 6 (*Berrut's Rational Interpolation [7, 8, 17]*).** *For a function $f$, $n$ distinct points $a < x_0 < x_1 < \cdots < x_{n-1} < b$ and the corresponding evaluations $f_0, f_1, \ldots, f_{n-1}$. The Berrut's rational interpolant of $f$ can be written in the form*

$$r(x) \triangleq \sum_{i=0}^{n-1} f_i l_i(x), \tag{6}$$

*where $l_i(x)$ for $i \in \{0, 1, \ldots, n-1\}$ are the basic functions are defined as*

$$l_i(x) \triangleq \frac{\frac{(-1)^i}{x - x_i}}{\sum_{i=0}^{n-1} \frac{(-1)^i}{x - x_i}}. \tag{7}$$

## 2.3  Problem Formulation

In this paper, we consider the problem of coded distributed computing in a master-worker distributed architecture consisting of a master nodes and $N$ worker nodes. Among the $N$ worker nodes, there are $S$ straggling workers and $T$ colluding workers. Notably, communication links between the master and workers are susceptible to eavesdropping, leading to unreliable communication. The presence of stragglers and colluding workers inevitably cause high computation latency and privacy issues, respectively.

To address these critical issues, we aim to design a secure and private approximated coded distributed computing (SPACDC) scheme using elliptic curve cryptography (ECC), which can ensures data security during the transmission process while reducing the recovery threshold and guaranteeing (information-theoretic) privacy protection of data.

## 3  Matrix Encryption Algorithm Based on ECC

In this section, we propose a matrix encryption algorithm based on ECC for CDC systems, abbreviated as MEA-ECC. First, we introduce ECC, which is a cost-efficient and high security encryption technique.

### 3.1  Background of ECC

ECC is a type of asymmetric public key encryption algorithm that based on elliptic curve theory. It uses the coordinate points of the elliptic curve over finite field $\mathbb{F}_q$ for cryptographic operations. The elliptic curve equation (4) over a finite field is specified by:

$$y^2 = \{x^3 + ax + b\} \bmod \{q\}, \tag{8}$$

which is called Weierstrass equation, the discriminant:

$$\{4a^3 + 27b^2\} \bmod \{q\} \neq 0. \tag{9}$$

ECC offers two fundamental mathematical operations: point addition and point multiplication. These operations take one or two distinct points on the curve as inputs and generate a new point on the same curve as output. As illustrated in Fig. 2, we given the graphical representation of the point addition and doubling operations.

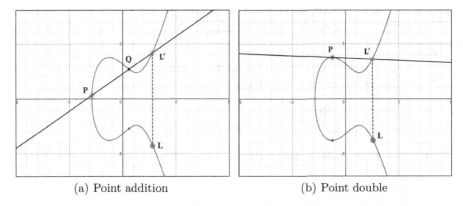

(a) Point addition                         (b) Point double

**Fig. 2.** Two visualized examples of point addition and double operations on elliptic curve $y^2 = x^3 - 5x + 10$. (a) Point addition: given two distinct points, $P$ and $Q$, draw a line passing through them and intersecting the curve at another point, $L'$. Then, draw a parallel line to the y-axis passing through $L'$, which intersects the curve at point $L$. (b)Point double: given a points, $P$, draw a tangent line passing through $P$ and intersecting the curve at another point, $L'$. Then, draw a parallel line to the y-axis passing through $L'$, which intersects the curve at point $L$.

1) **_Point Addition or Doubling:_** For two points, $P(x_1, y_1)$ and $Q(x_2, y_2)$ on the elliptic curve, the addition of the two points $P$ and $Q$ is defined as $P + Q = L(x_3, y_3)$, where

$$x_3 = \{\lambda^2 - x_1 - x_2\} \bmod \{q\}, \tag{10}$$

$$y_3 = \{\lambda(x_1 - x_3) - y_1\} \bmod \{q\}, \tag{11}$$

and

$$\lambda = \begin{cases} \{\frac{y_2 - y_1}{x_2 - x_1}\} \bmod \{q\}, & \text{if } P \neq Q; \\ \{\frac{3x_1^2 + a}{2y_1}\} \bmod \{q\}, & \text{if } P = Q. \end{cases} \tag{12}$$

2) **_Point Multiplication:_** For any point $P$ on the elliptic curve and an integer $n$, the point multiplication $n \cdot P$ is defined as

$$n \cdot P = \underbrace{P + P + \cdots + P}_{n \text{ times}}, \tag{13}$$

### 3.2   Matrix Encryption Algorithm Based on ECC

In this section, we introduce the proposed MEA-ECC. The master wants to securely send a confidential matrix $\mathbf{M}_i \in \mathbb{F}^{m \times d}$ to worker $W_i$ for $i \in \mathcal{N}$. The detailed encryption process of the MEA-ECC is described as follows:

1) **_Key generation:_** The master randomly generates an integer $sk_M < q$ as his private key, and then computes the public key $pk_M = sk_M \cdot G$, where $G$ is a generator point. Similarly, worker $W_i$ generates a private key $sk_{W_i} < q$ and a public key $pk_{W_i} = sk_{W_i} \cdot G$, respectively.

---

**Algorithm 1:** Matrix Encryption Algorithm

---

**Input:** $G, q, k, \mathbf{M}_i$
**Output:** $\mathbf{C}_i$

1   [ I ] **Key generation:** the master generates a private key $sk_M < q$;
2   The master computes the public key: $pk_M = sk_M \cdot G$;
3   **for** $i = 0 : N - 1$ **do**
4     |  Worker $W_i$ generates a private key $sk_{W_i} < q$;
5     |  Worker $W_i$ computes the public key: $pk_{W_i} = sk_{W_i} \cdot G$;
6   **end**
7   [ II ] **Key Exchanging:** the master and worker $W_i$ exchange their public keys $pk_M$ and $pk_{W_i}$;
8   **for** $i = 0 : N - 1$ **do**
9     |  The master computes share key $s_{K_i} = sk_M \cdot pk_{W_i}$;
10     |  Worker $W_i$ computes share key $s'_{K_i} = sk_{W_i} \cdot pk_M$;
11   **end**
12   $s_{K_i} = sk_M \cdot pk_{W_i} = sk_M(sk_{W_i} \cdot G) = sk_{W_i}(sk_M \cdot G) = sk_{W_i} \cdot pk_M = s'_{K_i}$;
13   We have $s_K = s'_K$;
14   [ III ] **Encryption:** the master generates a random integer $k$ where $1 < k < q$;
15   Ciphertext point: $\mathbf{C}_i = \{k \cdot G, \ \mathbf{M}_i + \Psi(k \cdot pk_{W_i})\mathbf{I}_{m,d}\}$;
16   **for** $i = 0 : N - 1$ **do**
17     |  The master sends ciphertext $\mathbf{C}_i$ to worker $W_i$;
18   **end**
19   [ IV ] **Decryption:** Worker $W_i$ receives $\mathbf{C}_i$ from the master;
20   Worker $W_i$ decrypts ciphertext $\mathbf{C}_i$ with private key $sk_{W_i}$;
21   **for** $i = 0 : N - 1$ **do**
22     |  Decryption: $\mathbf{M}_i + \Psi(k \cdot pk_{W_i})\mathbf{I}_{m,d} - \Psi[sk_{W_i}(k \cdot G)]\mathbf{I}_{m,d} = \mathbf{M}_i + \Psi[k(sk_{W_i} \cdot G) - sk_{W_i}(k \cdot G)]\mathbf{I}_{m,d} = \mathbf{M}_i$;
23   **end**
24   **Return:** $\mathbf{M}_i$

---

2) ***Key Exchanging:*** The master obtains the share key by computing $s_{K_i} = sk_M \cdot pk_{W_i}$. Similarly, worker $W_i$ obtains the share key by computing $s'_{K_i} = sk_{W_i} \cdot pk_M$. It can be observed that $s_{K_i} = sk_M \cdot pk_{W_i} = sk_M(sk_{W_i} \cdot G) = sk_{W_i}(sk_M \cdot G) = sk_{W_i} \cdot pk_M = s'_{K_i}$.

3) ***Encryption:*** The master sends confidential matrix $\mathbf{M}_i$ to worker $W_i$ for $i \in \mathcal{N}$. The ciphertext point is given by $\mathbf{C}_i = \{k \cdot G, \mathbf{M}_i + \Psi(k \cdot pk_{W_i})\mathbf{I}_{m,d}\}$, where function $\Psi(x, y) = x$, i.e., returns the value of the x-coordinate as the output. $\mathbf{I}_{m,d} \in \mathbb{F}^{m \times d}$ denotes the matrix with all elements being 1, and $k$ is a random integer while satisfying $1 < k < q$.

4) ***Decryption:*** Worker $W_i$ decrypts ciphertext $\mathbf{C}_i$ by computing $\mathbf{M}_i + \Psi(k \cdot pk_{W_i})\mathbf{I}_{m,d} - \Psi[sk_{W_i}(k \cdot G)]\mathbf{I}_{m,d} = \mathbf{M}_i + \Psi[k(sk_{W_i} \cdot G) - sk_{W_i}(k \cdot G)]\mathbf{I}_{m,d} = \mathbf{M}_i$.

The specific procedure of matrix encryption algorithm is given in Algorithm 1.

# 4 Secure and Private Approximated Distributed Computing Using ECC

In this section, we propose a secure and private approximated coded distributed computing scheme based on ECC, called SPACDC scheme. Before providing a general description, we firstly present an illustrating example to reveal the core idea of the SPACDC scheme.

## 4.1 Illustrating Example

Consider the function $f(\mathbf{X}_i) = \mathbf{X}_i \mathbf{X}_i^T$ in a distributed computing system consisting of a master node and $N = 8$ worker nodes. We set $K = 2$, $S = 1$, and $T = 1$. The master evenly divides the input matrix $\mathbf{X}$ into $K = 2$ submatrices as follows:

$$\mathbf{X} = \begin{bmatrix} \mathbf{X}_0' \\ \mathbf{X}_1' \end{bmatrix}, \tag{14}$$

where $\mathbf{X}_0'$ and $\mathbf{X}_1'$ both are with dimension of $\frac{m}{2} \times d$. Thus, the goal of the master is to obtain the computed results of $f(\mathbf{X}_0')$ and $f(\mathbf{X}_1')$.

The master encodes the input data $\mathbf{X} = \begin{bmatrix} \mathbf{X}_0' \\ \mathbf{X}_1' \end{bmatrix}$ using the following encoding function.

$$u'(z) = \frac{1}{(z-1)\phi(z)} \mathbf{X}_0' - \frac{1}{(z-2)\phi(z)} \mathbf{X}_1' + \frac{1}{(z-3)\phi(z)} \mathbf{Z}_0', \tag{15}$$

where $\phi(z) = \frac{1}{z-1} - \frac{1}{z-2} + \frac{1}{z-3}$, $\mathbf{Z}_0' \in \mathbb{F}^{\frac{m}{2} \times d}$ is a random matrix and generated independently of $\mathbf{X}$ by the master. All elements of $\mathbf{Z}_0'$ are selected uniformly independent and identically distributed (i.i.d.) from field $\mathbb{F}$. It can be noted that $u'(1) = \mathbf{X}_0'$, $u'(2) = \mathbf{X}_1'$ and $u'(3) = \mathbf{Z}_0'$. The master selects 8 distinct values $\{\alpha_i'\}_{i=0}^7$ from field $\mathbb{F}$ such that $\{\alpha_i'\}_{i=0}^7 \cap \{1, 2, 3\} = \varnothing$. Then, we obtain the encoded data $\{\tilde{\mathbf{X}}_i' = u'(\alpha_i')\}_{i=0}^7$ by employing encoding function (15).

To protect data security during the transmission process, the master encrypts the encoded data $\{\tilde{\mathbf{X}}_i' = u(\alpha_i)\}_{i=0}^7$ into ciphertext $\{\mathbf{C}_i'\}_{i=0}^7$ by the proposed MEA-ECC. Then, the master assigns encrypted data $\mathbf{C}_i'$ to worker $W_i$, for $i \in \{0, 1, 2, ..., 7\}$. When the worker $W_i$ receives the encrypted data $\mathbf{C}_i'$, it obtains the original encoded data $\tilde{\mathbf{X}}_i'$ by decrypting $\mathbf{C}_i'$ using the MEA-ECC.

Then, the worker $W_i$ performs the assigned computation task $\tilde{\mathbf{Y}}_i' = f(\tilde{\mathbf{X}}_i')$. Before returning the computed result back to the master, the worker node should encrypt the result $\tilde{\mathbf{Y}}_i'$ into $\tilde{\mathbf{C}}_i'$ by the MEA-ECC. This encryption step is essential to ensure the confidentiality and security of the computed result during the transmission process. Upon receiving the encrypted data $\tilde{\mathbf{C}}_i'$ from the worker $W_i$, the master decrypts it by MEA-ECC to obtain the original computed result $\tilde{\mathbf{Y}}_i'$. Let $\mathcal{F}'$ be the set of the indexes of the fastest workers that return the computed results back to the master. Hence, we have the interpolation points $(\alpha_i', \tilde{\mathbf{Y}}_i')$ for $i \in \mathcal{F}'$. After then, the master constructs a decoding function $\hbar(z)$

using Berrut's rational interpolant [17], as follows:

$$\hbar(z) = \sum_{i \in \mathcal{F}'} \frac{\frac{(-1)^i}{z-\alpha_i'}}{\sum_{j \in \mathcal{F}'} \frac{(-1)^j}{z-\alpha_j'}} \tilde{\mathbf{Y}}_i'. \tag{16}$$

Having this decoding function, the master approximately computes $f(\mathbf{X}_0')$ and $f(\mathbf{X}_1')$ by substituting $z = 1$ and $z = 2$ into Eq. (16), respectively. Hence, the master completes the computation task.

## 4.2   General SPACDC Scheme Design

In this section, we present the general description of the proposed SPACDC scheme. The SPACDC scheme is implemented in five steps that are described as follows:

   **1) Data Process:** The master divides the large-scale matrix $\mathbf{X} \in \mathbb{F}^{m \times d}$ into $K$ equal-sized blocks by row, i.e.,

$$\mathbf{X} = [\mathbf{X}_0^T, \mathbf{X}_1^T, ..., \mathbf{X}_{K-1}^T]^T, \tag{17}$$

where $\mathbf{X}_i \in \mathbb{F}^{\frac{m}{K} \times d}$. $K$ is a positive integer and the final block may be padded with zeros if $m$ is not divisible by $K$. Then, the goal of the master is to approximately compute $\mathbf{Y}_i \approx f(\mathbf{X}_i)$ for $i \in \mathcal{K}$.

   To provide data privacy against the colluding workers, the master selects $K + T$ distinct values $\beta_1, \beta_2, \ldots, \beta_{K+T-1}$ from $\mathbb{F}$ and encodes submatrices $\{\mathbf{X}_i\}_{i=0}^{K-1}$ using the following encoding function:

$$u(z) = \sum_{i=0}^{K-1} \frac{(-1)^i}{(z - \beta_i)L(z)} \mathbf{X}_i + \sum_{i=K}^{K+T-1} \frac{(-1)^i}{(z - \beta_i)L(z)} \mathbf{Z}_i, \tag{18}$$

where $L(z) = \sum_{j=0}^{K+T-1} \frac{(-1)^j}{z-\beta_j}$. $\{\mathbf{Z}_i\}_{i=K}^{K+T-1} \in \mathbb{F}^{\frac{m}{K} \times d}$ are random matrices and generated independently of $\mathbf{X}$ by the master. All elements of $\{\mathbf{Z}_i\}_{i=K}^{K+T-1}$ are selected uniformly i.i.d. from field $\mathbb{F}$. The master selects $N$ distinct values $\{\alpha_i\}_{i=0}^{N-1}$ from $\mathbb{F}$ such that $\{\alpha_i\}_{i=0}^{N-1} \cup \{\beta_i\}_{i=0}^{K+T-1} = \varnothing$. Thus, the master obtains the encoded data $\tilde{\mathbf{X}}_i = u(\alpha_i)$ for $i \in \mathcal{N}$. Moreover, it can be verified that $u(\beta_i) = \mathbf{X}_i$ for $i \in \{0, 1, \ldots, K - 1\}$.

   To ensure the data security during the transmission process, the master encrypts the encoded data $\{\tilde{\mathbf{X}}_i\}_{i=0}^{N-1}$ into ciphertext $\{\mathbf{C}_i\}_{i=0}^{N-1}$ by the proposed MEA-ECC. Then, the master sends encrypted data $\mathbf{C}_i$ to worker $W_i$ for $i \in \mathcal{N}$.

   **2) Task Computing:** After receiving the encrypted data $\mathbf{C}_i$ from the master, worker $W_i$ first decrypts the encrypted data $\mathbf{C}_i$ to obtain the original encoded data $\tilde{\mathbf{X}}_i$ by the MEA-ECC. Then, the worker $W_i$ computes the product $\tilde{\mathbf{Y}}_i = f(\tilde{\mathbf{X}}_i)$. After obtaining the computed result, worker $W_i$ encrypts the result $\tilde{\mathbf{Y}}_i$ into ciphertext $\tilde{\mathbf{C}}_i$ and return back to the master.

   **3) Result Recovering:** The master waits and collects returned encrypted data $\tilde{\mathbf{C}}_i$ from worker $W_i$ for $i \in \mathcal{N}$. By using the MEA-ECC, the master decrypts

**Table 2.** Comparison of complexity in six coding schemes

| Coded Scheme | Encoding Complexity | Decoding Complexity | Communication Complexity | | Computational Complexity | Data Security | Data Privacy |
|---|---|---|---|---|---|---|---|
| | | | Master to all workers | Workers to master | | | |
| Polynomial Codes [9] | $O(mdN)$ | $O(m^2 \log^2 K^2 \log\log K)$ | $O(mdN/K)$ | $O(m^2)$ | $O(dm^2/K^2)$ | No | No |
| MatDot Codes [18] | $O(mdN)$ | $O(Km^2 \log^2 K \log\log K)$ | $O(mdN/K)$ | $O(Km^2)$ | $O(dm^2/K)$ | No | No |
| SecPoly Codes [10] | $O(mdN)$ | $O(m^2 \log^2 K^2 \log\log K)$ | $O(mdN/K)$ | $O(m^2)$ | $O(dm^2/K^2)$ | No | Yes |
| BACC scheme [7] | $O(mdN)$ | $O(|\mathcal{F}|)$ | $O(mdN/K)$ | $O(m^2/(|\mathcal{F}|K^2))$ | $O(dm^2/K^2)$ | No | No |
| LCC scheme [11] | $O(mdN)$ | $O(m^2 \log^2 K \log\log K)$ | $O(mdN/K)$ | $O(m^2/K)$ | $O(dm^2/K^2)$ | No | Yes |
| SPACDC (Our Scheme) | $O(mdN)$ | $O(|\mathcal{F}|)$ | $O(mdN/K)$ | $O(m^2/(|\mathcal{F}|K^2))$ | $O(dm^2/K^2)$ | Yes | Yes |

---

**Algorithm 2: SPACDC Algorithm**

**Input:** $\mathbf{X}, N, K, T, m, d$

**Output:** $\{\mathbf{Y}_i\}_{i=0}^{K-1}$

1 [ I ] **Data process:** the master encodes $\mathbf{X}$;

2 The master divides $\mathbf{X}$ into $K$ submatrices, as shown in Eq. (17);

3 **for** $i = 0 : N - 1$ **do**

4      $\tilde{\mathbf{X}}_i = \sum_{i=0}^{K-1} \frac{(-1)^i}{(z-\beta_i)L(z)}\mathbf{X}_i + \sum_{i=K}^{K+T-1} \frac{(-1)^i}{(z-\beta_i)L(z)}\mathbf{Z}_i$;

5      The master encrypts $\tilde{\mathbf{X}}_i$ into $\mathbf{C}_i$ by Algorithm 1;

6      The master sends $\mathbf{C}_i$ to worker $W_i$;

7 **end**

8 [ II ] **Task Computing:** worker $W_i$ computes $\tilde{\mathbf{Y}}_i = f(\tilde{\mathbf{X}}_i)$;

9 **for** $i = 0 : N - 1$ **do**

10      **if** $W_i$ has received $\mathbf{C}_i$ from the master **then**

11          Worker $W_i$ obtain $\tilde{\mathbf{X}}_i$ by decrypting $\mathbf{C}_i$ using Algorithm 1;

12          Worker $W_i$ computes $\tilde{\mathbf{Y}}_i = f(\tilde{\mathbf{X}}_i)$;

13          Worker $W_i$ encrypts $\tilde{\mathbf{Y}}_i$ into $\tilde{\mathbf{C}}_i$ by Algorithm 1;

14          Worker $W_i$ sends $\tilde{\mathbf{C}}_i$ back to the master;

15      **end**

16 **end**

17 [ III ] **Result Recovering:** the master recovers $\mathbf{Y}_i$;

18 The master decrypts returned data $\tilde{\mathbf{C}}_i$;

19 The master collects points $(\alpha_i, f(u(\alpha_i))$ for $i \in \mathcal{F}$;

20 Constructing a rational function $h(z) = \sum_{i \in \mathcal{F}} \frac{\frac{(-1)^i}{z-\alpha_i}}{\sum_{j \in \mathcal{F}} \frac{(-1)^j}{z-\alpha_j}} f(u(z))$;

21 The master computes $\mathbf{Y}_i = f(\mathbf{X}_i) \approx h(\beta_i)$ for $i \in \{0, 1, \ldots, K-1\}$;

22 **Return:** $\mathbf{Y}_i$

---

$\tilde{\mathbf{C}}_i$ to obtain the computed result $\tilde{\mathbf{Y}}_i$. We set $\mathcal{F}$ as the indexes of the faster workers that return the computed results back to the master. Then, we construct a rational function $h(z)$ to approximately interpolates $f(u(z))$ by received points

$(\alpha_i, f(u(\alpha_i)))$ for $i \in \mathcal{F}$, is given by

$$h(z) = \sum_{i \in \mathcal{F}} \frac{\frac{(-1)^i}{z - \alpha_i}}{\sum_{j \in \mathcal{F}} \frac{(-1)^j}{z - \alpha_j}} f(u(z)). \tag{19}$$

Thus, the master is able to obtain approximated results $\mathbf{Y}_i = f(\mathbf{X}_i) \approx h(\beta_i)$ for $i \in \{0, 1, \ldots, K - 1\}$.

The specific procedure of the SPACDC scheme is given in Algorithm 2.

## 5  Result and Complexity Analyses

In this section, we present our main result on information-theoretic privacy of the proposed SPACDC scheme. Then, we give the complexity analysis about the RSPCC scheme.

### 5.1  Some Theorems of the SPACDC Scheme

**Theorem 1.** *For a CDC system, each worker $W_i$ for $i \in \mathcal{P}$ ($\mathcal{P} \subseteq \mathcal{N}$) cannot obtain any information about matrix $\mathbf{X}$ from encoded matrices $\tilde{\mathbf{X}}_i$, i.e., the privacy constraint (3) is satisfied.*

*Proof.* We prove Theorem 1 in a manner similar to [15]. For any worker $W_i$ for $i \in \mathcal{N}$, we have the mutual information

$$\begin{align}
\mathbf{I}(\mathbf{X}; \tilde{\mathbf{X}}_\mathcal{P}) &= \mathbf{H}(\tilde{\mathbf{X}}_\mathcal{P}) - \mathbf{H}(\tilde{\mathbf{X}}_\mathcal{P}|\mathbf{X}) \tag{20a} \\
&= \mathbf{H}(\tilde{\mathbf{X}}_\mathcal{P}) - \mathbf{H}(\tilde{\mathbf{X}}_\mathcal{P}|\mathbf{X}) + \mathbf{H}(\tilde{\mathbf{X}}_\mathcal{P}|\mathbf{X}, \mathbf{Z}_K, \mathbf{Z}_{K+1}, \ldots, \mathbf{Z}_{K+T-1}) \tag{20b} \\
&= \mathbf{H}(\tilde{\mathbf{X}}_\mathcal{P}) - \mathbf{I}(\tilde{\mathbf{X}}_\mathcal{P}; \mathbf{Z}_K, \mathbf{Z}_{K+1}, \ldots, \mathbf{Z}_{K+T-1}|\mathbf{X}) \tag{20c} \\
&= \mathbf{H}(\tilde{\mathbf{X}}_\mathcal{P}) - \mathbf{H}(\mathbf{Z}_K, \mathbf{Z}_{K+1}, \ldots, \mathbf{Z}_{K+T-1}|\mathbf{X}) \\
&\quad + \mathbf{H}(\mathbf{Z}_K, \mathbf{Z}_{K+1}, \ldots, \mathbf{Z}_{K+T-1}|\mathbf{X}, \tilde{\mathbf{X}}_\mathcal{P}) \tag{20d} \\
&= \mathbf{H}(\tilde{\mathbf{X}}_\mathcal{P}) - \mathbf{H}(\mathbf{Z}_K, \mathbf{Z}_{K+1}, \ldots, \mathbf{Z}_{K+T-1}) \tag{20e} \\
&\leq \mathbf{H}(\tilde{\mathbf{X}}_\mathcal{P}) - \sum_{i=K}^{K+T-1} \mathbf{H}(\mathbf{Z}_i) \tag{20f} \\
&= \mathbf{H}(\tilde{\mathbf{X}}_\mathcal{P}) - T \frac{md}{K} \log |\mathbb{F}| \tag{20g} \\
&\leq \sum_{i=1}^{T} \mathbf{H}(\tilde{\mathbf{X}}_i) - T \frac{md}{K} \log |\mathbb{F}| \tag{20h} \\
&= T \frac{md}{K} \log |\mathbb{F}| - T \frac{md}{K} \log |\mathbb{F}| \tag{20i} \\
&= 0,
\end{align}$$

where (20b) follows the fact that $\tilde{\mathbf{X}}_{\mathcal{P}}$ is a deterministic function of $\mathbf{X}$ and $\{\mathbf{Z}_i\}_{i=K}^{K+T-1}$; (20e) is due to the fact that random matrices $\{\mathbf{Z}_i\}_{i=K}^{K+T-1}$ are independently generated of $\mathbf{X}$ by the master. (20f) and (20h) follow from upper bounding of the joint entropy; (20g) follows i.i.d. uniform random elements of $\{\mathbf{Z}_i\}_{i=K}^{K+T-1}$; (20i) follows from an argument similar to (20g). This completes the proof.

**Theorem 2.** *For a CDC system, each worker $W_i$ for $i \in \mathcal{N}$ cannot obtain any information about the final product $\mathbf{Y}$ from computed sub-product $\tilde{\mathbf{Y}}_i$, i.e.,*

$$\mathbf{I}(\tilde{\mathbf{Y}}_i; \mathbf{Y}) = 0. \tag{21}$$

*Proof.* For any worker $W_i$ for $i \in \mathcal{N}$, we have the mutual information

$$
\begin{aligned}
\mathbf{I}(\mathbf{Y}; \tilde{\mathbf{Y}}_i) &= \mathbf{I}\big(f(\mathbf{X}); f(\tilde{\mathbf{X}}_i)\big) \\
&= \mathbf{H}\big(f(\mathbf{X})\big) - \mathbf{H}\big(f(\mathbf{X})|f(\tilde{\mathbf{X}}_i)\big) & \text{(22a)} \\
&\leq \mathbf{H}\big(f(\mathbf{X})\big) - \mathbf{H}\big(f(\mathbf{X})|f(\tilde{\mathbf{X}}_i), \tilde{\mathbf{X}}_i\big) & \text{(22b)} \\
&= \mathbf{H}\big(f(\mathbf{X})\big) - \mathbf{H}\big(f(\mathbf{X})|\tilde{\mathbf{X}}_i\big) & \text{(22c)} \\
&= \mathbf{H}\big(f(\mathbf{X})\big) - \mathbf{I}\big(f(\mathbf{X}); \mathbf{X}|\tilde{\mathbf{X}}_i\big) - \mathbf{H}\big(f(\mathbf{X})|\tilde{\mathbf{X}}_i, \mathbf{X}\big) & \text{(22d)} \\
&= \mathbf{H}\big(f(\mathbf{X})\big) - \mathbf{I}\big(f(\mathbf{X}); \mathbf{X}|\tilde{\mathbf{X}}_i\big) & \text{(22e)} \\
&= \mathbf{H}\big(f(\mathbf{X})\big) - \mathbf{H}(\mathbf{X}|\tilde{\mathbf{X}}_i) + \mathbf{H}\big(\mathbf{X}|\tilde{\mathbf{X}}_i, f(\mathbf{X})\big) & \text{(22f)} \\
&= \mathbf{H}\big(f(\mathbf{X})\big) - \mathbf{H}(\mathbf{X}) + \mathbf{H}\big(\mathbf{X}|f(\mathbf{X})\big) & \text{(22g)} \\
&= \mathbf{H}\big(f(\mathbf{X})\big) - \mathbf{I}\big(f(\mathbf{X}); \mathbf{X}\big) & \text{(22h)} \\
&= \mathbf{H}\big(f(\mathbf{X})|\mathbf{X}\big) & \text{(22i)} \\
&= 0, & \text{(22j)}
\end{aligned}
$$

where (22b) follows from the conditioning reduces entropy; (22e) and (22j) follow from the fact that $f(\mathbf{X})$ is a deterministic function of $\mathbf{X}$; (22g) follows from (3) which has been proved in Theorem 1. This completes the proof.

### 5.2 Complexity Analysis of the SPACDC Scheme

In this section, we investigate the computational complexities of the proposed SPACDC scheme for encoding, decoding, checking, communication and per-worker computation.

1) ***Encoding Complexity:*** Recalling the encoding phase of the SPACDC scheme, the overall encoding complexity depends on the encoding function $h(z)$ in Eq. (18). We observe that $u(z)$ is the sum of $K + T$ matrices, each of which with dimension $\frac{m}{K} \times d$. Hence, the computational complexity of the encoding function $u(z)$ for each worker is $\mathcal{O}(md(K+T)/K) = \mathcal{O}(md)$. For $N$ workers, the overall encoding complexity of the SPACDC scheme is $\mathcal{O}(mdN)$.

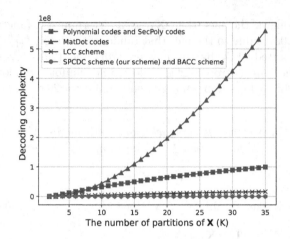

**Fig. 3.** Comparison of decoding complexity achieved by the Polynomial codes [9], Mat-Dot codes [18], SecPoly codes [10], BACC scheme [7], LCC scheme [11] and SPACDC scheme (our scheme) in distributed computing systems under parameter $m = 1000$ while varying $K$ from 1 to 36.

2) **Decoding Complexity:** Note that the result recovering phase of the SPACDC scheme, the master interpolates the polynomial $f(u(z))$ to decode the final result $\mathbf{Y}$ by Eq. (19). Similar to [7], the decoding complexity of the SPACDC scheme is $\mathcal{O}(|\mathcal{F}|)$.

3) **Communication Complexity:** The communication complexity of the SPACDC scheme includes two aspects: (1) master-to-worker and (2) worker-to-master. First, the master transmits $\mathcal{O}(md/K)$ symbols to each worker. Hence, the total number of symbols that the master transmits to $N$ workers is $\mathcal{O}(mdN/K)$. Second, each worker returns $\mathcal{O}(m^2)$ symbols to the master. Thus, the total number of symbols that the workers return back to the master is $\mathcal{O}(m^2/|\mathcal{F}|)$.

4) **Computational Complexity of Each Worker:** In the task comput-ing phase, worker $W_i$ for $i \in \mathcal{N}$ compute the product $\tilde{\mathbf{Y}}_i = f(\tilde{\mathbf{X}}_i)$, e.g., $\tilde{\mathbf{Y}}_i = \tilde{\mathbf{X}}_i \tilde{\mathbf{X}}_i^T$, where $\mathbf{X}_i$ with dimension $\frac{m}{K} \times d$. Then, we obtain that the computational complexity of each worker is $\mathcal{O}(dm^2/K^2)$.

As shown in Table 2, we give a summary of complexity analysis in terms of encoding, decoding, computation, and communication on the proposed SPACDC scheme and the existing coding schemes (polynomial Codes [9], Mat-Dot codes [18], SecPoly codes [10], BACC scheme [7], and LCC scheme [11]). The complexity comparisons among these coding schemes utilize identical parameter settings. From Table 2, we observe that our SPACDC scheme has the same cod-ing complexity as the other existing schemes. It is noteworthy that the SPACDC scheme achieves security and privacy protection with nearly identical complexity as the other coding schemes. Additionally, the communication complexity of the SPACDC scheme is equal to that of other coding schemes in term of master-to-

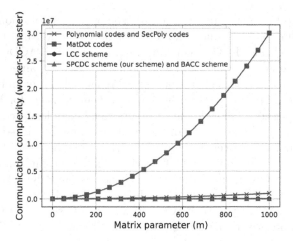

**Fig. 4.** Comparison of communication complexity (worker-to-master) of the Polynomial codes, MatDot codes, SecPoly codes, BACC scheme, LCC scheme and SPACDC scheme (our scheme) in distributed computing systems under parameter $K = 30$, $|\mathcal{F}| = 10$ while varying $m$ from 1 to 1000.

worker communication. It is mainly determined by the similarity and consistency of the matrix partitioning method of these coding schemes.

Figure 3 shows a comparison of the decoding complexity among the Polynomial codes, MatDot codes, SecPoly codes, BACC scheme, LCC scheme and SPACDC scheme (our scheme) under parameter $m = 1000$ while varying $K$ from 1 to 36. It is evident that the decoding complexities of the SPACDC and BACC schemes are smallest among these coding schemes, while MatDot codes exhibit the highest decoding complexity. The decoding complexities of the Polynomial and SecPoly codes are higher than those of the LCC, BACC and our SPACDC scheme. Both SPACDC and BACC schemes employ Berrut's rational interpolant for decoding the final result, constructing low-degree rational functions to significantly reduce computational complexity. The decoding complexity of the well-known coding scheme LCC is slightly higher than that of our scheme. As the degree of a polynomial function to be evaluated increases, the decoding complexity of LCC scheme will increase proportionally. The decoding complexity of LCC scheme will be much higher than that of our scheme due to a high polynomial degree.

In Fig. 4, we compare the communication complexity (worker-to-master) of Polynomial codes, MatDot codes, SecPoly codes, BACC scheme, LCC scheme and SPACDC scheme (our scheme) under parameter $K = 30$, $|\mathcal{F}| = 10$ while varying $m$ from 1 to 1000. The communication complexity of the SPACDC and BACC scheme are smallest among these coding schemes. The communication complexity (worker-to-master) of MatDot codes is the highest among all coding schemes. In fact, the communication complexity (worker-to-master) is largely related to the dimension of returned result matrices.

As shown in Fig. 5, we present a comparison of the computational complexity of various coding schemes, including Polynomial codes, MatDot codes, SecPoly codes, BACC scheme, LCC scheme, and our proposed SPACDC scheme. The parameters used are $m = 5000$ and $d = 1000$, with varying values of $K$ from 1 to 36. From the results, it is evident that our SPACDC scheme exhibits comparable computational complexity to the other coding schemes, except for MatDot codes. Notably, MatDot codes show higher computational complexity compared to the rest of the coding schemes. This discrepancy is primarily caused by the larger size of the assigned matrices in the workers when employing MatDot codes [18].

As discussed above, our SPACDC scheme exhibits significantly lower complexity compared to existing coding scheme, such as the Polynomial codes, MatDot codes, SecPoly codes, and LCC scheme. Although the SPACDC scheme has the same complexity with BACC scheme, BACC scheme is unable to provide security and privacy protection for data. Therefore, our SPACDC scheme outperforms all other coding schemes.

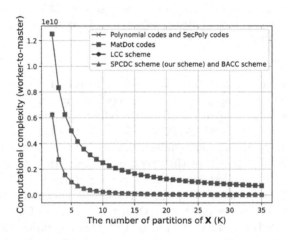

**Fig. 5.** Comparison of computational complexity of the Polynomial codes, MatDot codes, SecPoly codes, BACC scheme, LCC scheme and SPACDC scheme (our scheme) in distributed computing systems under parameter $m = 5000$, $d = 1000$ while varying $K$ from 1 to 36.

## 6  Conclusions

In this paper, we proposed a secure and private approximated coded distributed computing (SPACDC) scheme, which jointly addressed the issues of stragglers and colluding workers. It is worth noting that the SPACDC scheme is able to ensure data security during the transmission process using the proposed matrix encryption algorithm, i.e., MEA-ECC. Then, the theoretical proofs for the information-theoretic privacy protection of input data were given. Finally, we provided comprehensive performance analysis to demonstrate the effectiveness of our SPACDC scheme.

# References

1. Wu, Z., Sun, J., Zhang, Y., Wei, Z., Chanussot, J.: Recent developments in parallel and distributed computing for remotely sensed big data processing. Proc. IEEE **109**(8), 1282–1305 (2021)
2. Güler, B., Avestimehr, A.S., Ortega, A.: TACC: topology-aware coded computing for distributed graph processing. IEEE Trans. Sig. Inf. Process. Netw. **6**, 508–525 (2020)
3. Guo, Y., Zhao, R., Lai, S., Fan, L., Lei, X., Karagiannidis, G.K.: Distributed machine learning for multiuser mobile edge computing systems. IEEE J. Sel. Top. Sig. Process. **16**(3), 460–473 (2022)
4. Schlegel, R., Kumar, S., Rosnes, E., i Amat, A.G.: Privacy-preserving coded mobile edge computing for low-latency distributed inference. IEEE J. Sel. Areas Commun. **40**(3), 788–799 (2022)
5. Ng, J.S., et al.: A comprehensive survey on coded distributed computing: fundamentals, challenges, and networking applications. IEEE Commun. Surv. Tut. **23**(3), 1800–1837 (2021)
6. Yu, Q., Maddah-Ali, M.A., Avestimehr, A.S.: Straggler mitigation in distributed matrix multiplication: fundamental limits and optimal coding. IEEE Trans. Inf. Theor. **66**(3), 1920–1933 (2020)
7. Jahani-Nezhad, T., Maddah-Ali, M.A.: Berrut approximated coded computing: straggler resistance beyond polynomial computing. IEEE Trans. Pattern Anal. Mach. Intell. **45**(1), 111–122 (2023)
8. Jahani-Nezhad, T., Maddah-Ali, M.A.: Optimal communication-computation trade-off in heterogeneous gradient coding. IEEE J. Sele. Areas Inf. Theor. **2**(3), 1002–1011 (2021)
9. Yu, Q., Maddah-Ali, M.A., Avestimehr, A.S.: Polynomial codes: an optimal design for high-dimensional coded matrix multiplication. In: Proceedings of the 31st International Conference on Neural Information Processing Systems, pp. 4406–4416 (2017)
10. Yang, H., Lee, J.: Secure distributed computing with straggling servers using polynomial codes. IEEE Trans. Inf. Forensics Secur. **14**(1), 141–150 (2019)
11. Yu, Q., Li, S., Raviv, N., Kalan, S.M.M., Soltanolkotabi, M., Avestimehr, S.A.: Lagrange coded computing: optimal design for resiliency, security, and privacy. In: The 22nd International Conference on Artificial Intelligence and Statistics, pp. 1215–1225 (2019)
12. Ozfatura, E., Ulukus, S., Gündüz, D.: Coded distributed computing with partial recovery. IEEE Trans. Inf. Theor. **68**(3), 1945–1959 (2021)
13. Jiang, Y., et al.: Secure data transmission and trustworthiness judgement approaches against cyber-physical attacks in an integrated data-driven framework. IEEE Trans. Syst. Man Cybern. Syst. **52**(12), 7799–7809 (2022)
14. Byrne, E., Gnilke, O.W., Kliewer, J.: Straggler-and adversary-tolerant secure distributed matrix multiplication using polynomial codes. Entropy **25**(2), 266 (2023)
15. Aliasgari, M., Simeone, O., Kliewer, J.: Private and secure distributed matrix multiplication with flexible communication load. IEEE Trans. Inf. Forensics Secur. **15**, 2722–2734 (2020)
16. Sadhukhan, D., Ray, S., Biswas, G., Khan, M.K., Dasgupta, M.: A lightweight remote user authentication scheme for IoT communication using elliptic curve cryptography. J. Supercomput. **77**, 1114–1151 (2021)

17. Berrut, J.P.: Rational functions for guaranteed and experimentally well-conditioned global interpolation. Comput. Math. Appl. **15**(1), 1–16 (1988)
18. Dutta, S., Fahim, M., Haddadpour, F., Jeong, H., Cadambe, V., Grover, P.: On the optimal recovery threshold of coded matrix multiplication. IEEE Trans. Inf. Theor. **66**(1), 278–301 (2020)

# A Novel Semi-supervised IoT Time Series Anomaly Detection Model Using Graph Structure Learning

Weijian Song[1], Peng Chen[1(✉)], Juan Chen[1(✉)], Yunni Xia[2], Xi Li[1], Qinghui Xi[1], and Hongxia He[1]

[1] School of Computer and Software Engineering, XiHua University, Chengdu, China
{chenpeng,chenjuan}@mail.xhu.edu.cn
[2] School of Computer Science, Chongqing University, Chongqing, China

**Abstract.** Internet of Things (IoT) is an evolving paradigm for building smart cross-industry. The data gathered from IoT devices may have anomalies or other errors for various reasons, such as malicious activities or sensor failures. Anomaly detection is thus in high need for guaranteeing trustworthy execution of IoT applications. Existing IoT anomaly detection methods are usually built upon unsupervised methods and thus can be inadequate when facing complex IoT data regularity. In this article, we propose a semi-supervised approach for detecting IoT time series anomalies based on Graph Structure Learning (GSL) using multi-layer perceptron Graph Convolutional Networks (GCN) and the Mean Teachers (MT) mechanism. The proposed model is capable of leveraging a small amount of labeled data (1% to 10%) to achieve high detection accuracy. We adopt Mean Teachers to utilize unlabeled data for enhancing the model's detection performance. Moreover, we design a novel graph structure learning layer to adaptively capture the IoT data features among different nodes. Experimental results clearly suggest that the proposed model outperforms its competitors on two public IoT datasets, achieving 82.85% in terms of F1 score and 22.8% increase.

**Keywords:** IoT Time Series · Anomaly Detection · Graph Structure Learning · Graph Convolutional Networks · Semi-supervised · Mean Teachers

## 1 Introduction

The Internet of Things (IoT) is an emerging means that consists of collaborative terminals and sensors connected through the Internet. The IoT can be applied in different application domains, such as smart homes, wearable devices, smart

This research is supported by the National Natural Science Foundation under Grant No. 62376043 and Science and Technology Program of Sichuan Province under Grant No. 2020JDRC0067, No. 2023JDRC0087, and No. 2020YFG032662376043, and Chunhui Project of Ministry of Education of China under Grant No. Z2011085.

H. Gao et al. (Eds.): CollaborateCom 2023, LNICST 562, pp. 375–391, 2024.
https://doi.org/10.1007/978-3-031-54528-3_21

cities, healthcare, agriculture, transportation, and industry. The major strength of the IoT is that it helps to make appropriate decisions based on the data collected by sensors, and tracks devices in a smart way.

A typical IoT environment involves a large number of interconnected sensors, such as those found in water treatment plants, power plants, or transportation systems. Generally, real-time data collected from these sensors are processed and stored as IoT multivariate time series. The variables in these time series are often interrelated; for example, in a water treatment plant, if sensor data monitoring water flow rate exhibits anomalies, the sensor data monitoring water pressure is also likely to show abnormalities. Due to the a mass of sensors and the complexity of their relationships, performing anomaly detection in more intricate and large-scale IoT systems is generally more difficult.

IoT anomaly detection [1] holds significant importance and value in modern society. IoT devices are typically distributed across various geographical locations, monitoring a large amount of device status and operational data aids in predicting potential failures or damages By continuously monitoring anomalies in real-time, it becomes possible to forecast potential device failures in advance and carry out timely maintenance, thereby reducing maintenance costs and downtime, while enhancing equipment reliability and availability [2]. IoT systems involve extensive data transmission and processing, often operating in resource constrained environments (such as sensor nodes, embedded devices, etc.) [3,4]. Anomaly detection can help identify abnormal data flows, energy consumption, and more, optimizing resource allocation and improving system efficiency and performance [5]. IoT anomaly detection not only ensures the stability, security, and efficiency of IoT systems but also enhances user experience, providing robust support for data analysis and intelligent decision-making. As such, it holds crucial significance and value in IoT applications. Figure 1 depicts an example of IoT time series anomaly detection, where the highlighted red portion indicates the detected anomaly. Notably, methods for anomaly detection in IoT data have undergone extensive research and development, resulting in widespread exploration.

The methods for anomaly detection have evolved from classical approaches initially to machine learning and deep learning methods in recent years, achieving significant advancements. For instance, as early as 1979, Tukey [5] introduced a statistical method for detecting anomalies in time series. In the past decade, machine learning and deep learning methods have achieved tremendous success in computer vision tasks, leading researchers to apply these approaches to anomaly detection. For example, Autoregressive model (VAR) [6], Long Short-Term Memory (LSTM) [7], Variational Autoencoder (VAE) [8], Generative Adversarial Networks (GAN) [9]. Graph Neural Networks (GNNs) have attracted considerable attention in the realm of anomaly detection for time-series data [10]. Their ability to capture relationships and dynamic changes within time-series data has led to superior performance. They are capable of capturing relationships and dynamic changes in time-series data. GNNs can be mainly divided into Convolutional Graph Neural Networks (GCN), Graph Attention

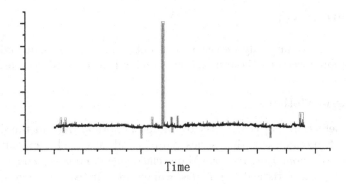

**Fig. 1.** A typical anomaly detection scenario of IoT time series.

Networks (GAT) [11], and Graph Neural Networks with gated updates, among others.

Despite the achievements mentioned above, when it comes to multidimensional time series anomaly detection in the context of IoT, there are still the following difficulties and challenges: (1) The detection accuracy of unsupervised methods remains insufficient; (2) Extracting and representing precise spatiotemporal data features from complex multi-dimensional IoT time series data is still a challenge.

To address such problems, we propose the semi-supervised Mean Teachers [12] based Graph Convolutional Network Model for IoT time series anomaly detection (MTGCN). The main contributions are summarized as follows:

- To address the challenge of data labeling difficulty, we introduce the Mean Teachers model, which enables leveraging unlabeled data for semi-supervised training, thereby enhancing the model's generalization ability and performance.
- To improve the detection accuracy of the model, we employ a multi-layer perceptron graph convolutional network (GCN) based on adaptive graph structure learning as the foundational framework. Compared to traditional distance-defined graph structures, this adaptive graph structure learning method enables us to acquire superior graph relationships, thereby boosting the performance of our model.
- The experimental results demonstrate that this approach still outperforms the majority of unsupervised methods in anomaly detection on two publicly collected real-world datasets, even when using a very small amount (1%–10%) of labeled data.

The rest of the paper is organized as follows. Section 2 reviews the existing research on anomaly detection based. In Sect. 3, we propose the semi-supervised model based on GSL and give a detailed description of each module. In Sect. 4, we conduct experiments and provide experimental results and analysis. Finally, we conclude and elaborate on future work in Sect. 5.

## 2   Related Work

We briefly review anomaly detection methods for time series, including both classical approaches and those based on machine learning and deep learning.

### 2.1   Classic Methods

Anomaly detection [13] is the task of finding abnormal data in the data. The detection of anomalies in time-series data has always held a crucial position in the field of anomaly detection. Many classical methods for anomaly detection are based on statistical techniques, while in recent years, numerous scholars have developed machine learning-based approaches for anomaly detection. Subsequently, methods based on deep neural networks have also become increasingly popular.

There are many traditional methods for time series anomaly detection, such as AR (AutoRegressive), MA (Moving Average), and ARMA (AutoRegressive Moving Average). Autoregressive model (AR) [14] is one of the fundamental models for univariate time series and is a linear model. AR model predicts a variable's future values by regressing on its own past values, assuming that the relationship between past and future values is consistent over time. The anomaly score is determined by the difference between the predicted value and the observed value [15]. The AR model is a classic statistical method used in time series anomaly detection. However, the AR model assumes that the data is stationary, so using AR for time series anomaly detection requires certain data requirements or necessitates necessary data preprocessing. The Moving Average model (MA) and AutoRegressive model (AR) are both linear models, but they differ in that AR uses past observed values as differences, while MA uses past residual errors as differences. The AutoRegressive Moving Average model (ARMA) is a combination of AR and MA and is commonly used for univariate time series.

### 2.2   Methods Based on Machine Learning and Deep Learning

**ML-Based Methods.** Different from statistical methods, the purpose of using machine learning methods for anomaly detection is to make the most accurate predictions or detections by inferring relationships between variables. Currently, there are many popular machine learning anomaly detection methods such as K-Means [16] clustering, Principal Component Analysis (PCA) [17], Isolation Forest, Feature Bagging, and more. K-Means is one of the classical clustering methods used for anomaly detection in machine learning. It calculates the distance between targets based on Euclidean distance [18]. The principle is to divide the sample set into K clusters based on the distances between samples. The goal is to have points within the same cluster as close together as possible and points from different clusters as far apart as possible. Principal Component Analysis (PCA) is a common data analysis technique often used for dimensionality reduction in high-dimensional data. It is also employed for anomaly detection by extracting the main feature components of the data. The primary steps of PCA for anomaly detection involve reducing the dimensions and then calculating the differences between the vectors obtained after dimensionality reduction and the original vectors. Isolation Forest [19] is an anomaly detection algorithm that isolates anomalies by constructing binary trees and measuring the number of steps required to isolate data points from the majority of the dataset.

**DL-Based Methods.** Based on deep learning, various methods have gained significant popularity recently, such as Variational Autoencoders (VAE) [20], Generative Adversarial Networks (GAN) [21–23], Unsupervised Adversarial Training of Autoencoders (USAD) [24], LSTM-based Time Series Anomaly Detection (LSTM-AD), and OmniAnomaly using Random Recursive Neural Networks [25]. The Variational Autoencoder (VAE) compresses input data into a code through an encoder and then decodes the code back into the input through a decoder. Through continuous learning, the output becomes increasingly similar to the input. VAE can learn the latent variables in the data, allowing it to generate entirely new samples rather than simply replicating the input data. The anomaly score of VAE is determined by the difference between the input (original data) and the output (reconstructed data). The primary challenge of VAE is that the generated samples can often be blurry or less precise. This is because the generation process is random, and VAE cannot guarantee that every generated sample is of high quality.

Generative Adversarial Networks (GANs) train the generator and the discriminator in an adversarial manner, ultimately making it difficult for the discriminator to distinguish the data generated by the generator. The challenge of GANs lies in achieving Nash equilibrium during training, where sometimes it can be accomplished using gradient descent, while in other cases, it may be difficult to achieve. The Unsupervised Adversarial Training of Autoencoders (USAD) combines the advantages of both autoencoders (AE) and Generative Adversarial Networks (GAN). It achieves this by continuously training two AE networks in an adversarial manner. Long Short-Term Memory Network for Time Series Anomaly Detection (LSTM-AD) utilizes LSTM, which is a type of Recurrent Neural Network (RNN) architecture. Compared to Convolutional Neural Networks (CNN), data in LSTM flows only forward, making it a type of feedforward neural network. A major issue with RNNs is the problem of vanishing gradients, which LSTM addresses by using gated units. LSTM-AD typically involves making predictions using Long Short-Term Memory (LSTM) networks and then computing the prediction errors to detect anomalies. LSTM can learn time dependencies, but learning long-term dependencies in lengthy time series can be quite challenging. OmniAnomaly employs Random Recursive Networks and flat normalization to generate reconstruction probabilities. This method outperforms many deep learning approaches, but its training time is relatively large.

The application of GNN in time series anomaly detection has been gradually attracting attention as they can capture relationships and dynamic changes between sequences. GNNs can be used to construct time-dependent graph structures and detect anomalous behavior by learning representations of nodes and edges in time series.

Graph Neural Networks (GNN) use network embedding to represent network nodes as low-dimensional vectors while preserving the network topology and node information. They then perform subsequent tasks such as classification, clustering, etc. For instance, Graph Convolutional Networks (GCN) aggregate neighboring nodes' features to represent the node's characteristics. Other classic graph neural networks include Graph Attention Networks (GAT), Spatio-Temporal Graph Convolutional Networks (ST-GCN) [26], and more. GNNs have found significant applications in time series anomaly detection. For instance, the Graph Deviation Network (GDN) [27], based on GAT, has achieved excellent results in anomaly detection for IoT multivariate time series. MTGNN [28], which uses GCN, also exhibits remarkable performance in anomaly detection for multivariate time series.

# 3   Proposed Framework

## 3.1   Architecture

The structure of MTGCN is illustrated in Fig. 2, where both the Student and Teacher models share identical architectures. Initially, input data is divided based on their labeling into labeled and unlabeled data. The training data for the Student model consists of both labeled and unlabeled data, while the Teacher model only receives unlabeled data. The graph structure learning module is trained and updated in conjunction with the training of the Student model, continuously updating the neural network's parameters. For the Student model, the labeled data is processed through multiple layers of Graph Convolutional Networks (GCNs) to obtain output results, which are then compared with the data labels to compute the cross-entropy loss (Cross-Entropy Loss (Crit)). Additionally, the unlabeled data processed by the Student model's GCNs is compared with the unlabeled data processed by the Teacher model's GCNs to compute the mean squared error (Mean Squared Error Loss (MSE)). Finally, the Student model's parameters are optimized based on the combined loss (weighted sum of Crit and MSE), while the Teacher model updates its parameters using the parameters of the Student model.

## 3.2   Graph Structure Learning

Our framework for anomaly detection follows a process where, firstly, the Internet of Things (IoT) dataset is transformed into graph-structured data. Next, we use Graph Convolutional Networks (GCN) to learn the relationships between sensors in this data. Finally, we employ the learned GCN for anomaly detection (Fig. 3).

In GCN, the spatial dependency between nodes is represented by the adjacency matrix A. However, existing methods for constructing an adjacency matrix

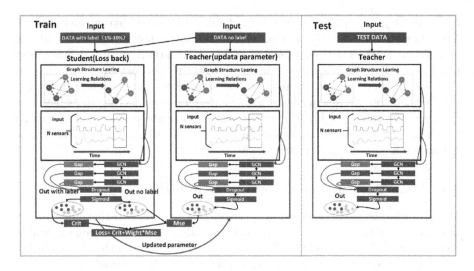

**Fig. 2.** Overview

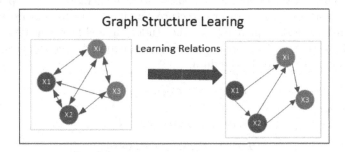

**Fig. 3.** Graph Structure Learning

for a graph typically involve computing the similarity between nodes using distance metrics like Euclidean distance. This approach can be computationally and spatially expensive, especially for large graphs, and the effectiveness of the adjacency matrix constructed through distance computation may not always be optimal. To address these limitations, we propose a neural network-based approach to learn the adjacency matrix [29].

$$M_1 = \tanh\left(Embedding_1\left(Node_n\theta_1\right) * \alpha\right) \tag{1}$$

$$M_2 = \tanh\left(Embedding_2\left(Node_n\theta_2\right) * \alpha\right) \tag{2}$$

$$A = Relu\left(\alpha * \left(M_1 M_2^T - M_2 M_1^T\right)\right) \tag{3}$$

$$For\ i = 1, 2, 3 \cdots n \tag{4}$$

$$I = argtopk\left(A\ [i, :\ ]\right) \tag{5}$$

$$A\left[i, -I\right] = 0 \tag{6}$$

$M_1$ and $M_2$ are matrices with randomly initialized parameters. Where $Embedding_1$ and $Embedding_2$ represent randomly initialized node embeddings, and $Node_n$ represents the number of nodes in the graph. $\theta_1$ and $\theta_2$ are model parameters, and $\alpha$ is a hyperparameter representing network saturation. As the relationships between sensors may not be symmetric, our adjacency matrix is transformed non-symmetrically using Formula 3. $i$ represents the top $i$ edges with the highest selected weights. Finally, we utilize the $argtopk$ operation to sparsify the adjacency matrix, selecting the top K edges with the highest correlations to obtain the final adjacency matrix $A$ [30,31].

### 3.3   Mean Teacher Semi-supervised Learning

Mean Teacher is an effective semi-supervised learning method that fully utilizes unlabeled data to improve model performance. It performs exceptionally well in scenarios with limited labeled data. In our model, we leverage the Mean Teacher semi-supervised approach for training and detection, where a small amount (1%–10%) of training data is labeled. The idea behind Mean Teacher is that the model serves as both a teacher and a student. The teacher model is a replica of the student network with the same architecture, and its parameters are exponentially averaged from the student network. The student model learns using the targets generated by the teacher model, and its parameters are continually updated during training to adapt to the data.

$$Loss_{crit} = Crit\left(S_{X_L}, L\right) \tag{7}$$

$$Loss_{mes} = Mes\left(S_X, T_X\right) \tag{8}$$

$$Loss = Loss_{crit} + \beta Loss_{mes} \tag{9}$$

$$\theta_t' = \alpha\theta_{t-1}' + (1 - \alpha)\theta_t \tag{10}$$

$S_{X_L}$ represents the output of the student model for labeled data, $L$ represents the labels of the labeled data, $S_X$ and $T_X$ represent the outputs of the student and teacher models for unlabeled data, respectively. The specific steps are as follows: input the data, both labeled and unlabeled, into the student model to obtain $S_{X_L}$, $S_X$, and $T_X$ outputs. Calculate the loss terms: $Loss_{crit}$ and $Loss_{mes}$ [32]. Finally, update the parameters of the student model based on the combined loss using Formula 9. Then, use formula 10 to update the parameters of the teacher model, leveraging the parameters of the updated student model.

## 4   Experiments

### 4.1   Datasets

In this paper, we utilized two sensor datasets based on a water treatment physical testbed system: SWat (Secure Water Treatment) and WADI (Water Distribution). In both datasets, operators simulated scenarios where real-world water treatment plants were subjected to attacks, and the recorded anomalies represent genuine occurrences. The SWat dataset originates from a water treatment testbed coordinated by the Public Utilities Board of Singapore (Mathur and Tippenhauer [33]). It consists of six interlinked processes, forming a representation of a small-scale IoT system mirroring real-world scenarios. In this study, the SWat dataset comprises data from 51 sensors, with anomalies accounting for 12.2% of the data. On the other hand, the WADI dataset is an extension of SWat, consisting of data from 127 sensors in total.

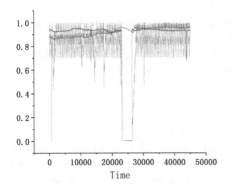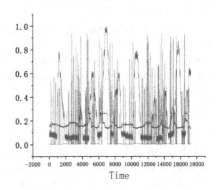

**Fig. 4.** The left (a) shows the feature representation of the WADI dataset, and the right (b) shows the feature representation of the SWaT dataset.

Figure 4 depict the feature representations of the two datasets, revealing significant differences in the feature distributions between them (Table 1).

**Table 1.** Datasets

| Datasets | Features | Train | Test | Anomaly Rate |
|----------|----------|-------|------|--------------|
| SWaT | 51 | 36000 | 8992 | 12.2% |
| WADI | 127 | 13824 | 3456 | 5.76% |

The types of anomalies in time series data mainly include point anomalies, contextual anomalies, long-term trend anomalies, seasonal anomalies, cyclic anomalies, and so on. This paper focuses on the detection of point anomalies. Point anomalies are one of the most common anomaly types in time series data and are typically caused by sudden, unusual events, or errors. Point anomalies can lead to one or more data points deviating significantly from the normal data pattern. These anomalies can have a significant impact on businesses or systems, so timely detection and handling are essential.

## 4.2   Evaluation Metrics

We adopt widely-used precision (Prec), recall (Rec), and F1-Score (F1) as the evaluation metrics for our experiments.

## 4.3   Experimental Setup

We implement our method in PyTorch version 1.13 with CUDA 11.6 and PyTorch Geometric Library version 2.2.0, and train them on a server with AMD Ryzen 7 5800H with Radeon Graphics @ 3.20 GHz and NVIDIA RTX 3070 graphics cards.

We compared machine learning and deep learning methods in our study. For machine learning, the methods included K-Means and PCA. As for deep learning, the compared methods were VAE, USAD, LSTM-AD, MAD-GAN, and OmniAnomaly based on Random Recursive Neural Network.

## 4.4   Experimental Studies

"MTGCN-0.1", "MTGCN-0.08"... in Tables 2 and 3 respectively represent the MTGCN model at different data annotation rates, with bold numbers indicating the maximum value in that column. In the SWaT dataset, the highest F1 score is achieved by MTGCN with a 10% data annotation rate, reaching 87.8%. The highest Recall (Rec) score is attained by OmniAnomaly, reaching 99.9%, while the highest Precision (Prec) score is achieved by MTGCN with a 1% data annotation rate, reaching 99.8%. In Table 3, with a 10% data annotation rate, MTGCN achieves a 77.9% F1 score. The highest Recall scores are obtained by LSTM_AD and USAD, reaching 8%. The highest Precision score is achieved by MTGCN with a 10% data annotation rate, reaching 82%.

## 4.5   Result Analysis

Tables 2 and 3 provide the precision (Prec), recall (Rec), and F1-Score (F1) of the MTGCN and baseline models on the SWaT dataset and WADI dataset. All the baseline models and MTGCN perform worse on the WADI dataset compared to the SWaT dataset. We compared classical machine learning methods and deep learning methods, where the machine learning methods included K-Means, PCA, and FeB, while the deep learning methods consisted of VAE, USAD, MAD GAN, OmniAnomaly, and LSTM AD.

MTGCN achieves significantly higher F1-Scores (F1) at 10% data labeling rate on both datasets compared to the state-of-the-art baseline models. Among the baseline models, USAD performs the best on both datasets, achieving an F1 of 0.812 on the SWaT dataset and an F1 of 0.634 on the WADI dataset. MTGCN outperforms the state-of-the-art baseline models by 8.1% on the SWaT dataset and 22.8% on the WADI dataset at 10% data labeling rate. Furthermore, MTGCN's performance on the SWaT dataset is 2.2% higher than the state-of-the-art baseline models at a 4% data labeling rate, and on the WADI dataset, it is 4.2% higher at a 5% data labeling rate.

**Table 2.** Experimental Results on the SWaT Dataset.

| Data | Method | Rec | F1 | Prec |
|------|--------|-----|-----|------|
| SWat | K-Means | 0.495 | 0.373 | 0.3 |
| | PCA | 0.445 | 0.318 | 0.247 |
| | FeB | 0.19 | 0.153 | 0.128 |
| | VAE | 0.475 | 0.335 | 0.259 |
| | USAD | 0.915 | 0.812 | 0.73 |
| | MAD_GAN | 0.764 | 0.674 | 0.602 |
| | OmniAnomaly | **0.999** | 0.806 | 0.675 |
| | LSTM_AD | 0.764 | 0.676 | 0.606 |
| | MTGCN-0.1 | 0.837 | **0.878** | 0.923 |
| | MTGCN-0.08 | 0.781 | 0.832 | 0.891 |
| | MTGCN-0.06 | 0.773 | 0.839 | 0.918 |
| | MTGCN-0.05 | 0.764 | 0.828 | 0.904 |
| | MTGCN-0.04 | 0.775 | 0.83 | 0.893 |
| | MTGCN-0.02 | 0.684 | 0.767 | 0.876 |
| | MTGCN-0.01 | 0.583 | 0.733 | **0.988** |

**Table 3.** Experimental Results on the WADI Dataset.

| Data | Method | Rec | F1 | Prec |
|------|--------|-----|-----|------|
| WADI | K-Means | 0.495 | 0.373 | 0.3 |
| | PCA | 0.445 | 0.318 | 0.247 |
| | FB | 0.19 | 0.153 | 0.128 |
| | VAE | 0.475 | 0.335 | 0.259 |
| | USAD | **0.81** | 0.634 | 0.519 |
| | MAD_GAN | 0.584 | 0.549 | 0.519 |
| | OmniAnomaly | 0.615 | 0.565 | 0.522 |
| | LSTM_AD | **0.81** | 0.525 | 0.388 |
| | MTGCN-0.1 | 0.744 | **0.779** | **0.82** |
| | MTGCN-0.08 | 0.68 | 0.72 | 0.767 |
| | MTGCN-0.06 | 0.648 | 0.693 | 0.748 |
| | MTGCN-0.05 | 0.625 | 0.661 | 0.705 |
| | MTGCN-0.04 | 0.433 | 0.545 | 0.739 |
| | MTGCN-0.02 | 0.295 | 0.412 | 0.7 |
| | MTGCN-0.01 | 0.288 | 0.367 | 0.518 |

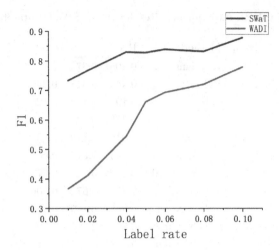

**Fig. 5.** MTGCN performance on two datasets.

Figure 5 displays the experimental results of MTGCN on the SWaT dataset and WADI dataset at different data labeling rates. Overall, the F1 scores of MTGCN on both datasets decrease as the data labeling rate decreases. Notably, MTGCN performs better on the SWaT dataset compared to the WADI dataset. This suggests that MTGCN is more effective in utilizing labeled data on the SWaT dataset, resulting in higher F1 scores, even as the amount of labeled data decreases. However, on the WADI dataset, MTGCN's performance suffers more when the data labeling rate is reduced. This difference in performance between the two datasets indicates that the characteristics and challenges of the datasets may play a role in influencing MTGCN's effectiveness under limited labeled data conditions.

From Fig. 6, Among the various models evaluated on the SWat dataset, we observe that MTGCN consistently demonstrates strong performance across different levels of data annotation, with F1 scores ranging from 0.878 at a 10% annotation rate to 0.733 at a 1% annotation rate. This consistent high performance suggests that MTGCN is particularly robust and effective in anomaly detection tasks with varying levels of labeled data. The decreasing trend in F1 score as the annotation rate decreases is less pronounced for MTGCN compared to other models in the list. This indicates that MTGCN has a notable advantage in handling scenarios with limited labeled data, making it a promising choice for anomaly detection tasks in real-world situations where labeled data may be scarce or expensive to obtain.

Figure 7 illustrates the comparison between MTGCN and the baseline models on the WADI dataset. From Fig. 7, it can be observed that at a data labeling rate of 5%, MTGCN outperforms all baseline models. Additionally, at a data labeling rate of 4%, MTGCN's performance is only surpassed by the USAD, MAD_GAN, and OmniAnomaly baseline models.

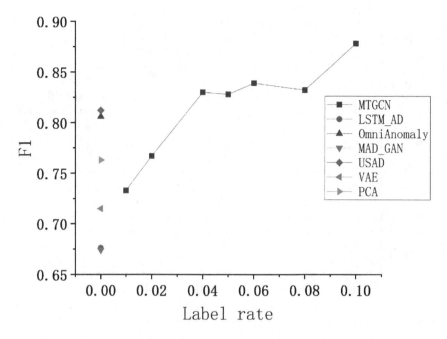

**Fig. 6.** Comparison of MTGCN on SWaT data set and baseline model.

## 4.6 Ablation Study

To validate the effectiveness of Graph Structure Learning (GSL), we conducted ablation experiments and observed the changes in F1 scores on both datasets (Fig. 8).

**Table 4.** Results of GSL ablation experiments on SWaT datasets.

| label | 0.1 | 0.08 | 0.06 | 0.05 | 0.04 | 0.02 | 0.01 |
|-------|-----|------|------|------|------|------|------|
| MTGCN + GSL | 0.878 | 0.832 | 0.839 | 0.828 | 0.83 | 0.767 | 0.733 |
| MTGCN | 0.869 | 0.836 | 0.821 | 0.806 | 0.82 | 0.763 | 0.732 |

From the data analysis in Table 4, it can be concluded that MTGCN, when using Graph Structure Learning (GSL), shows an average performance improvement of 1% on the SWaT dataset across all data labeling rates. The highest performance improvement, reaching up to 2.7%, is observed when the data labeling rate is 5%. From the data analysis in Table 5, it can be concluded that MTGCN, when using Graph Structure Learning (GSL), exhibits an average performance improvement of 4.5% on the WADI dataset across all data labeling rates. The highest performance improvement, reaching up to 8.7%, is observed when the data labeling rate is 5%.

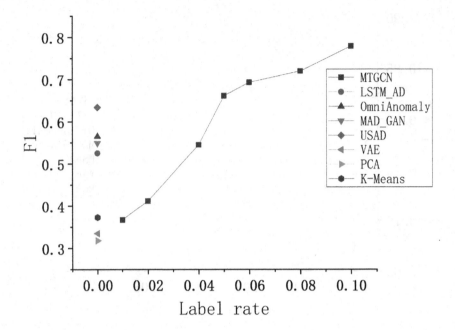

**Fig. 7.** Comparison of MTGCN on WADI data set and baseline model.

**Table 5.** Results of GSL ablation experiments on WADI datasets.

| label | 0.1 | 0.08 | 0.06 | 0.05 | 0.04 | 0.02 | 0.01 |
|---|---|---|---|---|---|---|---|
| MTGCN + GSL | 0.779 | 0.72 | 0.693 | 0.661 | 0.545 | 0.412 | 0.367 |
| MTGCN | 0.77 | 0.718 | 0.669 | 0.608 | 0.511 | 0.347 | 0.35 |

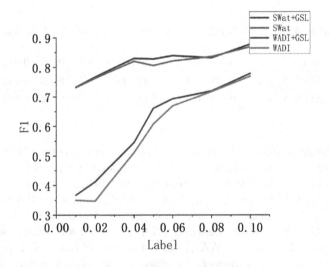

**Fig. 8.** Comparison of Ablation Experiments for GSL Learning on Two Datasets.

## 5    Conclusion and Future Work

MTGCN has demonstrated its effectiveness in anomaly detection on both the SWaT dataset and WADI dataset. Through a series of experiments and analyses, the introduction of Graph Structure Learning (GSL) in the MTGCN model has shown significant benefits. On the SWaT dataset, MTGCN outperforms all baseline models at a data labeling rate of 4%. Notably, at a lower data labeling rate of 2%, MTGCN's performance is only surpassed by the USAD and OmniAnomaly baseline models. The experimental results reveal that MTGCN effectively leverages the Graph Structure Learning (GSL) component, resulting in an average performance improvement of 1% on the SWaT dataset across all data labeling rates. The maximum performance gain of 2.7% is achieved at a data labeling rate of 5%. This indicates that the introduction of graph structure information significantly enhances MTGCN's anomaly detection capabilities on the SWaT dataset. Similarly, on the WADI dataset, MTGCN exhibits significant performance improvements with the inclusion of Graph Structure Learning (GSL). With an average performance gain of 4.5% across all data labeling rates, MTGCN consistently outperforms the baseline models. At a data labeling rate of 5%, MTGCN achieves its highest performance boost of 8.7%, demonstrating its superiority over the baseline methods. These findings emphasize the importance of Graph Structure Learning (GSL) in enhancing MTGCN's anomaly detection capabilities on both datasets. MTGCN effectively utilizes graph structure information, enabling it to adapt and excel even with limited labeled data, making it a competitive and effective approach in practical anomaly detection scenarios. The experimental results validate MTGCN's superiority over baseline models and underscore the significant role of Graph Structure Learning (GSL) in improving anomaly detection performance, establishing MTGCN as a competitive and effective method in anomaly detection research.

In future research, we intend to attempt more datasets and explore alternative methods to adapt to Mean Teachers

## References

1. Pang, G., et al.: Deep learning for anomaly detection: a review. ACM Comput. Surv. (CSUR) **54**(2), 1–38 (2021)
2. Sharma, B., Sharma, L., Lal, C.: Anomaly detection techniques using deep learning in IoT: a survey. In: 2019 International Conference on Computational Intelligence and Knowledge Economy (ICCIKE), pp. 146–149. IEEE (2019)
3. Chen, P., et al.: A probabilistic model for performance analysis of cloud infrastructures. Concurr. Comput. Pract. Exp. **27**(17), 4784–4796 (2015)
4. Pan, Y., et al.: A novel approach to scheduling workflows upon cloud resources with fluctuating performance. Mob. Netw. Appl. **25**, 690–700 (2020)
5. Tukey, J.W.: Exploratory Data Analysis, vol. 2 (1977)
6. van den Oord, A., et al.: WaveNet: a generative model for raw audio. arXiv preprint arXiv:1609.03499 (2016)

7. Filonov, P., Lavrentyev, A., Vorontsov, A.: Multivariate industrial time series with cyber-attack simulation: fault detection using an LSTM-based predictive data model. arXiv preprint arXiv:1612.06676 (2016)
8. Bodin, E., et al.: Nonparametric inference for auto-encoding variational Bayes. arXiv preprint arXiv:1712.06536 (2017)
9. Goodfellow, I., et al.: Generative adversarial networks. Commun. ACM **63**(11), 139–144 (2020)
10. Kipf, T.N., Welling, M.: Semi-supervised classification with graph convolutional networks. arXiv preprint arXiv:1609.02907 (2016)
11. Veličković, P., et al.: Graph attention networks. arXiv preprint arXiv:1710.10903 (2017)
12. Tarvainen, A., Valpola, H.: Mean teachers are better role models: Weight-averaged consistency targets improve semi-supervised deep learning results. In: Advances in Neural Information Processing Systems, vol. 30 (2017)
13. Braei, M., Wagner, S.: Anomaly detection in univariate time-series: a survey on the state-of-the-art. arXiv preprint arXiv:2004.00433 (2020)
14. Bali, T.G., Mo, H., Tang, Y.: The role of autoregressive conditional skewness and kurtosis in the estimation of conditional VaR. J. Bank. Financ. **32**(2), 269–282 (2008)
15. Chandola, V.: Anomaly detection for symbolic sequences and time series data. University of Minnesota (2009)
16. Angiulli, F., Pizzuti, C.: Fast outlier detection in high dimensional spaces. In: Elomaa, T., Mannila, H., Toivonen, H. (eds.) PKDD 2002. LNCS, vol. 2431, pp. 15–27. Springer, Heidelberg (2002). https://doi.org/10.1007/3-540-45681-3_2
17. Shyu, M.-L., et al.: A novel anomaly detection scheme based on principal component classifier. In: Proceedings of the IEEE Foundations and New Directions of Data Mining Workshop, pp. 172–179. IEEE Press (2003)
18. Li, Y., et al.: Diffusion convolutional recurrent neural network: data-driven traffic forecasting. arXiv preprint arXiv:1707.01926 (2017)
19. Liu, F.T., Ting, K.M., Zhou, Z.-H.: Isolation forest. In: 2008 Eighth IEEE International Conference on Data Mining. IEEE (2008)
20. Kingma, D.P., Welling, M.: Auto-encoding variational Bayes. arXiv preprint arXiv:1312.6114 (2013)
21. Li, D., Chen, D., Jin, B., Shi, L., Goh, J., Ng, S.-K.: MAD-GAN: multivariate anomaly detection for time series data with generative adversarial networks. In: Tetko, I.V., Kůrková, V., Karpov, P., Theis, F. (eds.) ICANN 2019. LNCS, vol. 11730, pp. 703–716. Springer, Cham (2019). https://doi.org/10.1007/978-3-030-30490-4_56
22. Chen, P., et al.: Effectively detecting operational anomalies in large-scale IoT data infrastructures by using a GAN-based predictive model. Comput. J. **65**(11), 2909–2925 (2022)
23. Qi, S., et al.: An efficient GAN-based predictive framework for multivariate time series anomaly prediction in cloud data centers. J. Supercomput. **80**, 1–26 (2023)
24. Audibert, J., et al.: USAD: unsupervised anomaly detection on multivariate time series. In: Proceedings of the 26th ACM SIGKDD International Conference on Knowledge Discovery & Data Mining, pp. 3395–3404 (2020)
25. Su, Y., et al.: Robust anomaly detection for multivariate time series through stochastic recurrent neural network. In: Proceedings of the 25th ACM SIGKDD International Conference on Knowledge Discovery & Data Mining, pp. 2828–2837 (2019)

26. Nicolicioiu, A., Duta, I., Leordeanu, M.: Recurrent space-time graph neural networks. In: Advances in Neural Information Processing Systems, vol. 32 (2019)
27. Deng, A., Hooi, B.: Graph neural network-based anomaly detection in multivariate time series. In: Proceedings of the AAAI Conference on Artificial Intelligence, vol. 35, no. 5 (2021)
28. Wu, Z., et al.: Connecting the dots: multivariate time series forecasting with graph neural networks. In: Proceedings of the 26th ACM SIGKDD International Conference on Knowledge Discovery & Data Mining, pp. 753–763 (2020)
29. Hamilton, W., Ying, Z., Leskovec, J.: Inductive representation learning on large graphs. In: Advances in neural Information Processing Systems, vol. 30 (2017)
30. Liu, Z., et al.: Rethinking the value of network pruning. arXiv preprint arXiv:1810.05270 (2018)
31. Vu, Q.H., et al.: A graph method for keyword-based selection of the top-k databases. In: Proceedings of the 2008 ACM SIGMOD International Conference on Management of Data, pp. 915–926 (2008)
32. Klinker, F.: Exponential moving average versus moving exponential average. Math. Semesterber. **58**, 97–107 (2011)
33. Mathur, A.P., Tippenhauer, N.O.: SWaT: a water treatment testbed for research and training on ICS security. In: 2016 International Workshop on Cyber-Physical Systems for Smart Water Networks (CySWater), pp. 31–36. IEEE (2016)

# Structural Adversarial Attack for Code Representation Models

Yuxin Zhang⬤, Ruoting Wu⬤, Jie Liao⬤, and Liang Chen⁽⊠⁾⬤

School of Computer Science, Sun Yat-sen University, Guangzhou, China
{zhangyx355,wurt8,liaoj27}@mail2.sysu.edu.cn, chenliang6@mail.sysu.edu.cn

**Abstract.** As code intelligence and collaborative computing advances, code representation models (CRMs) have demonstrated exceptional performance in tasks such as code prediction and collaborative code development by leveraging distributed computing resources and shared datasets. Nonetheless, CRMs are often considered unreliable due to their vulnerability to adversarial attacks, failing to make correct predictions when faced with inputs containing perturbations. Several adversarial attack methods have been proposed to evaluate the robustness of CRMs and ensure their reliable in application. However, these methods rely primarily on code's textual features, without fully exploiting its crucial structural features. To address this limitation, we propose STRUCK, a novel adversarial attack method that thoroughly exploits code's structural features. The key idea of STRUCK lies in integrating multiple global and local perturbation methods and effectively selecting them by leveraging the structural features of the input code during the generation of adversarial examples for CRMs. We conduct comprehensive evaluations of seven basic or advanced CRMs using two prevalent code classification tasks, demonstrating STRUCK's effectiveness, efficiency, and imperceptibility. Finally, we show that STRUCK enables a more precise assessment of CRMs' robustness and increases their resistance to structural attacks through adversarial training.

**Keywords:** Code Intelligence · Model Robustness · Code Representation Model · Adversarial Attack

## 1 Introduction

Recently, the integration of collaborative computing and artificial intelligence has facilitated the development of distributed deep learning (DL) training methods [5]. These methods leverage the power of multiple computing devices to train DL models, enabling the continuous expansion of model sizes and the enhancement of computational capabilities. Consequently, these models have demonstrated powerful data processing, analysis, and learning capabilities across various fields, including computer vision, natural language processing, and graphical data analysis [10,21,41]. Code intelligence field is also growing quickly as more

© ICST Institute for Computer Sciences, Social Informatics and Telecommunications Engineering 2024
Published by Springer Nature Switzerland AG 2024. All Rights Reserved
H. Gao et al. (Eds.): CollaborateCom 2023, LNICST 562, pp. 392–413, 2024.
https://doi.org/10.1007/978-3-031-54528-3_22

and more DL models benefiting from collaborative computing have been applied to various tasks such as source code processing and collaborative code development [14]. To further enhance the productivity of programmers in collaborative software development on platforms such as GitHub, numerous tools utilizing DL models have emerged, with typical examples including Copilot[1] and ChatGPT[2]. However, the widespread application of DL models in the code intelligence field faces a potential crisis due to their lack of robustness. Different programming styles and intentional modifications can result in the generation of adversarial example ($x_{adv}$) with the same semantics as the original code ($x$). Even the state-of-the-art (SOTA) DL models may produce completely inconsistent results for $x$ and $x_{adv}$ [24]. This lack of robustness, especially in security-sensitive tasks like malicious code classification [28], can lead to severe consequences, including system crashes. Furthermore, this issue hinders the development of deep learning models integrated with collaborative computing in the field of code intelligence.

The issue of non-robustness in DL models has received significant attention across various domains [6,19,20,32]. Researchers within the code intelligence field also recognize the importance of evaluating and improving models' robustness. To assess the robustness of DL models in code intelligence field, several adversarial attack methods against CRMs have been proposed [34–37]. However, most of them draw inspiration from the attack methods in NLP filed by renaming variable names in the code to obtain adversarial examples. For example, MHM [37] generates $x_{adv}$ by performing iterative variable name renaming based on Metropolis-Hastings sampling. We argue that these methods focus solely on textual features and overlook the crucial structural features of the code.

As a structured language, code's structural features contain a wealth of semantic information, rendering them an essential component for learning and comprehending code. These features can be obtained from code's structured representation, such as abstract syntax trees (AST) and data flow graphs (DFG). An increasing number of CRMs use the structural features of code to learn its semantics and thus improve the performance in downstream tasks [31]. It is necessary to consider the structural features of code when designing the attack methods for CRMs. While methods such as S-CARROT$_A$ [36] and CLONEGEN [40] attempt to generate adversarial examples using code's structural features, they have not yet fully exploited these structural characteristics. This results in limitations in accurately assessing model robustness and generating naturally adversarial examples. The substantial potential to utilize code structure for devising potent adversarial attacks against CRMs merits further academic exploration.

To compensate for the lack of prior attack methods that insufficiently exploit structural features of code and to further explore the potential of these features in developing attack methods, we present STRUCK (**Struct**ural adversarial atta**ck**). STRUCK is an attack method that uniquely capitalizes on the structural features of code. As a non-targeted, black-box attack method, it solely utilizes the original inputs and outputs of target models during the attack process.

---

[1] https://github.com/features/copilot.

[2] https://openai.com/blog/chatgpt.

By thoroughly leveraging the structural features of code, STRUCK facilitates a more accurate evaluation of the robustness of CRMs compared to previous non-targeted, black-box attack methods.

Inspired by research in graph attack [9] and considering the hierarchical structural features of code, STRUCK incorporates two perturbation levels: global (STRUCK$_G$) and local (STRUCK$_L$). Each perturbation level contains multiple perturbation methods. Similar to graph attack methods that modify connected edges in graph data, the perturbation methods in STRUCK$_G$ perturb the code's structural features at the global level by refactoring the code. Furthermore, similar to the graph attack methods which add dummy nodes and corresponding connected edges to the graph data, the perturbation methods in STRUCK$_L$ perturb the structural features of the code at the local level by adding code statements of different sizes to insertable positions.

To demonstrate the performance of STRUCK, we conduct a comprehensive evaluation of two representative source code classification tasks: functionality classification and defect prediction. Three categories of CRMs are assessed in the evaluation process: traditional sequential models (LSTM, GRU), classical structural models (GGNN [4], GCN [18]), and high-performing pre-trained models (CodeBERT [11], GraphCodeBERT [15], UniXcoder [14]). The experimental results demonstrate that STRUCK can effectively generate adversarial examples. Specifically, it induces an average relative performance degradation of 82.9% and 99.92% in functionality classification and defect prediction tasks respectively for target models, outperforming advanced adversarial attack methods such as MHM [37], S-CARROT$_A$ [36] and CLONEGEN [40]. Meanwhile, the average number of model invocations by STRUCK is only half of MHM's, indicating a more efficient generation of adversarial examples. Moreover, STRUCK demonstrates a lower average perturbation size (52) compared to S-CARROT$_A$ (55) and CLONEGEN (140) which also leverage code structural features. Our user study confirms that from programmers' perspective, STRUCK exhibits superior imperceptibility, rendering the generated adversarial examples more natural compared to those generated by S-CARROT$_A$ and CLONEGEN. Furthermore, we investigate the value of STRUCK for CRMs' robustness assessment and enhancement. The results reveal that STRUCK accurately evaluates the model's robustness and effectively improves its robustness against structural attacks through adversarial training. The contributions of this paper are summarized as follows:

1. We highlight the idea of fully utilizing the structural features of code to perform attacks on CRMs.
2. We propose an adversarial attack method (STRUCK) for CRMs. It comprehensively explores and exploits the structural features of code, integrating multiple perturbation methods to generate adversarial examples.
3. Extensive experiments demonstrate that STRUCK is superior in terms of its efficacy, efficiency, and imperceptibility when attacking CRMs.
4. We have demonstrated that STRUCK can accurately evaluate the robustness of CRMs and enhance their robustness to structural attacks via adversarial training, thereby improving their reliability.

# 2    Preliminary

## 2.1    Definitions for Codes

**Semantic Equivalence of Codes.** $x$ and $x'$ are considered semantically equivalent if $x$ can be transformed into $x'$ through a series of equivalence transformations. We use $F(x, k)$ to represent the result of applying $k$ equivalent transformations to $x$ and if $x' = F(x, k)$, $x$ and $x'$ are considered semantically equivalent.

$$F(x, i) = T(F(x, i - 1), t_i), i = \{1, 2, \ldots, k\} \tag{1}$$

with the initial condition $F(x, 0) = x$ and the constraint that $t_i \in T(x_{i-1})$. Here, $T(x)$ is a subset of all equivalence transformation types $T$, denoting the set of valid equivalence transformation types that can be applied to $x$. $T(x, t)$ represent the result of transforming $x$ using $t \in T(x)$.

**Code Distance.** We represent the differences between two semantically equivalent codes using the code distance $D(x, x')$, which measures the number of distinct tokens between them. For a transformation $t \in T(x)$, we denote its effect on $x$ as $d(x, t)$.The value of $d(t, x)$ is jointly determined by $t$ and $x$, representing the number of tokens changed, added, or deleted in $x$. Letting $x_0 = x$, we can obtain the following relationship:

$$D(x, x') = D(x, F(x, k)) \le \sum_{i=1}^{k} d(x_{i-1}, t_i). \tag{2}$$

$D(x, x')$ is bounded by the accumulated sum of the effects of $k$ equivalent transformations, as some transformations may counteract the changes introduced by previous ones. We can assume that the smaller the effects of the used equivalence transformations, the smaller the value of $D(x, x')$.

## 2.2    Code Representation

**Code Graph** is a significant structured representation of code based on AST and DFG, comprising essential structural information such as function calls and semantic flow. The left of Fig. 1 shows an example of converting a code snippet from text to graph representation, following the approach proposed by Allamanis et al. [4]. In the code graph, nodes serve as fundamental units that connect through various types of edges, such as Child Edges derived from the AST of code, to form subgraphs. Each subgraph corresponds to a unique statement or functional module in the code snippet. The combination of all these subgraphs results in the formation of the complete code graph.

**Code representation model (CRM)**, denoted as $R$, can map code snippets into low-dimensional dense real-valued vectors, which can be understood by other models. Learning code semantics through $R$ is essential for performing various downstream tasks. Different $R$ has distinct input format requirements and

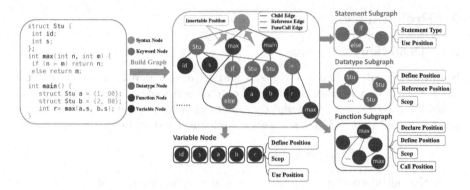

**Fig. 1.** Left: Conversion of C code to a graph representation. Right: Extraction of code graph structural information using *Extract*.

uses different code features [31]. Sequential models [2] leverage textual features to comprehend the semantics of code sequences, while structural models [4] learn from structured representations of code, such as AST, DFG, and code graphs.

**Code classification task** we focused on is a fundamental task that aims to predict the type of a given code. This task relies on a labeled code dataset $\mathcal{D} = \{(x_i, y_i)\}_{i=1}^{N}$. We use $\mathcal{D}_{\text{train}}/\mathcal{D}_{\text{dev}}/\mathcal{D}_{\text{test}}$ to respectively denote the train/valid/test set used, and $(x, y)$ represents a code-label pair. Code classification model $(M = R \mid C)$ is obtained by combining $R$ with a classifier $(C)$. The $C$ takes the code representation vector $(r = R(x))$ as input and outputs the prediction type of $x$.

### 2.3  Adversarial Learning

**Adversarial attack** aims to mislead DL models by generating adversarial examples through minute input perturbations, leading to unexpected outcomes. A trained model $(M)$ that excels at the downstream classification task can correctly identify $x$ as $y$ $(y = M(x))$. A successful attack obtains $x_{adv}$ by perturbing $x$ so that $y =\neq M(x_{adv})$, thereby misleading $M$. We call $M$ the target model of attack, and name $x$ and $x_{adv}$ the original and adversarial example, respectively.

Given the significant impact of adversarial attacks on the deployment of DL models, a variety of attack methods have been proposed [3,39]. Attack methods can be classified into targeted and non-targeted types depending on if they have a specific target or not. We focus on the non-targeted attack, which we consider as the foundation for targeted attacks. Based on the accessibility of information related to the target model, attack methods also can be classified into white-box, gray-box, and black-box [33]. In white-box configurations, attackers have access to all target model parameters. Black-box settings limit attackers to model outputs. Gray-box settings are between the two. DL models are frequently remotely deployed, attackers can only access models through API to call them and receive the outputs. So we focus on the more practical black-box type.

We use $\mathcal{A}((x,y)|M,\delta)$ [7] to denote the set of all non-targeted adversarial examples of the $(x,y)$ that mislead $M$ under the restriction of perturbation $\delta$.

$$\mathcal{A}((x,y)|M,\delta) = \{x_{adv} \mid M(x_{adv}) \neq M(x) \wedge D(x,x_{adv}) < \delta\}. \tag{3}$$

We focus on $(x,y)$ satisfies $M(x) = y$. Simultaneously, we employ the distance between $x$ and $x_{adv}$ ($D(x,x_{adv})$) to measure the perturbation size (**Psize**) generated by attackers during the generation of $x_{adv}$, considering only the adversarial examples produced under the perturbation size constraint $\delta$ as valid.

**Model Robustness.** A robust DL model's outputs should remain unchanged after input perturbations. $Rob.(M|(x,y))$ [36] indicates if $M$ is robust to $(x,y)$.

$$Rob.(M \mid (x,y)) = \begin{cases} 1, & \text{If } \mathcal{A}((x,y)|M,\delta) = \varnothing, \\ 0, & \text{Otherwise.} \end{cases} \tag{4}$$

The model is robust to $(x,y)$ when $Rob.(M \mid (x,y)) = 1$, indicating that attackers cannot use $(x,y)$ to generate $x_{adv}$ that mislead $M$. Further, we denote by $Rob._{adv}(M|(x,y)) = 1$ that the attacker $adv$ cannot generate $x_{adv}$ for $M$ using $(x,y)$. We count the examples in $\mathcal{D}$ for which the model is robust and use the proportion of robust examples to measure the model's robustness.

$$Rob.(M \mid \mathcal{D}) = \frac{\sum_{(x,y) \in \mathcal{D}_M} Rob.(M \mid (x,y))}{|\mathcal{D}_M|}, \tag{5}$$

where $\mathcal{D}_M = \{(x,y)|M(x) = y\}$. We estimate DL models' robustness using different attack methods. $Rob._{adv}(M \mid \mathcal{D})$ gives the proportion of examples with $Rob._{adv}(M|(x,y)) = 1$ in $\mathcal{D}_M$. And $M$'s robustness cannot exceed this proportion, i.e. $Rob.(M \mid \mathcal{D}) \leq Rob._{adv}(M \mid \mathcal{D})$. The precision of assessing $M$'s robustness correlates positively with the effectiveness of the attack methods used.

**Adversarial training** is an efficient way to boost DL models' robustness. It first update $\mathcal{D}_{\text{train}}$ with adversarial examples generated by $adv$ for $M$ to obtain $\mathcal{D}_{\text{adv}}$, then train $M$ from scratch with $\mathcal{D}_{\text{adv}}$. In general, $M$ achieves somewhat improved robustness against $adv$ after adversarial training [37].

## 3    Present Work: STRUCK

In this section, we first give an overview of STRUCK Subsect. (3.1), followed by the introduction of the extracted **structural information** (*codeinfo*) from codes by STRUCK Subsect. (3.2). Subsequently, we provide a detailed exposition of the equivalent perturbation methods at the global Subsect. (3.3) and local Subsect. (3.4) levels. Finally, we will go over the *controller* used by STRUCK during the attack in detail Subsect. (3.5).

## 3.1   Overview

STRUCK is a non-targeted, black-box attack method that generates adversarial examples by fully utilizing the structural features of original examples. Algorithm 1 gives the specific operation for $M$ using $(x, y)$, while Fig. 2 illustrates a single iteration of the process, which can aid in understanding the algorithm.

Before starting an iterative attack, preparations are needed (Line 1–4). STRUCK extracts the *codeinfo* from $x$ and obtains the Psize limitation $\delta$. The $\delta$ is based on the number of $x$'s tokens and $\alpha$ (perturbation limitations factor). STRUCK then initializes the *controller* to select the perturbation methods.

---

**Algorithm 1: STRUCK Algorithm.**

**Input:**
Target Model $M$, Code-label pair $(x, y)$, s.t. $y = M(x)$;
Max attack iteration $m$, Max candidate number $n$, Perturbation limitations factor $\alpha$.
**Output:**
Adversarial example $x_{adv} \in \mathcal{A}((x, y) \mid M, \delta)$, or None.

1  $x_0 = x$, $prob = \mathrm{Prob}(x, y; M)$;
2  $codeinfo = Extract(x)$;
3  $\delta = codeinfo.nums \times \alpha$;
4  $controller = Controller(codeinfo, m)$;
5  **for** $i$ **in** $\{0, 1, \cdots, m-1\}$ **do**
6  $\quad$ $t_{adv} = controller.choose(codeinfo, i, \delta)$;
7  $\quad$ **if** $t_{adv}$ **is** $\varnothing$ **then**
8  $\quad\quad$ | $\quad$ return None;// Fail
9  $\quad$ **end**
10 $\quad$ $\{x'_{i,1}, \cdots, x'_{i,n}\} = t_{adv}(x_i, codeinfo, n, \delta)$;
11 $\quad$ **for** $j$ **in** $\{1, 2, \cdots, n\}$ **do**
12 $\quad\quad$ **if** $x'_{i,j}$ **in** $\mathcal{A}((x, y) \mid M, \delta)$ **then**
13 $\quad\quad\quad$ | $\quad$ return $x'_{i,j}$;// Success
14 $\quad\quad$ **end**
15 $\quad$ **end**
16 $\quad$ $ind = min\ \mathrm{Prob}(\{x'_{i,1}, \cdots, x'_{i-1,n}\}, y; M)$;
17 $\quad$ $prob_{ind} = \mathrm{Prob}(x'_{i,ind}, y; M)$;
18 $\quad$ **if** $prob_{ind} < prob$ **then**
19 $\quad\quad$ $x_{i+1} = x'_{i,ind}$;
20 $\quad\quad$ $prob = prob_{ind}$;
21 $\quad\quad$ $codeinfo = Extract(x'_{i,ind})$;
22 $\quad\quad$ $\delta = \delta - D(x_i, x'_{i,ind})$;
23 $\quad$ **else**
24 $\quad\quad$ | $\quad$ $x_{i+1} = x_i$;
25 $\quad$ **end**
26 $\quad$ $controller.update(t_{adv})$;
27 **end**
28 return None;// Fail

---

In Algorithm 1 (also see Fig. 2), at each iteration, STRUCK first utilizes the *controller* to choose the equivalent perturbation method $t_{adv}$. Then the selected $t_{adv}$ uses *codeinfo* to generate $n$ candidate examples ($\mathcal{S} = \{x'_{i,1}, \cdots, x'_{i,n}\}$) for the current code snippet $x_i$, and $\forall x' \in \mathcal{S}$ satisfies $D(x_i, x') < \delta$. Next, STRUCK tests $\mathcal{S}$, if $\mathcal{R} = \mathcal{S} \cap \mathcal{A}((x, y) \mid M, \delta) \neq \varnothing$, the attack process will be completed, and $\forall x' \in \mathcal{R}$ is an adversarial example for $M$. Otherwise, STRUCK tests the candidate example $x'_{i,ind}$ with the lowest predicted probability value of the original label $y$ from $\mathcal{S}$. If the predicted probability value $\mathrm{Prob}(x'_{i,ind}, y; M)$ is less than the saved predicted probability value *prob*, it means $t_{adv}$ is valid since $t_{adv}$ misleads $M$, so update the relevant information (line 19–22). Whether the perturbation is valid or not, the *controller* records $t_{adv}$ (line 26), preventing the same perturbation method from being performed indefinitely. STRUCK assures the diversity of perturbations through *controller* recording. The attack process terminates when: I. an adversarial example is generated (line 13); II. no perturbation method is available (line 8); III the attack reaches $m$ iterations (line 28).

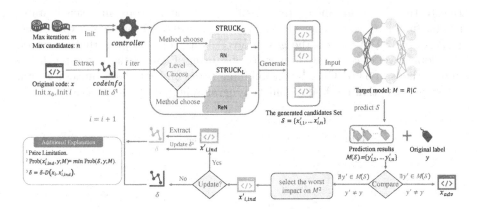

**Fig. 2.** Workflow of STRUCK (start at the top left).

## 3.2  Code Information

To more effectively exploit the structural features of code when attacking target models, STRUCK employs *Extract* to comprehensively extract structural information of varying granularity from the input code prior to attacking. $codeinfo = Extract(x)$ represents the extracted structural information. In particular, *Extract* analyzes the structure of the code and extracts its essential information, which is then organized within *codeinfo*. As illustrated on the right side of Fig. 1, *Extract* can draw out different substructures from the code graph of the example, including Variable Nodes, Statement Subgraphs, Datatype subgraphs, and Function Subgraphs. It also captures key information within these substructures, such as the definition position and scope (valid range) of variable nodes.

Although the code graph includes various types of nodes, STRUCK focuses on variable nodes (such as "Stu" nodes) because they are nodes defined by programmers and possess more uncertainty than keyword nodes (such as "if" nodes) and other types of nodes. STRUCK also pays attention to conditional/loop statement subgraphs which often play key roles in the code. The user-defined datatype subgraphs and function subgraphs extracted by STRUCK are very helpful to the analysis of the code graph. STRUCK also uses the isolation of subgraphs in the code graph to collect information on insertable positions, denoted as *Pos*. The isolation of subgraphs implies that there is no node intersection between two adjacent subgraphs. Inserting customized nodes or subgraphs between these two subgraphs will not affect their semantics. For example, in Fig. 1, there are no node intersections between the "Stu datatype subgraph" and the "Max Function Subgraph", indicating that the position marked by the arrow is an insertable location for perturbations and belongs to *Pos*.

### 3.3    STRUCK$_G$

Due to the code's specificity, its semantics can remain constant even if statements, functions, and other elements modify their positions and expressions. STRUCK$_G$ (STRUCK on the global level) is a proposed perturbation set on the global level of code based on code refactoring. Figure 3 shows the perturbation methods in STRUCK$_G$ by recombining nodes and subgraphs in code graph. These perturbation methods simulate programming development situations.

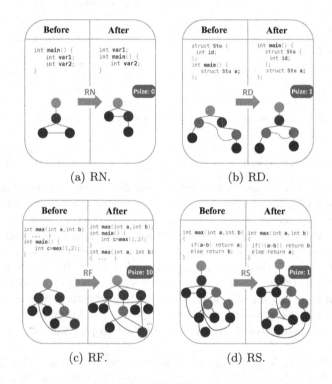

**Fig. 3.** Perturbation methods in STRUCK$_G$ performing on example codes.

**Reconstruct-Node (RN)**, **Reconstruct-Datatype (RD)**, and **Reconst ruct-Function (RF)** take advantage of uncertainty in the location of variables, user-defined datatypes, and user-defined functions, respectively, to perform perturbations. **Reconstruct-Statement (RS)** utilizes the diversity of loops and conditional statements to accomplish code refactoring, as previously implemented in CLONEGEN [40]. And these perturbation methods make use of *codeinfo* to complete code's refactoring, ensuring $\forall t \in$ STRUCK$_G$ satisfies $t \in \mathcal{T}(x)$. The perturbable objects for RN, RD, RF and RS are variables, user-defined datatypes, user-defined functions and conditional/loop statements, respectively. The idea behind STRUCK$_G$ is to refactor code without introducing new information, which leads to perturbation methods with negligible Psize. Specifically, the RN, RD and RF achieve a minimum perturbation size $d_{min}$ of 0 on the code, denoted as $\forall t \in \{RN, RD, RF\}$, $d_{min}(t) \approx 0$. For RS, some auxiliary identifiers will be added, such as Fig. 3(d) by adding "!" to reconstruct the conditional statement, so $d_{min}(t_{RS}) = 1$. Since the lower minimum Psize, the modification to the input code caused by the perturbation method in STRUCK$_G$ has high imperceptibility.

## 3.4    STRUCK$_L$

Redundant code refers to unnecessary segments of code that do not influence the semantics of it. STRUCK$_L$ (STRUCK on the local level) is a perturbation set based on the redundant code mistakes made by programmers. The perturbations in STRUCK$_L$ perturb the local level by inserting redundant subgraphs at any $p \in Pos$, as shown in Fig. 4. It is noteworthy that $\forall t \in$ STRUCK$_L$, $d_{min}(t) \geq 3$.

**Repeat-Node (ReN)** is inspired by the Copy-Move attack in the image processing field [8]. As shown in Fig. 4(a), ReN first copies "var1" and then pastes it twice at the insertable position near "var1" to introduce perturbation. **Change-Node-Decl (CND)** generates a new declaration statement subgraph for a variable node in code graph and inserts the new subgraph outside the scope of the variable node. Figure 4(b) illustrates the process of CND using "var1" for perturbation. **Change-Recover-Node (CRN)** takes advantage of the property that the value of a variable node in an inactive state does not change the code semantics and achieves perturbation by changing and recovering the value of variables in pairs. Figure 4(c) illustrates the process of CRN changing and recovering the value of "var1". **Redundant-Node (RedN)** uses common idempotent operations (self-assignment, self-division, bitwise operations, etc.) to generate a new assignment statement subgraph for a variable node in code graph without changing its value, and then inserts it at a insertable position. Figure 4(d) illustrates the process of RedN for "var". **Generate-Node (GN)** introduces a declaration statement subgraph of a new variable at any insertable location. Figure 4(f) shows the process of GN inserting a new variable "a" declaration subgraph into the code graph. **Generate-Statement (GS)** uses redundant conditional expressions to perturb the original examples. It generates redundant expressions and the corresponding loop/conditional statement subgraphs with imperceptibility according to the characteristics of each code at different locations. Figure 4(f) shows that GS first generates a redundant conditional expression "var != 1" using the variable node "var". Then it generates a redundant loop statement subgraph in combination with the existing declaration statement subgraph ("var = 1").

The perturbable objects of ReN, CND, CRN, and RedN are user-defined variables. GN and GS generate redundant subgraphs based on *Pos*, so their perturbable objects are *Pos*.

### 3.5   Controller

**Controller Initialization.** The *controller* initializes with the extracted *codeinfo* from $x$ and the maximum attack iteration $m$ (Line 4 in Algorithm 1). Based on the types of perturbable objects for different perturbation methods described in Sect. 3.3 and Sect. 3.4, the *controller* first initializes the specific perturbable objects for perturbation methods in STRUCK$_G$ and STRUCK$_L$. We use $objects(t, x)$ to denote the set of specific perturbable objects of perturbation method $t$ on $x$. In Fig. 4(b), $objects(t_{CND}, x) = \{var1, var2\}$ means CND can perturb $x$ by generating and inserting a new declaration statement subgraph for $var1$ or $var2$. If $objects(t, x) = \varnothing$, the *controller* removes $t$ from its corresponding perturbation level. Otherwise, the *controller* initializes the number of times that $t$ can be performed using $objects(t, x)$ and the hyperparameter attack amplification factor *scale*.

$$times_t = \mid objects(t, x) \mid \times scale. \tag{6}$$

Since there are always *Pos* in code, $t_{GN}$ and $t_{GS}$ can always be executed, allowing for the application of STRUCK$_L$. The *controller* maintains the perturbable levels of $x$, denoted as $L_c$. When $L_c = \{STRUCK_L\}$, $m_L = m$ is STRUCK$_L$'s

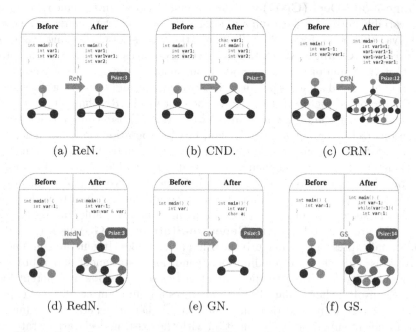

(a) ReN.          (b) CND.          (c) CRN.

(d) RedN.          (e) GN.          (f) GS.

**Fig. 4.** Perturbation methods in STRUCK$_L$ performing on example codes.

maximum perturbation iterations. When $L_c = \{\text{STRUCK}_G, \text{STRUCK}_L\}$, the $\text{STRUCK}_G$'s maximum iterations of perturbations is $m_G = m \times \theta$ by using the hyperparameter $\theta \in (0,1)$. Correspondingly, $m_L = m - m_G$.

**Controller Choose.** In each iteration of STRUCK, the *controller* is used to choose the perturbation method $t_{adv}$. Only if $t_{adv}$ is selected successfully can STRUCK continue to perturb $x$. Otherwise, STRUCK attack $x$ for $M$ fails. In this part, we only discuss the case of $L_c = \{\text{STRUCK}_G, \text{STRUCK}_L\}$. As shown in Fig. 2, the *controller* first selects the perturbation level $T_L$ from $L_c$. The perturbation methods in $\text{STRUCK}_G$ exhibit higher imperceptibility due to their low $d_{min}$, so the *controller* gives priority to $\text{STRUCK}_G$ when choosing. Only when there is no perturbation method available in $\text{STRUCK}_G$, or the current number of perturbation iteration $i$ exceeds $m_G$, the *controller* will choose $\text{STRUCK}_L$. After the *controller* selects $T_L$, it will further choose $t_{adv}$ from $T_L$.

We consider that the more perturbable objects are, the more candidate examples can be generated, and the higher the likelihood of successfully generating adversarial examples is. Therefore, when the *controller* uses the sampling method to select a perturbation method from $T_L$, the probability of each perturbation method being selected is as follows:

$$chance(t) = \frac{|objects(t,x)|(1 + \frac{|\delta - d_{min}(t)|}{\delta - d_{min}(t) + 1e\text{-}8})}{2\sum_{i=1}^{|T_L|}|objects(t_i,x)|(1 + \frac{|\delta - d_{min}(t_i)|}{\delta - d_{min}(t_i) + 1e\text{-}8})}. \tag{7}$$

$\forall t \in T_L$, when $d_{min}(t) < \delta$, the larger $objects(t,x)$ is, the greater the chance that *controller* selects $t$ is. For example, in the code graph of Fig. 1, there are four variables and one user-defined datatype. Therefore $chance(t_{RN}) > chance(t_{RD})$.

**Controller Update.** If *controller* successfully selects $t_{adv}$ in the iteration, it records $t_{adv}$ regardless of whether $t_{adv}$ is valid or not. When the number of perturbations of $t_{adv}$ exceeds $times_{t_{adv}}$ (calculated using Eq. (6)), *controller* removes $t_{adv}$ from the corresponding perturbation level. Also, if all perturbation methods within a perturbation level in $L_c$ are removed, the *controller* will remove that perturbation level from $L_c$. This updating process enables the *controller* to choose the appropriate perturbation method in the next iteration.

## 4  Experiment Setup

### 4.1  Dataset

We choose the source code classification task as the downstream task of the code representation, which serves as the foundation for more complex tasks. Specifically, we have chosen the Open Judge function classification dataset (OJ) [38] and the code defect prediction dataset (CC) [1] as our research objects. The OJ consists of 52,000 executable C/C++ code snippets categorized into 104 classes with 500 snippets per class. The CC includes 34,174 executable C/C++ code snippets classified into four categories based on their execution results on the CodeChef platform. Prior to in-depth analysis, we preprocess the C/C++ code snippets in both datasets based on [37]. Following TBCNN [22], we divide each dataset into $\mathcal{D}_{train}$, $\mathcal{D}_{dev}$, $\mathcal{D}_{test}$ in the ratio of 3.2:0.8:1. On the OJ, following [22], we employ Accuracy (Acc) as the performance metric to evaluate different models. And on the CC, which is a 4-class classification problem, we employ Precision (Prec), Recall, and F1 score (F1), with F1 as the primary performance metric.

## 4.2   Target Models

When selecting target models, we consider input format, generalizability, and performance. Our selection includes: fundamental sequential models such as LSTM and GRU; classical structural models like GGNN [4] and GCN [18]; popular pre-trained models including CodeBERT [11], GraphCodeBERT [15] and UniXcoder [14]. **LSTM** and **GRU** are routinely employed as the backbones of well-performing models to tackle various downstream tasks [17,30]. **GGNN** is the first graph representation model adopted in the code intelligence field and widely utilized as a fundamental component in complex models [12,16]. **GCN** is a conventional graph model included in our study to explore the robustness of graph models in learning code representations. **CodeBERT (CB)** is the first bimodal pre-trained model for programming language and natural language. **GraphCodeBERT (GCB)**, based on CB, leverages a semantic-level structure of code, i.e., DFG, in the pre-training stage. **UniXcoder (UX)** is a unified cross-modal pre-trained model for programming language that incorporates semantic and syntax information from code comment and AST.

Such comprehensive selection of target models not only can reveals the robustness levels of current advanced models, but also provides essential references for assessing and enhancing the robustness of future models with collaborative computing. We have implemented these models according to their original papers, and their performance on the OJ and CC datasets is presented in Table 1.

**Table 1.** Performance of the Target Models(%).

| Model | OJ | CodeChef | | |
|-------|------|-------|--------|-------|
|       | Acc  | Prec  | Recall | F1    |
| LSTM  | 96.88 | 77.06 | 75.46 | 76.19 |
| GRU   | 96.54 | 76.08 | 75.40 | 75.68 |
| GGNN  | 95.68 | 66.59 | 64.33 | 65.05 |
| GCN   | 94.54 | 58.55 | 55.54 | 55.30 |
| CB    | 98.30 | **85.40** | 82.61 | **83.80** |
| GCB   | 97.70 | 82.92 | 80.69 | 81.69 |
| UX    | **98.47** | 83.99 | **82.65** | 83.26 |

## 4.3  Baselines

To demonstrate the superiority of STRUCK, we compare it with popular non-targeted, black-box attack methods that emphasize either textual features (MHM, I-CARROT$_A$-S and ALERT [34]) or structural features (S-CARROT$_A$ [36] and CLONEGEN [40]). We implement these baseline based on official descriptions.

**MHM** is a SOTA black-box attack method for CRMs that generates candidate examples by iteratively renaming variable nodes and accepting suggestions based on an acceptance probability. I-CARROT$_A$-S is a simplified version of the SOTA white-box attack method I-CARROT$_A$ [36], which uses random sampling to obtain candidate replacement tokens without exploiting gradient information. **ALERT** is a SOTA black-box attack method for pre-trained models that uses another pre-trained model to generate natural-meaning substitutions when renaming user-defined variables in target code. However, ALERT is limited to attacking pre-trained models because it requires both the target and pre-trained models to use the same vocabulary to maintain the validity of replacement nodes. S-CARROT$_A$ focuses on exploiting code's structural features by inserting and deleting fixed redundant code snippets, with a Psize limitation for fair comparison with STRUCK. **CLONEGEN** evaluates the robustness of clone detection models by generating adversarial examples using 15 simple transformation operators and a deep reinforcement learning-based strategy. We have made appropriate modifications to ensure a fair comparison with STRUCK.

## 4.4  Metrics

**Effectiveness.** We use Relative performance degradation (RPD) to measure the effectiveness of attack methods, which is defined as follows:

$$\text{RPD} = \frac{P_{\text{before}} - P_{\text{after}}}{P_{\text{before}}}. \tag{8}$$

**Table 2.** Performance of Attackers on Target models (%).

| Attacker | LSTM | | GRU | | GGNN | | GCN | | CB | | GCB | | UX | |
|---|---|---|---|---|---|---|---|---|---|---|---|---|---|---|
| | OJ | CC | OJ | CC | OJ | CC | OJ | CC | OJ | CC | OJ | CC | OJ | CC |
| MHM | 55.20 | 99.92 | 69.54 | 99.91 | 62.94 | 97.70 | 75.95 | 90.54 | 19.41 | 87.15 | 34.39 | 94.35 | 22.30 | 89.84 |
| I-CARROT$_A$-S | 52.03 | 99.73 | 67.16 | 99.66 | 61.47 | 97.00 | 69.56 | 90.15 | 18.97 | 85.79 | 18.97 | 92.91 | 21.96 | 87.82 |
| ALERT | - | - | - | - | - | - | - | - | 24.04 | 80.23 | 19.24 | 84.43 | 19.93 | 91.77 |
| S-CARROT$_A$ | 57.04 | 96.25 | 44.66 | 98.03 | 26.09 | 75.54 | 76.85 | 76.56 | 6.85 | 93.33 | 6.85 | 86.98 | 8.45 | 83.18 |
| CLONEGEN | 27.08 | 67.75 | 16.30 | 53.35 | 51.72 | 47.94 | 24.42 | 52.07 | 65.96 | 70.40 | 71.00 | 77.64 | 59.18 | 84.00 |
| STRUCK$_G$ | 13.10 | 37.79 | 8.45 | 39.72 | 8.43 | 34.99 | 29.36 | 29.49 | 1.98 | 20.19 | 3.27 | 29.33 | 1.69 | 24.49 |
| STRUCK$_L$ | 77.05 | 100.0 | 81.57 | 99.83 | 81.25 | 97.66 | 89.11 | 99.41 | 85.12 | 99.01 | 77.29 | 98.69 | 68.24 | 99.32 |
| STRUCK | **80.06** | **100.0** | **83.28** | **100.0** | **88.95** | **98.48** | **92.15** | **99.52** | **86.85** | **99.37** | **79.67** | **99.60** | **69.59** | **99.76** |

**Table 3.** Average number of invocations (Invos) of attackers in OJ.

| Invos#↓ | LSTM | GRU | GGNN | GCN | CB | GCB | UX |
|---------|------|-----|------|-----|-----|-----|-----|
| MHM | 507 | 455 | 407 | 300 | 530 | 544 | 583 |
| I-CARROT$_A$-S | 372 | 342 | 300 | 303 | 426 | 409 | 445 |
| ALERT | – | – | – | – | 439 | 520 | 596 |
| S-CARROT$_A$ | 148 | 156 | 154 | 112 | 138 | 170 | 120 |
| CLONEGEN | 96 | 104 | 97 | 99 | 100 | 96 | 96 |
| STRUCK$_G$ | **60** | **62** | **53** | **44** | **39** | **74** | **68** |
| STRUCK$_L$ | 103 | 98 | 89 | 85 | 109 | 96 | 105 |
| STRUCK | 212 | 217 | 209 | 175 | 252 | 234 | 265 |

For OJ, the $P$ refers to Acc, while for the CC, it represents the F1. The relative performance change of the target model before and after the adversarial attack can visually demonstrate the effectiveness of the attacker. A larger RPD indicates a higher effectiveness of the attacker.

**Efficiency.** We evaluate the efficiency of $adv$ based on the average number of model invocations (Invos) during the attack. Given that $M$ is typically deployed remotely, multiple invocations can be time-consuming and expensive. Thus, a more efficient attack method requires fewer invocations of $M$.

**Imperceptibility.** Adversarial examples should have hard-to-detect perturbations [29]. We evaluate the imperceptibility of attack methods from two angles: code imperceptibility (Code-I) and programmer imperceptibility (Programmer-I). For Code-I, we calculate the average Psize (APsize) of generated adversarial examples; a smaller APsize indicates higher Code-I, offering a simple and clear evaluation. To assess Programmer-I for attack methods using code structural features, we conduct a questionnaire survey asking programmers to identify perturbations in code snippets. By analyzing the proportion of detected perturbations, we evaluate the Programmer-I of attack methods.

## 5  Experiment Results and Analysis

This section will answer the following questions.

RQ1 **Attack Performance**: How successful are the STRUCK attacks on CRMs?

RQ2 **Imperceptibility Evaluation**: Are the adversarial examples generated by STRUCK imperceptible?

RQ3 **Ablation Study**: Is it necessary for STRUCK to employ different perturbation levels and methods?

RQ4 **Robustness Assistance**: Does STRUCK effectively assess and improve the robustness of models?

## 5.1   RQ1: Attack Performance

**Effectiveness.** Table 2 presents the RPD of all baselines, STRUCK$_G$, STRUCK$_L$, and STRUCK. STRUCK outperforms all other attackers in all datasets and target models, demonstrating its generalizability. In the OJ, STRUCK achieves an average RPD of 82.93% on the target models, which is a significant improvement over MHM (48.53%) and S-CARROT (36.05%), with improvements of 70.89% and 130.30%, respectively. Despite the high susceptibility of target models in the CC dataset to adversarial attacks, STRUCK still achieves the best average RPD of 99.53%. Compared to MHM (94.20%) and S-CARROT (87.12%), STRUCK shows improvements of 5.66% and 14.24%, respectively.

**Efficiency.** Table 3 shows the Invos needed for various attackers to generate successful adversarial examples on the OJ. Notably, STRUCK$_G$ has the lowest Invos (57). In earlier attack methods, higher attack performance often required more Invos. However, STRUCK's Invos for all target models are lower than MHM, with an average of 223, a 54.35% decrease compared to MHM (489).

> **Answers to RQ1:** STRUCK's success in attacking CRMs shows that it is both effective and efficient, making it a practical and feasible method.

**Table 4.** Structural attackers' Imperceptibility evaluation in OJ.

| Attacker | APsize↓ | Unnatural | | Avg. unnatural blocks | |
|---|---|---|---|---|---|
| | | Prop.(%) | △(%)↓ | # | △(%) ↓ |
| None | 0 | 40.74 | – | 1.52 | – |
| S-CARROT$_A$ | 55 | 89.81 | 1.20 | 1.89 | 0.24 |
| CLONEGEN | 140 | 95.37 | 1.34 | 4.62 | 2.04 |
| STRUCK$_L$ | 66 | 78.70 | 0.93 | 1.75 | 0.15 |
| STRUCK | **52** | 75.93 | **0.86** | 1.56 | **0.03** |

For Unnatural, $\triangle = \frac{\text{Prop.}-\text{Prop.}_{None}}{\text{Prop.}_{None}}$, while for Avg. unnatural blocks, $\triangle = \frac{\#-\#_{None}}{\#}$. Lower $\triangle$ is better programmer-I.

## 5.2   RQ2: Imperceptibility Evaluation

Since STRUCK mainly uses code's structural features for adversarial attacks, directly comparing it with methods like ALERT, which focus on textual features, would be unfair. Structural perturbations are usually more noticeable than textual ones. In order to demonstrate the superior imperceptibility of STRUCK at the structural level, we compare it to S-CARROT and CLONEGEN.

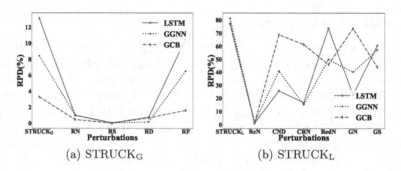

**Fig. 5.** RPD of different perturbation methods in STRUCK$_G$ and STRUCK$_L$.

**Code-I.** As shown in Table 4, STRUCK achieves an APsize of 52 on the target models, resulting in a reduction of 4.68% and 62.67% compared to S-CARROT (55) and CLONEGEN (140), respectively.

**Programmer-I.** To evaluate Programmer-I for attackers using code structural features, we conduct a user study. We sample code snippets from the OJ that can be successfully attacked by all selected attackers and generate adversarial examples for the questionnaire. We create 18 questionnaires with 30 test code snippets each, including original code and adversarial examples. Each test code is divided into five blocks for readability. We invite 18 programmers with at least four years of experience to participate and identify unnatural code blocks. Table 4 shows that even the original 108 codes (None) have a 40.74% Unnatural Proportion (Prob.) and 1.52 average unnatural blocks. This is due to different programming habits. We use the performance of the adversarial example sets obtained from the selected attackers relative to None ($\triangle$) to more accurately measure attackers' Programmer-I. STRUCK has the lowest $\triangle$ among the comparative methods. Compared to S-CARROT$_A$, the Unnatural Prob. and Avg. unnatural blocks of STRUCK are reduced by 28% and 89% respectively.

> **Answers to RQ2:** Compared to other attackers that leverage code structural features, STRUCK demonstrates the highest level of Code-I and Programmer-I, providing strong evidence of its high imperceptibility.

### 5.3   RQ3: Ablation Study

STRUCK includes two perturbation levels, STRUCK$_G$ and STRUCK$_L$, which draw inspiration from successful attack strategies in the graph data analysis field [9] while incorporating code-specific graph features. Table 4 shows that STRUCK has superior imperceptibility compared to STRUCK$_L$ in both the Code-I and Programmer-I, highlighting the importance of designing perturbation methods at both global and local levels. Moreover, the multiple perturbation levels in

STRUCK ensure scalability and allow for the incorporation of new structural perturbation methods in future iterations.

To compare the performance of perturbation methods used in $STRUCK_G$ and $STRUCK_L$, we conduct an ablation experiment. The experiment uses a single perturbation method in $STRUCK_G$ or $STRUCK_L$ to attack on representative models in OJ. Figure 5 shows the RPD of different perturbation methods. It can be seen that the RPD of any single perturbation method is lower than that of its corresponding level. STRUCK designs multiple perturbation methods for each level to enhance the effectiveness and diversity of perturbations.

> **Answers to RQ3:** The design of two levels and multiple perturbation methods at each level ensure the effectiveness, imperceptibility, diversity and scalability of STRUCK.

**Table 5.** Model's Robustness on OJ Assessed by Attackers (%).

| Robust | LSTM | GRU | GGNN | GCN | CB | GCB | UX |
|---|---|---|---|---|---|---|---|
| MHM | 44.80 | 30.46 | 37.07 | 24.05 | 80.59 | 65.60 | 77.70 |
| I-CARROT$_A$-S | 47.97 | 32.84 | 38.53 | 30.44 | 81.03 | 68.78 | 78.04 |
| ALERT | – | – | – | – | 75.96 | 80.76 | 80.07 |
| S-CARROT$_A$ | 42.96 | 55.34 | 48.28 | 23.15 | 93.15 | 69.34 | 91.55 |
| CLONEGEN | 72.92 | 83.70 | 73.91 | 75.58 | 34.04 | 29.00 | 40.82 |
| STRUCK$_G$ | 86.90 | 91.55 | 91.57 | 70.64 | 98.03 | 96.73 | 98.65 |
| STRUCK$_L$ | 22.95 | 18.43 | 18.75 | 10.89 | 14.88 | 22.71 | 31.76 |
| STRUCK | **19.94** | **16.72** | **11.05** | **7.85** | **13.15** | **20.33** | **30.41** |

**Table 6.** Results of Structural Adversarial Training in OJ (%).

| Model | Acc. | S-CARROT$_A$ | | CLONEGEN | | STRUCK | |
|---|---|---|---|---|---|---|---|
| | | Rob.↑ | Improv.↑ | Rob.↑ | Improv.↑ | Rob.↑ | Improv.↑ |
| LSTM | 96.88 | 42.96 | – | 72.91 | – | 19.94 | – |
| +S-CARROT$_A$ | 96.56 | 77.33 | 80.00 | 76.04 | 4.29 | 20.07 | 15.72 |
| +CLONEGEN | 96.73 | 51.72 | 20.38 | 91.67 | 25.71 | 18.84 | −0.05 |
| +STRUCK | 97.00 | 63.53 | 47.89 | 81.25 | 11.43 | 71.83 | 260.2 |
| GGNN | 96.54 | 48.28 | – | 73.91 | – | 11.05 | – |
| +S-CARROT$_A$ | 95.85 | 78.72 | 63.03 | 73.91 | 0 | 22.62 | 104.6 |
| +CLONEGEN | 96.25 | 44.56 | −0.08 | 90.21 | 22.06 | 19.04 | 72.23 |
| +STRUCK | 95.90 | 62.87 | 30.22 | 72.22 | −0.02 | 78.26 | 608.0 |
| GCB | 97.90 | 69.34 | – | 29.00 | – | 20.32 | – |
| +S-CARROT$_A$ | 97.69 | 91.55 | 32.03 | 36.00 | 24.13 | 8.84 | −56.49 |
| +CLONEGEN | 97.86 | 63.27 | −0.09 | 60.20 | 107.6 | 22.11 | 8.87 |
| +STRUCK | 97.91 | 83.51 | 20.43 | 31.00 | 6.90 | 86.87 | 336.3 |

## 5.4   RQ4: Robustness Assistance

Table 5 shows the robustness assessment of models on $\mathcal{D}_{\text{test}}$ using different attackers, with lower values indicating greater accuracy. The results demonstrate that STRUCK is more precise.

To explore whether adversarial training with STRUCK helps to improve the robustness of target models, we conduct experiments using LSTM, GGNN, and GCB as representative models. Our focus is on attackers that exploit code structural features. The adversarial training results are shown in Table 6. We can see that adversarial training with STRUCK effectively improves the robustness of target models against both STRUCK and S-CARROT$_A$. There is also some improvement in the robustness of LSTM and GCB against CLONEGEN. However, adversarial training with S-CARROT$_A$ or CLONEGEN has tiny effect on STRUCK. This shows that STRUCK is a more comprehensive method to attack using code structural features, and adversarial training with it can improve the robustness of models to structural attacks effectively.

---

**Answers to RQ4:** The target models' robustness can be assessed more accurately using STRUCK. And STRUCK adversarial training can be used to strengthen the robustness of models against structural attacks.

---

## 6   Related Work

DL models in code intelligence, particularly in the context of collaborative computing where multiple models or systems may interact, face robustness issues, prompting research to assess their robustness. We focus on the CRM target model. While works [26,36] show excellent performance in target models, such white-box attackers are less practical and not universal, as target models are typically unknown to attackers. We are more interested in black-box attack methods. MHM [37] and ALERT [34] are known SOTA black-box attack methods. They mainly modify user-defined variable names, with perturbations at the token level, ignoring structural features. They cannot generate different, higher-level perturbations and require multiple invocations to target models, lacking efficiency. S-CARROT$_A$ [36] and CLONEGEN [40] attempt adversarial attacks on CRMs using code structural features but have low RPD and imperceptibility.

There are a few more relevant studies for the robustness of CRMs available here. Rabin et al. [24] evaluate the generalizability of CRMs. Gao et al. [13] propose a framework based on counterfactual inference to mitigate naming bias in CRMs. Pour et al. [23] propose a testing framework that embeds source code into DL models. However, it has minimal impact on the performance of the target model. Works such as [25,27] perform poisoning attack on CRMs during the training phase by making changes to the training dataset.

# 7  Conclusion and Future Work

In this paper, we propose STRUCK, a novel method for attacking CRMs using code structural features. The objective of STRUCK is to advance the development of reliable DL models in the code intelligence field, and effectively evaluate the robustness of these DL models when applied to collaborative code development, automated code analysis, and other collaborative computing scenarios. To our best knowledge, STRUCK is the first work to attack using code structural features systematically and comprehensively. STRUCK utilizes global-level and local-level perturbations to generate adversarial examples, highlighting the idea of using code structural features to perform attacks. The experimental results show that STRUCK has higher effectiveness, efficiency and imperceptibility than the existing black-box attack methods in terms of sequential, structural, and pre-trained models. We also explore the value of STRUCK on the robustness of target models. STRUCK can more accurately assess the robustness of CRMs, and adversarial training using STRUCK can effectively improve the robustness of models against structural attacks. We have open sourced STRCUK at the GitHub repository https://github.com/zhanghaha1707/STRUCK to provide the support for further systematic robustness research of DL models for the field of code intelligence.

In the future, we will continue to improve STRUCK's imperceptibility and incorporate more perturbation methods using code structural features. And we aim to test the performance of STRUCK in more complex tasks and more datasets, expanding its applicability to a wider range of scenarios.

**Acknowledgment.** The research is supported by the National Key R&D Program of China under grant No. 2022YFF0902500, the Guangdong Basic and Applied Basic Research Foundation, China (No. 2023A1515011050). Liang Chen is the corresponding author.The research is supported by the National Key R&D Program of China under grant No. 2022YFF0902500, the Guangdong Basic and Applied Basic Research Foundation, China (No. 2023A1515011050). Liang Chen is the corresponding author.

# References

1. Codechef (2022). https://codechef.com/
2. Ahmad, W.U., Chakraborty, S., Ray, B., Chang, K.W.: A transformer-based approach for source code summarization. arXiv preprint arXiv:2005.00653 (2020)
3. Akhtar, N., Mian, A., Kardan, N., Shah, M.: Advances in adversarial attacks and defenses in computer vision: a survey. IEEE Access **9**, 155161–155196 (2021)
4. Allamanis, M., Brockschmidt, M., Khademi, M.: Learning to represent programs with graphs. In: ICLR 2018 - Conference Track Proceedings (2018)
5. Ben-Nun, T., Hoefler, T.: Demystifying parallel and distributed deep learning: An in-depth concurrency analysis. arXiv: Learning (2018)
6. Cao, H., et al.: Prevention of gan-based privacy inferring attacks towards federated learning. In: Collaborative Computing: Networking, Applications and Worksharing (2022)

7. Carlini, N., Wagner, D.: Towards evaluating the robustness of neural networks. In: IEEE Symposium on Security and Privacy (2017)
8. Christlein, V., Riess, C., Jordan, J., Riess, C., Angelopoulou, E.: An evaluation of popular copy-move forgery detection approaches. IEEE Trans. Inf. Forensics Secur. **7**(6), 1841–1854 (2012)
9. Dai, H., Li, H., Tian, T., Huang, X., Wang, L., Zhu, J., Song, L.: Adversarial attack on graph structured data, pp. 1115–1124. PMLR (2018)
10. Dong, S., Wang, P., Abbas, K.: A survey on deep learning and its applications. Comput. Sci. Rev. **40**, 100379 (2021)
11. Feng, Z., et al.: Codebert: a pre-trained model for programming and natural languages. In: Empirical Methods in Natural Language Processing (2020)
12. Fernandes, P., Allamanis, M., Brockschmidt, M.: Structured neural summarization. In: ICLR (2019)
13. Gao, S., Gao, C., Wang, C., Sun, J., Lo, D.: Carbon: a counterfactual reasoning based framework for neural code comprehension debiasing (2022)
14. Guo, D., Lu, S., Duan, N., Wang, Y., Zhou, M., Yin, J.: Unixcoder: unified cross-modal pre-training for code representation. In: ACL 2022, Dublin, Ireland (2022)
15. Guo, D., et al.: Graphcodebert: pre-training code representations with data flow. In: Learning (2020)
16. Hellendoorn, V.J., Sutton, C., Singh, R., Maniatis, P., Bieber, D.: Global relational models of source code. In: 8th International Conference on Learning Representations, ICLR 2020, Addis Ababa, Ethiopia, 26–30 April 2020 (2020)
17. Iyer, S., Konstas, I., Cheung, A., Zettlemoyer, L.: Summarizing source code using a neural attention model. In: Proceedings of the 54th Annual Meeting of the Association for Computational Linguistics, pp. 2073–2083 (2016)
18. Kipf, T., Welling, M.: Semi-supervised classification with graph convolutional networks. arXiv: Learning (2016)
19. Li, J., Peng, J., Chen, L., Zheng, Z., Liang, T., Ling, Q.: Spectral adversarial training for robust graph neural network. IEEE Trans. Knowl. Data Eng. **35**, 9240–9253 (2022)
20. Li, J., Xie, T., Chen, L., Xie, F., He, X., Zheng, Z.: Adversarial attack on large scale graph. IEEE Trans. Knowl. Data Eng. **35**(1), 82–95 (2021)
21. Li, S., Zheng, X., Zhang, X., Chen, X., Li, W.: Facial expression recognition based on deep spatio-temporal attention network. In: Collaborative Computing: Networking, Applications and Worksharing (2022)
22. Mou, L., Li, G., Zhang, L., Wang, T., Jin, Z.: Convolutional neural networks over tree structures for programming language processing. In: National Conference on Artificial Intelligence (2014)
23. Pour, M., Li, Z., Ma, L., Hemmati, H.: A search-based testing framework for deep neural networks of source code embedding. In: ICST (2021)
24. Rabin, M.R.I., Bui, N.D.Q., Wang, K., Yu, Y., Jiang, L., Alipour, M.A.: On the generalizability of Neural Program Models with respect to semantic-preserving program transformations. Inf. Softw. Technol. **135**, 106552 (2021)
25. Ramakrishnan, G., Albarghouthi, A.: Backdoors in neural models of source code. arXiv: Learning (2020)
26. Ramakrishnan, G., Henkel, J., Wang, Z., Albarghouthi, A., Jha, S., Reps, T.: Semantic robustness of models of source code. arXiv: Learning (2020)
27. Schuster, R., Song, C., Tromer, E., Shmatikov, V.: You autocomplete me: poisoning vulnerabilities in neural code completion. In: Usenix Security Symposium (2021)
28. Sun, X., Tong, M.: Hindom: a robust malicious domain detection system based on heterogeneous information network with transductive classification. ArXiv (2019)

29. Szegedy, C., et al.: Intriguing properties of neural networks. arXiv preprint arXiv:1312.6199 (2013)
30. Vasic, M., Kanade, A., Maniatis, P., Bieber, D., Singh, R.: Neural program repair by jointly learning to localize and repair. arXiv: Learning (2019)
31. Wu, R., Zhang, Y., Peng, Q., Chen, L., Zheng, Z.: A survey of deep learning models for structural code understanding. arXiv preprint arXiv:2205.01293 (2022)
32. Wu, X.: Blackbox adversarial attacks and explanations for automatic speech recognition. In: ESEC/FSE 2022 (2022)
33. Wu, Z., Pan, S., Chen, F., Long, G., Zhang, C., Philip, S.Y.: A comprehensive survey on graph neural networks. IEEE Trans. Neural Netw. Learn. Syst. **32**(1), 4–24 (2020)
34. Yang, Z., Shi, J., He, J., Lo, D.: Natural attack for pre-trained models of code. In: ICSE 2022, New York, NY, USA (2022)
35. Yefet, N., Alon, U., Yahav, E.: Adversarial examples for models of code. In: Proceedings of the ACM on Programming Languages, vol. 4, no. OOPSLA, pp. 1–30 (2020)
36. Zhang, H., et al.: Towards robustness of deep program processing models-detection, estimation, and enhancement. TOSEM **31**(3), 1–40 (2022)
37. Zhang, H., Li, Z., Li, G., Ma, L., Liu, Y., Jin, Z.: Generating adversarial examples for holding robustness of source code processing models. In: Proceedings of the AAAI Conference on Artificial Intelligence, vol. 34, pp. 1169–1176 (2020)
38. Zhang, J., Wang, X., Zhang, H., Sun, H., Wang, K., Liu, X.: A novel neural source code representation based on abstract syntax tree. In: ICSE. IEEE (2019)
39. Zhang, W.E., Sheng, Q.Z., Alhazmi, A., Li, C.: Adversarial attacks on deep-learning models in natural language processing: a survey. ACM Trans. Intell. Syst. Technol. (TIST) **11**(3), 1–41 (2020)
40. Zhang, W., Guo, S., Zhang, H., Sui, Y., Xue, Y., Xu, Y.: Challenging machine learning-based clone detectors via semantic-preserving code transformations. IEEE Trans. Softw. Eng. **49**(5), 3052–3070 (2023)
41. Zhou, Y., Shi, D., Yang, H., Hu, H., Yang, S., Zhang, Y.: Deep reinforcement learning for multi-UAV exploration under energy constraints. In: Collaborative Computing: Networking, Applications and Worksharing (2022)

# An Efficient Authentication and Key Agreement Scheme for CAV Internal Applications

Yang Li[1], Qingyang Zhang[2,3,4,5]([⊠]), Wenwen Cao[2,3,4,5], Jie Cui[2,3,4,5], and Hong Zhong[2,3,4,5]

[1] Anhui Province Key Laboratory of Cyberspace Security Situation Awareness and Evaluation, Hefei 230037, China

[2] School of Computer Science and Technology, Anhui University, Hefei 230039, China
qyzhang@ahu.edu.cn

[3] Anhui Engineering Laboratory of IoT Security Technologies, Anhui University, Hefei 230039, China

[4] Institute of Physical Science and Information Technology, Anhui University, Hefei 230039, China

[5] Key Laboratory of Intelligent Computing and Signal Processing of Ministry of Education, Anhui University, Hefei 230039, China

**Abstract.** The data of applications in connected and autonomous vehicles are important, which is usually collected by service providers to improve their services, such as object detection model. But, wireless communication is susceptible to various kinds of attacks. Thus, the data of the application module needs to be securely shared to the corresponding service provider. However, current schemes are with limited performance while a service provider collects multiple application data at the same time. By adopting signcryption and chaotic map, an efficient authentication and key agreement scheme is proposed, while batch authentication is achieved for efficient message authentication of multiple applications, and the efficient revocation is realized based on Chinese remainder theorem under the assistance of trusted execution environment supported vehicle computing/communication unit. The formal security proof shows that the scheme is secure under the random oracle model, and the experiment results shows that the scheme is more efficient than related schemes and can meet the requirements of CAV.

**Keywords:** Connected and autonomous vehicles · Signcryption · Chaotic map · Chinese remainder theorem

## 1 Introduction

The number of vehicles has soared in the past few years, creating new problems for transportation, such as traffic jams and accidents. As a potential solution, connected and autonomous vehicles (CAVs) can make real-time decisions based

H. Gao et al. (Eds.): CollaborateCom 2023, LNICST 562, pp. 414–434, 2024.
https://doi.org/10.1007/978-3-031-54528-3_23

on the surrounding environment so as to control the secure driving of vehicles [1,2]. Typically, the CAV consists of five parts: positioning, perception, planning, vehicle control, and system management [3,4]. The positioning system can identify the vehicle's real-time position on the map. The perception system could identify surrounding objects, such as other surrounding vehicles, traffic signals, and surrounding obstacles. The planning system inputs the data from the perception system and positioning system. It determines the driving path and specific driving behaviors, such as lane changes. The control system indicated by the planning system could convert the control actions into vehicles, such as steering. The management system supervises the operation status of all systems and provides the human-computer interface. The CAV deployed with a large number of sensors can provide accurate perception data. These data can be processed inside the vehicle to enable the vehicle to make real-time decisions. These data are also very important to the SP. For example, a CAV can share data with traffic authorities and service providers (SP) to improve congestion across the entire traffic network [5]. In addition, an SP needs to collect a large amount of reliable data to train the artificial intelligence (AI) model to improve their services [6]. AI model requires a large amount of reliable data as input. Models trained on large amounts of data are more effective.

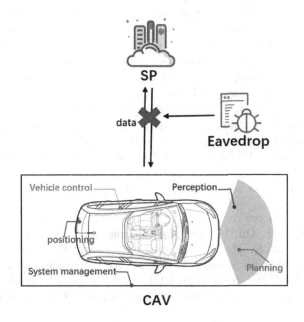

**Fig. 1.** Data leakage model for CAV data transmission

The data transmission between SP and CAV applications[1] is transmitted via the insecure public channel, which poses threats to privacy and security

---

[1] The applications here can also be in-vehicle modules connected by CAN bus.

[7–9]. The network communication may be subject to various attacks, such as impersonation attack, modification attack [10–13]. A malicious attack can cause the SP to collect incorrect data, which will lead to incorrect analytical decisions. Such attacks, as shown in Fig. 1, are fatal to the communication security of CAV. Therefore, it is necessary to take the authentication and key agreement (AKA) protocol [14,15] to protect the security of communication.

These applications share the same computing unit, i.e., vehicle computing/communication unit (VCU), and most of the computing workloads are occupied by autonomous driving applications. For driving safety, the additional algorithms, protocols, and schemes, such as the security scheme designed in this paper, should be as efficient as possible. In this case, some schemes are proposed. For example, some schemes adopt signcryption [16,17] and chaotic map [18,19] to implement authentication. They are based on a single AKA between the user and the server. However, an SP might collect a mass of data from multiple applications at the same time in one vehicle or an application for a while. Hence, these schemes need multiple AKA protocols or protocol executions are required, which is inefficient for CAVs.

In addition, anonymity makes sense for some scenarios, such as collecting data for AI model training. Adopting real identities may pose security and privacy threats for the participants [20]. Moreover, the efficient member management and key update of these applications also require to be considered.

Nowadays, many computing units have a trusted execution environment (TEE), which could isolate the targeted application from other applications. In this case, to address the aforementioned issues, we propose an efficient authentication and key agreement scheme for CAV internal applications with a TEE-supported VCU. The proposed scheme is adopted by the signcryption and chaotic map to realize security data transmission. On this basis, the scheme can generate signcryption to guarantee the security transmission of the application data. The SP can achieve efficient batch message authentication. Moreover, it could manage keys in one CAV based on the Chinese remainder theorem (CRT) with efficient revocation for the compromised application module, and the key can be updated periodically or when a compromised application module is detected.

- The scheme can realize key agreement between multiple applications and corresponding SP. On this basis, applications generate signcryption to send data to SP securely. The SP can verify and decrypt the message.
- When a large number of messages are received, batch message authentication can be realized. Benefiting from CRT, this scheme can realize efficient key updates. Moreover, for compromised applications, VCU can achieve efficient revocation.
- The related computing and communication costs indicate that the proposed scheme can achieve more efficient authentication. Under the random oracle model, the unforgeability of our scheme has been proved formally.

We will review the related works in Sect. 2 and provide some short preliminaries on the technologies we used, such as signcryption, chaotic maps, and CRT, as well as the system model of the proposed scheme in Sect. 3. Then, we introduce the proposed scheme in detail in Sect. 4. After that, we prove the security of the proposed scheme. In Sect. 6, the performance of the proposed scheme is evaluated. Finally, we conclude this work.

## 2 Related Works

In this section, we describe the related schemes of signcryption for the Internet of Things (IoT), and the related schemes of the AKA protocols based on the chaotic map will be illustrated. The CRT scheme will be described. The related comparison is shown in Table 1.

Ting *et al.* proposed the signcryption scheme [16] to achieve secure communication for an unsecured network in wireless sensor networks. This scheme proposed heterogeneous online/offline signcryption to achieve confidentiality, integrity, and unforgeability based on computational Diffie-Hellman and elliptic curve discrete logarithm assumption. The key agreement may not be optimal, and its computational overhead can be further reduced. At the same time, for higher security, key update and compromised sensors revocation can also be further considered.

In order to access real-time information from the IoT devices, Mandal *et al.* proposed a scheme [17] to achieve authorization, authentication, and revocation for participants, which is based on a three-factor certificateless-signcryption-based to achieve secure access between the user and smart devices with the help of the gateway. The computation and communication costs of this scheme are low. This scheme takes into account the revocation of users and the addition of smart devices. But for multiple smart devices, users need to conduct multiple key agreements. Moreover, the key in this scheme may be further considered for updating.

To achieve authentication and key agreement, Roy *et al.* proposed a provably secure three-factor anonymous authentication protocol [18] with fuzzy extractor crowdsourced IoT, in which the chaotic maps have been used to ensure session-key security. But the protocol is vulnerable to offline guessing, key compromise, and user impersonation attacks.

To achieve secure access and communication mechanism for various applications, Qiu *et al.* proposed a protocol [19] based on extended chaotic maps, which could achieve secure communication between the user and server. The security of this scheme is based on the Computational Diffie-Hellman (CDH) problem. The overall calculation and communication overhead of the scheme is low. However, for the authentication between multiple IoT users and servers, the authentication overhead will increase linearly.

In addition, Cui *et al.* proposed an authentication and key agreement scheme using chaotic mapping and three-factor mutual authentication [21], and the experimental results show that the scheme is suitable for the connected vehicle environment. Similarly, this scheme does not consider multi-user scenarios. In order to achieve a faster network service for users while ensuring confidentiality and authentication of data transmission, Xu *et al.* proposed a certificateless sign-cryption mechanism [22]. However, the scheme includes time-consuming bilinear pairing operations that can reduce the efficiency of authentication.

**Table 1.** Pros and Cons of Various Schemes

| Schemes | Main tech | Advantages | Disadvantages |
|---|---|---|---|
| [16] | ECDLP | Online/offline signcryption | Fail to achieve key update and revocation |
| [22] | Signcryption | Resist various common attacks | Time-consuming pairing operations |
| [17] | Three-factor, signcryption | authorization, authentication, and revocation | Fail to achieve key update |
| [18] | Three-factor, chaotic maps | Low costs, achieve revocation | Cannot resist off-line guessing attack, impersonation attack |
| [19] | Three-factor, chaotic maps | Revocation and key update | Fail to take into account multiple users |
| [21] | Three-factor, chaotic maps | Revocation | Fail to take into account multiple users |

## 3   Preliminaries and Background

We will introduce the related preliminaries, i.e., chaotic maps, and CRT, in this section. And then, the system model and threat model are described in detail, as well as the security requirements of the proposed scheme.

### 3.1   Preliminaries

**Chaotic Maps.** Assuming that $n, x \in_R Z_q^*$ are positive integer, $T_n(x)$ represents the Chebyshev polynomial [23–25] and is expressed as $T_n(x) = cos(n \cos^{-1}(x))$. The recurrence relation of Chebyshev polynomial is as follows:

$$T_n(x) = \begin{cases} 1, & if \ n = 0 \\ x, & if \ n = 1 \\ 2xT_{n-1}(x) - T_{n-2}(x), & if \ n \geq 2 \end{cases}$$

**Chinese Remainder Theorem.** We start with the construction of an integer $a$ whose modulus set is $k$. Let $a$ be the integer to be constructed, and $X$ the remainder of $a_i$ modulo $k_i$, i.e.,

$$X \equiv a_i \bmod k_i, where \ i = 1, ..., n$$

That is, all remainders $a_i$ modulo $k_i$ have the same value, named common remainder $X$. According to traditional CRT [26–28], X can be uniquely reconstructed as

$$X = a_1 + a_2 + \dots + a_n = \sum_{i=1}^{n} a_i \beta_i \gamma_i (\mathrm{mod}\, \zeta)$$

where $\zeta = k_1 k_2 \dots k_n$, $\beta_i = \frac{\zeta}{k_i}$, $\beta_i \gamma_i \equiv 1 \mod k_i$.

## 3.2   System Model

Figure 2 demonstrates the system model of the proposed scheme. The main entity includes Vehicle Computing/Communication Unit, Service Provider, and Application.

Vehicle Computing/Communication Unit (VCU): VCU is a trusted entity deployed inside the vehicle. The credibility of the VCU can be achieved through an embedded trusted execution environment [29,30] such as Intel SGX, AMD SEV, or ARM TrustZone.

Service Provider (SP): SP can provide personalized services for vehicle internal applications, including assisting in providing vehicle peripheral information and providing entertainment services.

Application: The internal applications can obtain real-time information of the vehicle. This information will be further securely transmitted to the corresponding application provider for further processing. For example, the surrounding road condition information is reported to the traffic authority, and the traffic congestion has been improved.

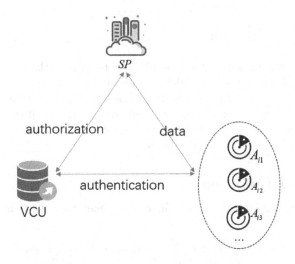

**Fig. 2.** System model of the proposed scheme

### 3.3  Threat Model

In our scenario, it is assumed that two participants, i.e., CAV and service provider, communicate through the public channel. Adversary A can modify, eavesdrop or delete the message transmitted between CAV and service provider. In addition, we assume that adversary A can adopt analysis attacks to extract all sensitive information for legitimate participants.

### 3.4  Security Objectives

**Message Authentication and Integrity.** For a received message, the message receiver must first determine that the message is sent by a legitimate sender, and judges whether the message has been tampered with or forged by an adversary.

**Identity Privacy Preserving.** The SP and A can not adopt real identity to communicate directly, and they could use a pseudo-identity to achieve identity privacy. Apart from the VCU, any third party can not track the true identity of the message sender.

**Traceability.** After receiving the request from the SP, the VCU have the ability to recover the real identity to achieve trace from the message of its $App_i$ pseudo-identity.

**Resistance to Ordinary Attacks.** The typical attacks, such as modification, replay and impersonation, should be withstood by the proposed scheme, thus the communication is secure.

## 4  Proposed Scheme

This part presents our proposed in detail. The proposed scheme mainly includes six parts, namely the system initialization phase, pseudonym generation phase of $App_i$ and $SP_j$, the session key generation phase, the message signcryption phase, the message decryption and verification phase, the traceability and revocation phase. The notations used in this scheme are shown in Table 2. Figure 3 shows the whole phase of the proposed scheme.

### 4.1  System Initialization

VCU generates system parameters, including generating the paired private and public keys.

1) VCU sets the elliptic curve $E$. The generator $P$ of $E$ is randomly chosen.
2) VCU chooses the hash functions $H : 0, 1^* \rightarrow Z_q^*$ and $w, r_E \in_R Z_q^*$. Then it computes $P_{pub} = wP$, $R_E = r_E P$, and then $s_E = r_E + wH(R_E)$.
3) VCU publishes the system parameters $P, H, P_{pub}, R_E$.

**Table 2.** Notations

| Notations | Definitions |
| --- | --- |
| VCU | Vehicle Computing/Communication Unit |
| $SP_j$ | Service Provider $j$ |
| $App_i$ | The application $i$ of the corresponding $SP_j$ |
| $ID_i, AID_i$ | The real identity and pseudonym of $App_i$ |
| $ID_j, AID_j$ | The real identity and pseudonym of $SP_j$ |
| $H(.)$ | The secure cryptographic hash operation |
| $a_i$ | The secret number of $App_i$ |
| $x, r_E$ | The secret number of VCU |
| $w, P_{pub}$ | The secret key and the public key of VCU |
| $s_E$ | The secret number for legitimate group $App_i$ |
| $SK$ | The session key for legitimate group member $App_i$ and $SP_j$ |
| $T_n(x)$ | Chaotic maps polynomial |
| $\oplus$ | The exclusive-OR operation |
| $\|$ | Concatenation operation |

### 4.2  Pseudonym Generation

In this phase, VCU achieves authorization to the $SP_j$, and it achieves authentication for legal applications, then it sends the secret value to the corresponding applications.

1) $App_i$ sends $ID_i$ to VCU through a secure channel, and VCU chooses the positive prime number $a_i \in_R Z_q^*$, and sends $a_i$ to $App_i$.
2) $App_i$ computes $AID_{i1} = a_iP, AID_{i2} = ID_i \oplus H(a_iP_{pub})$, and saves the $AID_i = (AID_{i1}, AID_{i2})$.
3) $SP_j$ sends $ID_j$ to VCU through a secure channel, and VCU chooses a number $x \in_R Z_q^*$, and computes $T_{S_E}(x)$. Then VCU securely sends $x, T_{S_E}(x)$ to $SP_j$.
4) $SP_j$ chooses random number $u \in_R Z_q^*$, computes $AID_{j1} = uP, AID_{j2} = ID_j \oplus H(uP_{pub})$, and saves the $AID_j = (AID_{j1}, AID_{j2})$. At the same time, the VCU calculates the hash values of multiple SPs $H(ID_j)$, adds them to the hash list of SP $H_{list}$, and broadcasts the list.

### 4.3  Key Agreement

When an $SP_j$ wants to access the data for some corresponding applications $App_i$, it needs to initiate a request.

1) $SP_j$ computes $C_1 = T_u(x), C_2 = T_u(T_{S_E}(x)), C_3 = H(ID_j) \oplus H(C_2)$, and $C_4 = H(AID_j\|C_1\|C_2)$. Then it computes the session key $SK = H(AID_j\|C_2)$. Finally, $SP_j$ sends $AID_j, C_1, C_2, C_3, C_4$ to $App_i$ for verifying.

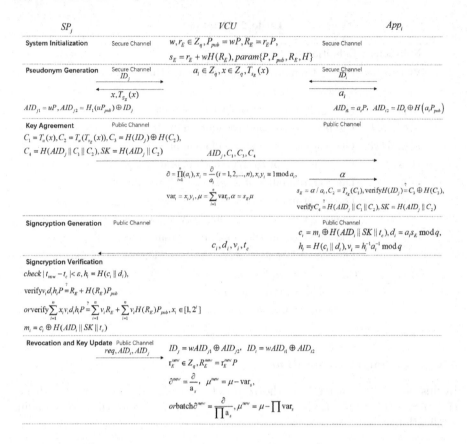

**Fig. 3.** Interaction Phase of the Proposed Scheme

2) VCU will compute $\partial = \prod_{i=1}^{n}(a_i), x_i = \frac{\partial}{a_i}(i = 1, 2, ..., n), x_i y_i \equiv 1 \bmod$ $a_i, \mathrm{var}_i = x_i y_i, \mu = \sum_{i=1}^{n} \mathrm{var}_i$. Then VCU computes $\alpha = s_E \mu$. VCU will send $\alpha$ to $App_i$ on the public channel.

3) After receiving $AID_j, C_1, C_3, C_4$ and $\alpha$, $App_i$ first computes $s_E = \alpha/a_i$, and $C_2 = T_{s_E}(C_1)$. It computes $H(ID_j) = C_3 \oplus H(C_2)$, and then checks whether $H(ID_j)$ exist in the list $H_{list}$. If existing, then it could verify $C_4 = H(AID_j \| C_1 \| C_2)$ equals or not. If the equal holds, then it computes $SK = H(AID_j \| C_2)$.

### 4.4 Signcryption Generation

The $App_i$ could encrypt the message $m_i$ by computing $c_i = m_i \oplus H(AID_i \| SK \| t_c)$. And it computes the signcryption as $d_i = a_i s_E \bmod q, h_i =$

$H(c_i||d_i), v_i = h_i^{-1}a_i^{-1} \bmod q$ where $t_c$ represents the timestamp. Then $App_i$ send $c_i, d_i, v_i, t_c$ to $SP_j$ through VCU.

### 4.5  Signcryption Verification

After receiving the encrypted message, the $SP_j$ needs to verify and decrypt the message.

1) It first checks the timestamp by $|t_{now} - t_c| \leq \varepsilon$, where $t_{now}$ represents the current time.
2) The $SP_j$ verifies the signcryption by computing $h_i = H(c_i||d_i)$. For one message, it could verify whether this equation $v_i d_i h_i P = R_E + H(R_E)P_{pub}$ holds. For n messages, it could achieve batch verification by check whether this equation $\sum_{i=1}^{n} x_i v_i d_i h_i P = \sum_{i=1}^{n} v_i R_E + \sum_{i=1}^{n} v_i H(R_E)P_{pub}, x_i \in [1, 2^t]$ holds.
3) If the signcryption is verified, it then gets the message by calculating $m_i = c_i \oplus H(AID_i||SK||t_c)$.

### 4.6  Revocation and Key Update

When the batch authentication is failed, $SP_j$ needs to execute a binary search to find the $AID_i$ that generated the signcryption. It can send a request to the VCU to trace the true identity, which generate the signcryption.

After receiving the request and $AID_i, AID_j$, the VCU verifies the authenticity of the request and follows these steps:

1) VCU could reveal the real identity of $SP_j$ by calculating $ID_j$ while $ID_j = H(wAID_{j1}) \oplus AID_{j2}$, and checks if $ID_j$ is a valid participant. If valid, continues, or else reject the request.
2) VCU receives the request, it could reveal the real identity of $App_i$ by calculating $ID_i = H(wAID_{i1}) \oplus AID_{i2}$.
3) When the VCU detects a malicious application, it needs to update the key. In addition, the key can be updated regularly even when the system is running normally. VCU updates the new secret value $r_E^{new} \in {_R}Z_q^*$, and compute $R_E^{new} = r_E^{new}P$.
4) VCU checks the $ID_i$ in the database, and it realizes the revocation of malicious applications through the following operations:
   For a malicious application, it could compute $\partial^{new} = \frac{\partial}{a_s}\mu^{new} = \mu - var_s$ to replace the $\partial, \mu$.

For some malicious applications, it could achieve batch revocation by computing $\partial^{new} = \frac{\partial}{\prod a_s}, \mu^{new} = \mu - \prod var_s$.

## 5  Security Analysis

We prove that the proposed scheme is secure under the random oracle model through a formal security proof, in this section. Then, we analyze in detail how the proposed scheme could achieve the aforementioned security requirements in Sect. 3.

## 5.1  Formal Security Proof

**Theorem 1.** *Assuming A2S be an event that A may violate the secure commu-nication process between Application and Service Provider. $D_{id}$ and $D$ are the identity dictionary of size $|D_{id}|$ and $|D|$ respectively, and both follow the regu-lar of uniform distribution. Assume that $Adv_A^{CMDLP}$ is the advantage of A in solving chaotic map-based discrete logarithm problem (CMDLP) in polynomial time.*

*Proof.* Let A represent the adversary who opposes the secure communication procedure. Within the time complexity limit $t$, the query is executed only at most $q_e$ times, the query is sent $q_s$ times, and the hash query is executed $q_h$ times. Hence,

$$Adv_{A2S}^{AKA}(A) \le \frac{2(q_s + q_e)}{|D_{id}|} + \frac{q_h^2 + q_s}{2^l} + \frac{(q_s + q_e)^2}{p}$$
$$+ 2q_s \max\{\frac{1}{|D|}, \varepsilon\} + 2q_h((q_s + q_e)^2 + 1)$$
$$* Adv_A^{CMCDH}(A)(t + (q_s + q_e)t_m) \tag{1}$$

Experiment $Exp_0$: In this experiment, the real simulated attack is performed in a random oracle model. A has access to all oracles. So we have

$$Adv_{A2S}^{AKA}(A) = 2Pr[E_0] - 1 \tag{2}$$

Experiment $Exp_1$: This experiment simulates random predictions H through the management of the hash list. Since all predictions are simulated as real attacks, the experiment cannot be distinguished from the actual execution of the protocol. Thus, we have

$$F_1 = |Pr[E_1] - Pr[E_0]| = 0 \tag{3}$$

Experiment $Exp_2$: This experiment also demonstrates all oracle's predictions Send, Execute, Reveal, Corrupt, and Test. Once A obtains the true identity of A or SP from the identity space, we stop simulating these guessed identity attacks. If this is not the case, $Pr[E_1]$ and $Pr[E_2]$ are indistinguishable:

$$F_2 = |Pr[E_2] - Pr[E_1]| \le \frac{q_s + q_e}{|D_{id}|} \tag{4}$$

Experiment $Exp_3$: In this experiment, all oracles are also simulated. There are two conflicting styles in $Exp_3$. If both collisions occur, the adversary A will launch a replay attack to win the game. According to the birthday paradox, we can draw the possibility of collision. The probability of hash collision is $\frac{q_h^2}{2^{l+1}}$, and probability of random number collision is at $\frac{(q_s+q_e)^2}{2p}$. Hence, the distinguished probability for $Pr[E_2]$ and $Pr[E_3]$ can be represented as:

$$F_3 = |Pr[E_3] - Pr[E_2]| \le \frac{q_h^2}{2^{l+1}} + \frac{(q_s + q_e)^2}{2p} \tag{5}$$

Experiment $Exp_4$: Here, all the predictions model in $Exp_3$ are also used in this experiment. When Corrupt(S) is queried, adversary $A$ can extract the information $C1$, $C3$, $C4$ and $s_E$ stored in the legitimate application. To get the session key, $A$ needs to know the secret value $x$, $r_E$, and $u$. It is difficult to recover $x$ and $s_E$ from the messages $C1$, $C3$ and $C4$. The adversary cannot obtain the correct session key because there is no useful secret value in the entire communication message. So we have

$$F_4 = |Pr[E_4] - Pr[E_3]| \leq q_s \max\{\frac{1}{|D|}, \varepsilon\} \tag{6}$$

Experiment $Exp_5$: In this experiment, we considered the probability $A$ forged authentication value $c_i, d_i, v_i$, but do not use the random oracle to make corresponding queries. Oracle can stop the game with the correct value, and $Exp_5$ becomes indistinguishable from $Exp_4$ to A. So we will have

$$F_5 = |Pr[E_5] - Pr[E_4]| \leq \frac{q_s}{2^l} \tag{7}$$

Experiment $Exp_6$: In experiment $Exp_6$, after the previous Test query, we assume that adversary $A$ is Corrupt(A). Similar to the aforementioned experiments, in the hash oracle, the probability of $u$ and $s_E$ in the same session is $\frac{1}{(qs+qe)^2}$ if the session key $SK$ can be obtained. We define adversary $A$'s advantages as $Adv_A^{CMDH}(A)(t + (q_e + q_s)t_m)$, and $t$ is the longest time. In addition, $t_m$ is point multiplication time in Elliptic Curve Cryptography. Thus, the game could be won with minimum $q_h$ hash queries. Hence, we have

$$\begin{aligned} F_6 &= |Pr[E_6] - Pr[E_5]| \\ &\leq q_h(q_s + q_e)^2 Adv_A^{CMDH}(A)(t + (q_e + q_s)t_m) \end{aligned} \tag{8}$$

In addition, if the Test query randomly returns real bit guesses, $A$ will successfully against the oracle. So, we will get

$$Pr[E_7] = Pr[E_6] = 1/2 \tag{9}$$

Therefore, we will get the equal from $F_1, F_2, F_3, F_4, F_5, F_6$

$$|Pr[E_0] - 1/2| = |Pr[E_6] - Pr[E_5]|$$
$$\leq |Pr[E_1] - Pr[E_0]| + |Pr[E_2] - Pr[E_1]|$$
$$+ |Pr[E_3] - Pr[E_2]| + |Pr[E_4] - Pr[E_3]|$$
$$+ |Pr[E_5] - Pr[E_4]| + |Pr[E_6] - Pr[E_5]|$$
$$= F_1 + F_2 + F_3 + F_4 + F_5 + F_6$$
$$\leq \frac{(q_s + q_e)}{|D_{id}|} + \frac{q_h^2}{2^{l+i}} + \frac{q_s}{2^l} + \frac{(q_s + q_e)^2}{2p}$$
$$+ q_s \max\{\frac{1}{|D|}, \varepsilon\} + q_h((q_s + q_e)^2 + 1)$$
$$* Adv_A^{CMCDH}(A)(t + (q_s + q_e)t_m) \tag{10}$$

Finally, according to Game $E_0 - E_6$, we could get

$$Adv_{A2S}^{AKA}(A) \leq \frac{2(q_s + q_e)}{|D_{id}|} + \frac{q_h^2 + q_s}{2^l} + \frac{(q_s + q_e)^2}{p}$$
$$+ 2q_s \max\{\frac{1}{|D|}, \varepsilon\} + 2q_h((q_s + q_e)^2 + 1)$$
$$* Adv_A^{CMCDH}(A)(t + (q_s + q_e)t_m) \tag{11}$$

## 5.2 Security Analysis

**Message Authentication.** This scheme can realize single message authentication by judging whether this equation $v_i d_i h_i P = R_E + H(R_E)P_{pub}$ holds. It could achieve batch message authentication for massive messages by judging whether this equation $\sum_{i=1}^{n} x_i v_i d_i h_i P = \sum_{i=1}^{n} v_i R_E + \sum_{i=1}^{n} v_i H(R_E)P_{pub}, x_i \in [1, 2^t]$ hold.

**Identity Privacy Preserving.** SP only needs to collect reliable data of real applications, and there is no need to obtain its real identity. This scheme can realize anonymous communication between SP and the application. For application $App_i$, only itself and the VCU can obtain his real identity. The $a_i$ and $w$ are kept securely, and the attacker cannot overcome the $ECDLP$ problem within a polynomial time, so the pseudonym is security.

**Traceability.** When necessary, the ECU can recover the true identity. Since $w$ is only unique to ECU, it can obtain the real identity of the application by calculating $ID_i = H(wAID_{i1}) \oplus AID_{i2}$.

**Resistance to Ordinary Attacks.** Here, the security of the proposed scheme will be evaluated based on the evaluation criteria and threat model.

**Impersonation Attack.** In order to pretend to be a server, an adversary $A$ must calculate the effective $AID_j, C_1, C_3, C_4$. Because of $C_1 = T_u(x)$, $C_2 = T_u(T_{s_E}(x))$, $C_3 = H(ID_j) \oplus H(C_2)$, $C_4 = H(AID_j \| C_1 \| C_2)$, and then $SK = H(AID_j \| C_2)$ is computed by $AID_j \| C_2$, it is protected by the one-way hash function. $A$ must obtain these secret parameters or guess the correct value in polynomial time. In order to obtain these secret parameters, $A$ needs to have $ID_j, u, x$. However, it is computationally difficult for an adversary $A$ to guess these values in polynomial time. At the same time, the scheme can achieve anonymity and cannot restore the real identity of the $SP_j$. An adversary $A$ cannot calculate a valid message. Therefore, the program can resist impersonation attacks.

**Modificaiton Attack.** Suppose that adversary $A$ initiates a message modification attack, and $A$ successfully calculates the session key on the premise that $T_{s_E u}$ is calculated. However, our formal security proof shows that if the forged message is successfully verified, the difficult problem of $CMCDH$ can be solved in polynomial time. However, it is generally accepted that it is difficult to calculate $CMCDH$ in polynomial time. Therefore, the scheme can resist modification attacks.

**Replay Attack.** Assume that the adversary $A$ obtains the request message $AID_j, C_1, C_2, C_3$ and $c_i, d_i, v_i, t_c$ on the public channel. If $A$ re-sends to the application. Due to the existence of the time stamp, the time difference between the time when the message is received and the time when the message is generated is first verified each time. Therefore, the replayed message cannot pass the verification of the message receiver. That is, this scheme could resist replay attacks.

**Session Temporary Information Attack.** In the proposed scheme, if temporary information is leaked, $A$ can calculate $SK = H(AID_j \| C_2)$. $A$ needs to calculate $C_2 = T_{us_E}(x)$. Since $A$ has no way to point out the correct $C_2$, which is calculated from the chaotic map. Therefore, the scheme can resist the session's temporary information attack.

**Man-in-the-Middle Attack.** In this scheme, we assume that the adversary $A$ gets the message $AID_j, C_1, C_2, C_3$ in the public channel. In order to successfully launch a man-in-the-middle attack, $A$ must forge a new message $AID_j^*, C_1^*, C_2^*, C_3^*$ or replay the previous message. As we discussed before, impersonation attacks and replay attacks can be resisted in the proposed scheme. Therefore, the forged message of $A$ cannot be verified by the verifier. Therefore, the scheme can resist man-in-the-middle attacks.

**Traceability.** This scheme can achieve traceability for malicious applications $A_i$ and $SP_j$. We assume that there is an application whose message authentication fails. At this time, the message verifier feeds the message back to the VCU. VCU can trace malicious applications by calculating $ID_i = H(wAID_{i1}) \oplus AID_{i2}$ from $AID_i$.

**Conditional Anonymous Provision.** The proposed scheme can realize the anonymity of $SP_j$ and applications $A_i$ during message transmission. At the same time, the pseudonym can be updated regularly, such as a period of time or the discovery of malicious applications. As described earlier, while ensuring anonymity, traceability can be achieved when needed.

**Session Key Security.** Adversary $A$ could get the all necessary parameters in the public channel, but the session keys must be secured. We assume that $A$ can obtain $AID_j, C_1, C_2, C_3$, $A$ want to compute the correct $SK$. However, in order to calculate the session key $SK$, $A$ needs to calculate $T_{us_E}$. But it is considered difficult for $A$ to extract random numbers $u$ and $s_E$ from $T_{us_E}$. Therefore, even if these secret parameters are leaked, $A$ cannot calculate $SK$. That is, the scheme can achieve session key security.

**Efficient Session Key Update.** In order to ensure the security of the session key and the secure transmission of the message, this scheme can realize periodic key update. When the VCU detects a malicious application, it immediately executes the key update operation as $r_E^{new} \in _R Z_q^*, R_E^{new} = r_E^{new} P$. At last, the $r_E^{new}, R_E^{new}$ could replace the $r_E, R_E$.

**Mutual Authentication.** Mutual authentication can be achieved in our proposed scheme between the application $App_i$ and the service provider $SP_j$. The application $App_i$ could use the list $H_{list}$ to check whether the service provider $SP_j$ is legal, and it could calculate $C_4 \overset{?}{=} H(AID_j \| C_1 \| C_2)$. $SP_j$ could calculate $v_i d_i h_i P \overset{?}{=} R_E + H(R_E) P_{pub}$ to verify the message sent by the application $App_i$.

**Efficient Revocation.** The proposed scheme can realize the efficient revocation of malicious applications. If the $SP_j$'s message authentication fails, it sends a message to the VCU. If the VCU confirms the message, it can achieve revocation as $\partial^{new} = \frac{\partial}{a_s}, \mu^{new} = \mu - \text{var}_s$ for the application. Moreover, this scheme can realize batch revocation as $\partial^{new} = \frac{\partial}{\prod a_s}, \mu^{new} = \mu - \prod \text{var}_s$ of the group of malicious applications.

## 6   Performance Evaluation

In this section, we analyze the security and computational cost of some schemes [16–19], and demonstrate the result in the form of tables.

The communication costs of different schemes are compared based on the same parameters. The related security parameters we used are as follows. We chose a 160-bit identity for all participants. For the prime number $p$, the length is 256 bits. And the random number is 128-bit in length, as well as the elliptic curve point is 160-bit in length. The hash function we used is SHA-160. The packet size of the symmetric encryption algorithm is 128-bit. Finally, the timestamp is a length of 16 bits.

CC represents communication cost, CMF represents the round number of communication message flows. We should note that some low-cost operations, such as XOR operations and concatenation operations, are ignored. And we use the following notations in this paper. The notation $T_c$ is the calculation time overhead for expansion chaotic maps, and the notation $T_m$ is the time overhead for point multiplication calculation on an elliptic curve. In addition, the notation $T_s$ is the calculation time overhead for the symmetric cryptographic operation, such as AES. Moreover, the notation $T_h$ is the calculation time overhead for the one-way hash operation.

As shown in Table 3, Ting *et al.*'s scheme [16] and Mandal *et al.*'s scheme [17] could achieve signcryption, but their scheme uses real identities, so transmission on a public channel cannot guarantee higher security. Their scheme cannot achieve efficient key update. Ting *et al.*'s scheme [16] does not provide resisting replay attack and efficient revocation. Ray *et al.*'s scheme [18] and Qiu *et al.*'s scheme [19] could achieve security authentication based on extended chaotic maps. Similarly, these schemes are constructed using real identities $ID$. Using real identities on public channels may reveal personal privacy information. Qiu *et al.*'s scheme [19] does not support efficient session key update.

**Table 3.** Security and Functionality Comparison

|  | [16] | [17] | [18] | [19] | Our scheme |
|---|---|---|---|---|---|
| Impersonation attack | √ | √ | √ | √ | √ |
| Modificaiton attack | √ | √ | √ | √ | √ |
| Replay attacks | × | √ | √ | √ | √ |
| Session temporary information attack | √ | √ | √ | √ | √ |
| Man-in-the-middle attack | √ | √ | √ | √ | √ |
| Traceability | × | × | × | × | √ |
| Conditional anonymous provision | × | × | × | × | √ |
| Session key security | √ | √ | √ | √ | √ |
| Efficient session key update | × | × | √ | × | √ |
| Mutual authentication | √ | √ | √ | √ | √ |
| Efficient revocation | × | √ | √ | √ | √ |

Table 4 shows the cost overhead for the scheme in the authentication phases. Ting *et al.*'s scheme [16] will cost $2T_m + 2T_h + 3T_m + 3T_h = 5T_m + 5T_h$ to generate and verify signcryption. Mandal *et al.*'s scheme [17] will cost $8T_m + 12T_h + 3T_m + 8T_h = 11T_m + 20T_h$ to generate and verify signcryption, which requires slightly more computational cost. But this scheme can realize the authentication of users and smart devices with the assistance of the gateway. Roy *et al.*'s scheme [18] will cost $9T_h + 2T_c + 6T_h + T_c = 15T_h + 3T_c$ to achieve user authentication. Qiu *et al.*'s scheme [19] will cost $10T_h + 3T_c + 8T_h + 3T_c = 18T_h + 6T_c$ to achieve secure authentication. During the authentication phases, the total computational cost of the proposed scheme is $6T_h + 2T_c + 2T_m + 5T_h + T_c = 2T_m + 11T_h + 3T_c$. We can see that more computational cost is required by our proposed scheme slightly than Qiu *et al.*'s scheme [19], but, compared with other schemes, the scheme in this paper can achieve more functions and better security.

**Table 4.** Cost comparison

| Protocols | User cost | Server cost | Total cost | CC | CMF |
|---|---|---|---|---|---|
| [16] | $2T_m + 2T_h$ | $3T_m + 3T_h$ | $5T_m + 5T_h$ | 672 bits | 1 |
| [17] | $8T_m + 12T_h$ | $3T_m + 8T_h$ | $11T_m + 20T_h$ | 1728 bits | 2 |
| [18] | $9T_h + 2T_c$ | $6T_h + T_c$ | $15T_h + 3T_c$ | 960 bits | 2 |
| [19] | $10T_h + 3T_c$ | $8T_h + 3T_c$ | $18T_h + 6T_c$ | 1376 bits | 2 |
| Ours | $6T_h + 2T_c + 2T_m$ | $5T_h + T_c$ | $2T_m + 11T_h + 3T_c$ | 1056 bits | 2 |

Ting *et al.*'s scheme [16] will cost $160 + 128 * 2 + 128 * 2 = 672bits$ to send $c, R_s, K1, d, v$ to receiver. the communication cost of Mandal *et al.*'s scheme [17] is $(160*3 + 128*2 + 160 + 16 + 128*2) + (128*2 + 160 + 16 + 128) = 1728bits$. The total communication cost of Roy *et al.*'s scheme [18] is $(160 + 128 + 160*2 + 16) + (160 * 2 + 16) = 960bits$. The communication cost of Qiu *et al.*'s scheme [19] is $(160 + 128 + 160*3) + (128 + 160*3) = 1376bits$. The total communication cost of the proposed scheme is $(160 + 128 + 160 + 160) + (160 + 128*2 + 16) = 1056bits$. The communication overhead of the proposed scheme is slightly higher than that of Roy *et al.*'s scheme [18], but it is significantly lower than Mandal *et al.*'s scheme [17] and Qiu *et al.*'s scheme [19].

The overhead of signature generation and verification for different schemes is shown in Fig. 4. The signature generation cost of the proposed scheme is higher than that of Ray *et al.*'s scheme [18] and Qiu et al.'s scheme [19]. However, the signature verification cost of the proposed scheme is lower than that of the compared schemes. In addition, the communication overhead is shown in Fig. 5.

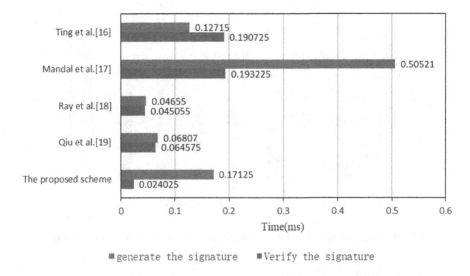

**Fig. 4.** The computational overhead of generating and verifying signatures

This scheme can realize batch message authentication and its computational overhead is shown in Fig. 6. The results show that the scheme can be used in the case of a large number of messages. The scheme has good performance for the application of large amounts of data security communication in CAV.

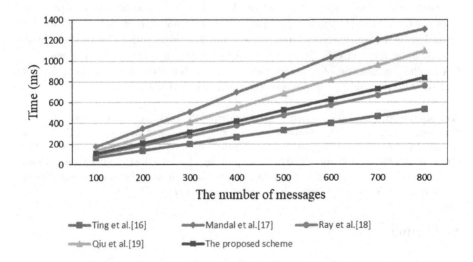

**Fig. 5.** The communication overhead of multiple messages

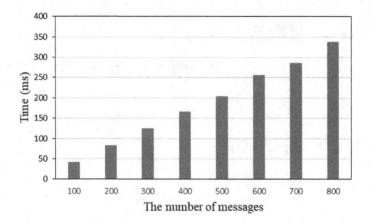

**Fig. 6.** The computational overhead of massive message authentication

## 7 Conclusion

To solve the secure data transmission between the CAV internal application module and the corresponding SP, this paper proposes a signcryption scheme based on the chaotic map, which realizes the secure transmission of data between the application module and SP with the assistance of VCU. SP can realize batch message authentication, which could achieve efficient message authentication. This scheme is based on conditional anonymity to achieve mutual authentication between applications and SP. When the VCU knows that there is a compromised application, It could revoke the application module and update the key. The formal security proof shows that the scheme is secure under the random oracle model. Security analysis shows that the scheme can meet the requirements of CAV. The comparison of related schemes shows that the scheme is more efficient and may be applied to the secure communication of CAV.

**Acknowledgments.** The work was supported in part by Open Fund of Anhui Province Key Laboratory of Cyberspace Security Situation Awareness and Evaluation, in part by the National Natural Science Foundation of China under Grant 62272002, Grant 62202005, and Grant 62202008, in part by the Excellent Youth Foundation of Anhui Scientific Committee under Grant 2108085J31, in part by the Natural Science Foundation of Anhui Province, China under Grant 2208085QF198.

## References

1. Kim, K., Kim, J.S., Jeong, S., Park, J.H., Kim, H.K.: Cybersecurity for autonomous vehicles: review of attacks and defense. Comput. Secur. **103**, 102150 (2021)
2. Zhang, Q., et al.: Openvdap: an open vehicular data analytics platform for cavs. In: 2018 IEEE 38th International Conference on Distributed Computing Systems (ICDCS), pp. 1310–1320 (2018)

3. Sroka, P., Kliks, A.: Towards edge intelligence in the automotive scenario: a discourse on architecture for database-supported autonomous platooning. J. Commun. Netw. **24**(2), 192–208 (2022)
4. Liu, S., Tang, J., Zhang, Z., Gaudiot, J.: Computer architectures for autonomous driving. Computer **50**(8), 18–25 (2017)
5. He, J., et al.: Cooperative connected autonomous vehicles (CAV): research, applications and challenges. In: 2019 IEEE 27th International Conference on Network Protocols (ICNP), pp. 1–6. IEEE (2019)
6. Ma, Y., Wang, Z., Yang, H., Yang, L.: Artificial intelligence applications in the development of autonomous vehicles: a survey. IEEE/CAA J. Automatica Sinica **7**(2), 315–329 (2020)
7. Wei, W., Yang, R., Gu, H., Zhao, W., Chen, C., Wan, S.: Multi-objective optimization for resource allocation in vehicular cloud computing networks. IEEE Trans. Intell. Transp. Syst. **23**(12), 25536–25545 (2021)
8. Cui, J., Wei, L., Zhang, J., Xu, Y., Zhong, H.: An efficient message-authentication scheme based on edge computing for vehicular ad hoc networks. IEEE Trans. Intell. Transp. Syst. **20**(5), 1621–1632 (2018)
9. Zhang, Q., Wu, J., Zhong, H., He, D., Cui, J.: Efficient anonymous authentication based on physically unclonable function in industrial internet of things. IEEE Trans. Inf. Forensics Secur. **18**, 233–247 (2023)
10. Li, T., Shang, M., Wang, S., Filippelli, M., Stern, R.: Detecting stealthy cyber-attacks on automated vehicles via generative adversarial networks. In: 2022 IEEE 25th International Conference on Intelligent Transportation Systems (ITSC), pp. 3632–3637. IEEE (2022)
11. Zhang, Q., Zhong, H., Cui, J., Ren, L., Shi, W.: Ac4av: a flexible and dynamic access control framework for connected and autonomous vehicles. IEEE Internet Things J. **8**(3), 1946–1958 (2021)
12. Mousavinejad, E., Yang, F., Han, Q.L., Ge, X., Vlacic, L.: Distributed cyber attacks detection and recovery mechanism for vehicle platooning. IEEE Trans. Intell. Transport. Syst. **21**, 3821–3834 (2019)
13. Chattopadhyay, A., Lam, K.Y., Tavva, Y.: Autonomous vehicle: security by design. IEEE Trans. Intell. Transport. Syst. **22**, 7015–7029 (2020)
14. Wazid, M., Das, A.K., Kumar, N., Vasilakos, A.V., Rodrigues, J.J.: Design and analysis of secure lightweight remote user authentication and key agreement scheme in internet of drones deployment. IEEE Internet Things J. **6**(2), 3572–3584 (2018)
15. Bagga, P., Das, A.K., Wazid, M., Rodrigues, J.J., Choo, K.K.R., Park, Y.: On the design of mutual authentication and key agreement protocol in internet of vehicles-enabled intelligent transportation system. IEEE Trans. Veh. Technol. **70**(2), 1736–1751 (2021)
16. Ting, P., Tsai, J., Wu, T.: Signcryption method suitable for low-power IoT devices in a wireless sensor network. IEEE Syst. J. **12**(3), 2385–2394 (2018)
17. Mandal, S., Bera, B., Sutrala, A.K., Das, A.K., Choo, K.R., Park, Y.: Certificateless-signcryption-based three-factor user access control scheme for IoT environment. IEEE Internet Things J. **7**(4), 3184–3197 (2020)
18. Roy, S., Chatterjee, S., Das, A.K., Chattopadhyay, S., Kumari, S., Jo, M.: Chaotic map-based anonymous user authentication scheme with user biometrics and fuzzy extractor for crowdsourcing internet of things. IEEE Internet Things J. **5**(4), 2884–2895 (2018)
19. Qiu, S., Wang, D., Xu, G., Kumari, S.: Practical and provably secure three-factor authentication protocol based on extended chaotic-maps for mobile lightweight devices. IEEE Trans. Depend. Secure Comput. **19**(2), 1338–1351 (2022)

20. Tangade, S., Manvi, S.S., Lorenz, P.: Decentralized and scalable privacy-preserving authentication scheme in vanets. IEEE Trans. Veh. Technol. **67**(9), 8647–8655 (2018)
21. Cui, J., Yu, J., Zhong, H., Wei, L., Liu, L.: Chaotic map-based authentication scheme using physical unclonable function for internet of autonomous vehicle. IEEE Trans. Intell. Transp. Syst. **24**(3), 3167–3181 (2023)
22. Xu, G., Dong, J., Ma, C., Liu, J., Cliff, U.G.O.: A certificateless signcryption mechanism based on blockchain for edge computing. IEEE Internet Things J. (2022)
23. Bergamo, P., D'Arco, P., De Santis, A., Kocarev, L.: Security of public-key cryptosystems based on Chebyshev polynomials. IEEE Trans. Circuits Syst. I Regul. Pap. **52**(7), 1382–1393 (2005)
24. Zhang, L.: Cryptanalysis of the public key encryption based on multiple chaotic systems. Chaos Solitons Fractals **37**(3), 669–674 (2008)
25. Abbasinezhad-Mood, D., Ostad-Sharif, A., Mazinani, S.M., Nikooghadam, M.: Provably-secure escrow-less Chebyshev chaotic map-based key agreement protocol for vehicle to grid connections with privacy protection. IEEE Trans. Ind. Inf. **16**, 7287–7294 (2020)
26. Lu, R., Heung, K., Lashkari, A.H., Ghorbani, A.A.: A lightweight privacy-preserving data aggregation scheme for fog computing-enhanced IoT. IEEE Access **5**, 3302–3312 (2017)
27. Zhang, J., Cui, J., Zhong, H., Chen, Z., Liu, L.: PA-CRT: Chinese remainder theorem based conditional privacy-preserving authentication scheme in vehicular ad-hoc networks. IEEE Trans. Depend. Secure Comput. **18**, 722–735 (2019)
28. Xiong, H., Chen, J., Mei, Q., Zhao, Y.: Conditional privacy-preserving authentication protocol with dynamic membership updating for vanets. IEEE Trans. Depend. Secure Comput. **19**, 2089–2104 (2020)
29. Maene, P., Götzfried, J., De Clercq, R., Müller, T., Freiling, F., Verbauwhede, I.: Hardware-based trusted computing architectures for isolation and attestation. IEEE Trans. Comput. **67**(3), 361–374 (2017)
30. Zhang, Q., Zhong, H., Shi, W., Liu, L.: A trusted and collaborative framework for deep learning in IoT. Comput. Netw. **193**, 108055 (2021)

# Processing and Recognition

# SimBPG: A Comprehensive Similarity Evaluation Metric for Business Process Graphs

Qinkai Jiang, Jiaxing Wang, Bin Cao$^{(\boxtimes)}$, and Jing Fan

Zhejiang University of Technology, Hangzhou 310023, China
{jiangqinkai,wjx,bincao,fanjing}@zjut.edu.cn

**Abstract.** Measuring the similarity between two business process models holds significant importance across various applications. At present, there are many different similarity calculation methods, such as structural similarity based on the graph edit distance(GED), text similarity based on task node description, and behavioral similarity calculation based on path matching. However, existing similarity computation methods cannot produce reliable results since: (1) To apply GED, business process graphs will be simplified to homogeneous graph where the heterogeneity as well as the routing semantics of the business process is removed. (2) To derive comprehensive similarity evaluation, linear weighted sum of different similarity metrics is a common way, but the final result strongly depends on the weighting coefficients that are empirically assigned. In this paper, we fuse multidimensional metrics to compensate for the sole reliance on structural similarity based on GED. To address the limitations of comprehensive evaluation, we propose a novel multidimensional process similarity evaluation method based on the entropy weight method and the Technique for Order Preference by Similarity to an Ideal Solution (TOPSIS) method. We also design a experimental method to verify the effectiveness of our method, leveraging an open source dataset. The experiment shows that our method can better represent the similarity of business process graphs than other methods.

**Keywords:** business process graphs · evaluation metric · similarity calculation · heterogeneous graphs · KM algorithm

## 1 Introduction

Business process management [1] technology has been applied in many enterprises, and more and more enterprises have built their own business process library. With the development of business, the scale of the business process library is also getting larger and larger, how to calculate the business process similarity has become an important link in the management of these business process libraries [2–4]. In general, business processes are often modeled as business process graphs, which are used to describe the business relationship between various units and personnel in the management system, the sequence of operations and the flow of management information [5,6].

© ICST Institute for Computer Sciences, Social Informatics and Telecommunications Engineering 2024
Published by Springer Nature Switzerland AG 2024. All Rights Reserved
H. Gao et al. (Eds.): CollaborateCom 2023, LNICST 562, pp. 437–457, 2024.
https://doi.org/10.1007/978-3-031-54528-3_24

In the field of business process similarity calculation, most of the previous work [7–9] have proposed to measure business process graphs similarity according to different business process requirements, such as structural similarity based on the graph edit distance(GED) [10], text similarity based on task node description [11,12], and behavioral similarity calculation based on path matching [13,14]. However, this single-dimension similarity measure cannot reflect the overall similarity of the business process graph. As far as we know, with the rise of graph neural networks (GNN) [15], more and more methods use graph embedding and graph matching methods [16,17] to train a deep learning model to calculate the similarity score between graphs. But they still use the calculation results of GED as the Ground Truth of the similarity between the two graphs, they do not essentially consider whether the true value of the model fitting is reliable, which will lead to the inaccuracy of the trained model. Actually, GED need to simplify the original business process graph into an isomorphic graph, which does not distinguish between the types of task nodes and the different execution sequences between them. This simplification ignores the important characteristic that the business process graph is essentially a heterogeneous graph [18,19], which makes the routing semantics of the original business process graph lost, and cannot accurately describe the control flow semantics of the original process graph, resulting in low reliability of the similarity calculation results. Therefore, adopting a multi-dimensional comprehensive evaluation method is more helpful to obtain the similarity between business process graphs.

Furthermore, there are some works [20,21] that consider process similarity information from multiple dimensions comprehensively, the existing multi-dimension evaluation fusion methods employ a linear weighted sum of different similarity metrics, which depends on the weighting coefficients that are empirically assigned. Although these methods combine information from multiple dimensions, they lack the adaptability to capture complex relationships and nuances in the data. Therefore, the reliability and robustness of the overall similarity assessment may be compromised. To address these challenges, there is an increasing urgency to develop a more complex and adaptable approach that holistically integrates multidimensional process similarity information while alleviating the reliance on empirically defined weights.

In this paper, we disassemble the heterogeneous information of the business process graph, separate the similarity metrics of different dimensions, and perform effective fusion to obtain the similarity score. Specifically, our method consists of the following two parts:(1) *Adaptive Weights Assignment*. We evaluate the similarity of business process graphs from multiple dimensions, and calculate the similarity scores of different dimensions, such as structural similarity based on GED method and behavioral similarity based on path matching [13]. Then we use the entropy weight method [22] to objectively assign weights to metrics of multiple dimensions to remove the influence of human subjectivity. (2) *Comprehensive Evaluation with TOPSIS*. Based on the similarity metrics of different dimensions obtained in the previous phase. Then use the ideal solution similarity ranking technique (TOPSIS) method [23] to fuse the similarity of multiple dimensions to get the final similarity score.

In the experimental part, since it is impossible to define the real similarity scores of two graphs, there is no Ground Truth process similarity calculation dataset. So we designed an experiment to verify the effectiveness of our method. Our experimental data comes from real business process models collected by IBM [24], which involve different domains and different versions of models. Based on the characteristics of this dataset, we particularly designed a set of experiments to verify the proposed comprehensive similarity measuring method. Specifically, our experimental design involves following three assumptions: (1) *The two business processes in different domains are likely to be dissimilar.* For example, the insurance claims process is different from the bank loan process. (2) *The similarity between different business processes is smaller than that of different versions of the same business process.* For example, different versions of a bank loan process will contain some common sequence of execution steps. (3) *The closer the version number, the smaller the change, and the greater the difference between the version numbers, the greater the change.* Then we conduct three sets of experiments for validation, confirming the reliability of our assumptions.

We summarize our contributions as follows:

- We comprehensively evaluate the similarity of different dimensions of business process graphs using the entropy weight method and the Technique for Order Preference by Similarity to an Ideal Solution (TOPSIS).
- In order to verify the proposed method, we propose three assumptions based on real datasets, and design cross-domain experimental to verify the effectiveness of evaluation metrics.
- Proven by extensive experiments, our method can better characterize the similarity measurement problem of business process graphs than traditional GED or behavioral similarity only.

The remainder of this paper is organized as follows. Section 2 gives the related work. Section 3 presents some preliminaries for our work. Section 4 provides a detailed description of our algorithm. The experimental and concludes are given in Sect. 5 and Sect. 6 respectively.

## 2    Related Work

As far as we know, no in previous studies has proposed a standard for measuring the similarity of heterogeneous graphs. A lot of work has only focused on representation learning for heterogeneous graphs [18,19,25,26]. However, in the field of business process graph similarity measurement, a lot of work focuses on the similarity calculation of business process model, which mainly divide into three aspects: (1) Text similarity considering task semantics information. Pamungkas E W et al. [11] attempted to use word sense disambiguation to improve the accuracy of business process similarity calculations. Akkiraju et al. [12] measured similarity of business process models only based on the number of equally labeled activities. (2) Structural similarity based on business process model. The most popular approach is to use Petri nets [27] to model and calculate the structural similarity between them. Li J et al. [8] used the greedy algorithm to calculate the GED between different process models based on the Petri net. Sebu et al. [9] compared the graphs considering the composition of the subgraphs and extracted the business process similarity factor. (3) Behavior similarity based on process mining. Cao B et al. [13] introduced the idea of fundamental path testing from the field of software testing and proposed an effective method to detect differences in workflow behavior. Wang Z X et al. [14] expressed the behavior of the process model by defining a transitional marker graph, refine the graph editing operation and the calculation method of the GED according to the behavior characteristics. However, they are all only consider one aspect of business process similarity, therefore, their method can only be calculated for the similarity of a particular business process requirement, and is not universal and accurate.

A small number of methods have tried multi-dimension fusion. Cao B et al. [7] proposed a query method based on the Hungarian algorithm, which defines the contextual similarity of a pair of place nodes from different process models by considering common paths and common transitions, and maps to the classic assignment problem that the Hungarian algorithm can effectively solve. They integrate structural similarity and behavioral similarity, but their methods only consider the behavioral similarity of local optimal matching, not the global behavior of the business process, which has an impact on evaluating the similarity of the entire business process. Aisyah et al. [20] and Zhou et al. [21] conducted a comprehensive evaluation of the similarity of business process graphs. They considered the weight differences between different branches and performed simple addition or linear changes to obtain comprehensive considerations of similarity in different dimensions. However, this method relying on empirical weights cannot reflect the similarity in the real multi-dimension space.

## 3    Preliminaries

This section we introduce the concepts of *Business Process Graph*, *Basic Path* and *Edit Distance*, which help to understand our method.

### 3.1    Business Process Graph

Business process model is often used to help identify, describe and decompose business processes. It can be modeled in many ways, including Event-driven Process Chains (EPC), UML Activity Diagrams, Business Process Modeling Notation (BPMN) and Petri nets [5,28]. In this paper, we only consider the similarity calculation between the two business process, trying to find a general graph similarity evaluation metric, the previous business process model representation method is too complex and the detail representation is too specific, which is not suitable for the similarity calculation of the business processes, so we define a new representation similar to Petri nets [29], but simpler and clearer than Petri nets.

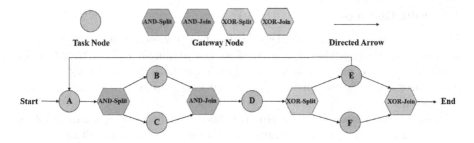

**Fig. 1.** Example of a business process graph.

*Definition 1:* a business process graph (BPG) is a 3-tuple *BPG = (T,G,E)*, where (1) *T* is a set of the task nodes, (2) *G* is a set of gateway nodes, (3) *E* is a set of directed arrows.

The gateway node has four types: AND-Split, AND-Join, XOR-Split and XOR-Join. When multiple tasks need to be executed in parallel, AND-Split and AND-Join need to be used. When mutually exclusive selection needs to be made, XOR-Split and XOR-Join need to be used. And the direction of the arrow indicates the direction of sequential execution. A example is shown in Fig. 1.

### 3.2  Basic Path

In the field of software testing [30], the basic path is based on the program control flow graph, by analyzing the loop complexity of the control structure, deriving the set of basic executable paths, and then designing the corresponding test cases [31] [32]. Inspired by basic path testing, we can extract independent paths from business process graphs and treat them as behavioral information of the graph. We calculate the cyclomatic complexity [33] to measure the complexity of the entire business process, and use this measure as the number of basic paths. The calculation method is as follows:

$$V(G) = |E| - |V| + 2 \tag{1}$$

where *V(G)* denotes the cyclomatic complexity, $|E|$ denotes the number of edges, the $|V|$ denotes the number of nodes.

Since there are many loops in the business process graph, we have specially processed these paths, that is, adding the *'loop'* string and the next task node after the loop starts. For example, for the business process graph in Fig. 1, we can find two basic paths, which are $\{A, B, C, D, E,' loop', A\}$ and $\{A, B, C, D, F\}$. These two paths represent the process of business process execution. Here, for the sake of convenience, we put the *B* and *C* tasks of parallel operations into the basic path in sequence, but this does not have a great impact on the execution process of the entire business process graph, because both tasks *B* and *C* have completed their execution process before task *D*.

### 3.3   Edit Distance

The edit distance is used to calculate the distance between two isomorphic graphs or two linear basic paths, it is defined as the minimum cost of transforming a graph (or basic path) into another graph (or basic path) through various transformations. The edit distance is divided into graph edit distance and path edit distance.

*Graph Edit Distance(GED)* [10] has been widely used in many applications, such as graph similarity search, graph classification, handwriting recognition, image indexing, etc. For two graphs $G_1$ and $G_2$, the graph edit distance $GED(G_1,G_2)$ refers to the minimum number of operations required to complete the mutual conversion between them through the insert, delete, and substitute operations of nodes and edges. Figure 2 shows an example of GED between two simple graphs. The GED between the graph to the left and the graph to the right is 3, as the transformation needs 3 edit operations: (1) delete an edge, (2) insert an edge, and (3) relabel a node.

*Path Edit Distance(PED).* Similar to GED, for two basic paths $P_1$ and $P_2$, we define $PED(P_1,P_2)$ as the minimum number of operations for converting $P_1$ to $P_2$, and the operation is only for inserting, deleting and substituting nodes. For example, suppose $P_1 = \{A, B, C, D, E, M\}$, $P_2 = \{A, G, B, C, D, F\}$, the basic path $P_1$ to $P_2$ require 3 edit operations: (1) insert node $G$, path converted to $\{A, G, B, C, D, E, M\}$, (2) delete node $E$, path converted to $\{A, G, B, C, D, M\}$, (3) replace node $M$ with $F$, path converted to $\{A, G, B, C, D, F\}$.

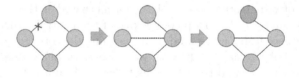

**Fig. 2.** Example of Graph Edit Distance.

## 4   Method

In this section, we introduce our proposed method SimBPG in detail. The input is any two business process graphs, while the output is the similarity score between them. Since there are multiple node types in the business process graph, we can regard it as a special heterogeneous graph. Our method is divided into two steps: *Adaptive Weights Assignment* and *Comprehensive Evaluation with TOPSIS*. The overall framework is shown in Fig. 3. First, calculate the similarity of different dimensions of two business process graphs by different methods, such as structural similarity based on GED [10] and behavioral similarity based on global semantic routing [13]. Then use the method based on entropy weight method [22] and the Technique for Order Preference by Similarity to an Ideal Solution (TOPSIS) [23] method to effectively fuse the features of each dimension.

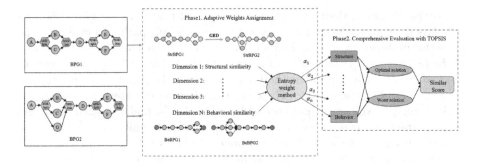

**Fig. 3.** An overview of SimBPG.

## 4.1    Phase1. Adaptive Weights Assignment

**Multidimensional Similarity Calculation.** The evaluation of the similarity of business process graphs can be carried out from multiple perspectives, which helps to provide valuable information for the optimization, improvement and comparison of business processes. For example, structural similarity helps to understand the basic framework and logic of business processes, and behavioral similarity is very important for identifying differences between different versions of graphs. We will detail the calculation methods of structural similarity and behavioral similarity we used in our experiments in the section, so that readers can have a more vivid understanding of our method.

**Structural Similarity Calculation.** In previous work, the structural similarity of graphs is usually calculated using graph edit distance (GED) [10]. The GED mainly measures the matching degree between graphs by measuring the dissimilarity between graphs, and the dissimilarity is measured by the distance value. The larger the distance value is, the greater the dissimilarity is, and the lower the matching degree is. However, they are suitable for isomorphic graphs and not for heterogeneous graphs. Therefore, we regard all nodes in the graph as nodes of the same type, and only consider the label information of nodes. Then we calculate the structural similarity of two graphs by the following formula:

$$Structure(G_1, G_2) = \frac{1}{1 + GED(G_1, G_2)} \qquad (2)$$

where $GED(G_1, G_2)$ represents the graph edit distance between $G_1$ and $G_2$.

For BPG1 and BPG2 in Fig. 3, we convert them into StrBPG1 and StrBPG2 respectively, calculate the GED between them as 7, that is, adding 2 edges and 1 node, relabeling 4 nodes and substitution formula (2) can calculate the structural similarity between them as 0.125.

**Behavioral Similarity Calculation.** Inspired by workflow difference detection based on basis paths method [13] [30], we think that the execution path of the business process graph can cover all node and edge information, so it can be used to represent global behavior information. We find out basic paths in the two graphs, and use path edit distance to represent the difference distance of two paths. However, there are different numbers of paths in each graph, how to calculate the composite similarity score between multiple paths is a challenge. To solve this problem, we use the KM algorithm [34] to search for the best mapping of the two path set paths, and finally calculate the behavioral similarity score of the two graphs. The specific method is divided into the following three steps.

*Step1. Find the basic path:* There are the following two steps for finding the basic path: (1) Add start and end nodes. In order to find the path, we must find the start and end nodes, so we define a start node uniformly and look for all paths from this node until the end node. (2) Delete the gateway node, and add the nodes after the AND gateway in order. For the path, the gateway node is not important, we need to focus on the execution path of the task node. At the same time, in order to improve the computational efficiency, we arrange the nodes after the AND gateway in order, which may shorten the path edit distance and thus reduce the overhead.

According to the above calculation method, we can use formula (1) to get $V(G)$ independent paths, which represent the behavior characteristic information of each business process graph. For example, BeBPG1 and BeBPG2 in Fig. 3 are converted from BPG1 and BPG2. for BeBPG1, we can get two paths: $\{A, B, C, D, E\}$ and $\{A, B, C, D, F\}$. For BeBPG2, we can get three paths: $\{A, B, D, E, F\}$, $\{A, C, D, E, F\}$ and $\{A, G, D, E, F\}$.

*Step2. Construct Behavioral Distance Matrix:* We get two different sets of basic paths from two different graphs, and when calculating the similarity, we establish a connection between two different basic paths for all possible combinations. So, we construct a behavioral distance matrix to measure the similarity of independent paths in different business process graphs, which is critical for us to find the maximum matching of the basic paths of two graphs later. Assume that the basic path sets of two graphs are $P$, $Q$. We compute the behavioral distance matrix W as follows:

$$W[i][j] = \frac{1}{1 + PED(P_i, Q_j)} \quad (3)$$

where $P_i \in P$ and $P_j \in Q$. $PED(P_i, Q_j)$ represents the path edit distance between the $i$ th path in $P$ and the $j$ th path in $Q$. $W[i][j]$ represents the behavioral similarity between the $i$ th path in $P$ and the $j$ th path in $Q$.

Now, we can compute the behavioral distance matrix for BeBPG1 and BeBPG2 as show in Table 1. Since BeBPG1 has 2 paths and BeBPG2 has 3 paths, a $2 \times 3$ behavioral distance matrix is constructed with a total of 6 distance values.

**Table 1.** The behavioral distance matrix for BeBPG1 and BeBPG2

|  | {A, B, D, E, F} | {A, C, D, E, F} | {A, G, D, E, F} |
|---|---|---|---|
| {A, B, C, D, E} | 0.33 | 0.33 | 0.2 |
| {A, B, C, D, F} | 0.33 | 0.33 | 0.2 |

*Step3. Optimal Matching Based on KM Algorithm:* By calculating the behavioral similarity matrix, we get the behavioral difference score between different independent paths in the two business process graphs, which is equivalent to establishing all possible connections of the two sets. However, there are many possibilities for their combination, and we want to find the best mapping with the largest behavioral difference score to measure the behavioral similarity between two business process graphs. This is actually the optimal matching problem of a weighted bipartite graph [35], which we solve through the KM algorithm [34].

We optimally match the basic path difference scores of the two graphs. Suppose the path set $P$ has $i$ nodes, and $Q$ has $j$ nodes. We match the nodes in $P$ with the nodes in $Q$, so that the sum of $W[i][j]$ in the matching is the largest, which is defined as *MaxWeight* and obtained by the km algorithm [34]. Next, we calculate the behavioral similarity of the two graphs as:

$$Behavior(G_1, G_2) = \frac{MaxWeight}{min(i,j)} \qquad (4)$$

where *MaxWeight* is the weight sum of the best match.

In the example, the $\{A, B, C, D, E\}$ and $\{A, B, C, D, F\}$ of BeBPG1 are matched with $\{A, B, D, E, F\}$ and $\{A, C, D, E, F\}$ in BeBPG2 respectively, where $MaxWeight = 0.33$ and the behavioral similarity between them is 0.33.

**Entropy Weight Method.** Now, we get similarity scores in multiple dimensions, namely structural similarity $Structure(G_1, G_2)$ and behavioral similarity $Behavior(G_1, G_2)$. It is inaccurate to simply add two values together to get the final similarity score. Structural similarity focuses on the static structure of business processes, such as the way nodes and edges are connected, while behavioral similarity focuses on the dynamic execution trajectory of business processes, such as the execution order of different nodes. Simply adding them up will make the structure and behavior information be treated equally in the similarity calculation, which may lead to information redundancy. Also, simple addition may result in loss of information. Because the structural and behavioral similarities may take values on different magnitudes, simple summing will make the similarity with high values have a greater impact on the final result, thereby ignoring the similarities with low values. In order to avoid information redundancy and information loss, the method of fusing structural and behavioral similarities needs to consider their weight and importance.

Due to the complexity of business processes, the business differences of different datasets may lead to different contributions of similarity metrics in different dimensions to the final similarity score. Therefore, we objectively weight the similarity indicators of different dimensions based on specific datasets. We draw on the idea of information entropy [22], which calculates the information entropy of the indicator, and determines the weight of the indicator according to the impact of the relative change degree of the indicator on the overall system. Indicators with a large degree have a greater weight. The specific implementation scheme is as follows.

Suppose we have $n$ groups to calculate structural similarity and behavioral similarity, so we get the following matrix X of $n \times 2$, where $x_{ij}$ represents the value of the $j$ th evaluation index of the $i$ th sample. We calculate the final weight by the following formula.

$$p_{ij} = \frac{x_{ij}}{\sum_{i=1}^{n} x_{ij}} \tag{5}$$

$$e_j = -\frac{1}{\ln n} \sum_{i=1}^{n} p_{ij} \ln p_{ij}, e_j \in [0,1] \tag{6}$$

$$d_j = 1 - e_j \tag{7}$$

$$\alpha = \frac{d_1}{d_1 + d_2} \tag{8}$$

$$\beta = \frac{d_1}{d_1 + d_2} \tag{9}$$

where $p$ represents the probability matrix, $e$ represents the information entropy of each metric, and $d$ represents the information utility value. We get the weight of structural similarity as $\alpha$ and the weight of behavioral similarity as $\beta$.

## 4.2    Phase2. Comprehensive Evaluation with TOPSIS

Next, we need to comprehensively consider multiple dimensions and take into account the weights and values of each dimension to provide a comprehensive evaluation score for the current sample, which can reflect the differences between different pairs of business process graphs. In fact, the similarity of business process graphs is a relative concept and needs to be referenced based on a maximum and minimum value. Therefore, how to quantify the relative distance between each sample and the maximum and minimum values to provide a relatively objective score is a challenge. We use the Technique for Order Preference by Similarity to an Ideal Solution (TOPSIS) [23] method for multi-dimensional fusion, which sorts by comparing the similarity between the sample and the optimal solution and the worst solution, which can comprehensively consider the influence of each dimension, and convert the evaluation criteria of multiple dimensions into a comprehensive sorting result. The value range of the similarity of the comprehensive evaluation is [0,1], where 0 and 1 indicate that the two graphs are completely different and exactly the same, respectively. In general, the optimal solution of the same dimension of two business flow charts is 1, and the worst solution is 0. So, we calculate the distances of the obtained $Structure(G_1, G_2)$ and $Behavior(G_1, G_2)$ from the optimal solution and the worst solution respectively:

$$d^+(G_1, G_2) = \sqrt{(1 - \alpha Structure(G_1, G_2))^2 + (1 - \beta Behavior(G_1, G_2))^2} \tag{10}$$

$$d^-(G_1, G_2) = \sqrt{\alpha Structure(G_1, G_2)^2 + \beta Behavior(G_1, G_2)^2} \tag{11}$$

where $d^+$ represents the distance between the two dimensions and the optimal solution, $d^-$ represents the distance between the two dimensions and the worst solution. $\alpha$ and $\beta$ represent the weights of each dimension, and their values are between $[0,1]$, and $\alpha + \beta = 1$.

Finally, we calculate the score based on the optimal solution and the worst solution:

$$SimilarScore(G_1, G_2) = \frac{2d^-(G_1, G_2)}{d^+(G_1, G_2) + d^-(G_1, G_2)} \tag{12}$$

In the example, when $\alpha = 0.5$ and $\beta = 0.5$, then $d^+ = 1.26$, $d^- = 0.25$, the final similarity score is 0.33. The proposed method calculation process is summarized as Algorithm 1.

---

**Algorithm 1:** SimBPG calculation method

---

**Input:** A pair of business process graphs $G_1$, $G_2$
**Output:** The similarity between two business process graphs: $SimilarScore$

1   $Structure(G_1, G_2) \leftarrow$ Calculate structural similarity;
2   $P_1 \leftarrow$ get the basic path from $G_1$;
3   $P_2 \leftarrow$ get the basic path from $G_2$;
4   $W \leftarrow$ initialize the behavior distance matrix;
5   **for** $i \leftarrow 0$ **to** $P.length()$ **do**
6      **for** $j \leftarrow 0$ **to** $Q.length()$ **do**
7         $PED(P_i, Q_j) \leftarrow$ Calculate the path distance;
8         $W[i][j] \leftarrow \frac{1}{1 + PED(P_i, Q_j)}$;
9      **end**
10 **end**
11 $MaxWeight \leftarrow KM(P, Q, W)$;
12 $Behavior(G_1, G_2) \leftarrow$ Calculate behavioral Similarity;
13 $\alpha, \beta \leftarrow$ Entropy weight method;
14 $d^+ \leftarrow \sqrt{(1 - \alpha Structure(G_1, G_2))^2 + (1 - \beta Behavior(G_1, G_2))^2}$;
15 $d^- \leftarrow \sqrt{\alpha Structure(G_1, G_2)^2 + \beta Behavior(G_1, G_2)^2}$ ;
16 $SimilarScore(G_1, G_2) \leftarrow \frac{2d^-(G_1, G_2)}{d^+(G_1, G_2) + d^-(G_1, G_2)}$;
17 **return** $SimilarScore(G_1, G_2)$

---

Algorithm 1.shows the flow of our method. The input is two business process graphs $G_1$, $G_2$, and the output is Comprehensive similarity score $SimilarScore$. First, calculate the structural similarity of two business process graphs (line 1). Second, obtain the basic paths of the two graphs and construct a behavioral distance matrix (lines 2-10), using the KM algorithm for optimal path matching (line 11) and calculate the behavioral similarity of two business process graphs (line 12). Third, calculate the weight of each dimension based on the entropy weight method (line 13), and calculate the final similarity score based on the TOPSIS method (lines 14-16).

# 5   Experiment

In this section, we design experiments to prove the effectiveness of the proposed method. There are two major challenges with this experiment. (1) We do not know the true similarity scores of the two business process graphs, so even if we use our method to calculate the similarity between them, we still cannot prove whether the results of the calculation are accurate. (2) Since we do not know the accuracy of the calculation results, we can not compare them with other methods to prove whether the proposed method is effective. In fact, there is no good solution to the above challenges. We can manually judge the similarity between two graphs, but the specific similarity score between them cannot be quantitatively determined, so we propose a cross-domain and multi-dimension experimental design scheme to qualitatively analyze whether our method is effective. Based on the dataset publicly available from IBM Corporation [24], one of the most commonly used datasets in the field of business process modeling, which originates from business processes in different domains. We put forward three assumptions and proved our conjecture through experiments. We also discuss in detail the reasonableness of parameter settings in the method and the influence of the number of nodes and the number of basic paths on the results. All experiments ran on a Windows 11 machine that used AMD Ryzen 9 5900HX with Radeon Graphics, 3.30 GHz, and 16 GB of RAM.

## 5.1   Dataset

The dataset publicly available from IBM Corporation [24] is a real-world dataset which has more than 3,000 business process models. Due to the incompleteness of some models in the dataset, we extracted more complete 845 different models from the dataset in the fields of insurance, banking, customer relations, and construction and automotive supply chains. We transform these models into the business process graphs we need, and anonymize the data in these models, because we do not consider the textual semantics information. There are 5 libraries in this dataset, including A, B1, B2, B3, and C, and each library represents a model in a different domain. Among them, libraries B1, B2, and B3 have partial overlap, they represent a series of models created in the same field in two years. One of the libraries is changed to the next by adding more process models and further refining all models, B3 is the latest library. We count the number of business process models in the dataset used, including 216 models in library A, 103 models in library B1, 136 models in B2, 255 models in library B3, and 135 models in library C. Table 2 calculates the average number of task nodes and the average number of basic paths in each library.

Table 2. Experimental data

|  | A | B1 | B2 | B3 | C |
|---|---|---|---|---|---|
| Graphs number | 216 | 103 | 136 | 255 | 135 |
| Node-total avg | 28.64 | 19.04 | 19.36 | 20.34 | 12.3 |
| Path-total avg. | 2.02 | 2.28 | 1.92 | 2.03 | 5.21 |

## 5.2  Design of Experiments

We make three assumptions as follows:

**Assumption 1.** Assume that business process graphs within the same domain are more similar than between different domains, because the business process graphs in the same domain have similar application scenarios, the semantics information of their nodes and the process execution process have a strong correlation. We define domain similarity as the average similarity score of all business process graphs between domains, and use this value to represent the degree of similarity between domains.

**Assumption 2.** In the dataset, the same business process graph will be updated into different versions over time, which we name as initial version, intermediate version and final version. Assume that for the same business process graph, it is more similar to other versions than it is to other business process graphs. This is because the same business process graph is created and updated for a specific task requirement, and the structure and behavior information of the business process is only partially adjusted, obviously there is a greater similarity.

**Assumption 3.** Based on the second assumption, we can assume that the initial and final versions of the same business process graph are less similar than the intermediate versions and other versions. Because the current version of the business process graph is updated and improved based on the previous version of the business process graph, there is a stronger relationship between adjacent versions.

**Domain Similarity Experiment.** Based on the Assumption 1, we will calculate the average business process graph similarity between the same domain and different domains. Since GED calculation takes a lot of time [7], especially for graphs with a large number of nodes, it is obviously unnecessary to calculate all graphs in the dataset. So we randomly select some graphs for testing. We randomly repeat multiple times to select $\mu$ models from different libraries, and construct $\mu^2$ pairs of graphs between the same library and different libraries respectively, and take the average value as the final experimental result. As shown in Fig. 4. Sample represents the sampling data, and total represents the total data. Figure 4(a) and Fig. 4(b) respectively represent the frequency distribution histograms of the number of nodes and the number of paths in library A. We can see that the curves of the two are roughly the same, so we suppose that the sampled data can objectively display the information of all data.

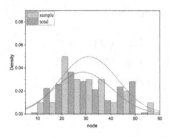    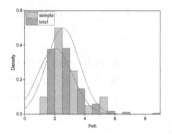

(a) Node number distribution       (b) Path number distribution

**Fig. 4.** When $\mu = 20$, node and path distribution of sampled data and overall data in library A

Specifically, we calculate the structural similarity (*Structure-Sim*), behavioral similarity (*Behavior-Sim*) and comprehensive evaluation similarity (*Comp-Sim*) between library A and library A, library A and library B3, library A and library C, library B3 and library B3, library B3 and library C, library C and library C respectively, and the results are shown in Table 3. Here, we designed three sets of experiments, which are $\mu = 20$, $\mu = 30$ and $\mu = 40$, for the business process graph of a certain library, its similarity with the graph in its own library is often higher than that between different libraries. For example, when $\mu = 20$, the average similar score in library A is 0.0865, which is higher than the average similar score with B3 of 0.0479 and the average similar score with C of 0.0667. All the results show a higher degree of similarity between the same libraries, which is in line with our perception that business process graphs in the same domain will be more similar.

Since the structure and behavior information of business process graphs in the same domain are more similar, the calculation using GED can also prove the approximate result of the first assumptions. However, our method has obvious advantages in different domain similarity measures. Since there is no positive relationship between structural and behavioral similarities across domains, the overall difference between the two graphs cannot be accurately measured if only GED is used. For example, when $\mu = 20$, in library A, their average *Structure-Sim* with library B3 graphs is higher than that of library C, and if only measured by GED, the graph of library A and library B3 is more similar. But in fact, whether in terms of the number of task nodes or the complexity of the graph, we tend to think that library A is more similar to library C. So when we consider behavioral similarity, plus *Behavior-Sim*, we find that library A has a higher average similarity score to library C.

**Table 3.** Domain similarity calculation results between different libraries

|  | metric | A-A | A-B3 | A-C | B3-B3 | B3-C | C-C |
|---|---|---|---|---|---|---|---|
| $\mu = 20$ | Structure-Sim | 0.0686 | 0.0265 | 0.0249 | 0.0952 | 0.0416 | 0.2407 |
|  | Behavior-Sim | 0.2363 | 0.2269 | 0.2292 | 0.3464 | 0.2969 | 0.3431 |
|  | Comp-Sim | **0.0865** | **0.0479** | **0.0667** | **0.1208** | **0.0893** | **0.2680** |
| $\mu = 30$ | Structure-Sim | 0.0527 | 0.0250 | 0.0202 | 0.0616 | 0.0291 | 0.2431 |
|  | Behavior-Sim | 0.2332 | 0.2078 | 0.2278 | 0.2375 | 0.2400 | 0.3421 |
|  | Comp-Sim | **0.0686** | **0.0394** | **0.0408** | **0.0815** | **0.0790** | **0.2649** |
| $\mu = 40$ | Structure-Sim | 0.0435 | 0.0352 | 0.0228 | 0.1032 | 0.0393 | 0.1834 |
|  | Behavior-Sim | 0.2307 | 0.2338 | 0.2248 | 0.2918 | 0.2694 | 0.3029 |
|  | Comp-Sim | **0.0571** | **0.0480** | **0.0507** | **0.1240** | **0.0975** | **0.2074** |

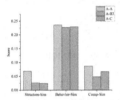 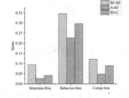 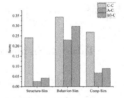

(a) Domain similarity be-  (b) Domain similarity be-  (c) Domain similarity between A and others        tween B3 and others        tween C and others

**Fig. 5.** When $\mu = 20$, the similarity between a library and other libraries compares the results

**Different Graph Similarity Experiments.** Based on the Assumption 2, we need to find different versions of the same business process graph. However, due to the anonymization of the task nodes of the dataset, it is impossible to find an updated iterative version of each graph, so we define an error value to determine whether both graphs are the same graph by the following formula.

$$Error(G_1, G_2) = \frac{|(node(G_1) - node(G_2)|}{max(node(G_1), node(G_2))} \tag{13}$$

where $node(G_1)$ and $node(G_2)$ represent the number of nodes in business process graph $G_1$ and $G_2$.

We assume that the error of the two business process graphs within the range of $\sigma$ represents the same business process graphs. Then, we can find different business process graphs in the same library and the different versions of the same business process graph in different libraries. Due to the similar structure of the experiments in different groups, we randomly select data $\mu = 20$ for experimentation, we first randomly select 20 business process graphs in library B1, and then find one different version in library B2 and B3. We calculate the average similarity of 20 different graphs in library B1 and the average similarity of these 20 graphs between different versions in library B2 and library B3, and the results are shown in Table 4. We set three error values, $\sigma = 0.05$, $\sigma = 0.10$ and $\sigma = 0.15$, and we find that no matter how we set the error values, the results are in line with our assumptions.

However, our assumptions cannot be obtained using only GED. As shown in Fig. 6(a), When $\mu = 20$, $\sigma = 0.05$, the *Structure-Sim* between different graphs in library B1 is higher than the *Structure-Sim* between these graphs and different versions in library B3, and the opposite is true for the final similarity *Comp-Sim*. This is because in the same domain, the application scenarios of the process business graphs are roughly the same, and it is likely to have similar structural information, but the specific execution process in the graph is different. If only GED is used for calculation, then the The similarity of is likely to be greater than the similarity between different versions. However, due to the difference in behavioral information, the final similarity between the two graphs weakens the structural similarity information, and will not be completely dominated by structural similarity, so our method is more reasonable.

**Table 4.** Similarity calculation results between different versions

|  | metric | B1-B1 | B1-B2 | B1-B3 | B2-B2 | B2-B3 | B3-B3 |
|---|---|---|---|---|---|---|---|
| $\sigma = 0.05$ | Structure-Sim | 0.1097 | 0.3519 | 0.0959 | 0.0702 | 0.1731 | 0.0719 |
|  | Behavior-Sim | 0.2041 | 0.2585 | 0.2145 | 0.2242 | 0.2544 | 0.2072 |
|  | Comp-Sim | **0.1100** | **0.3597** | **0.1247** | **0.0935** | **0.1827** | **0.0934** |
| $\sigma = 0.10$ | Structure-Sim | 0.1097 | 0.3212 | 0.1023 | 0.0634 | 0.1649 | 0.0933 |
|  | Behavior-Sim | 0.2041 | 0.2364 | 0.2174 | 0.2456 | 0.2456 | 0.2086 |
|  | Comp-Sim | **0.1100** | **0.3263** | **0.1283** | **0.0898** | **0.1983** | **0.0954** |
| $\sigma = 0.15$ | Structure-Sim | 0.1097 | 0.3084 | 0.0824 | 0.0547 | 0.1573 | 0.0806 |
|  | Behavior-Sim | 0.2041 | 0.2156 | 0.2032 | 0.2318 | 0.2358 | 0.2013 |
|  | Comp-Sim | **0.1100** | **0.2983** | **0.1269** | **0.0654** | **0.1828** | **0.0864** |

**Version Similarity Experiment.** Based on the Assumption 3, we believe that the longer the time span of different versions of the same business process graph, the less similar. We do the same as in the second experiment, which is actually implemented in the second experiment, and we analyze the results of Table 4. We select 20 graphs in library B1 and different versions of the same graph in library B2 and B3, where library B1 and library B3 have the longest time span, and library B2 is sandwiched between the two. When $\mu = 20$, $\sigma = 0.05$, Fig. 6(b) shows the similarity between different versions of the plot over different time spans, we find that for the same business process graph, whether it is *Structure-Sim* or *Behavior-Sim* or *Comp-Sim*, the similarity between library B1 and library B3 is less than the similarity between library B1 and library B2 or between library B2 and library B3.

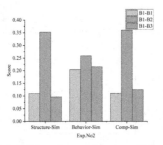
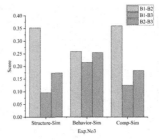

(a) Different graphs vs. different versions

(b) different versions

**Fig. 6.** When $\mu = 20$, $\sigma = 0.05$, the similarity between different graphs and the similarity between different versions of the same graph

## 5.3   Ablation Experiments

In this part, we discuss in detail the determination of parameters $\alpha$ and $\beta$ in equations (8) and (9). We also discuss the influence of the number of nodes and paths on the experimental results.

**The Influence of Parameter Settings.** In our proposed method, we give different weights to structural similarity and behavioral similarity, and we arrive at a relatively comprehensive assessment by balancing the relationship between the two. In the settings, if $\alpha = 0$, the evaluation only considers behavioral similarity, whereas if $\beta = 0$, the evaluation considers only structural similarity.

In the experiment, we set $\mu = 20$, that is selecting 20 business process graphs in libraries A, B3 and C. We calculate the comprehensive evaluation similarity of $\alpha = 0$, $\beta = 1$ and $\alpha = 1$, $\beta = 0$ and $\alpha = 0.5$, $\beta = 0.5$, and obtain the results as shown in Table 5. In our dataset, due to the large number of nodes and the relatively small number of paths, the *Structure-Sim* is relatively small, and the *Behavior-Sim* is relatively large, in this case, if we assign the weight of both metrics to 0.5, the final result will be closer to the behavioral similarity, that is, the result is dominated by behavioral similarity, which loses the meaning of behavioral similarity. However, using our method, the metrics we end up with are not dominated by behavioral similarity, so our weighting method is more comprehensive and objective to the final result.

**Table 5.** The effect of different parameter settings on the experimental structure

|  | A-A | A-B3 | A-C | B3-B3 | B3-C | C-C |
|---|---|---|---|---|---|---|
| $\alpha = 0, \beta = 1$ | 0.2363 | 0.2269 | 0.2292 | 0.3464 | 0.2969 | 0.3431 |
| $\alpha = 1, \beta = 0$ | 0.0686 | 0.0265 | 0.0249 | 0.0952 | 0.0416 | 0.2407 |
| $\alpha = 0.5, \beta = 0.5$ | 0.1802 | 0.1593 | 0.1599 | 0.2593 | 0.2072 | 0.3209 |
| **ours** | **0.0865** | **0.0479** | **0.0667** | **0.1208** | **0.0893** | **0.2680** |

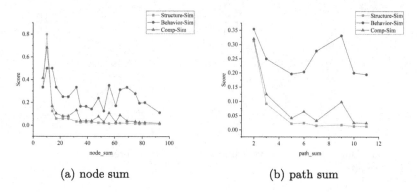

(a) node sum            (b) path sum

**Fig. 7.** The influence of the number of nodes and the number of paths on the similarity of the graphs

**The Influence of the Number of Nodes and Paths.** We explore the impact of different number of task nodes and different number of paths on the result. Since different groups of experiments have similar results, we select one of them for visual analysis, when $\mu = 20$, $\sigma = 0.05$, we calculate *Structure-Sim*, *Behavior-Sim* and final *Comp-Sim* between library B1 and library B3, and plot the transformation of each metric with the total number of nodes and the total number of basic paths. For the case where there is the same total number of nodes and basic paths for different pairs of graphs, we calculate the average of all pairs of graphs under the same total. It can be seen from the Fig. 7 that the number of nodes and the number of paths are roughly negatively correlated with *Structure-Sim*. This is because when the structure of the graph is more complex, more editing operations are required to achieve the conversion between the two graphs, which leads to The graph edit distance increases exponentially, so the *Structure-Sim* value will also become smaller. However, there is no absolute linear relationship between the number of nodes and the number of paths on the value of *Behavior-Sim*, the behavioral similarity of two graphs is more correlated with the semantics information of path execution. Since the final result is a comprehensive evaluation of *Structure-Sim* and *Behavior-Sim*, *Comp-Sim* integrates the information of the two, and basically decreases with the increase of the number of nodes and the number of paths, but there are individual points that are affected by *Behavior-Sim* and deviate.

## 6    Conclusion

In this paper, in order to solve the problem that the isomorphic abstraction simplification of the process graph model makes the original control routing semantics lost, and the original comprehensive evaluation method cannot reflect the real multidimensional space. We proposed a comprehensive evaluation method for business process similarity, which combines the multidimensional similarity features of the business process graph through the TOPSIS method, and uses the entropy weight method on a specific dataset to objectively empower the metrics of the two dimensions, eliminating the subjective judgment of artificial. In order to verify the validity of the evaluation metric, we boldly make three assumptions and explain the rationality of our method by designing a cross-domain and multi-dimension experimental protocol. Through experiments, we verified our assumptions and improved the shortcoming of the traditional use of GED lack of behavioral semantics information.

**Acknowledgments.** This work was partially supported by the National Natural Science Foundation of China (Grants No. 62276233, 62102366), Key Research Project of Zhejiang Province (2023C01048) and the Natural Science Foundation of Zhejiang Province (Grant No. LQ22F020010).

# References

1. Weber, P., Gabriel, R., Lux, T., Menke, K.: Business process management. In: Basics in Business Informatics, pp. 175–206 (2022)
2. Reijers, H.A.: Business process management: the evolution of a discipline. Comput. Indust. **126**, 103404 (2021)
3. Dijkman, R., Dumas, M., Van Dongen, B., Kää, R., Mendling, J.: Similarity of business process models: metrics and evaluation. Inf. Syst. **36**(2), 498–516 (2011)
4. Thaler, T., Schoknecht, A., Fettke, P., Oberweis, A., Laue, R.: A comparative analysis of business process model similarity measures. In: Dumas, M., Fantinato, M. (eds.) BPM 2016. LNBIP, vol. 281, pp. 310–322. Springer, Cham (2017). https://doi.org/10.1007/978-3-319-58457-7_23
5. Schoknecht, A., Thaler, T., Fettke, P., Oberweis, A., Laue, R.: Similarity of business process models-a state-of-the-art analysis. ACM Comput. Surv. **50**(4), 1–33 (2017)
6. Liu, C., Zeng, Q., Cheng, L., Duan, H., Cheng, J.: Measuring similarity for data-aware business processes. IEEE Trans. Autom. Sci. Eng. **19**(2), 1070–1082 (2021)
7. Cao, B., Wang, J., Fan, J., Dong, T., Yin, J.: Mapping elements with the Hungarian algorithm: an efficient method for querying business process models. In: IEEE International Conference on Web Services, pp. 129–136 (2015)
8. Li, J., Wen, L.J., Wang, J.M.: Process model storage mechanism based on petri net edit distance. Comput. Integr. Manuf. Syst. **19**(8), 1832–1841 (2013)
9. Sebu, M.L., Ciocârlie, H.: Similarity of business process models in a modular design. In: IEEE 11th International Symposium on Applied Computational Intelligence and Informatics, pp. 31–36 (2016)
10. Gao, X., Xiao, B., Tao, D., Li, X.: A survey of graph edit distance. Pattern Anal. Appl. **13**, 113–129 (2010)
11. Pamungkas, E.W., Sarno, R., Munif, A.: Performance improvement of business process similarity calculation using word sense disambiguation. IPTEK J. Proc. Series, 2(1) (2016)
12. Akkiraju, R., Ivan, A.: Discovering business process similarities: an empirical study with SAP Best practice business processes. In: Maglio, P.P., Weske, M., Yang, J., Fantinato, M. (eds.) ICSOC 2010. LNCS, vol. 6470, pp. 515–526. Springer, Heidelberg (2010). https://doi.org/10.1007/978-3-642-17358-5_35
13. Cao, B., Hong, F., Wang, J., Fan, J., Lv, M.: Workflow difference detection based on basis paths. Eng. Appl. Artif. Intell. **81**, 420–427 (2019)

14. Wang, Z.X., Wen, L.J., Wang, S.H., Wang, J.M.: Similarity measurement for process models based on transition-labeled graph edit distance. Comput. Integr. Manuf. Syst. **22**(2), 343–352 (2016)
15. Wu, Z., Pan, S., Chen, F., Long, G., Zhang, C., Philip, S.Y.: A comprehensive survey on graph neural networks. IEEE Trans. Neural Netw. Learn. Syst. **32**(1), 4–24 (2020)
16. Bai, Y., Ding, H., Bian, S., Chen, T., Sun, Y., Wang, W.: Simgnn: a neural network approach to fast graph similarity computation. In: Proceedings of the Twelfth ACM International Conference On Web Search And Data Mining, pp. 384–392 (2019)
17. Li, Y., Gu, C., Dullien, T., Vinyals, O., Kohli, P.: Graph matching networks for learning the similarity of graph structured objects. In: International Conference on Machine Learning, pp. 3835–3845 (2019)
18. Sun, Y., Han, J.: Mining heterogeneous information networks: a structural analysis approach. ACM SIGKDD Explorations Newsl **14**(2), 20–28 (2013)
19. Wang, S., et al.: Heterogeneous graph matching networks for unknown malware detection. In: Proceedings of the 28th International Joint Conference on Artificial Intelligence, pp. 3762–3770 (2019)
20. Aisyah, K.N., Sungkono, K.R., Sarno, R.: A new similarity method based on weighted-linear temporal logic tree and weighted directed acyclic graph for graph-based business process models. Int. J. Intell. Eng. Syst. 13(5) (2020)
21. Zhou, C., Liu, C., Zeng, Q., Lin, Z., Duan, H.: A comprehensive process similarity measure based on models and logs. IEEE Access **7**, 69257–69273 (2019)
22. Zhu, Y., Tian, D., Yan, F.: Effectiveness of entropy weight method in decision-making. Math. Probl. Eng. **1–5**, 2020 (2020)
23. Yoon, K., Hwang, C.L.: Topsis (technique for order preference by similarity to ideal solution)-a multiple attribute decision making, w: Multiple attribute decision making-methods and applications, a state-of-the-at survey. Berlin: Springer Verlag, **128** 140 (1981)
24. Fahland, D., Favre, C., Jobstmann, B., Koehler, J., Lohmann, N., Völzer, H., Wolf, K.: Instantaneous soundness checking of industrial business process models. In: Dayal, U., Eder, J., Koehler, J., Reijers, H.A. (eds.) BPM 2009. LNCS, vol. 5701, pp. 278–293. Springer, Heidelberg (2009). https://doi.org/10.1007/978-3-642-03848-8_19
25. Wang, Y., Huaibo Sun, Yu., Zhao, W.Z., Zhu, S.: A heterogeneous graph embedding framework for location-based social network analysis in smart cities. IEEE Trans. Industr. Inf. **16**(4), 2747–2755 (2019)
26. Xiao Wang, Deyu Bo, Chuan Shi, Shaohua Fan, Yanfang Ye, and S Yu Philip. A survey on heterogeneous graph embedding: methods, techniques, applications and sources. IEEE Transactions on Big Data, 2022
27. Eshuis, R., Wieringa, R.: Comparing petri net and activity diagram variants for workflow modelling – a quest for reactive petri nets. In: Ehrig, H., Reisig, W., Rozenberg, G., Weber, H. (eds.) Petri Net Technology for Communication-Based Systems. LNCS, vol. 2472, pp. 321–351. Springer, Heidelberg (2003). https://doi.org/10.1007/978-3-540-40022-6_16
28. Owen, M., Raj, J.: BPMN and business process management. Introduction to the new business process modeling standard, pp. 1–27 (2003)
29. Peterson, J.L.: Petri nets. ACM Comput. Surv. **9**(3), 223–252 (1977)
30. Westfall, L.: The certified software quality engineer handbook. Quality Press (2016)
31. Watson, A.H., Wallace, D.R., McCabe, T.J.: Structured testing: a testing methodology using the cyclomatic complexity metric. NIST Special Public. **500**, 235 (1996)

32. Botman, P.: Testing object-oriented systems: models, patterns and tools. Softw. Qual. Profess. **4**(1), 47 (2001)
33. Agarwal, S., Godboley, S., Krishna, P.R.: Cyclomatic complexity analysis for smart contract using control flow graph. In: Computing, Communication and Learning: First International Conference, pp. 65–78 (2023)
34. Kuhn, H.W.: The Hungarian method for the assignment problem. Naval research logistics quarterly, **2**(1–2), 83–97 (1955)
35. Asratian, A.S., Denley, T.M., Häggkvist, R.: Bipartite graphs and their applications. Cambridge University Press (1998)

# Probabilistic Inference Based Incremental Graph Index for Similarity Search on Social Networks

Tong Lu[1,2], Zhiwei Qi[1,2(✉)], Kun Yue[1,2], and Liang Duan[1,2]

[1] School of Information Science and Engineering, Yunnan University,
Kunming, China
mckinleylu@mail.ynu.edu.cn, {kyue,duanl,maryqizhiwei}@ynu.edu.cn
[2] Yunnan Key Laboratory of Intelligent Systems and Computing, Yunnan University,
Kunming, China

**Abstract.** To find $k$ neighbor users on social networks, the efficient approximate nearest neighbor search (ANNS) is useful. Existing graph index methods have shown attractive performance, but suffer from inaccuracy w.r.t. unindexed queries. To achieve both indexed and unindexed queries for graph-index methods, we propose an incremental graph index based method for ANNS on social networks. First, graph convolutional network based on attention mechanism is adopted to embed the social network into low-dimensional vector space, on which the graph index is constructed efficiently. To add the unindexed queries to the graph index incrementally, we propose Bayesian network (BN) learned from social interactions to represent dependency relations of unindexed queries and their neighbors, and perform probabilistic inferences in BN to infer the closest neighbors of unindexed queries. Extensive experiments show that our proposed method outperforms the state-of-the-art methods on both execution time and precision.

**Keywords:** Social network · Similarity search · Incremental graph index · Bayesian network · Probabilistic inference

## 1 Introduction

Millions of people use various social networks to connect with friends and family, and share private information. A key issue in social network is to find out the prospective friends of users so as to extend the users' social cycles. For example, Facebook has a friend finding page that suggests people you may know based on factors like mutual friends, shared workplaces or similar social interactions. Approximate nearest neighbor search (ANNS), as a similarity search method, is more widely utilized to find $k$ neighbors of users by constructing efficient index on large-scale and high-dimensional social networks, striking a better trade-off between accuracy and efficiency [24]. As shown in Fig. 1 (a), ANNS starts with a navigating node and takes a greedy routing strategy to find the query's $k$

H. Gao et al. (Eds.): CollaborateCom 2023, LNICST 562, pp. 458–473, 2024.
https://doi.org/10.1007/978-3-031-54528-3_25

($k = 3$) neighbors by calculating the similarity based on Euclidean distance among nodes.

Graph-index ANNS [7,8,23] methods show attractive performance for indexed queries (queries in graph index). However, these methods do not support unindexed queries (queries not in graph index) that lead to the curse of inaccurate search results. For example, although indexed query is closer to unindexed query than other indexed nodes, indexed query's neighbors do not include unindexed query in Fig. 1 (a). When unindexed query is added into graph index, it becomes indexed query's neighbor in Fig. 1 (b) that improves the accuracy of search results. Besides, graph-index ANNS cannot be directly fulfilled on social network but feature vectors [18], where the feature vectors, i.e. node embeddings of a social network, are commonly used to construct graph index. To this end, we will address the following problems to update unindexed queries into graph index: 1) how to map social network to obtain node embeddings and construct graph index on node embeddings; 2) how to describe the dependency relations of nodes by making fully use of social interactions; 3) how to add the edges of unindexed queries and their neighbors efficiently and accurately.

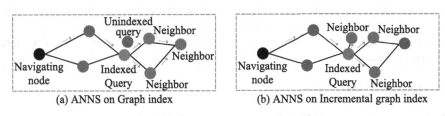

(a) ANNS on Graph index          (b) ANNS on Incremental graph index

**Fig. 1.** Search results of the indexed query on graph index vs incremental graph index. (a) the search results (green circles) of indexed query do not include the unindexed query. (b) the search results of indexed query include the unindexed query. (Color figure online)

To address the aforementioned problems and improve the performance of ANNS, our **P**robabilistic **I**nference based **I**ncremental **G**raph **I**ndex (PI-IGI) for similarity search on Social Networks is proposed. The graph index could be constructed efficiently on node embeddings rather than the social network itself. To map the social network into vector space while preserving network structure, an two-layer graph convolutional network (GCN) is proposed to generate node embeddings by adding a masked graph attention mechanism. Based on the similarity calculation of node embeddings, the initial graph index, also named KNNG, could be easily constructed. To keep the neighbors distributed around the nodes of KNNG, we prune the edges by constraining the angles of edges. A depth-first-search (DFS) tree is also built to keep the connectivity of graph index.

As shown in Fig. 1 (b), the increment graph index could improve the accuracy of search results. To update the unindexed queries into graph index, a candidate selection method is proposed to generate enough candidate neighbors to connect with unindexed queries. The Bayesian network (BN), including a directed acyclic graph (DAG) and conditional probability tables (CPTs), is used to qualitatively and quantitatively describe the dependency relations of random variables [16,22]. To describe the dependency relations between unindexed queries and their candidate neighbors based on social interactions, we propose the concept of query neighbor based Bayesian network (QNBN) and learn the DAG and CPTs of QNBN by rule-based method. The nodes of QNBN correspond to unindexed queries and their candidate neighbors, and edges correspond to the dependency relations of unindexed queries and their candidate neighbors. On the learned QNBN, we perform approximate inferences to infer the potential edges of unindexed queries and their candidate neighbors to be added into the graph index. Furthermore, a neighbor evaluation function is proposed to estimate which edges are added into the graph index, where the function combines Euclidean distance and posterior probabilities of nodes. Finally, the top $k$ neighbors of each unindexed query could be obtained by performing ANNS on the graph index.

The experimental results demonstrate that our PI-IGI improves the search precision by at least 5% and the search speed by at least 10% compared with the state-of-the-art methods.

The rest of this paper is organized as follows: Sect. 2 shows the related work. Section 3 presents our method PI-IGI. Section 4 provides the experimental results of PI-IGI compared to state-of-the-art methods. We give the conclusion and future work in Sect. 5.

## 2    Related Work

**Non-graph-index ANNS.** The non-graph-index methods mainly include tree-based, permutation-based, and hashing-based methods in Fig. 2. Tree-based methods partition data by their dimensions, including KD-tree [3], PM-tree [30], and NV-tree [15]. Hashing-based methods divide the data by hash functions and map the divided data into hyper-surfaces, including locality-sensitive hashing [4], spectral hashing [11] and minwise hashing [17]. Permutation-based methods use codebooks to encode data that could reduce memory consumption, including variance-aware quantization [20] and product quantization [19]. However, non-graph-index methods are much less efficient than graph-index ones when performing ANNS on large-scale social networks, due to traversing more nodes than graph-index methods. Therefore, we need to propose a graph-index ANNS method to improve the search efficiency.

**Graph-index ANNS.** Graph-index methods in Fig. 2 are more efficient and effective than non-graph-index methods for ANNS [24]. The state-of-art methods [7,8,18,23] improve the performance of ANNS by using different edge-select strategies. HCNNG [18] uses a hierarchical clustering algorithm to build graph index with a balanced tree structure, decreasing the memory consumption of graph index. NSG [8] builds a monotonic graph index to shorten the search path and obtains better performance of ANNS compared to HCNNG. GI-DSNE [23] is constructed by pruning edges on pre-built KNNG [21] and employs depth-first-search (DFS) trees to keep the connectivity of index, but suffers the curse of search precision of unindexed queries. NSSG [7] constrains the edges between two nodes to adjust the sparsity of index to guarantee the monotonicity of the search path of unindexed queries. However, these graph-index methods ignore the incremental updates of graph index.

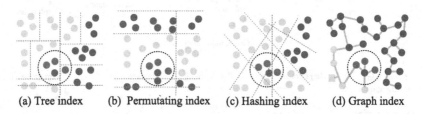

(a) Tree index    (b) Permutating index    (c) Hashing index    (d) Graph index

**Fig. 2.** Different base indexes on the identical dataset. The red circle represents query node, while dark green, light green and blue circles represent the nearest neighbors, checked and unchecked nodes, respectively. (Color figure online)

## 3    Methodology

In this section, we introduce our proposed method PI-IGI in Fig. 3 that includes graph index construction, QNBN learning, incremental graph index construction, and ANNS on graph index.

### 3.1    Graph Index Construction of Social Network

The formal definitions of social network, social network embedding and graph index are presented at first.

**Definition 1.** A social network is denoted as $G = (V, E)$, where $V = \{v_i\}_{i=1}^n$ is a set of nodes representing users, $E = \{e_{ij}\}_{i,j=1}^n$ is a collection of edges. $\mathbf{A} = \{a_{ij}\}_{i,j=1}^n$ is an adjacency matrix of $G$, where $a_{ij} = 1$ if and only if there is an edge $e_{ij}$ between $v_i$ and $v_j$, vice versa, $a_{ij} = 0$.

**Definition 2.** The embedding $\mathbf{Y} = \{y_i\}_{i=1}^n$ of $G$ is a mapping $f: v_i$ to $\mathbf{y}_i \in \mathbb{R}^d$, where $d \ll n$ and the function $f$ preserves the structure of $G$.

**Definition 3.** A index $G^I(V^I, E^I, \delta)$ is built on $\mathbf{Y}$ by graph-index methods, where $V^I = \{v_i^I\}_{i=1}^n$ is a set of nodes, $E^I = \{e_{ij}^I\}_{i,j=1}^n$ is a set of edges, and $\delta_{i,j} \in \delta$ is the similarity function based on the Euclidean distance ($l_2$ norm) between $v_i^I$ and $v_j^I$ in Eq. 1.

$$\delta_{i,j} = \delta(v_i^I, v_j^I) = \left(\sum_{l=0}^{d-1}(v_{il}^I - v_{jl}^I)^2\right)^{\frac{1}{2}} \tag{1}$$

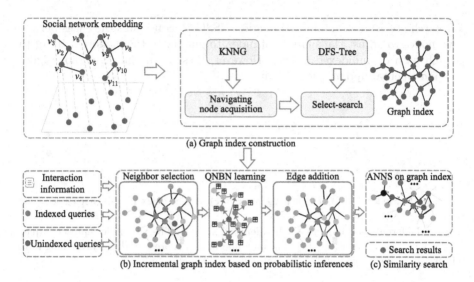

**Fig. 3.** Overview of our proposed PI-IGI. (a) the graph index is constructed on social network embedding. (b) the QNBN is learned on selected candidate neighbors of unindexed queries (red circles) and edges of incremental graph index are added by performing probabilistic inferences in QNBN. The cyan, pink and yellow circles represent the nearest candidate neighbors of unindexed queries, one-hop and two-hop neighbors of cyan circles, respectively. (c) the search results (green circles) of unindexed queries and indexed queries is obtained by ANNS on graph index. (Color figure online)

**Definition 4.** Social interactions characterizing a set of node pairs $\Omega = \{<v_i, v_j > | v_i, v_j \in V, i \neq j\}$ is denoted as an adjacency matrix $\mathbf{M}$, where $<v_i, v_j>$ denotes an social interaction between $v_i$ and $v_j$.

To construct graph index for ANNS on low-dimensional vector space, graph convolutional network (GCN) based on attention mechanism is proposed to map social network to generate node embeddings. In order to preserve the structure of social network effectively, the social network is transformed to a node degree matrix $\mathbf{D}$ and adjacency matrix $\mathbf{A}$ as inputs of two-layer GCN. In real social network, the neighbors of a node should be assigned to different weights because of different relationship strengths among nodes. To ensure important neighbors obtain large weights, the masked graph attention mechanism [29] concatenated to GCN aims to allocate weight to different neighbors. The node embedding $\mathbf{y}_i$ is generated by averaging aggregated features from each attention head as follows

$$\mathbf{y}_i = \sigma \left( \sum_{j \in \mathcal{N}_i} \beta_{ij} \mathbf{W} \cdot \mathbf{z}_j \right) \tag{2}$$

where $\mathbf{Z} = \text{GCN}(\mathbf{D}, \mathbf{A})$, $\mathbf{z}_j \in \mathbf{Z}$ denotes the initial node embedding, $\mathbf{W} = \text{GCN}(\mathbf{M}, \mathbf{A})$, $\mathbf{W}$ denotes weight matrix, $\mathcal{N}_i$ denotes the neighbor set of $\mathbf{z}_i$, and $\beta_{ij}$ denotes attention coefficient between $\mathbf{z}_i$ and $\mathbf{z}_j$.

To speed up the construction of graph index, we construct a graph index based on KNNG. Considering that the KNNG has plenty of edges that give rise to detours in the search path and memory consumption. In order to improve the efficiency of ANNS and guarantee the monotonicity of search path, we prune the edges of KNNG, cut long edges and control the angles among edges from $0°$ to $60°$ by ANNS starting from navigating nodes that is the centroid of data. To ensure the connectivity of graph index, DFS tree is spanned to merge possible connected indexes.

## 3.2   QNBN Learning on Social Interactions

To add unindexed queries into graph index efficiently, the enough candidate neighbors of unindexed queries are first obtained from graph index. Then, QNBN is learned from frequent itemset based on social interactions to describe the dependency relations of unindexed queries and their candidate neighbors. The frequent itemset and QNBN are defined as

**Definition 5.** The frequent itemset $F$ consists of items in social interactions and satisfies the following condition

$$Support(F) = P(F; \Omega) \geq min_{support} \tag{3}$$

where $\Omega$ is a set of social interactions, $P(F; \Omega)$ denotes the frequency of $F$ occurred in $\Omega$, and $min_{support}$ denotes the threshold of minimum support.

**Definition 6.** $B = (\mathcal{G}, \theta)$ represents a QNBN with a directed acyclic graph $\mathcal{G}$ and conditional probability parameters $\theta$, where

- $\mathcal{G} = (\mathcal{V}, \mathcal{E})$ is a DAG, $\mathcal{V} = \{X_i\}_{i=1}^{n_\varepsilon}$ is a collection of nodes of DAG, $\mathcal{E} = \{r_{ij}\}_{i,j=1}^{n_\varepsilon}(i \neq j)$ is a set of edges of DAG, $X_i$ represents a node or a conjuction of nodes and $X_i$ takes the values of 0 or 1.
- $\theta$ is a collection of probability parameters of nodes $\mathcal{V}$.

**Candidate Neighbor Selection of Unindexed Queries.** To generate the candidate neighbors of unindexed query $v_q$, we propose a candidate neighbor selection method based on NN-Descent [5]. The node $v_p^I$ having the minimum Euclidean distance with $v_q$ is first obtained by traversing the nodes in graph index and the one-hop and two-hop neighbors (orange nodes and yellow nodes in Fig. 3 (b)) of $v_p^I$ are considered as candidate neighbors of $v_q$, that is, the neighbors' neighbors of $v_p^I$ are also its neighbors, defined as

$$V_s^I(v_p^I) = \{v_i^I | v_i^I \in G^I \wedge \delta(v_p^I, v_i^I) <= \max(\delta(v_p^I, v_i^I))\}, \ v_p^I \in V_s^I(v_p^I). \tag{4}$$

where $V_s^I$ denotes a set of candidate neighbors of $v_p^I$, $\delta(v_p^I, v_i^I)$ represents the Euclidean distance between of pair node, $\max(\delta(v_p^I, v_i^I))$ denotes the maximum Euclidean distance of node $v_p^I$ and its one-hop neighbor.

The number of candidate neighbors of $v_q$ is further reduced by clustering its candidate neighbors to improve the efficiency of the update of graph index. To cluster candidate neighbors efficiently, k-means++ algorithm is adopted due to its better convergence and possessing a more intelligent initialization strategy for centroid placement [6].

Social interactions imply the dependency relations of unindexed queries and their neighbors, which are used to obtain query neighbor rules (QNRs) to learn the structure of QNBN. The QNBN learning includes structure learning and parameter learning, where the QNR needs to satisfy two properties:

1) The more frequently between two nodes of $G^I$ interact, the stronger the dependency relations between nodes are, i.e., the more frequent interactions $< v_i^I, v_j^I >$ between $v_i^I$ and $v_j^I$ are, the more possibly QNR $v_i^I \rightarrow v_j^I$ between them is occurred.

2) The shorter hop between two nodes of $G^I$ are, the more possibly QNR $v_i^I \rightarrow v_j^I$ between them is occurred, i.e., if there exists $v_i^I \rightarrow v_j^I$ and $v_i^I \rightarrow v_k^I \rightarrow v_j^I$, the more possibly QNR $v_i^I \rightarrow v_j^I$ exists.

**Structure Learning.** To generate QNRs to learn the structure of QNBN, a set of frequent itemsets $F$ is first obtained by Eq. 3, where each QNR $l_s \rightarrow (l - l_s)$ extracted from $F$ satisfies $\frac{support(l)}{support(l_s)} \geq \alpha$, and $\alpha$ is the threshold of the minimum confidence of QNR. The confidence of a QNR $v_i^I \rightarrow v_j^I$ could be formulated as

$$confidence(v_i^I \rightarrow v_j^I) = P(v_j^I | v_i^I) = \frac{support(v_i^I \cup v_j^I)}{support(v_i^I)} \tag{5}$$

where $support(v_i^I \cup v_j^I)$ is number of social interactions of $v_i^I$ or $v_j^I$, $support(v_i^I)$ is the number of social interactions of $v_i^I$.

Further, each QNR between unindexed query $v_q$ and its candidate neighbors is viewed as

$$v_1^I \wedge v_2^I \wedge \ldots \wedge v_n^I \rightarrow v_q \tag{6}$$

On the basis of logical implication, QNR $v_1^I \wedge v_2^I \wedge \ldots \wedge v_n^I \rightarrow v_q$ is equivalently transformed into Horn clause $\overline{v_1^I} \vee \overline{v_2^I} \vee \ldots \overline{v_n}^I \vee v_1^I \wedge v_2^I \wedge \ldots \wedge v_n^I \vee v_q$. Once all Horn clauses are transformed into DAGs, we merge DAGs to generate the ultimate DAG of QNBN.

**Parameter Learning.** To calculate the dependency relations between unindexed queries and their candidate neighbors quantitatively, we learn the CPTs of each node in DAG. If the nodes have no parents, their prior probabilities are evaluated by normalizing the number of frequent nodes in social interactions. If the nodes have parents, we employ logical constraints represented by Boolean expressions to evaluate their conditional probability

$$P(X_i = k^i | \pi(X_i)) = (b_1, ..., b_z) = f_{X_i \pi(X_i)} = \begin{cases} 1, & k^i = b_1 \vee \ldots \vee b_z \\ 0, & otherwise \end{cases} \tag{7}$$

where $\pi(X_i)$ denotes the parents of $X_i$, $k^i, b_j \in \{0, 1\}(1 \leq i, j \leq z)$.

### 3.3   Probabilistic Inferences for Incremental Graph Index

To connect unindexed query with its candidate neighbors in the graph index efficiently, approximate inference based on random sampling [22] is employed to calculate posterior probability to quantitatively describe their dependence relations. The posterior probability $P(X_{ik^i}|X_{jk^j})$ is formulated as

$$P(X_{ik^i}|X_{jk^j}) \approx \frac{\#(X_i = k^i)}{n_s} \tag{8}$$

where $k^i \in (0, 1)$ is the set of possible values of $X_i$ and $n_s$ represents the sample size. $X_{ik^i}$ corresponds to $v_i^I$ of $G^I$ or unindexed query, if a node $v_i^I$ is in the graph index, then the value $k^i$ of $X_i$ is 1, i.e., $X_i = 1$.

To add the unindexed query into graph index accurately, a nearest neighbor evaluation is proposed to measure the similarity of unindexed query and its nearest neighbors of graph index. The nearest neighbor evaluation $\Delta'(v_i^I, v_q)$ includes evaluations of structural similarity and conditional probability of unindexed query and its nearest neighbors, formulated as

$$\Delta'(v_i^I, v_q) = \delta(v_i^I, v_q) + W \tag{9}$$

where $W$ is the penalty term defined as

$$W = -\frac{P(X_q = 1|X_{v_i^I} = 1)\delta(v_i^I, v_q)}{n_{v_i^I v_q}} \tag{10}$$

where the numerator part of the penalty term consists of posterior probability and Euclidean distance among nodes, $n_{v_i^I v_q}$ denotes the number of social interactions of $v_i^I$ or $v_q$, and $P(X_q = 1|X_{v_i^I} = 1)$ denotes the probability of unindexed query $X_{v_q} = 1$ given $X_{v_i^I} = 1$.

According to Eq. 8, $P(X_q = 1|X_{v_i^I} = 1)$ could be rewritten as $\frac{\#(X_q=k^q)}{n_s}$ and $k^q$ is set to 1, the neighbor evaluation function is formulated as

$$\Delta'(v_i^I, v_q) = \delta(v_i^I, v_q) + W \approx \delta(v_i^I, v_q) - \frac{\#(X_q = 1)\delta(v_i^I, v_q)}{n_s \cdot n_{v_i^I v_q}} \tag{11}$$

The neighbor relationships between unindexed queries and their candidate neighbors are calculated by Eq. 11. The top $k$ neighbors of each unindexed query could be obtained via the calculation results. Thus, the incremental graph index is built by adding edges between unindexed queries and their top $k$ neighbors.

## 3.4   ANNS on Graph Index

For indexed queries, their $k$ nearest neighbors are obtained by performing ANNS on the graph index. For unindexed queries, we incrementally connect them into the graph index and perform ANNS to find their $k$ nearest neighbors. The ideas of PI-IGI are presented in Algorithm 1.

---

**Algorithm 1.** ANNS on incremental graph index$(G^I, v_p^I, v_q, H)$

---

**Input:** Graph index $G^I = (V^I, E^I, \delta)$, navigating node $v_p^I$, query node $v_q$, social interactions set $H$;

**Output:** $k$ nearest neighbors of $v_q$;

1: traverse the nodes to judge whether $v_q$ is an unindexed query or not.
2: **if** $v_q$ is an unindexed query **then**
3:     $v_i^I \leftarrow$ the node of index has nearest neighborhood relationship with $v_q$.
4:     obtain candidate neighbor set $C_s^I$ of $v_q$.
5:     learn QNBN on $C_s^I$.
6:     perform probability inferences on QNBN to obtain the nodes set $S$ having dependency relations with $v_q$.
7:     **for all** each node $v_i^I$ in $S$ **do**
8:         **if** $\Delta'(v_q, v_i^I) < \Delta'_{max}$ **then**
9:             add edge $e_{qi}$ into $G^I$.
10:            $\Delta'_{max} \leftarrow \Delta'(v_q, v_i^I)$.
11:            **if** the number of $v_i^I$'s neighbors $> l$ **then**
12:                remove the node that has the minimum similarity with $v_i^I$.
13:            **end if**
14:        **end if**
15:    **end for**
16: **end if**
17: return $k$ nearest neighbors by performing ANNS over graph index.

---

The time complexity of steps $3 \sim 4$, steps $5 \sim 6$, steps $7 \sim 16$ and step 17 is $O(n) + O(k) + O(k^3 d + T_1 k^3 d)$, $O(|\sum|) + O(|S|)$, $O(|S|)$ and $O(\log n)$, respectively. $T_1$ is the number of iterations of k-means++ algorithm, $|\sum|$ is the number of QNRs. The complexity of Algorithm 1 is $O(|n|)$.

## 4   Experiments

In this section, our approach PI-IGI is compared with existing non-graph-index and graph-index methods. Two sets of experiments are conducted on social networks: 1) the efficiency of social network embedding and graph index updating; 2) the effectiveness and efficiency of ANNS on PI-IGI. Each experiment was repeated for five times, we exhibit the average evaluations of social network embedding, graph index updating and ANNS.

## 4.1 Experimental Setting

**Datasets.** Real-world social networks such as Facebook[1], soc-Reddithyperlink (Soc)[2], Twitter[3] and Weibo[4] are employed and all network datasets contain social interactions. Facebook describes communication among people over time. Soc is generated by extracting available Reddit data. Twitter and Weibo contain lots of social interactions among users, such as comments and retweeted posts. Table 1 provides more details, where $\#(Interaction)$ represents the number of social interactions, $\#(Edge)$ represents the number of edges and $\#(Query)$ represents the number of unindexed queries.

**Table 1.** Details of social networks.

| Dataset | $\#(Interaction)$ | $\#(Edge)$ | $\#(Query)$ |
|---------|-------------------|------------|-------------|
| FaceBook | 33,720 | 7089 | 10 |
| Soc | 2,712,512 | 858,490 | 700 |
| Twitter | 4,012,396 | 1,003,564 | 1000 |
| WeiBo | 4,178,974 | 1,054,196 | 1000 |

**Comparison Methods.** Our method PI-IGI was compiled by using C++14 to compare with existing graph-index methods and non-graph-index methods. GI-DSNE has an extra step to embed social network into low-dimensional vector space, while other comparative methods construct indexes on low-dimensional vectors directly. We performed the experiments on a machine running the Ubuntu operating system, equipped with a ten-core Intel Core i9-10900X CPU operating at 3.7 GHz and 128GB of main memory.

- **GI-DSNE** [23] embeds social network into low dimensional vector space, constructs the graph index on node embeddings, and cuts redundant edges of graph index to improve the construction time of graph and precision of ANNS.
- **NSSG**[5] [7] prunes the edges via constraining angle between two edges and guarantees search path being monotonic.
- **NSG**[6] [8] constructs a monotonic graph index based on MRNG and regards the global centroid of the graph index as the navigating node.
- **FANNG**[7] [10] selects more discretely distributed neighbors from more than $k$ nearest vertices based on RNG.

---

[1] https://nrvis.com/download/data/dynamic/.
[2] https://snap.stanford.edu/data/soc-RedditHyperlinks.html.
[3] https://www.aminer.cn/data-sna#Twitter-Dynamic-Net.
[4] https://aminer.org/Influencelocality.
[5] https://github.com/ZJULearning/SSG.
[6] https://github.com/ZJULearning/nsg.
[7] https://github.com/ZJULearning/efannagraph.

- **HCNNG**[8] [18] constructs graph index based on MST and its navigating node is obtained on building KD-tree.
- **FAISS**[9] [12] is a non-graph index based permutation, which has both CPU and GPU versions, with the CPU version being employed.
- **FALCONN**[10] [1] based on locality-sensitive hashing (LSH) has excellent search performance on low-dimensional datasets.
- **ANNOY**[11] [2] is a tree-based index built by constructing an elegant binary space partition (BSP) tree.

**Evaluation Metrics.** We used $t$ to evaluate the efficiency of network embedding. The parameters $d$, $\alpha$ and $m$ were varied to evaluate the update time of PI-IGI. The search performance of PI-IGI was evaluated by calculating the queries per second (QPS) and the search precision of ANNS. Precision is defined as $precision = \frac{|R \cap G|}{|G|}$, where $R$ denotes query result set and $G$ denotes the real result set.

## 4.2   Experimental Results

**Efficiency of Social Network Embedding and Graph Index Updating.** We recorded the execution time of social network embedding and graph index updating on different datasets by varying the dimension $d$ of embeddings and the confidence threshold $\alpha$ of QNRs selection, respectively, to evaluate their efficiency.

*Exp-1.1 Impacts of $d$ on the execution time of social network embedding.* PI-IGI is compared with GI-DSNE because of these methods including extra embedding step. To estimate the execution time of embedding on different datasets in Table 1, $d$ was varied from 128 to 512. Table 2 shows the results of embedding execution time. For each dataset, we found that the larger the dimension is, the longer the time of embedding is, such as $d = 512$ taking about 0.48 times more embedding time than that of $d = 128$ on Facebook, since the more the dimension of embeddings, the longer the time of embedding computation. Besides, the larger the dataset is , the more time the embedding takes, such as Soc taking about 150 times more embedding time than that of FaceBook on the same dimension $d = 128$. Moreover, our embedding method is more efficient than GI-DSNE under the same condition. This is because the masked graph attention mechanism incorporates linear transformations of features to map the original high-dimensional features to a lower-dimensional space, learning to reduce the computational complexity of embedding.

To demonstrate the efficiency of graph index updating on all datasets in Table 1, we evaluated the impacts of different confidences $\alpha$ of QNR selection and various embedding dimensions $d$ of datasets on the update time of PI-IGI.

---

[8] https://github.com/jalvarm/hcnng.
[9] https://github.com/facebookresearch/faiss.
[10] https://github.com/FALCONN-LIB/FALCONN.
[11] https://github.com/spotify/annoy.

**Table 2.** Impacts of data size and date dimension on the execution time of graph embedding methods.

| Dataset | Embedding time(s) | | | | | | |
|---|---|---|---|---|---|---|---|
| | d=128 | d=192 | d=256 | d=320 | d=384 | d=448 | d=512 |
| Facebook(GI-DSNE) | 17.0637 | 33.63 | 54.25 | 68.94 | 92.31 | 103.23 | 115.48 |
| Facebook(PI-IGI) | **2.49** | **2.66** | **2.79** | **3.04** | **3.24** | **3.58** | **3.71** |
| Soc(GI-DSNE) | 9264.246 | 10581.97 | 15962.47 | 27994.11 | 33427.21 | 40892.55 | 52911.96 |
| Soc(PI-IGI) | **347.95** | **369.60** | **403.90** | **429.00** | **462.77** | **502.63** | **549.70** |
| Twitter(GI-DSNE) | 13278.47 | 20742.23 | 26117.31 | 37945.17 | 50720.07 | 59429.64 | 72145.37 |
| Twitter(PI-IGI) | **1180.26** | **1297.54** | **1387.17** | **1483.39** | **1561.77** | **1683.47** | **1767.71** |
| WeiBo(GI-DSNE) | 13496.97 | 22717.90 | 29047.47 | 38125.68 | 51990.84 | 61294.23 | 74001.23 |
| WeiBo(PI-IGI) | **1206.19** | **1305.00** | **1415.49** | **1492.68** | **1574.51** | **1694.82** | **1789.40** |

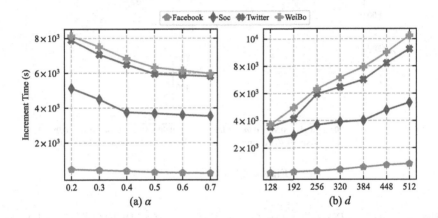

**Fig. 4.** Impacts of $\alpha$ and $d$ on the execution time of graph index updating.

*Exp-1.2 Impacts of confidence $\alpha$ of QNR selection on the update time of graph index.* The confidence $\alpha$ of QNR selection affects the update time of graph index. We find in Fig. 4 (a) that the time will be longer when $\alpha$ becomes smaller. This implies that the smaller the confidence threshold $\alpha$ is, the more QNRs are utilized to learn QNBN.

*Exp-1.3 Impacts of embedding dimension $d$ on the update time of graph index.* To discover the impact of different dimensions of datasets on the update time of graph index, $d$ was varied from 128 to 512. The results show that the larger the dimension is, the more time the update of graph index costs in Fig. 4 (b). This is because the higher the dimension of embeddings is, the longer time the PI-IGI takes to train GCN and masked graph attention mechanism.

**Effectiveness and Efficiency of ANNS.** To demonstrate the effectiveness and efficiency of ANNS on PI-IGI, we adopted QPS vs search precision to compare PI-IGI with five graph-index methods and three non-graph-index methods.

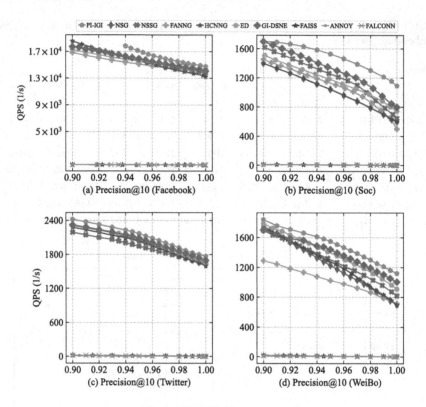

**Fig. 5.** QPS Vs Precision.

*Exp-2.1 Queries Per Second vs Search Precision.* For PI-IGI, NSG and NSSG, the quality and the size of graph indexes were set to 100 and 50, respectively. Meanwhile, the angles between two edges were set to 50 and the maximum candidate pool size was set to 100. For all compared methods, the dimension of datasets, the quality of search results and the number of neighbors were set to 256, 20 and 15, respectively. The QPS vs search precision of each indexing method is reported in Fig. 5. The results are as follows:

1) The search efficiency of PI-IGI is higher than that of other methods. For instance, the QPS of PI-IGI is higher by about 20% than that of GI-DSNE on Twitter when the precision attains 0.90. This is because that PI-IGI is an incremental graph index, the search path of unindexed queries' $k$ neighbors becomes shorter.

2) Given same QPS and dataset, the precision of PI-IGI is higher than that of other methods. For example, the precision of PI-IGI is about 5% higher than that of GI-DSNE on Facebook by fixing the QPS as 500, since unindexed queries could be found in search results.

3) It is not difficult to find that graph-index methods achieve much better ANNS performance than non-graph-index methods.

*Exp-2.2 Ablation Experiment.* To verify the effectiveness and efficiency of PI-IGI, we conducted incremental graph index method based on Euclidean distance (ED) to compare with PI-IGI. As shown in Fig. 5, the QPS of PI-IGI is higher than that of ED at the same precision, such that the QPS of PI-IGI is approximately 10% higher than that of ED on WeiBo when the search precision attains 0.98. This implies that PI-IGI takes shorter path to search neighbors of unindexed queries. Moreover, the search precision of PI-IGI is higher than that of ED at the same QPS, such that the precision of PI-IGI is approximately 3% higher than that of ED on WeiBo by fixing the QPS as 1200. This is because that PI-IGI obtains more accurate neighbors by calculating the dependency relations of unindexed queries and their candidate neighbors.

## 5 Conclusion and Future Work

We present a probabilistic inference based incremental graph index for ANNS, which improves search precision by at least 5% and search efficiency by 10% compared to the state-of-the-art methods. The improvements are due to the addition of unindexed queries into the graph index. Besides, we propose QNBN to describe the dependency relations between unindexed queries and their candidate neighbors and perform approximate inference in QNBN to infer the potential edges of graph index. Theoretical analysis and extensive experiments manifest the advantages of our method. In the future, we will propose a novel method based on Bayesian neural network to obtain accurate dependency relations of nodes to improve the precision of ANNS on PI-IGI.

**Acknowledgments.** This paper was supported by the National Natural Science Foundation of China (62002311), Major Project of Science and Technology of Yunnan Province (202202AD080001), Yunnan Key Laboratory of Intelligent Systems and Computing (202205AG070003), Research Foundation of Educational Department of Yunnan Province (2023J0022).

## References

1. Andoni, A., Indyk, P., Laarhoven, T., Razenshteyn, I., Schmidt, L.: Practical and optimal lsh for angular distance. In: Advances in Neural Information Processing Systems, 28 (2015)
2. Bernhardsson, E.: Annoy at github. GitHub. Repéré à https://github.com/spotify/annoy (2015)
3. Bi, W., Ma, J., Zhu, X., Wang, W., Zhang, A.: Cloud service selection based on weighted KD tree nearest neighbor search. Appl. Soft Comput. J. **131**, 109780 (2022)
4. Cheng, D., Huang, J., Zhang, S., Wu, Q.: A robust method based on locality sensitive hashing for k-nearest neighbors searching. Wireless Networks, pp. 1–14 (2022)
5. Dong, W., Moses, C., Li, K.: Efficient k-nearest neighbor graph construction for generic similarity measures. In: Proceedings of the 20th international conference on World wide web, pp. 577–586 (2011)

6. Ezugwu, A.E., et al.: A comprehensive survey of clustering algorithms: State-of-the-art machine learning applications, taxonomy, challenges, and future research prospects. Eng. Appl. Artif. Intell. **110**, 104743 (2022)
7. Fu, C., Wang, C., Cai, D.: High dimensional similarity search with satellite system graph: Efficiency, scalability, and unindexed query compatibility. IEEE Trans. Pattern Anal. Mach. Intell. **44**(8), 4139–4150 (2021)
8. Fu, C., Xiang, C., Wang, C., Cai, D.: Fast approximate nearest neighbor search with the navigating spreading-out graph. Proc. VLDB Endow. **12**(5) (2019)
9. Gorunescu, F.: Data Mining: Concepts, models and techniques. Springer Science, San Francisco (2011)
10. Harwood, B., Drummond, T.: Fanng: Fast approximate nearest neighbour graphs. In: Proceedings of the IEEE Conference on Computer Vision and Pattern Recognition, pp. 5713–5722 (2016)
11. Hu, D., Nie, F., Li, X.: Discrete spectral hashing for efficient similarity retrieval. IEEE Trans. Image Process. **28**(3), 1080–1091 (2018)
12. Johnson, J., Douze, M., Jégou, H.: Billion-scale similarity search with gpus. IEEE Trans. on Big Data **7**(3), 535–547 (2019)
13. Kosuge, A., Yamamoto, K., Akamine, Y., Oshima, T.: An soc-fpga-based iterative-closest-point accelerator enabling faster picking robots. IEEE Trans. Industr. Electron. **68**(4), 3567–3576 (2020)
14. Lejsek, H., Amsaleg, L.: Nv-tree: an efficient disk-based index for approximate search in very large high-dimensional collections. IEEE Trans. Pattern Anal. Mach. Intell. **31**(5), 869–883 (2008)
15. Lejsek, H., Amsaleg, L.: Nv-tree: nearest neighbors at the billion scale. In: Proceedings of the 1st ACM International Conference on Multimedia Retrieval, pp. 1–8 (2011)
16. Li, J., Yue, K., Li, J., Duan, L.: A probabilistic inference based approach for querying associative entities in knowledge graph. In: Proceedings of the Web and Big Data: 5th International Joint Conference, pp. 75–89 (2021)
17. Li, P., Shrivastava, A., Moore, J., König, A.: Hashing algorithms for large-scale learning. In: Advances in Neural Information Processing Systems 24 (2011)
18. Munoz, J.V., Gonçalves, M.A., Dias, Z., Torres, R.d.S.: Hierarchical clustering-based graphs for large scale approximate nearest neighbor search. Pattern Recognition **96**, 106970 (2019)
19. Pan, Z., Wang, L., Wang, Y., Liu, Y.: Product quantization with dual codebooks for approximate nearest neighbor search. Neurocomputing **401**, 59–68 (2020)
20. Paparrizos, J., Edian, I., Liu, C., Elmore, A.J., Franklin, M.J.: Fast adaptive similarity search through variance-aware quantization. In: 2022 IEEE 38th International Conference on Data Engineering, pp. 2969–2983 (2022)
21. Paredes, R., Chávez, E.: Using the k-nearest neighbor graph for proximity searching in metric spaces. In: Proceedings of the String Processing and Information Retrieval: 12th International Conference, pp. 127–138 (2005)
22. Qi, Z., Yue, K., Duan, L., Hu, K., Liang, Z.: Dynamic embeddings for efficient parameter learning of Bayesian network with multiple latent variables. Inf. Sci. **590**, 198–216 (2022)
23. Qi, Z., Yue, K., Duan, L., Liang, Z.: Similarity search with graph index on directed social network embedding. In: Web Engineering: 22nd International Conference, pp. 82–97 (2022)
24. Wang, M., Xu, X., Yue, Q., Wang, Y.: A comprehensive survey and experimental comparison of graph-based approximate nearest neighbor search. Proc. VLDB Endowment **14**(11), 1964–1978 (2021)

25. Welling, M., Kingma, D.P.: Auto-encoding variational bayes. In: ICLR (2014)
26. Xu, X., Wang, M., Wang, Y., Ma, D.: Two-stage routing with optimized guided search and greedy algorithm on proximity graph. Knowl.-Based Syst. **229**, 107305 (2021)
27. Yap, G.E., Tan, A.H., Pang, H.H.: Explaining inferences in bayesian networks. Appl. Intell. **29**, 263–278 (2008)
28. Yu, S., Sun, Y., Guo, Z.: Graph regularized unsupervised deep hashing for large scale image retrieval. In: 2020 5th IEEE International Conference on Big Data Analytics, pp. 292–297 (2020)
29. Zhang, T., Liu, B., Niu, D., Lai, K., Xu, Y.: Multiresolution graph attention networks for relevance matching. In: Proceedings of the 27th ACM international conference on information and knowledge management, pp. 933–942 (2018)
30. Zheng, B., Zhao, X., Weng, L., Nguyen, Q.V.H., Liu, H., Jensen, C.S.: Pm-lsh: a fast and accurate in-memory framework for high-dimensional approximate nn and closest pair search. VLDB J. **31**(6), 1339–1363 (2022)

# Cloud-Edge-Device Collaborative Image Retrieval and Recognition for Mobile Web

Yakun Huang[1($\boxtimes$)], Wenwei Li[1], Shouyi Wu[1], Xiuquan Qiao[1], Meng Guo[2], Hongshun He[2], and Yang Li[2]

[1] Beijing University of Posts and Telecommunications, Beijing 100876, China
{ykhuang,wwli,sywu,qiaoxq}@bupt.edu.cn
[2] China Mobile Communications Research Institute, Beijing 100053, China
{guomeng,hehongshun,liyangyw}@chinamobie.com

**Abstract.** Efficient image retrieval and recognition are pivotal for optimal mobile web vision services. Traditional web-based solutions offer limited accuracy, high overhead, and struggle with vast image volumes. Transferring images for real-time cloud recognition demands stable communication, and large-scale concurrent requests strain computational and network resources. This paper introduces a distributed recognition approach, leveraging cloud-edge-device collaboration through edge computing's low latency and high bandwidth. We present a lightweight image saliency detection model tailored for mobile web, enhancing initial image feature extraction. Additionally, we introduce an edge-based, deep learning-driven method to amplify image retrieval speed and precision. We incorporate a location and popularity-based caching system to alleviate strains on cloud resources and network bandwidth during extensive image requests. Our real-world tests validate our approach: our saliency detection model outpaces the benchmark by reducing the model size by up to 94%, making it suitable for mobile web deployment. The proposed method improves retrieval accuracy by 40% over cloud-based counterparts and cuts response latency by over 60%.

**Keywords:** Cross-platform · Edge computing · Image retrieval

## 1 Introduction

Web browsers remain a primary gateway for mobile internet applications, facilitating seamless access to cross-platform services via browsers and integrated apps. With the progress in artificial intelligence and computer vision, image search and recognition have become crucial for leading mobile services, notably in browser-driven augmented reality (AR) and mini-programs [1,2]. These services often encompass tasks such as capturing frames, image preprocessing, detecting feature points, and matching against image databases. Hence, proficient and precise image recognition is essential for mobile web visual services.

Currently, there are two dominant techniques for image recognition in mobile web browsers: **(1) Browser-Based Image Recognition:** Utilizing frontend

© ICST Institute for Computer Sciences, Social Informatics and Telecommunications Engineering 2024
Published by Springer Nature Switzerland AG 2024. All Rights Reserved
H. Gao et al. (Eds.): CollaborateCom 2023, LNICST 562, pp. 474–494, 2024.
https://doi.org/10.1007/978-3-031-54528-3_26

frameworks like JSFeat, this approach leverages JavaScript computation libraries for image matching via algorithms such as SIFT [3], ORB [4], and AKAZE [5]. Though these conventional algorithms ensure robustness and accuracy, they are sluggish in matching speeds. The computational capacity of mobile web platforms is constrained, posing difficulties for extensive image recognition. **(2) Cloud-Based Image Recognition:** Here, resource-intensive tasks, including feature point detection and matching, are transferred to the cloud, accommodating large-scale mobile visual recognition demands [6]. Cloud servers adeptly enhance mobile web platforms' computational prowess. However, regular data and model exchanges introduce considerable communication latency. High-resolution media, such as images, audio, or video, under inconsistent communication conditions disrupts real-time visual computation and portrayal. Also, the cloud grapples with increased resource and bandwidth usage during extensive simultaneous requests, restricting the broad applicability of the mobile web.

This paper proposes a cloud-edge cooperative architecture for distributed mobile web image retrieval and recognition. This approach comprises a saliency detection-based image preprocessing module and an edge-conscious image retrieval acceleration. Developing this efficient method presents two challenges:

- **Image Resolution Increase.** Improved terminal camera performance leads to higher image resolutions. As image resolution increases, the time required for feature extraction using the same algorithm grows longer. Direct compression of real-time image frames can reduce feature extraction and retrieval accuracy. To address this challenge, we introduce a lightweight image saliency detection module tailored for lightweight mobile web platforms. This algorithm effectively localizes and segments the main subject in images. Notably, in mobile web AR applications, it efficiently extracts regions of interest from high-resolution images, reducing image frame transmission, accelerating subsequent feature point extraction and matching computations, and thus enhancing image recognition efficiency.
- **Traditional Image Matching Limitations.** Conventional image-matching algorithms with handcrafted local features offer robustness against viewpoint and lighting variations but necessitate geometric verification. As the volume of images in a template library grows, real-time recognition becomes challenging. Our study introduces an edge-aware retrieval acceleration module that enhances edge server image retrieval efficiency and optimizes computational resources. We combine deep learning-driven image retrieval with traditional matching methods, using deep learning to extract feature vectors and pre-screen large image datasets, thus improving retrieval efficacy. Furthermore, we propose an image caching strategy based on geography and popularity, facilitating cloud collaboration. This strategy alleviates cloud computational and bandwidth demands, reduces mobile web latency, and bolsters edge server resource utilization, allowing for faster, more accurate large-scale image recognition.

To further validate the proposed cloud-edge collaborative distributed mobile web image retrieval and recognition method, we developed a prototype system for large-scale image retrieval and recognition based on the KubeEdge framework. We conducted experiments and analyses in actual business scenarios. The primary contributions of this paper are:

- We designed a cloud-edge-device collaborative architecture to enhance the efficiency of large-scale concurrent web retrieval and recognition requests, especially boosting the efficiency of large-scale concurrent web retrieval and recognition requests.
- We proposed extracting the main area from real-time images to accelerate subsequent feature extraction speed and improve image recognition accuracy.
- We combined deep learning-based image retrieval with matching algorithms to further boost the accuracy and efficiency of mobile web image recognition requests.
- We designed a caching mechanism based on geographical location and popularity, reducing the pressure on the cloud layer and enhancing the speed and accuracy of recognition.

## 2    Design of Proposed Collaborative Architecture

### 2.1    Problem Description

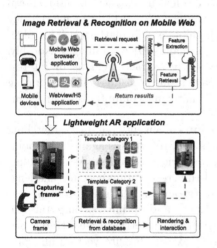

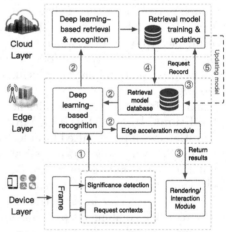

**Fig. 1.** Schematic of the mobile web image retrieval and recognition

**Fig. 2.** Proposed architecture of mobile web image retrieval and recognition

Figure 1 depicts the sequence of steps taken when a mobile web application (encompassing browser apps and WebView/H5-based applications) sends an image retrieval and recognition request to a cloud server. Once the cloud server receives this request, it deciphers the API interface, proceeds with image feature extraction, and juxtaposes these features with its image database. After performing the match and search, it arrives at the definitive retrieval and recognition outcome.

For a clearer perspective, let's consider the example of cross-platform mobile web AR recognition: (a) **Image Capture:** Through a browser, a user snaps a camera frame. (b) **Request Initiation:** The captured frame then sets off a retrieval and recognition petition to the cloud. (c) **Image Retrieval:** The cloud server contrasts the frame with its template library. (d) **Recognition & Rendering:** Upon finding a match, a 3D model tied to the identified object is displayed on the user's device. (e) **User Interaction:** This rendering culminates the user interaction, serving content or a service pertinent to the identified object. At its core, the primary aim of image retrieval and recognition activities is to methodically and promptly locate and align a target image from a designated image library, paving the way for subsequent operations and interactions. In contrast, the mission of image object recognition endeavors primarily hinges on ascertaining the category of the present object. The efficiency of retrieval and recognition is notably impacted by the size of the image library and the variations in features among targets of the same category. This paper zeroes in on the crucial challenge of streamlining precise image retrieval and recognition within resource-limited and cross-platform web applications, especially as it relates to immersive AR experiences and mobile multimedia visual services.

### 2.2 Overview of System Architecture Design

As depicted in Fig. 2, our proposed system utilizes a distributed computational structure spanning the mobile device, edge cloud, and remote cloud layers. Specifically, the device layer employs a saliency detection module to minimize data transmission, boosting the retrieval efficiency of both edge and remote clouds. Furthermore, richer context from the request enhances retrieval by providing personalized user data. Edge layer incorporates a deep learning-based image retrieval module, and an edge acceleration recognition module and synchronizes with the remote cloud's model library to improve retrieval accuracy. The acceleration module applies advanced techniques tailored to the user context. Emulating the edge layer's functionalities, the remote cloud layer houses a deep learning retrieval module, offering precise image results. Crucially, it hosts offline training for these models. Based on user request patterns, updated models are distributed to edge servers, optimizing efficiency and service quality.

For system edge node collaboration, we introduce a streamlined KubeEdge framework. It segments cluster operations for edge computing into two distinct components: Cloud Core (remote cloud) and Edge Core (edge side). The operational process for mobile web image retrieval and recognition unfolds as follows: **STEP 1:** Users activate the camera interface in browser apps to capture real-time frames. Using a saliency detection model, the primary subject is extracted from the image. This cropped image, together with the relevant context, triggers a retrieval request to the edge cloud. **STEP 2:** The edge cloud server processes the request, employing its deep learning recognition module to search its cached image library. If a match is found, results are sent back. If not, the task moves to the remote cloud server. A successful remote retrieval results in the corresponding image being cached in the edge library. **STEP 3**: The edge server conveys the recognized results to the mobile web. This specific request record is saved and periodically synced with the remote cloud. **STEP 4**: Cloud servers, equipped with robust computational and GPU resources, periodically assimilate user-uploaded query images into training sets. This data assists in training deep learning image retrieval models. **STEP 5**: Based on real-time needs, edge servers regularly fetch updated models from the remote cloud, refining the model's adaptability and enhancing retrieval accuracy.

## 3    Methods of Proposed Collaborative Architecture

### 3.1    Image Preprocessing Based on Saliency Detection

The efficiency of image retrieval and recognition, based on frames captured by mobile devices and sent to servers, is predominantly affected by: (1) High-

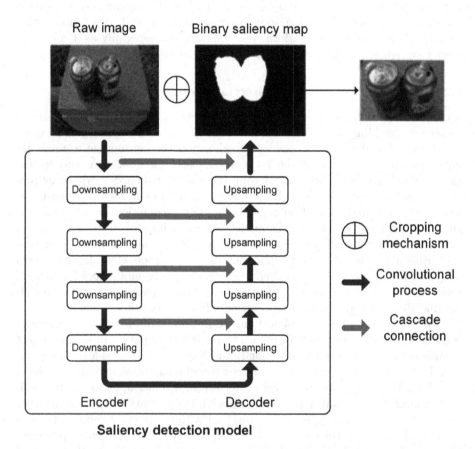

**Fig. 3.** Image preprocessing based on saliency detection

resolution Frames: Such frames necessitate a consistent, high-speed network, inducing considerable transmission lags. (2) Complex Backgrounds: Camera-captured keyframes often have a cluttered backdrop, impeding retrieval accuracy and speed. Employing deep learning for target segmentation intensifies computational demands, exacerbating retrieval and recognition delays.

Addressing the aforementioned challenges, we present a nimble saliency detection model optimized for widespread mobile web platforms. This model refines images captured by the camera, bolstering the accuracy and speed of server-side retrieval and recognition. Its core function is to identify, trim, and forward the primary subject portion of the image for server-side operations. As depicted in Fig. 3, the image preprocessing module, anchored on saliency detection, functions as follows: (1) The camera-captured raw image is inputted into the saliency detection model. (2) Using the derived binary saliency map, a region-centric cropping mechanism extracts the image's central subject. (3) Substituting the initial image, this refined version is relayed to the server, cutting down on data transmission and amplifying the efficiency and accuracy of the image retrieval and recognition.

**Lightweight Saliency Detection.** Fig. 4 delineates a saliency detection model tailored for the mobile web, addressing its inherent computational constraints. This model is structured to refine the clarity of saliency maps, featuring: (a) Foundation on Proven Architectures. Using the HED (Holistically-Nested Edge Detection) blueprint [7], the model augments the saliency map's resolution. The convolutional tiers of ShuffleNet V2 [8] lay the foundational network. (b) Multi-Scale Context Module (MSCM): It outputs a comprehensive saliency forecast. (c) Resolution Augmentation. Recognizing the global saliency map is merely 1/32 the resolution of the original, enhancing measures are adopted. Specifically, branches are integrated post the culminating layers of particular modules in ShuffleNet v2: Conv1, MaxPool, Stage 2, and Stage 3. These branches

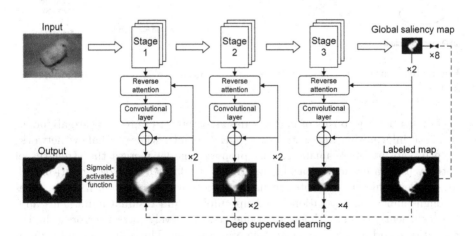

**Fig. 4.** Network structure of the saliency detection model

learn residual nuances at varying resolutions. Sequentially, features discerned from each layer aid in saliency map refinement. Final Projection: The superficial branch result from Stage 1 steers into a Sigmoid tier, culminating in the final predictive outcome. This design strikes a balance between elevating saliency map quality and ensuring a resource-conscious, nimble model apt for the mobile web.

Using ShuffleNet V2 in the backbone structure reduces the RAS [9] model size (initially based on VGG16) from 81MB to 3.5MB, but with a notable accuracy decrease. To counter this, we integrated a feature pyramid into ShuffleNet V2, including parallel 3×3, 5×5, and 7×7 depthwise separable convolutions. This efficiently processes spatial data from various target scales, improving accuracy. Figure 5 compares this revised structure to the original ShuffleNet, where "DWConv" denotes the depthwise convolution, splitting standard convolutions into channel-wise and point-wise tasks.

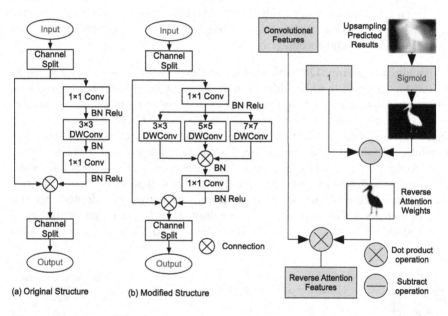

**Fig. 5.** Structure of the feature pyramid

**Fig. 6.** Reverse attention module

Furthermore, in terms of network design, deep structures capture abundant semantic information but often miss spatial details, whereas shallow networks adeptly capture these nuances. The proposed model merges the strengths of both by using a branched learning approach. It adopts a top-down multi-branch residual learning strategy, integrating predictions with ground truth across scales through bilinear interpolation-based upsampling and residual units. This approach efficiently trains with fewer parameters, adaptively corrects errors at higher resolutions, and produces a more streamlined model. The computation for residual units is denoted in Eq. (1) and Eq. (2). Here, $R_i$ symbolizes the current branch's residual feature, and $B_{i+1}$ represents the subsequent branch's saliency feature map. By upscaling and summing $R_{i+1}$ and $B_{i+1}$ by two, we obtain the saliency feature map $B_i$ for the current branch, with $G$ signifying the ground truth. Each branch $i$ outputs a feature map upsampled by $2^i$, which is then matched with the ground truth, effectuating deep supervised learning.

$$\{B_{i+1}\}^{up \times 2^{i+1}} \approx G \tag{1}$$

$$\{B_{i+1}^{up} + R_i\}^{up \times 2^1} = \{B_i\}^{up \times 2^i} \approx G \tag{2}$$

The branched structure incorporates a reverse attention module [9] tailored to discern details at diminished resolutions, thereby facilitating more accurate high-resolution predictions. As depicted in Fig. 6, this module generates reverse attention weights from the branch's prediction results, which are then multiplied by the original convolutional features, producing reverse attention features. This mechanism steers the multi-branch network's top-down learning, incrementally refining missing areas in saliency prediction to produce a map enriched in spatial detail.

As described in Eq. (3) and Eq. (4), $A$ denotes the reverse attention weight, while $T$ signifies the lateral output feature. The spatial position in the feature map is indicated by $z$, and the feature dimension is marked by $c$. The output feature $F$ emerges from the point-wise multiplication of the original lateral output feature and the reverse attention weight. During this process, the prediction result from the $(i+1)^{\text{th}}$ branch lateral output is upsampled, then deducted from the Sigmoid-activated function of the upsampled output minus 1, forming the reverse attention weight $A_i$.

$$F_{z,c} = A_z \cdot T_{z,c} \tag{3}$$

$$A_i = 1 - Sigmoid(B_{i+1}^{up}) \tag{4}$$

**Model Loss Function.** For efficient training of the lightweight saliency detection model shown in Fig. 3, deep supervision is essential for each branch network. This research considers the output layer of each branch as a pixel-level binary classifier, utilizing the cross-entropy loss function to compute the loss for the $i^{\text{th}}$ branch. The formula is:

$$\ell_{\text{side}}^{(m)}\left(I, G, W, w^{(m)}\right)$$
$$= -\sum_{x=1}^{|I|} G(z) \log \Pr\left(G(z) = 1 \mid I(z); W, w^{(m)}\right) \tag{5}$$
$$+ (1 - G(z)) \log \Pr\left(G(z) = 0 \mid I(z); W, w^{(m)}\right)$$

Here, $Pr(z)$ denotes the probability of pixel activation at position 'z' in the $i^{\text{th}}$ branch. $W$ encompasses parameters across all network layers, with $i$ and $G$ representing input and ground truth for each branch. The total loss function in equation (4) aggregates losses from individual branches and the global saliency map, where $M$ indicates the number of sub-loss functions.

$$c_x = \frac{M_{10}}{M_{00}}, c_y = \frac{M_{01}}{M_{00}} \tag{6}$$

**Clipping Mechanism Based on Region Generation.** Following the application of the saliency detection model, the original image produces a binary saliency map. Using the region generation mechanism [10], the cropping region's coordinates are determined. From this map, we derive the centroid coordinates $(c_x, c_y)$, calculated as follows:

$$L_{\text{side}}(I, G, W, w) = \sum_{m=1}^{M} \ell_{\text{side}}^{(m)}\left(I, G, W, w^{(m)}\right) \tag{7}$$

Subsequently, the standard deviation of the centroid coordinates is as follows:

$$\sigma_x = \sqrt{\frac{M_{20}}{M_{00}} - c_x^2}, \sigma_y = \sqrt{\frac{M_{02}}{M_{00}} - c_y^2} \tag{8}$$

wherein, the calculation methods for $M_{00}, M_{10}, M_{01}, M_{20}, M_{02}$ are as follows:

$$M_{00} = \sum_{i,j} S_{i,j}, M_{10} = \sum_{i,j} i \cdot S_{i,j}, M_{01} = \sum_{i,j} j \cdot S_{i,j}$$
$$M_{20} = \sum_{i,j} i^2 \cdot S_{i,j}, M_{02} = \sum_{i,j} j^2 \cdot S_{i,j}. \tag{9}$$

Following this, the primary subject area is defined by the top-left and bottom-right corner coordinates, calculated using the following:

$$(x_1, y_1) = (c_x + \alpha\sigma_x, c_y + \alpha\sigma_y),$$
$$(x_2, y_2) = (c_x - \alpha\sigma_x, c_y - \alpha\sigma_y). \tag{10}$$

Here, $\alpha$ is a hyperparameter that controls the comprehensiveness of the cropped primary subject. We set $\alpha$ to 0.3, ensuring the inclusion of the majority of the main subject while limiting background noise.

### 3.2   Edge Acceleration Recognition Module

**Deep Learning-Based Image Recognition Acceleration.** The image recognition module is pivotal for servers in image retrieval and identification. Dominant methods employ algorithms like SIFT, AKAZE, and ORB to extract image features and determine recognition based on matching points. Yet, with expanding image databases, these algorithms falter in real-time identification on mobile platforms. Recently, deep learning models for feature vector extraction and similarity calculations have demonstrated rapidity in extensive image databases. Table 1 juxtaposes the speed of SIFT-based image matching with that of the ResNet deep learning model [11], both evaluated under consistent conditions using images of 500×500 dimensions across varying library sizes.

In the image recognition sequence, features are first extracted from the uploaded image and then matched with features from the image library. The table reveals that as the library size grows, the time disparity between traditional and deep learning feature-matching algorithms increases, underscoring the inadequacy of traditional algorithms for real-time retrieval on constrained mobile platforms. For optimal efficiency in large-scale image retrieval and recognition, we propose a deep learning-driven image retrieval acceleration technique comprising two essential phases. The initial phase involves computing the similarity of image feature vectors, swiftly procuring the top-K analogous images from a vast image library in relation to the input image. In the subsequent phase, feature points from these K images and the input image are derived using the SIFT methodology. Post geometric verification, the final results are ascertained by the count of matched points, ensuring accurate recognition. Notably, SIFT has garnered traction across diverse visual tasks for its dual strengths: efficiency and precision.

**Table 1.** Comparison of SIFT with deep learning-based features

|                    | Number of Images | SIFT-Based | ResNet-Based |
|--------------------|------------------|------------|--------------|
| Feature Extraction | 1                | 0.0880     | 0.1440       |
| Feature Matching   | 1                | 0.0126     | 0.0001       |
|                    | 50               | 0.6371     | 0.0005       |
|                    | 500              | 6.3270     | 0.0012       |
|                    | 1000             | 12.5413    | 0.0018       |

Figure 7 elucidates this deep learning-centric acceleration method. The preliminary module, designated for image retrieval, begins by crafting a training dataset tailored to the present recognition context, succeeded by data refinement. Following this, a deep learning classification task, with ResNet as its core network, trains the model. The feature vector for the input image is sourced from the Softmax layer's input tensor within this network, leading to the extraction of a 2048-dimensional vector for every image. In an offline environment, feature vectors from the entire template image database (Gallery) are derived and cataloged in a matrix within a dictionary. In real-time usage, when a query arises, features from only the query image are extracted. Via matrix operations, distances between the query's feature vectors and those of the template library are gauged. Images are then sequenced based on these distances, with the top-K most similar images designated as the primary retrieval set.

The assessment of similarity among distinct images often leverages measures like the Euclidean distance and cosine similarity to gauge vector resemblances.

The Euclidean distance quantifies the length between two vector endpoints, as illustrated in Eq. (11). Conversely, cosine similarity represents the cosine value of the angle separating two vectors. Owing to its appreciable computational speed, outpacing that of the Euclidean distance, this paper opts for cosine similarity as its benchmarking metric. The methodology for computing this similarity is elucidated in the ensuing equation:

$$d(a,b) = \sqrt{\sum_{i=1}^{n}(a_i - b_i)^2} \tag{11}$$

$$Sim = \frac{\sum_{i=1}^{n}(a_i \times b_i)}{\sqrt{\sum_{i=1}^{n}(a_i)^2} \times \sqrt{\sum_{i=1}^{n}(b_i)^2}} \tag{12}$$

To enhance the recall speed of the pre-selection module, this paper adds a network layer during training to condense the dimensionality of image feature vectors, improving computational efficiency and recognition speed. Furthermore, we

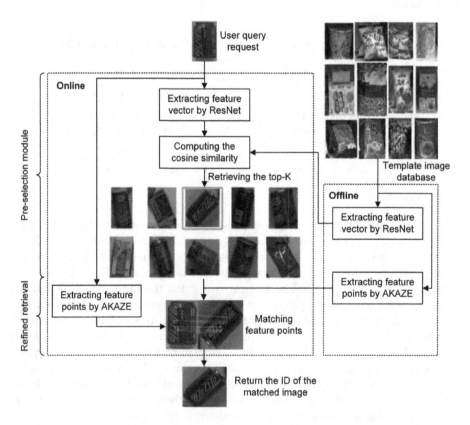

**Fig. 7.** Deep learning-based image recognition acceleration

employ the Hierarchical Navigable Small World (HNSW) algorithm for approximate nearest-neighbor searches. By indexing large-scale image feature vectors and prioritizing the most similar images, our approach significantly quickens image retrieval while maintaining search precision.

For the refined retrieval of the pre-selected image set, AKAZE features are utilized. These features, derived from the Hessian determinant's local maxima across scales, utilize binary descriptors to lessen computation and optimize real-time performance [12]. This paper incorporates an image recognition module on the cloud server, paralleling the edge server's capabilities. In real-world scenarios, the cloud server continuously receives user query images. With these fresh datasets, it refines and updates deep learning models, periodically syncing model parameters on both the cloud and edge, enhancing the adaptability of the deployed models.

**Retrieval Caching Mechanism Based on Location and Popularity.** Edge servers vary in service offerings based on user locations and application contexts. For instance, in museums, users predominantly request historical artifacts and renowned paintings, whereas in supermarket settings see frequent requests for everyday items. This suggests that template image retrieval frequency in databases correlates with both user location and image popularity. Consequently, the likelihood of querying the same template image can differ substantially across locations, resulting in varying access rates for identical data objects.

Given edge nodes' constrained cache capacity, formulating an adept cache replacement tactic is paramount when cache limits are met. Classical replacement strategies like Least Recently Used (LRU), First In First Out (FIFO), and Least Frequently Used (LFU) often underperform in terms of hit rates in dynamic contexts. Addressing this, our study proposes a cache replacement scheme anchored in content popularity. Specifically, we gauge the popularity of user-demanded content via its recent access frequency. Let $f_i(k)$ represent the instances content $k$ is requested from node $i$ within time $T$. Content $k$'s access frequency, $F_i(k)$, is articulated in Eq. (13), where $\sum_{j=1}^{k} f_{i,j}$ tallies all content requests on node $i$ during time $T$.

$$F_i(k) = \frac{f_i(k)}{\sum_{j=1}^{k} f_{i,j}} \tag{13}$$

Furthermore, the recency of a data request also influences the popularity calculation. If $T(k)$ denotes the time elapsed since the last request for content $k$, a smaller $T(k)$ indicates higher popularity. Considering the factors mentioned above, the popularity $P(k)$ of a cached data object in edge node $i$ is defined as Eq. (14).

$$P(k) = \mu F_i(k) + (1 - \mu)\frac{1}{T(k)} \tag{14}$$

$\mu \in (0, 1)$ acts as a modulation factor, dictating the balance between recent access time and access frequency. Initially set at 0.5, $\mu$ might necessitate adjustments aligned with real-world use. When cache data on an edge node hits its limit, data items with smaller $P(k)$ values are prioritized for replacement based on popularity. Users' geographical positions are typically sourced from their mobile devices' location systems, directing them to the closest edge node. However, in real scenarios, privacy-conscious users might opt out of location sharing. In these cases, a default method is employed: user queries are directly relayed to cloud servers for handling.

## 4   Experimental Analysis

### 4.1   Performance Analysis

**Experimental Settings.** Both cloud and edge service nodes utilize servers operating within Docker containers orchestrated by KubeEdge. Each server boasts an Intel®Xeon®Gold 5118 CPU @ 2.30GHz, 128 GB of RAM, and runs on Ubuntu 18.04.5 LTS. The system employs KubeEdge V1.3.0, Docker V19.03.12, and Mosquitto V1.6.12. Our infrastructure leveraged China Unicom's MEC service in Beijing, while cloud servers were based in Qingdao and Guizhou using Alibaba Cloud. Table 2 showcases transmission latency between server nodes for test requests originating from Beijing, with latencies averaged across 100 requests. It's clear that edge nodes markedly decrease transmission latency-a benefit that amplifies as the geographical gap between the cloud server and user widens.

**Table 2.** Experimental environment deployment

| Access Node) | Location | Distance (Km) | Delay(ms) |
|---|---|---|---|
| Edge Node | Beijing | 10 | 6 |
| Cloud Node1 | Qingdao | 660 | 10 |
| Cloud Node2 | Guiyang | 2083 | 78 |

**Analysis of Experimental Results.** In this section, we contrast the performance of our proposed methodology with cloud-based services within the aforementioned collaborative cloud environment. Table 2 presents a comparison of processing delay performance across different methods, considering varying data sizes. Notably, the edge server caches 500 images, while the cloud computing center retains the complete image dataset. During practical testing, user-initiated image retrieval requests are first addressed by the proximate edge node. If the recognition result meets expectations, it's promptly relayed to the user terminal. However, if the search query doesn't find a match in the edge node's cached image database, the request is rerouted to the cloud center. Subsequently, the cloud center's search outcome is dispatched to the device.

**Table 3.** Retrieval time comparison of different methods. Unit: Milliseconds (ms).

| | Number of Images | Data Fetch | Model Loading | Image Retrieval | Image Matching | Processing Delay | Total Delay |
|---|---|---|---|---|---|---|---|
| Only Edge | 500 | 24 | 157 | 0.4 | 185 | 6 | 372.4 |
| Only Cloud | 10000 | 25 | 178 | 7.3 | 183 | 78 | 471.3 |
| | 100000 | 23 | 200 | 53.1 | 191 | 78 | 545.1 |
| Collaboration | 10000 | 26 | 179 | 7.5 | 184 | 81 | 477.5 |
| | 100000 | 26 | 200 | 54.6 | 188 | 81 | 549 |

The key takeaways from our experimental results are: (1) For cloud computing centers with image databases of 10,000 and 100,000 images, relying solely on edge nodes for request handling yields reduced latencies compared to alternative techniques. Nonetheless, this approach isn't optimal for larger databases, positioning it as ideal for swift retrieval within more confined image sets. (2) Central cloud centers, while capable of accommodating expansive image searches, entail a longer processing delay, diminishing user satisfaction. (3) Our suggested cloud-edge collaboration technique effectively addresses a considerable chunk of user queries at the edge. By refining edge data caching tailored to specific business dynamics and user query trends, the majority of requests are catered to at the edge. This strategy retains its potency even amidst significant shifts in business demands, ensuring uninterrupted user services. Notably, for extensive image retrievals, the use of edge nodes significantly trims user request response durations.

### 4.2 Saliency Detection Analysis

After showcasing the efficacy of our cloud-edge collaboration in previous experiments, we now delve into evaluating the image preprocessing module's performance, which is rooted in saliency detection and implemented on the mobile web. This section outlines the datasets and experimental configurations, contrasts our method with standard benchmarks, and ends by gauging the module's performance on diverse mobile web platforms.

**Datasets and Configuration.** We quantitatively validate our model on three key datasets often used in saliency detection: **MSRA-B** [13]: A dataset of 5,000 images, divided into 3,000 for training and 2,000 for testing. **HKU-IS** [14]: A collection of 4,447 images. **ECSSD** [15]: It contains 1,000 images. Training of the saliency model was expedited using the NVIDIA TITAN XP GPU on the PyTorch framework with the Stochastic Gradient Descent (SGD) optimizer. The initial learning rate was set at $1 \times 10^{-8}$, with crucial parameters like batch size, momentum, and learning rate decay coefficient held constant. As training loss reached a certain level, the learning rate was judiciously reduced. To counteract overfitting, strategies such as horizontal flipping were integrated into our data augmentation, bypassing the use of a validation set.

**Analysis of Experimental Results.** We examined the efficiency of saliency detection models, comparing with methods like DRFI [16], DCL+ [17], DSS [18],

ASNet [19], PicaNet [20], and RAS [9] using the MSRA-B training set. Metrics analyzed encompassed model size, time overhead, F-Measure, and MAE, with F-Measure representing the harmonic mean of precision and recall. Figure 8 shows the overhead of different saliency detection methods on the web. Results reveal our proposed lightweight model is 3.5MB, marking a 95.7% reduction from the second-ranking RAS. In comparison, the ASNet model is 363MB, introducing notable latency for mobile web.

As shown in Fig. 9, we compared the average processing time of our method with benchmark saliency algorithms on the MSRA-B test dataset using 500×500 images. Our method improved inference efficiency by about 92.3%, 97.9%, and 65.6% over RAS, DRFI, and DCL+ methods, respectively. This indicates our lightweight model's suitability for real-time mobile web use, whereas traditional methods lag in performance. In saliency detection, this work introduces an innovative lightweight method optimized for mobile web platforms, transferring some computational tasks from the cloud, thereby boosting cloud computing center throughput.

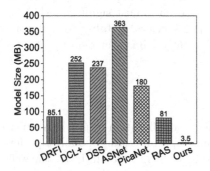

**Fig. 8.** Analysis of model sizes of several saliency detection algorithms

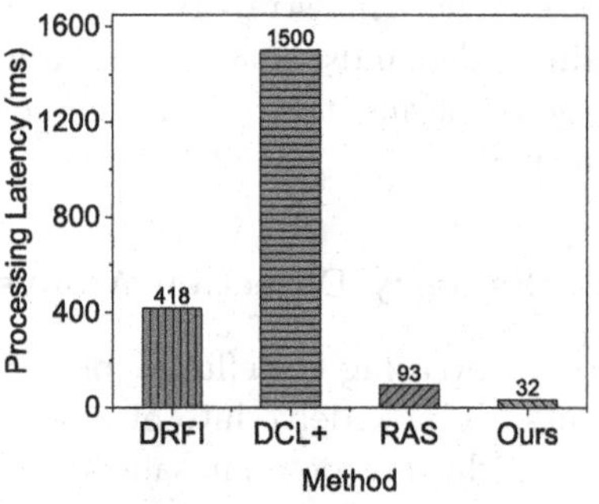

**Fig. 9.** Execution time of different saliency detection algorithms

Experiments on the MSRA-B, HKU-IS, and ECSSD datasets evaluated model accuracy. Figure 10 and Fig. 11 juxtapose the performance of the DRFI, DCL+, and RAS algorithms with our proposed lightweight saliency detection method using the F-Measure and MAE metrics. Ideally, a high F-Measure and low MAE are sought. The results reveal that our lightweight model boasts a 94% size reduction compared to the advanced RAS model and reduces inference latency by 62%. The inclusion of a pyramid structure further curtails accuracy loss. Notably, our method's F-Measure and MAE scores surpass those of leading methods, proving its efficiency and precision for practical use on mobile web.

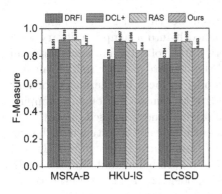

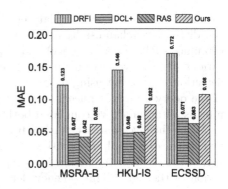

**Fig. 10.** F-Measure performance    **Fig. 11.** MAE performance

For deployment and performance, the crafted lightweight saliency detection model is readily deployable and executable on common mobile web browsers. During implementation, we transitioned the model from Keras's h5 format to a mobile web-friendly JSON format using the TensorFlow.js Converter. Table 3 showcases the inference durations and frame rates when using our model on diverse mobile devices, with test images at a 500×500 resolution in the Chrome browser. All results reflect the average of ten independent tests.

The results suggest that the mobile device's performance significantly impacts the model's inference time and frame rate. For example, a more basic device like the Xiaomi6 achieves about 5 frames per second. In contrast, the Samsung Galaxy Note20 reaches roughly 10 frames per second, and the iPhone 13 Pro hits around 15 frames per second. While there's a performance variation across devices with diverse specifications, the model ensures real-time image processing even on less advanced devices, handling multiple frame inferences within a second.

**Table 4.** Test on different mobile devices.

| Device (CPU) | Image Size | Running Time (ms) | Frame Rate |
|---|---|---|---|
| Xiaomi6 | 500×500 | 180–200 | 5–5.5 |
| Honor p20 pro | 500×500 | 122–149 | 6.7–8.2 |
| Galaxy Note20 | 500×500 | 95–108 | 9.3–10.5 |
| iPhone X | 500×500 | 103–120 | 8.3–9.7 |
| iPhone 11 | 500×500 | 96–109 | 9.2–10.4 |
| iPhone 13 Pro | 500×500 | 63–79 | 12.6–15.9 |

### 4.3 Analysis of Image Retrieval Acceleration

**Deep Learning-Based Image Recognition.** To assess the effectiveness and efficiency of the deep learning-based image recognition method, we employed the Retail Product Checkout dataset [21] from Megvii, consisting of images for 200 distinct merchandise items. We partitioned it into a template library with 600 images (three per category) and a query library of 8,397 images taken from various perspectives. We further evaluated the benefits of the terminal saliency detection module by using a lightweight model to focus on the main portions of the query images. Unneeded backgrounds were removed through a cropping process, after which we compared both the original and processed images.

Using the given dataset, this study assesses the saliency detection model using two metrics: "Recall/Recognition Accuracy" and "Image Recognition Time." Fig. 12 shows the outcomes for images processed both before and after the application of the lightweight saliency detection model. For image retrieval, cosine distances are calculated from the image feature vectors, which are then ranked to pinpoint the most similar images. The model's efficacy is gauged using TOP-K recall accuracy, as outlined in the following formula.

$$Accuracy_{recall} = \left( \sum_{i=1}^{N} y_i \right) /N. \tag{15}$$

Let $N$ denote the number of images in the test set. The indicator variable $y_i$ is set to 1 if at least one of the top $k$ images retrieved by the model matches the query image's category; otherwise, it's 0. In the experiments, 8,397 query images were matched against a set of 600 template images.

Figure 12 highlights several key findings: (1) The saliency detection module effectively isolates the main subject in user images, removing extraneous background details. As a result, vital information dominates the feature vectors, leading to a marked increase in recall accuracy across Top-1, Top-5, Top-10, and Top-20 retrievals. The "retrieval + matching" approach involves refining the top-10 recalled images with a precise image-matching algorithm, with final identification based on the number of matching points. (2) Introducing the proposed image matching technique enhances recall accuracy beyond that of sole image recognition, evident in the Top-1 column. Post saliency detection, the image recognition accuracy rises to 0.8378, an over 40% surge from before and a significant jump from the original 0.2847. (3) After preprocessing, our method consistently outperforms in recall accuracy for all Top-K categories, highlighting the efficiency of the deep learning-based recognition approach. This translates to enhanced performance in mobile web search and recognition, thereby elevating user experience.

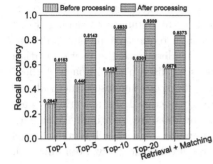
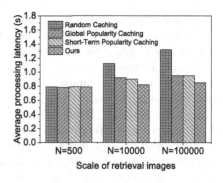

**Fig. 12.** Image recognition accuracy

**Fig. 13.** Performance of different image retrieval cache strategies

Table 5 details the time overhead associated with image recognition computations on mobile Web platforms across various stages. Notably: (1) Saliency Detection Overhead: Using the lightweight saliency detection model on a mobile Web browser introduces an overhead of 180–200ms, increasing the preprocessing time from 10ms to 210ms. For single-image matching, the saliency detection module efficiently eliminates extraneous background, decreasing the feature point extraction and descriptor generation time using the AKAZE algorithm from 123ms to 51ms. The aggregate processing time for matching the top 10 images retrieved shows a marked difference in comparison to the preprocessed duration. (2) Image Retrieval Overhead: As images are standardized to a consistent size before feature vector extraction, the expected processing time stays relatively stable pre and post-preprocessing, with slight variances. The overall time for the image recognition service drops from 1352ms to 824ms, a 39% decrease in service response time. Such a refined strategy optimizes computational requirements, leading to an enhanced user experience on mobile Web platforms.

**Table 5.** Cost of image recognition on the mobile web. Unit: Milliseconds (ms).

| | Terminal Preprocessing | Image Retrieval | Single Image Matching Time | Total Image Matching Time | Total Time |
|---|---|---|---|---|---|
| Pre-processing | 10 | 112 | 123 | 1230 | 1352 |
| Post-processing | 210 | 104 | 51 | 510 | 824 |

**Cache Strategy Analysis Based on Location and Popularity.** This section assesses the efficacy of our caching strategy, which emphasizes geographical location and image popularity in real-world situations. We maintain consistent network topology, computational nodes, and experimental parameters as in prior experiments. Figure 13 examines the average request processing latency across various user request volumes, comparing multiple caching strategies: (1) Random Caching. Images are cached at edge nodes from the cloud randomly.

(2) Global Popularity Caching. Edge nodes cache images based on their overall request frequency and popularity. (3) Short-Term Popularity Caching. Edge nodes cache images that have recently shown high request frequency and popularity. (4) Proposed Method. This strategy considers both the user's location and image request popularity. The objective is to discern the impact of these strategies on latency and to highlight the benefits of our suggested method.

Key observations include: (1) Scale of Image Retrieval. At a retrieval scale of 500 images, the latency differences across methods are marginal. All images can be cached at edge nodes, resulting in comparable average latencies across strategies. (2) Elevated Retrieval Scale. As retrieval scale grows, our method, which merges geographical and short-term popularity considerations, primarily addresses user requests at edge caches, negating the need to contact the distant cloud. This delivers superior latency performance. (3) Popularity-Centric Strategies. Although popularity-focused methods (global, short-term, and our proposed) surpass random caching in latency, they might compromise retrieval rates for less-demanded images, necessitating more cloud interactions. Conclusively, our geography and popularity-centric caching method predominantly meets user retrieval needs, optimizing the average processing latency.

## 5    Conclusion

This paper discusses the challenges of mobile web image retrieval and recognition services, notably prolonged latency and decreased accuracy in real-world settings. We introduce a cloud-edge collaborative computing architecture that uses edge computing for timely request responses. Algorithms are deployed on both cloud and edge nodes via Docker containers, centrally managed from the cloud to reduce the strain on cloud-based services. We present a lightweight saliency detection model that increases computational efficiency by distinguishing the primary subject in user images, eliminating background noise, and facilitating feature point extraction with region-based cropping. Edge-based caching, designed around geographical location and popularity, maximizes the restricted cache capacity of edge nodes to elevate content accessibility. Integrating image retrieval with image matching, we compare feature vectors to quickly pinpoint the top-K images from a vast library, then use the AKAZE algorithm to extract feature points from a reduced candidate pool, finalizing matches based on point congruence. Tests reveal our approach improves accuracy by 47% and reduces response times by over 60% compared to standard methods.

**Acknowledgment.** This research was funded in part by the National Natural Science Foundation of China under Grant 62202065, in part by the Project funded by China Postdoctoral Science Foundation 2022TQ0047 and 2022M710465, and in part by Beijing University of Posts and Telecommunications-China Mobile Research Institute Joint Innovation Center.

# References

1. Qiao, X., Ren, P., Dustdar, S., Liu, L., Ma, H., Chen, J.: Web ar: a promising future for mobile augmented reality-state of the art, challenges, and insights. Proc. IEEE **107**(4), 651–666 (2019)
2. Qiao, X., Ren, P., Nan, G., Liu, L., Dustdar, S., Chen, J.: Mobile web augmented reality in 5g and beyond: Challenges, opportunities, and future directions. China Commun. **16**(9), 141–154 (2019)
3. Lowe, D.G.: Distinctive image features from scale-invariant keypoints. Int. J. Comput. Vision **60**, 91–110 (2004)
4. Rublee, E., Rabaud, V., Konolige, K., Bradski, G.: Orb: an efficient alternative to sift or surf. In: 2011 International Conference on Computer Vision, pp. 2564–2571. IEEE (2011)
5. Alcantarilla, P.F., Solutions, T.: Fast explicit diffusion for accelerated features in nonlinear scale spaces. IEEE Trans. Patt. Anal. Mach. Intell **34**(7), 1281–1298 (2011)
6. Qiao, X., Ren, P., Dustdar, S., Chen, J.: A new era for web ar with mobile edge computing. IEEE Internet Comput. **22**(4), 46–55 (2018)
7. Xie, S., Tu, Z.: Holistically-nested edge detection. In: Proceedings of the IEEE International Conference on Computer Vision, pp. 1395–1403 (2015)
8. Ma, N., Zhang, X., Zheng, H.-T., Sun, J.: ShuffleNet V2: practical guidelines for efficient CNN architecture design. In: Ferrari, V., Hebert, M., Sminchisescu, C., Weiss, Y. (eds.) Computer Vision – ECCV 2018. LNCS, vol. 11218, pp. 122–138. Springer, Cham (2018). https://doi.org/10.1007/978-3-030-01264-9_8
9. Chen, S., Tan, X., Wang, B., Lu, H., Hu, X., Fu, Y.: Reverse attention-based residual network for salient object detection. IEEE Trans. Image Process. **29**, 3763–3776 (2020)
10. Lu, P., Zhang, H., Peng, X., Jin, X.: An end-to-end neural network for image cropping by learning composition from aesthetic photos. arXiv preprint arXiv:1907.01432 (2019)
11. Jian, S., Kaiming, H., Shaoqing, R., Xiangyu, Z.: Deep residual learning for image recognition. In: IEEE Conference on Computer Vision & Pattern Recognition, pp. 770–778 (2016)
12. Prakash, C.S., Panzade, P.P., Om, H., Maheshkar, S.: Detection of copy-move forgery using akaze and sift keypoint extraction. Multimedia Tools Appli. **78**, 23535–23558 (2019)
13. Liu, T., Yuan, Z., Sun, J., Wang, J., Zheng, N., Tang, X., Shum, H.Y.: Learning to detect a salient object. IEEE Trans. Pattern Anal. Mach. Intell. **33**(2), 353–367 (2010)
14. Li, G., Yu, Y.: Visual saliency detection based on multiscale deep cnn features. IEEE Trans. Image Process. **25**(11), 5012–5024 (2016)
15. Shi, J., Yan, Q., Xu, L., Jia, J.: Hierarchical image saliency detection on extended cssd. IEEE Trans. Pattern Anal. Mach. Intell. **38**(4), 717–729 (2015)
16. Jiang, H., Wang, J., Yuan, Z., Wu, Y., Zheng, N., Li, S.: Salient object detection: a discriminative regional feature integration approach. In: Proceedings of the IEEE Conference on Computer Vision and Pattern Recognition, pp. 2083–2090 (2013)
17. Li, G., Yu, Y.: Deep contrast learning for salient object detection. In: Proceedings of the IEEE Conference on Computer Vision and Pattern Recognition, pp. 478–487 (2016)

18. Hou, Q., Cheng, M.M., Hu, X., Borji, A., Tu, Z., Torr, P.H.: Deeply supervised salient object detection with short connections. In: Proceedings of the IEEE Conference on Computer Vision and Pattern Recognition, pp. 3203–3212 (2017)
19. Wang, W., Shen, J., Dong, X., Borji, A.: Salient object detection driven by fixation prediction. In: Proceedings of the IEEE Conference on Computer Vision and Pattern Recognition, pp. 1711–1720 (2018)
20. Liu, N., Han, J., Yang, M.H.: Picanet: learning pixel-wise contextual attention for saliency detection. In: Proceedings of the IEEE Conference on Computer Vision and Pattern Recognition, pp. 3089–3098 (2018)
21. Wei, X.S., Cui, Q., Yang, L., Wang, P., Liu, L.: Rpc: a large-scale retail product checkout dataset. arXiv preprint arXiv:1901.07249 (2019)

# Contrastive Learning-Based Finger-Vein Recognition with Automatic Adversarial Augmentation

Shaojiang Deng[1], Huaxiu Luo[1], Huafeng Qin[2], and Yantao Li[1(✉)]

[1] College of Computer Science, Chongqing University, Chongqing, China
yantaoli@cqu.edu.cn
[2] Chongqing Technology and Business University, Chongqing, China

**Abstract.** In finger-vein recognition tasks, obtaining large labeled datasets for supervised deep learning is often difficult. To address this challenge, self-supervised learning (SSL) provides a solution by first pre-training a neural network using unlabeled data and subsequently fine-tuning it for downstream tasks. Contrastive learning, a variant of SSL, enables effective learning of image-level representations. To address the issue of insufficient labeled data for vein feature extraction and classification, we propose CL3A-FV, a Contrastive Learning-based Finger-Vein image recognition approach with Automatic Adversarial Augmentation in this paper. Specifically, CL3A-FV consists of the dual-branch augmentation network, Siamese encoder, discriminator, and distributor. The training process involves two steps: 1) training the Siamese encoder by updating its parameters while keeping other components fixed; and 2) training the dual-branch augmentation network with a fixed Siamese encoder, integrating a discriminator to distinguish views generated by the two branches, and a distributor to constrain the distribution of the augmented data. Both networks are updated adversarially using the stochastic gradient descent. We conduct extensive experiments to evaluate CL3A-FV on three finger-vein datasets, and the experimental results show that the proposed CL3A-FV achieves significant improvements compared to traditional self-supervised learning techniques and supervised methods.

**Keywords:** Contrastive learning · Automatic adversarial augmentation · Finger-vein recognition

## 1 Introduction

Due to its high security and reliability, finger-vein recognition has garnered considerable attention as a promising biometric identification technology. Finger-vein patterns are unique and highly distinctive, which can be captured by non-invasive imaging techniques, making finger-vein recognition a convenient and user-friendly biometric identification method [1].

In recent years, there has been a surge in the development of finger-vein recognition techniques. These approaches encompass both traditional methods that rely on handcrafted features [2,3], as well as deep learning-based methods [4,5]. Traditional

H. Gao et al. (Eds.): CollaborateCom 2023, LNICST 562, pp. 495–513, 2024.
https://doi.org/10.1007/978-3-031-54528-3_27

methodologies, such as repeated line tracking [6], maximum curvature points [7], and local binary pattern [8], have been proposed and demonstrated impressive recognition performance for finger-vein image recognition. However, compared to the rapid evolution of deep learning methods, these traditional handcrafted methods are constrained by their reliance on the prior knowledge. Consequently, an increasing number of deep learning techniques are employed in vein recognition. Recent works have explored various approaches for finger-vein recognition, such as those based on deep separable convolution [9], frequency-spatial coupling network [10], and the utilization of locality-constrained consistent to fuse multiple features [11]. Within deep learning-based methodologies, contrastive learning has risen as a potent technique for acquiring meaningful feature representations in the absence of negative samples [12–14]. Contrastive learning-based approaches have demonstrated exceptional performance in diverse computer vision areas, i.e., object detection, segmentation, and image classification, achieving state-of-the-art results. The typical approach in contrastive learning is to apply two different transformations to the original image, generate two views as inputs, and then learn the feature representation by minimizing the distance between them in a latent space. The success of contrastive learning heavily relies on predefined transformations [15]. However, for finger-vein data, deformation changes may cause the loss of some fine-grained details in vein images after transformations, potentially impacting the performance of contrastive learning methods.

In order to tackle the aforementioned issues, we present a novel Contrastive Learning-based Finger-Vein image recognition with Automatic Adversarial Augmentation, namely CL3A-FV. Instead of the predefined data augmentation operations, our method utilizes a neural network to learn augmented views by training the network in an adversarial manner between the contrastive learning network and the augmentation network. In the proposed CL3A-FV, we use a neural network-based data augmentation method that learns to generate more effective and diverse augmented samples for finger-vein images. Specifically, we train two different generator networks to create two augmented images from an input image, and a discriminator network to distinguish views by two different generator networks. The primary goal of optimizing the generator network is to generate samples that can effectively evade detection by the discriminator network. Conversely, the main objective of optimizing the discriminator network is to precisely classify images originating from two separate enhancement branches. The output of the generator network is used as the augmented input for the contrastive learning network, which learns to produce effective feature representations for finger-vein recognition. We assess the effectiveness of CL3A-FV on three publicly-available finger-vein recognition datasets, and the experimental results demonstrate that CL3A-FV achieves the state-of-the-art performance, and outperforms existing contrastive learning methods that rely on predefined data augmentation operations, thereby improving the accuracy and robustness of finger-vein recognition. The proposed method has several advantages over existing contrastive learning methods. First, it has the capability to acquire enhanced data augmentation techniques tailored specifically for finger-vein images, thereby enhancing the robustness and generalization capabilities of finger-vein recognition models. Second, it can reduce the manual effort required to define data augmentation operations, which is particularly important for large-scale datasets. Finally, it can seamlessly integrate into current contrastive learning frameworks with minimal adjustments or modifications.

This work can be summarized by the following contributions:

- We propose CL3A-FV, a contrastive learning-based finger-vein recognition with automatic adversarial augmentation to address the issue of insufficient labeled data for vein feature extraction and classification. CL3A-FV consists of four components, namely the dual-branch augmentation network, Siamese encoder, discriminator, and distributor.
- CL3A-FV trains the encoder and augmentation network alternately by stochastic gradient descent in an adversarial manner, thereby improving the recognition accuracy and robustness of the model.
- We conduct extensive experiments on three public finger-vein datasets, by comparing CL3A-FV with traditional supervised learning methods as well as contrastive learning methods. The experimental findings substantiate that CL3A-FV attains the highest level of performance in tasks related to finger-vein image recognition.

The rest of this work is organized as follows. We review the related work in Sect. 2. In Sect. 3, we detail the proposed CL3A-FV in terms of the contrastive learning, dual-branch augmentation network, augmentation discriminator, distribution divergence minimization, and adversarial training, and access the performance of CL3A-FV in Sect. 4. We conclude this work in Sect. 5.

## 2 Related Work

### 2.1 Deep Learning Based Vein Recognition

In recent years, deep learning has demonstrated remarkable expertise in extracting meaningful features, resulting in its successful deployment across diverse computer vision tasks. Image classification stands out as a notable instance of its application [16]. Upon this success, researchers have employed deep learning techniques to analyze finger-vein images for various tasks. These tasks encompass the image classification [17–22], feature extraction [23–29], image enhancement [30–35], and image segmentation [36,37]. For *vein image classification*, various approaches have been explored. In [17], ResNet is directly applied to the images for classification, and [19] combines the deep belief network with histograms of uniform local binary patterns derived from curvature gray images for finger-vein recognition. Notably, a joint attention module is introduced in [22] to enhance the vein pattern contribution in the feature extraction. In addition to Convolutional Neural Networks (CNNs), alternative neural network architectures have been employed. For instance, [20] utilizes the Graph Neural Network (GNN) for classification, taking advantage of the graph-like structure inherent in intricate vein textures. Moreover, [18] employs the supervised discrete hashing to improve the matching speed, while [21] incorporates bias field correction and spatial attention to enhance the optimization of CNN-based finger-vein image recognition. For *vein feature extraction*, researchers have employed different strategies. Some studies [23,25,27] follow a similar workflow, where a CNN structure is employed to extract features from finger-vein images, and then are analyzed by traditional machine learning algorithms. On the other hand, novel approaches have also been explored. For instance, [26] utilizes a combination of autoencoder and convolutional network to learn feature codes from finger vein images. In [28], a capsule neural network-based method is proposed to extract the region of interest (ROI) in finger veins. [24] introduces a lightweight two-channel network with three convolution layers to extract image features efficiently, followed by the verification using a support vector machine. Lastly, [29] presents a multi-modal biometric authentication system based on the deep fusion of electrocardiogram and finger-vein image data. For *vein image enhancement*, Generative Adversarial Networks (GANs) are commonly employed to recover missing vein patterns caused by various factors during the image capture process [32]. For severely-damaged finger-vein images, [33] introduces a modified GAN that utilizes neighbors-based binary pattern texture loss. To address the issue of motion blur in the finger-vein image recognition, [34] proposes a modified DeblurGAN to restore motion-blurred finger-vein images, thereby enhancing the identification performance. Apart from GANs, other modules are also utilized for image restoration in finger-vein image recognition. For instance, [30] presents a method that utilizes a deep CNN with a deconvolution sub-net to recover the original image and a modified linear unit to enhance finger vein texture details. Another study [31] employs a convolutional autoencoder (CAE) to restore venous networks in finger vein images by extracting effective features. In terms of enhancing finger vein image quality, [35] introduces a novel network architecture based on the pulse-coupled neural network. This architecture aimed to improve image quality and make finger vein image recognition more practical. For *vein image segmentation*, [36] proposes a finger vein segmentation algorithm based on LadderNet. This algorithm leverages the concatenation of feature channels from the expanding and contracting paths in the network to obtain comprehensive semantic information from vein images. Furthermore, traditional finger vein segmentation networks often have excessive parameters, making them challenging to use in mobile terminals. To address this issue, [37] proposes a lightweight real-time segmentation network specifically designed for finger vein image recognition on embedded terminals. This network achieves comparable performance to more complex networks while meeting the requirements of embedded mobile terminals.

The application of deep learning methods has further advanced the development of vein recognition, but there are still some drawbacks. For example, from a modeling perspective, due to the complexity of deep learning models, they often perform well on the training set, but their performance on the test set may decrease, which constrains the capacity of model generalization. This may be due to the difference between the training set and test set, such as different acquisition devices or environmental conditions. From a data perspective, issues such as poor quality of finger-vein images (e.g., blur, uneven lighting, spatial position changes, etc.) and sparse single-class images can also affect the robustness of feature extraction.

## 2.2    Contrastive Learning

Contrastive learning is a specific form of self-supervised learning, which strives to acquire meaningful representations by comparing samples that are similar with ones that are dissimilar [38–40]. The criterion for defining positive and negative samples is an important part of the contrast paradigm, which directly determines whether a good representation can be learned. Traditionally, contrastive learning uses a set of positive and negative pairs to train the model. Positive pairs are samples that are similar, while negative pairs are samples that are dissimilar. The model learns to push the negative pairs apart in the embedding space while pull the positive pairs together. This approach has been used in many successful contrastive learning methods, such as InfoNCE [41] and SimCLR [39]. More recently, some researchers have proposed to use only positive samples in contrastive learning, without negative samples. These methods rely on the idea that samples from the same class are inherently similar, therefore can be used as positive examples. Examples of such methods include SimSiam [13] and BYOL [12], which have achieved the state-of-the-art performance on several benchmark datasets. Overall, the choice of positive and negative samples is an important aspect of contrastive learning, and both approaches have shown promising results in various applications.

## 2.3    Automatic Augmentation

Automatic augmentation has recently gained popularity in the field of supervised learning [42–46]. [42] uses reinforcement learning to learn data augmentation policies and searches for the optimal augmentation strategy. [43] proposes a search algorithm based on weak data augmentation policies, which significantly reduces the search time. In [44], a search algorithm based on backpropagation finds a balance between computation time and performance. [45] proposes a straightforward yet effective data augmentation strategy that leverages random combinations of operations to enhance data. [46] proposes a population-based optimization algorithm that efficiently learns data augmentation policies. Typically, these methods establish a search space in advance and then search for augmentation policies within that space for the target tasks. However, the search cost of these methods is typically high and not suitable for contrastive learning. To address this limitation, we propose a new self-supervised learning (SSL) strategy in this paper.

## 3    Proposed Method

This paper introduces CL3A-FV, a contrastive learning-based approach for finger-vein recognition that employs automatic adversarial augmentation to enhance the performance of finger-vein recognition in scenarios with limited labeled data. Figure 1 illustrates the architecture of the proposed CL3A-FV, which consists of four components, namely the Dual-Branch Augmentation Network, Siamese Encoder, Discriminator, and Distributor. The training process is divided into two steps: 1) train the Siamese Encoder, where the other parts of CL3A-FV are fixed and only the parameters of the encoder are updated. The Siamese Encoder learns feature representations by minimizing the similarity between different views of the same image, generated by two learnable neural networks; and 2) train the Dual-Branch Augmentation Network, where the Siamese Encoder is fixed and a Discriminator is introduced to distinguish the views generated by the two branches. To constrain the distribution of the generated data, a Distributor is introduced to produce discriminative augmentations, i.e., more dissimilar sample pairs. Both networks are updated by the stochastic gradient descent in an adversarial manner. The proposed CL3A-FV can be incorporated into any contrastive learning method, which will further improve the performance of the corresponding contrastive learning method. In the following, we first introduce some prior knowledge about contrastive learning, and then detail each component of CL3A-FV.

### 3.1   Contrastive Learning

Contrastive learning is a commonly-used image self-supervised learning method, which learns generic features of images by minimizing the distance between different augmented versions of the same image. Specifically, for a given encoder network $f(\cdot)$ and an exponential moving average (EMA) encoder $f'(\cdot)$, the similarity loss used in SSL does not exploit negative samples, which can be written as Eq. (1):

$$\mathcal{L}_C = \frac{1}{2}\mathcal{D}(f(x_1), f'(x_2)) + \frac{1}{2}\mathcal{D}(f(x_2), f'(x_1)), \tag{1}$$

In the given context, $\mathcal{D}$ represents a similarity distance, while $x_1$ and $x_2$ refer to two transformed versions of the image, specifically $x_1 = t_1(x)$ and $x_2 = t_2(x)$. These transformations, as previously demonstrated in [39,40,47,48], involve techniques such as cropping the image followed by the application of color transformations.

### 3.2   Dual-Branch Augmentation Network

The augmentation types can be categorized into illumination augmentation, geometric augmentation, and noise augmentation, which address the uneven illumination or occlusion, incomplete images or positional displacement of the vein curve, and noise introduced by device-related factors during image acquisition, respectively. Inspired by these categories, we construct our dual-branch augmentation network. As illustrated in Fig. 2, one vein image is first normalized and resized to obtain $x$, which is then fed into two augmentation networks, namely $T_{\theta_1}$ and $T_{\theta_2}$. Each augmentation network applies three enhancement blocks to $x$, resulting in two transformed samples: $x_1 = T_{\theta_1}(x)$ and $x_2 = T_{\theta_2}(x)$. Finally, the contrastive loss between $x_1$ and $x_2$ is calculated by Eq. (2):

**Step 1. Update Contrastive Network**

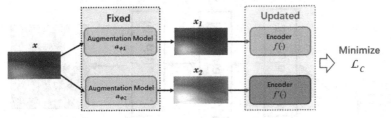

**Step 2. Update Augmentation Network**

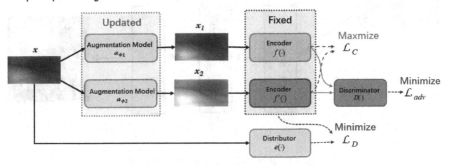

**Fig. 1.** Architecture of CL3A-FV.

$$\mathcal{L}_C = \frac{1}{2}\mathcal{D}(f(T_{\theta_1}(x)), f'(T_{\theta_2}(x))) + \frac{1}{2}\mathcal{D}(f(T_{\theta_2}(x)), f'(T_{\theta_1}(x))). \qquad (2)$$

In particular, the augmentation network $T_\theta$ is composed of three modules: a geometric transformation module $g_\theta$, an illumination transformation module $c_\theta$, and a noise transformation module $p_\theta$, which are designed to learn transformations suitable for vein images. The three modules are elaborated as follows:

*Geometric Augmentation*: Spatial transformation functions commonly employed at present, including rotation, scaling, and translation, can be generalized into more comprehensive functions known as affine transformations. Inspired by STN [49], we design a geometric network $g_\theta$ to learn the affine transformation parameters. The network structure can be a multilayer perceptron (MLP) or a convolutional network with the input of an image itself or Gaussian noise. Since geometric transformations are universal for different images, we use MLP due to the generality and transferability as expressed in Eq. (3):

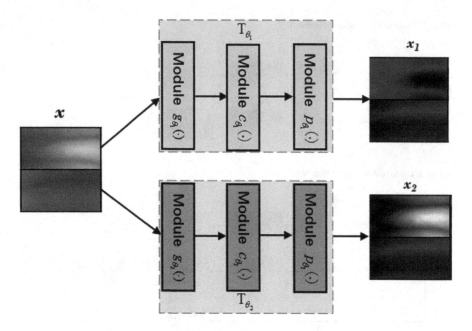

**Fig. 2.** Dual-branch augmentation network.

$$x' = Augg(x, A + I), A = g_\theta(z), \tag{3}$$

where $Augg(x, A + I)$ is an affine transformation that includes the most geometric transformations applicable to vein images and $A \in R^{2\times 3}$ is the learned transformation parameters. $I \in R^{2\times 3}$ is represented by a matrix, where $I_{ii} = 1$ or $0$, making the affine transformation an identity mapping, and $z$ is an $N$-dimensional Gaussian noise.

*Illumination augmentation*: For a given vein image $x$, the illumination transformation module is defined as Eq. (4):

$$x'' = Augc(x', c), c = c_\theta(x, z), \tag{4}$$

where $Augc$ is a color transformation function with parameters $c$, and $c_\theta$ is a small convolutional network. $z \sim N(0, I_N)$, where $N(0, I_N)$ is an $N$-dimensional Gaussian distribution.

*Noise Augmentation*: Additive noise is a commonly-used tool for generating adversarial examples [50,51], and thus we explore it in the image data augmentation. While adversarial examples can be utilized as augmented data during adversarial training, their primary objective revolves around enhancing the model's robustness rather than solely focusing on improvement. Some evidence [52] suggests that adversarial training often sacrifices the model's generalization to clean data. However, our adversarial augmentation model can improve its generalization performance through the online training. Recently, AdvProp [50] has successfully used PGD attack [51] and OnlineAugment [53] has used a learning perturbation for data augmentation. In this work, we design an adversarial augmentation model to generate additive noise. Specifically, the adversarial augmentation network $p_\theta$ takes the original image $x$ as its input and generates additive noise $x_z$. By adding the generated noise to the original image, we obtain an adversarial perturbed image $x'''$. We use a variational autoencoder (VAE) network to learn to generate noise, as shown in Eq. (5):

$$x''' = Augp(x'', x_z), x_z = p_\theta(x), \qquad (5)$$

where the shape of $x_z$ is the same with the input $x$.

The above three types of augmentations basically cover all possible variations of the samples. In order to further improve the performance of this method, we also adopt a strong augmentation strategy in this paper, which applies multiple augmentations to the original image. The learning objective of the two augmentation networks is to obtain pairs of samples with large difference. Therefore, we update the augmentation networks by maximizing the distance between the generated sample pairs, which is opposite to the learning objective of the encoder. At the same time, inspired by the approach of generating images with GANs, we introduce a discriminator to distinguish images generated by two different branches, further achieving the goal of generating dissimilar pairs of samples.

### 3.3 Augmentation Discriminator

In the existing GAN models, a discriminator is introduced to supervise the generator by performing binary classification on generated images and real images, in order to train a generator that can create images close to the real distribution. In the proposed CL3A-FV, we adopt a similar approach to GANs to ensure that the augmentation network produces two "dissimilar" augmented images. Specifically, we introduce a discriminator to perform binary classification on the augmented images from the two branches. The output loss of the discriminator is used as the adversarial loss to update the augmentation network.

We assign different pseudo-labels to the augmented images from the two branches. The input space is denoted as $X = \{X^{aug1}, X^{aug2}\}$, and the set of possible labels is denoted as $Y = 0, 1$, where 0 and 1 are the labels assigned to the augmented images from the two branches. Therefore, the adversarial loss for the two augmentation networks is defined as Eq. (6):

$$\mathcal{L}_{adv}(D(f(x_i)), d_i) = -[d_i log \frac{1}{D(f(x_i))} + (1 - d_i)log\frac{1}{1 - D(f(x_i))}], \qquad (6)$$

where $D(\cdot)$ is the introduced discriminator, and $d_i$ denotes the binary variable (augmentation label) for the $i$th example, which indicates whether $x_i$ comes from augmentation $T_{\theta_1}(x_i \sim X^{aug1}, if\ d_i = 0)$ or from the augmentation $T_{\theta_2}(x_i \sim X^{aug2}, if\ d_i = 1)$.

### 3.4 Distributional Divergence Minimization

To align the images before and after augmentation and prevent harmful augmentation that may affect downstream tasks, we introduce the maximum mean discrepancy

(MMD) to constrain the distribution. The MMD is utilized to quantify the discrepancy between two distributions within the reproducing kernel Hilbert space. The distance between two distributions is calculated as Eq. (7):

$$L_{MMD}(x^{original}, x^{aug}) = \|\frac{1}{n}\sum_{i=1}^{n} g(x_i^{original}) - \frac{1}{m}\sum_{j=1}^{m} g(x_j^{aug})\|_H^2, \qquad (7)$$

where $x^{original}$ represents the image before enhancement, and $x^{aug}$ represents the image after augmentation. $m$ and $n$ are the batch sizes, and $g$ is the Gaussian kernel function which maps $x$ to the reproducing Hilbert space. It is worth noting that for the three augmentation networks, we only need this regularization term to ensure that the augmentation networks perform image transform without destroying the original data distribution. Specifically, we input both the original image $x$ and augmented images $x_1$ and $x_2$ into a distributor $e(\cdot)$, which is an encoder version of $f(\cdot)$ without the MLP head. During the training, its weights are not directly updated, but inherited from the encoder $f(\cdot)$. We calculate the distribution difference $\mathcal{L}_D$ between the original distribution and the transformed distributions, and use it as the distribution supervision signal for the augmentation network to avoid excessive transformation. The term used to constrain the augmentation networks can be represented as Eq. (8):

$$\mathcal{L}_D = \frac{1}{2}(L_{MMD}(e(x), e(x_1)) + L_{MMD}(e(x), e(x_2))). \qquad (8)$$

### 3.5 Adversarial Training

For the augmentation network, its task is to generate dissimilar pairs of samples, which can force the contrastive network to learn more robust representations. Therefore, when guiding the learning of the augmentation network, we consider three aspects: maximizing the contrastive loss, minimizing the discriminator loss, and minimizing the distribution loss, which can be formulated as Eq. (9):

$$\mathcal{L}_{aug} = \lambda\mathcal{L}_D + \mathcal{L}_{adv} - \mathcal{L}_C, \qquad (9)$$

where $\lambda$ is a hyper-parameter used to constrain the augmentation network. To generate "dissimilar" pairs of samples, we train the model in an adversarial manner. The training process is partitioned into two components: training the augmentation network and training the encoder. These two parts are updated in an alternating manner. The encoder's parameter update is achieved by minimizing $\mathcal{L}_C$, which minimizes the distance between two transformed views. The augmentation network's parameter update is achieved by minimizing $\mathcal{L}_{aug}$, which encourages the two branches to generate more "dissimilar" views and better helps the learning of the encoder.

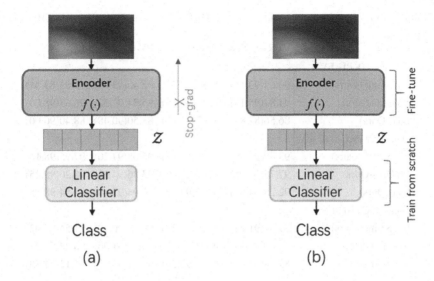

**Fig. 3.** Linear evaluation protocol (a) and fine-tuning evaluation (b).

## 4   Experiments

### 4.1   Experiment Setting and Datasets

**Experiment Settings.** We conduct extensive linear evaluation experiments on CL3A-FV using the commonly-adopted evaluation methods for self-supervised methods. In addition, to demonstrate the superiority of CL3A-FV over supervised methods, we conduct fine-tuning experiments. In the linear evaluation experiments, we first pre-train the model on an unlabeled dataset, and then further evaluate the trained encoder on a labeled dataset with the fixed encoder weights. In the fine-tuning experiments, we further fine-tune the trained encoder on a labeled dataset with a very small learning rate. We evaluate the proposed CL3A-FV with three different SSL objectives: BYOL [12], SimSiam [13], and Barlow Twins (BT) [14]. In our experiments, the state-of-the-art finger-vein classifiers, i.e. FVRAS-Net [54], FV-CNN [55], PV-CNN [56], and LW-CNN [57] are used to test our approach. We split each dataset into a training set and a testing set with a ratio of 6 : 4 for evaluation.

**Datasets.** To assess the effectiveness of the proposed CL3A-FV, we conduct extensive experiments on three finger-vein databases:

(1) **HKPU-FV:** The Hong Kong Polytechnic University finger-vein database [58] comprises a total of 3,132 contactless and opening images from 156 subjects. These images include 2,520 finger images taken from 105 subjects across two separate sessions, with an average interval of 66.8 d between sessions. Each subject provided 12 images per session, with six images captured from their index and middle fingers, respectively. The remaining 612 images were captured from 51 subjects in the first session only. For testing purposes, we utilized the sub-database containing the first 105

**Table 1.** Top-1 Classification Accuracy (%) on HKPU-FV, MMCBNU-FV, and CTBU-FV.

| Method | FVRAS-Net | FV-CNN | PV-CNN | LW-CNN |
|---|---|---|---|---|
| Dataset: HKPU-FV | | | | |
| SimSiam(+Ours) | 90.68(93.56) | 90.88(93.75) | 92.46(93.05) | 85.03(87.41) |
| BYOL(+Ours) | 94.84(95.14) | 92.17(93.16) | 95.34(96.52) | 96.63(98.00) |
| BT(+Ours) | 86.56(87.80) | 91.67(91.97) | 88.50(90.48) | 88.40(90.00) |
| Dataset: MMCBNU-FV | | | | |
| SimSiam(+Ours) | 93.80(97.04) | 96.29(96.95) | 96.08(97.20) | 97.95(98.16) |
| BYOL(+Ours) | 97.75(97.98) | 97.04(97.69) | 93.36(94.23) | 98.20(98.25) |
| BT(+Ours) | 92.25(94.56) | 96.33(97.25) | 97.04(97.84) | 98.54(98.85) |
| Dataset: CTBU-FV | | | | |
| SimSiam(+Ours) | 89.12(91.23) | 89.25(92.56) | 88.16(90.78) | 91.54(93.02) |
| BYOL(+Ours) | 92.83(94.56) | 89.12(91.25) | 90.83(91.96) | 90.08(91.33) |
| BT(+Ours) | 89.98(90.75) | 89.00(90.56) | 90.37(92.02) | 94.12(94.86) |

subjects' finger images from the first session, which more accurately replicates a two-session scenario.The images are grayscale and have a resolution of $256 \times 513$.

(2) **MMCBNU-FV:** The MMCBNU6000 fingerprint database [59] comprises 6,000 images, derived from 100 volunteers who provided six fingers each. During the data capture process, each volunteer placed their fingers - the index, middle, and ring fingers of both the left and right hands on the sensor 10 times, resulting in 10 images being collected for each finger.

(3) **CTBU-FV:** The Chongqing Technology and Business University finger-vein dataset [60] comprises 6,000 images obtained from 100 subjects (66 males and 34 females). Each subject contributed six fingers, namely the index, middle, and ring fingers from both the left and right hands. For each finger, there were ten images with a size of $240 \times 320$ pixels. These images were cropped to extract the region of interest (ROI) images, which were then normalized to $55 \times 127$ pixels.

### 4.2    Evaluation of Representations

The commonly employed method for assessing learned representations during the SSL pre-training process is the linear evaluation protocol [61]. In this protocol, a linear classifier, such as SVM or Logistic Regression, is trained on the frozen backbone network. The image representations, obtained from the final or penultimate layers of the backbone network as a feature vector, are utilized. The test accuracy serves as a proxy for the quality of the representations (Fig. 3(a)). In this work, to assess the learned representations of the proposed method, we conduct experiments on three datasets employing four classifiers within the linear evaluation protocol of self-supervised learning. The experimental results are presented in Table 1.

In Table 1, the results in parentheses represent the performance of CL3A-FV architecture applied to the corresponding SSL objectives, while the results outside the parentheses represent the baseline results of the original SSL methods. For instance, in the first row, the results are shown for four different backbones on three original SSL methods (outside the parentheses) and on our corresponding method (inside the parentheses) in the HKPU-FV dataset. From Table 1, it can be observed that there is an improvement across all four classifiers for the HKPU-FV dataset, with the highest margin in recognition accuracy being approximately 3%. However, the improvement effects are generally less pronounced for the MMCBNU-FV dataset. In contrast, for the CTBU-FV dataset, the proposed CL3A-FV method performs better compared to the MMCBNU-FV dataset under the same settings. We speculate that this difference may be attributed to variations in the sample quality. Our approach might be more effective for coarsely-processed data. Models using the proposed framework consistently outperform their respective SSL baselines beyond the margin of error.

### 4.3    Fine-Tune Evaluation

Fine-tuning [62] is a method that allows us to reuse a pre-trained model and adapt it to a new task. It involves unfreezing some of the top layers of the pre-trained neural network model, which is initially used for feature extraction. As a result, we can jointly train these unfrozen layers along with the newly-added part of the model, such as a fully-connected classifier. This process helps the model to specialize in and adapt to the specific requirements of the new task. This technique is referred to as fine-tuning because it involves making subtle adjustments to the higher-level representations of the pre-trained model (Fig. 3(b)). These adjustments are made to align the model more closely with the specific problem being addressed, thereby increasing its relevance and effectiveness for the task. Only the top layers of the convolutional base are possible to be fine-tuned once the classifier on top has already been trained so as to train a randomly-initialized classifier, freezing of pre-trained convolutional networks like VGG16 [63]. The solution lies in utilizing a smaller learning rate for the weights undergoing fine-tuning, and a higher one for the randomly initialized weights, such as those in the softmax classifier. Pre-trained weights are already good, but they need to be fine-tuned.

To demonstrate that SSL methods can improve the classifier performance without increasing the amount of data, we compare the results of training the entire network from scratch on a labeled dataset with the results of fine-tuning the pre-trained feature extractor using our method with a smaller learning rate. Fine-tuning evaluation results are listed in Table 2. From the table, it can be observed that all classifiers show improved recognition accuracy on different datasets after comparative learning with pre-training and fine-tuning, including the top-performing LW-CNN classifier. Particularly the CTBU-FV dataset has lower sample quality, because the supervised training with LW-CNN exhibits overfitting. However, this issue is significantly alleviated through pre-training and fine-tuning. To more intuitively observe the difference between the results with and without pre-training, we present the fine-tuning results in Fig. 4 on datasets of HKPU-FV, MMCBNU-FV, and CTBU-FV. In Fig. 4, the CTBU-FV dataset may suffer from overfitting due to its more homogeneous sample data and the powerful LW-CNN classifier. Pre-training and fine-tuning can significantly alleviate the overfitting. For the other two datasets, most of them show a significant improvement compared to traditional fully-supervised one-stage training under the same settings, while a small

**Table 2.** Classification Accuracy (%) of Fine-tuning on HKPU-FV, MMCBNU-FV, and CTBU-FV.

| Method | HKPU-FV | MMCBNU-FV | CTBU-FV |
|---|---|---|---|
| Classifier: FVRAS-Net | | | |
| SimSiam(+Ours) | 95.54(96.23) | 96.91(97.58) | 95.00(95.70) |
| BYOL(+Ours) | 96.13(97.02) | 98.20(98.25) | 96.33(96.98) |
| BT(+Ours) | 95.35(96.33) | 94.62(97.50) | 95.58(96.70) |
| Scratch | 95.44 | 96.20 | 93.37 |
| Classifier: FV-CNN | | | |
| SimSiam(+Ours) | 94.05(95.34) | 96.12(96.75) | 90.33(91.30) |
| BYOL(+Ours) | 93.85(96.43) | 96.04(96.98) | 91.08(91.79) |
| BT(+Ours) | 94.74(94.84) | 96.54(97.00) | 91.20(91.83) |
| Scratch | 94.15 | 95.95 | 89.62 |
| Classifier: PV-CNN | | | |
| SimSiam(+Ours) | 95.56(96.63) | 97.05(97.75) | 92.79(93.50) |
| BYOL(+Ours) | 95.90(96.33) | 97.56(97.91) | 94.29(95.05) |
| BT(+Ours) | 92.48(95.44) | 96.33(97.08) | 93.87(94.52) |
| Scratch | 90.78 | 95.91 | 91.86 |
| Classifier: LW-CNN | | | |
| SimSiam(+Ours) | 98.81(99.00) | 98.29(99.13) | 93.95(94.88) |
| BYOL(+Ours) | 98.61(99.23) | 98.33(98.60) | 93.50(95.14) |
| BT(+Ours) | 98.70(98.80) | 98.45(98.86) | 94.87(95.35) |
| Scratch | 98.00 | 97.87 | 85.12 |

portion may have limited improvement due to factors, such as the model and the dataset itself.

## 4.4 Ablation Study

To investigate the effectiveness of the proposed distributor, we conduct four comparative experiments on the HKPU-FV dataset for each of the three methods (SimSiam+Ours, BYOL+Ours, and BT+Ours), by removing the distribution constraint MMD or replacing it with Jensen-Shannon (JS) distance, Kullback-Leibler (KL) divergence, and Wasserstein distance, respectively. The results are shown in Table 3. The results in the second row of Table 3 correspond to the unconstrained augmentation network, and when compared to the first row, it can be observed that the MMD distance improves the performance across all three frameworks, where the BYOL+Ours showing the most significant improvement. However, the other three constraint conditions do not yield improvements in every method. We speculate that this may be due to excessive constraints, which results in the augmentation network learning ineffectively.

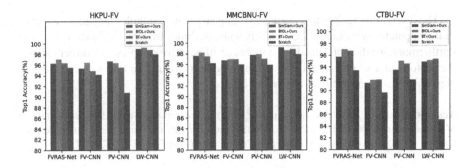

**Fig. 4.** Fine-tuning evaluation on HKPU-FV, MMCBNU-FV, and CTBU-FV.

**Table 3.** Classification Accuracy (%) of Ablation Study on HKPU-FV.

| Condition | Method | | |
|---|---|---|---|
| | SimSiam+Ours | BYOL+Ours | BT+Ours |
| MMD (Ours) | 93.56 | 95.14 | 87.80 |
| None | 93.06 | 91.17 | 87.02 |
| JS | 93.16 | 87.61 | 86.35 |
| Wasserstein | 91.77 | 90.28 | 87.88 |
| KL | 93.26 | 89.79 | 87.65 |

# 5    Conclusion

In this paper, we proposed a novel contrastive learning-based finger-vein image recognition with automatic adversarial augmentation, namely CL3A-FV. Our method addresses the limitations of traditional contrastive learning methods by using a neural network-based data augmentation method that generates more effective and diverse augmented samples of finger-vein images. The proposed CL3A-FV achieves the state-of-the-art performance on three finger-vein datasets, outperforming the existing contrastive learning methods that rely on predefined data augmentation operations. The proposed CL3A-FV has several advantages: 1) it is capable of learning more effective data augmentation operations specifically designed for finger-vein images; 2) it reduces the manual efforts required to define data augmentation operations; and 3) it is easy to be integrated into existing contrastive learning frameworks. Moreover, our approach enables the learning of adaptive enhancement pairs for finger-vein images, which improves the performance and robustness of the model. We conduct extensive experiments on three finger-vein datasets and show that CL3A-FV achieves state-of-the-art performance and robustness in vein image recognition tasks, compared to traditional supervised learning methods and the existing contrastive learning methods. Overall, the proposed method provides a novel and effective solution for improving finger vein recognition in scenarios with limited labeled data. We believe that this work will inspire further research in the field of self-supervised methods for biometric identification and have a significant impact on the development of more accurate and reliable biometric identification systems.

However, training the model and generating augmented samples may require significant computational resources, particularly when dealing with large-scale target datasets. Furthermore, we did not consider the inclusion of negative samples. To further enhance the performance of our model, we will investigate methods to introduce negative samples at a lower computational cost in the future.

**Acknowledgment.** This work was supported in part by the National Natural Science Foundation of China under Grants 62072061 and 61976030, and in part by the Funds for Creative Research Groups of Chongqing Municipal Education Commission under Grant CXQT21034.

# References

1. Shaheed, K., Liu, H., Yang, G., Qureshi, I., Gou, J., Yin, Y.: A systematic review of finger vein recognition techniques. Information **9**(9), 213 (2018)
2. Yang, J., Zhang, X.: Feature-level fusion of global and local features for finger-vein recognition. In: IEEE 10th International Conference On Signal Processing Proceedings, pp. 1702–1705. IEEE (2010)
3. Liu, Y., Ling, J., Liu, Z., Shen, J., Gao, C.: Finger vein secure biometric template generation based on deep learning. Soft. Comput. **22**, 2257–2265 (2018)
4. Zhang, D., Zuo, W., Yue, F.: A comparative study of palmprint recognition algorithms. ACM Comput. Surv. (CSUR) **44**(1), 1–37 (2012)
5. Yang, L., Yang, G., Wang, K., Hao, F., Yin, Y.: Finger vein recognition via sparse reconstruction error constrained low-rank representation. IEEE Trans. Inf. Forensics Secur. **16**, 4869–4881 (2021)
6. Miura, N., Nagasaka, A., Miyatake, T.: Feature extraction of finger-vein patterns based on repeated line tracking and its application to personal identification. Mach. Vis. Appl. **15**, 194–203 (2004)
7. Miura, N., Nagasaka, A., Miyatake, T.: Extraction of finger-vein patterns using maximum curvature points in image profiles. IEICE Trans. Inf. Syst. **90**(8), 1185–1194 (2007)
8. Lee, E.C., Jung, H., Kim, D.: New finger biometric method using near infrared imaging. Sensors **11**(3), 2319–2333 (2011)
9. Shaheed, K., et al.: Ds-cnn: a pre-trained xception model based on depth-wise separable convolutional neural network for finger vein recognition. Expert Syst. Appl. **191**, 116288 (2022)
10. Huang, J., Zheng, A., Shakeel, M.S., Yang, W., Kang, W.: Fvfsnet: frequency-spatial coupling network for finger vein authentication. IEEE Trans. Inf. Forensics Secur. **18**, 1322–1334 (2023)
11. Yang, L., Liu, X., Yang, G., Wang, J., Yin, Y.: Small-area finger vein recognition. IEEE Trans. Inf. Forensics Secur. **18**, 1914–1925 (2023)
12. Grill, J.B., et al.: Bootstrap your own latent-a new approach to self-supervised learning. Adv. Neural. Inf. Process. Syst. **33**, 21271–21284 (2020)
13. Chen, X., He, K.: Exploring simple siamese representation learning. In: Proceedings of the IEEE/CVF Conference on Computer Vision and Pattern Recognition. pp. 15750–15758 (2021)
14. Zbontar, J., Jing, L., Misra, I., LeCun, Y., Deny, S.: Barlow twins: self-supervised learning via redundancy reduction. In: International Conference on Machine Learning, pp. 12310–12320. PMLR (2021)
15. Zhang, J., Ma, K.: Rethinking the augmentation module in contrastive learning: learning hierarchical augmentation invariance with expanded views. In: Proceedings of the IEEE/CVF Conference on Computer Vision and Pattern Recognition, pp. 16650–16659 (2022)

16. Krizhevsky, A., Sutskever, I., Hinton, G.E.: Imagenet classification with deep convolutional neural networks. In: Advances in Neural Information Processing Systems 25 (2012)

17. Kim, W., Song, J.M., Park, K.R.: Multimodal biometric recognition based on convolutional neural network by the fusion of finger-vein and finger shape using near-infrared (nir) camera sensor. Sensors **18**(7), 2296 (2018)

18. Xie, C., Kumar, A.: Finger vein identification using convolutional neural network and supervised discrete hashing. Pattern Recogn. Lett. **119**, 148–156 (2019)

19. Fang, Z.M., Lu, Z.M.: Deep belief network based finger vein recognition using histograms of uniform local binary patterns of curvature gray images. Inter. J. Innovative Comput. Inform. Control **15**(5), 1701–1715 (2019)

20. Li, J., Fang, P.: Fvgnn: a novel gnn to finger vein recognition from limited training data. In: 2019 IEEE 8th Joint International Information Technology and Artificial Intelligence Conference (ITAIC), pp. 144–148. IEEE (2019)

21. Huang, Z., Guo, C.: Robust finger vein recognition based on deep cnn with spatial attention and bias field correction. Int. J. Artif. Intell. Tools **30**(01), 2140005 (2021)

22. Huang, J., Tu, M., Yang, W., Kang, W.: Joint attention network for finger vein authentication. IEEE Trans. Instrum. Meas. **70**, 1–11 (2021)

23. Qin, H., El-Yacoubi, M.A.: Deep representation for finger-vein image-quality assessment. IEEE Trans. Circuits Syst. Video Technol. **28**(8), 1677–1693 (2017)

24. Fang, Y., Wu, Q., Kang, W.: A novel finger vein verification system based on two-stream convolutional network learning. Neurocomputing **290**, 100–107 (2018)

25. Nguyen, D.T., Yoon, H.S., Pham, T.D., Park, K.R.: Spoof detection for finger-vein recognition system using nir camera. Sensors **17**(10), 2261 (2017)

26. Hou, B., Yan, R.: Convolutional auto-encoder based deep feature learning for finger-vein verification. In: 2018 IEEE International Symposium on Medical Measurements and Applications (MeMeA), pp. 1–5. IEEE (2018)

27. Kamaruddin, N.M., Rosdi, B.A.: A new filter generation method in pcanet for finger vein recognition. IEEE Access **7**, 132966–132978 (2019)

28. Ma, N., Li, Y., Wang, Y., Ma, S., Lu, H.: Research on roi extraction algorithm for finger vein recognition based on capsule neural network. In: International Conference on Frontiers of Electronics, Information and Computation Technologies, pp. 1–5 (2021)

29. El-Rahiem, B.A., El-Samie, F.E.A., Amin, M.: Multimodal biometric authentication based on deep fusion of electrocardiogram (ecg) and finger vein. Multimedia Syst. **28**(4), 1325–1337 (2022)

30. Zhu, C., Yang, Y., Jang, Y.: Research on denoising of finger vein image based on deep convolutional neural network. In: 2019 14th International Conference on Computer Science & Education (ICCSE), pp. 374–378. IEEE (2019)

31. Guo, X.J., Li, D., Zhang, H.G., Yang, J.F.: Image restoration of finger-vein networks based on encoder-decoder model. Optoelectronics Lett. **15**(6), 463–467 (2019)

32. Yang, S., Qin, H., Liu, X., Wang, J.: Finger-vein pattern restoration with generative adversarial network. IEEE Access **8**, 141080–141089 (2020)

33. He, J., et al.: Finger vein image deblurring using neighbors-based binary-gan (nb-gan). IEEE Trans. Emerging Topics Comput. Intell. (2021)

34. Choi, J., Hong, J.S., Owais, M., Kim, S.G., Park, K.R.: Restoration of motion blurred image by modified deblurgan for enhancing the accuracies of finger-vein recognition. Sensors **21**(14), 4635 (2021)

35. Lei, L., Xi, F., Chen, S.: Finger-vein image enhancement based on pulse coupled neural network. IEEE Access **7**, 57226–57237 (2019)

36. Zeng, J., Wang, F., Qin, C., Gan, J., Zhai, Y., Zhu, B.: A novel method for finger vein segmentation. In: Yu, H., Liu, J., Liu, L., Ju, Z., Liu, Y., Zhou, D. (eds.) ICIRA 2019. LNCS (LNAI), vol. 11741, pp. 589–600. Springer, Cham (2019). https://doi.org/10.1007/978-3-030-27532-7_52

37. Zeng, J.: Real-time segmentation method of lightweight network for finger vein using embedded terminal technique. IEEE Access **9**, 303–316 (2020)

38. Wu, Z., Xiong, Y., Yu, S.X., Lin, D.: Unsupervised feature learning via non-parametric instance discrimination. In: Proceedings of the IEEE Conference on Computer Vision and Pattern Recognition, pp. 3733–3742 (2018)

39. Chen, T., Kornblith, S., Norouzi, M., Hinton, G.: A simple framework for contrastive learning of visual representations. In: International Conference on Machine Learning, pp. 1597–1607. PMLR (2020)

40. Tian, Y., Krishnan, D., Isola, P.: Contrastive multiview coding. In: Vedaldi, A., Bischof, H., Brox, T., Frahm, J.-M. (eds.) ECCV 2020. LNCS, vol. 12356, pp. 776–794. Springer, Cham (2020). https://doi.org/10.1007/978-3-030-58621-8_45

41. Oord, A.v.d., Li, Y., Vinyals, O.: Representation learning with contrastive predictive coding. arXiv preprint arXiv:1807.03748 (2018)

42. Ho, D., Liang, E., Chen, X., Stoica, I., Abbeel, P.: Population based augmentation: efficient learning of augmentation policy schedules. In: International Conference on Machine Learning, pp. 2731–2741. PMLR (2019)

43. Lim, S., Kim, I., Kim, T., Kim, C., Kim, S.: Fast autoaugment. In: Advances in Neural Information Processing Systems 32 (2019)

44. Hataya, R., Zdenek, J., Yoshizoe, K., Nakayama, H.: Faster autoaugment: learning augmentation strategies using backpropagation. In: Vedaldi, A., Bischof, H., Brox, T., Frahm, J.-M. (eds.) ECCV 2020. LNCS, vol. 12370, pp. 1–16. Springer, Cham (2020). https://doi.org/10.1007/978-3-030-58595-2_1

45. Cubuk, E.D., Zoph, B., Shlens, J., Le, Q.V.: Randaugment: practical automated data augmentation with a reduced search space. In: Proceedings of the IEEE/CVF Conference on Computer Vision and Pattern Recognition Workshops, pp. 702–703 (2020)

46. Cubuk, E.D., Zoph, B., Mane, D., Vasudevan, V., Le, Q.V.: Autoaugment: learning augmentation policies from data. arXiv preprint arXiv:1805.09501 (2018)

47. Bachman, P., Hjelm, R.D., Buchwalter, W.: Learning representations by maximizing mutual information across views. In: Advances in Neural Information Processing Systems 32 (2019)

48. Dosovitskiy, A., Springenberg, J.T., Riedmiller, M., Brox, T.: Discriminative unsupervised feature learning with convolutional neural networks. In: Advances in Neural Information Processing Systems 27 (2014)

49. Jaderberg, M., Simonyan, K., Zisserman, A., et al.: Spatial transformer networks. In: Advances in Neural Information Processing Systems 28 (2015)

50. Xie, C., Tan, M., Gong, B., Wang, J., Yuille, A.L., Le, Q.V.: Adversarial examples improve image recognition. In: Proceedings of the IEEE/CVF Conference on Computer Vision and Pattern Recognition, pp. 819–828 (2020)

51. Madry, A., Makelov, A., Schmidt, L., Tsipras, D., Vladu, A.: Towards deep learning models resistant to adversarial attacks. arXiv preprint arXiv:1706.06083 (2017)

52. Raghunathan, A., Xie, S.M., Yang, F., Duchi, J.C., Liang, P.: Adversarial training can hurt generalization. arXiv preprint arXiv:1906.06032 (2019)

53. Tang, Z., Gao, Y., Karlinsky, L., Sattigeri, P., Feris, R., Metaxas, D.: OnlineAugment: online data augmentation with less domain knowledge. In: Vedaldi, A., Bischof, H., Brox, T., Frahm, J.-M. (eds.) ECCV 2020. LNCS, vol. 12352, pp. 313–329. Springer, Cham (2020). https://doi.org/10.1007/978-3-030-58571-6_19

54. Yang, W., Luo, W., Kang, W., Huang, Z., Wu, Q.: Fvras-net: an embedded finger-vein recognition and antispoofing system using a unified cnn. IEEE Trans. Instrum. Meas. **69**(11), 8690–8701 (2020)
55. Das, R., Piciucco, E., Maiorana, E., Campisi, P.: Convolutional neural network for finger-vein-based biometric identification. IEEE Trans. Inf. Forensics Secur. **14**(2), 360–373 (2018)
56. Qin, H., El-Yacoubi, M.A., Li, Y., Liu, C.: Multi-scale and multi-direction gan for cnn-based single palm-vein identification. IEEE Trans. Inf. Forensics Secur. **16**, 2652–2666 (2021)
57. Shen, J., et al.: Finger vein recognition algorithm based on lightweight deep convolutional neural network. IEEE Trans. Instrum. Meas. **71**, 1–13 (2021)
58. Kumar, A., Zhou, Y.: Human identification using finger images. IEEE Trans. Image Process. **21**(4), 2228–2244 (2011)
59. Lu, Y., Xie, S.J., Yoon, S., Yang, J., Park, D.S.: Robust finger vein roi localization based on flexible segmentation. Sensors **13**(11), 14339–14366 (2013)
60. Qin, H., Hu, R., El-Yacoubi, M.A., Li, Y., Gao, X.: Local attention transformer-based full-view finger-vein identification. IEEE Trans. Circuits Syst. Video Technol. **33**(6), 2767–2782 (2023)
61. Kolesnikov, A., Zhai, X., Beyer, L.: Revisiting self-supervised visual representation learning. In: Proceedings of the IEEE/CVF Conference on Computer Vision and Pattern Recognition, pp. 1920–1929 (2019)
62. Peng, P., Wang, J.: How to fine-tune deep neural networks in few-shot learning? arXiv preprint arXiv:2012.00204 (2020)
63. Simonyan, K., Zisserman, A.: Very deep convolutional networks for large-scale image recognition. arXiv preprint arXiv:1409.1556 (2014)

# Multi-dimensional Sequential Contrastive Learning for QoS Prediction

Yuyu Yin, Qianhui Di, Yuanqing Zhang, Tingting Liang[(✉)], Youhuizi Li,
and Yu Li

School of Computer Science, Hangzhou Dianzi University, Hangzhou, China
{yinyuyu,dqh_2021,yuanqingzhang,liangtt,huizi,liyuconp}@hdu.edu.cn

**Abstract.** Quality of service (QoS) is the main factor in service selection and recommendation, and it is influenced by dynamic factors, such as network condition and user location, and static factors represented by the invocation sequence at a fixed time slice. In order to jointly consider these two factors, this work proposes a multi-dimensional sequential contrastive learning framework named MDSCL, which applies contrastive learning method to learn the sequence representations of both user and time dimensionalities. An overlap crop augmentation strategy is proposed to obtain positive examples for user sequences and time sequences, respectively. Besides, MDSCL includes an integrated feature extractor that combines WaveNet and BiLSTM to facilitate the long short-term feature capturing. Extensive experiments on WSDREAM have been conducted to verify the effectiveness of our approach.

**Keywords:** QoS prediction · Multi-dimensional contrastive learning · Multi-task training

## 1 Introduction

The continuous advancement of Service-Oriented Architecture (SOA) motivates the rapid growth of the number of Web services or Web APIs, which drives the production of software applications with more complex functions and accelerates the development of interoperable interaction through the Internet. The proliferation of Web services makes it difficult for consumers to effectively discover the high-quality services that meet their requirements. Therefore, how to provide the satisfactory service recommendation for consumers is becoming an imperative task.

For those Web services with similar functionalities, the traditional semantic matching based service selection methods are no longer operative. In this case, Quality of Service (QoS), which describes the non-functional characteristics of Web service, such as response time, reliability, throughput, becomes the main factor in service selection and recommendation. QoS prediction is the essential preparation for service recommendation which aims at providing the

H. Gao et al. (Eds.): CollaborateCom 2023, LNICST 562, pp. 514–531, 2024.
https://doi.org/10.1007/978-3-031-54528-3_28

appropriate services for consumers to satisfy both functional and non-functional requirements.

There exist many approaches of predicting unknown service QoS values by modeling the historical invocation information. Generally, these approaches can be categorized into three groups, which are memory-based, model-based, and context-aware methods. The memory-based methods [1,2] usually compute the similarity between users or Web services and predict the missing QoS values depending on the historical values of similar users or services. The model-based approaches [3,4] learn the potential characteristics of consumers and Web services with the machine learning algorithm for prediction. The context-based approaches [5,6] incorporate the contextual information, *e.g.*, geographical information, time, trustworthiness to facilitate QoS prediction, among which the temporal-aware methods have attracted great attention. Considering that a consumer might receive different QoS experiences when invoking the same service at different points of time, a deep learning based approach called DeepTSQP is proposed to learn the temporal feature representations by modeling the user-service invocation changes across different temporal slices [7]. Besides, a dynamic graph neural collaborative learning approach is utilized to model user-service historical temporal interactions and extract latent features of users and services at each time slice [8].

Although the aforementioned approaches improve the performance of service QoS prediction, most of them focus on the modeling of user invocation sequence while neglect the importance of sequential information in time dimensionality. Generally, many previous work models the user invocation sequence to predict the QoS values on all the services in the next time slice considering that the invocation conditions (*e.g., network condition, user location*) might be different across different time slices. However, besides the dynamic factor, the static factor represented by the invocation sequence at a fixed time slice should also be considered. The underlying intuition is that service state is consistent and user-service interactive features would be more prominent.

To compensate for this shortcoming, this work proposes a Multi-Dimensional Sequential Contrastive Learning framework named MDSCL for QoS prediction. Specifically, MDSCL performs contrastive learning on service invocation sequences from both user and time dimensionalities to learn the discriminative representations of user behaviours and temporal conditions. An overlap crop strategy is proposed for the sequence augmentation which generates two positive examples for the user sequence and temporal sequence, respectively. Furthermore, in order to obtain the representative sequential features, we integrate the WaveNet [9] and BiLSTM [10] to capture both long and short information for contrastive learning.

The main contributions of this work can be summarized as follows:

- We propose a multi-dimensional sequential contrastive learning framework named MDSCL for QoS prediction which considers invocation sequences of both user and time dimensionalities.

– We equip MDSCL with a overlap crop augmentation strategy for positive sequence generation and an integrated feature extractor for long short-term feature capturing.
– We conduct comprehensive experiments on a real-world dataset and compare the proposed MDSCL with the well-known existing methods. Experimental results demonstrate the effectiveness of our MDSCL.

## 2   Related Work

Among various research topics related to dynamic service QoS prediction, the prediction and estimation of actual QoS values of dynamic QoS attributes have been widely studied, and the methods are mainly classified into factor analysis-based methods, time-series-based methods, and hybrid-based methods that combine the above two methods.

Factor analysis is a variable simplification technique that starts from analyzing the correlation of multiple original variables, mainly by studying the correlation matrix of multiple variables and identifying a limited number of potential variables that govern the correlation to achieve the purpose of explaining complex problems with a few variables. In the field of QoS prediction, tensor decomposition methods can be used [11], which can extract user-specific, service-specific, and time-specific potential features from a three-dimensional matrix based on user-service-time, and then perform QoS prediction based on the potential features. On the basis of the basic matrix decomposition and tensor decomposition, it can be improved. For example, the biased non-negative latent factor decomposition model models the linear bias (LB) of users, services, and time points and uses LB vectors of the same dimensionality to form a first-order tensor of LB [12]. It applies additive GD and LB for each latent factor and controls the learning rate to offset the negative terms with the initial state of the corresponding parameters.

The essence of the factor analysis algorithm is to find potential factors in the data and apply the potential factors to explain the phenomena shown by the original variables. However, in practice, potential factors are difficult to extract accurately, and the potential characteristics of users are dynamically changing, as shown by the fact that the QoS values of users in a specific time interval will be influenced not only by the QoS values of similar users, but also by the QoS values in previous time intervals. Therefore, QoS prediction of dynamic services can be performed by time series. The method is divided into a statistical based method and a neural network based method. Statistical based time series methods include by ARIMA model [13–15]. The neural network based time series method mainly includes the prediction by using recurrent neural network RNN [3,16].

The hybrid approach is to choose two or more of the most suitable methods among the single methods of factor analysis and time series mentioned above. However, it is not the case that the more methods there are, the better the final prediction performance. Rather, its key factors should be considered, for example, if the prediction accuracy is considered, i.e., the method with the lowest prediction error. A typical approach is to combine matrix decomposition with other methods. For example, it can be combined with network embedding, where a reputation-aware network embedding is used to learn the hidden representation of the user [17]. Then a user-based matrix decomposition method is used to predict the unknown QoS values. Also, it can be combined with convolutional neural networks [18] to extract QoS features through a joint deep network of potential factor embedding methods, matrix decomposition, and convolutional neural networks [19]. In addition, it can also be combined with graph networks [20] to first deep mine potential relationships based on the QoS matrix [21], and then combine multi-source information from user-aware context and service-aware context with graph networks to adaptively combine the QoS values by cutting irrelevant edges into several subgraphs and establishing a Gaussian mixture model (GMM) of QoS values as a fusion method based on the local information of the subgraphs and the global information of the integral graph. Local and global information to complete the final QoS prediction. Meanwhile, it can also be combined with deep neural network DNN [22,23], with LSTM [24–26], etc. Although all of the above methods take the time factor into account in QoS prediction, they tend to extract dynamic features on user sequences at different time slices and thus utilize it for QoS prediction to improve the final prediction accuracy. However, these methods do not consider the sequence information on fixed time slices, which is also important and reflects the user interaction information in the same external state.

## 3    Proposed Model

In this section, we start with stating the problem formulation of prediction task, and then describe the overall framework of MDSCL and the details of different components.

### 3.1    Problem Formulation

Suppose the QoS prediction scenario includes $N$ users $\mathcal{U} = \{u_1, u_2, \cdots, u_N\}$ and $M$ services $\mathcal{S} = \{s_1, s_2, \cdots, s_M\}$. If user $u_i \in \mathcal{U}$ invokes service $s_j \in \mathcal{S}$ at time slice $t$, the QoS value would be recorded. These QoS values generated by the $N$ users invoking $M$ services at multiple time slices forms a three-dimensional QoS matrix $Q \in \mathbb{R}^{N \times M \times T}$, where $T$ denotes the number of time slices. Fix the user dimensionality and concatenate the invocation sequences in different time slices to form a one-dimensional user invocation sequence $Seq^u = [Seq_1^u, Seq_2^u, \cdots, Seq_t^u]$, where $Seq_t^u = [(u, s_1, t, q_{u,s_1,t}), (u, s_2, t, q_{u,s_2,t}), \cdots, (u, s_M, t, q_{u,s_M,t})]$ is the invocation sequence of user $u$ at time slice $t$. $q_{u,s,t}$ is an element of matrix $Q$ which denotes the QoS value of user $u$ on service $s$ at time slice $t$. The values of services that users do not invoke at each time slice are filled in using the padding technique. In an analogical manner, the sequence of time dimensionality can be constructed as $Seq^t = [Seq_1^t, Seq_2^t, \cdots, Seq_m^t]$, where

$Seq_m^t = [(u_1, s_m, t, q_{u_1, s_m, t}), (u_2, s_m, t, q_{u_2, s_m, t}), \cdots, (u_N, s_m, t, q_{u_N, s_m, t})]$ is the invocation sequence of service $s_m$ at time slice $t$. In this work, given the historical invocation sequence of both user and time dimensionalities, $Seq^u$ and $Seq^t$, the goal is to precisely predict QoS values for the invocation on the $t+1$ time slice.

## 3.2    MDSCLFramework

This paper proposes a multi-dimensional sequential contrastive learning framework MDSCL, aiming at better extracting the user dynamic and time static features from service invocation data for accurate QoS prediction. Figure 1 shows the overview of the proposed framework. MDSCL consists of three phases: sequential data filtering, multi-dimensional sequential contrastive learning, and joint training. Firstly, the sequences of two different dimensionalites are transformed from the historical invocation data and inputted into the Kalman filter layer to get the smoothed QoS sequences. In the second step, the sequences are inputted into a multi-dimensional sequential augmentation module including the overlap crop to generate two positive sequence representations and an integrated feature extractor to obtain the representative sequential embeddings. Finally, we combine the contrastive learning losses of different dimensionalities and one prediction loss for model training.

## 3.3    Sequential Data Filtering

As shown in Fig. 1, the sequences of two different dimensionalities are generated from the historical invocation data. Specifically, the invocation sequence of user and time dimensionalities are respectively denoted by $Seq^u$ and $Seq^t$ as mentioned in Sect. 3.1. Since some interfering factors are present in the QoS sequence, the Kalman algorithm, as a state-space model-based filtering algorithm, could be chosen to filter the noise in the QoS data.

The original sequences $Seq^u$ and $Seq^t$ could be transformed into $KSeq^u = KalmanSmoother(Seq^u)$ and $KSeq^t = KalmanSmoother(Seq^t)$ through the Kalman smoother. The Kalman smoothing algorithm includes forward filtering algorithm and reverse filtering algorithm [27]. Specifically, the Kalman filter has the following state and measurement definitions:

$$\mathbf{x}_{k+1} = \mathbf{F}_{k+1,k}\mathbf{x}_k + \mathbf{W}_k, \mathbf{y}_k = \mathbf{H}_k\mathbf{x}_k + \mathbf{V}_k, \tag{1}$$

where $\mathbf{x}_k$ and $\mathbf{y}_k$ are the state and measurement at moment $k$, $\mathbf{F}_{k+1,k}$ and $\mathbf{H}_k$ are the transition and measurement matrix, $\mathbf{W}_k$ and $\mathbf{V}_k$ are the process and measurement matrix which are assumed to be white, zero mean Gaussian, and the covariance matrix of $\mathbf{V}_k$ is $\mathbf{R}_k$. In the forward filtering algorithm, the one-step prediction of the state, and the state estimationare respectively as follows:

$$\hat{\mathbf{x}}_{k/k-1} = \Phi\hat{\mathbf{x}}_{k-1}, \hat{\mathbf{x}}_k = \hat{\mathbf{x}}_{k/k-1} + \mathbf{K}_k(\mathbf{y}_k - \mathbf{H}_k\hat{\mathbf{x}}_{k/k-1}), \tag{2}$$

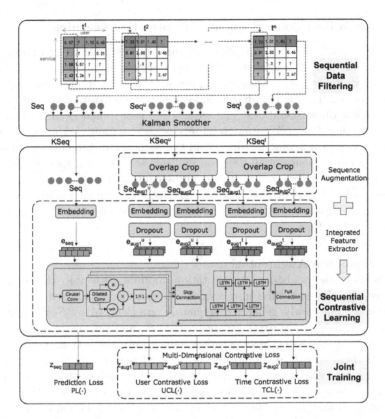

**Fig. 1.** The overall framework of MDSCL. The red and blue dots represent the sequences of user and time dimensionalities derived from the original invocation records. The gray dots represent the invocation sequence of user $u$ on the first $t$ time slices being used to predict the QoS values on the $t + 1$ time slice, which are actually the same as the red dots.

where $\hat{\mathbf{x}}_{k/k-1}$ is the *a priori estimate* of $\mathbf{x}_k$, $\hat{\mathbf{x}}_{k-1}$ is the *a posteriori estimate* of $\mathbf{x}_{k-1}$, $\Phi$ is the $k - 1$ moment to $k$ moment one-step transfer matrix. The mean square error of the one-step prediction $\mathbf{P}_{k/k-1}$ and estimation $\mathbf{P}_k$ can be calculated, and the Kalman gain $\mathbf{K}_k$ could be obtain. Continuously iterating the above calculation process, the state vector estimation $\{\hat{\mathbf{x}}_k\}_{(k=1,2,\cdots,t)}$ can be finally obtained. In the inverse filtering algorithm, the smoothing equation is:

$$\hat{\mathbf{x}}_{k/t} = \hat{\mathbf{x}}_k + \mathbf{A}_k(\hat{\mathbf{x}}_{k+1/t} - \hat{\mathbf{x}}_{k+1/k}), \tag{3}$$

where $\mathbf{A}_k = \mathbf{P}_k \Phi^T \mathbf{P}_{k+1/k}^{-1}$, and the smoothed mean square error $\mathbf{P}_{k/t}$ can be calculated. Suppose $\hat{\mathbf{x}}_{t/t} = \hat{\mathbf{x}}_t$, the above process is integrated on the basis of forward filtering, and the smoothed state vector estimate $\{\hat{\mathbf{x}}_{k/t}\}_{(k=t-1,t-2,\cdots,0)}$,i.e., the output $KSeq^t$ is obtained recursively from the state vector estimate $\{\hat{\mathbf{x}}_{k/t}\}$.

## 3.4  Multi-dimensional Sequential Contrastive Learning

In order to learn the discriminative sequence representations containing both dynamic and static characteristics, this paper proposes a multi-dimensional contrastive learning which is the core component of MDSCL framework. The multi-dimensional contrasitve learning includes separate contrastive learning in both user and time dimensionalities. The sequence of user dimentionality is the invocation sequence of a specific user on all services across multiple time slices, which contains the user dynamic features. And the sequence of time dimensionality is the invocation sequence of all users on multiple services at a specific time slice, from which the service static features can be captured.

Specifically, the multi-dimensional contrastive learning module consists of three parts: sequence augmentation, integrated feature extraction, and contrastive loss function.

### 3.4.1  Sequence Augmentation

In this part, the sequence augmentation module generates two invocation sequences for the smoothed user sequence $KSeq^u$ and time sequence $KSeq^t$, respectively. The newly generated sequences are denoted by $Seq^u_{aug1}$, $Seq^u_{aug2}$ and $Seq^t_{aug1}$, $Seq^t_{aug2}$. Since the sequences of user and time dimensionalities are processed with the same augmentation and feature extraction operations, we represent them with $KSeq$ uniformly in the next sections for simplicity. Specifically, each smoothed sequence $KSeq$ is fed into two successive layers, overlap crop and embedding layer with dropout, to obtain two representations for the augmented invocation sequences which contain the similar sequential characteristics. These augmented representations are used as positive pairs for the following multi-dimensional sequential contrastive learning.

The previous sequence augmentation methods [28,29] usually use the ordinary crop method, where some sub-objects of the original object are randomly selected as the augmented object. However, the ordinary crop method is only applicable to the domain where the original object is simple, such as computer vision. In the QoS prediction task, the QoS sequences have their unique time distributions, it is prone to destroy the time distribution of original sequence with the traditional crop method adopted, resulting in a low correlation between the time distributions of the two augmented sequences after cropping. Such augmented sequences are less referable and less effective for the subsequent contrastive learning.

To alleviate this problem, this work designs an overlap crop method for the QoS sequence augmentation, as shown in Fig. 2. Firstly, a segment of QoS subsequence $[q_{start}, \cdots, q_{end}]$ is arbitrarily selected as the overlap region in the smoothed invocation sequence $KSeq = [q_0, \cdots, q_t]$. The length of the subsequence is decided by a preset parameter $\alpha$, i.e., $|[q_{start}, \cdots, q_{end}]| = \alpha \cdot |KSeq|$. Here we only use the symbols of QoS values to denote the invocation record for simplicity. $q_{start}$ and $q_{end}$ can be the same as $q_1$ and $q_t$. Next, one of the augmented sequences $Seq_{aug1} = [q_i, \cdots, q_{end}]$ is generated, where $i = \beta \cdot start$. The other augmented sequence $Seq_{aug2} = [q_{start}, \cdots, q_j]$ can also be determined,

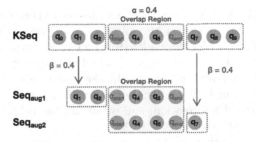

**Fig. 2.** A description of the overlap method.

where $j = end + \beta \cdot |t - end|$. Fig. 2 shows an example of overlap crop. Once the overlap region is decided, two augmented sequences are derived by expanding the region in different directions with the parameter $\beta$.

With the proposed overlap crop method, part of the time distribution $[q_{start}, \cdots, q_{end}]$ in the original sequence $[q_0, \ldots\ldots, q_t]$ is preserved, making the two augmented sequences contain common temporal characteristics and facilitating the subsequent multi-dimensional contrastive learning.

### 3.4.2 Integrated Feature Extractor

*3.4.2.1 Embedding-Dropout Layer*

The augmented sequences $Seq_{aug1}$, $Seq_{aug2}$ generated by the overlap crop are fed into the subsequent embedding layer with dropout to capture the sequential features of the augmented samples from two dimensionalities.

$$\mathbf{E}_{aug1} = Dropout(F(Seq_{aug1})), \tag{4}$$

$$\mathbf{E}_{aug2} = Dropout(F(Seq_{aug2})), \tag{5}$$

where $F(\cdot)$ denotes the embedding layer and $Dropout(\cdot)$ is the dropout operation. $\mathbf{E}_{aug1} = [e_{aug1,1}, \cdots, e_{aug1,l}] \in \mathbb{R}^{l \times d}$ is the embeddings of the augmented sequence $Seq_{aug1}$, where $l$ denotes the length of the sequence and $d$ is the embedding size. Here the dropout is introduced to add some noise by randomly setting input units to 0 with a frequency of rate to the augmented representations, which is able to improve the robustness of the model.

*3.4.2.2 Long Short-Term Feature Extractor*

Considering that the sequences augmented by the proposed overlap crop are usually not too short, it requires a feature extractor that has the ability of capturing both long-term and short-term sequential information. WaveNet [9] is originally proposed for speech recognition and generation and achieves the impressive performance on sequential feature learning. Compared with the basic convolutional neural network (CNN), the casual and dilated convolutions of WaveNet effectively expands the receptive field, which increases its ability to handle long sequences. Since WaveNet processes the sequence only in one direction and might loses the sequential features of another direction, we propose to integrate it with Bidirectional LSTM (BiLSTM) model [10]. LSTM is a type of recurrent neural network (RNN) which maintains memory of the input internally, making it well suited for solving long continuous data like time series. The performance of BiLSTM is better than LSTM in the series prediction problem [30] as it considers more contextual information, and we utilize the BiLSTM model as long short-term feature extractor in this work.

Since the representations of the augmented sequences, namely $\mathbf{E}_{aug1}$, $\mathbf{E}_{aug2}$ are going to pass through the same layers, in this section, we denote the representation with $\mathbf{E}_{aug}$ uniformly. The augmented sequence embedding $\mathbf{E}_{aug}$ is firstly fed into a casual convolutional layer, which ensures to keep the ordering of the input sequence. Subsequently, this filtered tensor is fed into a stacked dilated convolutional layer. Each layer performs the same operation, which is formulated as follows:

$$\mathbf{v}_k = tanh(\mathbf{W}_{f,k} * \mathbf{u}_k) \otimes \sigma(\mathbf{W}_{g,k} * \mathbf{u}_k), \tag{6}$$

where $\mathbf{W}_{f,k}$ and $\mathbf{W}_{g,k}$ are the learnable dilated convolution filters, $f$ and $g$ denote 'filter' and 'gate', $k$ denotes the layer index, $\mathbf{u}_k$ denotes the input of the $k$-th layer, and the input for the first layer is the output of causal convolution layer. $*$ denotes the convolution operator, $\otimes$ is the element-wise multiplication operator, $\sigma(\cdot)$ is the sigmoid activation function.

After the gated activation unit, $\mathbf{v}_k$ is processed with a $1 \times 1$ convolution layer and residual operation, and the output is the input of the next dilated convolutional layer, while the sikp connection is used to obtain the output of WaveNet: :

$$\mathbf{u}_{wave} = \mathbf{u}_0 + \sum_{k=1}^{d} \mathbf{u}_k = \mathbf{u}_0 + \sum_{k=0}^{d-1}(\mathbf{W} * \mathbf{v}_k + \mathbf{u}_k) \tag{7}$$

The sequential feature representations filtered by WaveNet are used as the input to the BiLSTM module for further extraction of long short-term features, and the calculation process is as follows:

$$\mathbf{h}_t = LSTM(\mathbf{g}_t, \mathbf{h}_{t-1}), \mathbf{h}_t = LSTM(\mathbf{g}_t, \mathbf{h}_{t-1}), \mathbf{h}_t = \mathbf{W}_t^f \mathbf{h}_t + \mathbf{W}_t^b \mathbf{h}_t + \mathbf{b}_t, \tag{8}$$

where $\mathbf{g}_t$ denotes the input of the BiLSTM network at time slice $t$, the input of the first moment of the network is the output of WaveNet $\mathbf{u}_{wave}$. $\mathbf{h}_t$ denotes the forward output of BiLSTM at time slice $t$ and $\mathbf{h}_t$ is the reverse output of BiLSTM at time slice $t$. $\mathbf{W}_t^f$ and $\mathbf{W}_t^b$ are the weight matrices, and $\mathbf{b}_t$ is the bias. We choose the last hidden vector $\mathbf{h}_t$ as the final output of the BiLSTM and perform a full connection layer $FC(\cdot)$ of this output as the representation of one augmented sequence $\mathbf{z}_{aug}$:

$$\mathbf{z}_{aug} = FC(\mathbf{h}_t) \tag{9}$$

### 3.4.3  Multi-dimensional Contrastive Loss

The multi-dimensional contrastive loss function is designed to minimize the difference between the augmented sequence pair and maximize the distance between the negative sequence pair. Here we use the inner product of sequence representations to measure the difference between sample pairs.

Given a training batch with size $BN = BN^u + BN^t$, where $BN^u$ is the number of sequences of user dimensionality and $BN^t$ is the number of sequences of time dimensionality, we can get $2BN^u$ positive sequences of user dimensionality and $2BN^t$ those of time dimensionality. For each augmented sequence pair of user dimensionality $(Seq_{aug1}, Seq_{aug2})$, the rest $2(BN^u - 1)$ is used as the negative samples. The contrastive loss function of user dimensionality can be defined as:

$$\mathcal{L}_{cl}^u = -\log \frac{\exp((\mathbf{z}_{aug1}^u \cdot \mathbf{z}_{aug2}^u)/\tau)}{\exp((\mathbf{z}_{aug1}^u \cdot \mathbf{z}_{aug2}^u)/\tau) + \sum \exp((\mathbf{z}_{aug1}^u \cdot \mathbf{z}^{u-})/\tau)}, \tag{10}$$

where $\tau$ is a temperature hyper-parameter [31]. In the same manner, the contrastive loss function of time dimensionality can be defined as follows:

$$\mathcal{L}_{cl}^t = -\log \frac{\exp((\mathbf{z}_{aug1}^t \cdot \mathbf{z}_{aug2}^t)/\tau)}{\exp((\mathbf{z}_{aug1}^t \cdot \mathbf{z}_{aug2}^t)/\tau) + \sum \exp((\mathbf{z}_{aug1}^t \cdot \mathbf{z}^{t-})/\tau)}. \tag{11}$$

### 3.5  Joint Training

The task of the proposed multi-dimensional contrastive learning aims at learning the discriminative representations for service invocation sequences of both user and time dimensionalites by closing the augmented positive sequence pairs and separating the negative ones. The aforementioned two contrastive losses $\mathcal{L}_{cl}^u$ and $\mathcal{L}_{cl}^t$ well serve this purpose.

For the QoS prediction task, as mentioned in the problem formulation, the goal is to precisely predict the QoS values on the next time slice $t+1$. The original sequence $Seq^u = [Seq_1^u, Seq_2^u, \cdots, Seq_t^u]$ is fittered by the Kalman smoother and input into the integrated feature extractor to generate the sequential representations in the same manner with that of the augmented sequences. The target service $s_{target}$ to be predicted at time $t+1$ is fed into the embedding layer to obtain the representation $\mathbf{e}_{target}$. With the learned representation of the original sequence $\mathbf{z}_t$ and $\mathbf{e}_{target}$, the final QoS value can be predicted by $\mathbf{z}_t \cdot \mathbf{e}_{target}$. To effectively learn the QoS prediction task, we adopt the squared loss as objective function:

$$L_{pred} = \frac{1}{|\mathcal{D}_{t+1}|} \sum_{i \in \mathcal{D}_{t+1}}^{N} (\hat{y}_i - y_i)^2, \tag{12}$$

where $\mathcal{D}_{t+1}$ denotes the set of observed QoS values of all users on all services at the $t+1$ time slice. $y_i$ is the true QoS value, and $\hat{y}_i$ is the predicted QoS value.

To jointly learn the QoS prediction task and the additional multi-dimensional contrastive learning task, we combine the predictive loss and the constrastive learning loss of two dimensionalites to obtain the final objective function as follows:

$$\mathcal{L}_{total} = \mathcal{L}_{pred} + \lambda(\mathcal{L}_{cl}^u + \mathcal{L}_{cl}^t), \qquad (13)$$

where $\lambda$ denotes the fixed coefficient for sequential contrastive loss function of the user and time dimensionalies.

## 4 Experiments

### 4.1 Datasets

We conduct all experiments on a publicly available dataset WSDREAM[1], which was collected from real-world Web services and suitable for large scale experiments. The dataset is a time-aware dataset consisting of 27,392,643 response time records obtained from 142 users from different regions sending requests to 4500 real-world Web services over 64 consecutive time slices. Since each time period is 16 h, according to a time interval of every 15 min, there are a total of 64 time slices per user. We select response time as a typical QoS values for our study.

### 4.2 Expermimential Setup

#### 4.2.1 Implementation Details

In reality, since a user may invoke only a small number of services, the corresponding QoS values contain a large number of missing values, leading the user-service QoS matrix with high sparsity. In order to simulate the actual service invocation scenario, we remove some QoS values randomly on the basis of the original data to generate eight datasets of different sparsity levels, namely $1\% - 5\%$, $10\%$, $15\%$, and $20\%$. When dividing the dataset, $60\%$ of the QoS values are used as the training set, and the remaining $40\%$ are used for model testing. In addition, in order to eliminate the coincidence of experimental results, each experiment is conducted 5 times for each data density and the average result is used as the final result.

For all the baseline methods, we take the same modeling approach for sequencial input, i.e., the sequencial modeling approach in our MDSCL for the user dimension. In addition, we take the same window size and number of samples to control the sequence length and optimize the computational cost. We adjust the parameters of the baselines according to the guidelines of the original paper, so that the model parameters are different for different baselines, but the parameters are the same for each baseline at different sparse. For our MDSCL, we adjust the parameter settings to achieve optimal predictions. We utilize the Adam optimizer with a batch size of 256 and set the learning rate to 0.001. The temperature for the multi-dimensional contrastive learning is set to 0.04 and the weights of contrastive losses are set to 0.1. We use an early stopping technique to train the model.

---

[1] https://github.com/wsdream/wsdream-dataset.

#### 4.2.2 Metrics

We use Mean Absolute Error (MAE) [2] and Root Mean Square Error (RMSE) [2] as the metrics for the evaluation, which are defined as:

$$MAE = \frac{\sum_{i=1}^{n} |real_i - predicted_i|}{n}, RMSE = \sqrt{\frac{\sum_{i=1}^{n} (real_i - predicted_i)^2}{n}},$$

(14)

where $n$ is the number of predicted QoS values i.e. the response time, and $real_i$ and $predicted_i$ are the true and predicted values.

#### 4.2.3 Baselines

We compare the proposed MDSCL with the following sequential prediction models and QoS prediction methods:

- TASR [32] is based on a time-aware service prediction method that combines an enhanced time-aware similarity-based collaborative filtering approach with an ARIMA model.
- CTF [33] is a QoS prediction method based on matrix decomposition, which reduces outliers and increases the robustness of outliers through Corsi loss, while taking the time factor into account in the matrix decomposition.
- RNN [34] is a recurrent neural network for processing serial data.
- LSTM [35] is long short-term memory network that improves the problem of gradient disappearance and gradient explosion in RNN and has long-term dependence.
- Trsfm [36] is based on a self-attentive mechanism deep learning model.
- RNN + Trsfm incorporates the Transfomer mechanism into RNN temporal prediction.

### 4.3 Performance Comparison

To verify the effectiveness of the proposed MDSCL in QoS prediction task, we compare it with the baseline methods. We use the same training, testing datasets and the same form of data input to run all these methods. Table 1 summarizes the performance of MDSCL and the baseline methods at different sparsity in terms of MAE and RMSE. The best results are shown in bold. Generally, our MDSCL achieves the best prediction accuracy for all sparsity. It shows the adaptability of the realistic QoS environment, which learns sequential features from both user and time dimensionalities and optimizes the prediction model and contrasive learning by the multi-task joint training.

Specifically, our MDSCL consistently outperforms the baselines at each sparsity, especially the extremely sparsity of 1%, with MAE of 0.626 and RMSE of 0.949. When the sparsity is between 1% and 5%, the performance of our method tends to be stable in terms of both metrics, benefiting from the robustness of our model for sparse data processing. When the sparsity exceeds 5%, our method decreases slightly, it is probably because the sequences of both dimensionalities would become complex and noisy when the training data gets denser, which might increases the probability of randomly overlap cropping invalid sequence. Thus, the proposed MDSCL is more suitable for the situation where the training QoS data is sparse.

It is observed that our method performs better than the most efficient sequential model LSTM which obtains the highest prediction accuracy in all baselines. On the one hand, we improve the feature extraction by combining the WaveNet and BiLSTM. Compared to LSTM, the proposed integrated feature extractor has the stronger extraction capability in handling long sequences as they expand the receptive field and leverage the more contextual information. More importantly, we improve the feature optimization by replacing the traditional prediction task with a joint task of prediction and contrastive learning, so that the final learned features are more representative and thus achieve higher prediction accuracy. In addition, the other time series-based methods, such as RNN, exhibit lower prediction accuracy. A possible reason is that RNN is deficient for extracting long-term dependencies, while QoS data are usually long-term correlated, making it the worst performer with a MAE of 1.505 at 1% sparsity. It also leads to the effect of the combination of RNN and transformer with the highers values of MAE on 4%, 10%, 15%, and 20%, reaching 1.159, 1.233, 1.195, and 1.208, respectively. Traditional-based methods, such as CTF, which relies on matrix decomposition, consistently exhibit lower prediction accuracy on RMSE, especially at a low sparsity of 1% sparsity, with an RMSE of 2.951. However, in general, it can be seen that the time series-based prediction methods consistently outperform the traditional prediction methods.

## 4.4   Ablation Study

We conduct an ablation study for the proposed MDSCL to explore the performance of each module. Table 2 shows the predicted results of the variants which removes components for multi-dimensional sequential contrastive learning module and joint training one by one.

The results show that the composition of each part leads to the best performance. In particular, both MAE and RMSE are significantly higher after we use the traditional augmentation method, which randomly applies two of crop, mask, and random order to generate positive samples. It indicates that our proposed overlap crop could be used to generate effective positive samples for the multi-dimensional contrastive learning.

In the joint training module, it can be seen that both contrastive losses are effective in reducing MAE and RMSE. Particularly, the contribution of contrastive loss of user dimensionality is more significant than that of time dimensionality. We further validate that removing the contrastive loss function leads to the worse performance. Overall, both contrasive loss of user dimensionality and contrastive loss of time dimensionality are able to facilitate the learning of sequence representations and further improve the prediction performance.

**Table 1.** Performance comparison for different sparsity (Best results in bold numbers).

| Sparsity | | TASR | CTF | RNN | Trsfm | RNN + Trsfm | LSTM | MDSCL |
|---|---|---|---|---|---|---|---|---|
| 1% | MAE | 1.107 | 1.239 | 1.505 | 1.193 | 1.183 | 1.125 | **0.626** |
| | RMSE | 1.897 | 2.951 | 2.435 | 2.233 | 2.218 | 2.151 | **0.949** |
| 2% | MAE | 1.058 | 1.218 | 1.314 | 0.881 | 1.149 | 0.882 | **0.647** |
| | RMSE | 1.695 | 2.764 | 2.256 | 1.868 | 2.165 | 1.848 | **0.954** |
| 3% | MAE | 1.071 | 1.197 | 1.163 | 0.926 | 1.118 | 0.846 | **0.646** |
| | RMSE | 1.661 | 2.653 | 2.263 | 1.927 | 2.219 | 1.808 | **0.956** |
| 4% | MAE | 1.077 | 1.087 | 1.118 | 0.935 | 1.159 | 0.842 | **0.645** |
| | RMSE | 1.655 | 2.674 | 2.171 | 1.921 | 2.224 | 1.784 | **0.960** |
| 5% | MAE | 1.173 | 1.071 | 1.124 | 0.934 | 1.130 | 0.846 | **0.652** |
| | RMSE | 1.663 | 2.636 | 2.228 | 1.954 | 2.217 | 1.810 | **0.993** |
| 10% | MAE | 1.059 | 1.045 | 1.171 | 0.980 | 1.233 | 0.833 | **0.732** |
| | RMSE | 1.639 | 2.593 | 2.253 | 1.997 | 2.360 | 1.811 | **1.111** |
| 15% | MAE | 1.132 | 1.019 | 1.160 | 0.963 | 1.195 | 0.871 | **0.767** |
| | RMSE | 1.605 | 2.671 | 2.241 | 2.002 | 2.301 | 1.854 | **1.181** |
| 20% | MAE | 1.015 | 1.021 | 1.166 | 0.933 | 1.208 | 0.842 | **0.801** |
| | RMSE | 1.590 | 2.592 | 2.252 | 1.975 | 2.308 | 1.800 | **1.232** |

## 4.5 Parameter Sensitivity

We conduct sensitivity analysis on two hyperparameters, namely *DropoutRate* and $\lambda$. *DropoutRate* denotes the hyperparameters in the dropout layer in the module of integrated feature extractor, which decides the percentage of neurons to be randomly deleted. $\lambda$ is the coefficient of multi-dimensional contrastive loss in the joint training phase. To make the results more convincing, dataset with $d$ of 1% is used to simulate the data in sparse environment.

For *DropoutRate*, Fig. 3(a) shows the results in terms of MAE and RMSE with different parameter values. It can be observed that different *DropoutRate* has essentially no effect on the results for MAE, while RMSE reaches a minimum at 0.4 and then tends to increase gradually, peaking at 0.7. It might be because the dropout of the embeddings of the augmented sequences prevents the model from overfitting and improves the robustness, and the MAE is basically steady. However, when the *DropoutRate* is too large and too much information is lost in the augmented sequences, it leads to a decrease in RMSE. Overall, we choose *DropoutRate* = 0.4 to get the best performance on both metrics.

**Table 2.** Ablation study of MDSCL on WSDREAM with 1%.

| Method | | MAE | RMSE |
|---|---|---|---|
| Multi-Dimensional Sequential Contrastive Learning | w/o Overlap Crop | 0.661 | 1.032 |
| | w/o Embedding Drop | 0.656 | 1.030 |
| | Traditional Augmentation | 0.684 | 1.054 |
| | w/o WaveNet | 0.640 | 0.997 |
| | w/o BiLSTM | 0.642 | 1.001 |
| Joint Learning | w/o User Contrastive Loss | 0.646 | 1.011 |
| | w/o Time Contrastive Loss | 0.643 | 0.998 |
| | w/o Contrastive Loss | 0.647 | 1.005 |
| MDSCL | | **0.626** | **0.949** |

For $\lambda$, Fig. 3(b) shows the performance with different $\lambda$. It can be seen that with the increase of $\lambda$, both MAE and RMSE show a slowly increasing trend. This is because the prediction task still dominates in QoS prediction, and the multi-dimensional contrastive learning task is only an auxiliary task to improve the prediction accuracy by learning the more representative sequence feature embeddings. If the weight of the multi-dimensional contrastive learning task is too high, it would lead to overfitting of the model and thus reduce the prediction performance. Therefore, we choose to set $\lambda = 0.1$ to obtain the optimal prediction results.

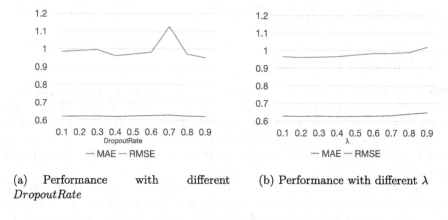

(a) Performance with different *DropoutRate*

(b) Performance with different $\lambda$

**Fig. 3.** Parameter sensitivity of *DropoutRate*, $\lambda$ in MDSCL with d=1%.

## 5   Conclusion

In this paper, we propose a multi-dimentional sequential contrastive learning framework (MDSCL). Specially, a augmentation strategy of overlap crop is proposed in order to generate positive sequence pairs, and an integrated feature extractor with an embedding layer with dropout, WaveNe module, and BiL-STM module is designed to capture long short-term sequential features. Finally a contrastive learning framework that considers both the user and time dimensionalities is combined with the original prediction objective to facilitate the task of QoS prediction. The experimental evaluation demonstrate the effectiveness of our MDSCL. In the future, we will further work on the representation of QoS and learn more fine-grained information to improve the accuracy of QoS prediction.

**Acknowledgements.** This work is supported in part by National Key R&D Program of China under grant 2022YFF0903300, National Natural Science Foundation of China under grant U20A20173 and 62002088, Natural Science Foundation of Zhejiang Province under grant LY22F020009.

# References

1. Shao, L., Zhang, J., Wei, Y., Zhao, J., Xie, B., Mei, H.: Personalized qos prediction forweb services via collaborative filtering. In: IEEE International Conference on Web Services (ICWS 2007), pp. 439–446. IEEE (2007)
2. Zheng, Z., Ma, H., Lyu, M.R., King, I.: Qos-aware web service recommendation by collaborative filtering. IEEE Trans. Serv. Comput. **4**(2), 140–152 (2010)
3. White, G., Palade, A., Clarke, S.: Forecasting qos attributes using lstm networks. In: 2018 International Joint Conference on Neural Networks (IJCNN), pp. 1–8. IEEE (2018)
4. Yin, Y., Chen, L., Xu, Y., Wan, J., Zhang, H., Mai, Z.: Qos prediction for service recommendation with deep feature learning in edge computing environment. Mobile Netw. Appli. **25**, 391–401 (2020)
5. Lo, W., Yin, J., Deng, S., Li, Y., Wu, Z.: Collaborative web service qos prediction with location-based regularization. In: 2012 IEEE 19th International Conference on Web Services, pp. 464–471. IEEE (2012)
6. Zhu, X., et al.: Similarity-maintaining privacy preservation and location-aware low-rank matrix factorization for qos prediction based web service recommendation. IEEE Trans. Serv. Comput. **14**(3), 889–902 (2018)
7. Zou, G., et al.: Deeptsqp: temporal-aware service qos prediction via deep neural network and feature integration. Knowl.-Based Syst. **241**, 108062 (2022)
8. Hu, S., Zou, G., Zhang, B., Wu, S., Lin, S., Gan, Y., Chen, Y.: Temporal-aware qos prediction via dynamic graph neural collaborative learning. In: Service-Oriented Computing: 20th International Conference, ICSOC 2022, Seville, Spain, November 29-December 2, 2022, Proceedings, pp. 125–133. Springer (2022). https://doi.org/10.1007/978-3-031-20984-0_8
9. Oord, A.v.d., Dieleman, S., et al.: Wavenet: a generative model for raw audio. arXiv preprint arXiv:1609.03499 (2016)
10. Schuster, M., Paliwal, K.K.: Bidirectional recurrent neural networks. IEEE Trans. Signal Process. **45**(11), 2673–2681 (1997)
11. Zhang, Y., Zheng, Z., Lyu, M.R.: Wspred: A time-aware personalized qos prediction framework for web services. In: 2011 IEEE 22nd International Symposium on Software Reliability Engineering, pp. 210–219. IEEE (2011)
12. Luo, X., Wu, H., Yuan, H., Zhou, M.: Temporal pattern-aware qos prediction via biased non-negative latent factorization of tensors. IEEE Trans. Cybern. **50**(5), 1798–1809 (2019)

13. Li, M., Hua, Z., Zhao, J., Zou, Y., Xie, B.: ARIMA model-based web services trustworthiness evaluation and prediction. In: Liu, C., Ludwig, H., Toumani, F., Yu, Q. (eds.) ICSOC 2012. LNCS, vol. 7636, pp. 648–655. Springer, Heidelberg (2012). https://doi.org/10.1007/978-3-642-34321-6_51

14. Xia, Y., Ding, J., Luo, X., Zhu, Q.: Dependability prediction of ws-bpel service compositions using petri net and time series models. In: 2013 IEEE Seventh International Symposium on Service-Oriented System Engineering, pp. 192–202. IEEE (2013)

15. Rahman, Z.U., Hussain, O.K., Hussain, F.K.: Time series qos forecasting for management of cloud services. In: 2014 Ninth International Conference on Broadband and Wireless Computing, Communication and Applications, pp. 183–190. IEEE (2014)

16. Chen, D., Gao, M., Liu, A., Chen, M., Zhang, Z., Feng, Y.: A recurrent neural network based approach for web service qos prediction. In: 2019 2nd International Conference on Artificial Intelligence and Big Data (ICAIBD), pp. 350–357. IEEE (2019)

17. Keshavarzi, A., Toroghi Haghighat, A., Bohlouli, M.: Online qos prediction in the cloud environments using hybrid time-series data mining approach. Iranian J. Sci. Technol. Trans. Electrical Eng. **45**, 461–478 (2021)

18. Xia, Y., Ding, D., Chang, Z., Li, F.: Joint deep networks based multi-source feature learning for qos prediction. IEEE Trans. Serv. Comput. **15**(4), 2314–2327 (2021)

19. Iandola, F.N., Han, S., Moskewicz, M.W., Ashraf, K., Dally, W.J., Keutzer, K.: Squeezenet: Alexnet-level accuracy with 50x fewer parameters andj 0.5 mb model size. arXiv preprint arXiv:1602.07360 (2016)

20. Grover, A., Leskovec, J.: node2vec: scalable feature learning for networks. In: Proceedings of the 22nd ACM SIGKDD International Conference on Knowledge Discovery and Data Mining, pp. 855–864 (2016)

21. Chang, Z., Ding, D., Xia, Y.: A graph-based qos prediction approach for web service recommendation. Appli. Intell. 1–15 (2021)

22. Zou, G., Chen, J., He, Q., Li, K.C., Zhang, B., Gan, Y.: Ndmf: neighborhood-integrated deep matrix factorization for service qos prediction. IEEE Trans. Netw. Serv. Manage. **17**(4), 2717–2730 (2020)

23. Xu, J., Xiao, L., Li, Y., Huang, M., Zhuang, Z., Weng, T.H., Liang, W.: Nfmf: neural fusion matrix factorisation for qos prediction in service selection. Connect. Sci. **33**(3), 753–768 (2021)

24. Xiong, R., Wang, J., Li, Z., Li, B., Hung, P.C.: Personalized lstm based matrix factorization for online qos prediction. In: 2018 IEEE International Conference on Web Services (ICWS), pp. 34–41. IEEE (2018)

25. Chen, X., Li, B., Wang, J., Zhao, Y., Xiong, Y.: Integrating emd with multivariate lstm for time series qos prediction. In: 2020 IEEE International Conference on Web Services (ICWS), pp. 58–65. IEEE (2020)

26. Sahu, P., Raghavan, S., Chandrasekaran, K., Usha, D.: Time-aware online QoS Prediction Using LSTM and Non-negative Matrix Factorization. In: Sheth, A., Sinhal, A., Shrivastava, A., Pandey, A.K. (eds.) Intelligent Systems. AIS, pp. 369–376. Springer, Singapore (2021). https://doi.org/10.1007/978-981-16-2248-9_35

27. Georgiadis, S.D., Ranta-aho, P.O., Tarvainen, M.P., Karjalainen, P.A.: Single-trial dynamical estimation of event-related potentials: a kalman filter-based approach. IEEE Trans. Biomed. Eng. **52**(8), 1397–1406 (2005)

28. Chen, T., Kornblith, S., Norouzi, M., Hinton, G.: Simclr: a simple framework for contrastive learning of visual representations. In: International Conference on Learning Representations, vol. 2 (2020)

29. Xie, X., et al.: Contrastive learning for sequential recommendation. In: 2022 IEEE 38th International Conference on Data Engineering (ICDE), pp. 1259–1273. IEEE (2022)
30. Siami-Namini, S., Tavakoli, N., Namin, A.S.: The performance of lstm and bilstm in forecasting time series. In: 2019 IEEE International Conference on Big Data (Big Data), pp. 3285–3292. IEEE (2019)
31. Wu, Z., Xiong, Y., Yu, S.X., Lin, D.: Unsupervised feature learning via non-parametric instance discrimination. In: Proceedings of the IEEE conference on computer vision and pattern recognition, pp. 3733–3742 (2018)
32. Ding, S., Li, Y., Wu, D., Zhang, Y., Yang, S.: Time-aware cloud service recommendation using similarity-enhanced collaborative filtering and arima model. Decis. Support Syst. **107**, 103–115 (2018)
33. Ye, F., Lin, Z., Chen, C., Zheng, Z., Huang, H.: Outlier-resilient web service qos prediction. In: Proceedings of the Web Conference 2021, pp. 3099–3110 (2021)
34. Medsker, L.R., Jain, L.: Recurrent neural networks. Design Appli. **5**, 64–67 (2001)
35. Graves, A.: Long short-term memory. Springer, Heidelberg (2012). https://doi.org/10.1007/978-3-642-24797-2_4
36. Vaswani, A., et al.: Attention is all you need. In: Advances in Neural Information Processing Systems 30 (2017)

# Author Index

**A**

Angelis, Ioannis  I-18
Antonopoulos, Christos  I-3

**B**

Besimi, Adrian  III-154
Bi, Zhongqin  III-134
Blasi, Maximilian  III-229

**C**

Cang, Li Shan  II-265
Cao, Bin  II-437
Cao, Cong  II-205
Cao, Dun  III-79
Cao, Wenwen  II-414
Cao, Ya-Nan  II-321
Chang, Jiayu  II-131
Chen, Hui  II-115
Chen, Juan  II-173, II-375, III-100
Chen, Kaiwei  II-79
Chen, Liang  II-242, II-392
Chen, Mingcai  II-20
Chen, Peng  II-173, II-375, III-100, III-118
Chen, Shizhan  II-281
Christopoulou, Eleni  I-18
Cui, Bo  I-207
Cui, Jiahe  III-23
Cui, Jie  II-414

**D**

Dagiuklas, Tasos  III-41
Deng, Shaojiang  II-495
Di, Qianhui  II-514
Ding, Weilong  III-329
Ding, Xu  I-187, I-365, I-385
Ding, Yong  I-167, I-243, II-301, II-321
Du, Miao  I-54
Duan, Liang  II-458
Duan, Yutang  III-134

**F**

Faliagka, Evanthia  I-3
Fan, Guodong  II-281
Fan, Jing  II-437
Fan, Yuqi  I-187
Fan, Zhicheng  II-20
Fang, Cheng  I-54
Feng, Beibei  II-341
Feng, Lin  III-308
Feng, Shilong  I-385, III-273
Feng, Xiangyang  III-291
Feng, Zhiyong  II-281, III-208
Fichtner, Myriel  III-249
Fu, Jianhui  II-205

**G**

Gan, Yanglan  III-291
Gao, Chongming  III-191
Gao, Jinyong  III-365
Gao, Min  III-191, III-365
Guo, Linxin  III-191
Guo, Meng  II-474
Guo, Ming  II-20
Guo, Zhenwei  II-321

**H**

Han, Dingkang  III-347
Han, Jianghong  III-308
Hao, Junfeng  III-100
He, Hongshun  II-474
He, Hongxia  II-173, II-375
He, Yunxiang  III-23
Henrich, Dominik  III-249
Hu, Bowen  II-96
Hu, Haize  I-284, I-303, I-343
Hu, Qinglei  III-23
Hu, Zekun  I-128
Huang, Jie  I-225
Huang, Jihai  III-329
Huang, Kaizhu  III-3
Huang, Xingru  II-96

H. Gao et al. (Eds.): CollaborateCom 2023, LNICST 562, pp. 533–536, 2024.
https://doi.org/10.1007/978-3-031-54528-3

Huang, Yakun  II-474
Huang, Yi  III-3

**I**

Idoje, Godwin  III-41
Iqbal, Muddesar  II-265, III-41

**J**

Jablonski, Stefan  III-249
Jelić, Slobodan  I-38
Ji, Rui  I-385, III-273
Jian, Wenxin  I-93
Jiang, Qinkai  II-437
Jiang, Xinghong  I-93
Jiang, Yujie  III-173
Jiao, Liang  III-347
Jin, Yi  I-265
Jin, Zhifeng  I-187
Ju, Zixuan  I-225

**K**

Keramidas, Giorgos  I-3
Knežević, Milica  I-38
Kraft, Robin  III-229
Kuang, Li  I-265, II-131

**L**

Lei, Nanfang  III-79
Li, Baoke  II-205
Li, Bing  I-54
Li, Dongyu  III-23
Li, Fan  I-77
Li, Jiaxin  II-39
Li, Min  II-281
Li, Mingchu  I-421, II-3
Li, Peihao  I-225
Li, Peisong  III-3
Li, Qi  I-323
Li, Shuai  I-421, II-3
Li, Wenwei  II-474
Li, Xi  II-173, II-375
Li, Xiang  II-341
Li, Yang  II-96, II-414, II-474
Li, Yantao  II-495
Li, Yin  I-77, III-118
Li, Yixuan  II-96
Li, Youhuizi  II-514
Li, Yu  II-514
Li, Zhehao  I-365, III-273

Liang, Hai  I-167, I-243, II-321
Liang, Qingmi  I-265
Liang, Tian  II-131
Liang, Tingting  II-514
Liang, Weiyou  I-167
Liao, Jie  II-392
Liu, Donghua  III-208
Liu, Feng  I-365
Liu, Jianxun  I-284, I-303, I-323, I-343
Liu, Jinyuan  I-243
Liu, Lingmeng  II-79
Liu, Peiyu  II-39
Liu, Qingyun  III-347
Liu, Ruiqi  III-365
Liu, Xiangzheng  I-284
Liu, Xu  I-207
Liu, Yanbing  II-205
Liu, Yi  I-284
Liu, Yilin  II-301
Liu, Yumeng  II-223
Long, Teng  I-303
Lu, Tong  II-458
Luo, Huaxiu  II-495
Lyu, Zengwei  III-308

**M**

Ma, Jingrun  II-341
Ma, Yong  I-77, I-93, II-79
Mei, Tianyu  I-207
Mihaljević, Miodrag J.  I-38
Mo, Dikai  III-347

**N**

Nanos, Nikolaos  I-3
Ni, Mingjian  II-96
Niu, Xianhua  III-100

**O**

Oikonomou, Konstantinos  I-18
Ouyang, Zhaobin  III-118
Ouyang, Zhenchao  III-23

**P**

Peng, Chao  III-208
Peng, Qinglan  I-77, II-79, III-118
Peng, Xincai  II-265
Peng, Yang  I-225
Pryss, Rüdiger  III-229

## Q

Qi, Chufeng I-149
Qi, Wanying I-421, II-3
Qi, Zhiwei II-458
Qian, Shuwei II-20
Qiao, Xiuquan II-474
Qin, Huafeng II-495
Qiu, Houming II-357

## R

Reichert, Manfred III-229
Ren, YongJian III-59
Riedelbauch, Dominik III-249

## S

Schickler, Marc III-229
Selimi, Mennan III-154
Ševerdija, Domagoj I-38
Shan, Meijing III-134
Shao, Shiyun II-79
Sheng, Yu I-265
Sherratt, Robert Simon III-79
Shi, Lei I-187, I-365, I-385, III-273
Shi, Yukun III-385
Shkurti, Lamir III-154
Shu, Xinyue I-111
Song, Qihong I-343
Song, Weijian II-173, II-375
Song, Yi II-115
Song, Yulun II-96
Spournias, Alexandros I-3
Su, Jiajun II-79
Su, Majing II-205
Sucker, Sascha III-249
Sun, Haifeng I-403
Sun, Maoxiang III-329
Sun, Yong III-347

## T

Tchernykh, Andrei III-3
Todorović, Milan I-38
Tsipis, Athanasios I-18
Tu, Jiaxue I-77

## V

Voros, Nikolaos I-3

## W

Wan, Jian II-151
Wan, Zihang II-223

Wang, Bin II-39
Wang, Bo II-115
Wang, Chongjun II-20
Wang, Chunyu II-189
Wang, Fan II-39
Wang, Gongju II-96
Wang, Hongan II-223
Wang, Huiyong I-167, II-301
Wang, Jiaxing II-437
Wang, Jin III-79
Wang, Peng II-57
Wang, Pengwei I-128
Wang, Quanda II-96
Wang, Shiqi III-191
Wang, Shunli II-189
Wang, Xi II-341
Wang, Xiaowen I-225
Wang, Xin III-59
Wang, Xinheng III-3
Wang, Xu III-118
Wang, Yang III-100
Wang, Yongjie II-57
Wang, Yujue I-167, I-243, II-301, II-321
Wei, Zhen III-273
Wei, Zhenchun III-308
Wen, Baodong I-243
Wu, Hongyue II-281
Wu, Quanwang I-111
Wu, Ruoting II-242, II-392
Wu, Shouyi II-474
Wu, Yujiang III-365

## X

Xi, Qinghui II-173, II-375
Xia, Yunni I-77, I-93, II-79, II-375, III-100, III-118
Xiao, Wang III-208
Xiao, Wanzhi II-131
Xiao, Ziren III-3
Xie, Qi I-265
Xie, Qilin I-93
Xie, Yibin I-365
Xing, Weiwei I-149
Xiong, Jiasi III-79
Xiong, Xinli II-57
Xu, Chaonong III-173
Xu, Fuyong II-39
Xu, Jie II-151
Xu, Juan I-385
Xu, Junyi III-308

Xu, Lei   III-100
Xu, Peiran   III-385
Xu, Xiaolin   II-341
Xue, Meiting   III-385
Xue, Xiao   II-281, III-208

**Y**
Yan, Cairong   III-291
Yan, Long   II-96
Yan, Xiangpei   III-208
Yang, Changsong   I-167, I-243, II-301,
     II-321
Yang, Ke   II-115
Yang, Peng   I-54
Yang, Yuling   II-205
Yao, Qian   II-57
Yao, Xinwei   I-149
Yi, Chen   II-301
Yi, Meng   I-54
Yin, Yuyu   II-514
Yu, Qi   III-329
Yuan, Fangfang   II-205
Yuan, Xiaohui   III-308
Yue, Kun   II-458
Yue, Lupeng   III-385

**Z**
Zang, Tianning   II-341
Zeng, Jie   III-365
Zeng, Kaisheng   III-385
Zeng, Yan   III-59

Zeng, Yanguo   III-385
Zhan, Baotong   I-385
Zhang, Beibei   III-59
Zhang, Changjie   III-23
Zhang, Daqing   I-403
Zhang, Jia   III-365
Zhang, Jilin   III-59, III-385
Zhang, Jun   I-187, II-189
Zhang, Lihua   II-189
Zhang, Lu   II-281
Zhang, Qingliang   I-111
Zhang, Qingyang   II-414
Zhang, Shuai   II-265
Zhang, Weina   III-134
Zhang, Xiangping   I-303, I-323
Zhang, Xin   II-151
Zhang, Yiwei   III-291
Zhang, Yuanqing   II-514
Zhang, Yuedong   III-347
Zhang, Yuxin   II-242, II-392
Zhang, Zhaohui   I-128
Zhao, Han   II-79
Zhao, Peihai   I-128
Zhao, Yijing   II-223
Zheng, Haibin   I-243
Zheng, Hui   III-59
Zhong, Hong   II-414
Zhou, Mingyao   III-59
Zhou, Sirui   I-225
Zhu, Dongge   I-77
Zhu, Kun   II-357
Zhu, Yujia   III-347

Printed in the United States
by Baker & Taylor Publisher Services